A
Love Letter
to the Many

This abridged edition first published by Jacana Media (Pty) Ltd in 2024

10 Orange Street
Sunnyside
Auckland Park 2092
South Africa
+2711 628 3200
www.jacana.co.za

Vishwas Satgar, 2024
All rights reserved.

ISBN 978-1-4314-3482-4

Cover design by publicide
Editing by Christopher Merrett
Proofreading by Lara Jacob
Indexing by Ali Parry
Set in Ehrhardt MT Std 10/14.5pt
Printed and bound by ABC Press, Cape Town
Job no. 004156

See a complete list of Jacana titles at www.jacana.co.za

A Love Letter to the Many

Arguments for Transformative Left Politics in South Africa

Selected Writings

Vishwas Satgar

Praise for
A Love Letter to the Many

ANC-led Alliance national liberation politics is exhausted. It is anti-worker, unjust, corrupt and a danger to our democracy. If you are interested in trail-blazing people and worker-led alternatives that can secure a transformative future, engage with these writings by Vishwas Satgar. He is one of our most consistent, thoughtful and critical left intellectuals at the frontline of contemporary struggles.

Ruth Ntlokotse is the president of the South African Federation of Trade Unions (SAFTU) and the erstwhile second deputy president of the National Union of Metal Workers of South Africa (NUMSA)

Vishwas Satgar has passion. and commitment for the people and life. His work dreams in a way that closes distance, ends the borders in our hearts and sow seeds of peace and freedom. Take the bold step and read this love letter addressed to you.

Knorke Leaf is an award-winning Bolivian muralist

With his own long-Covid precarity serving as a personal-is-political metaphor, through this collection of highly insightful and reflective writings rooted in praxis, Vishwas Satgar challenges – and indeed dares – us to re-imagine and actively work for a more just, more humane, more planet-affirming world, not through ideological orthodoxy or short-term expediency, but driven By that most revolutionary of forces: love! Love for humanity, love for our lifegiving Earth, rooted in an ethics of care.

Mike van Graan is a playwright

What do you do when your dreams turn to dust? How do you live your life when the movement you have built degenerates in a murky maze of contradictions, concessions and even betrayal? Where do you go when there is a painful parting of the ways? So many activists in South Africa, who fought a long struggle to bring a liberation movement to power, only to see it capitulate to capital, have asked these questions. In this book, Vishwas Satgar bravely takes them on, telling his own story while examining the deepest issues about our movements, our species, our planet. He takes us through four decades of activism from a school boycott through grassroots organising in the UDF through holding a leading position in the SACP to building an alternative left outside the ANC-SACP. This book is a moving and insightful contribution to the current and future left.

Helena Sheehan is emeritus professor at Dublin City University and author of books such as Marxism and the Philosophy of Science, The Syriza Wave, Navigating the Zeitgeist **and** Until We Fall

Vishwas Satgar is a fearless fighter for social justice. Whether you agree with him or not his voice is an important one to read and hear.

Jay Naidoo was the founding general secretary of COSATU and a minister in President Mandela's Cabinet

A moving and inspiring volume emerging from over four decades of activism and scholarship, this love letter to future generations chronicles histories of struggle and hope, but also of betrayal by those in power. It frames a new decolonial and emancipatory politics of the left, oriented towards solidarity of the many, and centred on ecological justice. Intellectually profound and oriented towards a transformative politics that challenges ecocidal capitalism. This book is ultimately a celebration of collective strength and the will to bring about new worlds.

Nivedita Menon is professor at the Centre for Comparative Politics and Political Theory, Jawaharlal Nehru University, New Delhi

For decades now, Vishwas Satgar has been rethinking and advancing the socialist project. This collection of essays shows his rigorous, historical analysis of left politics in South Africa, his commitment to democratic ecofeminist socialism as an active force for its renewal, and his hallmark, defiant lucidity. Satgar provides a crucial foundation for transformative strategies to accelerate and deepen the just transition from below. This volume speaks to the exigencies of our time and is profoundly relevant to a failing state, and the next generation, in a boiling world.

Janet Solomon, director of Becoming Visible, co-founder of Oceans Not Oil

This is an amazing book: it bears witness to the hopes and struggles of countless activists for a new and progressive South Africa, and the disappointments of a revolutionary generation in this country and around the world. Vishwas Satgar has offered important contributions, for many years, to the struggles for justice, social change and ecosocialism; and in this book he offers another powerful motivating force towards the recovery of a transformative left imagination and the dreams of freedom which are essential, so we can live in a world free of the threats posed by a hyper-destructive globalised and financialised capitalism.

Alfredo Saad Filho is professor of Political Economy and International Development, King's College London

This volume illustrates the making, the breaking and the re-awakening of an activist. It illustrates the transformative potential of a politics that is willing to learn, evolve and be shaped by struggle. The volume uses the history of an individual to reflect the history of a nation. It perfectly balances the factual with the felt; it demonstrates the impact of individual struggle and how this informs the role one plays in collective struggle. Written with passion and conviction, and with radical love for the many, this is worth a read – and a re-read.

Courtney Morgan is a climate justice activist and ecofeminist

A timely collection of conjunctural and against-the-grain interventions. It will rouse all those who mistakenly believe that retreats and defeats of the last three decades unhinged everyone and robbed the political left of all options. These writings remind us that ongoing renewal and involvement in struggle are the lifeblood of emancipatory politics, and a worthwhile insurance against political ossification.

Dinga Sikwebu is a retired educator of NUMSA, the metalworkers' union in South Africa

Vishwas Satgar has long demonstrated the possibility of combining radical theory with praxis. In this book, coming at a time when our society is not only ravaged by manifold crises but above all paralysed by a dearth of political imagination, Satgar reminds us that the starting point of any emancipatory vision must be love: love for humanity, love for nature, and love for life itself.

William Shoki is the editor of *Africa is a Country*

Vishwas Satgar writes from his personal experience of South Africa and his perspective on the failure of left politics. He challenges us to think of how to re-imagine a leftist vision that bridges divides and strives for transformative change for a just and inclusive society. Satgar eloquently articulates our shared purpose for urgent collective action, social and ecological justice in a world facing unprecedented challenges in our current poly-crisis, especially the climate crisis. His profound insight shows the path towards a more equitable, sustainable and compassionate future.

Francesca de Gasparis, executive director of Southern African Faith Communities' Environment Institute (SAFCEI)

Contents

Acronyms and abbreviations ... xiii
Acknowledgements ... xix
Preface: Writing among, with, and for the many ... xxi
Introduction ... 1

Part I: Resisting revolutionary orthodoxy, neoliberal market democracy and emergent neofascism

Contributing to a democratic imaginary in the SACP
Workplace forums and autonomous self-management from below ... 45
The visible hand of development planning in India: Lessons for South Africa ... 57
Worker-owned co-operatives, development and neoliberal economic adjustment ... 63
Be partisan for peace ... 82
Socialism and sustainable local economic development ... 85

Rejecting the fraud of the National Democratic Revolution
A critique of government's macro-economic strategy: Growth, employment and redistribution (with Langa Zita and Dale McKinley) ... 103
Neoliberalised South Africa: Labour and the roots of passive revolution ... 109
The Marikana massacre and the South African state's low-intensity war against the people ... 135
Beyond Marikana: The post-apartheid South African state ... 139

Opposing Zumafication in the SACP and outside
Reflections: the age of barbarism ... 165
We need a truly transformative democracy ... 188

'No!' tells the ANC enough is enough 192
It's up to us to make sure Zuma goes 196
Protests mustn't harm our future 200
Fees protests: History shows true revolution lies not in violence 203
The EFF's wrecking ball politics is fascist rather than left 205
Zuma's Cabinet reshuffle inaugurates South Africa's Zimbabwe moment .. 209
South Africa must resist another captured president, this time by
    the markets 213
Trump may be gone, but neofascism remains alive and kicking in
    mainstream American society 217
South Africa is turning on itself (with Awande Buthelezi) 220
International Mandela Day: Respondent to keynote address of President
    Cyril Ramaphosa, 18 July 2021 224
Without a serious challenge from the left, the political field in South Africa
    could see the emergence of an extreme right 230

The challenge of left renewal in the context of worsening capitalist crisis
The left project and post-national liberation politics 237
There is a democratic left response to the global crisis 242
Occupying the economy 245
Reclaiming a vision of hope and a life of dignity 249
NUMSA moment leads left renewal 256
Between crisis and renewal: Where to for South Africa's left? 260

Part II: Decolonial critique of ecocidal capitalism

Perspectives on ecocide
Marx and the International 277
Seven theses on radical non-racialism, the climate crisis and deep, just
    transitions: From the national question to the ecocide question 284
The coloniality of the scientific Anthropocene: Towards decolonial
    futures of North–South relations 304
Crises, socio-ecological reproduction and intersectionality: Challenges
    for emancipatory feminism 322

Part III: Building mass resistance to climate injustice

For people and worker-driven climate politics
The World Social Forum and the battle for COP17 339
The climate is ripe for social change 343

Worsening climate crisis and the challenge of red-green alliances for labour: Introducing the Climate Justice Charter alternative in South Africa ... 347
The geopolitics of vaccine apartheid ... 357

Raising the alarm louder against climate injustice
Light a fire under SA's climate policy ... 363
South Africa's carbon democracy is going over the cliff ... 367
Covid-19, the climate crisis and lockdown: an opportunity to end the war with nature ... 372
Where have all the flowers gone?: A final climate crisis warning ... 380
Party politicians fiddle about with climate change while SA burns ... 384
South Africa, the climate pariah, needs to change its ways ... 387
An open letter to Hosken Consolidated Investments and Minister Gwede Mantashe: A beginner's guide to poppycock (with Janet Solomon) ... 390
US, Russia and Ukraine: The death trap beyond the new Cold War and World War 3 ... 400
The ANC needs a wake-up call on the urgency of the climate crisis ... 406

Part IV: For a democratic ecosocialist South Africa and world

Democratic ecosocialism through democratic systemic reforms
The climate crisis and systemic alternatives ... 413
Climate ecocide and democratic ecosocialism in South Africa ... 429
Why ecosocialism for a red-green future ... 434
Marx, the commons and democratic ecosocialism ... 437
End ecocidal capitalism or exterminate life on Planet Earth: A South African contribution to ecosocialist strategy ... 453

Transformative politics and the new global left imaginary
Alternatives to neoliberal globalisation ... 471

Co-operative development and worker co-operatives
NUM worker co-ops are dead! long live worker co-ops? ... 493
A co-operative movement response to the crisis of civilisation: Choosing to sustain life! ... 498

Solidarity economy
With, against and beyond the state: A solidarity economy through a movement of movements ... 509

Food sovereignty
  Break the food chain to build our humanity ... 529
  South Africa's food system in dire straits ... 533
  Food sovereignty: The viable alternative to ANC and EFF land solutions ... 535
  Civil society: The state has failed and cannot be trusted, let us help solve
    the hunger crisis ... 539

Universal basic income grant
  The South African precariat, Covid-19 and #BIGNOW ... 545

The Climate Justice Charter pluri-vision
  No short cuts for a deep, just transition: Towards a Climate Justice
    Charter for South Africa (with Jane Cherry, Courtney Morgan and
    Aaisha Domingo) ... 553

Annexure: Additional resources for transformative activism ... 559
Bibliography ... 563
Index ... 589

Acronyms and abbreviations

ACCOSCA	African Confederation of Savings and Credit Co-operatives
AMCU	Association of Mineworkers and Construction Union
ANC	African National Congress
ASGISA	Accelerated and Shared Growth Initiative for South Africa
AU	African Union
B-BEEE	Broad-Based Black Economic Empowerment
BC	Black Consciousness
BEE	Black Economic Empowerment
BIFR	Board for Industrial and Financial Reconstruction (India)
BIG	basic income grant
BLM	Black Lives Matter
BRICS	Brazil, Russia, India, China and South Africa
CACE	Centre for Adult and Continuing Education
CBDA	Co-operative Banks Development Agency
CBDR	common but differentiated responsibilities
CC	Competition Commission
CCMA	Commission for Conciliation, Mediation and Arbitration
CCUL	Cape Credit Union League
CDL	Conference of the Democratic Left
CDM	clean development mechanism
CEO	chief executive officer
CFCs	chlorofluorocarbons
CFF	contingency financing facility
CJC	Climate Justice Charter
CJCM	Climate Justice Charter Movement
CO_2	carbon dioxide
CODESA	Convention for a Democratic South Africa

COP	Conference of the Parties
COPAC	Co-operative and Policy Alternative Centre
COPE	Congress of the People
COSATU	Congress of South African Trade Unions
DA	Democratic Alliance
DM	Democratic Marxism series
DMA	Disaster Management Act
DTI	Department of Trade and Industry
EFF	Economic Freedom Fighters
ESSET	Ecumenical Service for Socio-Economic Transformation
EU	European Union
FAO	Food and Agriculture Organization
FDI	foreign direct investment
FEDUSA	Federation of Unions of South Africa
FSA	Financial Services Association
FSVC	Financial Services Village Co-operative
FTAs	free trade agreements
GATT	General Agreement on Tariffs and Trade
GCMs	general circulation models
GDP	gross domestic product
GEAR	Growth, Employment and Redistribution
GHG	greenhouse gas
GIS	geographic information system
GMOs	genetically modified organisms
GNR	Global Nutrition Report
GNU	Government of National Unity
GW	gigawatts
HCI	Hosken Consolidated Investments
HIV	human immunodeficiency virus
HIV/AIDS	human immunodeficiency virus/acquired immunodeficiency syndrome
ICA	International Co-operative Alliance
IDC	Industrial Development Corporation
IDP	integrated development plan
IEA	International Energy Agency
IEC	Electoral Commission of South Africa
IFIs	international financial institutions

IFP	Inkatha Freedom Party
ILO	International Labour Organization
IMF	International Monetary Fund
IPCC	Intergovernmental Panel on Climate Change
IRP	integrated resource plan
ISI	import substitution industrialisation
ISP	Industrial Strategy Project
JSE	Johannesburg Stock Exchange
LED	light emitting diode
LGBTI	lesbian, gay, bisexual, transgender and intersexed
LRA	Labour Relations Act
MEC	minerals-energy complex
NAFTA	North American Free Trade Agreement
NALEDI	National Labour and Economic Development Institute
NASA	National Aeronautics and Space Administration
NATO	North Atlantic Treaty Organization
NCASA	National Co-operative Association of South Africa
NDP	National Development Plan
NDR	National Democratic Revolution
NEDLAC	National Economic Development and Labour Council
NEPAD	New Partnership for Africa's Development
NGDP	net global domestic product
NGO	non-governmental organisation
NIC	Natal Indian Congress
NIEO	new international economic order
NMW	national minimum wage
NPA	National Prosecuting Authority
NPC	National Planning Commission
NUM	National Union of Mineworkers
NUMSA	National Union of Metalworkers of South Africa
OECD	Organisation for Economic Co-operation and Development
OPEC	Organization of the Petroleum Exporting Countries
PMBEJD	Pietermaritzburg Economic Justice and Dignity
PPE	personal protective equipment
PT	Workers' Party (Partido dos Trabalhadores, Brazil)
RDP	Reconstruction and Development Programme
SACCO	Savings and Credit Co-operative

SACCOL	South African Credit and Co-operative League
SACP	South African Communist Party
SACTU	South African Congress of Trade Unions
SACTWU	South African Clothing and Textile Workers Union
SADCC	Southern African Development Co-ordination Conference
SAFSC	South African Food Sovereignty Campaign
SAFTU	South African Federation of Trade Unions
SAHRC	South African Human Rights Commission
SALB	*South African Labour Bulletin*
SALDRU	Southern Africa Labour and Development Research Unit
SANCO	South African National Civic Organisation
SAP	structural adjustment programme
SARB	South African Reserve Bank
SAWPA	South African Waste Pickers Association
SDGs	sustainable development goals
SERT	socio-ecological reproduction theory
SETA	Sector Education and Training Authority
SMEs	small and medium-sized enterprises
SOEs	state-owned enterprises
SRC	Student Representative Council
SRT	social reproduction theory
STEM	science, technology, engineering and mathematics
SWOP	sociology of work project
TAC	Treatment Action Campaign
TIC	Transvaal Indian Congress
TRC	Truth and Reconciliation Commission
TRIMS	trade-related investment measures
TRIPS	trade-related aspects of intellectual property
UBIG	universal basic income grant
UBIGNOW	universal basic income grant now
UDF	United Democratic Front
UK	United Kingdom
UKZN	University of KwaZulu-Natal
UN	United Nations
UNCTAD	United Nations Conference on Trade and Development
UNFCCC	United Nations Framework Convention on Climate Change
UN-IPCC	United Nations Intergovernmental Panel on Climate Change

UNITA	União Nacional para a Independência Total de Angola (National Union for the Total Independence of Angola)
UPM	Unemployed People's Movement
US	United States
UWC	University of the Western Cape
V20	Vulnerable 20
VFSC	Village Financial Services Co-operatives
WEF	World Economic Forum
WHO	World Health Organization
WMO	World Meteorological Organization
WSF	World Social Forum
WSSD	World Summit on Sustainable Development
WTO	World Trade Organization

Acknowledgements

IT WAS IN MY EXTENDED and communal family that the seeds of love for the many were sown. While this communal family world is disappearing in the storm of modernity and progress, I am deeply grateful to all of you for contributing to making me who I am. My mother and father gave me the best examples of how to bring courage to my convictions. There is undying love in these communal ties that I shall always cherish.

Central to my transformative praxis is a belief in the collective intellectual. Transformative knowledge is co-created in the social relations of activism, movement building and mass politics. Hence some of these writings are also co-written. I want to thank all co-authors for some of the writings in this book. I want to thank all the trade unionists, grassroots women, workers, community activists, students, movements, networks and radical academics who contributed to the tacit knowledge of transformative politics in these writings, including in the Democratic Marxism series and my Emancipatory Futures Studies in the Anthropocene project.

The Co-operative and Policy Alternative Centre (COPAC) has been a space to nurture, evolve and deepen transformative praxis. I have worked with many amazing young people in the COPAC team over the years, both as employees and volunteers. They are too numerous to mention but I want them all to be acknowledged for their contributions to programmes of the organisation. In the recent period I want to thank Athish Satgoor, Andrew Bennie, Courtney Morgan, Aaisha Domingo, Sunanda Mathis and Alexia Daoussis. Also, an immense gratitude has to be expressed to all board members, past and present, but specifically Annie Sugrue who has been consistent, ever willing to give advice and proffer encouragement. For this book the comments and engagements from Charles Simane, Awande Buthelezi, Stacey Hope-Bailie and Ferrial Adam are appreciated. Jane Cherry played a crucial role in compiling the materials, securing permissions and putting it all together. Her support role made all the difference.

The Rosa Luxemburg Foundation has always been true to the spirit of Red Rosa. They have supported COPAC and my transformative praxis work for over a decade, including during precarious times. I thank them for their support for this book. I also want to thank the Emancipatory Futures Studies project at Wits University, for assisting with writing retreats as well as a contribution to the publication costs of this book.

To the woman who recognised that I was not a political Frankenstein despite being a Marxist and, at the time we met, a South African Communist Party (SACP) member and leader. Michelle Williams, my partner, has been an immeasurable pillar of strength and intellectual support during my journey. Her uncompromising care labour during my debilitating Covid-19 infection brought me back from a horrific place. There is certainly a love for the many in my life but there is a special love for her. For more than 20 years we have revelled in our authentic connection and had many wonderful adventures. There's a lot more to come.

My appreciation also goes out to the Wits University Historical Papers Research Archive for establishing and housing the Vishwas Satgar Papers, which contains many of my writings.

Finally, I acknowledge the team at Jacana, particularly Bridget Impey, Lara Jacob, Maggie Davey, Lucille Koch and Mbalenhe Simelane for their production support, editorial assistance and promotion of this book.

Preface
Writing among, with, and for the many

> *What we need in South Africa is for egos to be suppressed in favour of peace. We need to create a new breed of South Africans who love their country and love everybody, irrespective of their colour.*
>
> Chris Hani

INFINITY IS THE OPPOSITE of the time- and space-bound mortality of human and non-human life. It is a protean concept that brings into sharp relief how transient, finite and limited our lives are. The moment we are born, the laws of biology start working on our end. Yet in this evolutionary unmaking we have life, contingent and shaped by socio-ecological conditions, but also our own ethical choices. While societies attempt to condition us, socialise us and even define our identities, we are not empty vessels to be programmed like robots. We are able to think beyond our class locations, beyond oppressive belief systems and are capable of constituting human agency to transform the world. The human journey has been remarkable in demonstrating that when we choose to work together, co-operate, share and build solidarities we can survive extreme threats and overcome serious challenges including violence, greed and oppression. We can engage in emancipatory world and life making as Chris Hani invites us to do based on love. This book is anchored in this premise. It is about more than four decades of activist commitment and intervention to transform South Africa.

In deciding to publish this contribution, I was prompted by a haunting question: has the end of human and non-human life begun? A question like this evokes deep trepidation if you understand what is happening in the capitalist life world we inhabit, while at the same time, it has a profound millenarian ring to it.

It almost sounds like a sound bite from end-of-times prophecy. However, used as a heuristic, a tool, it challenges us to think about the socio-ecological evidence, the nature of time (such as social, geological, climate), beyond simple cause and effect and to reach for deeper explanations and generate further questions such as whether or not these processes can be reversed. Is there hope and prospects for an emancipated South Africa and world? The end of life (human and most of non-human life) and how we survive are increasingly debated in parts of the more critical academy, among climate scientists, activists, informed publics and ordinary people – the human many, if you like – as crises of socio-ecological reproduction (climate shocks, hunger, unemployment and failing market democracies, for instance) engulf our fragile lives. In the twentieth century, the threat of nuclear annihilation brought such concerns to the fore. Today it is the historical specificity of a triumphant ecocidal (mass-scale destruction of human and non-human life) capitalism that threatens everything and pushes all forms of life towards extinction. There is no red threat or Communist spectre to blame this time. Capital has everything it wants, its free market utopia including having states bail it out with immense resources, rather than assisting the people. Yet, this same system threatens to destroy everything; it is the harbinger of catastrophe everywhere. Despite the harms and consequences, capitalists and ruling classes are failing to save capitalism even from itself; it is like a runaway train that can only be stopped if it is derailed. A big but necessary challenge that has to be confronted.

In this context, the post-apartheid transition to democracy, once vaunted as a miracle is now a living nightmare. Our narration of ourselves as the rainbow nation, historical myths about the African National Congress (ANC) and Mandela and certainties about the importance of democracy are all in question. South Africa is a country that has gone horribly wrong, with polarisation, social misery and institutional collapse becoming normalised. The greatest paradox of all is having an African majority government, given incredible legitimacy, support and a mandate to transform South Africa, but failing spectacularly for almost three decades to bring about meaningful change in the lives of the many. What happened? Why has South Africa been pushed into a disaster spiral? What kind of post-apartheid socio-ecological order and democracy has really been constructed? Were there alternative choices and paths that could have been taken? With the climate crisis worsening and the more general civilisational crisis of capitalism intersecting with South African capitalist realities, the stakes are extremely high. For the many left outside and behind by the exclusionary rationalities of national liberation politics, there is a need for a genuine reckoning with these questions. My contribution to political economy/ecology analyses of the post-apartheid transition, particularly the rejection of the fraud of the ANC-led Alliance's NDR, seeks to contribute to this national conversation. It provides a macro-level explanation for how African nationalism defeated working-class left alternatives and has degenerated into criminalised politics.

However, South Africa did not have to end up where it is. As a young person at the beginning of the transition to democracy in South Africa, I chose to work for COSATU's think tank, NALEDI, and do political education work in the SACP, which gave me a vantage point and strategic positioning within the power configuration at the heart of post-apartheid South Africa. My generation of decolonial-Marxist-feminist-ecologists chose the SACP so we could re-imagine socialism beyond its stultified and authoritarian version constructed in the Soviet Union, strengthen the gains of our hard-fought-for democracy, clarify what 'Our Marxism' is and transform South Africa. I lived through, observed and acted in the midst of key conjunctural moments that defined the post-apartheid trajectory: the adoption of homegrown Afro-neoliberal macro-economic policy, the moment of democratic socialist renewal inside the SACP until the return of a dogmatic Marxism-Leninism, the closing of ranks in the SACP and COSATU behind Zuma, the Marikana massacre, the failure of the national liberation left to stand firm against a resurgent racism after apartheid even its populist Africanist and patriarchal Zumafied version, #FeesMustFall, a dogmatic left outside the ANC-led Alliance failing to converge around a new transformative imaginary, an uncaring and inadequate ANC government response to the Covid-19 pandemic, the July 2021 violence and a power structure normalising the most dangerous threat we face: the climate crisis. As both an activist (for over 40 years) and academic (for over a decade) I have intervened intellectually, sometimes together with others, in each of these key conjunctural moments to try to open up other possibilities for mass practice and transformative change. My grounding in a transformative praxis meant going against the grain of defeat but with an unapologetic positioning among, with and for the many.

I made existential life choices, walked a political path and made contributions that can largely be considered part of the invisible archive of the South African left; a defeated left. While South Africa has had a vibrant left intelligentsia, a radical labour movement, the oldest communist party on the continent and a tradition of mass movements, these social forces have largely been eclipsed, tamed and I would argue delegitimised. Some of this has to do with the continuity of a propagandistic *rooi gevaar* (red threat) imaginary, the profoundly reactionary nature of ANC-led national liberation politics, the normalising of an exclusionary market democracy and also the failures of the left itself.

At the same time, the historically specific nature of contemporary capitalist crisis has posed a serious challenge to social science (including the academy more generally with its specialisations), to dominant left understandings of crisis, to activists and to public discourse. A total crisis of socio-ecological reproduction, with specific historical dynamics, registers in complex ways in our economy, in the state, in our ecosystems, including the biosphere, and in everyday life worlds. We tend to reduce the crisis to discreet, specific and individual aspects: the hunger crisis, the climate crisis, the economic crisis, the democracy crisis and more. These reductionist modes of thinking crisis are limited. On the other extreme, self-paralysing discourses are evoked such as collective suicide and end of times extinction that engender abstention and agential confusion, suggesting that the many are responsible for this scary predicament. Yet we are experiencing an unprecedented systemic and conjunctural crisis that has been socially constructed; it is an interconnected poly-crisis which can be explained and overcome. Ruling class interests, ideas and policies in South Africa and the world have engendered this total crisis. Many of these ideas are integral to a supremacist paradigm of thinking that reproduces an unviable Euro-American civilisation. It is the continuity of coloniality, of imperial domination, to reproduce an ecocidal capitalism that has brought us to the brink of extinction. My writings in this volume contribute to a decolonial critique and understanding of this civilisational crisis. In this regard, I draw on my own reading of Marx and other critical thinkers to clarify a decolonial approach to understand the deeper logic of ecocidal capitalism and the disciplinary role of imperialism.

As mentioned, the climate crisis is the most dangerous systemic crisis tendency we face; it can wipe out planetary life. It is imperative we all understand the worsening climate crisis, its complexity and its challenges for socio-ecological transformation. The climate crisis has a history and a politics. Ruling class climate politics has been failing human and non-human life for almost three decades. Today the climate crisis has shifted planetary conditions such that we are living on a new planet. A 1°C overshoot in 2015, since prior to the Industrial Revolution, has inaugurated a world facing climate-induced weather extremes (for instance, floods, droughts, heatwaves and cyclones) that are having disproportionate impacts on workers, the poor, grassroots women, peasants, poorer countries and non-human life. The many are the victims of climate injustice. Activists at the frontline of the climate crisis have been making the case for a long time for people and worker-led just transitions to happen speedily. Work has also been done on bottom-up visioning, transformative politics and the amplification of systemic alternatives, by the many themselves, that can preserve human and non-human life, if we act collectively now through a mass-based climate justice movement. If we fail, the end of the many – human and non-human life – will be realised.

While my political formation in the 1980s gave me an orientation to human ecology through the work of several critical thinkers and particular life experiences, it was in the 1990s that I developed a more grounded concern for ecological questions, both as part of a younger generation rethinking socialism in the SACP and with my embrace of environmental justice politics. By the 2000s I was deeply immersed in township communities seeking to make the practical link between ecological justice and transformative change. The climate crisis became an issue of concern during this time. My contributions to highlighting the urgency of the worsening climate crisis and the need for people and worker-led climate justice politics are shared in this volume. Hopefully, these arguments will convince many more to take a stand for climate justice.

The current world order, system and civilisation is broken and in chaos. After the Cold War, the triumphalism of US-led Western capitalism even declared the end of history; we were all conscripts to an imposed set of liberal Euro-American universals, a linear unfolding of world history, and our destinies were collapsed into mimicking Americans wherever we lived; their market democracy which has given inordinate power to corporations over the state and society was meant to be our version of democracy. The hegemony of this supremacist world view, embedded within deep globalisation, was so strong and successful some even declared it is easier to imagine the end of the world rather than the end of capitalism. This is a false realism, defeatist and a fatalistic perspective, devoid of an appreciation of the remaking of left politics in South Africa and in the world. For over three decades there have been global cycles of resistance re-inventing the left imaginary, politics and resistance. My own contribution to the renewal of socialism as democratic ecosocialism began in the SACP and has continued beyond. These intellectual interventions were informed by the imperative of overcoming neoliberal dogma (even indigenised as Afro-neoliberalism) including the importation of shallow US-style market democracy that constitutionalised the power of corporations, such that economic policy choices were in lock-step with the wishes of credit rating agencies, the World Economic Forum (WEF), the International Monetary Fund (IMF) and World Bank and more generally the business press. My concern for deepening the constitutional democratic project weaved its way into debates about a renewed worker control politics, the role of co-operatives (including co-operative banks and worker co-operatives), democratic planning, local economic development, demilitarisation, rethinking food systems and even arguments for the SACP to contest elections to secure the future of South Africa's multi-party democracy and keep open the logic of a politics driven from below.

Beyond the SACP my commitment to transformative alternatives made the connection between systemic change and the deep, just transition in a heating world. For me this meant rethinking the relationship between a decolonial Marxism, democracy, ecology and feminism for a renewed socialism as democratic ecosocialism through the realisation of people- and worker-driven democratic systemic reforms. Underpinning this has been an elaboration of transformative themes, ideas and practices such as the commons, co-operative-based systems, worker co-operatives, the solidarity economy, food sovereignty, a universal basic income grant (BIG), democratic public utilities and the importance of a climate justice pluri-vision to anchor activism in the deep, just transition. The idea of a pluri-vision is encapsulated in the Climate Justice Charter. It is about confronting the legacies of oppression, the current crises of socio-ecological reproduction and building a liveable, just and democratic future; it speaks to the challenges of our past, present and future as we struggle for deep transformation. The importance and relevance of these transformative systemic alternatives for a renewed left politics are contained in the writings in this book.

A life-changing and debilitating Covid-19 infection also prompted me to put this book together. This is not an autobiography nor a memoir, but rather a curation of one small part of post-apartheid intellectual and political history that has existed at the margins of what is considered the political mainstream circus in South Africa. It is offered as an intellectual resource, a compass and an expression of commitment to support and enrich the mass-scale movement building and resistance the many have to wage to prevent the end of everything. In essence this volume provides arguments, grounded in a transformative praxis over several decades, for a new left politics: post-national liberation, post-Soviet and post-social democratic. This is about a transformative left politics and imaginary homegrown in the shadows of South Africa's shallow, criminalised and exclusionary market democracy. Inspired by Chris Hani, this volume is a love letter; an expression of radical love for the many to achieve a genuine constitutional democracy and substantive transformation. I may not be able to continue the fight as I have for many decades, due to compromised health, but I hope this intellectual resource assists present and future generations displace a dangerous ecocidal capitalism in South Africa and the world, before it is too late. Deracialising a dehumanising, patriarchal, ecocidal and racist capitalism, for the few, was never the horizon of change envisaged in the South African struggle. From the Freedom Charter to the Climate Justice Charter there is a yearning, a burning desire for more, by the many. This I believe can be achieved by advancing people- and worker-led democratic systemic reforms from below that deepen, strengthen and wield our unrealised constitutional democratic project against the insanity of contemporary capitalism, while providing the moorings for a democratic ecosocialist alternative.

A note on texts and terminology

These writings span 27 years but are arranged thematically in four parts to capture synchronous lines of thought developing out of transformative praxis, the consistent underlying thread. At the same time, each theme is arranged with its own chronology and can be explored independently as part of a holistic body of work.

This is the title used for an article published in the *Daily Maverick*: 'Without a serious challenge from the left the political field in South Africa could see the emergence of an extreme right.' The words 'extreme right' replace 'neoliberal right' contained in the published version. Chapters derived from the Democratic Marxism series, that served as framing chapters, have been edited to remove synoptic overviews of other chapters in those volumes. The longer version of the article for *Monthly Review* 'End eco-cidal capitalism or life on Planet Earth: a South African contribution to ecosocialist strategy' has been used in this book.

As praxis-centred writings implicated in resistance and activism these writings are diachronic; language has changed over time and depending on the context, either inside the SACP or outside, particular language registers express themselves, informed by particular considerations. Hence, the following words need to be clarified upfront including their usage. The term National Democratic Revolution (NDR) derives from the SACP's strategic thinking on a two-stage approach to the transition to socialism. The term also has common currency within national liberation discourse. It is a crucial political category denoting inclusion, deep democracy and transformation of social relations. In formal SACP documents it has particular attributed meanings. In this book the term passive revolution is used to dissect the unravelling of the NDR. It is an analytical category derived from the work of the Italian Marxist, Antonio Gramsci, and refers simply to a form of non-hegemonic rule, a type of fraud; a class project to hide real interests, agendas and processes of change as part of making capitalism. The passive revolution is not transformative and fails to change power and socio-ecological relations in furtherance of the interests of the many.

Third World was used in some of these writings in the 1990s to capture the uncertainty of political alignment in the post-Cold War world. Generally, Third World is more than geographic specification but about a common project amongst anti-colonial and non-aligned countries. A lot has changed since then. Hegemonic revolutionary reforms is a language used to refer to the building of elements of socialism through the SACP's political programme and linked to its leading role. After the SACP, the term democratic systemic reforms comes to the fore as part of clarifying transformative strategic politics. This is a central category in this new mode of left politics to emphasise the leading role of peoples and workers in constituting, championing and achieving such reforms. The SACP did not resolve whether it was a mass or vanguard party in the transition to democracy. The use of the term vanguard is used deliberately in some of these writings to confront the factionalising of the SACP through dual membership with the ANC. The evoking of the term was meant to draw attention to this problem and the loss of its independence.

Zumafication is about more than the individual Jacob Zuma, but refers to an ethno-nationalist, authoritarian and criminalised class project. Neoliberalism is used to define a US-led class project and an accumulation model transnationalising monopoly capital. Finance has been pivotal in this process. Afro-neoliberalism is about indigenising this class project and giving it African characteristics. Neoliberalisation is the process to give more power to corporations, finance and deep globalisation.

There is also a variegated vocabulary used to reference transformative politics that can be considered interchangeable. This includes generative, anti-capitalist, emancipatory practice, emancipatory politics, systemic alternatives, democratic systemic reforms, deep, just transition and counter-hegemony, for instance.

Introduction

IN THE RESISTANCE TO apartheid and in the early years of transition to a constitutional democracy, it was commonplace to imagine a South Africa in which exploitation, racism and patriarchy could be overcome. A rich tradition of left politics shaped the horizons of change and there were legitimate popular hopes and dreams. Moreover, with apartheid being the last holdout of institutionalised and systemic racism on the African continent, the world had high expectations for a democratic South Africa. The anti-apartheid movement legitimately expected an ANC-led South Africa to keep its promises; it would be a beacon of a country rooting out all forms of racism to achieve a liberated society. For the left internationally, South Africa was imagined as a place that could buck the trend towards further neoliberalisation (more power to corporations, finance and deep globalisation) on the African continent, given the need to address racialised legacies. There was certainly political space, despite US triumphalism after the Cold War, for more strategic engagements with global capitalism and for transformative change to happen. In this context, brimming with hope and a sense of destiny, Chris Hani could call for a new South African way of being, centred in love: a civic love, a radical non-racial love to overcome centuries of dehumanisation.

Today, after almost three decades of ANC-led Alliance rule, based on utilising one of the most inhumane and oppressive capitalist systems in the twentieth century to bring about social change, the country and its young democracy are on a destructive trajectory. This has been in the making for a while as the country has lurched from one crisis to the next. One outcome of this historical process, with almost three decades of deep globalisation, concessions to capital and integration into global markets, is that the shallow and corrupt market democracy created turns on itself, given its exclusionary logic; accumulation of privilege for a minority based on accumulation of suffering for the many. Everything from burning community public infrastructure, food riots, the Marikana massacre, violent protests at South Africa's universities and the July 2021 violence portend such a future. An unliveable society was turned into an unviable society under ANC rule. Yet its creators like Thabo Mbeki, the all-knowing nationalist intellectual who force-marched a collective project with his transnationalising faction and who weaned the ANC on Afro-neoliberal dogma, fear the coming Arab Spring in public discourse but fail, in typical disingenuous fashion, to admit how damaging their policy choices have been since 1996. Domesticating neoliberalism (a US-led class project and an accumulation model transnationalising monopoly capital) as Afro-neoliberalism (with African characteristics) was not a very original project. Comparatively, most countries in Latin America and Africa, since the 1980s, have structurally adjusted on the terms of transnationalising capital with disastrous consequences. In South Africa more Afro-neoliberal dogma merely confirms the haunting presence of Fanon's ghost and his warning against a venal nationalism, and in this case an African nationalism. This project of market-led social engineering of a deeply divided country has increased racial polarisation, precarity and exclusion. Of course, for the insiders sitting on boards of companies, transacting Black Economic Empowerment (BEE) deals, wielding worker money through union investment companies and benefiting from state corruption, these harsh realities are not a major concern. These embourgeoised-elites did not 'struggle to be poor', as they reminded us, but to enrich themselves at the expense of the many.

The conditions of desperation and inequality, and a criminalised market democracy, have given rise to a violent, revanchist and exclusionary nationalism expressing itself through xenophobia, coloured nationalism, resurgent extreme white nationalism and post-apartheid majoritarian black neofascism. Racism after apartheid is in the mainstream of political life. This is an outcome of the policies and politics of deradicalisation imposed by the ANC-led Alliance. Again, a comparative perspective shows how the second coming of fascism, with historical continuities and discontinuities, has been underway as neoliberalisation and its market logic have been resisted in the US (the most affluent liberal democracy), Europe, Brazil (the largest democracy in Latin America) and India (the largest democracy in the world), for instance. The new fascism of exclusionary nationalism is about a politics of hate, authoritarian rule, scapegoating and violence while maintaining the key institutions of capitalism. South Africa will not survive this. Another possible outcome of ANC-led Alliance rule is a country overcome by worsening crises of socio-ecological reproduction, given its criminalised and weak state. Covid-19 ravaged South Africa with over 300,000 excess deaths, among the highest in the world. South Africa is not prepared for the worsening climate crisis. The drought (2014–2021), the flash flooding in KwaZulu-Natal during April 2022, more flooding in parts of the country in 2023 and the onset of heatwaves have affirmed climate injustice for the many. The next big climate induced drought is going to push South Africa beyond its limits. These shocks coupled with key socio-ecological system collapse – water, energy, food and local government service delivery – could push the country into an irreversible process of decline; a failed country.

With the ANC-led Alliance at the helm, the future of South Africa looks bleak. A degenerate revolutionary nationalism, re-Stalinisation of the oldest communist party in Africa and a deradicalised labour movement have produced the dismal state of affairs in the country. National liberation politics is exhausted. There is nothing self-reflexive about these forces. Under apartheid, officially 69 people were shot during the Sharpeville massacre; under ANC rule 144 people died during the Life Esidemeni tragedy. During the Soweto uprising about 500 children were mercilessly killed by the apartheid regime; under ANC rule almost 5 million came close to losing their lives due to HIV/AIDS denialism and an unresponsive government. In the July 2021 violence more than 350 people lost their lives and during the floods in KwaZulu-Natal in 2022 about 461 people lost their lives. The lives of the many did not matter under apartheid and still do not matter under ANC rule; there isn't even a sense of shame or remorse for the harms done and the crisis-ridden country the ANC has created. The distance between rulers and ruled is wide, such that the legitimation crises confronting these forces is brushed aside by hubris and a crude majoritarianism. Despite the propaganda, performative politics of a NDR and orthodox certainties of the national liberation left, all they have to offer is degeneration into a dead end for the many. The African majority and the working class more generally, the many, have a raw deal and the stakes are high for all. In my activist life (for over four decades) and as a radical academic (since 2010), I have wanted the many to have dignity, conditions for human flourishing, happiness and justice (for human and non-human life forms); this is certainly not the reality in contemporary South Africa. Like many committed activists and as a consistent South African leftist (a democratic ecosocialist), I struggle deeply with what South Africa has become and where it is headed.

This volume is an invitation to continue the struggle through a new transformative left politics; to build on ground broken over decades of activism in townships, in relationships with community organisations, unions, unemployed people's movements, solidarity economy networking, food sovereignty pathway building and climate justice campaigning. Nothing short of tackling the root causes of South Africa's crises will suffice and this is the crux of the new politics being argued for: a post-national liberation, post-Soviet and post-social democratic left politics. The rest of this introduction provides more historical context to arguments for a new transformative left politics and the background conditions of intellectual production that produced these diachronic writings, including its intellectual roots. It situates the material – journal articles, discussion documents, book chapters, newspaper articles and popular magazine pieces – around two axes of intellectual intervention to influence mass practice for different scales of socio-ecological transformation: (i) resisting revolutionary orthodoxy (national liberation, Marxist-Leninist and Trotskyist), neoliberal dogma (even as third-way social democracy or Afro-neoliberalism) and emergent neofascism; and (ii) anchoring left renewal in the making of transformative politics. This body of work is praxis centred, seeking a unity of theory and mass practice, and can be considered part of an epistemology of experimental knowledge. It is about connecting ethical values, knowledge production and being in struggle for an emancipated South Africa and world.

Nature pulls the brake

Walter Benjamin, an original Marxist thinker in the twentieth century, who committed suicide in 1940 before he could be handed over to the Nazi regime, provoked us all to rethink human history. He did not embrace a crude materialism and ideology of progress so deeply embedded in everyday common sense and productivist thought. In 1940 he wrote a set of theses on *The Concept of History*, which provided a critique of Western capitalist modernity by looking at the past as a detour to a new future. As Löwy (2006: 4) highlights, Benjamin's text is 'one of the most important philosophical and political texts of the twentieth century'. Benjamin in his conception of historical temporality made a plea for historical discontinuity and called for the brake to be pulled on the 'march of progress' and its illusions.[1] He was concerned about the immanent dangers and catastrophes of his time: the rise of fascism, militarism and techno-

---

1   Benjamin highlights in thesis 8 the importance of the permanent 'state of emergency' of the oppressed and which has to be given primacy. In thesis 9 Benjamin indicts the storm of 'progress' and the dangers of catastrophe.

industrialism. He died just before gas chambers became the industrial tool of Nazi mass extermination. What Benjamin did not envisage or reckon with was the revenge of nature and Earth's response to the rupture of the climate system through ongoing use of coal, oil and gas. Covid-19, a biological disaster on a planetary scale pulled the brake on capitalism and brought the system temporarily to a grinding halt. The power and revenge of nature prevailed over everything. Capitalism's ecocidal logic, expressed through globalisation, more growth and even more extraction has encroached on all fragile ecosystems, unleashing the spread of zoonotic diseases. This contradiction is here to stay and worsen with climate change feedbacks and shocks. South Africa's corrupt ruling class had to feign concern and it came short. After three years of experiencing the Covid-19 pandemic, South Africa had 100,000 direct fatalities.

After escaping Covid-19 infection for over two years, it finally caught up with me in May 2022. Fortunately, I was vaccinated months earlier and without a vaccination I could certainly have been much worse. The first three days of my infection had all the symptoms of typical flu, but then my body descended into hell: widespread inflammation, burning sensations, uncontrolled shivers, paralysis in my hands and feet, and overwhelming fatigue. Covid-19 also exploited a weakness in my body. I lived with mild psoriasis for over 20 years; stressful living and activism exacerbated it. Covid-19 took my psoriasis into overdrive and I lost my skin twice. Doctors could not diagnose my condition. Opinions varied from vasculitis (an attack on my blood vessels), to an overactive immune system to just simply an unexplained Covid-19 infection. One of the specialists consulted reduced it to systemic psoriasis. I have had two more relapses since then and come to terms with Covid-19 induced damage to my immune system and debilitating inflammation. The care, fortitude and uncompromising love from my partner, Michelle Williams, was decisive for my recoveries. Her selflessness and dedication have made all the difference in these moments. However, a biophysical limit had arrived in my life; my frenetic academic and activist work ground to a halt. A small pathogen, a consequence of human attempts to dominate nature, had now pulled the brake on my life like many others afflicted with long Covid. This has been life changing. In their book *Inflamed: Deep Medicine and the Anatomy of Justice* Rupa Marya and Raj Patel situate this kind of micro-scale lived experience in a larger context by arguing that 'the inflammatory diseases we are seeing today are not the cause of the body's dysfunctional reactions. They are the body's correct responses to a pathological world' (2021: 13).

The steroids I was put on helped suppress my immune system for a short while, but did not solve the problem. Hence, I have looked to alternative medical practices and scientific traditions to cope with long Covid-19, not because these traditions are good and allopathic is bad; but rather because the complexity of my condition exposed the limitations of reductionist medical science. Moreover, allopathy actually does not know how to deal with the immune system as part of a mind/body relationship and through a holistic approach to healing. Thus, my journey to find holistic healing included a functional medicine doctor (who worked on root causes and mind/body therapies), a traditional healer (who advised that my body was carrying blockages because I worry too much about the state of the world) and Ayurveda.[2] The last is the oldest recorded holistic healing practice in the world. It is part of the civilisational history of India (poly-religious), which the British tried to erase (Shroff, 2000: 219–220). Fortunately, despite even Ayurvedic universities being shut down by British colonial authorities, this indigenous scientific tradition continued in the shadows of empire. You don't have to be religious to appreciate the value of Ayurveda. It approaches healing with an emphasis on prevention, homeostasis (balance) and holistic (mind/body/inner self and material) context. A crucial premise for Ayurveda is the idea that we are cosmological beings, integrally connected to and part of the web of life. We are made up of space, air, water, fire and earth, the material elements of life. When these elements are in a state of imbalance, in our biophysical selves, sickness takes root. Using its own classificatory system Ayurveda provides treatments for each individual's constitution. All treatments attempt to tackle illness internally and externally, support mind/body balance, and include herbal medication, massages, a strict diet (food is treated as medicine) and yoga,[3] among other practices.

Ayurveda has mitigated my health challenges and has helped me manage my damaged immune system.[4] It has prompted me to ask deeper questions about the crisis of allopathic healthcare systems; increasingly commodified, abstracting individuals from larger socio-ecological relations and tackling symptomatic conditions. With public healthcare underfunded, medical aids and private healthcare as dominant modes of health provisioning for those who can afford it, healthcare is in crisis; it is broken. The ANC government's

---

2 I have also been visiting a psychologist, for the first time in my life, to help me deal with the anxieties and rage I have about the worsening climate crisis. I struggle with the nightmare we are being pushed into by corrupt and mindless ruling classes.

3 Many of the yoga poses are based on observing the behaviour of animals.

4 Ayurveda is not available in the public healthcare system, nor does medical aid cover it. I have had to cover these costs out of pocket.

National Health Insurance scheme is going to make this worse. A crisis-ridden healthcare system also met the Covid-19 pandemic with tragic consequences for many. We need a new paradigm of public-based, ethical, holistic, preventative and integrative healthcare (bringing together allopathic and holistic indigenous scientific traditions). However, this is a battle that transformative social forces have to wage. Ayurveda has also thrown up a challenge for how I live with a damaged immune system: it requires me to slow down. Slow living can certainly be a subversive approach to a hyper-busy capitalist life world in which the noise of infotainment, the speed of the microchip, fast food culture, competitive productivism and the cult of 'now' is overcome. With my health constraints, I do not know how far I can go with my political commitments. Hence this volume, which documents 27 years of unbroken commitment to transformative praxis, is a contribution to the reconstruction of the South African left imaginary and ideological orientation in a context in which we face the extinction of human and most of non-human life because of an ecocidal capitalism.

A child of the South African national liberation struggle

I answered the door, with one of my aunts. It was a cold evening in 1980. There were two burly and menacing Afrikaner men at the door and there were blue lights everywhere. I had never seen such persons before in my neighbourhood or at our house door, in the Indian suburb of Pietermaritzburg. They demanded to know the whereabouts of my elder brother. We told them we did not know where he was. They said they had come to arrest him because he was organising school boycotts. My elder brother, together with another comrade of his, ended up in detention for 14 days without trial. I was enraged and fearful when they took him away. My family feared for his life given that many activists had been killed in detention in the late 1970s. As an eleven-year-old I did not understand apartheid and went to school, after my brother's arrest, and attempted my first school boycott. I gathered my friends together and explained my brother's arrest to them and that we needed to make a statement about this. We stood at the back end of the school ground after the school assembly. The school principal marched at us with his infamous cane in hand. This life-changing moment of defiance ended in tears for me and my parents coming to school. But through all of this the lyrics from Bob Marley's album *Survival* were an important reference and still are. My elder brother used to blast it in his car as he took me to school every morning.

After my short-lived school boycott my life changed. It wasn't the last time I would be involved with school boycotts, but my political formation took a decisive turn. I was drawn into the world of the Natal Indian Congress (NIC), an affiliate of the United Democratic Front (UDF), in Pietermaritzburg. It was my political home throughout the 1980s. It inducted me into the practice of mass grassroots organising, movement building and strategic politics: student, youth, community and civic. Developing pamphlets, painting banners, talking to workers in the early hours of the morning or in the evening in their homes and organising meetings all became part of my activist training. It was also where I learned the basics of how to chair a meeting, engage in debate, take minutes and write reports; I learned very quickly that a big part of struggle and resistance politics was being a professional meeting goer. Nonetheless, it was a wonderful training experience surrounded by politically mature adults, who kept us on a tight leash. There were a few books shared such as *Revolutionary Thought in the Twentieth Century* or *Selections from the Prison Notebooks* (by Antonio Gramsci) but in the main the activist intellectual milieu was largely oral. Looking back, several heuristic tools shaped my consciousness: storytelling about the history of the movement, sharing historical examples (Russian, Cuban and Nicaraguan revolutions) and long discussions. Robben Island, Mandela and the ANC in exile all became mythical.

Sometimes out of frustration I wondered why this movement was not more militant and audacious but also balanced this with a realisation of how powerful the apartheid regime was. There was a strong bolshevised Marxist influence in the activist milieu, due to the SACP underground presence in the NIC, with some embracing the Russian Revolution as the template for left politics. It was in this experience I developed an antipathy to those with a dogmatic adherence to Marxism-Leninism. The tension centred on methods and tactics of struggle and took me on a journey to affirm and elaborate a more ethical political subjectivity. This has been part of my praxis throughout my activist life. I was never convinced then nor now that ends justified means. When I went to university in 1988, despite a lot of the Marxist books being banned and in a special collection, I read whatever I could. One of the highlights of my young activist life and journey through the cauldron of mass politics in the 1980s was as one of the youngest members of the NIC-TIC (Transvaal Indian Congress) delegations that met the leadership of the ANC and SACP in the early 1990s to discuss the future of the Indian congresses. Many heavyweights such as Walter Sisulu, Pallo Jordan, Joe Slovo and others engaged. I listened and sat very quietly. Over the two meetings the one issue that was not clearly and compellingly resolved was the question of jumping a step from the mass UDF to the Tripartite Alliance.

Moreover, in discussions I held with a senior activist I was closest to in Pietermaritzburg there was another question that some of us wondered about: should the ANC revive the Congress movement (the white Congress of Democrats and Coloured People's Congress, together with the existing Indian congresses) as in the 1950s and let that institutional configuration lead the transition, anchored by the UDF. After all, the racialised geographies of apartheid necessitated separate organising and this developed into a strategic essentialism of black (African, coloured and Indian) solidarity together with anti-apartheid whites. These could be the building blocks for genuine and inclusive nation building. Despite high-level debate, these questions were not fully engaged nor entertained. Instead, the ANC-led Tripartite Alliance quickly became the institutional mould for providing political leadership in the transition. And before we knew it black and white solidarity was replaced with the language of minorities in the ANC's electoral rhetoric. The dangers of making nationalism red rather than nationalising socialism were beginning to show.

My immediate and extended communal family is where my political formation also deepened. A dear aunt of mine was a former trade unionist. As a strong feminist and committed activist, harassed by the security police in the 1970s, she ended up retreating into a small library in the Indian working-class community of Northdale in Pietermaritzburg. Here she made every effort to build a reading culture. Every week she brought books to our home. She exposed me to Franz Fanon, Paulo Freire, Ivan Illich and ecofeminists like Vandana Shiva. She loved Gabriel Garcia Marquez, Kahlil Gibran, Chinua Achebe, Bessie Head, Nadine Gordimer, Christopher Hope and many others. These also became some of my favourite writers.[5]

The other important political and ideological influence in my life was an uncle who was in the political military underground of the ANC and SACP (including being involved with an underground SACP printing press inside the country). He was trained in the Soviet Union and from the mid-1980s increasingly operated deep underground as part of Operation Vula (an attempt to build a military infrastructure in the country to take on the apartheid state). Despite all the risks, our families provided a support network for him, moving him around

---

5   In the post-apartheid period, whenever I visited my family home in Pietermaritzburg, she always reminded me of Fanon's warning about the pitfalls of national consciousness. Empirically it became hard to argue against as things started falling apart under ANC rule.

to different homes and keeping him safe. He was a constant guide in my political journey. He was always reading and we had long engaged conversations when we had time together. One day when we met, he was reading Merle Lipton's *Capitalism and Apartheid: South Africa 1910 to 1984*. I knew the book as a liberal political economy interpretation of South Africa that argued capitalism did not need apartheid. When I asked him what was valuable about it, he said, 'We have to understand how the other side thinks.' He was one of those mature adults who kept my militancy in check, exposed me to a wide body of literature and helped me understand why working among the people and workers was essential for us to overcome apartheid. These arguments and guidance also prevented me from joining the armed struggle in exile. Working organically and consistently among the people and workers is a political truth that has shaped my activist journey including in the post-apartheid period. These selected writings bear testimony to this premise for my ethical political praxis.

With my parents being teachers, early in their careers, and part of a progressive neo-Hindu movement, the Arya Samaj, they consciously brought their faith into resistance against apartheid. They actively supported the UDF and inter-faith dialogue to build solidarity bridges and opened their temples to the mass movement. My elder sister was extremely active in inter-faith dialogue work as part of organising faith communities to resist apartheid. The Arya Samaj supported women's emancipation, was anti-caste and believed in political freedom. Their founder in India, in the nineteenth century, was a freedom fighter and ardent anti-colonialist. For my parents and my maternal grandmother this meant stepping forward to resist apartheid. Both my mother and grandmother showed their bravery when we were engaged in a school boycott in the mid-1980s and they stood between us and the police. They actually prevented the police from baton charging us; while at another school the police brutally injured students.[6]

Following on the heels of the defeat of the apartheid military machine in Angola in 1988, mass resistance served as a powerful internal pincer to rock the apartheid power structure and ruling class. In that year I was also elected secretary of the Black Students Society at the University of Natal (Pietermaritzburg). It was the first time I was interacting with white students and professors. I always looked at them and wondered if they were superior

---

6 In 1988 while at university I also attempted to organise boycotts in schools. The police got wind of what I was doing and I was interrogated for a few hours at the Alexandra Road police station. I still recall how one of the police officers cocked a gun and pointed it at point blank range into my face to intimidate me.

to me but my political consciousness always mediated this dehumanisation of myself; my radical non-racialism affirmed in me that I was not inferior. I was a human being and had conscious agency to resist racism in me and and racist supremacy if it attempted to dehumanise me. As a result, I made enduring black and white friendships at the university. With the struggle boiling over, 1989 exploded with mass resistance. At my university we mobilised across races, gender and the division of labour. We held a mass protest with professors, workers and students. We blocked the entrance to our university, sitting peacefully in rows on the ground.[7] The police arrested all of us. This was anti-apartheid intersectional praxis alive in struggle decades before the American academy spewed out the idea of intersectionality. As resistance to unban the Mass Democratic Movement intensified in 1989 the bravery of the powerful women in my life, my grandmother and mother, was on full display during mass street demonstrations. As activists we all rallied but my grandmother, mother and father were among the leaders, leading the mass march in the city of Pietermaritzburg. This moment of mass power in the streets of many big cities in South Africa was part of a tenuous but courageous arc of resistance going back to and punctuated by the following: the resurgence of black trade unionism in the early 1970s, the 1976 Soweto uprising by schoolchildren and the mass resistance led by the UDF (1983–1984) to the tricameral parliament. These mass demonstrations of people's power contributed to making apartheid rule unworkable, despite its states of emergency, and propelled our democratic opening and transition. However, thousands on the streets in South Africa were part of similar democratic assertions of mass power in Germany (and other parts of eastern Europe) and Tiananmen Square.

In the larger context and layers of world history, 1989 was a bookend to 1968. It was the end of two decades of resistance, both in the heartlands of capitalism and in the peripheries. Its world historical significance expressed itself as a yearning for deep democracy at the barricades – as worker control, people's power, women's power, anti-imperialism, anti-war, anti-colonialism and anti-apartheid. Essentially, more democracy not less. My generation was shaped by this commitment to deep democracy. However, unbeknown to the crowds, a new wave of capitalist expansion was well underway to undercut all these subaltern world-making moments such that Soviet socialism crashed into

---

7   This kind of counter-hegemonic organising was very different from the crowd politics of #FeesMustFall and war waged against universities between 2014 and 2017. I failed academically in 1989, for the first time in my life, due to my activist commitments including addressing student financial exclusions.

Wild West American-style shock therapy capitalism rather than democratic socialism; while Chinese socialism through tank battalions continued its march towards globalised authoritarian state capitalism with Chinese characteristics. In South Africa the ANC-led Alliance would be the main harbinger of this capital-led expansionist process utilising self-inflicted economic adjustment to meet the needs of transnationalising monopoly capital rather than the needs of the people and working class.

Discovering radical love for the many

As Marx's Marxism teaches us, we are products of socialisation and history; in historical materialist terms we are made in the life worlds we inhabit. Nonetheless we are not hostages to class, race, gender and ecologically located consciousness. It is in struggle, as part of organising the resistance of the many, that we find the moral conception of ourselves and higher consciousness; the ethical practices that guide our actions. This has not been theorised by Marx because Marx was not a moral philosopher but he certainly had an ethics grounded in his humanist and ecological critique of capitalism.[8] In the ecohumanist Marx the biological human with essential needs, the human with potential for all rounded development, the human outside nature but dependent on nature, the human separated from the fruits of their labour, taken together the alienated human within capitalism, needed to be emancipated. These foundational ideas also formed the basis for more than a scientific critique of capitalism but also furnished the resources for a moral critique of unfreedom and an ethics of care, love and solidarity, to guide political praxis. Put differently, Marx's ethics of care, in my view, relates to a deep love for humanity and non-human life, the need for solidarity in resistance and the need for freedom to explore the all-round development of each one of us.

Che Guevara was echoing a version of Marx's ethics of care when he said, 'At the risk of seeming ridiculous, let me say that the true revolutionary is guided by a great feeling of love. It is impossible to think of a genuine revolutionary lacking this quality.'[9] Guevara speaks to a noble love, a love of the wretched of

---

8   In Marxist theory the search for ethics in Marx has related to debates about human nature, freedom and to some extent care labour related to Marxist feminism. A lot more has to happen in relation to Marx's ecology, care labour and ethics, an area I am deeply interested in. The dogmas of revolutionary Marxism brushed democracy and even ethics aside and never thought about these issues. See Geras (1983), Sayer (2003) and more recently Blackledge (2012).

9   This quote has been synonymous with the iconic version of Guevara and has travelled the world on posters, stickers and t-shirts and is now available on the internet.

the Earth, the exploited and the victims of capitalism. The altruism of this kind of love is akin to Marx's, but Guevara's is also about sacrificing for the many through paying the ultimate price. For Guevara this was vanguard love, while for Marx this was about a movement of the many, including in the *Communist Manifesto*. For Guevera the advanced, the conscious revolutionary, would work in small armed groups and intervene in history to catalyse the masses into action. This was called his *foco* theory of armed struggle. It did not work despite its moral foundation. Moreover, the archetypal twentieth-century revolutionary was capable of immense violence and harm. In the Soviet Bolshevik tradition all means justified the ends. The cause of vanguard socialism meant everything could be sacrificed to achieve these ends even if it meant famines, mass killings, gulags and even inflating the threat of mutual destruction through nuclear annihilation. I always had reservations about the twentieth-century version of revolutionary love. It had ethical and moral deficits which I could not reconcile with, but yet I did not believe in capitalism. Hence my activist and existential journey took me down a path that found a different grounding for radical love, inspired by Marx's ethics of care and more.

Love is central to life, human and non-human, but yet we never really pause to reflect on what it is. There are not many studies on love. It probably featured in the lives of the first humans, across civilisations, certainly exists among non-humans and has different forms and cultural conceptions. My embrace of radical love for the many, human and non-human, grew out of three important conditions. First, from my family and my cultural upbringing in a working-class community. Being part of a large communal family with many parents and cousins, an ethics of service to society (part of the neo-Hinduism I grew up with), and alternative culture that I was exposed to and searched for nurtured this ethics of care and love. Looking back, beyond books, it is clear that music, poetry and later visual cultural forms such as photography and cinema shaped this consciousness. One of my mother's brothers was a photographer. I used to enjoy spending time at his studio and watching him work in his darkroom. It was magical to watch people of different colours come to life in photos. This kind of everyday photography transgressed the racialised boundaries of apartheid. I also enjoyed cultural experiences that deepened my political consciousness. It started with a factory worker that lived down the road from my house. Every week he bought a vinyl LP (long playing record) and I was the privileged guest of one who had to sit absolutely silently and enjoy the music. It is in this experience that I learned about Motown, blues, jazz and reggae.

As I grew up in the 1980s, I learned more about the South African greats: Miriam Makeba, Dollar Brand, Hugh Masekela and many others. This was music outside the mainstream and which provided a counter to oppression. Similarly, I discovered Charlie Chaplin, particularly *The Tramp*, on 16mm during family movie get togethers and later the captivating poetry of Pablo Neruda and magical vignettes of Eduardo Galeano.

Love was different in this extended set of kinship relations compared to the nuclear family.[10] Every aunt or uncle was a parent figure and there was always a connection of care and feeling. Communal love transcended the gender division of labour; aunts always shared whatever was cooking on their stoves and working-class uncles shared every cent they could spare to bring us modest pleasures: sweets, movie tickets or a simple cool drink. Girls and boys gained from this communal love. Even discipline, when it was enforced, was for the collective benefit. In the end, these many parents socialised us into a love and affective bonds that gave us a refuge from a world of racial hatred. Communal love sowed the seeds of love for the many.

Second, Bollywood took love in a different direction. Growing up on a diet of romantic Indian films (with its morally choreographed love scenes and songs), I discovered love was about wholeness; two parts need to be joined to be complete. It had its roots deep in Indian philosophy in which feminine and male power were complementary. Bollywood also gave us a form of courtly love that Europe experienced in the Middle Ages (Ackerman, 1995: 56–60). There were moral limits, physical consummation was forbidden and even if secretive, marriage was the endgame. In secondary school, at the age of 16, I fell in love. This was Bollywood courtly love but in a South African context with all moral unboundedness. In my being this was idealised love; the object of love was perfect; almost godlike. It became mutually obsessive and the physics of this brought an inferno to my heart. The passion enraptured, scared and thrilled both of us. It took us to places we did not understand, emotional horizons beyond comprehension and a wild eroticism. This teenage love was clearly out of its depth. When this became known to our parents courtly moral love kicked in. Families met and our futures were being discussed. My dear librarian aunt took the moment to thrust Gabriel Garcia Marquez's *Love in the Time of Cholera* into

---

10 My father was the second eldest in a family of ten siblings. The two eldest died young and he and his elder sister played a pivotal role in their family. In addition, my father's side was closely intertwined with eight other cousins through marriage (two sisters, one being my father's mother, married two brothers, with one being my father's father). On my mother's side she was the second eldest among eight siblings.

my hands with the words: 'Don't end up like this.' She knew I was not caught in the grips of a Cleopatra-like siren or being manipulated. This was about me not losing myself in passionate love that would steer my life in a direction of regret. She appreciated I was young and needed to overcome this idealised love. My first love and I did overcome and it was painful. I learned that my heart loved love but I needed to ensure its raw dangers did not destroy me.

At university, the library was an interesting place. Among all the books including the Marxist ones (not on the banned list), I crossed paths with another which got my heart racing again. This time it was gladiatorial in the sense that it was me, the woman and her parents. The beautiful being with whom I bonded was upper middle class and I was considered unacceptable to the parents. I was politically too radical – a Marxist – and was considered unsuitable. Even studying to be a lawyer was deemed insufficient; in their words, 'he will be an ambulance chaser.' This was class prejudice and the height of bourgeois love. The one I loved was deemed a commodity by her parents and I was clearly not worthy of delivering on the price. In its conceit it also othered me; I was a political freak, a Frankenstein as in Mary Shelley's classic. This got me self-doubting and as I loved and gave, it was like a knife going deeper and deeper. When the parents rendered it unworkable and my heart broke, I took my passion deeper into the struggle. If I was going to be an outsider, a Marxist and Communist freak, so be it. If I was going to find a partner, it had to be someone who loved me for who I was; not someone that thought in the words of musician Rodriguez, from his 1973 album *Cold Fact*, 'Cos I was born for the purpose that crucifies your mind.' I also understood from this experience that my political commitments and my Marxist ideological disposition made me an outsider; I was on a political path that meant I had to live between class structures and worlds. For a young person this was difficult but for many years these experiences helped mature my love of love, but as part of a larger struggle in which love had a deeper meaning.

As a politically conscious human being and deeply committed, I knew I could give love to the many and not be considered a freak. Actually, the living praxis of non-racialism was about love; this is what Chris Hani called for in terms of a new breed of South Africans grounded in love. This meant finding an affective, intellectual and political connection to the oppressed in the course of struggle and more generally all with whom we co-existed. This was about a love based on a genuine inter-subjective connection that transcended skin colour, ethnicity, genders and I would stretch it further to include other species. A country of hate could only endure if its opposite did not triumph.

Third, the embrace of a tangible working-class and more generally subaltern humanism; a radical humanism, influenced my love of the many. This was largely shaped by Marx's ethics of care as I became a Marxist at the age of 15. The late nineteenth century and the greater part of the twentieth century was marked by this radical humanism. It was shaped by workers' parties, trade unions, social democratic parties, communist parties, socialist parties, national liberation movements, anti-imperial movements and the great revolutions of the twentieth century. The subaltern universals in these movements affirmed collective class solidarity, anti-racism, women's power and internationalism. Some of these movements went further than others and made important historical gains. The South African struggle did not escape this and neither did I. Radical humanism placed the anti-apartheid struggle on anti-capitalist ground to the extent that it appreciated that apartheid and its colonial antecedents were integrally connected to the dehumanisation and forms of alienation engendered by capitalism. To emancipate the many, capitalism had to be transformed in South Africa; not deracialised to have a few black Oppenheimers (or Stellenbosch billionaires) and monopoly capitalists. On this journey, carried by the tides and currents of history, I also met my partner Michelle as I was leading (2001–2007) the SACP in Gauteng province. I was not a radical freak to her and she was not a white American woman to me. Our shared radical ecohumanism, engaged intellectual conversations into early hours of the morning, and commitment to left renewal forged a partnership of equals for many wonderful years now. This adventure of authentic love and mutual care gave me the necessary anchor to go further with the love for the many.

Against the grain of defeat: Transformative intellectual praxis and left renewal

In my engagement with and reading of Marx, the notion of praxis connects and runs through everything.[11] It is about the interconnection of theory and practice, guided by an ethics of care; a use value to realise the de-alienation of human life in its relationship with non-human life. Put differently, the notion of praxis is at the core of Marxist politics seeking to be part of mass collective consciousness and resistance. It is deeply embedded in Marx's philosophical dialectic, his theory of history (historical materialism) and his humanist and

---

11 Other readings of Marx, particularly with an academic bent de-emphasise this.

ecological critique of capitalism. To overcome exploitation and oppression, mass resistance practice is imperative for world and history making. Hence the itinerary of Marxism ended up in setbacks, failures, crises and dead ends over a period of more than 150 years.[12] However, a praxis-centred Marxism did provide intellectual scaffolding for the three main left projects that defined the twentieth century: Soviet socialism (and its satellites); social democracy; and revolutionary nationalism (Amin, 1994). These projects shaped four generations in the world, including in South Africa, and gave them an orientation towards mass organising, movement building and strategic politics.

As a young person, getting politicised in the 1980s in South Africa, exposed me to this mass praxis; it politically schooled the last anti-apartheid generation. However, this was overshadowed by the world historical defeat of Soviet socialism, social democracy and revolutionary nationalism. This was largely due to internal contradictions and weaknesses, but also the onslaught of imperialism. This was amplified through the neoliberal class project (1980 until the present) which remade the world in the image of American capitalism. A degenerate Soviet socialism easily succumbed to full-blown neoliberal adjustment, social democracy through third-way politics was co-opted, and revolutionary nationalism, locked into debt, abandoned the project of sovereignty for deep globalisation. South Africa's democratic opening was being realised in this context. However, South Africa compared to most places in the world had the conditions to navigate neoliberalisation differently at the end of the 1980s. It had a mass resistance movement (the UDF, ANC, SACP and COSATU), international anti-apartheid solidarity, legitimate expectations from the many to address the legacies of apartheid, a consensus across society to do so, a divided white monopoly capitalist class and an incredible pool of national talent to ensure the state and economy had capacity.

In the long Cold War, from 1917 to 1993, many left breakthroughs faced invasions, internal destabilisation, coups, mass killings, assassinations, torture and isolation. In places like Germany (1918), Latin America (after coups and military dictatorships such as the toppling of Arbenz in Guatemala in 1954 or Allende in Chile in 1973), Indonesia (1965–1966) and Iran (1979), the left was physically annihilated. During the short Cold War (after World War 2) more than ten million people lost their lives and there has been no reckoning with the role of Euro-American violence in this brutal suppression. Most historians claim the Cold War ended with the dissolution of the Soviet Union in 1991.

---

12 See Therborn's (2008 [2018]) mapping of the twentieth century as the 'century of Marxism'.

Actually, the end of the Cold War in Africa happened on 10 April 1993, with the callous and cowardly assassination of Chris Hani. This was the world historical significance of Chris Hani's assassination; it drew the curtain on a global fault line that haunted the twentieth century. Moreover, domestically the implications of Hani's assassination became clear over time, in key post-apartheid conjunctures. His assassination inaugurated the neutralisation of the national liberation movement left. While the process of dealing with the national liberation left did not go the route of physical annihilation, it certainly, from within the ANC-led Alliance, led to the evisceration of transformative potentials and possibilities.[13] How the SACP and COSATU were turned into instruments for the shallow deracialisation and deep globalisation of post-apartheid South Africa is central to these writings, as an insider for over a decade. The writings in these pages seek to explain how the much-vaunted NDR became a fraud and how instead of being emancipatory became a passive revolution for the benefit of a criminalised and greedy few. The unravelling of working class-led national liberation hegemony in the context of conjunctural shifts is dissected to reveal its deeper relational dynamics. The test of South Africa's democratic transition proved the existence of a garden variety of ANC-centred nationalism that took the path of least resistance, lost its nerve for leading fundamental transformation, and became corrupt.[14]

As a Marxist from age 15 and with the influence of the SACP underground in my own political formation, joining the SACP after its unbanning was an obvious thing to do. However, I consciously chose not to join the SACP immediately after its unbanning, although I made an SACP and ANC banner after the unbannings were announced in 1990, and waved it from our cavalcade of cars as we drove through the streets of Pietermaritzburg. With the collapse of the Soviet Union and with a strong commitment to a democratic socialist politics, I watched the SACP closely for the first few years after its unbanning and tracked its internal debates, mapping the key intellectual interventions made in response to Joe Slovo's 'Has Socialism Failed'. I was disturbed by the likes of Harry Gwala and Blade Nzimande, who were defending an unreconstructed Marxism-Leninism.[15] Nonetheless, more than the academic, labour and even

---

13 Praxis-centred Marxist theory appreciates that collective class and popular power has to be built and institutionalised to make history, keeping open potentials and possibilities. Even this basic function of the national liberation movement was lost in post-apartheid South Africa. Today corrupt factions dominate the inner worlds of the ANC-led Alliance.

14 Ebrahim Harvey (2021) in his hard-hitting critique of the ANC refers to the 'Great Pretenders'.

15 Both Gwala and Nzimande came from my home town, Pietermaritzburg. I considered them to be warlords as we lived through the Seven Day War in KwaZulu-Natal in March 1990 which

independent left, the SACP was attempting to re-find its ideological vision after the wreckage and disaster of the Soviet Union. There was an opportunity, given its Marxist epistemology, to learn lessons from the historical failures of the Soviet Union and renew a new horizon for a socialism within South African conditions, rethink its Marxism beyond the dogmas of Marxism-Leninism, and elaborate an innovative programmatic response to transform post-apartheid South Africa. In addition, the SACP was a pioneer of non-racial politics and had as legitimate a claim on the historical inheritance of national liberation politics as the ANC. Instead of being swept up in the euphoria, I wanted to confirm that I could dedicate my life to a SACP firmly committed to left renewal; as a child of the national liberation struggle, I wanted to be like Ruth First, Yusuf Dadoo, Bram Fischer and of course Chris Hani. Hani's assassination clinched my commitment to the SACP and I joined its ranks soon after.[16] Existentially, it meant going against the grain of defeat but anchoring praxis in the potentials and historical possibilities of left renewal underway inside the SACP. Hence by 1995, instead of choosing to become a labour lawyer in Cape Town after completing my course work for my Masters in Labour Law, I chose to work for COSATU's think tank, the National Labour and Economic Development Institute (NALEDI), on labour market reform. This positioned me at the heart of COSATU as well as the SACP. Once in COSATU House I consciously sought out the SACP head office, which was in the same building, and I committed to supporting national political education.[17] This was an exciting time in my young adult life particularly being in Johannesburg, providing technical support to dismantle one of the most racialised and gendered labour markets in the world while also living my political commitments.

My journey of transformative intellectual praxis and left renewal commenced in the SACP but did not end there. With the world historical defeats endured by the twentieth-century left, there was global introspection going on among the left. Hence while doing national political education in the SACP, together with a dear comrade (who was the national political education officer), we travelled to

---

took the lives of many including young people. I was helping build the ANC Youth League and lost a comrade who was shot, according to witness accounts, at point blank range in Richmond. Many of us coming out of KwaZulu-Natal live with these traumas.

16 I was so moved by Hani's assassination I ensured I got to Johannesburg for his funeral. I stayed with comrades in one of the East Rand townships. This was my first visit to the big city of Johannesburg.

17 I also wasted no time in buying a full set of the *African Communist*. If I was going to make a lifelong commitment to the SACP, I wanted to understand its ideological history. Some of it is very revealing in how it also policed and perceived other currents of national liberation politics.

several countries (December 1999–January 2000) to have a dialogue with leading left intellectuals and leaders about the future of the left. We visited Brazil, the US, Japan, India, Russia, Sweden, Germany, Italy and the UK. The book *New Frontiers for Socialism: Conversations on a Global Journey* was only published a decade later after I was breaking with the SACP. I was expelled in 2009 from the SACP for my final reflections in that volume, entitled: 'Reflections: The age of barbarism' and which is included in this selection.[18] We did not publish the *New Frontiers* book on our return because Blade Nzimande became the general secretary of the SACP in 1998 and one of his first acts of reversing the project of socialist renewal was firing the head of political education in the SACP; the dear comrade I travelled with to different countries.[19]

Nonetheless the battle to ensure democratic socialist and left renewal continued inside the SACP when I became the Gauteng secretary of the SACP (2001–2007). Gauteng is the industrial heartland of South Africa, with 50% of COSATU's membership. We were not going to let the SACP get straightjacketed into dogma, so attempted from below to elaborate the notion of 'Our Marxism', shape the democratic socialist programmatic horizons of the SACP, and deepen praxis around the strategic slogan: 'Socialism is the future, build it now!' The import of this slogan was such that it took us beyond two-stage national liberation revolutionary dogma; it also challenged social democracy which merely wanted to manage capitalism, including its globalising neoliberal variant; and dogmatic Marxist-Leninist (even Trotskyist) ruptural positions of revolution, in which the next society only starts being built when the old order is swept away. The strategic orientation of the SACP was novel and provided warrant for a transformative political orientation to work interstitially; in the nooks and crannies, outside and within contradictions of post-apartheid capitalism. My transformative intellectual praxis in the SACP tested this thesis to its limits but even beyond, as I exited the snake pit of a Zumafied SACP and ANC-led Alliance, and further deepened my connections with the global cycles

---

18 Mazibuko Jara, a Young Communist League leader, was also expelled for a document he wrote against Zumafication. His document was entitled: 'What colour is our flag? Is it red or JZ?.'

19 Before Nzimande became general secretary I was invited to a meeting to discuss his ascendancy. He, a leading trade unionist, another senior woman party leader and the national political education officer of the SACP were present. I was very clear in that meeting that he was not my preferred candidate and rather argued for a younger person, given that we had a young population in the country. I wanted the national political education officer of the SACP to be the next leader. What I did not verbalise was my concerns about his unreconstructed Marxism-Leninism and my fears of a re-Stalinisation of the SACP. Of course this is what happened under Nzimande's leadership as he made himself the indispensable leader for almost two decades. His generation and Thabo Mbeki's generation has failed the many.

of resistance to neoliberalisation.[20] In this ferment from the Caracazo (1989) in Venezuela to anti-WTO, IMF and World Bank protests, to the pink tide in Latin America (from 1998) to Occupy Wall Street (2011) to #StandingRock (2016) a new transformative left praxis was in the making.[21] It has a longer history, over the past 500 years, going back to indigenous peoples resisting ecocide; slave rebellions, the Haitian Revolution and building of runaway slave communities; peasants resisting enclosures in the global North and South; workers taking over factories and setting up co-operatives in the nineteenth century; workers and soldiers building soviets during the Russian Revolution; and anti-colonial and anti-imperial movements.

In the resistance to neoliberalisation, the frontiers of transformative politics expanded geographically in the imaginary of the new global left and institutionally; from the party-movement form of the Workers Party in Brazil, to the network of movements-of-movements of the World Social Forum (WSF), to horizontalism in recovered factories in Argentina, to La Via Campesina and food sovereignty alliances, participatory democracy in peoples budgeting in Kerala, India, climate justice forces and more. A new transformative global left strategic politics grew, incubated and evolved for about four decades in resistance to the dogmas of neoliberalisation. It certainly had its ebbs and flows, ups and downs, but it clearly contributed to remaking the left. For me this meant translating, adding to and amplifying the recasting of left politics in the South African context practically in relation to worker control, participatory township development, co-operative development work, solidarity economy network building, food sovereignty campaigning and climate justice campaigning.[22] Transformative strategic politics is an alternative to the reform versus revolution binary of the twentieth century left. Both these strategies have proven to be inadequate to

---

20 I attended two WSF meetings, published two edited collections on the solidarity economy (the first volume included leading thinkers from Brazil, UK and Italy), engaged numerous food sovereignty forces on the African continent through the South African Food Sovereignty Campaign, provided a platform for dialogue between Marxist and broader anti-capitalist forces in the world through the Democratic Marxism series I edit and through my Emancipatory Futures Studies project, and deepened global solidarity links with leading climate justice forces in the world through the Climate Justice Charter process. I also attended two UN-COP meetings over the years and cemented links with key climate justice activists.

21 As the cycles of global resistance unfolded, I have had engaged dialogues with some of the leading left thinkers who have been part of the making of the new global left: Samir Amin, Hilary Wainwright, Marta Harnecker and Michael Lebowitz among others.

22 See annexure in this volume for activist tools developed for over two decades to ground transformative politics in everyday resistance.

go beyond capitalism and create emancipated societies.

Reform approaches are associated with the social democratic experience. Key enabling conditions gave rise to this form of reformism: strong labour movements, the geopolitics of the Cold War particularly the importance of redistributive reforms to stave off the spectre of revolution, and class compromises with nationally bounded big capital. These conditions no longer exist. In the neoliberal context social democratic reform politics has been undermining the conditions of its own existence: dis-embedding capital from national regulation, contributing to the precariatisation of the working class and dismantling parts of the welfare state, exacerbating social reproduction challenges for many. Many Western countries, once vaunted as shining examples of social democracies, are now revealing the coloniality and exclusionary nationalism at the foundation of the welfare states constructed, as migrants and refugees are kept out or treated badly. These conditions have also given birth to a new extreme right and in some Western countries, for the first time since World War 2 neo-fascists are in power or are sitting in national parliaments. Crucially though social democratic reform has failed to utilise capitalist crisis against capital. In other words, to survive the worsening poly-crisis, and specifically the climate crisis, the dogmatic mould of top-down gradualism and evolutionary pragmatism central to social democratic politics is not up to the task of accelerating the deep, just transition.

Revolution as strategy is associated with the 1917 October Russian Revolution, the first attempted worker revolution. It is about smashing the capitalist state (even if it is a long drawn-out process and not an event) to transform its social relations and transfer power to the working class. It requires a general crisis of capitalism and in the case of Russia the conflagration of World War 1, a vanguard party of elite revolutionaries, mass discontent and a divided ruling class. The main modes of politics produced are: a class alliance, an authoritarian grip on power by a vanguard party, planning mechanisms and a militarised state bureaucracy. Coercion, its calibration and deployment, is the crux to determine the trajectory and policy choices of society. This model was exported and universalised as a template for successful revolution. In the end, the Soviet Union, China and Vietnam have not produced transitions to socialism, but transitions back to capitalism. Cuba is struggling to survive with its geographic contiguity to the US, China with its current rivalries with the US-led bloc faces constraints on its super exploitation, export-led and coercion-centred accumulation process.

Transformative left politics is about overcoming the dogmas of the twentieth century left. These dogmas are religious, in the sense that they are based on faith, fossilised thinking and incapable of thinking through a politics relevant to the challenges and realities of our time. In simple terms, such capsuled thinking would argue, in a doctrinaire way Lenin led a successful revolution therefore I want to follow Lenin's way and formulas. In other words, they work with a transhistorical conception of the political and hence under all circumstances the Leninist mode of politics is appropriate. Transformative strategic politics is self-reflexive about the strategic pitfalls of these modes of politics and thus learning hard lessons about the limits of reformism and revolutionary modes of politics, examining the nature of contemporary capitalist crisis, being self-reflexive about agency, elaborating a new power paradigm, utilising utopia as collective emancipatory method, rethinking political forms (including the political instrument), innovating on the accumulation of capacities (even rethinking forms of knowledge), developing new approaches to aggregating mass power (anti-capitalist intersectionality), and clarifying the modalities of democratic ecosocialist transition. In summary, the renewal of left politics as transformative strategic politics, as elaborated in these praxis-centred writings and its arguments, is about ensuring a decolonial-Marxist-ecofeminism in dialogue with frontline anti-capitalisms, explains our material conditions, provides generative alternatives to the destruction of our planetary life world by an ecocidal capitalism, and affirms a praxis of struggle-driven democratic systemic reforms.

Such democratic systemic reforms address key limitations of reformist and revolutionary politics. Reforms can be reversed, neutralised or constrained in the implementation process and this has been demonstrated in the history of social democracy and its current crisis. Democratic systemic reforms are driven through struggle by peoples and workers; their making begins from below, and therefore class and popular power will determine whether such reform is weak, strong or truly transformative such that social relations and power dynamics change to lock these reforms in. Revolutionary politics, with its elitist top-down rationality, does not prepare society for its grand scale changes; its big leaps and millenarian ambitions solicit counter-revolution and engender chaos. On the other hand, democratic systemic reforms are based on utilising all forms of democratic practice and logics of democratisation to build consent in society for systemic transformation (particularly complex socio-ecological systems) to accelerate the deep, just transition. It is informing, preparing, prefigurative, guided by and affirming of democratic societal consensus. Societal limits rather than vanguard limits are crucial. Democratic systemic reforms position transformative politics to the left of social democratic reformism and add to Antonio Gramsci's notion of hegemony/counter-hegemony in ways that he also did not imagine.[23] To arrive at these conclusions two axes of transformative intellectual engagement enabled this journey: (i) resisting revolutionary orthodoxy (revolutionary nationalist, Marxist-Leninist and Trotskyist), neoliberal dogma (including co-opted third way social democracy and an indigenised Afro-neoliberalism) and emergent neofascism in the slip stream of everyday struggle; and (ii) anchoring left renewal in the making of transformative politics. This is elaborated on further below.

Resisting revolutionary orthodoxy, neoliberal dogma and emergent neofascism

Tom Lodge in his history of the SACP (2021) does not explore the socialist renewal debates and praxis inside the SACP nor its inability to dislodge the Afro-neoliberal trajectory of the ANC government.[24] The last chapter of his book deals superficially with the SACP in the post-apartheid period and provides a thin political sociology analysis (not even class analysis), betraying his own normative desire for a social democratic mutation in the SACP. The process of rethinking socialism inaugurated by Joe Slovo's 'Has socialism failed?' was a bold first step to question the primacy of the Russian Revolution in the national liberation left imagination and its problems. However, Slovo's intervention occluded and failed to confront the SACP's own bolshevised praxis and the national liberation orthodoxies it engendered. Besides the orthodoxy of the NDR and which was subverted from within the ANC-led Alliance (what I analyse as a passive revolution in these writings) because of an over-determining and dangerous place given to ANC nationalism and leadership, Slovo did not question dual membership, the state centrism of the national liberation imagination and the productivist mould of the SACP's Marxism-Leninism. Put differently, he underestimated the authoritarian and anti-ecological mould of the

---

23 This claim is not based on a Leninist reading of Gramsci.

24 Williams (2008) provides a more rigorous analysis. She identifies three ideological orientations (grassroots tendency, trade union tendency and statist tendency) shaping the SACP in the post-apartheid period and theorises the potentials of counter-hegemonic generative politics. I was in the grassroots tendency.

SACP's Marxism-Leninism and its impact on national liberation politics.

While Slovo was triumphalist in the early days of South Africa's transition about how the country avoided a Yugoslavia scenario of balkanisation and civil war, he assumed that dual membership, with communists as members of the ANC, was a guarantee of SACP influence on the ANC, on the terrain of state power. Many in the SACP I worked with also vaunted this golden link. In practice, it proved to be a disaster in two respects. First, as ANC dominance kicked in and its electoral machine practices subordinated its allies, the SACP became factionalised; those co-opted by the ANC into the state had their own material interests and agendas in the SACP and COSATU. While doing national political education in the SACP and as Gauteng secretary of the SACP, in the early 2000s I came to realise that dual membership was a threat to the independence of the SACP and its programmatic commitments; it was unworkable. Communists behaved more nationalist than nationalists in the ANC to prove their loyalty to a degenerating ANC inside the SACP. Moreover, it became a potent danger with the rise of Zumafication (an ethno-nationalist, authoritarian and criminalised class project). Zumafication and its consequences belie this criticism of 'dual membership'. Essentially, the Zumafication of national liberation politics, in which Nzimande's leadership of the SACP was a crucial factor, inaugurated the criminalised hollowing out of the constitutional democratic state. The July 2021 violence fomented by Zuma allies, mainly in KwaZulu-Natal, came close to Slovo's Yugoslavia scenario.[25] Inside the SACP I made every effort to argue for a different way forward for the SACP to deepen socialist renewal rather than support Zumafication. In these writings I also make the case for the SACP to consider electoral contestation, as part of mass politics.[26] The state power debate and option was the alternative to Zumafication but was spiked by the SACP leadership at a 2005 State Power Conference in Durban.[27] The SACP could have chosen to mature South Africa's democracy by opting for a strategic electoral option, including to regain lost ground for the working class

---

25 I was invited to be part of a panel to respond to President Cyril Ramaphosa's Nelson Mandela Day address after the July 2021 violence. My input and my speaking notes are published here and posed from a place of deep-seated anger at the ANC: when did it lose its non-racialism?

26 I wrote two documents for the theoretical magazine of the SACP, the *African Communist*. In one of these arguments, I openly argue against a central committee document.

27 The Gauteng province I was leading had a vibrant debate on state power and we wanted this option to come to the fore at the 2005 conference. While I did not believe in a full-blown maximalist break with the ANC, I did believe that a well-calibrated electoral option was necessary and feasible. However, before the conference could start, a special convening of the central committee took place. I was warned and told not to table any electoral contestation resolution at the conference. I knew then the SACP was no longer about the unemployed and workers who supported it. Moreover, there was no space for strategic debate.

given the impacts of Afro-neoliberalism. Hence after the 2005 Durban State Power Conference, and after several attacks in the central committee of the SACP, including crude racialisation of my minority status and a reminder that I was not African, I broke with the SACP; it was committing political suicide through its opportunism and as it threw its weight behind the dubious messiah of the working class, Jacob Zuma. This had serious dangers for South Africa.[28] Dual membership conscripted the SACP to the worst of African nationalism. However, this degenerate shift by the SACP did not stop me from continuing to resist Zumafication outside the SACP. Several key moments, captured in these writings, speak to this resistance: speaking out against the Marikana massacre of mineworkers; the Vukani-Sidikiwe campaign formed with Ronnie Kasrils, Louise Colvin and Nozizwe Madladla-Routledge and others during the 2014 elections (which earned a declaration by the Zuma Cabinet that we were all treasonous); organising an encampment outside the Treasury; and supporting a mass march to the Union Buildings in April 2017 to demand #ZumaMustGo and during #FeesMustFall when the Economic Freedom Fighters (EFF) instigated violence and war on our universities that threatened to destroy them. The EFF is a product of Zumafication and like the extreme white right portends the making of a neo-fascist politics as part of the shift to authoritarian neoliberalism in many countries. Many on the left misrecognise the EFF and what it represents.

Second, Slovo's Yugoslavia scenario for South Africa has also been given material grounding with the transition to a market democracy in which a few gain while the many live under conditions of marketised neo-apartheid. The growth of the African middle class (about six million) has been based on the highest income inequality and structural unemployment rates in the world.[29] This has been constructed through ANC government policy choices to ensure deep globalisation. Dual membership did not stop the great leap into Afro-neoliberalism and the undermining of South Africa's constitutional

---

28 I have wondered over the years if Hani, Ruth First, Bram Fischer or Yusuf Dadoo were sitting in the SACP central committee how they would have reacted to these racist attacks. It's in this context I also decided to publish *New Frontiers for Socialism* and openly attacked the opportunism of the SACP in my final reflections. I was expelled in 2009 for these, although politically I disengaged from a serious commitment to the SACP after the 2005 State Power Conference. I remember the sadness of the SACP comrade who came to deliver my expulsion notice. I was clear that the SACP was being led by African nationalists and not communists. Anyway, for me, the dialectic of transformative praxis was immature in the muddled and opportunistic leadership of the SACP. I needed to move on.

29 In many parts of the world such as India, Brazil and the US, for instance, such consumerist middle classes have not been the bulwarks of democracy but have actually supported the rise of extreme right-wing, even neo-fascist, political forces.

democracy through the constitutionalising of a market democracy in which credit rating agencies, the World Bank, IMF, WTO, foreign direct investors and the business press have more power than the voting public. Such a country is deeply polarised, tenuous and not viable. The dogmas of neoliberalism and its market-centred reason were confronted head on by those committed to socialist renewal inside the SACP. In the first left critique of the Growth, Employment and Redistribution (GEAR) macro-economic strategy adopted in 1996 by the ANC government, which we wrote as part of the national political education secretariat of the SACP, we make the point that GEAR would lead to the de-industrialisation of South Africa; it was not an accumulation strategy appropriate for the country.[30] A selective and biased reading of economic history was underpinning this strategy: market-based export led industrial development guided by market competition; neoliberal economic dogma. The conjunctural transformation of the post-apartheid state according to Afro-neoliberal strictures remade the forms, functions, capacities and relationality of the state. Even the declaratory developmental state discourse of the early 2000s was too late to stop the actual transnationalising of the state. Understanding how the post-apartheid accumulation model, state and constitutional democracy has been squeezed and captured by the global power structure, markets and capital is a central preoccupation of some of these political economy/ecology writings. Neoliberal and homegrown Afro-neoliberal dogma has been detrimental to the strengthening of post-apartheid constitutional democracy and in these writings, there is a consistent attempt to critique shallow and exclusionary market democracy and keep alive a deep democracy imaginary, inside and beyond the SACP.

State centricism is a central dogma of both the national liberation left and the Trotskyist left in South Africa.[31] While the Freedom Charter calls for the people to govern, it is shot through with prescriptions to ensure state control of the commanding heights of the economy. In Slovo's critique of the democratic deficits in state centric Soviet socialism he failed to challenge state

---

30 This critique of GEAR is published in this volume. Jeremy Cronin refused to publish it in the *African Communist* and hence we published it in the first issue of *Debate*. Moreover, by 1998 as the SACP leadership came around to appreciate aspects of this critique, the ANC unleashed Mandela to give us a dressing down at the 1998 congress. I loved Madiba but I remember sitting at the congress listening to him and feeling deep revulsion. He and the ANC were wrong about GEAR.

31 The Trotskyist left has made important contributions to left thinking in South Africa about racial capitalism and Marxist historiography. However, it has not rethought its classical revolution approach and therefore its practical presence in struggles is minimal and entryist.

centricism or nationalisation dogma in the South African context. This is not about rejecting a strategic role for the state, but recognising that the democratic ecosocialist transition does require democratising logics from below to be determining and not top-down state control. Moreover, emancipatory and democratic ecosocialist property relations cannot be reduced merely to state property. The commons, co-operatives, democratic public utilities and self-management are all forms of socialised property relations that deepen a democratic ecosocialist logic.

Failure to unhinge the spectre of nationalisation has meant that the SACP and the ANC have looked to Chinese state dirigisme as a new source of inspiration. This lazy state-model thinking fails to recognise that Chinese authoritarian state capitalism is shaped by very specific historical conditions and dynamics; and thus it is not reproducible.[32] Moreover, China is not about democratic socialism. Its cheap labour industrialisation was premised on the precariatisation of the global working class; it actually contributed significantly to the global crisis of socio-ecological production inflicted on workers of the world. After the SACP, I made every effort to find convergence with the left outside the national liberation movement. However, they clearly did not understand the process of socialist renewal that inspired and shaped some of us. There was a lot of distrust given that the SACP was perceived as a Stalinist organisation.[33] Nonetheless, an attempt was made to build convergence through the Democratic Left Front (DLF) which was meant to deepen analysis of the crisis of national liberation politics and society, elaborate alternatives and build solidarities in struggle.[34] South Africa's leading Trotskyist intellectuals came into this process. However, a state-centric imagination loomed large among these unreconstructed Trotskyists. When the tragic Marikana massacre happened, they wanted to call for the nationalisation of the mines rather than support the demands of the rock drill operators for R12 500. When the EFF came on the scene, they were also enamoured by nationalisation rhetoric. The dogmas of some of South Africa's left are twentieth century dogmas,

---

32 In 2008, when I was director of the Co-operative and Policy Alternative Centre, we convened a workshop with leading developmental state scholars to rethink the notion of the developmental state from a deep democracy perspective. The arguments made by leading China scholar Chin Kwan Lee (2014) need to be heeded about why China as a model is not reproducible. China is the product of class struggles from below, centre-state fiscal relations and the monopoly of power held by the Chinese Communist Party. The latter has some of the wealthiest in its leadership ranks.

33 Such a perception obviated the need to be self-critical of the authoritarianism of revolutionary Trotskyism.

34 My journey to co-found the DLF started in 2007 but ended in 2012.

frozen in time: left politics begins and ends with the Soviet Union. It is stuck in an instrumentalist paradigm of state power rather than embracing a transformative paradigm of power.

Slovo's 'Has socialism failed?' did not deal with the ecological problems with Soviet socialism. When I decided to actively commit to the SACP, I was already shaped by the lived experience of human ecology, particularly communal family food production and food culture that I grew up with, and the ecological thought of Gandhi, Andre Gorz, Ivan Illich and Vandana Shiva.[35] It is from this perspective I developed an aversion to militarism and wrote against the infamous arms deal and US militarism. At the same time, as we were thinking through the renewal of socialism, including on the international trip (in late 1999) to meet leading left intellectuals, parties and movements, the ecological dimension of capitalism and crisis was something we probed. My embrace of environmental justice politics including serving on the board of the Greenhouse project in Joubert Park (around the mid-1990s) and working with the Ecocity project in Ivory Park township (from 1999 to 2012) deepened my ecological perspective. However, bringing this into the SACP, after Blade Nzimande became general secretary in 1998, was a challenge given his unreconstructed Marxism-Leninism. Nonetheless as soon as I became Gauteng secretary of the SACP (2001) there were three key focus areas to start elaborating an ecological dimension to 'Our Marxism': a public transport campaign in response to the elitist Gautrain,[36] a focus on food systems, and participatory sustainable local economic development.[37] However, all these efforts did not culminate in an effective critique of productivist Marxism and capitalist thought and a democratic ecosocialist orientation in the SACP. This line of transformative thought was developed after the SACP and is related to the Democratic Marxism series, solidarity economy, food sovereignty, climate justice and my Emancipatory Futures Studies project. The elaboration of democratic ecosocialism as a political project is central to the renewal of left

---

35 On my paternal side my grandmother was a garden farmer and she pushed a cart to sell vegetables. My grandfather on my maternal side believed in self-reliance. He had a food garden and fruit trees at their home.

36 We had a million signatures campaign. Within a few months after engaging commuters and building an alliance of environmental organisations, trade unions and commuter organisations we had about 250,000 signatures. The central committee misdirected this campaign to the national Minister of Transport for its Red October campaign and thus ended the campaign. South Africa and Gauteng still do not have an effective, affordable, clean energy and inter-modal public transport system.

37 These ideas were presented to a Gauteng SACP Conference on Socialism and Sustainable Local Economic Development, 20 July 2003 at Wits University.

transformative politics but this again has meant praxis centred intellectual elaboration. I turn to that below.

Towards left renewal through transformative politics

Working at COSATU's think tank NALEDI (1995–1999) gave me an incredible vantage point to understand COSATU and its positioning in the transition to democracy. My work on labour market reform was exciting. Dismantling the apartheid labour market regime and replacing it with new laws – Labour Relations Act (LRA), Basic Conditions of Employment Act and the Employment Equity Act – meant the lives of millions working in the South African economy could be transformed. Next to the Constitution these were important laws for post-apartheid democracy. However, sharp debates happened with African nationalist trade unionists and social democrats. The African nationalists did not want labour to have wall-to-wall collective bargaining, although such a reform could have skewed industrial relations and macro-economic power towards labour. Much later and after NALEDI these arguments made clearer political sense; with hindsight this moderation of labour's positions on labour standards was actually tied to the Afro-neoliberal agenda inside the ANC to ensure the labour market could be precariatised and left fragmented. We needed a language to characterise the dominant COSATU consensus and so at NALEDI I theorised it as a new paradigm of regulated flexibility. Nonetheless, labour made important gains with these labour market reforms, given the global trend towards deregulation. The challenge has been to strengthen union densities, ensuring dynamic worker control and building a transformative strategic capacity to harness these laws and deepen these reforms as democratic systemic reforms.

While at NALEDI I also wondered about how as a think tank we were contributing to COSATU's agenda for socialism. COSATU had several resolutions on socialism and I felt strongly that NALEDI could help elaborate this with policy ideas and proposals. The neoliberal shift was happening and NALEDI could have been a strategic resource. However, my arguments did not make much headway. There was a strong social democratic undertow at NALEDI and the push back was intense. I felt it in debates about the workplace forums provision in the LRA. The social democrats merely wanted to import the German model of co-determination. I was arguing that we needed to be more open about the spectrum of possibilities that could emerge from class struggle including self-management. I argued this position in the *African*

Communist and in a book chapter.[38] I believed that worker control was crucial to maintain labour's democratising role in the post-apartheid transition. Also, the Afro-neoliberal shift could be countered by renewing worker control politics with workplace forums including self-management. This could be central to a new transformative strategy for labour including harnessing worker pension funds. In 2015 I co-edited a volume *COSATU in Crisis: The Fragmentation of an African Trade Union Federation* based on interviews with 600 shop stewards. The picture at a shop steward level in COSATU was disastrous. Worker control was on its way out, shop steward councils were not meeting and COSATU was dying at its base. The book was banned by Sdumo Dlamini (the president at the time) at a COSATU congress. He waved the volume before the congress and called on workers not to read it.[39]

In 1999 I left NALEDI and co-founded a grassroots NGO, the Co-operative and Policy Alternative Centre (COPAC).[40] Several leading trade union general secretaries and senior SACP leaders supported its formation. COPAC was about exploring grassroots alternatives. The funding environment was difficult but COPAC became crucial for deepening transformative praxis. It pioneered post-apartheid co-operative development (about 300 co-operatives were established) including influencing the legislative agenda for the Co-operatives Act of 2005,[41] developed the notion of sustainable local manufacturing hives in township communities,[42] explored participatory sustainable development in peoples housing, contributed to the development of the Ivory Park township ecovillage, shaped the implementation of the Co-operatives Banks Act,[43] experimented

---

38 The social democratic co-editor of the volume called me into his office and attacked my chapter viciously. That day I left NALEDI very distraught and was driving down to KwaZulu-Natal to give a report to workers at the Workers College about the LRA negotiations. I had an accident at Van Reenen's Pass that almost killed me.

39 My chapter in that volume is published in this collection.

40 I was the director from 1999 to 2009. Since then I have chaired the board of COPAC.

41 In the early 2000s COPAC co-hosted a legislative agenda conference for a new Co-operatives Act in South Africa.

42 The first hive I designed was in Bophelong township near Sebokeng. Part of what it did was toilet roll manufacturing and coffin making. This provided a template for about 25 more hives on the East Rand in numerous township communities. These hives included bakeries, recycling operations, condom manufacturing and more. The idea was to upend racial geographies and create work where people lived. Start-up and working capital were a serious constraint for these co-operatives.

43 I was appointed to the board of the Co-operative Banks Development Agency and served on it for six years. We developed the legal and support tools to develop co-operative banks. My view was that they were a crucial democratic systemic reform to diversify the banking system and give people control of capital. A few co-operative banks have been established but the uptake has been slow.

with liveable urban living,[44] pioneered the idea of the solidarity economy, and co-founded the South African Food Sovereignty Campaign (2014 to the present) and the Climate Justice Charter process (2019 to the present).

In terms of my commitment to left and socialist renewal, I had come far but not far enough in the SACP, at NALEDI, the Greenhouse Project, the Ivory Park ecovillage, the COPAC and engagements with the new global left. It was becoming clear that through transformative praxis, more needed to be done to provide new ideological foundations for transformative politics in South Africa. While on this journey, I sometimes asked myself what was I doing in township communities: the ground was messy, many co-operatives failed, the state was working against independent co-operatives and bottom-up transformative practices, and the ANC patronage machine was having a toxic impact at the grassroots level. My ethics of care was being tested as well as my commitment to left renewal. Existentially it was a very lonely time. Also, my contemporaries, family and friends, were becoming upwardly mobile as professionals, starting families, and had savings and medical aid. My partner, very supportive of my grassroots work, also encouraged me to consider entering academia given that my income was erratic and my economic circumstances were precarious. The grounded transformative praxis I was engaged in with working-class communities, waste pickers and unemployed people's movements was not sexy enough for the liberal donor community, who wanted merely to construct a liberal civil society in their own image and give some credibility to an exclusionary market democracy that really did not work for the many. As they played with the lives of the poor, they created inequalities in progressive civil society.[45]

In my late thirties, all I wanted was an opportunity to think more deeply with Marxism, the new anti-capitalisms shaping the global left, and take

---

44 In this regard I lived in an old art deco building in Yeoville and refused to leave. As urban decay set in and banks redlined the area, my partner and I set up the Sunflower Project in our building. Through debt finance, given that delinquent owners were not investing, we turned the building around and made it a beacon of livability. I located the COPAC office in one of the units. My partner and I also did not want to be landlords because in the renewal process we ended up owning six out of nine units. For this reason after we made the building liveable we sold, at reasonable prices, most of the units to women and ensured the building remained mixed income. We turned down offers from investors.

45 From working in the NGO space for almost three decades I have come to the conclusion that South Africa needs wealth and inheritance taxes to end the feel-good philanthropy of the rich. These are actually ecojustice taxes given that the wealthy have the largest resource and carbon footprints. Of course, this requires a left government coming to power committed to accelerating the deep, just transition.

transformative political praxis to the level of a political project for the country. In this context I joined the academy at the age of 40 in 2010. I was disappointed at the intellectual culture at the university. Identity politics was rife, particularist histories were being churned out and political theory was reduced to figuring out the discursive subject. Postmodernism had ravaged the university and even academic Marxism was on the retreat or disavowed. While postmodernism declared the end of metanarratives in its language games, capitalism loomed large with a universal presence as a metanarrative. This was supported and purveyed by liberal theories of globalisation. Moreover, it was fashionable to claim that Marx was a white male and racist and therefore could not be taken seriously. The crisis of national liberation politics and its Marxism (revolutionary nationalism and Marxism-Leninism) fed into this disaffection. I felt strongly that without a critical grasp of capitalism, including an understanding of its structures (states, economies, classes and oppressions) and its fourth great polycrisis, we were doing a disservice to the next generation of critical intellectuals.

Hence, I continued the project of renewing Marxism and transformative left politics through teaching a social theory course to trade unionists on understanding global capitalism; and established the Democratic Marxism series (2013) and later my Emancipatory Futures Studies in the Anthropocene project (2019). The social theory course began in 2010 as a dedicated course for the National Union of Metalworkers of South Africa (NUMSA). Together with other colleagues and strategically minded comrades in NUMSA we built critical capacities at different levels of the union. By 2013 when NUMSA had a conference and resolved to stop supporting the ANC-led Alliance, build a movement for socialism and a worker's party, many of our graduates led and shaped those debates. The NUMSA moment was pivotal for left renewal and potentially a counter-hegemonic project to a degenerate national liberation politics. Unfortunately, it all descended into vanguardist dogma, sectarianism and business unionism. Those who wanted the NUMSA moment to renew left politics were defeated by another version of unreconstructed Marxist-Leninist politics. In this context, Irvin Jim, the Marxist-Leninist general secretary of NUMSA, unilaterally shut down our social theory course in 2016 despite workers and a NUMSA resolution wanting it to continue.[46] Nonetheless, we continued it and opened it up to all unions. It has been in existence for over a decade.

---

46 He publicly attacked me on Facebook and called me a 'frog lover'. I am guilty as charged. I make no apologies as a democratic ecosocialist for loving frogs, an endangered species, and other life forms.

The Democratic Marxism (DM) series (2014 to the present) has been about revisiting the Marxist canon in dialogue with contemporary anti-capitalisms to explain the conjunctural shifts and dynamics of a crisis-ridden capitalism. Marxism is no longer hegemonic in global resistance and has to earn its place in terms of its intellectual, political and strategic contributions. Moreover, a crucial premise has been recognising that democracy and democratic theory do not belong to capitalism and liberalism. Actually, the latter truncated and limited democracy in the course of its modern history and today has engineered market democracies that merely entrench the sovereignty of capital over states, people and nature. This form of democracy is at the heart of the legitimation crisis of contemporary capitalism, enabling conditions for the second coming of fascism and more generally the poly-crisis of capitalist civilisation. The DM series recognises this but also the authoritarian tendencies of left politics (vanguards, technocratic elites and lumpen ruling classes) and thus stakes out democracy in its processual, rights, institutional and agential forms as crucial for our our society; an expansive democratic imaginary is necessary and integral to transformative politics. The DM series has also challenged facile renderings of Marx as a racist particularly among some in #FeesMustFall.[47] While confirming the anti-racist role of praxis-centred Marxist theorising, including in South Africa, it has engaged Marx as a decolonial thinker (or anti-Eurocentric), his ecology and contributions to feminism. In other words, it has furnished a decolonial-ecofeminist-Marx as crucial for transformative politics. In this vein there has been an attempt to position a decolonial Marxist critique of capitalism highlighting the imperative of the ecocide question, the relationship between imperialism and ecocide, the rise of ecofascism, crises of socio-ecological reproduction and how accumulation through ecocide necessitates decolonial futures making from the global South.

As an academic I married my activist commitments to the knowledge project. The Afro-neoliberal shift brought tremors into the Tripartite Alliance, but after Polokwane the corrupt face of Zuma's ANC was in full view, Marikana happens, and the EFF breakaway from the ANC and the

---

47 Like all historical phenomena #Feesmustfall was contradictory. It was amazing to witness the post-apartheid generation assert itself and call for decommodifed higher education, decolonisation and insourcing, at least at Wits University. The role of the EFF and the violence it engendered began to overshadow its positive role. In this context I co-hosted a peace meeting at Wits and co-founded the Higher Education Crisis process which culminated in the Higher Education Crisis Conference at Megawatt Park. I raised R3 million through the Norwegian Embassy for this process, which was given to the Mandela Foundation, as a co-convenor. I was shocked when the EFF violently destroyed the peace meeting and conference platform. It gave me a face-to-face view of neofascism.

NUMSA moment takes place. We were all witnesses to serious alignments away from the national liberation bloc and the ANC-led national liberation movement was dying, mainly through its own self-inflicted wounds. I was also aware that this disintegration could go in any direction including further to the extreme right. In this context, through chairing the board (2010 till the present) of COPAC, we co-founded the South African Food Sovereignty Campaign (SAFSC) out of a national dialogue in 2014. In my grassroots transformative organising, over the years, I was struck by the depth of hunger in township communities and even at the university. Also, many co-operatives failed because people needed to meet their food needs, first and foremost. The SAFSC provided a crucial platform for convergence and translated the notion of food sovereignty into the South African context. From a transformative politics perspective we deepened the political ecology critique of the corporate-controlled food system; developed activist tools and a hub methodology to engage in food sovereignty commoning and pathway building to end hunger in communities, villages, towns and cities; supported local alliance building; and through several national food sovereignty festivals produced the People's Food Sovereignty Act, 2018, in response to the drought (2014–2021), high food prices and the collapsing commercial food system. We took the Act to parliament and seven government departments, but were ignored. Like the Co-operatives Act of 2005, which COPAC influenced and which provided a mechanism for bottom-up participation, the Peoples Food Sovereignty Act was an example of a democratic systemic reform to build, through people and worker power, the next food system.

Through my democratic ecosocialist concerns for ecological justice, I increasingly developed a concern for the worsening climate crisis. I embraced climate justice politics as an extension of environmental justice politics. During the World Summit on Sustainable Development (WSSD) in 2002, we had about a thousand visitors a day to the Ivory Park Township Ecovillage.[48] As mentioned, through the Gauteng province of the SACP we attempted to foreground an ecological dimension to the SACP's Marxism and socialist programme. In my engagements in the DLF, I also foregrounded the climate crisis. As an academic (from 2010) the first thing I did was design a course entitled 'Empire and the Crisis of Civilisation' to foreground the nature of contemporary crisis,

---

48 The Ecocity Trust, whose board I joined, secured a partnership with the city of Johannesburg to profile the Ivory Park Ecovillage during WSSD with the condition that they would support the next phase of ecohousing. They never did.

particularly the climate crisis, and in 2019 secured a grant to develop a body of knowledge around Emancipatory Futures Studies in the Anthropocene.[49]

Put simply, how do we survive in a heating world through subaltern action and future making? However, of deep concern was how to connect everyday struggles of peoples and workers to the worsening climate crisis to raise mass consciousness. In this context the SAFSC became a crucial platform to connect the drought, high food prices and worsening climate crisis. We also connected the day zero water challenge through drought speak outs to the climate crisis, had a bread march in the streets of Johannesburg, protested outside the Johannesburg Stock Exchange (JSE), built a human chain around SASOL's head office and occupied media offices. These advances, however, were not enough to incite a mass awareness and transformative movement building. In this context we engaged in deep constituency-based dialogues in 2019 to develop the world's first Climate Justice Charter (CJC). The CJC provides a pluri-vision to address the legacies of apartheid and the current poly-crisis and seeks to secure a liveable, just and democratic future. Even though we took it to parliament as per section 234 of the Constitution, which provides for charters to be adopted, we were ignored. Instead, the ANC government has continued its carbon addiction while normalising the most dangerous challenge human and non-human life face as a simple technocratic policy challenge to be solved by a business-driven Presidential Climate Commission.

Individual activism is not enough; celebrities and influencers are also not enough for the challenges we face with the worsening poly-crises of capitalism. The most powerful lesson from successful historical movements that have given dignity and hope to the many are all about collective mass power. Whether it was about the abolition of slavery, colonialism, apartheid, anti-war movements or even embedding capital within the imperative of societal needs in the twentieth century, it came down to mass organising, movement building and strategic power. In the post-apartheid context, the ANC-led Alliance has undermined our capacity for strategic and mass grassroots politics as it has surrendered to the whims of a transnationalising white global monopoly capitalism. Yet the vector of capitalist history is towards the total destruction of human and non-human life; carbon capitalism is deeply ecocidal in its logic. The crises it has engendered risk overwhelming our societies and unleashing global chaos, violence and socio-ecological systems collapse. Free market utopia is lived dystopia for the many;

---

49 In 2011, during the COP 17 Summit, I marched with about 120 of my students in the streets of Durban for climate justice.

there is no freedom in the globalised marketplace and in market democracies. We are all meant to be mere subjects of US imperial power and transnational corporations. As the climate crisis worsens, we have to invent hope in resistance. This means world making from below by the many. There is time, albeit limited, to make serious transformative choices and practise transformative politics to bring about systems change. My writings about the worsening climate crisis and its intersections have been about raising the alarm and hopefully will serve as a resource to awaken many more to the dangers we face as a species and country.

Today the Climate Justice Charter Movement (CJCM) is in a phase of transformative movement building. A new form of political instrument is being constructed with a transformative praxis committed to the constitution of power from below and accumulation of capacities. It is intersectional, advances people and worker-led democratic systemic reforms and is articulating transformative strategic politics on all terrains to accelerate the deep, just transition now.[50] In the South African context the emergent CJCM, formed out of the worst droughts in the history of the country, is the embodiment of left renewal and transformative praxis in post-apartheid South Africa. Two simple metaphors capture what it is all about. First, the idea of the lighthouse. As the shadow of the climate crisis grows, the CJCM stands tall in its shadow warning society about the unfolding and impending catastrophe. It holds aloft, for all to see, its pluri-vision to secure our survival, if we act together now. Second, the metaphor of the firefighter is apposite. To accelerate the deep, just transition many fires have to be fought. For the CJCM this does not mean bringing a water pistol to a forest fire or bucket to a flood. Rather, the CJCM is fighting strategically through a climate justice project for the country and a democratic ecosocialist programme to accelerate the deep, just transition now. If the many rally and build this people- and worker-driven movement, South Africa's trajectory of self-destruction can be displaced.

So why democratic eco (feminist) socialism as the world-making programmatic alternative of the CJCM? Put more starkly, these are the choices facing the many: extinction or climate justice? Ecocidal capitalism or democratic ecosocialism? Under capitalism human and most of non-human life do not have a future. The evidence of precariatised societies, destruction of ecosystems and the Earth system speaks for itself. As an alternative to ecocidal capitalism, democratic ecosocialism is not inevitable and the given next stage of history. Rather, it is what we have to fight for if we are going to stand any

---

50 Its strategic perspectives, policies and activist tools can be found on its webpage, https://cjcm.org.za

chance of survival. Such a reconstructed socialism is based on learning lessons from almost two centuries of alternative world making that have attempted to challenge capitalism and transition beyond it. It is not a newcomer to the struggle for an emancipated society and is certainly enriched by the deeper historical grounding of transformative politics.

Moreover, democratic ecosocialism is also not a blueprint but a compass for us to start creating the next society in the present; it has an ethics of care, values and a praxis we can work with to design and build institutions, develop laws, construct socio-ecological systems, and build capacities in society to take us in this direction. In other words, democratic systemic reforms to accelerate the deep, just transition now in our communities, workplaces, sectors and the state. Lastly, we have to locate the life-sustaining challenge in the long span of geological time. We have had 200,000 years of modern humans, walking upright, bipedal, and surviving on a hostile planet. The past 11,000 years of a relatively stable climate was an aberration in this long geological span. The key to our survival was co-operation, working collectively and in solidarity. We survive today because of the solidarities of old; we are products of co-operation. Yes, geography matters and yes, climate geography is going to change and very likely many nation states will vanish but if we weave in and practise these essential truths there is another horizon, another possibility, another tomorrow. We have the gift of life. It is not guaranteed in the long term for our species, but in our journey now let's make it count.

Our ancestors have been here before and they certainly made it count in their appreciation of the wonder of this planet and its delicate web of life. They lived through a way of life that was in nature and part of respectful inter-species relations; taking what they needed without destroying the vital rejuvenating cycles of place-based ecosystems. Humility marked their harmonious appreciation of a nature- and Earth-led world. Moreover, as the ecological and climate crisis worsens, we have to remake a decolonial self. The radical non-racial tradition with its commitment to a transformative intersectional politics: anti-capitalist, decolonial, anti-oppression and anti-ecocide is a crucial bridge to discover a post-imperial, post-productivist and post-anthropocentric way of being. Democratic ecosocialism takes this to a higher level through a new transformative politics and praxis. There is more to the argument in these writings. So, let's keep thinking together and keep the debate open.

The future as history

I am not sure, with my fragile health, how long my story will go on, but I am not about to give up; slow living in struggle is my next move. More importantly is the story of the many as history and their emancipatory future making. I offer three songs to complete my serenade of the many.

The love of the many is facing three versions of socially alienating modes of being that easily veer into being anti-human: (i) technotopian productivism which believes humans are masters of nature and earth. It is deeply supremacist and anthropocentric: technology, capital and markets will fix everything. This is magical thinking which creates false hopes, delaying decisive action, while many have already started perishing; (ii) elitist neo-Malthusianism increasingly underpinning exclusionary nationalisms and neofascism, in the global North and which blames the darker nations and their populations for the crises we face while they continue their carbon- and resource-intensive ways of life that are responsible for burning the planet and destroying ecosystems; (iii) symbolic idiocy related to mass consumerism of infotainment, celebrity culture, branding practices of the self, sporting brand name clothing, obsession with techno-gadgetry and addictions to cyber consciousness. These are hyper-individualised and selfish humans who are basically indifferent to the world around them and the dangers facing humanity. These forms of anti-humanism complement a carbon capitalism that is taking us into a terrifying nightmare. Together we need to start painting on the canvas of a new future but we have to do this without any guarantees. This message is part of John McLean's *Starry Starry Night*,[51] a celebration of the artist Vincent van Gogh and is apposite. It's a song about an artist upending the artistic mainstream and reaching for a post-impressionist aesthetic; bringing beauty to the canvas in ways that was not done before. It was a lonely and difficult path and it was not given the artist's message would be understood nor find traction amongst the many. Transformative praxis and politics faces the same challenge today as it seeks to get in front of the polycrises we face.

As millions get displaced by climate shocks, including an estimated 200 million Africans in the coming decade, we need to accelerate the deep, just transition now locally – in communities, workplaces, sectors and the state – but also work towards creating a new planetary basis for existence. Nation states

---

51 I was not allowed to use the actual lyrics of the songs *Starry Starry Night*, *Imagine* and *Stand By Me* because of property rights. I wonder in a world of climate chaos how long property rights as a colonial and capitalist construct, a myth that benefits a few, will continue to oppress us.

and nationalism will eventually become anachronistic as parts of the planet become unliveable. John Lennon helps us in his song *Imagine* to think beyond the container of nationalism, religious fundamentalism, militarism and other divisive ideologies that accentuate particularist difference, and which fail to appreciate our common universal humanness as part of a shared planetary consciousness and existence. A common planetary tomorrow is what we need to build today such that national struggle is a point of departure for a planetary commons. We must end the antagonism with Planet Earth, our common home and ark, in our everyday lives, in the biosphere and as part of the Earth system. We need to dream this and live it as John Lennon invites us to do.

Finally, we need to ensure intergenerational justice. We need to rise to the call of our children and youth to halt the destruction of the planetary conditions that have sustained life. The deep despair, anxiety and uncertainty amongst youth and children that are climate conscious is real. They know they are going into a terrifying world and that the relatively stable biophysical conditions of their parents and grandparents is disappearing. The song *Stand By Me* sung by Tracey Chapman (original by Ben E. King) helps appreciate their burning desire for justice and attentiveness to their concerns.

In the end, it comes down to a transformative praxis grounded in an ethics of care: love, solidarity and freedom for the many to become fully human as beings in and of nature.

PART I

RESISTING REVOLUTIONARY ORTHODOXY, NEOLIBERAL MARKET DEMOCRACY AND EMERGENT NEOFASCISM

*Contributing to a Democratic
Imaginary in the SACP*

Workplace Forums and Autonomous Self-Management from Below

This paper engages with Karl von Holdt's work in the *South African Labour Bulletin* and Langa Zita's unpublished paper on transformative unionism.

Introduction

WORK IN THE MODERN South African economy – whether in a factory, on a mechanised farm or in a hi-tech office environment – has generally been characterised by exploitation, hierarchical work arrangements and managerial dominance. Industrial democracy, supposedly realisable through collective bargaining did not, over the past few years, extend beyond a narrow bargaining agenda. Fundamental workplace issues like production planning, investment decisions and work organisation did not feature prominently on the bargaining agenda. However, for the first time in South Africa's industrial relations and labour law history there is an opportunity to fundamentally change decision-making and management within the workplace. This is as a result of the legal provision of a workplace democratisation institution, known as the workplace forum, in Chapter 5 of the new LRA of 1995.

With co-determination deeply embedded in the statutory make-up of Chapter 5, the subsequent debate pertaining to the transformative role of workplace forums has amounted to defending and promoting the co-determination thrust of statutory workplace forums. As a result, most mainstream industrial and labour market policy thinking is suggesting joint decision-making or co-management as the absolute horizon of democratisation. Other transformative possibilities are eclipsed. To reopen the debate, beyond equating Chapter 5 of the LRA to co-determination, the limitations of co-determination will be highlighted. This is not an exercise in verbal militancy, nor an attempt to trash co-determination, but rather an attempt to open up the ideological and political boundaries that surround it. It is only through this kind of critical engagement that creative thinking can emerge from the grassroots, within the union movement, to advance worker control and, ultimately, thorough-going workplace democratisation.

Finally, there is an attempt to locate workplace forums within a transformative vision of worker ownership and control; thus, opening up possibilities for worker-initiated workplace democratisation, to define a new model for workplace forums that goes beyond co-determination to embrace autonomous worker self-management.

The limits of co-determination

Most of the conceptual development of labour law in South Africa over the past decade and a half has been within a pluralist framework of industrial relations. The co-determination leap in the LRA of 1995, with its value-laden notion of co-operation, should be located within the realm of collective labour law and ultimately what can best be described as a neo-pluralist paradigm or framework of industrial relations. The main limitation of this paradigm is its inability to grasp the complexity of the state, both in its political and industrial relations roles. Substituting theoretical abstraction – the notion and assumption of a neutral state – for the complexities of a changing political situation, in which political re-alignments are firmly in motion, is clearly ideologically inappropriate and misleading. An additional limitation relates to the assumption of a power equilibrium as intrinsic to co-determination. This is blatantly blind to the asymmetries in power that emerge from ownership in a marketplace that is increasingly becoming transnational in terms of market share and equity.

An economistic Marxist response to the challenge of worker control in the Third World has often, in a very reductionist way, concluded that workers are not ready. The argument against the feasibility of worker control has been based largely on the simplistic conclusion that only workers in advanced capitalist countries have the cultured consciousness to embrace and advance worker control.

While reductionist approaches like the above rule out worker control in a country like South Africa, local advocates of co-determination, approaching matters from their own angle, concur in ruling out a more radical perspective for the South African working class. For a writer like Karl von Holdt, co-determination in the context of the workplace forum starts to be the ultimate horizon of economic democratisation. We have here the workplace equivalent of political transition as an exercise in nation building and reconciliation. The workplace forum becomes power-sharing co-determination.

The paucity of this perspective emerges when one looks at attempts at worker control in the Third World, which have taken different forms, but which have all been initiated by workers from below. According to Munck, an example of this is Chile during the 1970–1973 period when workers began to organise a form of workers' council later extended into an organisational form called the industrial belt (*cordones industriales*). Unfortunately, this worker control movement was crushed by the Pinochet-led coup. Similarly, in Algeria, during the Ben Bella period (1960–1965), workers established self-management committees to take over enterprises from fleeing French colonialists, but again this worker initiative was eclipsed by an authoritarian and bureaucratic political elite that emerged within the Algerian national democratic state. A similar fate confronted workers in Iran in 1981, when worker-established councils (*shoras*) were suppressed by Ayatollah Khomeni. A further rebuttal of economistic Marxism resides in the argument and historical fact that workers in South Africa have been at the forefront of fighting the apartheid regime and, but for organised workers in this country, dual power would not have emerged in the 1980s, enabling a negotiated transition. Even in the 1990s, if it were not for COSATU's mass action in 1992, the deadlock in the CODESA negotiations would not have been resolved. In short, South Africa has a tradition of working-class struggle, which has taken unions and workers beyond the factory, to engage on a political terrain that holds out the prospect of transforming society; hence there is immense potential among the working class to democratise the workplace and society beyond a narrow workerist or shopfloor conception of co-determination.

To pick up on the notion of workerist co-determination, or a narrow shopfloor-centred approach to workplace forums, it is apparent there are serious dangers lurking for the labour movement within this conception and approach to worker control. In explicit terms the labour movement could be co-opted into a paradigm of co-operation and finally integrated into the formalism of a legislated industrial relations system. Exacerbating this danger is the fact that in other countries collective bargaining is clearly separated from the co-determination channel. For instance, in Germany, Sweden and Italy collective bargaining takes place in national industrial bargaining forums, while co-determination takes place in the workplace. In the South African industrial relations system centralised bargaining exists in a few industries like clothing and textiles and metal and motor vehicles, but generally it is uneven with most bargaining arrangements prevailing at company and plant level. With the failure of the LRA to provide legislated centralised bargaining across sectors, while at the same time providing a duty to bargain over co-determination issues, it is likely the dividing line between bargaining and co-determination could become blurred, thus opening up the way for a co-optive co-determination system. In the end though, watching for this danger is not new to the labour and shop floor tradition in South Africa and was apparent in the opposition displayed by unions to works and liaison committees.

Beyond co-determination?: Workplace forums and transformation from below

The year 1989 was epic because the political geography of the world was fundamentally changed through the collapse of the Second World. Soviet-style bureaucratic and authoritarian socialism came to an end. In the wake of this historical turning point, the West has proclaimed the end of history and the vindication of the capitalist system. With this kind of ideological refrain, buttressed by the systemic hegemony of the United States over the new global political order, it has become difficult to advance a socialist alternative. Most left-wing governments are forced into a politics of survival, and in the South, the developmental challenge is defined simply as unbridling the market to catch up with the West.

For the new democratic South African state, with its democratic features of multi-parties, elections, a bill of rights, separation of powers and an independent judiciary, globalisation has presented serious constraints. Contestation of economic policy, and in the main the Reconstruction and Development Programme (RDP), has come from different forces within the global order – the G7, IMF and World Bank and multinationals. In addition, most large monopoly corporations, for instance Anglo American, have gone offshore which gives them added political leverage against the new state and together with the continued existence of the old apartheid bureaucracy and globalising pressures, it is politically rational to conclude the South African state is essentially under siege. It has not become, even in a classical sense, a state for itself. In short, it cannot, by itself, ensure the transformation of South African society and, most importantly, ensure a socialist advance (unless it radically transforms itself and asserts its national sovereignty as a nation state in the global order.)

For some South Africans, including previous anti-capitalist intellectuals who have decomposed ideologically and retreated from class engagement, the achievement and even suggestion of a socialist alternative might seem rhetorical. However, for the SACP – the leading political formation of the working class – and COSATU, socialism still remains a serious vision and alternative to globalising capitalism. Even at a strategic level the SACP has gone beyond a two-stage theory of revolution, initially developed and espoused by the Third Communist International formed after the Russian Revolution. This is evidenced in the following:

> The socialist transition may well be of long duration. The transition may also be marked by contradictions, stagnation and major reverses. History is never a smooth process, nor does it have a guaranteed outcome ... The socialist transition is opened up at the point at which there is a decisive development of ... popular democracy to a position of dominance in all spheres – political, economic, social and cultural (SACP, *African Communist*, first quarter, 1993: 15–16).

Simply, the SACP is not about to, now and in the future, smash the state and construct a socialist order on the ashes of the old. Instead, SACP theorisation, clearly, places the prospect of a socialist transition firmly on the national political agenda but it also reflects a commitment to achieving socialism through democratic contestation and process.

This places the SACP at the forefront of democratic thinking in South Africa by recognising power and ownership relations can only be transformed through thorough-going democratisation. Within the RDP this is echoed with explicit mention of democratising the state and a people-driven process of delivery. For industrial relations theory and labour law reform the challenge of thorough-going democratisation of the workplace opens up the way to revive and renew Marxist industrial relations theory. This paradigm shift suggests democratisation should contribute to the transcendence of the employer and employee relationship while at the same time ensuring workplace and community relations and workplace and state relations are transformed.

But, taking forward this challenge, to ensure socialist construction begins in South Africa, requires a transformative strategy that is driven by the democratisation of society from below. It is in trying to assert this that the worker movement has to change strategic gears while at the same time defining, in concrete terms, a new transformative vision and model of worker control.

Changing strategic gears?: The challenge of transformative unionism

In the new global context, the political transition in South Africa has spawned serious rethinking on revolutionary change. Unlike the past where the barrel of the gun served to distinguish paths to power and the strategic model of revolutionary transformation, there is currently a dominant perspective which goes beyond this. At times it is articulated as structural reform or radical reform, which attempts to locate general policy reform for social transformation within a wider process of struggle and contestation, beyond electoralism and parliamentary politics. It basically recognises that within a democratic society transformation is not just the prerogative of the state and solely implementable by the state, but instead at the grassroots, within civil society, social movements and forces also have power and responsibility to advance and deepen reform.

The strategic emphasis on democratisation within the SACP captures this notion. Within the worker movement, especially COSATU, this strategic understanding and perspective began to prevail with more coherence in 1992, under the rubric of strategic unionism. As conceived by Von Holdt, strategic unionism entails an emphasis on trade union unity, coalitions which extend beyond the factory floor and an alliance with the ANC. The thrust of this strategic emphasis is to try to position COSATU, and the worker movement generally, within the centre of economic policy making but in particular at the coalface of industrial restructuring, within the transition to democracy.

In political terms strategic unionism, as articulated by Von Holdt, with its emphasis on deepening a programme of radical reforms to advance working-class interests, is about engaging capital to foster a class compromise. It is essentially social democratic. Socialism is some kind of abstract future goal within this strategic perspective, which can only be achieved through two-stagism – social democracy then socialism. This becomes even more apparent when one scrutinises the reforms proposed by this framework to overhaul the industrial relations system and ultimately democratise the workplace. In this regard Von Holdt understands co-determination as the most feasible plank of a strategy of worker control that can be achieved, currently, in order to democratise the workplace. In his words,

> co-determination is a major breakthrough in the struggle for democracy at work, and for workers' influence in production. By building unions institutional power in the workplace, and developing workers' experience in production issues, co-determination provides the possibility for ongoing efforts to expand workers' control. This would be a long-term, gradual and continuous process, involving elements of struggle.

Co-determination in other words provides a vehicle for gradual transformation, for continually expanding the realm of democracy at work and in production.

Now, do history and workplace democratisation have to proceed in such an incremental, two-stagist kind of way? Is it possible that workplace forums, and Chapter 5, hold out possibilities for democratisation and transformation that include and go beyond co-determination? To pose the fundamental question and challenge, can workplace forums open up a socialist transition? This question can only be answered positively if strategic unionism is linked to a socialist conception of transformation that begins now. In other words, socialist construction and workplace democratisation can only happen if COSATU and the worker movement shift strategic gears away from social democratic strategic unionism to what Langa Zita calls a strategy of transformative unionism.

Transformative unionism does not reject the key strategic thrusts of strategic unionism but recognises that unionism cannot be limited to one model or concept, given that it is the level of worker consciousness that would define and realise potentialities within worker and union organisation broadly. Put differently, the extent to which unions utilise spaces to roll back managerial prerogative and ownership will depend on the capacity of those unions themselves. This means transformative unionism has a different grasp on history and what is feasible for the worker movement in the current South African context. Within Zita's conception this is expressed as follows:

> Even though the democratic space is never guaranteeable under capitalism, its continued expansion and defence remains the most potent weapon for the ultimate transformation of capitalism that in this democratic revolution the transformation takes for a lack of a better word an 'eclectic' form, a combination of various forms of struggle through varied agency, within a context of appreciating the various levels of determination. That the capitalist society in a democratic context is not irreconcilable with various forms of economic co-ordination.

In short, transformative unionism recognises that democratisation of society and the workplace cannot be limited to co-determination. In other words, there are a host of other forms of workplace democratisation, with different degrees of worker ownership and control, which could emerge and be asserted within the democratic South African political order. With this recognition, transformative unionism goes beyond the workerism of social democratic strategic unionism and opens up possibilities for breaking through and transcending capitalist relations, here and now, such that the system is finally negated. To further unpack this, it is necessary to define, as key strategic elements of transformative unionism, a vision and model of workers' control.

Defining a transformative vision?: Worker ownership and control

Socialism is dead, long live socialism! This is the paradox that accompanies the demise of the Soviet model of socialism. Central planning and complete public ownership of property has been discredited as a socialist development alternative. For the anti-capitalist left, throughout the globe, this has produced ideological insecurity and retreat. In this context, the triumphalism and proclamations by Western ideologues about the historical vindication of free market democracies has also limited the scope for development alternatives for countries in the South. Modernisation or catching up through export-led industrialisation, underpinned by free market policies, has become the new panacea. In addition, globalisation within this development discourse has become a politically partisan concept, suggesting the death of the nation state and as such the inevitable assimilation of countries into the global capitalist economy.

Notwithstanding the ideological crisis and political onslaught confronting the anti-capitalist left, the end of authoritarian and bureaucratic Soviet socialism heralds a new beginning for renewed and critical redefinitions of socialist practice and ideological concepts. It opens up the possibility to chart a socialist path that would take into account the specificities and historical circumstances that prevail in a particular society. In the South African context this has resulted in an intellectual questioning about the moral and ethical superiority of a socialist alternative, the role of the state, the market, planning and civil society. However, what has been lacking is a rethinking of the notion of property. This is essential because at the centre of Soviet socialism has been a concept of common ownership, which resolved itself as public or state ownership of everything. In political and policy terms this translated into an understanding of socialism as amounting to nationalisation and expropriation.

Within the SACP, for instance, state ownership and property relations have been fairly well theorised, such that public ownership is not counterposed to private ownership. Nonetheless, thinking through forms of socialised private ownership is only beginning. As a result, it is this lack of ideological clarity that has, to an extent, rendered the engagement of the worker movement with privatisation of state assets, industrial restructuring, de-industrialisation and land reform indecisive. Transformative vision and engagement have not made the shift away from state-centred socialism and as a result worker ownership and control is not coming to the fore. To open up possibilities for social justice, including economic efficiency and in the ultimate sense a socialist project driven from below, the challenge of socialising private ownership must be relocated at the centre of the democratisation of the workplace. According to Gamble and Kelly there is need to make a distinction between types of private ownership. They suggest that

> there is an important distinction in discussing private ownership between personal property, goods of final consumption, and impersonal or social property, which includes ownership of productive assets. Private ownership in respect of personal property is almost universally accepted and justified as a condition of personal identity and autonomy. It is the justification of private ownership of impersonal or social property that is contested (Gamble and Kelly, 1996).

Hence, it is only through this ideological breakthrough there can be a coherent vision that would inspire socialisation of non-personal property relations and ultimately worker ownership, through buy-outs, co-operatives and investments either as equity or employee stock option schemes.

But despite advancing a transformative vision, anchored in a new conception of worker ownership, democratisation of the workplace would be incomplete if it were not informed by an approach and model of worker control. This is so, because borne out by numerous examples, the modern joint stock company has effectively separated management functions from ownership.

Therefore, worker ownership by itself would not resolve the oppression that prevails within hierarchical work arrangements. The rationality of managerial dominance will still reign over the division of labour within the enterprise or even institutions in the public sector. Therefore, to democratise workplaces completely, worker ownership and even public ownership (sometimes referred to as state ownership) has to be accompanied by worker-initiated alternatives to managerial dominance or worker control. For Munck (1988),

> workers' control is thus essentially a slogan in a political strategy which advocates a gradual role by workers in contesting management's 'right

to manage'. Some of its forms may seem similar to co-management but it aims ultimately at workers self management and thus seeks to avoid integration within the industrial relations machinery.

Simply, worker control is a means to dislodge and democratise managerial prerogative such that workers are collectively responsible for running and managing the enterprise. This is integral to a transformative vision of worker ownership, although, in strategic terms, the theory of worker control cannot be realised in a big bang. Within the strategic framework of transformative unionism, a host of worker participation possibilities within the enterprise are possible and consistent with realising autonomous worker self-management. At the same time, this does not preclude the immediate realisation of autonomous worker self-management within certain situations.

What does this mean for Chapter 5 of the LRA and workplace forums? Alternatively expressed, how can workplace forums become organs of worker control? Essentially these questions enable a departure from theory into the realm of the practical and an attempt to define workplace forums as a worker control model.

Workplace forums as a worker control model?: Co-determination and autonomous self-management

The emergence of a new democratisation institution in the workplace is bound to be embroiled in struggle. Employers are definitely going to resist inroads into managerial prerogative and besides trying to thwart these initiatives, concerted attempts would be made to institutionalise workplace forums within a co-optive framework. Without a clear perspective on what should be achieved by the union movement, this could end in disaster, with institutions that are flawed and controlled by employers. With Chapter 5 of the LRA trying to strike a balance between legal regulation and voluntarism several models could emerge. The first is a statutory model with two variations, developed as follows:

(i) through prescription if the parties fail to reach a voluntarist agreement and which requires the Commission for Conciliation, Mediation and Arbitration (CCMA) to establish and define a workplace forum in terms of Chapter 5, read together with the 'Guidelines for establishing workplace forums' contained in Schedule 2;

(ii) through the statutory provisions for trade union-based workplace forums, which would allow the competencies of workplace forums to be conferred on shop steward structures.

According to Halton Cheadle, 'first prize should be a thousand voluntary workplace forums rather than statutory forums.' In other words, this is the second model that is envisaged by the LRA and it allows for collective agreements, outside of the statutory framework. It is this model that holds out the prospect of going beyond legislated co-determination and ultimately subverting the rationality of hierarchical management, in both the private and public sector. Essentially, it would allow parties to define a workplace forum that is trade union-centred, but which allows for autonomous self-management. In practice this could, broadly, have two variations.

The first is a completely autonomous self-management workplace forum, which would allow skilled and unskilled workers to run an enterprise, public service unit or co-operative. For example, in the public service an autonomously self-managed workplace forum can be established in a school. This would bring together skilled and unskilled workers into the managerial realm of the school. Besides this collective forum, interfacing with parents and other community participants, it could decide on work schedules and education policy issues relevant to the school and could also work out accountable, transparent and participatory ways of managing the administration of the school. Similarly, in a primary healthcare unit or even a police station, workers can self-manage their work. Another example is a de-industrialised plant, which if taken over by workers could be managed through a workplace forum that is designed to allow the workers to autonomously self-manage the plant. Internationally there are numerous examples of this kind of worker control. For instance, Lucas Aerospace was a company renewed by shop stewards who took over production by developing a corporate plan. In India, workers in a factory called Kamani Tubes took over ownership of an ailing factory and autonomously self-managed it into a viable industrial unit. Essentially, in this kind of situation the law of value is fundamentally changed. Labour power is no longer an exchange value and input into production for profit maximisation. Rather, it becomes a socialised outcome of production.

Another variation of an autonomous self-management workplace forum, is one that not only allows for co-determination over certain issues but at the same time also has an autonomous self-management competency and agenda for workers, within that particular enterprise. For example, in a parastatal or large conglomerate, like Anglo American, an autonomous self-management workplace forum can be agreed to that allows for co-determination on investment decisions, production planning, work re-organisation and technology use but autonomous self-management on affirmative action policy, training, and health and safety issues. The challenge with this variation of autonomous self-management is to struggle to achieve a full and complete self-management agenda that eventually transcends the co-determination competency. This would become likely if workers also address the ownership dimension of the enterprise at the same time.

Conclusion

State-centric socialism has been discredited. In the South African revolution this has been acknowledged and a new revolutionary model of structural reform has emerged. This does not deny a transformative role for the state, but recognises the political and transformative importance of forces in civil society.

In addition, given the present constraints on the emergent national democratic state, the imperative of a transformation agenda driven from below, as opposed to together with the state, becomes essential. In this regard, a transformative strategy for unionism with a vision for worker control and ownership and an autonomous self-management workplace forum model would fundamentally change the mode of production in South Africa. Socialism will not just be constructed by state ownership, which would also have to be democratised, but would have to be accompanied by democratisation and socialisation of production relations, from below, even if it is mapped unevenly within South African reality. This would open up space for a worker and community sector in the economy. In short, workers have to push boundaries beyond co-determination, now. There would be no guarantees of success but experiments, initiative and creative innovation by workers is what is required now and over time. It is the knowledge and experience accumulated from all of this that would make socialism the only viable alternative.

African Communist 147, Third quarter, 1997.

The Visible Hand of Development Planning in India: Lessons for South Africa

VISHWAS SATGAR VISITED India recently. He is a policy analyst working for NALEDI, a COSATU think tank. He is also part of the national political education secretariat in the SACP.

Towards the late eighties and early nineties, any discerning observer of India's economic performance would have identified an escalating foreign debt, acute import intensity and increased capital flight by non-resident Indians; essentially an unmanageable balance of payments situation was in the making. Strangely, decisive policy intervention did not occur. Around July 1991 India had two to three weeks' worth of foreign exchange reserves; de facto placing the Indian economy in the throes of a balance of payments crisis. In response, the Congress Party Finance Minister, a converted disciple of the Washington Consensus (also known as the neoliberal agenda), used this crisis as an alibi to impose simultaneously an IMF-designed macro-economic stabilisation programme and a World Bank structural adjustment programme (SAP), on the world's largest poor population. Although embracing a free market modernisation vision for India, with textbook economic policies – like privatisation, trade and exchange control liberalisation, fiscal austerity and conservative monetary policies – the National Planning Commission (NPC), which was responsible for five decades of post-independence development, rather anomalously continued to exist. Actually, its continued existence has rendered crude any juxtaposition of the plan with the market, primarily because it is the visible hand of the NPC that is at the forefront of planning and driving free market modernisation.

The NPC has its origins in an economic planning committee set up by the Congress Party during the thirties and which was chaired by Jawaharlal Nehru, subsequently the first Prime Minister of India. Since independence, in 1947, the NPC has produced nine five-year plans. For the first fifteen years of independence the general strategy and institutional design of the Indian development planning model was established. In this regard both Nehru and the first chairperson of the NPC, Professor Mahalanobis, were the main architects and hence the development planning model is sometimes referred to as the Nehru-Mahalanobis model. By the third five-year plan, India had firmly opted for a strategy of import substitution industrialisation (ISI), which was pivoted around three elements. The first was the achievement of self-reliant growth through industrial development protected by high tariffs and import restrictions. Second, was the removal of capital constraints in a manner that would allow savings to be easily converted into productive investment. Third, industrial development would be guided by an elaborate system of licensing and controls. To a large extent land reform and basic needs amelioration never emerged in a decisive way on the planning agenda.

In terms of the planning process, the commission of experts prepares an approach paper which is sent to the National Development Council, composed of chief ministers from the different states and chaired by the prime minister, for consideration. It then returns to the NPC for final formulation. All the plan documents have not stipulated policies but have mainly contained macro-economic and sectoral targets and detailed plan outlays for the public sector. Institutionally the NPC has been very centralised and has had a limited interface with state and union governments. Of late, consultation has become decentralised, mainly with constitutionally established grassroots participatory institutions, known as *panchayats* (very similar to RDP forums).

Development planning in India has succeeded in ensuring a diversified industrial base, food grain self-sufficiency and limited land reform. But most progressive economists would agree that even the most commonplace development indicators suggest an appalling development record. For instance, the number of people below the poverty line (about 288 million and with the recent SAP it has increased to 355 million) exceed the total population of the Soviet Union, the third largest country in the world. The infant mortality rate in the eighties was 121 per thousand (more than one and half times that of China). Two-thirds of the total population of India does not have access to safe drinking water. About half of the villages do not have a road or a single electricity connection. Nearly one-third of primary school age children are not enrolled in school (in contrast to one-third in China) and nearly two-thirds (in contrast to one-third in China) of the adult population are illiterate (female literacy lagging far behind male). Also, 8% of the population owns 48% of the assets. The exception to this is the state of Kerala, which has had a Communist Party-led government (in and out of power over several decades), and which according to Amartaya Sen (the world's leading economist on famine) and Jean Dreze (also an economist), has a social development record which not only surpasses that of South Korea but is an example for the rest of India and even the world. In short, using the advantage of hindsight it is apparent the political economy of India's development planning model has not benefited the majority of poor and working people but has merely benefited industrial capital, a bureaucratic elite and rich farmers.

Broadly speaking there are two important lessons that can be distilled out of India's development planning experience. The first lesson can best be framed as a question. Should South Africa establish a statutory development planning commission? Answering this question in the affirmative rests on three essential reasons:

1. Modern liberal states in configuring their institutions of law making and governance have ascribed to a doctrine of a separation of powers, primarily to protect the interests of citizens against the abuse and corrupt use of power. However, this doctrine is in serious crisis in the light of the degeneration of electoral political systems. Noberto Bobbio, a leading Western political philosopher, articulates this problem as the inability of political parties to translate electoral mandates into policy. In the South African context this has a resonance given the macro-economic policy introduced by the Department of Finance. Basically, it deviates from the RDP and supplants a vision of people-centred modernisation with a vision of free market modernisation. We have, in historical terms, moved from oppression under the apartheid regime to the tyranny of the fundamentalist free marketeers in the Department of Finance (which is analogous to the fallacy of omniscience displayed by Soviet central planners). This, however, is symptomatic of a wider problem, which is euphemistically referred to as the development industry. This includes other disciples of the Department of Finance like development consultants, planners and economists who are able to provide ready-made technocratic development solutions at exorbitant prices, which have had a draining effect on the fiscus and ultimately the taxpayer. To overcome this situation, the economic planning function and capacity within the state has to be democratised and in this sense an independent development planning commission, existing parallel to the state and working in a bottom-up manner, would be necessary.
2. The policy-making system in South Africa is at a critical point of maturity such that it requires more appropriate policy planning and co-ordination. The kernel of the policy-making environment is constituted of ministries, the National Economic Development and Labour Council (NEDLAC), which

is a necessary consensus-building institution, the Constitutional Court, particularly if it attempts to vindicate socio-economic rights, provincial and local government, participatory fora spawned through the Development Facilitation Act (and which are facilitating participatory budgeting) and workplace forums if they are established by the trade union movement. If a development planning commission exists, it could absorb the particular policy interests and demands of various constituencies and institutions and factor these into the broader development plan for South Africa. For example, a scenario that could emerge with a development planning commission is the following: a discussion paper on 'Macroeconomic policy and basic needs' is developed by the planning commission after bottom-up consultation and this is then presented to a restructured development chamber at NEDLAC, in which the public finance chamber and the development chamber are fused. From here the macro-economic policy document would proceed to the Cabinet and finally return to the planning commission to be encapsulated in a complete macro-economic strategy. Also, the implementation of the strategy would be annually monitored by the planning commission and a report presented to the restructured development chamber of NEDLAC and the Cabinet.

3. The intelligent economist, policymaker and development planner has realised the need to transcend the mythology of the free and perfect market. Lagging behind but eventually making the breakthrough has been economic theory, which has produced a body of knowledge on market failures, recognising that markets are prone, for instance, to conveying imperfect information, overconcentration, environmental externalities and unemployment. At the same time, state intervention has also generated distortions like bureaucratisation, supply-side inefficiencies, rent-seeking behaviour and corruption. To find the complementarity between markets and state intervention, spatially and within the different sectors of South Africa's economy, policies need to be planned by a development planning commission, driven by consensus and consultation.

In the second instance, India's development planning experience highlights the need to move away from defining the development problematic as a challenge of catching up with the West or rather the developed economies. India, like South Africa, over the past few decades attempted to catch up through a strategy of ISI, bordering on complete autarchy. Apparent in this industrialisation experiment is the failure to ensure wider socio-economic development. Tragically, the logic of this kind of modernisation is suggesting an economic trajectory that uses the diversified industrial base of ISI for an outward economic orientation. In other words, export-led industrialisation (ELI) buttressed by free market policies have become the new modernising panacea. This policy orientation has also taken root in South Africa. Without wanting to tackle the limits and weak-kneed assumptions of an export led take-off for South Africa, cutting to the bone of the logic of sequencing ISI and ELI reveals a shift from factories to Rooivalk attack helicopters and mega development projects, like the Maputo Corridor, being the new symbols of progress that co-exist incongruously with squatter settlements, illiteracy and widespread poverty. Essentially, the Maputo Corridor project is not only a trickle-down growth pole but a launch pad for South Africa's export-led take off which would ensure South Africa no longer blocks the development of its neighbouring countries through military destabilisation but through economic expansionism.

To argue against sequencing ISI with ELI is not to make a case for the continuity of ISI but rather to articulate the need for what political economist Samir Amin has conceptualised as a strategy of delinking, at least in the short to medium term. Delinking applied in the current set of circumstances prevailing in South Africa would present the development problematic as bridging the gulf between the First and Third World within South Africa. Put differently, it would allow political reconciliation to be accompanied by an economic transition that would ensure economic reconciliation. At a political level delinking is about asserting political will, not to compete with the US over a share of the international arms market, but to ensure the autonomy of South Africa's economic transition. Basically, it would have to amount to negotiating a hands-off peace with the economic agenda of the Washington Consensus or as a last resort consideration would have to be given to shutting South Africa's borders to it. At an economic policy level delinking would entail the prioritisation and planning of people-centred modernisation but it would not mean the end of trade; rather, trade policy would not be the main stimulus of growth. People-centred modernisation entails a planning agenda, with a fixed-time horizon, informed by the following key aspects of the RDP: basic needs policies (which includes education, health, housing infrastructure, electricity, sanitation and transport), land redistribution and agrarian reorganisation, and finally the development of and diffusion of home-grown intermediate technology, across sectors, which is environmentally friendly and which harmonises with the development needs of small, medium and microenterprises (including cooperatives). In this regard, immense potentialities would stem from the use of the computer chip and solar energy.

The tenacity of a democracy is measured by the extent to which it allows differences of opinion and dissent. Reflecting this notion is the impasse in the debate between free market fundamentalists and left-wing debunkers, around the government's macro-economic strategy. Nonetheless, moving beyond this impasse does not require hard-nosed implementation of the macro-economic strategy. Instead there is a need to recognise that no economic policy is irreversible particularly if it is inconsistent with the electoral mandate of a new government. At the same time there is a need to focus the minds of South Africa's nation builders, policy-makers, politicians and most importantly its citizens on constructive solutions that could advance economic reconciliation and a stable democracy. A reflection on India's development planning model has not only revealed its co-existence with the largest (and also the most tenuous) democracy in the world but has also made visible the extent to which most of the post-independence rulers of India used development planning to create a better life for a few more rather than for all. South Africa can avoid this if, for instance, it adopts a strategy of delinking, undergirded by a development planning commission driven by consensus building, participation and an agenda for people-centred modernisation.

African Communist 146, First quarter, 1997.

Worker-owned Co-operatives, Development and Neoliberal Economic Adjustment

Introduction

WHILE THE FIRST CONSUMER co-operative experiment in Rochdale, in 1844, inspired by the ideas of Robert Owen, is widely documented, it would seem the sociological study of co-operatives began in earnest from the 1960s onwards. While most of this literature was initially very descriptive (Spaul, 1965) it was only later that attempts were made to interrogate the development impact of co-operatives, the conditions necessary for success or those that contribute to failure, the role of the state in supporting the co-operative movement and other general approaches to co-operative development from below. A lot of this literature also used case studies to highlight experiences, practices and challenges.

At the same time, the Cold War also had a major impact on the literature and general discourse around co-operatives. From within the Soviet Union (Maslennikov, 1983) attempts were made to theorise the role of co-operatives in Asia and Africa and how this linked with the global socialist system. Emphasis was also placed on understanding class formation in co-operatives, the nature of co-operative property, co-operatives in exchange and production, government and co-operatives (both in states with or without a capitalist orientation) and finally the training of experts in socialist countries.

Later on, in the 1980s and 1990s, a policy-orientated literature began to emerge from the ILO, the World Bank and even the International Co-operative Alliance itself. With the advent of the internet, the debate and study of co-operatives has become more textured. Comparative information is more easily available. Worker-owned co-operatives have also been documented and these studies are available within this general pool of information. This literature review has drawn from all the above sources. At the same time the conclusions reached from this exercise are meant to stimulate discussion on some of the critical tasks the SACP has to consider in order to build a socialist co-operative movement in South Africa.

Conceptual issues

The ILO, in the Co-operative (Developing Countries) Recommendation, 1966 (no. 127) defines a co-operative as: 'an association of persons who have voluntarily joined together to achieve a common end through the formation of a democratically controlled organisation, making equitable contributions to the capital required and accepting a fair share of the risks and benefits of the undertaking, in which members actively participate.'

This definition by the ILO, while recognising that equity in a co-operative comes from within, from its members, unlike a public company, nonetheless obscures the ownership dimension of co-operatives.

This stands in contrast to the definition by the International Co-operative Alliance (ICA) which states that: 'A cooperative is an autonomous association of persons united voluntarily to meet their common economic, social, and cultural needs and aspirations through a jointly-owned and democratically-controlled enterprise.'

However, the notion of an 'association of persons' has tended to focus mainly on member owners and has excluded employees of the co-operative from ownership. This separation of ownership from employees in a co-operative is normally expressed in the classification of consumer and producer co-operatives. In the former, member owners contribute to the internal market of the co-operative, buy from the co-operative and also own shares in it. Workers or employees in the co-operative do not have shares in it and are de jure as per the statute, excluded from ownership.

Co-operatives also operate and exist at three levels – primary, secondary (sometimes referred to as central) and federal. Agricultural co-operatives are a good example of this. As primary economic enterprises these co-operatives produce a particular crop or fruit or livestock and so on. Their members are individual farmers who join the co-operative. Secondary or central co-operatives are made up of primary co-operatives as their members. Within branches of the agricultural sector, like maize for instance, secondary co-operatives have provided credit, cheaper inputs, transport, grading, cleaning and storage facilities, a marketing channel and processing facilities either downstream or upstream within the value chain. Sometimes primary and secondary co-operatives can be organised as multipurpose and handle several areas of economic activity. Also, all the primary and secondary agricultural co-operatives could organise themselves into federal or sectoral co-operatives involved in agriculture.

At a national level, apex bodies are constituted by sectoral or federal structures and sometimes organise themselves on national lines – as provincial and regional structures. Apex national bodies are meant to be the national voice of co-operatives in a country and are meant to represent members in policy formulation and to devise strategies and programmes for the development of co-operative activities. In many experiences apex bodies have failed to discharge their core function primarily because they have been controlled by government or have been the conduits for donor agendas. In Italy there are three national co-operative bodies. One was linked directly to the Communist Party and played an important role in the red belt area. The apex body is known as Lega Co-op (Philip, 1987).

Sometimes co-operatives are classified as formal or informal (Attwood, 1988). This distinction largely relates to the legal status of a co-operative. A formal co-operative is by definition legally registered in terms of co-operative legislation and has to comply with certain statutory requirements. An informal co-operative normally operates outside the ambit of the law but works with the values of a co-operative, has co-operative practices and might even have a voluntary constitution.

Worker-owned co-operatives

Robert Oakeshott's *Mondragon: Spain's Oasis of Democracy* (1973) and *The Case for Workers' Co-ops* (1978) were pioneering in terms of exposing the most sophisticated worker-owned co-operative complex to the world. The Mondragon worker-owned co-operatives have grown dramatically since their initial formation in 1956 – from 23 workers in one co-operative to 19,500 worker-owners in more than one hundred worker co-operatives in 1991.

They have also displayed a phenomenal record of success – of the 103 worker co-operatives that were created from 1956 to 1986, only three have been shut down (Whyte and Whyte, 1991). Worker-owner relations have impacted on Mondragon co-operatives in three important respects (Whyte and Whyte, 1991). First, management in Mondragon co-operatives do not have a right to vote. They are located alongside the board of co-operatives and merely participate in board meetings to make recommendations. The general policy direction of the co-operative is decided by the worker-owner board members; managers merely implement. In the second instance, worker-owners are at the core of all co-operatives. For example, the Co-operative Bank in Mondragon is a secondary co-operative but its employees also have ownership in the co-operative and are represented on the board and share in surpluses. In the third instance, worker-owner relations have incentivised the labour process. Workers do not require typical hierarchical work relationships to ensure productivity. Instead, shares in surpluses, participation in decision-making and commitment as worker-owners have ensured that worker co-operatives in Mondragon are more productive than their capitalist counterparts.

Other experiences of worker-owned co-operatives exist in situations where trade unions have attempted worker buyouts. In the Third World, the Kamani Tubes Experiment stands out. It is documented by Srinivas in *Worker Takeover in Industry: The Kamani Tubes Experiment* (1993). Set up in Bombay in 1959 by the Kamani family, Kamani Tubes was engaged in manufacturing non-ferrous products which enjoyed a good market. The death of the patriarch of the family in 1972 led to the decline of the Kamani empire. Internecine feuds among family members adversely affected the performance of the Kamani group of companies. The frequent siphoning off of funds along with inept and non-professional management spelt doom. During the early 1980s the unit suffered heavy losses and by 1985 these had accumulated to a large amount with increasing liabilities. Failing to respond to the crisis, the management abandoned the factory premises in September 1985. At this juncture, the workers of Kamani Tubes, through their union, explored various ways to revive the unit. A revival scheme prepared by the workers was presented to the Supreme Court which in turn directed the Board for Industrial and Financial Reconstruction (BIFR) to file a feasibility study of the workers' scheme. Based on the report submitted by BIFR, the Supreme Court gave an historic judgment in September 1988 favouring worker takeover of Kamani Tubes on a co-operative basis. This decision was consistent with the provisions of the Sick Industrial Companies Act, 1985, which facilitates the takeover of a sick company by its employees through formation of a co-operative.

Like Kamani, in South Africa the use of worker-owned co-operatives has also been used in defensive situations. In most instances during the 1980s, trade union-linked co-operatives used to provide subsistence employment to workers who lost their jobs. In general, the conclusions reached by Kate Philip (1987) from her case studies is that 'co-op collapse is common, degeneration is manifest, and those co-ops that do survive struggle economically. The case studies also illustrated some of the classic problems arising from these pressures: undercapitalisation, marketing difficulties, low productivity, uncompetitiveness and self-exploitation'. However, the focus by Philip on South African co-operatives was one-sided and did not take into account the dualistic character of the co-operative sector. Parallel to the worker-owned co-operatives in South

Africa were numerous white-owned agricultural co-operatives that were provided with a host of enabling, protective and incentive-based policy support from the state. This enabled them, particularly the seasonal grain co-operatives (see below) to become billion-rand economic operations.

The development process and co-operatives

Formal co-operatives were first introduced in sub-Saharan Africa by colonial governments, often for the purpose of promoting cash crops by peasant farmers. After independence, many governments adopted policies that further reinforced the role of co-operatives and other rural organisations in the agricultural sector. This one-sided approach to co-operatives, as instruments only for agricultural development, failed to draw on the potential of co-operatives to develop other sectors of the rural economy. In apartheid South Africa this was also the case with enabling legislation and incentive-based policy measures used to support the development of agricultural co-operatives (Amin and Bernstein, 1995).

In the main, the development potential of primary co-operatives resides in the following attributes:

- Internal capital formation: this happens by pooling member fees and share purchases into an internal capital pool. This is further enlarged if co-operatives re-invest a portion of their surplus or borrow from member surpluses. Within the wider movement, co-operative banks are essential to provide technical support, business advice, but most importantly start-up or venture capital. In Mondragon the co-operative bank, also known as the Caja Laboral Popular, has played a crucial role in financing the co-operative movement and planning the formation of new co-operatives or assisting with the conversion of private enterprises (Whyte and Whyte, 1991).
- Locally based asset formation and control: as the co-operative invests its capital in equipment and land or even inventory, it contributes to local asset formation that would be controlled by member owners in the co-operative rather than an outside stakeholder. These member owners would be responsible for these assets due to ownership but would also have the prerogative to dispense with them and even replenish them after depreciation sets in.
- Links land redistribution to productive economic activity: this is particularly the case with rural development. With this link, land reform policy can be implemented in a more sustainable manner and contribute to micro-economic activity and the efficacy of development strategies.

- Employment: to this extent, co-operatives can provide for self-employment for individual farmers or can contribute to fulltime employment or seasonal employment. In a context in which there is no proper state support or protection or no co-operative movement linked into a wider political programme, employment created through co-operatives would merely amount to survivalist jobs earning co-op members an income far less than a living wage and amounting to self-exploitation (Philip, 1987).
- Co-operative movement networks: these exist when the demand and supply side of the market are organised through co-operatives. This allows for needs to be met in a more planned way but also provides consumers with cheaper products or services. To this extent the market is socialised and controlled and co-ordinated by decisions made jointly by producers and consumers (Wainwright, 1994).

Within secondary or central co-operatives involved in development activity, the following positive contribution has been identified:
- They provide their members with the advantage of economies of scale. By combining their resources, producers can obtain needed goods and services at reduced costs, and market their produce in larger volumes, giving them a stronger bargaining position in dealing with traders.
- They can link small-scale producers to the national economy. By serving as a means to obtain inputs and marketing of produce for their members, the organisations can help to incorporate smaller producers into the national economy and contribute to higher productivity and improved farmer income in the smallholder sector.
- They can contribute to rural stability. By providing an institutional permanence for self-help, these community-based organisations can extend services to members over the long term. When collaborating with development projects, they can continue project-related activities after external assistance has been concluded.

In terms of the development approaches used vis-à-vis co-operatives as development instruments, the literature points broadly to three experiences. In the first, mainly in the Third World, co-operatives were used in primary export sectors, which were very important to the local economy. The rationality of centralised macro-planning gave politicians the power to decide policy ends and planners the power to decide means or policy interventions to realise these ends

(Hyden, 1988). Planners in the state provided blueprints or models for the role of co-operatives in agrarian reform and farmers on the ground were forced into these socially engineered co-operative relations. In the main these co-operatives were largely state controlled and were conveyor belts of state policy, rather than understood as institutions that needed to be nurtured in a wider web of political and economic relations.

In an attempt to reclaim the autonomy of co-operatives as development instruments, a key theme in the literature has pointed to a greenhouse approach (Hyden, 1988). In this approach, rather than organising people for purposes beyond their comprehension and interest, the greenhouse approach focuses on factors that help local efforts grow on their own. Thus, rather than insisting on implanting organisational models, irrespective of whether or not they fit the political economy of a given society, the greenhouse approach takes as its starting point what exists on the ground and encourages organisational development from below or from within. To this extent, this approach recognises the richness of institutional forms and origins that exist in the global co-operative movement. However, beyond this, greenhouse development of co-operatives is about a philosophy of incubating a self-help culture; informal co-operatives are nudged to become formal co-operatives. This would happen by reclaiming the autonomous nature of co-operatives, while at the same time, empowering and strengthening apex organisations to perform a host of support functions for primary co-ops.

From a Northern donor perspective, the greenhouse approach is useful and allows donors to work closely with national apex organisations in the Third World. Three problems emerge from this approach. First, the assumption that the organic knowledge of people outside any informal self-help group is less than those in it, is not necessarily the case. This means working with people who have not formed any kind of informal co-operative does not mean that a co-operative cannot grow even from very formal beginnings particularly if the process capacitating the co-operative is empowering. Second, the state cannot be ignored completely in the context of co-operative development. The state in any country is crucial for the development of a co-operative movement. However, the challenge is finding the right balance between state control and complete non-intervention. Finally, in the context of liberalisation the greenhouse approach to co-operative development produces weeds and sick plants that are basically capitalist enterprises that undermine the essential founding principles and philosophy of co-operatives.

A third approach in the literature to co-operatives in development can best be termed the transformation from below approach (Wainwright, 1994). This approach proceeds with the understanding that co-operatives are part of social movements in which the organic knowledge of members is crucial for co-operatives' development and existence. This, however, does not preclude political relationships with parties or new vanguards. This party-to-movement relationship is not one-sided or instrumentalised and it provides co-operatives with a political and strategic role to advance transformation from below such that control of the economy and development is a central driving force. Transformation through co-operatives means socialising economic relationships and changing the basis of overall economic co-ordination. In Lega Italy, this existed in the relationship between the Italian Communist Party and the co-operative movement. Together with support from the regional state, the co-operative movement was able to advance worker takeovers and buyouts and new co-operatives were established in a host of economic sectors. Also, in Brazil currently, the Workers Party is supporting the Landless Workers Movement by using its position in local and provincial state legislatures to open up blocked spaces for advance.

Neoliberal economic adjustment and the impact on co-operatives

Most of the current literature on the global co-operative movement reflects a serious ideological shift in support of neoliberalism. Three important themes emerge strongly to define the adaptation required by co-operatives to deal with liberalisation, privatisation and deregulation. The first theme emphasises the opportunity that neoliberalism offers co-operatives in the Third World and countries in the former Second World that are in transition to market economies (ILO, 1996), to reclaim their autonomy from the state. The end of state control and intervention in the economy inaugurates a new balance between state and market. Thus, co-operatives need to embrace the only logical economic space for their continued survival and renewal; that is, the market (Hussi et al., 1993; Rajapatirana, 1998; ILO, 1996). The use of terms like a co-operative sector or third sector are jettisoned and the economic viability and the general orientation of co-operatives is conflated with the market and ultimately the private sector.

A corollary to this theme is a minimalist state policy on co-operatives that merely provides a simple legislative framework, preferably in plain English, and which is enabling (Hussi et al., 1993; ILO, 1996). Policy incentives, protective measures and other training supports from the government are decried. The alternative being advanced by neoliberalism is greater emphasis on support for apex organisations to play a role in policy making, training and strategy development or full-blown conversion of co-operatives into companies. Most donor programmes are focusing on promoting this approach, even those in South Africa today (see below). The third theme complements this thrust by arguing for a new kind of management in co-operatives to ensure they are globally competitive. Co-operative experts (Davis, 1995) are arguing for the end of worker control and self-management and instead talk about the promotion of the new kind of co-operative manager who operates with the values of co-operatives but understands the efficiencies of the market. In addition, Davis (1996) goes further than this to argue for managers to be given voting (and possible ownership) rights in boards. In other words, it is only through embracing this new kind of co-operative management paradigm, it is argued, that co-operatives can deal with the global market and the necessary challenges of economic adjustment.

From the standpoint of the basic principles of co-operatives, the neoliberal appropriation of co-operatives into the globally competitive market, with minimal state support and typical managerial prerogatives, opens the way for degeneration and for co-operatives to be treated as businesses – profit maximisation and competitiveness become the sole goal of the co-operative, which supplants the wider social, cultural, developmental and spiritual needs of co-operators and co-operatives. However, at the same time as the global adjustment of advanced capitalist economies began in the 1970s and intensified through the 1980s and 1990s, Mondragon worker-owned co-operatives have proven the vitality and appropriateness of labour-management relations that are defined solely by worker ownership and decision-making power. Instead of shedding jobs during the adjustment of European economies or even changing worker-owner and management relations, the Mondragon co-operatives have created jobs during this period (Whyte and Whyte, 1991).

Worker-owners in the Mondragon complex responded to the adjustment threat in the 1990s by developing, on their terms, areas of strategic organisational restructuring but in the main drew on the strengths that were already established as part of the worker complex (Whyte and Whyte, 1991): education and training, a role for social councils involving the base of workers in decision-making and worker-owner exclusive power on boards to determine policy and strategy. In some cases, the Mondragon co-operatives very cautiously entered joint ventures with private firms but largely on terms that did not allow the private companies to take over or undermine their autonomy (Whyte and Whyte, 1991). The Mondragon complex stands out as a successful worker-owner-led co-operative response to global economic adjustment. Without detracting from its original philosophy, other worker-owner-led co-operative movements can do the same (Dumais, 1997). For Itkonen (1996) it is clear that the internal knowledge and the human centredness of co-operatives is what gives these institutions an edge over typical enterprises. This is further enhanced when women are treated equally in co-operatives. Following on these perspectives, it is possible to argue that a worker-owner-led co-operative movement that is linked into a dynamic party-to-movement relationship with a political vanguard and which has a clear ideological programme, can also achieve what the Mondragon worker-owned co-operatives have achieved.

Case studies

While the literature on co-operatives contains numerous case studies, we concentrate on two experiences; namely, dairy co-operatives in India and the white-owned seasonal grain co-operatives in South Africa. These case studies are meant to highlight the various institutional forms that co-ops can take, the diverse activities co-ops can be involved in, the role of the state and policy, the contributions of these co-operatives to rural development, and, finally, some of the problems encountered.

Dairy co-operatives in India

In India Amul co-operative dairy is located in the town of Anand which is part of the Kaira or Kheda district in Gujarat state (George, 1988). This dairy is part of a milk co-operative that began after World War 2, in 1946. Prior to this, dairy production was in private hands and given exclusive rights to supply the nearby Bombay market. In response to this, dairy producers came under the influence of Gandhian philosophy and nationalist revolutionaries which prompted the growth of the dairy co-operatives (Patel, 1988). In 1947 there were only eight village-based co-operatives with 432 milk producers. By 1983 this had increased dramatically to 895 villages involving 352,000 milk producers collecting about 183,820,076 litres per year (Patel, 1988). In terms of the organisational structure, it operates with three tiers (Baviskar, 1988): one at village level, which is a co-operative society and the other at district level, made up of numerous village co-operatives. Together the various districts form a federation at a state or provincial level. Farmer members of the co-operative sell milk to the co-op twice daily, in the morning and afternoon. The local co-operative supplies the district, which runs the Amul Dairy and is responsible for procuring and marketing the output and processing. Quality and grading are done by the district level co-operatives. Amul Dairy produces all the by-products of milk – cheese, butter, buttermilk. Amul also has a technology centre where scientific research and business feasibility studies are conducted to increase product diversity. In addition, the co-operative provides other services and supplies to co-operative members: a guaranteed market for milk at a fixed price, cattle feed at reasonable cost, and regular and efficient veterinary services in the village (Baviskar, 1988).

State policy support for the dairy and milk producing co-operatives has been at three levels. The first has been at the level of breeding technology for dairy cows. Local and indigenous species are crossbred for high milk output. Second, the nutrient content of cow fodder has been improved. Third, state policy has also contributed to transport linkages. In this regard the state has provided the necessary infrastructure for transportation like roads, vehicles and communication lines. Currently, the state is trying to replicate the Amul Dairy Co-operatives in other parts of India where there has been a dire shortage of milk. The extent to which the state can succeed will depend on it understanding the specific success factors of the Amul Co-operative.

As a vehicle for rural development the Amul Co-operative has had a differential impact. While the co-operative is open to everyone notwithstanding caste, class and religion, large landowners are in the majority and together with middle-level land owners have been the main beneficiaries of the benefits provided by the co-operative. Landless workers have not been able to gain directly. At the same time, the co-operatives have created jobs estimated at about 5000 in Gujarat state alone, with an average of six persons per co-operative (Apte, 1988). In addition, the dairy co-operatives generate employment in their plants as well as in the transport of milk and milk products, in the manufacture of cattle feed and in the financing agencies and infrastructural services (Apte, 1988).

Annually, after 50% of the annual profit is distributed among members, the remaining amount is allotted to various funds such as the reserve fund, charity fund, extension of co-operative fund, and so on (Patel, 1988). In the end these allocations of co-operative surpluses have contributed to local development through the establishment of schools and healthcare centres, construction of roads, and provision of water supplies and electricity connections to villages. Also, women have been educated and empowered in terms of family planning and a broader understanding of economic issues and processes (see below).

At the same time, while the dairy co-operatives have been hailed as the harbingers of the white revolution (following the green revolution) and been more successful in terms of contributing to rural development, several problems plague these co-operatives. First, land ownership is governed by the market and hence most people cannot afford to purchase land and engage in dairy farming activities. Second, women are mainly involved in tending cows and buffaloes in Indian villages and they deliver milk to the co-operatives, more so than men do in Indian villages (Apte, 1988). As a result, they have achieved an improved status through being involved in milk production and earning an income from it. Widows in particular have been able to increase household income. However, men still dominate the co-operatives and their leadership structures.

Most members are also faced with a lack of capital (Patel, 1988). The co-operatives don't provide credit and hence it is difficult for members to start up, expand and maintain their cows. After about a year or two a cow dries up and there is a need for another cow. In the end, if loans are taken it is difficult to repay credit institutions that have agreements with co-operatives to deduct a certain percentage of members' sales. This negatively affects mainly farmers who have one cow, as opposed to farmers with several cows who are able to rotate their cows, a farmer with a single cow overuses the cow such that it dries up before the loan can be paid. This creates debt.

A fourth problem facing these co-operatives is management. While the management has not been corrupt, it has been made up exclusively of upper-caste large landowners. They are literate, compared to the widespread illiteracy among most members, and have been able to manipulate and direct co-operatives according to their ideas and interests (Apte, 1988). This type of management, which completely undermines member participation in decision-making, is also referred to as paternal managerialism.

South African white-owned seasonal grain co-operatives

In the South African context white agricultural co-operatives have been used as important instruments of rural development. Currently, about 250 agricultural co-operatives have emerged in South Africa with around 142,000 members, total assets of some R12.7 billion, total turnover of some R22.5 billion, and annual pre-tax profits of more than R500 million (Amin and Bernstein, 1995). In addition, according to Amin and Bernstein, agricultural co-operatives handle all exports of citrus and deciduous fruit, handle and/or process the entire wool clip, and market 90% of dried fruit. On the input side, they provide and/or finance 90% of the fertiliser, 85% of the fuel, 65% of the chemicals, and a significant proportion of the machinery and implements used by white farmers. They also provide 25% of credit used by white farmers (Amin and Bernstein, 1995: 5). At the heart of this white-owned agricultural complex are eleven summer grain co-operatives. These are mainly concentrated in the north of the country and in the Free State and they dominate the rural agricultural economy. The two largest summer grain co-operatives, OTK and SWK, have an annual turnover of R2.374 billion and R2.22 billion respectively, which compares with some of South Africa's largest food corporations like Imperial Cold Storage with an annual turnover of R2.4 billion and Rainbow Chickens with a turnover of R1.5 billion in 1993.

These co-operatives provide a host of agri-services to their farmer members. These range from receiving, handling, grading, fumigating and storing controlled commodities. A levy is charged to members on the volume of business and this helps to finance other activities. The second important role of these co-operatives is the channelling of Land Bank funds (and those acquired from other financial institutions) to members. Funds are provided to members to purchase production inputs. Drought relief funds have also been channelled through these co-operatives to their members. The third service provided by these co-operatives to members is general trading of bulk-procured production supplies – seeds, fertilisers, pesticides, herbicides, farm implements, and machinery and equipment – as well as consumer goods. Increasingly trade is also happening with non-members. A fourth service provided by these co-operatives to members is an insurance brokering service for short-term cover and Sentraos for crop insurance. Some co-operatives also provide group schemes, pension funds and credit insurance for their personnel and for members. Finally, these co-operatives provide secondary processing of agricultural produce. This is mainly in downstream activities. Examples of such activities are: maize milling, peanut butter production, sunflower oil pressing and malting. A few co-operatives have specialised upstream into fertiliser blending and seed multiplication.

In terms of state support this came through agriculturally skewed co-operative legislation, the Co-operatives Act (91 of 1981), which was largely enabling for these co-operatives. However, they were also beneficiaries of government policy through the Land Bank Act and the Income Tax Act. In the terms of the Land Bank Act, summer grain co-operatives were designated agents of the Land Bank and have administered loans and drought relief for small fees to members. Drought relief provided farmers with major direct and indirect financial support. This included concessions for mortgage loans to assist with the consolidation of debt; consolidated carry-over debts to be repayable over a six-year period; and interest subsidy by government on new production credit. Although these concessions were modified and gave added benefits to summer grain co-operatives, in 1992 a massive emergency relief scheme involving the transfer of R2400 million to assist farmers and co-operatives was introduced by the government. The largest proportion of this finance went to summer grain co-operatives (that is, 88% which reduced the debt of summer grain co-operatives by 82%).

In terms of tax benefits, prior to 1977 agricultural co-operatives only paid income tax on profits from non-members' turnover. Later, due to pressure, co-operatives were taxed at the company rate of 35%. However, the Income Tax Act grants agricultural co-operatives special concessions ranging from allowances for purchase of buildings and machinery, general depreciation benefits and an allowance for losses as a result of damage to farm products from the control boards. Also, surpluses declared as bonuses six months after the year-end can be deducted for tax purposes.

At the same time, the recent changes in the tax laws which ended a ten-year tax holiday in 1987; the gradual movement of Land Bank lending towards market-related interest rates since the mid-1980s; the deregulation of the Maize Board and the end of the apartheid dispensation have posed serious challenges to the seasonal grain co-operatives. Instead of opening up membership to more African members, in particular, they have attempted to consolidate their positions as powerful white enterprises through a host of strategies. Amin and Bernstein (1995) note the following strategies adopted by these co-operatives: improving management practices; amalgamations (since 1990); diversifying activities, mostly into downstream processing; expanding non-member business, especially in the former homelands; converting to companies under the provisions of the Amendment Act 37 (1993); and entering maize marketing on their own account from the 1995–1996 season.

This poses serious challenges for rural development policy and for consideration to be given to breaking the monopoly position of these co-operatives and limiting their statutory privileges or alternatively building powerful black-owned secondary co-operatives in various branches of the rural agricultural economy to bolster the emergence of black farmers and ensure that they also draw on the policy benefits that are ensconced within the legal and policy framework that has supported white agriculture.

Main challenges for the SACP to build a socialist co-operative movement in South Africa

While the co-operative movement in South Africa is in its infancy, there can be no middle road on the ideological orientation of this movement. The onslaught of neoliberalism is appropriating co-operatives into the private sector. The implications of this are threefold. First, the enabling role of the state is limited and it basically should not provide the environment for a co-operative sector. Instead, co-operatives are seen as essential self-help complements to the state as it withdraws and shrinks due to privatisation, liberalisation and deregulation. Second, co-operatives are considered to be businesses like any other juristic entity – like a company, closed corporation and so on – and must compete with the same aggression and profit maximisation imperative. Third, the identity of co-operatives grounded in co-operation and mutuality between co-op members, the co-op movement and the rest of society is supplanted by the social Darwinism of market-driven competitiveness and fervour to marketise.

In South Africa the choice is simple: we either capitulate to the dominance of global capitalism and let co-operatives be treated as typical capitalist enterprises or we build a co-op movement on a scale and mass that induces the forces of capitalism to accept a contending logic of need, co-operation, solidarity, self-reliance and self-management. If the SACP takes the latter option and asserts co-operatives as one of many crucial programmatic thrusts to advance (even minimalist) socialist construction in South Africa, then some of the following tasks and questions need to be dealt with.

Building a party-movement relationship with NCASA

The SACP needs to clarify its relationship with the National Co-operative Association of South Africa (NCASA). This is an apex body that was developed through Canadian funding since 1996 and has brought in sectoral co-ops like the Savings and Credit Co-op League, Medical Co-op Association, Home Industry Co-op Association, National Community Co-op Association and the Agricultural Business Chamber. At the same time NCASA has attempted to build provincial structures and is even considering regional structures. All of this happened in a top-down way and has been contrary to international experience – co-ops do not have a sense of ownership of NCASA and also most of the developing co-operatives do not believe in the services and support it can provide them and hence do not affiliate. While the debate on the structural formation of NCASA is open and happening currently, the major issue is its orientation. Should NCASA become the greenhouse and be the backbone for capitalist co-operatives or should it foster a mass-based socialist co-operative movement that builds relationships of solidarity and co-operation between co-operatives and within society and ultimately constructs, together with the state, a co-operative sector?

Beating at the heart of this question is the relationship between the SACP and NCASA. International and historical experience points to one possible approach: NCASA becomes a front of the SACP and is controlled by it, conveyor-belt style. Alternatively, and more appropriately, a party-movement relationship can be forged which ensures that NCASA and the SACP develop joint programmes to mobilise and build the co-op movement, attempt to engage each other on strategic and tactical questions and debate ideological questions. While this approach will have communists emerging and working in NCASA, this would not undermine the organisational autonomy and independence of the co-operative movement. In short, with this approach NCASA would not have a socialist orientation by force or appendage status but by the strength of our arguments and mass-based practice.

Mobilising in key areas to ensure working-class leadership of the movement

Flowing from this is the need, both in theory and practice, to advance working-class leadership of NCASA – a leadership committed to the socialist orientation of NCASA. Practically speaking this means the SACP has to champion a worker-owner model as the generic model for co-operatives in South Africa; but more importantly, there is a need to organise the working class (both employed and unemployed, rural and urban) into the co-operative movement. This means working closely with trade unions, working-class communities, rural villages and former combatants as priorities of mass mobilisation to educate, organise and build the co-operative movement.

With trade unions, co-operatives should not just be used defensively but should also be part of an offensive strategic approach that promotes worker takeover and buyouts. In both working-class communities and rural villages there is a need to promote co-operatives as development institutions that can organise local labour, capital, land and other resources into a model of self-reliant and sustainable local economic development. In this regard it might be important to promote local co-operative movements made up of cornerstone co-operatives like a community co-operative bank, a labour and technology co-operative (which distributes work rights to the unemployed members within local economic development projects and refurbishes second-hand technologies that can be borrowed for productive purposes by co-op members), waste recycling co-operatives (that also engage in processing like recycled paper, toys and so on), arts and crafts co-operatives and organic farming co-operatives (with either of the latter co-ops running a local community market). All of this would stimulate dynamic local economic activity and a sustainable growth path. In Midrand within the Ecocity project most of these co-ops have been put into place and are attempting to achieve such a model of local sustainable development. With rural villages a similar co-operative complex can be experimented with to build self-reliance but with the possibility of building in a secondary co-operative that can procure inputs in bulk and even market produce both to the wider co-op movement and market.

With former combatants, most of them have been trained in Marxism-Leninism and have a very firm ideological orientation and commitment to socialism. This is very much part of the historical investment made by the SACP when it ensured many cadres in training camps obtained such ideological training. However, currently, many combatants are discontent in the army. From a political and strategic point of view it is important to work with these cadres and ensure that they take up the co-operative option both to ensure self-employment and re-integration into society. More importantly they can provide a bedrock political force for the co-operative movement. In Zimbabwe, for instance, such an approach was also used. However, current studies on the co-operative movement in Zimbabwe reveal a lack of a proper support environment and in most instances heavy-handed state control, in the context of rural transformation, which has contributed to their demise in many places (Louis, 1995: 162–177).

Building a SACP-linked co-operative bank

In many contexts, the need for capital is an important constraint on the development of co-operatives. While co-operatives can generate capital through membership fees, ownership shares, and re-injection of surpluses, sometimes this is not sufficient. In the Mondragon worker complex the co-operative bank was central to providing capital for the start up and expansion of co-operatives. This model also houses technical capacity which helps emergent co-operatives develop feasibility studies, co-operative business plans and advice for start-up operations. A lot of this groundwork takes about two to three years in

Mondragon and has ensured an almost zero failure rate. In the party-movement model in Italy the party was also crucial in providing finance to the co-operative movement. This is also the case and experience in Cyprus. The SACP could design and set up its own co-operative bank which can provide capital for the co-operative movement. This could mean working with the South African Credit and Co-operative League (SACCOL) model of credit unions but ensuring that finance is not only used for consumption but for productive capital. Alternatively, the SACP could design its own model, based on a common bond of party membership and attempt to secure an exemption from the registrar of banks for its co-operative bank. In short, the co-op bank of the SACP could become the central tool to facilitate a socialist co-operative movement from below.

Policy intervention on the Co-operatives Bill

The next major intervention by the SACP to ensure that a co-operative movement is promoted and a co-operative sector is buttressed through state regulation is by influencing the review of co-operative legislation. Consideration should be given to publicly calling on NCASA to host a national civil society conference on co-operative law. This event would not only assist progressive and left forces to define a firmer agenda on co-operative legal reform but would also give impetus to the movement and build a wider societal consciousness on co-operatives.

Analytically speaking there are many problems with the Co-operatives Bill. Some of the major substantive areas that the SACP should consider focusing include:

- Ensuring a worker-owner model is inscribed into the law that gives all employees of a co-operative membership, ownership and decision-making rights. In some co-operatives like consumer co-operatives employees are excluded from obtaining such rights, for instance.
- A separate law be passed for financial services co-operatives that removes the constraints contained in exemptions to the Banks Act. For instance, SACCOL credit unions cannot grow beyond a certain size and village co-operative banks have to use commercial banks as their link banks as per their exemptions. In short, these exemptions constrain the size of financial services co-operatives.
- A national policy forum/board is constituted with the power to influence co-operative policy, ensure standards and accreditation of training institutions, administer funds for co-operative capacity building, ensure

statistics are provided, inform regulations made by the minister; and with the power to sit as a special tribunal, to provide orders, based on feasibility studies and business plans presented before it, on worker-initiated takeovers and buy-outs.
- Provides for conversions of other juristic entities to co-operatives through a regulated process.
- A Department of Trade, Industry and Co-operatives is to be established. In many national governments, like Italy, India, St Lucia and Swaziland, or certain provincial governments in Canada (Ontario), ministers are given the responsibility to champion the interests of the co-operative movement. More importantly, the SACP has to ensure that the necessary institutional capacity is built in the DTI so that co-ops are not merely small and medium-sized enterprises (SMEs) and the role of the DTI reduced to administration of the Act by the registrar. A fully fledged co-operative department must be promoted in the DTI that mainstreams co-ops within industrial development but also houses the registrar, the loan guarantee fund, policy advisory forum and any other policy projects and programmes necessary to build co-operatives in the South Africa co-operative movement.

The SACP should also provide a more comprehensive submission on the new Co-operatives Bill. More importantly, this process should not be halted any longer. Thus far it has taken over two years to review this legislation. Progressive forces must push for this legislation to be passed in the course of this year and if there are other important policy issues these can be handled through the policy forum provided for in the law and the struggles waged by the co-operative movement on the ground.

African Communist 156, First quarter, 2001.

Be Partisan for Peace

THIS WEEK THE WORLD is poised at the edge of catastrophe: the United Nation's weapons inspectors, currently in Iraq, are meant to table their final report on Friday. From now until then the UN stands between a bellicose US government and a scared and ambivalent Iraqi regime. Put more starkly, the UN stands between a war that would intensify global chaos or the beginning of a new world order based on collective security and peace. What is going to happen?

One scenario is the US government, with or without UN consent, attacks Iraq and begins a war. According to US Secretary of State, Colin Powell, one of the reasons for the war is the alleged link the Iraqi regime has with Al Qaeda. To this extent it would seem the US is still seeking revenge to ensure the scales of retribution are balanced for September 11. While the horror of September 11 was a crime against humanity and requires justice to prevail, the use of war to achieve this has not been appropriate. Thus far the US military response to September 11 has been asymmetrical and disproportionate. The tonnes of bombs dropped on Afghanistan did not just defeat the Taliban but also shattered the lives of the Afghan people. Thousands of innocent people have been displaced or killed, commonly referred to by US propagandists as collateral damage.

The irony of all this carnage and devastation is that a defeat of the Taliban has not ended the threat of global terror. A Taliban defeat has only unleashed greater fear and uncertainty about the next terror attack/s in the world. A conventional military solution to global terror has not and will not work, including the successful capture of Bin Laden. Ironically, the US arrogantly persists on this path vis-à-vis Iraq. And even if Saddam Hussein is defeated by the US, a final victory against global terror cannot be claimed.

Another scenario argued by analysts and conflict resolution experts is a containment option for Iraq – continued military policing, accompanied by economic sanctions, overseen by the US and its allies, under the auspices of representing the UN. Such a solution can easily escalate into full-blown war and does not deal with the root causes of the current US/Iraq conflict. Most importantly, it would be the Iraqi people who would bear the brunt of containment. A third scenario is genuine demilitarisation and democratisation by the Iraqi regime which meets the requirements of UN resolutions – a peaceful settlement prevails. While this is the best case scenario and one that the UN is trying to achieve, including our own government, it is going to be extremely difficult to secure. The main obstacle facing the UN is not merely US unilateralism but the birth of the US imperial empire; euphemistically referred to as the American world order. Increasingly it would seem world history is not about what the left once called inter-imperialist rivalries or the Cold War fracture. Instead, it is about US global domination of any country outside its sphere of hegemonic influence and patronage. The US of today is shaped by an attitude that says: 'We won the Cold War, and so we are the most powerful country in the world and we can do what we want'. To overcome this obstacle facing the UN and to defend whatever prospect there is for world peace every citizen of the world – black, white, Muslim, Jew, communist, capitalist and so on – should take a visible stand against the US war in Iraq. The peace movement gathering in South Africa, against the war on 15 and 19 February must garner as many South Africans to stand united for world peace as possible. However, for this to happen we have all to put aside our fear and hatred. We have to shrug off millenarian ideas about a great levelling event taking place which would allow justice to prevail – the villains would be struck down by earthquakes or plague or floods or some other fatal happening and the world would be peaceful and we can all co-exist happily. We have to also resist becoming Darwinians of the sort who accept the world must be ruled by the most powerful. For contemporary international relations this means the US is justified in using whatever force is at its disposal to deal with its ostensible enemies (who are generally poorer and weaker than it). It also means the US is justified in policing any other country in the world that has acquired or produces weapons of mass destruction – nuclear, biological and chemical. It is time for South Africans to rise to the challenge of collective responsibility for the future of the world, as millions of people are doing, by taking a stand for world peace.

To take a stand for peace in the world today is more radical than mere opposition to a war. A stand for peace today recognises the world system of capitalism is no longer the harbinger of progressive change but is driven by an ideology of militarism and violence, which has become a way of life and a means of co-existing between the US and other nation states or non-state enemies. The media, the culture industry, academic think tanks and intellectuals all reinforce the grip of militarism. According to Robert D. Kaplan, an advisor to the US

Special Forces, in his recent book called *The Coming Anarchy* there is a need for greater military expenditure and increased development of intelligence capacity in the US in order to push back the 'revenge of the poor' in the world, among other threats. Taken further, a stand for peace means standing for an alternative society, not just the end of warmongering and militarism, which would place the needs of the powerless poor majority at the centre of society. To me this is what the ANC-led Alliance rallying slogan 'Peace for Development' means.

A stand for peace also means being willing to vindicate the promise of the Nuremburg Trial for global justice, if crimes against humanity are perpetrated. To this extent, the peace movement should not hesitate to call for George Bush and his Cabinet to be put on trial for crimes against humanity if the war with Iraq continues, primarily because this is a war that is no longer about mitigating September 11 and neither is it about weapons of mass destruction. This is a war about US domination. It is a war for which the Iraqi people and future victims of global terror will have to pay the price.

Finally taking a stand for peace means being partisan – against perpetrators of violence and war whether it is the US government or the Iraqi government. If both sides are driven by militarist ambitions, then both sides should be condemned. Also being partisan for peace means being genuinely disturbed by the loss of innocent lives. It means being disturbed by the tragedy of the victims; either through US aerial bombardment or those who perished on September 11. The politics of world peace, today, in the national and global peace movement cannot stand for anything less.

Sowetan, 11 February 2003.

Socialism and Sustainable Local Economic Development

Introduction

THE NATIONAL PROGRAMME of the SACP, including the national 2003 Programme of Action (POA), focuses the SACP on local economic development as one of the key thrusts to advance the challenge of building socialism now.

Consistent with this the SACP in Gauteng province has a minimum socialist programme to achieve elements of socialism within the provincial development process and accumulation path. Central to this emphasis is socialist local economic development. This is for three reasons:

(i) Trade and industrial strategy of the province, including the BLUE IQ investment projects, do not deal directly with poverty and in the end maintain a high skill, high tech and trickle-down growth development path which is not labour absorbing. The economic evidence indicates an increase in the unemployment rate from 29% to approximately 35%, over the past few years. The SACP in Gauteng province does not reject the trade and industrial strategy, but does not believe it is an adequate economic intervention to overcome the economic challenge of mass poverty in the province – it needs allied economic strategies.

(ii) There are 2.4 million people in the province suffering from absolute poverty and another 2 million from relative poverty, almost 50% of the provincial population.

(iii) Local economic development in Gauteng has not really taken off and most importantly has been uneven in its initiation. The trade and industrial strategy (particularly its BLUE IQ investment projects) of the province have excluded the poorest areas of the province, namely Metsweding, Sedibeng and West Rand.

Central to the relationship between socialism and sustainable local economic development is the following issue: is exiting from the industrial capitalist system an option for the 4 million poor in Gauteng province? Can we give poor people and working-class communities the option of socialist local economic development?

Placing the local township within the multi-level world system

The terrain on which we struggle and exist can best be described as the world capitalist system. It covers every expanse of the planet, albeit unevenly. If we periodise the development of industrial capitalism within the world capitalist system, it has gone through three important phases:

- Early modern colonial empire building by a few European countries;
- Monopoly-driven imperialism leading to two world wars; and now
- Global hegemonic imperialism, driven by transnational capital and embodied within the US regime and its militarism.

At the same time global hegemonic imperialism is dualistic. In one sense, it polarises or divides the world we live in between rich and poor countries or centres (obviously centres led by the US) and peripheries of capitalism. Within this there are also hierarchies of local spaces or cities. New York is more affluent, developed and powerful economically than Johannesburg. At the same time, the world system increasingly integrates and fosters interdependencies through markets, exchange, internet, culture and so on. In the end, the simultaneous polarisation and integration within the world system is on the terms set by the imperial hegemon and its satellites. The outcome, then, for countries in the periphery of the world capitalist system is greater destruction of local economic capacity, biodiversity, the environment and human beings (absolute poverty has increased dramatically over the past few decades). The periphery always loses.

What does this mean for local spaces? More importantly, what does this mean for the township? Should we aspire to be part of the globally competitive world system? Should we try to find our place within global hegemonic imperialism for and with township communities?

Some would answer yes and impose the idea of a shopping mall community for local townships. This usually means consumption of goods produced internationally without local resources (labour, physical and financial) contained in them. Townships are flooded with commodities, many adopt market determined cultural identities and, most importantly, many claim this as development – we are part of the global village! Yes, the township has to have commodities, but does it have to be Coca Cola, Palmolive, Kerrygold butter, McDonald's and so on?

In the end the township is part of a multi-level world system – household, township, city, province, national, continental and global. At each of these levels there is elbow room or space for an economy. At least, space for a local economy that meets basic needs through local resources. At the same time, local township economies do not have to be autarkic and cut off from the rest the world.

An alternative local economic development for townships is essentially about creating choices within local spaces – the city, the township and the household – for people to decide how they want to survive. For example, a household should be given the choice of solar and/or fossil fuel electricity, composting its waste or contributing to recycling. These choices impact on the household economy and ultimately the availability of resources in a household.

A community should have the choice of locally produced food or food produced thousands of miles away. A member of a community should have the choice between walking, cycling, using public transport or personalised motorised transport. A community should have the choice of being able to work and play (recreation) in its immediate environment and not be forced to travel great distances for this. In the end, these kinds of choices determine whether the township economy sustains and improves the quality of life or destroys both the quality of life and life itself.

The political economy of the township and the local government response

The historical development of capitalism has produced an urban and rural divide. Many people have been displaced from rural communities and forced to leave rural areas to find work in urban areas. South Africa has followed this pattern of development, except under colonialism of a special type it has also had the added feature of racially divided cities – affluent white neighbourhoods or suburbs and poverty-stricken black townships. Our cities, as we know, were designed to keep black people out and merely bring them in as transient workers.

White neighbourhoods or suburbs were mainly bourgeois or middle class in the extreme. These spaces were designed and planned to provide peaceful, safe, luxurious enclaves with shopping malls nearby. Most people have cars and have been able to easily move around to enjoy cultural experiences and other recreational activities within the wider expanse of the city. To a large extent the white suburbs were functional spaces not designed to foster a sense of community. They reinforced individualism and bourgeois privacy. Today, these suburbs are undergoing a major transformation with white business increasingly migrating from the city centre into suburbs. For example, the JSE moved from the inner city of Johannesburg to Sandton, the heart of white, affluent suburbia. To this extent these urban spaces are becoming mixed use – people live and work in the same spaces as opposed to travelling far distances to work – which perpetuates the apartheid legacy of affluent neighbourhoods conveniently located and townships relegated to the fringes of economic activity.

In contrast, the township has been a ghetto, a tragic dot designed to be invisible within the urban space. High concentrations of people live in densely populated townships, living almost on top of one another. These have been multi-class communities, mainly lower middle and working class. Often the housing settlements of townships have easily shaded into shack settlements – poverty within poverty – occupied mainly by the urban poor (employed and unemployed). In Gauteng alone it has been estimated that approximately 2.3 million people live in 583,966 shacks. This socio-economic reality has also been the breeding ground for the lumpen proletariat.

In the main, township communities are concentrations of extreme and absolute mass poverty. This poverty cannot just be explained in terms of socio-economic indicators. We need to ask what is causing the poverty – ultimately powerlessness. It is not just the legacy of apartheid-invented poverty, but a path of continued capitalist accumulation in post-apartheid South Africa. This accumulation path causes poverty and powerlessness in the following ways:

- It reinforces monopoly and transnational control and ownership of the means of production;
- It ensures the resource base of the economy still serves the needs of a minority;
- It fragments the labour market and depresses wage standards through casualisation and atypical employment;
- It supports the intensive and conspicuous consumption pattern of the minority;
- It limits and blocks access of the poor to assets; and
- It forces the poor to deplete and abuse their limited resources, which keeps them trapped in a cycle of poverty and environmental degradation.

Hardest hit by the juggernaut of absolute poverty in Gauteng and elsewhere are the urban poor and permanently unemployed working class who are increasing in numbers due to technological displacement from the labour process and labour market – machines and technology are replacing workers. These strata do not have the choice of work and wages. Put more sharply, having a job is not the means through which these people sustain their lives and ensure their reproduction – the ideology of wage labour, which is also patriarchal and fosters dependency on the capitalist system, is in crisis. Is there life and work after wage labour?

This question brings us back to the need to explain the space the urban poor and permanently unemployed working class has within the township for an alternative local economic development collectively determined by them. If the mainstream economy is increasingly job shedding and casting people away to perish in townships, this means the system has irreversibly excluded these people. In other words, their choice is not between trying to re-enter the system or breaking with the system. Rather they are pushed outside the system and have to face the necessity of surviving outside it. The system does not need them to survive and does not care about their existence. Thus, given their irrelevance to the system, alternative local economic development is the only viable option for the urban poor. Put differently, a result of their exclusion is the elbow room created for a collectively determined alternative local economic development in which the mode of organising production and work has to change.

However, such alternatives are not engendered without struggle. In Gauteng there are 15 municipal councils, three of which are metropolitan councils. Most of these councils are a terrain of national and class struggle. The local economic debate is polarising into two extremes:
- Neoliberal catch up local economic development (LED): this is characterised by an emphasis on the developed formal economy within most cities to the exclusion of the adjacent townships. Economic regeneration and support for the formal sectors of the local economy are meant to be the engine that would absorb labour from the townships and ensure wage remittances – trickle-down growth would happen. At the same time this LED option places a great deal of emphasis on place marketing to attract foreign investment, promote export and globally competitive businesses, tourism and other incentives to business. In the end, the core function of the municipal government is reduced to basic service delivery within a framework of cost recovery.
- Local corporatism: this is an economic consensus at a local level forged between the local council, local business and labour. In most instances, the economic consensus is also about using the local formal economy in a city as the engine for growth and development. However, in the end, all these

social partners have to make a contribution to achieve certain outcomes. This LED option also does not tackle the challenges of mass poverty and permanent unemployment in the township. In this vision, the local government does not lead the development process.

Are there alternatives to these two local economic development options that can ensure the township is developed collectively by the people? Are there alternative LED options that tackle mass poverty in the township directly, both in the short to medium term, and prioritise the creation of an alternative mode of production where work is organised to sustain life and the environment?

The global ecological crisis and mainstream local alternatives

Many global platforms have been created over the past four decades to deal with capitalism's destruction of non-renewable resources and the widespread pollution by its industrial system. The UN Commission (otherwise known as the Brundtland Commission or the World Commission on Environment and Development) on the environment produced in 1987 a report entitled *Our Common Future*. It makes some of the following observations:

> There are environmental trends that threaten to radically alter the planet, that threaten lives of many species upon it, including the human species (2).
>
> Nature is bountiful but it is also fragile and finely balanced. There are thresholds that cannot be crossed without endangering the basic integrity of the system. Today we are close to many of these thresholds; we must be mindful of the risk of endangering survival of life on Earth (32–33).

The Brundtland Commission provided a useful analysis of the world ecological crisis and concluded that the main causes of environmental degradation in the North can be attributed to patterns of high consumption. In the South environmental degradation was caused by poverty. In the end, the solution or alternative offered by the Brundtland Report was a paradigm of sustainable development.

The most generic definition of sustainable development is: meeting needs of the present generation while not compromising the needs of future generations. The concept of sustainable development is a host for many ideas and interpretations. The Brundtland Commission ultimately married sustainable development to catch-up capitalist modernisation. Simply put, capitalist growth economics, which ironically has been the cause of environmental degradation, was presented as the solution. In the words of Brundtland:

> It is essential that global economic growth be revitalised. In practical terms, this means more rapid economic growth in both industrial and developing countries, freer market access for the products of developing countries, lower interest rates, greater technology transfer and significantly larger capital flows, both concessional and commercial (89).

The sustainable development alternative of Rio (1992 UN Conference), commonly known as Local Agenda 21, and the 2002 WSSD (Johannesburg Implementation Plan) work with this same marriage to growth economics.

Outside of the sustainable local economic development alternative provided by Brundtland, Rio and the WSSD there have developed three important sustainable local economic development options within the global environmental and anti-capitalist movement. These local alternatives are the following:

- Localisation: this option emphasises the need to meet as many basic needs within the local community economy as possible. It does not reject having relations with the wider global economy where necessary. In the main the localisation alternative advocates local currencies, recycling, local food production, the use of renewable energy in communities, local savings schemes and co-operatives. It has a theoretical argument against the world capitalist system highlighting its failure in particular to achieve sustainable growth given the limits on fossil fuels – like oil. Its main argument explaining the existence of poverty is dependence on the mainstream cash economy. Alternatively put, the lack of money locally causes poverty. Hence it proposes local money systems that complement the national currency. Is the challenge more money or eradicating money systems? Besides the obvious self-help appeal of localisation, it has many other problems. In the first place, it is grounded in an issue-centred analysis of capitalism to point out its limits (like the end of crude oil resources) and/or the wider ecological destruction of capitalism (global warming, pollution, end of biodiversity and so on) as opposed to a deeper structural analysis of the crisis of capitalism. Hence it does not fully come to terms with (i) overproduction, (ii) the technological displacement effect and (iii) the class forces driving the system. In the second place, the agenda of localisation

does not have a conception of power that defines a role for the state – it believes in bypassing the state to achieve its objectives. It is also unclear about how to build a proper movement/s for localisation, except to be a voice within the anti-capitalist global movement.
- Bioregionalism: emphasises the need for local communities to be determined and organised around the biodiversity and physical resources in its spatial area. It also advocates an agenda similar to localisation. Ecovillages and the demonstration of an alternative lifestyle are important features of this approach. In the main, bioregionalism as a practical alternative attempts to change consumption patterns of the affluent to fit into a one planet lifestyle thus trying to fit the ecological footprint of people within the carrying capacity of the Earth. It does not have a structural analysis of capitalism and on the production side is willing to work within the overall market framework to achieve bio-advantage through trade. Most importantly the application of bioregionalism and its ecological footprint methodology has limited application in the South or periphery of capitalism where most people are existing under conditions of mass poverty.
- Green communes: this has been a proposal from green anarchists. They present communes and an alternative sub-culture based on co-operative and peaceful social relations as the local alternative to the world capitalist system. Again, there is no deeper analysis of the structural crisis of capitalism and state power is not seen as important.

Marxist socialism does not have and has not had a blueprinting approach to champion the concerns of humanity. At the same time, in its own prescriptions it does not have to reject all the above proposals for local alternatives. However, it has to work with its framework of (i) understanding the structural and class struggle determined conditions under which social change and local transformation has to happen; (ii) advancing socialist local economic development through a practice of revolutionary reforms; and (iii) placing the actual socialist alternatives within an understanding of historically determined material conditions.

Does Marxist socialism have a local alternative?

For Marxist socialism to present a local alternative to capitalism it has to confront the utopianism of the environmental and anti-capitalist global movement. At the same time, Marxist socialism has to address the four main intellectual attacks emanating from the anti-capitalist social movement and environmental movement, both in the world and in South Africa, against it playing a role in local transformation. The first argument against Marxist socialism is that it places human beings first as opposed to nature; that is, it is anthropocentric. This critique is best captured in the idea that Marx and Engels advocated the 'conquest of nature', at all cost, to ensure human survival. In the first place, Marx and Engels had an ecological conception and sensitivity within their work (for example, *Early Writings, Economic and Political Manuscripts, Capital, Anti-Dühring and Dialectics of Nature*).

Marx in *Capital* volume III explicitly refers to the necessary obligation human beings have to preserve the ecological preconditions of human life for future generations:

> From the standpoint of a higher socio-economic formation [i.e socialism] individual private ownership of the earth will appear just as much in bad taste as the ownership of one human being by another. Even a whole society, a whole nation, or all contemporary societies taken together are not the absolute owners of the earth. They are only its occupants, its beneficiaries, and like a good paterfamilias have to leave it in improved condition to following generations (Marx, 1991 [1984]: 911).

Engels, in his work on 'The role of work in transforming ape into man', provides the most important ecological lesson:

> As we have already indicated, animals modify the natural environment as do men, although to a lesser degree, and, as we have seen, the modifications which they have effected in their surroundings react in turn to transform the actors themselves. For nothing happens in isolation in nature. Every phenomenon reacts on the other, and inversely, and it is usually because they forget this dynamic and this reciprocal action that your scholars are prevented from understanding the simplest things. We have seen how goats impeded the reforestation of Greece ... The animal destroys the vegetation without knowing what it is doing. Man destroys it to plant grain on the available land, or to plant trees or vines which he knows will yield him a harvest several times greater than what he has sown, transfers the useful plants and domestic animals from one country to another, and he thus modifies the flora and fauna of whole

continents. There is more. Thanks to artificial selection, the agency of man transforms plants and animals to the point that they can no longer be recognised ... In brief, the animal only uses the external environment, modifying it simply by its presence; by the changes which he brings, man makes it serve his purposes. He conquers it (Engels, 1934 [1986]: 178–181).

All of this does not mean that Marx and Engels were the founders of modern ecology, but they did understand how the destructiveness of capitalism had an impact on human beings and nature. The second point to make in defence of a Marxist understanding of the relationship between human society and nature is that Marx and Engels believed in human consciousness being capable of liberating itself through class struggle and in this process having a dialectical relationship with nature – taking from nature what is necessary to meet human needs, ensure creativity, pleasure and beauty. In other words, a conscious society [i.e., socialist] and revolutionary movement have a dialectical relationship with nature as opposed to a domineering or antagonistic relationship. Engels observed:

Let us not, however, flatter ourselves too much as to our victories over nature. For each one of these, it takes its revenge. Initially, each victory certainly has the consequences which we anticipated, but at a second or third remove, it has effects that are so different, so unforeseen, that too often the initial achievement is destroyed (Engels, 1934 [1986]: 181).

The third point to make about Marxism is that it places one fundamental limit on the human use of nature: nature cannot be destroyed to the point where it threatens human survival. Put differently, Marxists understand human beings to be part of nature and if nature is destroyed then human beings cannot survive. The second argument against Marxist socialism is what is considered to be its obsession with the determining role of the forces of production and the abundance it creates. There are three important points to be made in defence of Marxist socialism. In the first place, reductionism and economic determinism are part of a vulgar Marxism which fails to understand the dialectical relationship between base and superstructure and more importantly the dialectic between forces and relations of production. Hence, the subject of attack by Greens is a crude version of Marxism. In the second place, the forces of production have been unevenly spread throughout the world and Marxists understand how the world capitalist system has created abundance for a few on a world scale as opposed to an abundance for the majority. In the third place, Marxists understand the forces of production as being composed of machinery, labour power, raw material and energy, for instance. It is consistent with this framework for Marxists to understand limits on the forces of production; if for example, crude oil supplies suddenly end. Put differently, it is within the ideological understanding of Marxists to even consider ecological limits on the forces of production and ultimately capitalism. The third argument made by Green critiques of Marxism is that the working class is dependent on the resource intensive industrial base of capitalism. In the world we live in today the working class is not unaware of the trans-class issues like global warming, ozone depletion, pollution and so on that affect their survival. Like everyone else it is in the objective interest of the working class to be supportive of alternatives that would sustain all our lives. In South Africa, COSATU unions were at the forefront of the WSSD NGO process and demonstrated an understanding of the threat capitalism poses to workers and the survival of nature, as well. This consciousness has to also be taken further as part of a programme for socialist development that would transform South African capitalism ecologically as well. This conference is part of that process.

Actually, existing socialism has destroyed the environment and has proved that socialism is not sustainable. This is the fourth critique normally wielded against Marxist socialism. In defence of Marxist socialism, the following has to be put across. In the first place in the golden years of the Soviet Revolution in the early to mid-1920s there was a strong environmental movement. It was influenced by the work of Bogdanov and taken up in policy terms by Lunacharsky and Bukharin. Many conservation reserves were set up from 1919 and were strongly supported by Lenin. However, by 1929 the rise of the environmental movement was stopped in its tracks by Stalin. He basically suppressed any preoccupations with the environment and launched his plan for forced march industrialisation. In the second place, Stalin's industrialisation was a disaster for the environment and produced catastrophic consequences for the resource base of the Soviet economy. To this extent, the Green critique of existing socialism is correct except that its target should be Stalinist socialism and not socialism in general.

Marxist socialism has an alternative that is also ecological within the NDR in South Africa. In this sense it has to proceed from the following premises: (i) a dialectic relationship between nature and society – as opposed to the domineering and antagonistic relationship under capitalism; (ii) a structural analysis of capitalism and how the class structure of capitalism exploits and alienates human beings and destroys the environment – the destructive power of capitalism does not just have consequences for human beings but also for nature; and (iii) a central role for the working class-led bloc of forces is to assert socialist demands that are also ecological demands.

Achieving sustainable local economic development through socialist transformation

The South African NDR has the space for socialist local economic development to be pursued both from above and below. Both the ANC resolutions adopted at Stellenbosch and the SACP's programme for Building Socialism Now advocate the need for poverty eradicating sustainable local economic development. This means the politics of achieving these results should not be lost in two extremes:

- An oppositional politics, which sees socialist local economic development as something to be fought for. While there might be a need to mobilise communities to ensure certain needs or concerns are heard, it does not mean that the ANC government is the enemy and all its policies are anti-people. In fact, many of the policies are progressive and consistent with the need for government to implement a framework to support poverty eradication and sustainable local economic development. Local communities do not have to ascribe to a go-it-alone logic.
- Pressure group politics, which is about flagging single issues in the country outside of an integrated programme. Socialist local economic development cannot succeed on these terms. Most importantly it is not just about changing lifestyles and values and education through ecological examples like ecovillages. It has to be about integrated and overall development that is participatory and controlled by working class and poor communities.

The politics for the SACP in Gauteng to achieve socialist local economic development is informed by a political understanding of revolutionary reforms, a theory of socialist transition (the content of which is a minimum socialist programme), and an approach to socialist local economic development that is sustainable in the ecological sense but also self-reliant in terms of the role of communities. On revolutionary reforms our starting point is recognition of the necessary preconditions for revolutionary reforms to attempt socialist local economic development:

(i) A role for developmental local government: This means local governments must plan, lead and give support to community-controlled and determined socialist local economic development. It would be important for local governments to form partnerships with township communities to ensure resources and other technical support can be properly channelled.

(ii) ANC-led Alliance as the vanguard of the community: This means while government has a leading role, it has to be complemented by a role that political structures play in local communities. This means top-down or statist delivery of programmes is not enough for sustainability. The ANC-led Alliance structures in communities have to be at the forefront of ensuring communities are organised to participate in government-supported programmes, as well as their own self-reliant initiatives. A good example is the SACP idea of community food security forums, which should ensure Alliance structures and other community structures are involved in solving the problem of local hunger and organising people into local food production projects.

(iii) Front for Socio-Economic Transformation or Popular Movement for Transformation: This means local co-operative movements, stokvels, burial societies, community projects and initiatives have to be organised into a movement, at least in local communities. This would ensure and maintain the momentum for local change and facilitate the building of people's power. In more concrete terms, it is about ensuring township communities become spaces for creating and sustaining life on terms of the people living and co-existing there. In short, collective working-class action is the central driver or motive force for transformation.

On the socialist transition, socialism has to contend with and contradict capitalist and statist tendencies within the NDR. The transformation of the township economy would require the socialist and statist tendencies of the NDR to prevail. This means the participatory impulses and thrusts within government delivery frameworks and mechanisms like integrated development plans (IDPs) and the bottom-up organisation of communities, through socialist practice, must work together to transform households, townships and cities.

Central to a socialist approach to local development is the concept of self-reliance. What is self-reliant local economic development?

Self-reliance is not about autarky, but about utilising the conditions and resources for human survival in a community to meet the basic needs of local communities on their terms. This means local communities would also meet other needs but not through local economic activity – a balance has to be struck between the township economy and the wider or external economy.

Self-reliance is about values of self-provisioning, self-sufficiency, autonomy and freedom – contra capitalism's individualism and opportunities for the few.

Self-reliant economic activity is about harnessing local savings, labour and physical resources for local production and consumption. It means organising local production for use values and need, using local resources. The knock-on consequences of this would be the stimulation of a community-controlled economy. This is different from labour and labour power being utilised to produce exchange values or commercial commodities. To this extent there is freedom in work, production of subsistence goods and creation of sustainable livelihoods.

Self-reliant local development is also about the cultural, political, economic, gender and spiritual development of individuals and a community. In other words, it is about all-rounded development grounded in the wisdom and knowledge of local communities.

In short, a socialist approach to local economic development must attempt to meet basic needs in the context of people already being rejected by the capitalist system. It is about ensuring a politics of revolutionary reforms prevails such that self-reliant township communities can be realised.

The programmatic challenges for building elements of socialism in the township and the household

The main programmatic challenges for the SACP in Gauteng to achieve socialist local economic development and ultimately elements of socialism are the following:

- Building local co-operative movements and sectors, integrated into production, consumption, savings and sustainable livelihoods;
- Championing food security/vulnerability and nutritional deficiency through food security forums and local food production;
- Shifting local government resources to the township economy, thus increasing per capita rand spend in the township economy through procurement, services and development;
- Making IDPs and ward committees people-driven such that resources are decentralised and participatory development happens;
- Renewing participatory governance – school governing boards, hospitals

and policing forums, local clinics and so on;
- Organising beneficiaries into the people's housing process to ensure integrated, self-reliant and ecologically informed communities take root;
- Encouraging walking, cycling and public transport;
- Promoting the use of efficient, clean and renewable energy technology and resources;
- Linking township communities with provincial and national interventions, such as GAUMAC enterprise development mechanism, sector education and training authorities (SETAs) and BLUE IQ infrastructure investments.

Conclusion

For the SACP in Gauteng NDR theory and socialist theory have to engage with the ecological question seriously. This discussion paper is one small step in that direction.

At the same time, we are also convinced that Marxist socialism has always been concerned about the future of humanity and nature. However, it also understands that it is the collective choices we make in the present that would determine the kind of future we all have. Socialist local economic development is therefore crucial to ensure human life and nature is protected and sustained at a time when capitalism is only characterised by destruction. The phase of imperialist empire building is essentially about defending a system in its death throes – capitalism can only become more moribund and reactionary as it comes up against the limits to conquering human beings and nature.

SACP Gauteng province, Conference on Socialism and Sustainable Local Economic Development, 20 July 2003, Wits University.

Rejecting the Fraud of the National Democratic Revolution

A Critique of Government's Macro-Economic Strategy: Growth, Employment and Redistribution
with Langa Zita and Dale McKinley

IN RESPONSE TO THE government's macro-economic strategy the national political education secretariat of the SACP has prepared this discussion paper. As a starting point, this document does not accept the government's macro-economic strategy as a framework within which the RDP can be delivered. Essentially, it places capitalist accumulation at the centre of growth and development, as opposed to the prioritisation of basic needs and redistribution as envisaged in the RDP. At a political level, it is indicative of a rightward shift by the ANC government. For this reason, it is time for the SACP to engage with political and economic development in a dispassionate and politically rigorous manner, to tease out its implications for the NDR and the socialist project in South Africa.

Introduction: The growth framework

While the document lays claim to advancing RDP delivery and ethos, the underlying rationale is in fact monetarist, based on further liberalisation inducing capital accumulation through the financial markets. Redistribution, therefore, only appears as a secondary outcome and of growth and employment generation. It is no longer a key element in the process and strategy:

- The document assumes market-oriented policies will yield the desired outcomes of significant job creation growth, reduced poverty and inequality. It is premised on an individualistic approach to accumulation and development. It seeks to create a market democracy, that is, one where everybody is notionally equal in the marketplace, subject to their existing access to, and control over resources. It does not challenge the inherited economic structure.
- There is nothing new about this framework, which represents a restating of the trickle-down approach, with growth first and redistribution subject to the cake increasing in size.
- Industrial development is envisaged based on winning and penetrating

export markets including southern Africa. The assumption is that South Africa will be transformed into the first African tiger through exploiting the opportunities in the global marketplace. The framework appears blind to the realities of world trade where competition is neither free or fair.
- At the kernel of the document is the reduction of inflation through constrained demand. Policies in the macro-economic framework are directed at reducing inflation through constraining demand as the fundamental condition for growth. Therefore, government policies are not directed towards growth itself, through the expansion of opportunities for the majority.

Fiscal policy

The strategy adopts the logic of deficit reduction and accepts existing political and economic constraints. This implies:
- Reduction of taxes, rather than setting out a framework of taxation to increase revenues available to government;
- Fiscal policy accepts the existing structures of production and ownership. This is obviously not neutral but instead means that fiscal policy serves middle- and upper-income earners who benefit from tax reductions, while the working class have to accept wage restraint;
- Judgement that the debt is too high, while in fact South Africa's debt is in comparison with most advanced capitalist economies.

The threat of structural adjustment is being used as a stick, while it is really an illusion. South Africa is instead in a relatively strong position. South Africa's debt is largely domestic, and a large portion is due to government commitments to a fully funded pension scheme. If South Africa had a 'pay as you earn' scheme similar to Britain, it would mean that the deficit would be recorded as less than half of the reported figures. For example, on this basis the 1994 deficit would have been just 2.9%. The accounting being used in this respect by the government is overstating the deficit and thus exaggerates the threat of debt trap from which the proposed strategy is meant to save us all.

The document relies on projections of relatively strong and sustained growth and foreign capital inflows to enable social spending and government infrastructure investment to be increased. In 1996, growth is projected at 3.5%. However, Central Statistical Services data for the first quarter of 1996 means that this is highly questionable. The growth performance reveals that, while there has been a strong post-drought spurt in agricultural production, total non-agricultural production grew at an annualised rate of just 0.6%, while manufacturing recorded zero growth. In short, the broad-based growth expected by the strategy has already faltered, and therefore, in order for the government to achieve the deficit-reduction targets, health and education spending will have to be restrained, mainly impacting the poor.

Monetary and foreign exchange policy

The two main elements are:

1. Monetary policy as key to controlling inflation:

- Real interest rates will only be reduced once the present low inflation levels have been maintained, and incomes policy constraining expenditure and government deficit reduction has taken effect. Real interest rates have been excessively high by international standards, and only impact on inflation through engineering a contraction in the economy. Far from being a platform for growth, the interest rate policy is a major constraint on domestic investment in housing, and by SMEs who cannot afford the cost of loans;

- High real interest rates attract short-term speculative capital relaxing the foreign exchange constraint but create instability in the medium term. It has also fuelled lending for consumption, as domestic banks borrowed on international markets at low rates to lend on at high domestic rates, for example, through in-store credit, such as Edgars cards. As soon as the short-term capital flows cease, the exchange rate collapses, but domestic banks have passed on the cost to consumers through higher interest rates to maintain their own profit levels.

2. Financial and exchange control abbreviation is assumed to create private-sector investment. But

- A vibrant industrial sector rather than completely unfettered markets stimulate investment, China being the obvious example of this. Government intervention is crucial in developing the foundation for profitable industries, and therefore, in attracting long-term investment.

- Exchange control liberalisation further increase South Africa's vulnerability to foreign capital flows and narrows the range of instruments available to the government. It encourages investors in short-term assets who are concerned about their ability to withdraw their money rather

than investors making long-term commitment and investing in increased productive capacity;
- It makes industrial development contingent on foreign investment, and allows investors to essentially hold the government to ransom. Instead, government policy should be directed at releasing the substantial domestic resources existing in the economy.

Labour market, employment and income policy

While the macro-economic framework proposed regulated flexibility, the institutional framework is not in place. Although the LRA went some way to setting this up, it does not go far enough. Legislated central bargaining in most sectors is not in place. In this context, the document opens the door to absolute flexibility and increased exploitation, alongside lower wages.

At present between 35–50% of wage earners earn less than the minimum living level of R970 per month. Workers in the South African economy are poor. Against this, the proposed macro-economic approach can only stabilise poverty, even if employment creation succeeds. Ironically, the document proposes a social accord hinged on wage restraint by the working class, while wages of middle- and upper-income earners continue to increase at disproportionate levels. The result will be an increased disparity in wages, in direct contradiction to RDP objectives.

Trade and industry

The export-led growth strategy, to be spurred by accelerated tariff reductions, will not generate the employment projected. The sectors that will benefit from this process are capital-intensive and high-skill, while in labour-intensive sectors workers are being retrenched and factories closing. This process is already underway with massive job losses in textiles and clothing, while electrical goods production has been expanding.

While trade liberalisation has put down pressure on inflation, it has done this through imports becoming progressively cheaper relative to domestically produced goods. This leads to unemployment as domestic factories cannot compete with imports, and the current account goes into deficit. This process is similar to the de-industrialisation experienced in Zimbabwe and is an ongoing spiral. As the current account deteriorates, interest rates are raised to attract foreign capital, further compounding the production crisis.

The strategy relies on supply-side measures and incentives to stimulate output growth. These measures are only slowly being put in place although the tariff reduction schedule has been underway for two years. Moreover, the incentives such as tax holidays and accelerated depreciation favour capital-intensive investments, and tax holidays mean that newly established and foreign owned enterprises will be able to undercut existing industries. This will have a double negative effect of retrenchment in the existing industries and a loss of tax revenue to the government.

Public investment and asset restructuring

It is proposed that the R173 billion required for infrastructure will be gained from a number of sources including privatisation revenues, loans from multilateral institutions and restructuring of fiscal expenditures.

However,

- as noted above, increasing infrastructure expenditure in the budget can only occur at the expense of other core items, given the acceptance of these existing constraints;
- the majority of government investment is planned, in the proposed strategy, to occur in the later years, and is contingent on growth trickling down. In this programme, government infrastructure investment follows the private sector. This is not consistent with the RDP, which envisaged public investment leading economic development;
- ironically, government fixed investment meant to pick up in the years 1999–2000 might represent part of the re-election strategy;
- privatisation will not yield the resources government requires and weakens the government's long-term position, as revenue is lost from enterprises which have been sold;
- privatised enterprises will not extend services to unprofitable areas such as rural areas;
- cost recovery is proposed as a means to fund infrastructure development, which implies that rates will rise significantly if infrastructure is to be extended. This will hit the poor most, and is not a framework within which RDP priorities and backlogs can be addressed.

Conclusion: The politics of process

The macro-economic strategy did not emerge out of a collective process of the Tripartite Alliance and as such, does not represent the constituency which voted the ANC into power. Consultation was mainly driven by the intention to dampen any misgivings of the Alliance partners. Leading elements in government used the technical skills of mainly old order economists and the World Bank, while progressive economists in NGOs and the broader Alliance were not part of the process. The outcome is therefore not surprising given the composition of the team.

The further pronouncement by Trevor Manuel that the parameters are non-negotiable contradicts the basis of the Alliance itself. It is imperative that the SACP seriously engage the ANC and COSATU on the future of the government's macro-economic strategy.

Debate 1, 1996.

Neoliberalised South Africa: Labour and the Roots of Passive Revolution

Introduction

POST-APARTHEID SOUTH AFRICA'S neoliberalisation was not inevitable. The project of national liberation led by the ANC and its allies, including the SACP, COSATU and other mass organisations, held out to South Africans and the world the possibility of fundamental change. The visions of a post-apartheid South Africa articulated by this national liberation movement were generally framed by left discourses ranging from revolutionary nationalism, left social democracy and a Sovietised scientific socialism. However, with the first democratic elections in 1994 the direction of change in South Africa veered to the right. The historical achievement of electoral and procedural democracy and the end of formal apartheid has not produced a radically transformed society. Instead, South Africa has experienced more than 14 years of neoliberalisation. In many instances the prestige of the ANC-led liberation movement, the Mandela factor and the disingenuous marrying of transnational neoliberalism with national liberation discourse has generally obscured attempts to understand what happened in post-apartheid South Africa.

This contribution attempts to find the origins of the right-wing shift in post-apartheid South Africa, and to look for its roots. This takes us to an earlier reception of neoliberalism in South Africa during the apartheid era when the initial moment of neoliberalisation was part of a response to a deep organic and conjunctural crisis. In this historical moment the restructuring of South Africa's accumulation path in accordance with the requirements of transnational neoliberalism inaugurated the beginning of a structural shift: a transition from monopoly capitalism to a transnationalised domestic capitalism. Such a form of capitalism is different from the inward-looking industrialisation South Africa experienced for the greater part of the twentieth century and was linked to its minerals-energy complex. Instead, a new transnationalising capitalism is grounded in transnationalised relations of production and an externally orientated accumulation model. At the same time the response of the labour movement, led by COSATU, a consistently left-wing trade union movement with a militant commitment to socialism proves to be inadequate. Its agenda of a democratic corporatist state is eclipsed by a deepening of neoliberal restructuring. This article attempts to explain labour's failure by locating South Africa's home-grown neoliberalisation in the context of a passive revolution.

The concept of passive revolution is taken from the work of Antonio Gramsci and refers to a historical possibility during times of hegemonic crisis. It refers to a non-hegemonic form of class rule, in which leadership of society is not based on consent and the moral, intellectual and strategic character of leadership. In the South African context, it points to a form of politics in which mass initiative is contained from above such that struggle around the post-apartheid state form, the globalisation of a deracialising import-substitution model, the unravelling of ANC hegemonic leadership and the rise of a transnational fraction of South Africa's ruling class, contributes to a limited process of historical change. The concept of passive revolution is utilised to interpret the nature of change in post-apartheid South Africa. The specificity of this comes through by historicising the first six years of South Africa's transition to democracy from 1990 to 1996, as the conjuncture of a democratic corporatist state. This conjuncture is made up of two phases: the phase of negotiations (1990–1993) and the phase of democratic advance (1994–1996).

The shift from National Democratic Revolution to passive revolution

The notion of National Democratic Revolution is an ideological linchpin within national liberation discourse in South Africa. Within the ANC-led liberation movement it has been a consistent practice to analyse the structural conditions of South Africa's political economy and the shifting balance of national and class forces within this frame. Prior to South Africa's transition to electoral democracy, the essence of the NDR was defined in a classical Marxist-Leninist way (SACP, 1989). The main content and meaning of revolution was the seizure of state power and its transfer from monopoly capital to the working class. Accompanying this conception of revolution was a strong commitment to the principle of working-class leadership. In its current articulation within the ruling party, the ANC, the concept of the NDR does not provide an analysis and understanding of the underlying structural changes within South Africa's post-apartheid political economy (ANC, 2007). Such a concept when brought in touch with contemporary reality is a false abstraction and a disciplinary concept. It does not assist with explaining and understanding current South African realities and the social forces shaping contemporary South Africa. For instance, the current framing of South African reality focuses on the salience of monopoly capital, a concept associated with a 'racialised Fordist accumulation regime' (Gelb, 1991: 13–19). In the context of a globalised South African economy the concept of monopoly capital lacks analytical precision. Moreover, the centrality of the principle of working-class leadership is rendered irrelevant in a context of Afro-neoliberal-led economic change which favours the interests of transnational capital.

The restructuring of South African capitalism into a transnational capitalism reflects a new stage in the development of its mode of production. Such a transnationalised stage links South African capitalism more deeply into global circuits of accumulation. Increasingly, South African monopoly capital has moved offshore and in most instances beyond the South African market, while the domestic economy has become increasingly geared and dependent on external flows of capital. This is not a conjunctural moment and neither was it inevitable. The emergence of a transnational capitalism is a rupture and a structural shift that has remade South Africa's political economy. National accumulation has been globalised (internally and externally) beyond the national space such that South Africa's internationalised economy is increasingly integrated into a transnational political economy. This economic transition coincided with and has shaped and has been shaped by the political transition.

While the democratic advance of a post-apartheid constitutionalism was historically fundamental, the implications of South Africa's deep organic crisis in terms of its underlying accumulation pattern expressed itself over the past 14 years through a politics of reformism, also understood as a passive revolution. Such a politics disabled mass initiative through a technocratic, elitist and top-down approach to economic reform. The politics of passive revolution embedded transnational neoliberalism in the South African context. Through its internalisation of transnational neoliberalism, the politics of passive revolution has informed and conditioned the class-based strategies and initiatives that have remade South Africa's political economy: its accumulation model, state forms, social forces, state–civil society relations and class formation, and has ensured a revolution in which a democratic South Africa has restored and advanced the power of capital over society, particularly of transnational capital. To understand this revolution without revolution it is necessary to clarify and distinguish the theoretical approach of this analysis.

The concept of passive revolution is very different from the notion of counter-revolution. Counter-revolution refers to the reversal of radical advances or breakthroughs, while the notion of passive revolution refers to the redirection of historical processes in order to reproduce capitalism. During the twentieth century the concept of counter-revolution was imbued with a meaning based on actual experiences of violent suppression of revolutionary change. In the context of the Cold War and superpower rivalry it referred to violent attempts to stop revolutionary advance. The Bay of Pigs in Cuba, the coup against Allende, and other violent counter-offensives against left forces in the twentieth century, were all important moments of counter-revolution.

The concept of passive revolution refers to a different kind of phenomena. In the first place it refers to a historical period with immanent possibilities for fundamental transformation of social relations of production and power in a particular society. However, in such moments progressive forces lose the initiative and things change but not in a radical direction. Structural change happens, like the form of the state is changed and the accumulation model, but this is not necessarily in the interests of radical social forces. To use a cliché: the more things change, the more they stay the same, in terms of social and power relations. In short, capitalism succeeds in reproducing itself, even as a new form.

Moreover, the concept of passive revolution refers to a type of politics in historical moments that are full of possibility for radical change, but that ultimately take the initiative away from radical social forces. In most instances, this is a top-down politics, which is about co-opting the leadership of progressive forces, accommodating particular demands of social forces to engender division, deploying a revolutionary rhetoric that espouses the aspirations of mass social forces and generally utilising tactics to neutralise progressive social forces. The politics of passive revolution is an anti-mass-based politics and it seeks to lead change away from mass influence and power. It is about the politics of reforms that do not seek to transform capitalism, but to ensure its survival (Sassoon, 1982: 127–128).

In utilising the concept of the passive revolution we shall attempt to think about the current political economy dynamics of contemporary South Africa that engendered an Afro-neoliberal project. This is different from Gramsci's attempt to utilise the concept to make sense of the degeneration of the Russian Revolution, for example. In this sense what follows is an attempt to think about post-apartheid South Africa in a Gramscian way and to go beyond.[1] More specifically, this means drawing on Gramsci's historicism (Morera, 1990: 67–127), but to understand social change in a neoliberalised South Africa. Gramsci's historicism accepts that the social order is not natural and neither is the social order merely determined by structural changes. Within Gramsci's historicism the dialectical relationship between structure and agency is central to understanding social change. This brings in a role for social agency and hence we can make and unmake the world we live in.

Three aspects of Gramsci's historicism are crucial to assist with understanding contemporary South Africa.[2] First, socio-historical time operates at various levels, each with its own tempos, from the historical event, to the conjuncture and the civilisational shift. These different levels are interconnected and assist with understanding change beyond the surface appearance of things. Gramsci's historicism assists with understanding structural movements at an organic level, to the terrain of rival projects and petty everyday politics. Second, Gramsci highlights that change happens within the limits of the possible. These limits (ideas, consciousness, institutions, power relations) are not fixed or immutable, but exist within social structures that are subject to the dialectic of historical change: contradiction. Ultimately while social action is shaped and conditioned by social structures, these structures are also transformed by such action. Third, Gramsci reminds us that knowledge and ideas are implicated in the process of social change through social agency. Knowledge and ideas have material effects and consequences. This link between ideas and social agency provides the basis for a normative belief of achieving a society better than capitalism within Gramsci's historicism.

Through thinking about post-apartheid South Africa in a Gramscian way we can locate the roots of passive revolution in three underlying dynamics. The first relates to the conjuncture that created the conditions for the rise and eclipse of a democratic corporatist state (1990–1996). Historicising this conjuncture begins with locating the relationship between apartheid and the

---

[1] See Hall (1982). In some quarters it might be easy to reduce the social and political thought of Antonio Gramsci to that of an Italian tradition, and for some the appropriations of Gramsci have reduced him to a theorist of revolution in the West. This further strengthens and feeds into Africanist dismissals of radical thought. Antonio Gramsci was a theorist of the political, and a non-economistic reading assists in recognising that for Gramsci the politics of hegemony – active consent for strategic, moral and intellectual leadership – is a challenge for ruling classes in developed and developing societies.

[2] Within critical international political economy, the work of Robert Cox, Stephen Gill and David Morton among others has popularised this understanding of Gramsci's historicism.

reception of neoliberal ideological currents and how this framed a response by the apartheid regime to South Africa's structural and conjunctural crisis: the neo-apartheid reform agenda. Coming out of resistance to these reforms and into South Africa's transition to democracy was a clearly articulated agenda by labour to define a democratic corporatist state solution to resolve South Africa's organic crisis. However, the struggle for a democratic corporatist state was eclipsed by the globalisation of South Africa's accumulation model and the articulation of an indigenised variant of neoliberalism: a South African variant of Afro-neoliberalism, a continental expression of neoliberalism with African characteristics.

The second dynamic underpinning South Africa's passive revolution relates to the unravelling of the hegemonic moment. Such an unravelling emerges out of the contradictions within an ANC-led Alliance transition to democracy in which the conjuncture of the democratic corporatist state brings to the fore certain party-based and, later, state practices that begin to disable civil society and truncate democracy into a narrow representative form. In historicising state–civil society relations in the conjuncture of the democratic corporatist state, through its phases of negotiations (1990–1993) and democratic advance (1993–1996), there is an attempt to show how a wider conception of participatory democracy was lost in post-apartheid South Africa.

The third dynamic underpinning South Africa's passive revolution relates to class formation and particularly the creation of a transnational fraction capable of advancing an Afro-neoliberal project in South Africa. Such a class fraction was structurally engendered through Afro-neoliberal restructuring. However, it developed a class consciousness through politico-ideological factors that ensured a convergence between a globalising white monopoly capital, a faction within the petty bourgeois political leadership of the ANC, key bureaucratic cadres in the state managing South Africa's adjustment, and other important social forces. This article will bring into view the factors that contributed to forming a transnational fraction of South Africa's ruling class and Afro-neoliberal historic bloc.

In short, this analysis pivots around an examination of the roots of South Africa's post-apartheid passive revolution in four respects: (i) the eclipsing of a democratic corporatist state form; (ii) the globalisation, from within and externally, of a deracialising accumulation model; (iii) the shift from hegemonic politics to the beginnings of a politics of dominance; and (iv) processes of class formation that engendered a transnational fraction of South Africa's ruling class and an Afro-neoliberal historical bloc. The understanding of the beginning of post-apartheid South Africa's passive revolution reflects a transitional politics related to the constitution of a transnationalised capitalism. However, to understand these historical structures and processes various elements of Gramsci's notion of a passive revolution are combined to assist with tracing the origins of and explaining change in the new South Africa.

Neoliberalism and apartheid

Jessop (1990: 198–199) defines an accumulation strategy or model as a

> specific economic 'growth model' complete with its various extra-economic conditions and also outlines a general strategy appropriate to its realisation. To succeed, such a model must unify the different moments in the circuit of capital (money or banking capital, industrial capital, commercial capital) under the hegemony of one fraction (whose composition will vary inter alia with the stage of capitalist development).

The underlying dynamics of South Africa's accumulation model (goals, policies, regulatory frameworks and institutions) in the twentieth century lent itself to concentrating capital into racialised monopolies. This model has undergone various changes in the course of the twentieth century. By the early 1970s, due to major changes in the international political economy, like the removal of the Gold Standard and oil price hikes, South Africa's racialised import-substitution strategy, premised on a regimented, cheap, unskilled labour force and buttressed by an Afrikaner-controlled strategic parastatal sector, began displaying serious structural weaknesses. Most importantly its export dependence on primary commodities such as gold also began to affect macro-balances negatively as the price of gold began fluctuating and even declining. These structural weaknesses crystallised into an organic crisis, requiring major adjustments and registering contradictions at the political and ideological levels. By the 1980s, South Africa's political economy was experiencing declining growth (1.9% by 1984 down to 1.5% for the rest of the decade and was in the negative range in the early 1990s), low rates of private investment, balance of payments crises (due to sanctions and import dependence for capital goods and fluctuating gold prices), increasing inflation, deepening structural unemployment, ballooning fiscal pressures due to soaring military costs and a major wave of struggles led by the working-class bloc of national liberation forces (Gelb, 1991; Marais, 2001: 30–33).

In responding to this mid-1970s crisis, the ruling National Party, by then the political instrument of Afrikaner capital, opted for reforms from above, a neo-apartheid solution. A crucial element included the introduction of neoliberal reforms aimed at globalising the apartheid economy both internally and externally, mirroring a trend on the African continent. This adjustment, however, was not done in a consistent way and brought together a mix of statist neo-mercantilist policy and neoliberalism. The neoliberal moment expressed itself mainly through firm monetary policy directed at curtailing inflation, liberalising exchange controls for a brief moment, and an attempt at restructuring bloated and inefficient state parastatals. However, in the midst of this, the globalisation of the South African economy through the mobility of capital (internal and external) became discernible. Capital flight out of the economy together with outward movement by finance capital towards the late 1980s and early 1990s, displayed the first signs of internally driven globalisation (Allen, 2006: 49). South African capital increasingly began displaying signs of having transcended national capitalism. This trend becomes even more sharply defined in the post-apartheid context. However, prior to the democratic transition, South Africa already had various global giants within its economy. Despite sanctions and widespread disinvestment campaigns, at the time of the unbanning of political movements in the early 1990s there were more than 450 firms within South Africa with foreign direct investment (FDI) liabilities at $8 billion and with 85% from Europe and 13% from North America (Gelb and Black, 2004: 8). This points, further, to South Africa being caught in globalising tides, from the outside coming in, as part of a process of transnational neoliberal restructuring emanating from capitalist centres from the 1970s.[3]

In addition, during the apartheid era South Africa was forced into a debt standstill in the mid-1980s when various payments became due. The apartheid regime failed to bring about economic growth and to service the debt without new capital; hence it took its debt obligations very seriously so as not to close off external sources. Allen (2006: 31–68) highlights how the moratorium on

---

3 It should be noted that in the 1980s Ronald Reagan came to power in the US and Margaret Thatcher in the UK. Both were committed to a transnational neoliberal project to solve the accumulation crisis experienced in Western economies since around 1973. They encouraged the transnationalising of capital to deal with declining profit rates. Moreover, we should not forget that neoliberalism's first experiment in a Third World country was in Chile after the 1973 coup. These doctrines were imposed in the context of military dictatorship. This should help shed some light on why Reagan and Thatcher were also extremely sympathetic to the apartheid regime. They did not encourage disinvestment despite important mass pressure from the anti-apartheid movement.

$13.62 billion owed to 233 banks only reached firm resolution by 1993, when the ANC was drawn into the final phase of these negotiations in which it accepted responsibility for the remaining debt obligations of the apartheid regime.

The main effect of the neoliberal moment during apartheid was to pass on adjustment costs to workers and the poor. Slower growth in the 1980s accompanied by a contractionary monetary policy led to retrenchments. Unions also refused to be bought off by wage productivity trade-offs but instead strikes for wages were frequent (Gelb, 1991: 28). At the same time, labour market reform deracialised collective bargaining and by 1986 influx control was abolished ensuring a steady supply of labour for monopoly capital. These economic reforms were necessary but not sufficient to address the structural weaknesses of South Africa's accumulation model. Most importantly, at a political level the neo-apartheid solution failed and from the latter half of the 1980s the ensuing dialectic of repression and resistance propelled South Africa into a negotiated transition and a new conjuncture: the conjuncture of the democratic corporatist state.

Labour's agenda: The democratic corporatist state solution

In the first half of the 1990s a clear pattern of democratic corporatism was established through the phases of negotiation (1990–1993) and democratic advance (1994–1996). The initiative for this was spurred on by two crucial factors. The first relates to the impact of the Mandela factor, which refers to the moral and ethical authority Mandela acquired through his 27 years in prison. Mandela's moral authority gave him a stature and leading role in South Africa's negotiated political settlement, which enabled compromise. This set in train a practice that increasingly understood negotiated compromise, at various levels of society, as being the same as reconciliation. Second, the labour movement, led by COSATU, had already engaged the apartheid state in struggles on the deregulation of labour law in the late 1980s. These engagements were subsequently institutionalised within the National Manpower Commission and then through a corporatist structure, the National Economic Forum. In the early 1990s, these tripartite engagements already began providing some scope for labour to impact on fiscal policy such as setting the value added tax and tariff reform.

Underlying these trends was a concerted push for a democratic corporatist state from the side of labour, premised on the assumption that labour had the strategic initiative in South Africa's transition. This came through in three important developments. First, the left social democratic element in labour, through NALEDI, the Sociology of Work Project (SWOP), various labour lawyers and key unions such as South African Clothing and Textile Workers Union (SACTWU) and NUMSA began elaborating a democratic corporatist state solution as part of a strategy of radical reform to achieve a class compromise with capital (Adler and Webster, 2000). This led to the formation of the National Economic Development and Labour Council (NEDLAC) in 1995. NEDLAC was legally institutionalised, through an Act of parliament, and provided for macro-level bargaining between the big three – government, labour and capital – on fiscal and monetary policy, trade and industrial policy and labour market reform. A community chamber was also added to the mix. The legal mandate given to NEDLAC compelled social partners to seek consensus in this process even before legislation and policy could reach parliament.

The second important development, linked to an initiative by labour was the Industrial Strategy Project (ISP). This project envisaged a process of industrial restructuring through co-determination. The ISP also rejected an understanding of competitiveness based on lower factor costs and preferred a much more sequenced approach to trade policy (Joffe et al., 1993: 91–126). Ultimately, it shared with the neoliberal thrust a commitment to a competitive economy that was export led and, in the end, found convergence and expression within the Afro-neoliberal shift in South Africa. Supporting this approach was a provision within the new LRA of 1995, in Chapter 5, for workplace forums. This chapter was designed to ensure plant-, firm- and even sectoral-level co-determination around industrial restructuring. Many within the left social democratic current of the labour movement envisaged this to be the German model transplanted into South Africa (Adler, 2000).

Finally, COSATU pushed for a reconstruction accord with its allies in the Tripartite Alliance to define the content of democratic governance. The reconstruction accord envisaged had three potential meanings from the side of the union federation: as a framework for ongoing action, as an election manifesto to be implemented by the new democratic government and as a very specific form of social contract (Gotz, 2000: 168–169). This reconstruction accord evolved into the RDP, which further reinforced the corporatist politics of labour. With the election of the new democratic government COSATU was well positioned to take forward its democratic corporatist solution with its former general secretary, Jay Naidoo, being given the portfolio of RDP Minister and one of its leading intellectuals, Alec Erwin, eventually becoming Minister for Trade and Industry.

Globalising the accumulation model in the conjuncture of a democratic corporatist state (1990–1996)

The integration/disintegration of the racialised accumulation model as part of global restructuring began in the apartheid era. However, after apartheid the Afro-neoliberal loosening and opening up from within gave further impetus to transnationalising South Africa's economy. In the conjuncture of the democratic corporatist state important reform happened to shift the accumulation model in a competitive direction with an exclusively export-led orientation. Ironically, this was done without having an integrated industrial policy framework in place. It would seem the economy was pushed over a cliff without a parachute except for the guidance of the Department of Trade and Industry policy (1995) document 'Support measures for the enhancement of the international competitiveness of South Africa's industrial sector'. However, prior to this and in some instances alongside it, various other major reforms came into effect to support this restructuring.

First, the new democratic government allowed the Bretton Woods institutions, the IMF and World Bank, to set the parameters for post-apartheid South Africa's accumulation path and hence started indigenising an Afro-neoliberalism through a South African voice. The IMF in 1993 intervened in public debate through its report 'Economic policies for a new South Africa' in which it argued for a trickle-down growth model which resonated with various sections of South African business. At the same time, it provided a $850 million compensatory and contingency financing facility (CFF) to the Transitional Executive Council, tied to conditions that would further liberalise the South African economy (Padayachee, 1994: 589). Padayachee (1994: 591–594) also highlights that this finds expression in the first democracy budget of 1994–1995, which shows clear signs that macro-economic stability was not being interpreted based on the ANC-led Alliance RDP but in line with IMF imperatives, despite the rhetoric from the Government of National Unity (GNU). The World Bank during this time engages civil society from below and draws left intellectuals into various projects. The bank also becomes the training ground for cadres from the liberation movement (Marais, 2001: 128).

Second, trade policy and tariff liberalisation, particularly, became a key lever for restructuring through import liberalisation. This was aimed at dismantling the protections that sheltered local industry. At the same time, trade policy was understood as a key priority for government given the balance of payments constraint. It was also a crucial instrument that could be used to send the right signals to the market. The zeal for securing and achieving pro-market credentials was expressed in the commitments government made to the WTO. South Africa's offer to the WTO committed it to liberalising its economy and its tariff phase-down schedule ensured that between 1994 and 1996 its average tariff declined from 11.7% to 6.8% (Cassim and Zarenda, 2004: 106–107). While this process was understood to be part of streamlining a cumbersome tariff system, it also had devastating sectoral impacts within the economy. In 1994 the new DTI, fixated with achieving market credibility, announced deep tariff cuts in clothing and textiles and automobile components that went far beyond what was demanded under the General Agreement on Tariffs and Trade (GATT) (Marais, 2001: 115).

Third, fundamental labour market reform began in this period. In late 1995 South Africa's democratic parliament passed into law a new LRA that fundamentally transformed collective bargaining and brought about a paradigm shift in industrial relations. While deepening deracialisation of the labour market, the LRA was a product of negotiated compromise and hence it steered clear of deregulation at the one extreme and full-blown re-regulation of collective employment relations at the other. Instead, it affirmed a paradigm of regulated flexibility (Baskin and Satgar, 1996: 102). This kept open the role for a power play between labour and capital to determine whether the emphasis would be towards flexibility and hence a limited scope for regulated collective bargaining or regulation with peak-level bargaining setting standards for all employees and employers in a sector. Unfortunately, as restructuring has occurred in the South African economy, accompanied by massive job shedding, the power balance of regulated flexibility has increasingly moved in favour of capital (Buhlungu and Webster, 2006).

Hence, for the social democratic politics of COSATU its dream of a democratic corporatist state, underpinned by a class compromise, was born in a global context in which social democracy was moving to the right and increasingly being assimilated by transnational neoliberalism. Similar shifts were already discernable in the South African context. By 1996 an Afro-neoliberal shift that was in the making for a few years (going back to talks about negotiations in the pre-1990 period) through the twists and turns and shifting relations of force underpinning South Africa's negotiated political settlement became more explicit. This was clearly expressed with the adoption of the GEAR macro-economic policy framework in 1996. Ironically, this Afro-neoliberal macro-economic framework was the result of self-induced change. An earlier move to begin reform of exchange controls prompted a run on and massive devaluation of the South African Rand, providing the ideal opportunity to impose GEAR without consultation within the ANC-led Alliance but even more broadly with stakeholders in NEDLAC. GEAR conformed not only to key prescriptions of transnational neoliberalism but also resonated with ideas put forward by monopoly capital.[4] This conservative macro-economic framework was more than a stabilisation package, but actually provided the most important and unambiguous signal to monopoly and transnational capital about the direction the new ANC government was taking the South African economy and further confirmed commitment to restructuring the economy according to the requirements of a globalising neoliberal capitalism.

The unravelling of ANC-led Alliance hegemony

This perspective on the roots of passive revolution is all about explaining why in the post-apartheid context things have changed, but have also stayed the same. That is how a working-class-led struggle for national liberation with its own projects for social transformation lost the initiative to lead post-apartheid transformation and was replaced by a top-down, technocratic and elitist Afro-neoliberal project.[5] It is about trying to understand how a national liberation movement with mass support, moral authority and a clear vision for social transformation turned its back on the historical possibility of fundamental transformation in the interests of the workers and the poor who supported it and instead chose to surrender the initiative to transform South Africa to a transnationalising white monopoly capitalist class. Hence, we have also to bring into view changes in the power dynamics that have affected civil society. Post-apartheid state–civil society relations have been recast and remade in various ways such that consent for the strategic, moral and intellectual leadership

---

4   In the Department of Finance summary document (1996: 1-2) there were eleven key elements in the proposed package. These contained commitment to privatisation to tariff reductions and inflation-driven monetary policy and so on.

5   Besides the democratic corporatist project of COSATU, other visions and projects for post-apartheid transformation also inhabited the national liberation movement. These ranged from Sovietised socialism in the SACP to revolutionary nationalism in the mainstream of the ANC.

of society has become increasingly passive and indirect. Mass initiative has increasingly become constrained and kept out of the policy and political process.

While the ANC has won three consecutive elections since the advent of narrow electoral democracy, this is not a gauge of hegemony. Liberal interpretations suggest that these elections are an indication of the depth of legitimacy and consent given to the government. From a Gramscian point of view, elections are not determining in obtaining consent to rule a society. While elections are important, it is the relationship between the masses and leaders, rulers and ruled in a dynamic process of articulating a political project that is defining of the authority to lead society. Legitimacy and consent crystalise in the process of organising hegemony on the terrain of civil society and then expressed through organs of the state. Breaking this link between leaders and led, between hegemony and civil society, opens the way for a different logic to politics. Instead of hegemony the logic of dominance prevails. What follows is an attempt to historicise state–civil society relations through two phases of the democratic corporatist conjuncture to show how ANC-led Alliance hegemony unravelled on the terrain of civil society as an indigenised variant of Afro-neoliberalism began defining the direction and content of change in post-apartheid South Africa.

The negotiations phase (1990–1993)

In the democratic corporatist conjuncture (1990–1996), the negotiation phase (1990–93) and the subsequent phase of democratic advance (1994–1996) witnessed state–civil society relations change from demobilisation to instrumentalisation to bureaucratisation. Mediating this was the hegemonic practices of the ANC-led Tripartite Alliance on the terrain of civil society and later expressed through political society. The first aspect of hegemonic practice asserted by the ANC-led Alliance since the release and unbanning of the ANC, SACP and other political organisations was the consolidation of the grassroots Congress movement organised through the UDF under the leadership of the ANC-led Tripartite Alliance.

Pre-1990 South African civil society was loosely bifurcated into two broad camps: anti-apartheid and pro-apartheid. The latter included civil society organisations incorporated into or aligned to institutions of the apartheid state. Within the anti-apartheid camp, a range of civil society organisations – religious, sports, youth, women's, activist groups and so on – developed counter-hegemonic capacities, including ideological coherence and participatory democratic practices through the leadership of the UDF (Seekings, 2000). The radical potential of this co-ordination was also expressed in the link between the factory floor and community struggles organised through trade unions and civic organisations. The South African National Civic Organisation (SANCO)-aligned civics were crucial in creating conditions of ungovernability in various townships in response to local government reforms; probably one of the most radical civic movements in the twentieth century. Moreover, political consciousness within the UDF ensured effective mobilisation of resistance to various tactics of repression and by 1988 the UDF was restricted but revived again from below through rolling mass mobilisation across all key major city centres in South Africa during 1989.

The stalemate in the shifting relations of coercion and mass mobilisation was a crucial factor that propelled South Africa into the phase of negotiation. However, the disbanding of the UDF, with the re-emergence of the exiled leadership and imprisoned leadership of the ANC, South African Congress of Trade Unions (SACTU) and SACP, while informed by various political and strategic considerations, had the consequence of undermining and disabling the participatory democratic impulse within civil society. At the same time, some of the radical leadership elements in the UDF leadership were either sidelined or selectively brought into the centre of the ANC-led Tripartite Alliance. This reorganisation of national liberation forces and leadership, inside the country, was enabled by the moral authority of those at the centre. This was a leadership that sacrificed by going to prison, working in the underground and going into exile. It had a tried and tested record in the eyes of the people. The demobilisation of anti-apartheid civil society through disbanding the UDF simultaneously re-channelled the activist and organic intellectual cadre into building ANC and SACP branch structures. The consolidation of ANC-led Alliance leadership over mass forces was completed and redefined the relationship between leaders and led, within a framework of a more commandist and bureaucratic centralist institutional practice.

A second important aspect of ANC-led Alliance hegemonic practice during this period related to the leveraging of mass power for negotiations. The bargaining and pacting going on at a leadership level increasingly instrumentalised civil society. The ANC-led Alliance deployment of the mass tactic assisted with winning gains at the negotiating table, as it was used to countervail violent initiatives by the regime and also realign forces in the apartheid homelands. For instance, during the negotiations the assassination of Chris Hani, general secretary of the SACP, on 10 April 1993, nearly brought

South Africa to the brink of civil war. This was averted by the leadership provided by the ANC-led Alliance. Mass anger and protest action were used as a pressure point in the negotiations process such that a date was set for the first democratic elections. This decision was then brought to the masses; emotions were pacified and elite pacting continued. Mass mobilisation was switched on and off at decisive moments.

A third aspect of ANC-led Alliance hegemonic practice related to organising civil society for the purpose of preparing to govern. Due to the insistence of COSATU a process to develop the RDP brought in an array of progressive forces. The RDP was a crucial programmatic platform to take on board concerns and interests from across civil society and built a consensus around economic transformation in and outside the Alliance. In the RDP's mix of objectives and Keynesian prescriptions, a prominent place was defined for participatory development and a people-driven RDP (ANC, 1994: 131–132).

Finally, the first democratic elections were used to consolidate strategic, moral and intellectual leadership over society. The ANC's election nomination lists brought in a non-racial mix, was sectorally balanced, and included top leadership from the Alliance including SANCO. The downside of this was a leadership, with years of experience and capacity, leaving mass organisations including the Alliance as they moved to parliament and into the government bureaucracy. The challenge of reproducing high calibre leadership within these organisations still remains a challenge particularly given that the electoralist dynamic and careerist impulses have increasingly come to the fore. This has been exacerbated by the subsequent emergence of a practice of co-option among mass forces even in the ranks of the once radical civic movement (Heller and Ntlokonkulu, 2001). In short, demobilisation of anti-apartheid mass forces began in the negotiations phase and a tendency towards centralising leadership and instrumentalising social forces became more discernible. Hegemonic leadership began showing morbid symptoms such that it increasingly became about centralising control through subordinating national liberation forces to the discipline of bureaucratic centralism, co-option of leadership and limiting room for participatory, bottom-up practices.

The phase of democratic advance (1994–1996)

With the democratic opening of 1994, through the first democratic elections in April, a shift in the political relations of force inaugurated a phase of democratic advance. The formation of the ANC-led GNU completed the moment of hegemony; that is the strategic, moral and intellectual leadership of society by the ANC Alliance was in place. However, hegemonic leadership of society is never static and as the underlying conditions shift, the struggle to maintain hegemony continues. In a mature political context rival hegemonic projects also disrupt established hegemonies. Moreover, the hegemonic leadership of society can also unravel, particularly when the mechanisms of hegemony, like political parties, degenerate such that the gap between leaders and the led, rulers and ruled widens. In such instances, active and direct consent rooted in civil society is attenuated. This increasingly became the reality after 1994 and until 1996, when the transition from an instrumentalised to a bureaucratised civil society became more apparent. Such a restructuring of state–civil society relations was not inevitable, given that freedom for associational activity was enhanced and legally buttressed by the Constitution; and coercive legal prohibitions were dismantled (Habib, 2003). Underlying this shift in state–civil society were four crucial factors related to hegemonic state practice and effects on civil society relations.

The first relates to what Gramsci would refer to as the educative function of the hegemonic state. In this regard the role of the Mandela factor is important. Some analyses on the left, with a Gramscian gloss, have treated the Mandela factor as a benevolent and positive Bonapartist/Caesarist factor that rises above class struggle to ensure progressive change; thus juxtaposing him with the negative or reactionary Mbeki presidency more closely aligned with capital.[6] The practical import of such analyses has lent itself to the search for a substitute: our benevolent Bonaparte/Caesar, with a disposition to the left mainly through an authoritarian populist politics. However, the Mandela factor in this analysis is understood as a moment in the educative function of the GNU and ultimately the democratic corporatist state. Such a function expressed itself positively and negatively.

On the one hand, the historical task and role played by the Mandela factor in national reconciliation can never be overestimated. This was an extremely positive educative function of the democratic corporatist state. The Mandela magic on rugby fields, in volatile hot-spots in the province of KwaZulu-Natal in which the prospects of civil war loomed large, through expressing the moral authority of the new South Africa in diplomatic engagements with the world and holding together a multi-party government was an essential ingredient in national consciousness. It took on iconic and mythological proportions in the national common sense. It epitomised the righteousness of national liberation and showed to South Africans and the world what non-racialism meant; this

---

6   This kind of analysis has been very common in the ranks of the SACP over the past few years.

was despite its appropriations into rainbowism and multiculturalism. This function was further buttressed by the role of the Truth and Reconciliation Commission (TRC) and the adoption of a new democratic constitution, enshrining human, civil and socio-economic rights of all South Africans and guaranteeing formal equality among all citizens. On the other hand, the stabilising role of the Mandela factor also impacted negatively on class struggles as the concerns and interests of business dovetailed with Mandela's role in calling on workers to support nation building by ending economic struggles. This fed into a practice of corporatist bargaining and deal-making and which points to the second factor of hegemonic state practice implicated in bureaucratising state–civil society relations.

This second factor relates to the institutionalising of macro-level decision-making through NEDLAC as a key element in labour's strategy to achieve a democratic corporatist state. Such corporatist arrangements have been disempowering to civil society given that these institutional arrangements are built around powerful, organised, resourced and capacitated interests. Actually, since its inception and throughout its existence, civil society representation in NEDLAC's community chamber was handled clumsily and based on arbitrary criteria, to say the least, and reflects the extent to which such an institutional space was merely an add-on. Moreover, the bureaucratisation logic of such neo-corporatist arrangements is pointedly captured by Friedman and Reitzes (1995: 10): 'Their purpose is not to empower civil society but to formalise the participation of interests which already have power and the demands of which the state needs to incorporate if it is to govern effectively.'

Such a bureaucratising logic fed into the third factor shaping state–civil society relations in this period: the RDP Ministry's promotion of local development forums. These committees were envisaged as 'coordinators of development' (Friedman and Reitzes, 1995: 4–5). However, in a context in which massive demobilisation had happened, particularly with the disbanding of the UDF, the political capacity of community-based organisations to effectively participate in such institutions was displaced. Moreover, key organic intellectual cadres from civil society were already being sucked into the state bureaucracy. Hence, a people-driven RDP increasingly took on a bureaucratic rationality. This bureaucratic flirtation, albeit with a top-down approach to participatory democracy, was short-lived in this period as the RDP Office was unceremoniously shut down as the Afro-neoliberal shift took hold and the finance department was positioned to be the state within the state. These developments also heralded the beginning of a move from bureaucratising civil society towards unleashing the market on society. With neoliberal reforms the market was increasingly disembedded. The logic of liberalisation, privatisation and deregulation re-allocated resources to more efficient and competitive parts of the economy. This meant cost-cutting and pressures against workers, it meant higher costs for services like water in some communities and higher food prices as the agricultural sector was completely deregulated through the dismantling of marketing boards. Ultimately, South Africa's version of Afro-neoliberalism began to foster a schism between the state and civil society. The state has increasingly become insulated from mass protests and from voices from below as a part of projecting the democratic state as pro-business, while at the same time, patronage has become the order of the day as part of fostering a new black capitalist class through BEE (Southall, 2005, 2006 and 2007).

In the conjuncture of the democratic corporatist state the restructuring of state–civil society relations denuded counter-hegemonic capacities in civil society. Mass demobilisation, instrumentalisation and bureaucratisation were shaped by ANC-led Alliance hegemonic practices and state effects. Most importantly, participatory democratic practices and tendencies within the anti-apartheid camp in civil society were eviscerated. At the same time, parts of the anti-apartheid camp in civil society were increasingly assimilated into institutional politics within the state. Furthermore, as an aggressive Afro-neoliberalism became more dominant a restructured civil society began to emerge in the context of a growing schism between state and civil society (Atkinson, 2007; Ndletyana, 2007). New interests, fault lines and organisational forms began to come to the fore in relation to the Afro-neoliberal state form: the internationalised competition state (1996 to the present).[7] Such a state form is different from the interventionist developmental state of East Asia or the Western welfarist state, for example. Instead, such a state form displays the following features: (i) it is co-opted within public and private transnational neoliberal institutions like the World Bank and WEF; (ii) it firmly embraces a monetarist macro-economic policy approach which has geared the economy around international financial markets and flows; (iii) it has dismantled self-sufficiency in strategic sectors of the economy and state responses are guided by the need to support competitive advantage; and (iv) micro-policy interventions foster business and reduce costs of doing business. In short, this is a state governed by the market, a product of global capitalism and a post-Westphalian imposition by transnational capital.

---

7   I draw on Soederberg et al. (2005) who have analysed the global convergence around the neoliberal state form: the competition state. However, I also bring into view the international dimension.

The rise of a transnational fraction of the South African ruling class and the Afro-neoliberal historical bloc

The politics of passive revolution that drove South Africa down an Afro-neoliberal path were not in full view even with the defeat of labour's democratic corporatist solution. The rhetoric of the NDR was trumpeted at high pitch in the midst of rolling back the working class. Neither did the politics of passive revolution spring automatically from an externally oriented accumulation model and a shift to a politics of dominance in state–civil society relations. Behind these shifts an important role has also to be given to social agency. In this respect our analysis has to take on board class formation in the post-apartheid context, within the process of transnationalising South African capitalism. The Afro-neoliberal class project in post-apartheid South Africa was championed by a transnational fraction of South Africa's ruling class. This fraction was engendered structurally in three ways.

First, through neoliberal reforms that gave South Africa's accumulation process an external orientation. The rush to be globally competitive adjusted all key sectors, reallocated resources and placed South Africa on an export-led trajectory, which has produced an enclave economy (Makgetla, 2004). The racialised import-substitution accumulation model, linked to South Africa's minerals-energy complex was dismantled. In key sectors, from agriculture, to mining and manufacturing deepening exports became key as part of building a competitive economy. Moreover, South Africa's parastatal sector was redirected as well. Restructuring through privatisation and commercialisation attempted to place all key parastatals on a globally competitive footing. All of this ruptured and displaced any commitment to an internally based accumulation model and development strategy. Neoliberal restructuring was not about the right balance between import-substitution and export-led accumulation; it turned its back on a national development strategy. Class forces emanating from these restructuring processes developed on outlook and interest beyond the South African market. This has contributed to transnational class formation and fractionation.

The second structural determinant of class formation, and transnational fractionation, relates to the movement of South African monopoly capital outward. This began in the early 1990s. According to the Edge Institute's database, outward expansion involves the full spectrum of South African business – 82 of the top 100 listed companies on the JSE are included in the 340 companies involved in outward investment, and a substantial majority of all JSE-listed companies, together with numerous major unlisted corporations and all major state corporations.[8] According to a survey done on Africa's top 500 companies operating on the continent, over 150, the majority are South African (*Africa Report*, 2008, 54–60 and 78–92). These giants are dominant in all sectors, from power, mining, logistics, retail and telecoms, except energy. Many of the leading companies are South African parastatals that are building a significant presence on the continent and which are at the vanguard of BEE in South Africa, in the context of parastatal restructuring.

Many of these transnationalised corporations have moved into Africa in the context of other African governments attempting to attract FDI, after their own experiences of Afro-neoliberalisation for almost three decades. However, at the same time, some of South Africa's former top companies have now listed offshore: Anglo American, Old Mutual, SA Breweries, Billiton, Dimension Data and Liberty Life have moved their financial listings and headquarters to London. This has led to massive outflows through profits, dividends and interest payments (Makgetla, 2004: 276). At the same time, with these company assets denominated in more secure hard currency their asset values and share prices have gone up (Carmody, 2002: 263). Moreover, many of South Africa's former monopolies that have transnationalised are now operating with the same risk concerns and interests as any other transnational. Various strategies and practices are evolving that bring globalisation in and extend it outward. This would include movements by financial capital out of South Africa as far afield as the US economy (like Old Mutual), mergers at a global scale (Billiton with Australian mining house BHP), outsourcing and strategic partnerships. Besides the transnationalising of the South African economy from within, over 30% of the JSE is foreign owned (Rumney, 2005: 415).

The third structural determinant of class formation, particularly transnational fractionation, has been through attracting FDI. In this regard fiscal policy has also aligned around tight management so as not to crowd out investors. The South African macro-economic policy framework's deficit reduction targets have ensured a decline in deficit spending and since 1999 has been kept below 3% of gross domestic product (GDP) (Gelb, 2005: 374). Complementing this effort to bring in investment has been the creation of numerous investment promotion agencies and initiatives in national, provincial and local government: all declaring 'South Africa is open for business'. Gelb and Black (2004: 8) suggest there are more than 35 incentive schemes for investors,

---

8   The Edge Institute is a leading economic policy think tank in South Africa. It has worked closely with the South African government on various economic and foreign policy initiatives.

commitments to treat all investors the same in South Africa regarding foreign exchange for import, export and access (based on commitments made by South Africa under trade-related investment measures, TRIMS) and there are over 30 bilateral investment treaties mainly with OECD countries. Despite this Afro-neoliberal approach to macro-economic management, FDI flows have been dismal in comparative terms and as a share of global flows (Gelb and Black, 2004: 9–10). However, this does not detract from the fact that South Africa has had various global giants already within its economy, even prior to the democratic transition. This point was alluded to earlier.

In the context of South Africa's political economy, engendering a transnational fraction and linking to global accumulation circuits through FDI was not sufficient for a right-wing shift in post-apartheid South Africa. Such a fraction had to foster consent for Afro-neoliberalism amongst key social and political forces. It had to utilise both its structural and direct power to constitute a historical bloc of social forces capable of advancing the Afro-neoliberal project and deepening South Africa's passive revolution. In this respect two historical factors are important. The first is dialogue with and contestation of the ANC. This happened in the 1980s when business began a dialogue with the exiled ANC about the future of South Africa and its economic policy options. In the 1990s monopoly capital went on the offensive and a flurry of scenario planning exercises were unleashed by key financial and mining houses mainly targeted at the ANC (Bond, 2000: 53–88). Key leaders of the ANC were brought into these processes and a consensus began to emerge about South Africa's economic choices. This fed into the second important historical factor that clinched support for an Afro-neoliberal solution in South Africa.

The second factor is the shift within the dominant faction in the ANC, a petty bourgeois element, towards embracing an Afro-neoliberal consensus. This is reflected in two important developments that reveal themselves in the conjuncture of macro-restructuring but evolve beyond. The first is a commitment to deracialising South African monopoly capitalism rather than transforming it in an anti-capitalist or socialist direction as envisaged in the ANC's historical programme, the Freedom Charter. Nationalisation, decommodification and socialised forms of ownership were key thrusts of the ANC's Freedom Charter. These policies were placed on the back burner and were replaced by various reforms that attempted to develop a new layer of black capitalists. The main policy framework to achieve this was BEE. It gained impetus from the mid-1990s as major South African conglomerates began unbundling and deconcentrating the ownership structure of the South African economy.

This BEE process has gone through various phases (Rumney, 2005). The first phase dates from the mid-1990s with private sector attempts to cut debt-financed ownership deals. By 1998, with over 230 such deals on the JSE, valued at R37 billion, the stock market crashed with most BEE ventures going down with it. A second phase was restarted in 1999, spearheaded by black business associations and government. This initiative led to the establishment of a non-statutory Black Economic Commission and a strategy. Deriving from this intervention has been a third phase which kicked in with BEE charters, the first being put in place in the liquid fuels industry and the subsequent promulgation of the Broad-Based Black Economic Empowerment Act (2004). This policy and process of BEE envisages various forms of empowerment including direct ownership and control of enterprises and assets, deracialising management at senior levels, human resource development and employment equity and indirect empowerment through procurement. By all accounts this process is not happening smoothly, with uneven deracialisation across sectors. This is happening in a context in which historically white monopoly capital has been moving offshore since the early 1990s (Carmody, 2002: 262; Daniel et al., 2003).

The second important development and shift within the dominant ANC faction, and which has been mentioned, is the embrace of neoliberal reforms for the purpose of macro-economic stabilisation and adjustment. This process began with the apartheid regime and was taken on board by the new democratic government. We can be generous and suggest that low growth rates and high unemployment necessitated some of these reforms in the short term. Unfortunately, these reforms continued as the basis of a clear class project. A virtue was made of necessity and South Africa's Department of Finance (now known as the Treasury) began wielding undue influence in government such that it defined government's approach to economic policy over the past 13 years. South Africa's Finance Minister, Trevor Manuel, performed his job so well he became a darling of the Bretton Woods institutions. He became the chair of the IMF/World Bank board of governors in 1999–2000 and chair of the IMF/World Bank development committee in 2001–2002. However, the reform strategy from within has not worked, even if there were revolutionary intentions lurking beneath the Afro-neoliberal consensus. Today, South Africa is locked into the global power structure rather than manoeuvring to secure space for a genuine national development project. South Africa is a member of the G20 group of countries, formed in Washington D.C. on 25 September 1999 by the G7. Soederberg (2004b: 81) concludes that this suggests that 'Taken together, the constitution of the G20 demonstrates renewed attempts at core-periphery coercion by inviting these countries into the highly exclusive G7/G8; or, put more bluntly, by co-opting them into the rules and standards of the core-alliance coercion by ensuring official, and thus more tightly integrated relations with the IMF and World Bank.' In short, South Africa's Afro-neoliberal reforms from within have ensured it a place within the process of managing a new international financial architecture for the world. It is one of the many poster nations that has to play a role in managing a complex and volatile global financial system in the interests of transnational but particularly finance capital.

Moreover, the Afro-neoliberal consensus that crystallised from these structural and politico-ideological shifts points to an elite bargain at the heart of South Africa's passive revolution. This bargain is made up of the following elements: (i) ensuring neoliberal reform such that South Africa's economy has an external orientation to ensure that monopoly capital can transnationalise to recover and increase profit rates and transnational capital can come in on its terms, with minimal risk; (ii) deracialising of monopoly capital to ensure an emergent black capitalist class has a stake in the economy. This consensus did not unfold smoothly but required policy reform trade-offs: more neoliberal reforms in exchange for a greater BEE stake in the transnationalisng commanding heights. At each stage of advancing BEE policy, the government had to provide signals through its economic reforms of moving in a neoliberal direction. For instance, the Afro-neoliberal macro-reform framework was complemented by a micro-reform agenda, the ASGISA (2006). This micro-reform agenda is mainly about cutting the costs of doing business in South Africa and tackling constraints that stand in the way of making South Africa globally competitive. In short, BEE policy was directly linked to transnationalising South African capitalism.

The interests of these class forces and their reproduction lies in a capitalist South Africa that is locked into the global economy on the terms of South Africa's transnational fraction and transnational capital. Hence, to advance its interests as the general interests of South African society, transnational capital in South Africa constituted an Afro-neoliberal class project. The social forces that come together to advance this project constitute a non-hegemonic historical bloc, led by the transnational fraction, and is made up of the following social elements:

- transnationalised South African corporations, private and parastatal;
- global transnationals operating within global production, financial and trade structures;
- technocrats within the state bureaucracy, particularly those departments at the interface with the global economy, as well as managers in provincial and local government wanting to globalise;
- the new black capitalist class (including managers) in both the private and public sectors;
- a faction within the ruling ANC, including various intellectuals that hover around the party giving advice, and other parties adhering to an agenda to promote global capitalism;
- a fraction of the working class whose interests are realised through union investment companies and through employment within transnational corporations and transnationalised South African corporations; and
- most mainstream corporate owned media, in particular financial journalists.

The passive revolution inaugurated by this transnational fraction, has brought about deep changes in South Africa's political economy that have engendered these class and social forces and created the conditions for its reproduction. Moreover, it is the shared articulation of an Afro-neoliberal solution for restructuring post-apartheid capitalism that brings this fraction and its historic bloc into existence.

Conclusion

South Africa's transition to democracy coincided with the second decade of global neoliberal restructuring. An analysis of the roots of South Africa's passive revolution reveals how the indigenisation of neoliberalism begins in the apartheid era and is deepened in the context of narrow electoral democracy. The conjunctural scale and depth of this is reflected in the eclipse of a democratic corporatist state solution articulated by the organised labour movement in response to the organic and conjunctural crisis of South African capitalism, the globalisation of a deracialising import-substitution model, the unravelling of ANC hegemony and the emergence of a transnational fraction of South Africa's ruling class. This has laid the basis for the emergence of an Afro-neoliberalism that sutures together elements of national liberation ideology and transnational neoliberalism.

This Afro-neoliberal class project has brought to the fore a passive revolution. This has, in the first place, redirected and co-opted South Africa's national liberation project and struggle for socialism. It has fostered a non-hegemonic historic bloc in support of this class project. This Afro-neoliberal historic bloc, led by the transnational fraction of South Africa's ruling class, has utilised Afro-neoliberal restructuring and the globalisation of the South African economy to advance its interests while at the same time blocking fundamental transformation. Second, it has unleashed a new form of elite politics on South African society. Such a politics has reduced democracy to narrow electoralism and leaves citizens disempowered beyond election processes, which has further fuelled deep-seated disaffection. Understanding the structural and politico-ideological roots of South Africa's passive revolution assists in understanding the right-wing shift in post-apartheid South Africa. It also assists in understanding how a racialised monopoly capital, that was nationally bounded, has now transnationalised.

Labour, Capital and Society 41, 2, 2008.

The Marikana Massacre and the South African State's Low-Intensity War Against the People

THE MASSACRE OF THE Marikana/Lonmin workers has inserted itself within South Africa's national consciousness, not so much through the analysis, commentary and reporting in its wake. Instead, it has been the power of the visual images of police armed with awesome firepower gunning down these workers, together with images of bodies lying defeated and lifeless, that has aroused a national outcry and wave of condemnation. These images have also engendered international protest action outside South African embassies. In themselves these images communicate a politics about official state power. It is bereft of moral concern, dehumanised, brutal and at odds with international human rights standards; in these ways it is no different from apartheid-era state-sponsored violence and technologies of oppressive rule. Moreover, the images of police officers walking through the Marikana/Lonmin killing field, with a sense of professional accomplishment in its aftermath, starkly portrays a scary reality: the triumph of South Africa's state in its brutal conquest of its enemies, its citizens.

At the same time, the pain and suffering of the gunned-down workers has become the pain of a nation and the world; this has happened even without the ANC government declaring we must not apportion blame but mourn the dead. In a world steeped in possessive individualism and greed, the brutal Marikana/Lonmin massacre reminds us of a universal connection; our common humanity. However, while this modern human connection and sense of empathy is important, it is also superficial. This is brought home by a simple truth: the pain of the Marikana/Lonmin workers is only our pain in their martyrdom. They had to perish for all of us to realise how deep social injustice has become inscribed in the everyday lives of post-apartheid South Africa's workers and the poor. The low wage, super-exploitation model of South African mining, socially engineered during apartheid, is alive and well, and thriving. It is condoned by the post-apartheid state. This is the tragic irony of what we have become as the much-vaunted rainbow nation.

New fault-line is revealed

Moreover, the spectral presence of the Marikana/Lonmin massacre speaks to us about another shadow cast by the rainbow fairy tale. It forces us to confront the hard edge of violence fluxing through our stressed social fabric. At one time, violent crime – car jackings, robberies, rapes, murders – defined our everyday understanding of violence. Our narration of these violent events constructed a sense of criminal violence as a major fault line running through South African society. Such violence spreads fear, racial division and a sense of siege. It has been our undeclared civil war. However, the social geography of violence changes with the Marikana/Lonmin moment. A new fault-line is revealed. Such a fault-line has been in the making deep inside South African society through xenophobic attacks, violent police attacks on striking transport and municipal workers (over the past few years), violence against gays and lesbians especially in township communities, and police complicity in thwarting legitimate protest action in poor communities and informal settlements. Through a failure to act decisively (in some instances like during xenophobic violence or by failing to provide policing in informal settlements) or through orchestrated violence, the South African state is at war with the working class within its borders; a low-intensity war. More specifically such a war spans shootings, intimidation, failure to allow communities to lay charges, failure to investigate crimes perpetrated against poor communities, failure to be responsive to the safety needs of poor communities, fabrication and smear campaigns against local leaders, complicity with goons linked to local politicians (particularly the ANC) and a failure to act, knowing that innocent lives are in danger.

A few examples of police-orchestrated low-intensity warfare working in cahoots with ANC goon squads or local politicians against communities illustrate this more clearly. This is based on testimony received from activists. First, after Abahlali baseMjondolo (shack dwellers movement) successfully challenged the Slums Act in the Constitutional Court, ensuring community participation to determine whether there can be relocation from an established community, they became the target of police-ANC violence. In early 2010 an ANC goon squad violently removed Abahlali from Kennedy Road informal settlement in Durban. This is also captured in a documentary entitled *Dear Mandela*. The police carried out arrests of Abahlali leadership on trumped-up charges and public violence which are eventually kicked out of court. Abahlali was not able to return to Kennedy Road informal settlement.

Second, a more recent example in Umlazi township, Durban also shows this police-political party nexus working in insidious ways to suppress community demands. The local Unemployed People's Movement (UPM) and ward 88 residents demanded a recall of their ANC councillor and democratisation of the ward committee. In their perception the ANC ward councillor was corrupt, failing to deliver and engaging in clientelistic control of development resources. This unleashed a series of reprisals. On 23 July the leader of the UPM was arrested under false charges. The complainants turned out to be incited by the councillor working in cahoots with the station commander at Umlazi police station. These charges could not stick but they held the leader of UPM for a day. It would seem these trumped-up charges were meant to prevent him from leading a community meeting being held on the same day. This story has many twists and turns with the police-ANC apparatus constantly trying to intimidate the UPM and residents of ward 88 in the course of this struggle.

What is striking about these examples is their challenge to mainstream academic and media explanations of community-based violence as being merely reducible to intra-ANC battles. In all these instances a conscious awakening and challenge by communities and movements to the ANC state unleashes a low-intensity destabilisation of these community forces through the police-ANC state nexus.

COSATU's challenge

Contrary to Zwelinzima Vavi, the general Ssecretary of COSATU, who believes South Africa is poised to experience the shock of a ticking time bomb rooted in deep inequality and unemployment, this bomb is already exploding in various locales. However, the response of the ANC state has been recourse to low-intensity violence. The Marikana/Lonmin massacre merely brings this trend into sharp relief. The challenge to COSATU is simple: does it want to remain a democratising force, with a proud history, and take a stand with the wider working class or does it want to be complicit in the low-intensity war against the broader working class and citizenry?

At a mass meeting on 22 August 2012 at the University of Johannesburg the Marikana workers and community passionately appealed for solidarity. Such solidarity actions are congealing into but not limited to:
- calls for a national and international day of solidarity action with Marikana workers (including three minutes of silence on 29 August at 1pm as a symbolic reference to the three minutes it took the callous South African Police Services to mow down 34 workers on 16 August 2012);

- support for solidarity strike action emerging within the platinum mining industry;
- a call for an independent people's commission of enquiry to ensure full transparency, testimony and justice for the Marikana workers and communities afflicted with state-ANC violence;
- calls demanding the withdrawal of all charges and the immediate release of miners held in police custody;
- calls for the dismissal of the head of the National Prosecuting Authority and the Minister of Police to be dismissed for trying to cover up police killings of the miners by utilising a common purpose provision in apartheid legislation to charge workers for murder and calls for an end to the police siege and harassment of the Marikana communities.

Marikana as a defining moment in post-apartheid politics is essentially about galvanising the battle to reclaim South Africa's democracy from below. It resonates with and expresses the desire of the majority to end the ugly reality of South Africa's deep-seated and racialised class-based inequality that has been widening under ANC rule.

Bullet 693, 5 September 2012: http://www.socialistproject.ca/bullet/693.php#continue

Beyond Marikana: The Post-Apartheid South African State

ON 16 AUGUST 2012 post-apartheid South Africa experienced what has been called the Marikana massacre. Striking mine workers were gunned down by police at the Lonmin platinum mine. Media and academic reports confirmed that most of the 34 miners were shot in the back while fleeing from the police, suggesting premeditated action. Moreover, the surviving workers were initially charged using apartheid-era legislation and deemed to have perpetrated the murder of their fellow workers. Due to civil society outrage, this charge has been temporarily suspended, and the government has also ordered heavy police and military presence along the platinum belt, effectively suspending constitutional rights to protest, undermining the constitutional right of mine workers to strike, and imposing an undeclared state of emergency. Throughout this tragic saga, key government ministers, including the Minister for Minerals and Energy and the Minister for Trade and Industry, have openly attempted to assure international investors that South Africa is a safe destination for investment and that investments in mining are very secure. What does the Marikana massacre, including the assuaging of foreign investors' concerns by ministers in the aftermath of this tragedy, mean for the character and role of the post-apartheid state? Put differently, is the Marikana massacre simply a manifestation of what the state has become in South Africa?

The post-apartheid state form is contested ideologically and politically in South Africa. National liberation ideology historically – particularly through the ANC's programmatic Freedom Charter – authorised state intervention as a crucial part of non-racial nation building. At the same time, legitimate grassroots expectations expressed the need for a national popular project in which the logic of state-centric development occupied a crucial place in economic transformation alongside other development logics. However, these conceptions of state-led development did not materialise with the election of the first post-apartheid democratic government in 1994. Instead, during nearly two decades of freedom, South Africa's liberation movement internalised a neoliberal approach to economic management, and after half a decade of such economic management it declared the post-apartheid state a developmental state.

This article questions the characterisation of the post-apartheid state form as a developmental state. To interrogate this question, it draws on neo-Gramscian global political economy, which is well established in the discipline of international relations and has two important starting points as a critical mode of analysis. First, it recognises that the state form cannot be treated as an ontological given existing outside history. In other words, the state as a crucial social actor has to be historicised to understand the origins of its various institutional forms and how it is constituted and shaped by social forces, both domestic and international. Second, social and theoretical analysis is never neutral and is always for someone and towards some end. In this regard, neo-Gramscian global political economy has a normative underpinning in pursuit of social justice and progressive transformation.

The article begins by highlighting what is at stake by characterising the post-apartheid state as a developmental state and explaining how this misrecognition is ideologically constituted. Second, the article argues for an approach to understanding the post-apartheid state by locating it within the context of the rise of transnational neoliberalism and the process of indigenising neoliberalism on the African continent. It examines how post-apartheid South Africa's choice to embrace global capitalist restructuring (otherwise known as globalisation) favoured the interests of transnational capital and created the conditions for transnationalising monopolistic relations of production beyond a nationally bounded mode of production. The embrace of neoliberalism and the deepening of South Africa's integration into global circuits of accumulation brought to an end a discourse of South African exceptionalism. Instead, South Africa became one of many laboratories of Afro-neoliberalism; that is, neoliberalism with African characteristics.

Moreover, this article examines the actual economic practices of the state that make it, more precisely, an Afro-neoliberal state. Such economic practices display a convergence between the actual post-apartheid state and the ideal type neoliberal state form in the context of global neoliberal restructuring. This article identifies and shows how the various economic management practices of the state recompose it into an Afro-neoliberal state form while engendering an extroverted, competitive and enclave-based accumulation model. This contribution historicises the economic management practices of the post-apartheid state form as part of the conjuncture of constituting the Afro-neoliberal state (1996 to the present).

The post-apartheid developmental state in question

The twentieth-century developmental state has been characterised as a state leading catch-up industrialisation, a state that uses intervention to bring about structural change and provide a basis for capital accumulation (Chang, 2002). Such states have shifted from high-growth, low-tech economies to high-growth and high-tech economies. In this regard, the developmental state literature has attempted to bring the state back in by looking closely at how developmental states have led such processes of structural change. This literature has constituted an iconic framing of successful Asian tigers such as Japan, South Korea, Taiwan and, more recently, China. While this literature has not framed developmental state models, it has pointed to crucial reforms and state practices that portend what is possible. Such experiences and literature point to various success or failure factors that could provide a basis for mimetic learning and diffusion (see Amsden 1989 and 2001; Evans 1995; Chibber 2003).

However, the experience of the developmental state is also about the relationship between visions of developmentalism, conceptions of the state and how these are articulated through nationalism. In a path-breaking text on the emergence of the developmental state and state-guided capitalist development in East Asia, Chalmers Johnson in *Miti and the Japanese Miracle* (1982), highlights how an effective institutional system evolved over time through a learning process and out of different crisis moments in Japanese capitalist development. While such a system was anchored in a prioritisation of developmentalism over time, it developed a repertoire of policy tools and mechanisms to actualise this. However, Johnson (1982: 307) provided a caution still relevant today: 'It may be possible to borrow Japan's priorities and institutions, but the situational nationalism of its people during the 1950s and 1960s is something another people will have to develop, not borrow.'

This point about the mobilising role of nationalism to achieve national economic goals is also underlined by Woo-Cumings. She writes, 'Johnson places the "binding agent" of East Asian development in both the context of "late development" and the East Asian setting of revolutionary nationalism – not a garden-variety nationalism but one that grew from war and imperialism and manifested itself variously: communism in China and North Korea, and the capitalist developmental state in Japan, South Korea and Taiwan' (Woo-Cumings 1999: 7).

Similarly, in France such a national consciousness after World War 2 was evoked not by appealing to growth or to some technical economic outcome.

Loriaux (1999: 252–253) shows how moral ambition played a substantial role in mobilising developmental ambitions within the national consciousness. Moreover, the study of various national histories about these ambitions makes it seem as if the 'developmental-state elite pursue moral goods whose definition is informed by a certain mythological construction of how the world works and what we can and should accomplish' (Loriaux, 1999: 253).

In the South African context, the nationalism of national liberation forged a national identity in the context of overcoming apartheid. A new South Africanness emerged through programmatic politics grounded in the adoption of the Freedom Charter in 1955 at the Congress of the People. While this nationalism declared a non-racial alternative to racialised oppression it also recognised that racial inequities had to be addressed through state-led transformation. In many ways, the utopian element of a non-racial nationalism for South Africa envisaged a state-centric developmental project: either social democratic, revolutionary nationalist or Soviet socialist. The state loomed large in the imaginary of national liberation despite its various ideological inflections. However, the narrative of state-led redistribution, industrial development and transformation lost its moorings in a post-apartheid context due to the shortcomings of the national liberation project and its neoliberalisation.

In the post-apartheid South African context, the mobilising role of nationalism to achieve a developmental state has been confused by different visions of the state and developmentalism. In other words, the form and functions of the state are cloaked in different ideological representations of the state. In this regard, the voice of South African labour and its project for the post-apartheid state has been central. The labour movement, particularly COSATU, envisioned a 'democratic corporatist state' (Satgar, 2008). Labour's support of a democratic corporatist state came out of intense struggles with the apartheid regime regarding labour market reforms. Between 1990 and 1996, the labour movement advanced three crucial elements that together, it was hoped, would form the basis of a democratic corporatist state: the RDP that promoted a redistributive agenda for government; the creation and formalisation of the NEDLAC as a macro-bargaining space over state policy; and the ISP that gave COSATU an opportunity to help shape industrial development. Like the progressive rhetoric of national liberation ideology, the progressive thrusts of these three demands coming from labour have merely obscured the actual character of the emergent post-apartheid state. Most of these demands did not come to fruition as South Africa's transition embraced neoliberalism. Today,

COSATU clings to the macro-bargaining space – NEDLAC – as the most important basis for driving state policy, while at the same time, this macro-bargaining space has been undercut by macro-economic adjustment and industrial restructuring led by the state (Buhlungu, 2010).

Moreover, the general approach to the developmental state has been propagandistic and declaratory. The first articulation of the developmental state emerged in the early 2000s after an intense period of political strife in the ruling ANC-led Alliance over the adoption of neoliberal macro-economic policy (Marais, 2011: 338–352). After achieving a degree of stabilisation of the South African economy, but while continuing neoliberalisation, the notion of a 'developmental state' entered South Africa's policy discourse. Under President Thabo Mbeki (1999–2008) – one of the key architects of South Africa's neoliberalisation – the South African state consistently declared itself a developmental state. Mbeki's State of the Nation addresses in parliament underlined this (cf. Buhlungu et al., 2006 and 2007). Using developmental-state rhetoric helped legitimate the state's contradictions: while many in the government claimed the state was developmental, it simultaneously pursued neoliberal policies that undermined the nation's developmental aspirations. This rhetorical move collapsed a normative ambition about what the South African state should be with the reality of the existing state. This was further reinforced at a major national conference in 2007, at which the ruling ANC firmly embraced a hybrid developmental state that would bring together the European welfare state and the East Asian developmental state. In his 2012 State of the Nation address (Zuma, 2012), President Jacob Zuma declared, 'As a developmental state that is located at the centre of a mixed economy, we see our role as being to lead and guide the economy and to intervene in the interest of the poor, given the history of our country.' Despite this declaration, the general contours of neoliberal macro-economic management have not shifted.

There have also been various declaratory voices from below claiming the South African state to be developmental: many journalists, commentators and academics argue that any kind of state intervention is evidence that the state is developmental or leaning towards being a developmental state (Gelb, 2006). Such arguments, however, ignore the fact that a great deal of state intervention focuses on creating conditions for externalised dynamics of accumulation and not the promotion of state-led industrialisation that was a hallmark of the earlier generation of developmental states.[1] Moreover, such a position inadvertently

---

1   This is not to argue for ecologically destructive industrialisation. Rather, in the twenty-first

legitimates a shift in neoliberal discourse that warrants state intervention. For example, the World Bank authorises state intervention, but in a way that supports marketisation (World Bank, 1997). In the case of industrial policy, 'neoliberalism is not just constraining industrial policy, it is redirecting it' (Evans, 2005: 203). Similarly, the current South African state supports regulatory interventionism to bolster market efficiency; the state does not retreat but is remade to buttress the rule of transnational capital and to provide conditions for its reproduction.

In short, the forces shaping the post-apartheid state are not pushing it towards being a developmental state, despite the state's discourse. At the same time, the declaratory developmental-state discourse has not suffused nation building in a way that mobilises social forces around common economic goals and a shared moral ambition. South Africa does not have a shared consensus and imaginary around advancing a developmental state, let alone a twenty-first-century conception: a state that is about widening popular democracy, ensuring ecocentric production, engendering bit-based sources of growth and building human capabilities to support such high-tech development (Evans, 2010). The practices of the state that most South Africans experience seem to undermine these pretensions. South Africa has been de-industrialising as the post-apartheid state has driven the globalisation of the economy and as it has remade itself in this conjuncture (Marais, 2011). So, if the post-apartheid state is not developmental, then what is it? To understand the ideological character of the South African state requires placing it squarely within the process of global neoliberal restructuring.

Neoliberalisation and the end of South African exceptionalism

The notion of South Africa has been inscribed with various meanings within the struggle for national liberation. In particular, mainstream liberation movement theory has consistently referenced the South African social formation as colonialism of a special type – a theoretical category utilised most prominently by the SACP. Due to an institutionalised and regulated form of racism perpetrated by the apartheid regime and white monopoly capital, South Africa occupied an exceptional place within the global consciousness. In the transition to democracy, liberal articulations of South Africa have continued to imbue it with atypical qualities. From the rainbow nation to the democratic miracle,

---

century a more ecocentric industrialisation is necessary and possible for countries in the global periphery as part of achieving structural transformation.

South African exceptionalism has been consistently affirmed (see Waldmeir, 1997). The much-vaunted ANC-led liberation movement has also exaggerated South African exceptionalism as it has neoliberalised South Africa through its rule; it has styled itself as the harbinger of a neoliberalism of a special type.

However, the approach to South Africa and the post-apartheid state in this contribution locates it within a global process of capitalist restructuring. According to Gill (1994: 170), this is a process shaped by a dialectic of disintegration/re-integration in what he describes as 'patterned disorder'. This means social, economic and political structures of the world order are being transformed or are breaking down but the new structures are only just beginning to become identifiable. In this context, placing in perspective the rise of transnational neoliberalism is crucial to understanding how transnational capital has been constituted, state forms remade and global processes of accumulation restructured. Transnational neoliberalism has three important aspects. First, it is an accumulation strategy, or growth model, which attempts to reproduce transnational relations of production. Underpinning this is a policy agenda that favours marketisation and financialisation through privatisation, liberalisation, deregulation and monetarist macro-economic policy consistent with adjusting national markets to get prices right and meet the imperatives of transnational capital.

Second, transnational neoliberalism is the ideology of transnational capital, a world view attempting to realise a global 'market civilisation' (Gill, 2003). Such a market civilisation is premised on possessive individualism and competition. As a class ideology it is also a material force that operationalises itself through its own mechanisms of discipline and control informed by specific class objectives within social relations of production. It also has material effects on social structures and practices. In this sense, it is implicated in class struggles and is constituted by transnationalising class forces. In short, transnational neoliberalism is a historical structure shaping the current world order through a US-led bloc of transnational class and social forces. Third, transnational neoliberalism has been referred to as a form of governmentality, governance and even class rule. However, underpinning these various conceptual approaches is the recognition that the contemporary state form is remade by transnational neoliberalism not to serve the political subjectivity of citizens but to ensure that the sovereignty of capital is protected from risk.

Transnational neoliberalism did not invent the global expansion of capital but has been articulated to it as part of capital's response to the accumulation crisis of the early 1970s. Over the past three decades, the process of global neoliberal restructuring has engendered four major structural shifts in the global political economy.[2] First, through liberalising financial markets, the structural power of finance capital has been enhanced. A global offshore financial market has been constituted, which allows for high-speed speculative flows in variable directions. Second, a post-Fordist global production structure has emerged and has reconfigured the spatial division of labour across and between national boundaries. Third, the past three decades have witnessed a rise of transnational firms, which have become the backbone of the global political economy. These firms provide the material and objective basis for the existence of a transnational capitalist class. Finally, global convergence around the neoliberal state form has also been a major structural shift – in the literature sometimes referred to as the competition state or internationalised state.[3] Such a conception of the state has changed in its role and functions to the extent that the state does not engage in strategic intervention in the economy. Instead, the state regulates economic processes such that market efficiencies can be enhanced. More specifically, the mode of state regulation is such that the state does not pursue outcomes but rather ensures that rules are established and enforced to create a 'balanced playing field' for market forces (Soederberg et al., 2005: 17).

Drawing on the internationalised state and competition state literature, it would seem the neoliberal ideal type state has taken on four key characteristics in practice:

1. It is internationalised in the sense that it is locked into global market structures that impact the national through multilateral processes, institutions and ideological structures shaped by a US-led transnational historical bloc of social forces;
2. It emphasises the use of monetary policy (supply-side economics) to manage inflation and to ensure fiscal and non-fiscal resources are allocated according to global market signals;
3. It dismantles self-sufficiency in ringfenced or strategic sectors and shifts towards organising state responses based on competitive advantage;

---

2   In this regard, there is an important global political economy literature that captures these trends. See, for instance, Strange (1994), Cox (1994), Gill (2003) and Sakamoto (1994).

3   The conception of a neoliberal/Afro-neoliberal state form draws on two important literatures: one deals with the conceptual and empirical aspects of an internationalised state in the global political economy. See Held and Mcgrew (1994), Hitti (1994) and Kamo (1994), for example. The other literature deals with the concept and theory of the competition state, in particular its theoretical pedigree, assumptions and empirical features. See Palan et al. (1999) and Soederberg et al. (2005).

4. It promotes a culture of capitalist accumulation on the terms of transnational capital and through private enterprise, individual initiative and a philosophy of enrichment.

It would also seem from the viewpoint of the neoliberal ideal type state that Africa has been deemed to have the greatest number of failed states. In the wider context of Africa, the idea of a failed state has various meanings and implications. In particular, it reinforces certain racialised stereotypes about African rule and is often associated with imperial representations of the postcolonial state within Western social science (Bilgin and Morton 2002: 55–80), thus justifying various forms of paternalistic intervention, from military incursions to aid and relief work. Furthermore, the notion of failed states has tended to flatten out the African reality and to conflate diverse experiences. Mkandawire (2001) points to an analytical literature in the 1980s and 1990s that claimed that African developmental states were not possible. However, he argues against this by historicising diverse postcolonial experiences and shows that many African countries from independence up until the mid-1970s displayed a developmental orientation. This was lost in the context of the great transformation of neoliberalisation.

The extent to which the post-apartheid state has taken on the characteristics of the neoliberal ideal type will be empirically highlighted to substantiate the conjuncture of the Afro-neoliberal state form since 1996. In this sense, South African exceptionalism has ended. While this perspective overlaps in some ways with the work of other critical political economists, it is distinctive. Fine (2010), for example, while noting the constraints of macro-economic policy on the realisation of a South African developmental state, as well as the inherent limits of the developmental state paradigm, concentrates his critique on the absence of the conditions necessary to realise a developmental state: institutional capacity and strategic state-capital engagements. His approach is grounded in an understanding of the minerals-energy complex (MEC) – which is about a symbiotic relationship between state and capital and core activities related to mining and energy such as minerals extraction, heavy metals, heavy chemicals and fossil fuel-generated electricity – and from this perspective recommends policy alternatives. This contribution highlights the limits of realising a developmental state in South Africa by trying to make intelligible what the state is and how it works in the context of global neoliberal restructuring. This relates directly to the next point about the end of South African exceptionalism.

More specifically, South African exceptionalism has ended in terms of how it indigenises transnational neoliberalism as the basis for an accumulation model. The end of South African exceptionalism began with the apartheid regime in the 1980s adopting firm monetary policy directed at curtailing inflation, liberalising exchange controls for a brief moment, and attempting to restructure bloated and inefficient state parastatals. In the midst of this, the globalisation of the South African economy through financial capital (internal and external) also became discernible. Capital flight out of the economy together with the outward movement by finance capital in the late 1980s and early 1990s were the first signs of internally driven globalisation (Allen, 2006: 49). South African monopoly capital increasingly began to display signs of having transcended national capitalism. This trend became more sharply defined in the post-apartheid context. With the ANC government taking on the debt obligations of the apartheid regime, macro-economic management was locked into a neoliberal trajectory.[4] After accepting a loan from the IMF, the first post-apartheid democracy budget (1994-1995) echoed the IMF's language of macro-economic stability.

By 1996, the neoliberal accumulation trajectory was further entrenched with the adoption of a monetarist macro-economic policy. The GEAR macro-economic policy framework was initially defended by ANC ideologues and ministers as a home-grown approach to restructuring and adjustment. It was even suggested that GEAR was necessary to stabilise South Africa's macro-economy. Ironically, an earlier, self-induced move by the ANC government created the conditions for instability. An attempted reform of exchange controls prompted a run on and massive devaluation of the South African rand, providing the ideal opportunity to impose GEAR. GEAR not only conformed to key prescriptions of transnational neoliberalism but also resonated with ideas put forward by monopoly capital.[5] This conservative macro-economic framework was more than a stabilisation package. It provided the most important and unambiguous signal to monopoly and transnational capital about the direction in which the new ANC government was taking the South African economy, further confirming the ANC government's commitment to globalising the economy from within.

---

4   Allen (2006: 31-68) highlights how the moratorium on $13.62 billion owed to 233 banks reached a firm resolution only in 1993, when the ANC was drawn into the final phase of these negotiations in which it accepted responsibility for the remaining debt obligations of the apartheid regime.

5   In the Department of Finance summary document (1996), there were eleven key elements in the proposed package, including a commitment to privatisation, tariff reductions, inflation-driven monetary policy, and so on. Also see Bond (2000) and Satgar (2008) in which the class dynamics of this ideological shift are further elaborated.

South Africa's choice of a neoliberal development path was not inevitable or necessary. In reality it is the outcome of class and social struggles in which an Afro-neoliberal state has been engendered.[6] Such an Afro-neoliberal state has been both cause and effect of the externalisation and restructuring of South Africa's political economy into an enclave-based accumulation model. Post-apartheid capitalism has emulated and innovated as it has encountered and internalised neoliberalism. In this process, national liberation ideology, as an articulation of ruling-party ideology, has been responsible for indigenising and giving an African voice to neoliberalism. This is not exceptional but merely an expression of a trend affecting every corner of the global political economy. In the African context, a nationally articulated variant of neoliberalism placed post-apartheid South Africa in a race to catch up ideologically with a neoliberalising Africa, tragically caught in the grip of Afro-neoliberalism.[7]

South Africa's neoliberalisation expresses this continental trend and is a version of continental Afro-neoliberalism, a neoliberalism with African characteristics. This kind of specificity helps bring into view the role of national class and social forces within neoliberalisation. It closes the gap where everything was blamed on the Washington Consensus and prompts us to look more holistically to also identify who domestically has gone to bed with transnational capital. According to a growing body of academic work, the ncoliberalisation of the world has prompted a conclusion regarding the end of national capitalisms (Soederberg et al., 2005). It is argued that we are witnessing the emergence of transnational neoliberal capitalism but with national and even regional varieties. National accumulation processes are being transnationalised such that monopoly capitalism is being reconstituted as transnational capitalism (Palan et al., 1999: 19). Hence, a neoliberalised post-apartheid South Africa is not exceptional but rather has brought the universal into the specific and the specific into the universal. It has been one of many national laboratories for neoliberalisation, which reproduces the rule of transnational capital such that it displays a historical specificity not outside of, but within a neoliberal global capitalist economy.

---

6   This article does not foreground these struggles from below given the focus on the ideological representation and constitutive economic practices of the state from above. See Bond (2000) and Satgar (2008).

7   This neoliberal catch up argument is different from Bond's (2004), as he argues that South African sub-imperialism was the harbinger of neoliberalisation on the African continent. On the contrary, Africa has been a laboratory for transnational neoliberalism since 1980. Also see Ferguson (2006), Satgar (2009b) and Harrison (2010). Harrison's book looks at neoliberalism as a form of social engineering on an African and global scale.

The conjuncture of the Afro-neoliberal state

The remaking of South Africa's state as an Afro-neoliberal state form since 1996 has fundamentally changed the relationship between the political and the economic. The mode of authority of the Afro-neoliberal state has been remade as it has retreated from and has re-regulated various aspects of state-market relations. In this process, the Afro-neoliberal state has remade national capitalism into a transnational capitalism. South Africa's mode of production is now driven by an externalised logic. The global market mechanism has become crucial for organising production, financing and consumption such that even in the state, commercialisation and commodification of public services have become standard. In the South African context, competitive restructuring has subsumed the state by way of a disembedded and deterritorialised market.

The state has become one of many actors within the market. The Afro-neoliberal state chose not to go down a path in which a national popular project could exist driven by statist, capitalist and socialist logics (Amin, 2009). Instead, the transnational fraction of South Africa's ruling class (including the ruling ANC-led Alliance) constructed a state geared towards facilitating and managing a transnational capitalist mode of production. This has solicited praise from the IMF, World Bank, WTO and WEF; most importantly, such praise has emerged from within the ranks of transnational capital. However, more than asserting that the post-apartheid state is Afro-neoliberal, it is necessary to show how it is constituted. More precisely, what are the practices of such an Afro-neoliberal state? What are the determining functions of the state that constitute it as an Afro-neoliberal form?

To answer these questions, we need to bring into view how state practice is structurally implicated in changing the underlying conditions of accumulation, which in turn shape and remake the state form. We need to show how the post-apartheid state is locked into the macro-restructuring and management of the economy in a manner that eclipses strategic developmental state interventionism – that is, it is necessary to examine what the main characteristics of the state are as an Afro-neoliberal state and as it has overseen a shift to a globalised, competitive and export-led growth model with trickle-down effects. Such a state is not developmental through its embrace of deep integration into global markets and a logic of global accumulation.

What follows traces how, since 1994 – but mainly with the adoption and deepening of a neoliberal macro-economic framework in 1996 – the post-apartheid state form and its practices are constituted through the restructuring of the Afro-neoliberal accumulation model: the dialectics of integration/ disintegration, external/internal globalisation and national/transnational capitalism are highlighted. This conjunctural historicising highlights a state form that was constituted in post-apartheid South Africa in the main during Mandela's and Mbeki's governments. While there are strong continuities with Zuma's government, it is still too early to conclude that this 18-year trajectory will change, despite the Zuma-led government's developmental state rhetoric.

The internationalised dimensions

To understand the shift to an Afro-neoliberal state, we must look at the internationalised dimension. This relates mainly to key apparatuses, public and private, within the US-led transnational historical bloc managing the consensus around transnational neoliberalism and its mechanisms of discipline and control. The Bretton Woods Institutions (the World Bank and the IMF), the WTO and the WEF developed an important presence in post-apartheid South Africa. In turn, South Africa also developed a presence in these institutions. Together, these institutions set parameters for South Africa's growth model. For example, in 1993 the IMF intervened in public debate through its report *Economic Policies for a New South Africa* in which it argued for a trickledown growth model, which resonated with various sections of South African business. At the same time, it provided an $850 million CFF to the Transitional Executive Council, conditional upon further liberalisation of the economy (Padayachee, 1994: 589).

The first democracy budget of 1994–1995 showed clear signs that macro-economic stability was not being interpreted based on the RDP, but rather in line with IMF imperatives, despite the rhetoric from the GNU (Padayachee, 1994: 591–594). At the same time, the World Bank engaged civil society and drew left intellectuals into various projects. The bank also became the training ground for cadres from the liberation movement (Marais, 2001: 128). In the WTO multilateral process, South Africa attained credentials as a firm proponent of tariff liberalisation and industrial adjustment based on competitive advantage. This was articulated in the GEAR policy, which promoted the restructuring of the accumulation model towards a competitive economy. Thus, trade liberalisation meant South Africa was leaving behind an era of racialised import-substitution industrialisation and instead was choosing a growth path driven by FDI and competitive advantage. Consistent with GEAR's targets for tariff reform, and the WTO's liberalisation commitments,

South Africa's average tariff declined from 6.1% in 1997 to 4.9% in 2004 (Cassim and Zarenda, 2004: 106–107). Import duties also declined for consumption of intermediate and capital goods, further confirming an emphasis on promoting domestic manufacturing through adjustment to global market pressures and ultimately competitive advantage.

Trade liberalisation triggered a major structural shift in the South African economy. Firms, industries and sectors began responding to market pressures through processes of right sizing, business re-engineering and downsizing (Buhlungu, 2010; Buhlungu and Webster, 2006). According to Nattrass (2003: 141–157), this process has not led to labour absorption as claimed by the state, but instead has shed jobs as part of increasing labour productivity.[8] Moreover, while labour-intensive import-substitution industries have been hardest hit, export industries have also not created jobs, but have become more capital-intensive in order to remain competitive. Due to rising imports and penetration by transnational capital in some sectors, local producers have been displaced in the production of capital goods, consumer equipment, dairy, pharmaceuticals and clothing (Makgetla, 2004: 273–276). At the same time as many sectors of the economy have been decimated, the state has continued to trumpet export successes such as the motor industry. However, as Makgetla (2004: 276) points out, while the motor industry has had some successes in attracting FDI and increasing exports dramatically over the past few years, it is still almost wholly owned by foreign transnationals and linked into a global commodity chain. It also has had substantial tariff incentives through the Motor Industry Development Programme. The actual effect of the motor industry's success must be further questioned as many domestic component manufacturers have been displaced (Carmody, 2002: 267). Similarly, foreign clothing firms are leading exports in the clothing and textile industry and financial market entrants have connected businesses in South Africa to global financial networks (Gelb and Black, 2004: 18–25). Taken together, the state's actions have not been those of a developmental state; rather, liberalisation and restructuring have produced an export-led enclave around which a structurally fragmented and disarticulated economy has had to adjust.

The South African state has actively participated in these state-centred global institutions and has argued that it is transforming these institutions from

---

8   South Africa's unemployment rate has been over 20% since the advent of democracy in 1994. In the context of the global economic crisis, this job-shedding trend has deepened. It is estimated that the secondary effects of the global economic crisis since 2008 have led to the loss of over one million jobs.

within (Bond, 2001). The Minister of Trade and Industry and the Minister of Finance come across as champions of a new global reform agenda, which is beneficial to South Africa. However, the empirical reality is that the reform from within strategy has not worked, as South Africa has engaged through the internalisation of transnational neoliberalism, rather than through a development strategy grounded in a national consensus. South Africa is locked into these global relations and has not manoeuvred to secure space for a genuine national development project. For example, South Africa's membership in the G20 group of countries, which emerged from the G7 post-1999, has reinforced its commitment to the controls of the IMF, WTO and World Bank. As Soederberg (2004b: 81) suggests 'Taken together, the constitution of the G20 demonstrates renewed attempts at core-periphery coercion by inviting these countries into the highly exclusive G7/G8, or, put more bluntly, by co-opting them into the rules and standards of the core-alliance coercion by ensuring official, and thus more tightly integrated relations with the IMF and World Bank.'

In short, South Africa's 'reforms from within' have ensured it a place within the process of managing a new international financial architecture for the world. It is one of the many poster nations playing a role in managing a complex and volatile global financial system in the interests of transnational capital, especially finance capital. Since the 2008 global economic crisis, South Africa has been increasingly drawn into global management of this crisis and has had to ensure its own macro-economic adjustments are in step with the global consensus it is part of.

The other important aspect of South Africa's international relations is the WEF, as it is one of the most important transnational private institutions in the world and, like other multilateral apparatuses, it organises and expresses the structural power of transnational capital. Since its formation over 30 years ago, the WEF has played a crucial role in ensuring the rise and articulation of transnational neoliberalism as a dominant ideology in the global political economy. The WEF is an agenda-setting institution for transnational capital (as it is composed of the top 1000 corporations in the world) and it is crucial to extending the reach, networks and links between a transnational business community and national classes. In a classical Gramscian sense, we can refer to the WEF as the modern prince of global capital.

South Africa has been a consistent participant in the WEF's Davos meetings since Nelson Mandela, F.W. de Klerk and Mangosuthu Buthelezi made a joint appearance in 1992. Subsequently, South Africa has hosted the WEF's

Africa Forum since 1999. There have been 18 Africa Forum meetings so far. Zuma, like Mbeki, has ensured that his Cabinet members continue to be diligent hosts of the WEF in Africa. Similar to its Davos Forum, which brings the top transnational business leaders together with world political leaders, the Africa Forum targets leading figures on the continent such as business leaders, political leaders, academics, journalists and other prominent personalities. These forums are extremely influential as they generate knowledge and serve as platforms to champion a brand of structural neoliberalism. In short, the WEF's vision of removing the obstacles to global competitiveness is pursued through these forums. The vital role it plays in co-ordinating a particular class project cannot be underestimated. It is no coincidence that its emphasis on competitiveness and its problem-solving methodology to unblock obstacles for markets resonates with Afro-neoliberalism.

In a similar vein, the South African state has created the President's International Investment Council, which brings together representatives of transnational capital and canvasses support for government reforms and policies (*BuaNews*, 2008). In this context, South Africa has won praise from the IMF and World Bank and has also earned a prestigious place in the WTO as an ardent supporter of trade liberalisation. Similarly, the WEF has increased its approval ratings of South Africa's global competitiveness. For example, using its competitive index (one of its main disciplinary and surveillance tools), the WEF declared that South Africa had moved up in the global competitiveness rankings from 46th to 44th, which won the state further praise in the ranks of transnational capital (WEF, 2006). While these approvals help cement the link between transnational and domestic capital, this does not mean that South Africa's Afro-neoliberal state is a success in development terms. Instead, it means the state is locked into managing an elite economic consensus rather than discharging a democratic mandate from its citizens to ensure economic transformation and self-determination. These institutions, together with other presidential working groups, have become the main macro-agenda-setting institutions in South Africa. Further, it is out of this nexus of relations that South Africa has put its weight behind the African Union's New Partnership for Africa's Development (NEPAD) agenda for continental Afro-neoliberal restructuring.

The primacy of monetary policy

The second dimension of South Africa's Afro-neoliberal state relates to how it has managed market perceptions through monetary policy and through inducing financial allocations consistent with the interests of transnational capital. To understand South Africa's monetary policy orientation, it is necessary to begin with the insulation of the South African Reserve Bank (SARB) from undue political pressure. The story begins with the constitutional autonomy given to the SARB in the new democracy. This has bolstered its conservative role and shift to neoliberal monetarism, which privileges capital mobility and low inflation (by controlling the money supply). Zuma's finance minister has continued this approach.

Tight monetary policy has not fostered employment creation but has traded this off by trying to attract capital inflows. This is reflected in exchange control liberalisation and inflation targeting. The former has happened incrementally with capital account liberalisation in 1995, which included the removal of the two-tier currency system, the removal of restrictions on foreign owners of capital, and deregulation to permit foreign banks to enter the economy. By 1998 most exchange control regulations on domestic investors were eliminated. The SARB's prioritisation of managing inflation was reflected in the formalisation of inflation-targeting in February 2000. Inflation targets are set by the Minister of Finance, and the SARB attempts to realise this target through interest-rate adjustments. All of this has helped in terms of good governance surveillance by credit-rating agencies and has led to improved ratings, affirming South Africa's consistency in embracing the global consensus around neoliberal economic management.

Fiscal policy has also been aligned around tight management so as not to crowd out financial flows, particularly investors. GEAR's deficit-reduction targets have ensured a decline in deficit spending and since 1999 this has been kept below 3% of GDP (Gelb, 2005: 374). Complementing this effort to bring in investment is the creation of numerous investment-promotion agencies and initiatives in national, provincial and local government, all declaring that 'South Africa is open for business'. Gelb and Black (2004: 8) suggest there are more than 35 incentive schemes for investors and commitments to treat all investors the same in South Africa regarding foreign exchange for import, export and access (based on commitments made by South Africa under the WTO Agreement on TRIMS), and that there are over 30 bilateral investment treaties, most with OECD countries. In addition, South Africa's Afro-neoliberal state has actively promoted development corridors and industrial development zones as a basis to attract FDI flows. In this regard, the lengths gone to provide sweeteners to FDI are rather telling. Hallowes (2011: 231–234) reveals the hefty energy and tax subsidy advanced to win the deal with Rio Tinto Alcan and secure their commitment to the Coega Industrial Development Zone. To sweeten the deal, the government had already spent R20 billion on Coega, which included R6.4 billion in high-voltage transmission infrastructure to supply power to the smelter and provided a R1.93 billion tax incentive. Hallowes points out this deal would have created only a thousand jobs at a cost of R5 million each, with at least 300 being available only to highly skilled professionals. After a decade, Alcan pulled out of the deal, claiming the government could not guarantee the power supply. The attempt to attract Rio Tinto Alcan into the Coega Industrial Development Zone is symptomatic of the state's desire to reproduce the competitive advantage of cheap electricity that underpins South Africa's MEC, and in the process the state is decrying South African commitments to address climate change, including the broader macro-challenge of ecocentric production and an ecological transition of the economy.

Ultimately, the Afro-neoliberal approach to macro-economic management has been dismal in terms of attracting FDI in comparative terms and as a share of global flows (Gelb and Black, 2004: 9–10; Mohammed 2010). However, this does not detract from the fact that South Africa has had various global corporations already within its economy, even prior to the democratic transition. Despite sanctions and disinvestment, at the time of the unbanning of political movements there were more than 450 firms within South Africa – 85% from Europe and 13% from North America – with FDI liabilities at $8 billion (Gelb and Black, 2004: 8). This points further to South Africa being caught in globalising tides, from the outside coming in, as part of a process of transnational neoliberal restructuring emanating from capitalist centres of the 1970s. The Afro-neoliberal loosening and opening up from within gave further impetus to the transnationalisation of South Africa's economy.

Dismantling self-sufficiency in strategic sectors

The third dimension of South Africa's Afro-neoliberal state relates to the dismantling of self-sufficiency and further configuring state responses based on competitive advantage. The first aspect of this relates to the restructuring of state assets. The apartheid regime built up a racialised import-substitution-industrialisation-accumulation model, supported by the export of minerals, but with a strong parastatal sector to buttress it. This form of state intervention affected the underlying cost structure of the South African economy, in terms of energy, transport, communications, fuel and other inputs for production. With the ANC's RDP envisaging massive public sector investment and the further development of the internal market as a platform from which to develop an external orientation, the role of reconfiguring South Africa's parastatals to support an endogenous-driven growth and development strategy was seen as crucial. In other words, such a parastatal sector was crucial in finding the right balance between import-substitution and export-led accumulation. The restructuring of state assets in post-apartheid South Africa through the Afro-neoliberal agenda was not guided by this imperative. Instead, it was informed by the imperative of raising fiscal resources by selling of state assets (Fine, 1995).

In this process it is estimated that at least 18 non-core assets have been sold off, including Sun Air, Transnet's Production House, Chemical Services and Transmed Administrator (Cassim, 2006: 73). However, this process is now left with core parastatal enterprises: ESKOM, South African Airways, Telkom, Transnet and Denel. Various BEE deals, through strategic equity partners, are changing the ownership patterns of these core parastatals and their assets. Increasingly, these enterprises are operating as quasi-private enterprises rather than state institutions guided by national development objectives. Moreover, the commercialising and competitive logic of restructuring has not seen a cut in costs from Eskom, the main electricity provider. Instead, electricity price increases are firmly on the agenda. In the case of Eskom as it is cut loose from sourcing capital expenditure from the national fiscus it has to pass on the costs of capital financing to its consumers. In short, South Africa's parastatals are not operating in accordance with national priorities and a co-ordinated development strategy.

A similar trend has emerged in agriculture. Historically, South Africa developed a highly commercialised and mechanised, though racialised and fossil fuel-driven, agricultural system. This agro-food economy was central in ensuring food security. Through big bang Afro-neoliberal restructuring, agriculture has been deregulated through the removal of all state-run marketing boards; farm subsidies have been cut; agriculture co-operatives have been forced into a process of conversion into equity-based companies; and land reform has been anchored within a willing seller, willing buyer model. The state justified these moves by arguing that regulation both raised the price of food and undermined efficiency (Makgetla, 2004: 273). In fact, the opposite has been witnessed, with ownership patterns concentrating in the context of liberalised agriculture and with food prices constantly increasing. In the case of bread, a staple for most working-class South Africans, four major milling and bread-producing companies have consistently colluded to push up the price of bread (Cock, 2006). In 2008 South Africa was a net importer of farm products like wheat and more recently even maize, as commodity speculation has had its impacts.

In general terms, the withdrawal and re-invention of state-market relations have permitted the state to promote prestige and mega-development projects while trying to ameliorate the deepening inequalities and precariousness gripping South African society. A mix of games and crumbs has come to the fore as the basis of state intervention. On the one side, the FIFA World Cup (estimated R30 billion), the high-speed Gautrain (estimated R30 billion) and South Africa's arms deal (estimated R70 billion) have all cost the South African taxpayer excessive amounts of money while being presented as crucial drivers of growth and job creation.[9] Despite the official rhetoric and expenditure, South Africa's growth rates were in a negative range by 2009, with modest improvements and reaching approximately 2% in 2012. In general terms, and given South Africa's link with the global economy, a period of stagnation is more the appropriate scenario. The room for counter-cyclical fiscal policy has been exhausted (unless the state wants to increase its debt-to-GDP ratio and its sovereign debt like Greece); FDI inflows have been dismal; there is growing tax fatigue amongst citizens; and domestic capital is not investing. Moreover, official unemployment has remained at approximately 25%, with one million jobs having been lost with the onset of the global crisis in 2008–2009 (Makgetla, 2010).

On the other side, the state has brought close to 14 million people onto the social grant system, provided indigent support for poor households at the municipal level, and built a million houses to address housing backlogs. In terms of the social grant system (child and elderly grants), this is a crucial buffer for households at the epicentre of the crisis of social reproduction; however, currently between eight and ten million people are not receiving any grants, wages or remittances in South Africa (Terreblanche, 2012: 101). Indigent-support policies in municipal governments, like that of Johannesburg, are a response to grassroots struggles. As Prishani Naidoo (2010: 186) points out,

---

9   It is estimated that the costs of the World Cup have generally been underestimated. Cornelissen (2010) shows that official projected expenditure on stadiums and infrastructure upgrades alone stood at R33 billion and projected income at R19 billion in 2008. Moreover, in the public discourse it has been suggested that South Africa allowed FIFA to take a larger share than any other host country ever had of income from the World Cup for spectator fees, food, media contracts and paraphernalia.

in practice '[these policies] move away from creating universal forms of access to decommodified services towards more targeted interventions that provide such access incrementally according to an individual's ability to pay' and that 'while [such policies are] portrayed as "pro-poor", [they] actually work towards moulding the behaviours of that population group in ways that further entrench inequality and differentiated standards of living'. While the state trumpets its building of over a million houses since 1994, the failure to provide jobs where people live has led to an increase in migration to urban areas. Housing demand and backlogs in this urban context have ballooned recently, with the state far from delivering what is really required. Currently, it is estimated the state needs to build another 2.1 million houses to address the needs of 12 million South Africans, a quarter of the population.

Underpinning this reality is a state incapable of stemming the tide towards deepening inequality. According to Terreblanche this is a trend consistent with comparative international experience of neoliberal forms of state rule; in South Africa, given inherited legacies, income inequality has become grotesque. He points out that 'over the past 18 years the Gini coefficient increased from 0.66 to 0.70. The richest 10 million South Africans received almost 75% of total income in 2008, while the poorest 25 million received less than 8 per cent' (Terreblance, 2012: 110).

In short, despite the ameliorative social protection provided by the state, this is premised on the deepening of poverty, unemployment and inequality. The state essentially prevails over an unviable society as it has remade strategic state intervention into pro-market efficiency practice.

Fostering a culture of capitalist accumulation on the terms of transnational capital

The final dimension and crucial legitimating practice of South Africa's Afro-neoliberal state relates to promoting a culture of capitalist accumulation on the terms of transnational capital. Former President Thabo Mbeki's characterisation of South Africa as being composed of two economies helped to engender this culture of accumulation. The first economy is relatively well developed and competitive, while the second economy is backward, underdeveloped and survivalist. The crucial challenge in the two-economies discourse is to deracialise the first economy while also creating a pathway or ladder from the second economy into the first economy. This discourse of two economies did not question South Africa's historically monopolised mode of production, but instead focused on the need to deracialise and broaden the first economy or transnationalised mode of production. All South Africans were meant to aspire to be part of transnational capitalism. The state effectively became a crucial enabler in this process.

Since 1996 government intervention has been informed by this characterisation of the economy in various ways (Hirsch, 2005: 193–256). First, the state has promoted small and medium enterprises as a way to unleash latent entrepreneurs into the first economy. In March 1995 the President's Conference on Small Business led to a white paper, a new small business law, and five new major institutions: the Centre for Small Business Promotion (policy unit in the DTI), the Centre for Small Business Promotion (a policy unit in the DTI), the Ntsika Enterprise Promotion Agency (to provide non-financial assistance to small entrepreneurs), Khula Enterprise Finance Ltd (to provide loan funds and loan guarantees) and the National Small Business Council. Alternative forms of enterprise such as co-operatives have been collapsed into this framework and are seen as stepping stones to just another business form in the transnationalised first economy (Satgar and Williams, 2011a).

Second, the state recognised that the first economy needed to be linked to the second economy through micro-reform interventions. The state's answer to this was ASGISA, which aims to achieve an annual average growth rate of 6% between 2010 and 2014.[10] The crux of ASGISA is to bring down the costs of doing business in South Africa by highlighting conditions for the first economy to be globally competitive particularly through state-led infrastructure spending.[11] In addition, the New Industrial Policy Framework adds the need for various measures such as public works, small and medium enterprises, procurement policy, and so on, to provide a ladder from the first to the second economy for the poor, excluded and marginalised. Under the Zuma government, this direction of industrial policy has not changed.

Finally, the culture of accumulation is linked to attempts to deracialise monopoly capitalism through BEE (Rumney, 2005). BEE gained impetus starting in the early 1990s as major South African conglomerates began unbundling and deconcentrating the ownership structure of the South African

---

10 Contained in 'Background document: A catalyst for Accelerated and Shared Growth-South Africa (ASGISA)', media briefing by Deputy President Phumzile Mlambo-Ngcuka, 6 February 2006.

11 In his 2012 State of the Nation address, President Zuma announced a R300 billion capital expenditure plan led by Transnet, South Africa's commercial rail parastatal, to build transport infrastructure to bring down costs of doing business.

economy. The BEE process has gone through various phases. In the mid-1990s the private sector attempted to cut debt-financed ownership deals. By 1998, with over 230 such deals on the JSE valued in aggregate at R37 billion, the stock market crashed, bringing most BEE ventures down with it. A second phase, spearheaded by black business associations and the government, began in 1999. This initiative led to the establishment of a non-statutory Black Economic Commission and a strategy. A third phase established BEE charters – the first was put in place in the liquid fuels industry – and the subsequent promulgation of the Broad-Based Black Economic Empowerment Act (2004).

This policy and process of BEE envisages various forms of empowerment including: direct ownership and control of enterprises and assets, deracialising management at senior levels, human resource development and employment equity, and indirect empowerment through procurement. By all accounts this process is not happening smoothly, with uneven deracialisation across sectors and in a context in which historically white monopoly capital has been moving offshore since the early 1990s (Carmody, 2002: 262; Daniel et al., 2003). Despite its challenges, the state has used these various mechanisms to develop a culture of accumulation which has also served to undermine the state. The rampant corruption engendered through BEE has led to the capture of the state bureaucracy in many instances by parasitic interests.

Corruption in the South African state has become endemic and reaches into the highest echelons (Sole, 2005; Southall, 2007). In many ways, BEE has provided a licence to loot state resources, with officials in government tied in with politicians and aspirant elites outside the state. In the province of Kwazulu-Natal alone, R1 billion has been lost to corruption. Most government departments have achieved qualified audits in terms of the Public Finance Management Act and according to the Auditor-General. This further confirms the abuse and misuse of fiscal resources. Over the past few years, South Africa's media outlets have blown the whistle on the 'looting of the Land Bank'; an arms deal involving South Africa's sitting president, Jacob Zuma; Oilgate, which involved ANC front companies and the illegal purchase of oil from Saddam Hussein's Iraq; Travelgate, which involved ANC parliamentarians and travel agencies; as well as some of the most high-profile BEE-related corruption scandals. Several national Cabinet ministers, provincial ministers and municipal councils have also been fingered in BEE-related corruption. The recent World Cup has also not escaped this dominant trend. Corruption has been exposed related to stadium building and ostensibly linked to the murder of eight politicians in the province of Mpumalanga. In most instances, criminal prosecution has been avoided and the Department of Finance has not blacklisted any BEE companies on its register for corruption. Instead of an overarching national vision and a clear directing role for the state, BEE accumulation is not about structural transformation but rather about facilitating parasitic class formation. More specifically, BEE policy is a crucial part of a trade-off with white monopoly capital to facilitate the globalisation of South Africa from within.

Conclusion

Post-apartheid South Africa resolved its globalisation dilemma by embracing the restructuring of global capitalism. This choice engendered an Afro-neoliberal state from above that undermines state capacity for strategic intervention and an endogenous accumulation path driven by various logics and a practice of embedded autonomy. Instead, the Afro-neoliberal state locks South Africa into economic management practices to ensure that the country is integrated into global financial, production and trade structures on the terms of transnational capital, including a transnational fraction of South African capital championing BEE. It constrains and closes off areas of autonomous economic policymaking.

In concrete terms, the South African economy has been structurally transformed into an extroverted and enclave-based accumulation model. Afro-neoliberal state practices have been the cause and effect of this. These features of the post-apartheid political economy confirm the end of South African exceptionalism and reduce South Africa to just another of many neoliberal experiments on the African continent and in the global political economy. Despite the rhetoric and declarations about being a developmental state, South Africa does not have such a state, even given the rise to power of Jacob Zuma – the champion of the working class according to the ANC left. Instead, national liberation and post-apartheid development is about reproducing the rule of transnational capital, free markets and possessive individualism. The Marikana massacre affirms this reality and the willingness of ruling elites to go beyond market mechanisms to the point that state violence is utilised to maintain and manage a deeply globalised economy. This does not bode well for the future of South African democracy.

Africa Spectrum 47(2–3), 2012: 33–62.

*Opposing Zumafication in
the SACP and Outside*

Reflections: The Age of Barbarism

Introduction

AT A COMMON-SENSE LEVEL, in everyday life the crisis of global capitalism has shattered hope and engendered a debilitating despair and uncertainty. When workers lose their jobs, when peasants are dispossessed of their land and when food prices go up bringing hunger into the lives of millions, the brutality and violence of capitalism looms large. Moreover, when ruling classes argue that a one or two degree change in planetary temperatures will mean adaptation, the reality is that these shifts in climatic conditions will be felt disproportionately by the working class and the poor. For many it would seem humanity is trapped and our circumstances cannot be changed.

However, as pointed out in the introduction to this book, immanent within the crisis of global capitalism are various historical possibilities. This requires a recognition that history is open, given the objective weaknesses and limits of global capitalism, and given that historical outcomes can be shaped if we choose to struggle. The global power structures of capitalism have been made by social forces and can be remade to support a new way of existence. Global capitalism is not a progressive force for the development of humanity and a non-destructive relationship with nature. This is confirmed by its ongoing destruction of the conditions that sustain life on Earth. It is an enemy of humanity and nature. In this context a failure to engage in conscious political action for an alternative is tantamount to complicity in the perpetuation of this irrational system of endless accumulation (that benefits a minority) and our self-destruction.

The poetic footprints I have shared, as part of this book, give glimpses into the destructiveness of capitalism, its barbarism, but also an appreciation and respect for the indomitable human spirit. Such a spirit is reflected in the courage of the left to stand up and fight against this barbarism in the twentieth century. Many like Luxemburg, Gramsci, E.M.S. Namboodiripad (the first elected Communist Party chief minister in Kerala, India, in the 1950s) and Allende are examples from the left who have struggled to keep history open. They chose not to surrender to capitalism but neither to revolutionary orthodoxy. As we try to use the contradictions of global capitalism to find exits and departure points for a democratic ecosocialist future, we need to recognise that the crucial lesson of twentieth-century socialism, in my view, is that barbarism cannot be used to fight barbarism.

This means we have to think much more deeply about means and ends in the context of transformative struggle. The Marxist tradition has not dealt with the question of means and ends adequately. In most instances, all means justify the scientifically defined ends. This is one kind of extreme. The other kind of unthinking Marxism is one in which certain strategies and tactics have been frozen as part of a successful revolutionary canon and therefore these tried and tested methods, under all historical circumstances, must prevail. Today, the context of global capitalist crisis provides fertile ground for reactionary ideologies to come to the fore, including doctrinaire left ideologies. The resurgence of revolutionary orthodoxies and dogmas such as neo-Stalinist populism poses as much of a threat to progressive change as does global capitalism. This is the crux of the reflections I would like to share.

US supremacy and barbarism

It was Rosa Luxemburg who posed the question: socialism or barbarism? In the context of the world in which we live today, of rampant global capitalism, the barbarism of this system is experienced differently from Rosa Luxemburg's time. We are in a civilisation that does not value the importance of human life, it is actually anti-human, and it does not value our relationship with the natural environment. Put differently, the logic of endless accumulation and global expansion is not merely about polarisation or exploitation but fundamentally about physical destruction. This is the characteristic feature of contemporary global capitalism and what defines its barbarism. This destruction is happening on a global scale. Central to driving the destruction of the world is US supremacy. After the Cold War US supremacy has been unrivalled on the planet even with the emergence of China as an important global economic player.

To understand the logic of destruction inherent in contemporary global capitalism we have to understand how US supremacy has engendered the conditions for this to prevail. There are three crucial ways in which US supremacy has prevailed over the world. The first is through the globalisation of a model of neoliberal capitalism. Neoliberalism is a global accumulation strategy of transnational capital and a world view about the primacy of market-led development. The primary objectives of neoliberalism are to ensure US supremacy in the world and ensure the realisation of the interests of transnational capital. This process of globalising a neoliberal model of capitalism began in the 1980s and was driven by the rise of finance capital. Concomitantly a process of global restructuring has ensued, which has wrenched open economies and displaced any kind of alternative political economy. This was spurred on by the end of the Cold War and in the twenty-first century through neoliberal restructuring we have a world that is being recreated in the image of the US and organised around the interests of transnational capital. The flip side of this market-led restructuring process are fundamental consequences for the reproduction of societies. Actually, most societies that have been forced to open their economies and integrate into global capitalism have lost a great deal of policy autonomy and control over national economic decision-making.

In this context food security has been compromised, de-industrialisation has been taking place with entire sectors disappearing, and financial markets have become volatile. Through market-led development, crashing and collapsing national economies have become a feature of global capitalism over the past three decades. In this sense the global crisis of capitalism did not begin with the collapse of the sub-prime housing market in the US but has actually been ongoing and an inherent feature of the neoliberal restructuring of societies in the periphery of capitalism. This has had crushing consequences for workers and the poor. Global growth has been encouraged without including the vast majority on this planet. We have become truly a planet of slums alongside enclaves of extreme concentrations of wealth. Moreover, globalised production structures have broken the link with reproduction. Wage-based employment as the means to ensure survival and the reproduction of households has become extremely difficult. Actually, with the global economic crisis job losses are deepening the horrors and destruction of everyday life.

The second way in which US supremacy is creating the conditions for the destruction of our world is through militarism. Militarism has been a key element of US foreign policy especially since the Spanish-American war. However, with the end of the Cold War US expansionism through the projection of military power did not abate. The expected demilitarisation and peace dividend did not materialise. The first invasion of Iraq in 1991 was a show of military power in a region with crucial geopolitical importance. Later through NATO the US also projected its power in Yugoslavia and began developing a military presence in eastern Europe. However, the barbarism of US violence is not only related to its expansionism but also with how it unleashes war. First, the cost of invading Iraq and Afghanistan after 9/11 is conservatively estimated by the Congressional Research Service as being $942 billion. Other economists place the costs at over $3 trillion. Whether the higher or lower figure is accepted, what is irrational about all this is that these large sums of money are being spent In the context of massive economic fallout both in the US and in the global political economy. While this massive military expenditure might be a part of the strategy for economic recovery, it still suggests war is more important than the over five million Americans who have lost their jobs in the economic crisis. The US stimulus package (about $700 billion) is not as large as the cost of financing these wars. In short, war and military spending is both at the expense of American workers and citizens, and also at the expense of the poor countries being destroyed by US military power. The second aspect of how the US wages war is not through evidence and legal rights. We have entered the age of a new kind of warfare in which war is akin to witch hunts. War is merely about the exercise of power; might is right. This comes through with regard to the reasons given for invading Iraq. The argument that Saddam Hussein had weapons of mass destruction has been proven to be false. Moreover, the new kind of drone warfare orchestrated through remote-controlled airplanes blasts and kills more than suspected terrorists. It kills innocent people that might be in the vicinity of a so-called target. This kind of techno-killing also reflects in a stark way the anti-human side of capitalism's contemporary barbarism. Finally, the use of torture has added to the almost feudal character of how the US wages war.

The third way in which US supremacy creates the conditions for the logic of destruction is through its opposition to being part of addressing the ecological crisis facing global capitalism. The US accounts for a quarter of the world's greenhouse gas emissions. It has the highest per capita emission levels of carbon dioxide per person on the planet. Following in a close second are the rest of the industrialised countries (or the G7). Essentially 684 million people and their patterns of production and consumption are driving global warming, threatening the biosphere and the future of the planet. Climate change science shows this and confirms that human activity is the cause of global warming. Despite this evidence the US government refused to sign the first-ever legal instrument, the Kyoto Protocol, that provided for legally binding restrictions in greenhouse gas emissions of 5.2% below 1990 levels, by 2008–2012, for all industrialised countries. The US was meant to bring down its greenhouse gas emission levels to 8%. The irony of this US reluctance is that the Kyoto Protocol was merely a symbolic gesture. In itself it fell far short of a more serious and aggressive approach to address climate change.

Stalinism through the eyes of William Kentridge

With global capitalism in crisis, the need for a renewed socialism to come to the fore as an alternative is critical. However, more likely in some places is a resurgence of revolutionary orthodoxies and dogmas. This derives from the Marxism that dominated the imagination of the twentieth century and emerged out of the Russian Revolution. It was canonised by Stalin and exported to the world as Marxism-Leninism. For Rosa Luxemburg, a supporter of the Bolsheviks led by Lenin, the turn to terror and undemocratic means after the capture of power in revolutionary Russia, sowed the seeds of destruction. Her argument that a virtue was made of necessity proved to be correct. Moreover, her perspective on revolutionary politics privileged the need to widen the democratic space and ensure conditions were created for mass self-organising and mass power from below. Instead, and as she observed, the revolutionary violence and authoritarianism that was utilised early on became the rule and not the exception. Karl Kautsky, the leading ideologue of the German Social Democrats, also critiqued the Bolshevik turn to terror but went further to argue that the conditions in Russia did not provide for a successful advance to socialism. In his view Russia was a backward country and therefore socialism could not be achieved. In the main he problematised ends, in this case a socialist project, by focusing on objective conditions. Both these arguments provide us with important ways of thinking about the means and ends challenge facing Marxist politics.

However, another way of thinking about means and ends relates to consequences. The choices made by the Bolsheviks led by Lenin and later by Stalin had fundamental consequences for their revolution. For Stalin's centrally planned socialism the justifications for this seem to derive from three Marxist-Leninist arguments or ways of thinking about social change. The first relates to harnessing the achievements of capitalism as the basis of socialism. In many ways the Soviet mass Fordist factory was part of this experiment. Big factories were symbols of building on the best of capitalism. It reflected the forward march of the forces of production. At the same time, Stalin's choices had destructive ecological consequences. Not only did the great industrial leap forward obscure the ecological aspects in Marx's Marxism but it also suppressed an ecological dimension to Soviet socialism. Such a dimension expressed itself through the golden years of the Soviet Revolution. In the early to mid-1920s there was a strong environmental movement. It was influenced by the work of Bogdanov and taken up in policy terms by Lunacharsky and Bukharin. Moreover, many conservation reserves were set up from 1919 and were even strongly supported by Lenin. However, by 1929 the rise of the environmental movement was stopped in its tracks by Stalin. He basically suppressed any preoccupations with the environment and launched his plan for forced-march industrialisation. Stalin's industrialisation was a disaster for the environment and produced catastrophic consequences for the resource base of the Soviet economy. To this extent the Green critique of actually existing socialism is correct except that its target should be Stalinist socialism and not socialism in general. This ecological critique is one of the many aspects absent in Joe Slovo's disengagement from the Soviet Union.

The second Marxist-Leninist argument justifying Stalin's centrally planned socialism derives from the scientism of Soviet Marxism (also present in Second International Marxism). This suggested that Marxism-Leninism has a superior understanding of how society was changing. The iron laws of history were clear on where society should end up even if it meant wiping out large parts of the peasantry through forced collectivisation of agriculture. The violence that transformed the class structures of rural Russia, under Stalin, was extremely brutal. Hunger, starvation on a mass scale and thousands of executions ensured the scientific certainties of a classless society prevailed through collectivised agriculture. The primitive accumulation and extraction of surplus from the peasantry laid the basis for what many we have interviewed refer to as state capitalism, bureaucratic state-led development, and so on. A third Marxist-Leninist argument advocated by Stalinism for the choices it made was anchored in the superiority of the knowledge that resided in the vanguard. The vanguard understood the past and the future. The vanguard had the monopoly of the class perspective. In practice this monopoly resided with Stalin and the power structures he built up to ensure his reign of terror.

The madness of this and its tragic consequences, in my view, is best captured by William Kentridge, one of South Africa's great artists, who has combined his painting, film making and training in theatre, to produce some of the most creative work we are seeing in the world today. In one of his most recent opera productions he explores the tragedy of the Russian Revolution through the device of absurdity. He places Comrade Nose (a fictional character derived from a short story written by Gogol) inside Stalin's crazy world and shows how the Bolshevik cream lost their noses. In other words, he shows how those who dared to question the monopoly of truth that resided in the party, and ultimately Stalin, were erased from history. He has a powerful scene in his opera in which Bukharin is defending his life in the central committee. Kentridge takes directly from the minutes of Stalin's central committee (recorded in its original to include reference to laughter) to show how inhumanity presented itself as revolutionary, how barbarism worked inside Stalin's party.

Bukharin:

The whole tragedy of my situation lies in this, that this Piatakov and others like him so poisoned the atmosphere, such an atmosphere arose that no one believes human feelings – not emotions, no the impulses of the heart, not tears. [Laughter] Many manifestations of human feeling, which had represented a form of proof – and there was nothing shameful in this – have today lost their validity and force.

Bukharin:

Comrades, I implore you not to interrupt me, because it is difficult for me, it is simply physically hard for me to speak. I will answer any question posed to me, but please do not interrupt me just now. I won't shoot myself, because then people will say I killed myself so as to harm the party. But if I die, as it were, from an illness, then what will you lose by it? [Laughter] Please permit me to finish and explain this whole business to the best of my ability.

Kaganovich:

You are not very good at explaining it – that's the whole point.

Bukharin:

Whether I explain it well or poorly, I am speaking sincerely, my thoughts are sincere.

Kaganovich:

Not every act of sincerity is correct.

Bukharin:

In any case, I am speaking sincerely.

Molotov:

And we are criticising you sincerely. [Laughter. Uproar in the room].

Voroshilov:

You scoundrel! Keep your trap shut! How vile! How dare you speak like that!

Bukharin:

But you must understand – it's very hard for me to die.

Stalin:

And it's easy for us to go on living?! [Noise in the room, prolonged laughter].

The brutal and violent consequences of particular means are another way of thinking critically about the appropriate means to achieve socialism. Such an argument assists in recognising that some means contain within them consequences that take away from socialism; actually, it reproduces what we should be against. Finally, another way of grappling with the challenge of means and ends, and engendering a self-aware practice and understanding of tactics, is through qualifying the means used. This means there are principles that come before our actions and should guide them. In this regard we can draw from the contribution made by Victor Serge, a Russian anarchist, who joined the Bolsheviks and later became part of the left opposition that was critical of Stalin and the increasing bureaucratisation of the Russian Revolution. It would seem he was the first to describe the Soviet regime as totalitarian and he also compared Stalin's regime to the Thermidorian reaction that followed the French Revolution. Serge was expelled from the Communist Party in 1928. In the 1930s he spent a few years in a gulag and eventually through international pressure the Stalinist regime was forced to let him leave the country. From his autobiography *Memoirs of a Revolutionary* he has this to say about qualifying the means to achieve particular ends:

I. Defence of man. Respect for man. Man must be given his rights, his security, his value. Without these, there is no Socialism. Without these, all is false, bankrupt and spoiled. I mean: man whoever he is, be he the meanest of men—"class enemy", son or grandson of a bourgeois, I do not care. It must never be forgotten that a human being is a human being. Every day, everywhere, before my very eyes this is being forgotten and it is the

most revolting and anti-Socialist thing that could happen ...
II. Defence of truth. Man and the masses have a right to the truth. I will not consent either to the systematic falsification of history or to the suppression of all serious news from the Press (which is confined to a purely agitational role). I hold truth to be a precondition of intellectual and moral health. To speak the truth is to speak of honesty. Both are the right of men.
III. Defence of thought ... I hold that Socialism cannot develop in the intellectual sense except by the rivalry, scrutiny and struggle of ideas; that we should fear not error, which is mended in time by life itself, but rather stagnation and reaction; that respect for man implies his right to know everything and his freedom to think.

The rise of neo-Stalinist populism in South Africa

The SACP was a child of both the Russian Revolution and the South African struggle. It was born in 1921 and fought for decades for a democratic South Africa. It was the first non-racial political organisation in the country. While it has had to navigate its relationship with the Soviet Union, including the Sovietisation of its own Marxist outlook during the greater part of the twentieth century, it was a party that mediated this through its moorings in the South African struggle for national liberation and socialism. In this struggle the working class in South Africa through its practices, struggles and ideological battles with the racist regime, were able to ensure that a profound democratic impulse prevailed. An African worker excluded from the franchise wanted the right to vote in the society of his/her birth and wanted to determine who the political leadership of South Africa should be (which also partly explains the high voter turn outs we still have in our democracy). Such a worker wanted the democratic means to organise, build mass movements, debate and influence the content of government policy even from the factory floor. Traditions of worker control and people's power were central to this home-grown South African Marxism. In many ways the abstractions of a Sovietised Marxism-Leninism such as the dictatorship of the proletariat and one-party state had to come to terms with this powerful democratic impulse and participatory logic in the South African struggle.

With the collapse of Eastern Europe the SACP more than most left political organisations in the world had fertile conditions to innovate and renew Marxist socialism. It had appropriate raw materials (indigenous Marxist impulses) to de-Stalinise and contribute to the renewal of socialism in the twenty-first century.

It had the opportunity to elaborate on 'Our Marxism' in theory and practice. This process was inaugurated by Joe Slovo through his pamphlet 'Has socialism failed?' but this found shallow roots inside the organisation. While important programmatic themes emerged inside the SACP during the 1990s that reflected a degree of rethinking and socialist renewal this was shortlived. The possibilities of a new conception of socialism and some of its themes are documented in a book entitled *Roots of Participatory Democracy: Democratic Communists in Kerala, India and South Africa*. My generation was part of this process and contributed to this renewal both theoretically and practically. So, what happened? Why was socialist renewal eclipsed inside the SACP? Why was socialist renewal replaced with neo-Stalinist populism?

In my view there are four crucial factors. First, the leadership that emerged at the helm of the SACP since 1998 did not believe in the project of socialist renewal. It preferred dogmatic and orthodox certainties but tolerated both the theoretical and programmatic shifts taking place around renewal. Moreover, as a mass party increasingly populated with various currents and tendencies it was difficult for them to ideologically straightjacket the organisation. However, this has happened gradually and over time; such that today political education is taken straight from the classic texts published by Progress Publishers. A Stalinised Marxism-Leninism is back and is the new gospel. These days with low production costs and super-exploitation of the workers in China, the sacred texts come to South Africa with the approval of the Chinese Communist Party.

The second factor that has rolled back the renewal of socialism in the SACP is a preoccupation with a statist conception of socialism. This is partly a knee-jerk response to neoliberalism's attack on the state and therefore statism, the opposite, has to be defended. Again, there is a failure to devise strategy by looking at the actual conditions underpinning the state and changing its form. Moreover, the rise of China has engendered a new enthusiasm for state-led development. The Chinese superpower and developmental state model holds a powerful attraction. Again, there is no critical appreciation of what the underlying dynamics of Chinese accumulation are. Aspects of China are selectively appropriated to support the case for a South African developmental state. One of the recent proposals to emerge from the SACP leadership called for a two-tier super-Cabinet with a strong centralising and commandist structure for governance. Feeding into state-centric conceptions inside the SACP has been a fixation among some in the trade union movement for neo-corporatist macro-policy making. Such a conception derives from an unreconstructed social democratic politics that believes elite deals at the apex of society can impact on redistribution and provide a social wage for workers. In short, a state capitalism has emerged as the project of the SACP under a neo-Stalinist leadership.

This relates to a third factor. Such a state capitalism (but dressed up in the rhetoric of socialism) is presented as an alternative to the neoliberalism of the Mbeki era. Under Thabo Mbeki South Africa experienced uninterrupted neoliberalisation, which began in the apartheid era. Mbeki's faction globalised the South African economy ensuring monopoly capital moves offshore while making concessions to deracialise the commanding heights through BEE. Mbeki consciously fostered a new transnational fraction of the South African ruling class and encouraged rapid class formation through the state. All of this constituted a passive revolution. A deracialising and globalising capitalism replaced radical transformation as the project for a post-apartheid South Africa. Global capitalism was understood as the path to emancipation and alternatives to capitalism were marginalised. In this process concessions were made to the working class to ensure some of their interests were realised through Mbeki's passive revolution. This included labour market reform, increasing social expenditure and empowerment deals for union investment companies.

Many of us on the left were marginalised, humiliated and contained in this process. These tactics were not only utilised at a national level but confronted us at various levels. Inside the SACP this manifested as an aggressive factionalism. Mbeki's forces contested and attempted to even contain the SACP from within. The response from the rank and file in the SACP was to push for the SACP to consider its own political future and secure this through marrying direct electoral contestation to socialist renewal. Such a strategic option had various permutations and possibilities and even included the possibility of the SACP renovating itself into a new left party aligned to a new bloc of left forces. Instead of ensuring and supporting a serious strategic debate on the question of state power, the dominant neo-Stalinist faction or the Nzimande/Cronin faction chose to manipulate and contain it. I was a provincial secretary at the time when at a special Durban conference in 2005 convened to discuss this question we were called into a backroom and told unambiguously by the SACP leadership led by the Nzimande/Cronin faction that the SACP was not going to take this question forward and resolve decisively on it. In short, the leadership was not interested in the rank and file and from behind their backs was going to control this process. Instead of allowing the unemployed and working-class base to determine the outcome at this conference, a vague and ambiguous resolution was passed that tried to placate the rank and file while the bureaucratic apparatus recaptured ground. This revealed that the state capitalist project of the Nzimande/Cronin faction had much in common with the BEE elites inside the ANC, the union investment companies and the personal interests of those in the SACP leadership who were in parliament and government positions benefiting from the largesse of the ANC.

The Nzimande/Cronin faction were clearly on a path to sell out the working class. This led to the fourth factor that fostered the rise of neo-Stalinist populism. Instead, of choosing the strategic option of entering the political system and realigning political forces to secure a future for the socialist project, this faction chose to feed into the divisions inside the ANC and gain an ascendancy. The SACP became a means to advance state capitalism and the personal interests of this faction. In this regard Mbeki's hubris and disconnection from the base played into their hands. The moment Mbeki fired the deputy president of the country because of his alleged corrupt involvement in the arms deal, Jacob Zuma became the trump card for the Nzimande/Cronin faction to settle scores with Mbeki but also pave the way for their project. Under the leadership of the Nzimande/Cronin faction the SACP became the main champion of Jacob Zuma's innocence.

A host of means were utilised to close ranks around the new hero of the working class: Jacob Zuma was a victim of a conspiracy, the real enemy of the revolution was the 1996 class project (which translates into the Mbeki faction), Zulu nationalism became a big part of discourse in the SACP during Zuma's rape trial, the courts were bourgeois and racism came to the fore against some of us who were non-African. A madness raged inside the SACP as this faction closed ranks and lined up behind hero Zuma. Those of us who tried to engage in a rational politics and focus the party on its programmatic commitments to the workers and the poor were dealt with viciously and harshly. The SACP was no longer about socialism, but had raised the flag of neo-Stalinist populism. A similar intolerance gripped the unions. Zuma became the Trojan horse for the ANC path to socialism. A neo-Stalinist populism was unleashed on the ANC-led Alliance and the country by the Nzimande/Cronin faction. Giving the working class new strategic options to advance a renewed socialist project and the means to build their capacity to lead genuine transformation from below was abandoned.

By 2007 Mbeki experienced a humiliating defeat at the Polokwane conference of the ANC and Jacob Zuma was installed as president of the ANC. This was hailed as a victory for democracy. However, in the course of 2008 an unrelenting attack was launched on the young institutions of our democracy. Our courts were maligned and judges were declared counter-revolutionary from the streets as Zuma's legal team tried every trick in the book to prevent him from appearing before our courts on charges of corruption. The special crime fighting unit, the Scorpions, was disbanded by a Zuma-controlled legislature; Mbeki was recalled as president of the country by September 2008 before concluding his term; and finally Zuma was let off the hook when charges were dropped by a politically embattled and compromised National Prosecuting Authority (NPA). Since the ANC Polokwane conference (2007) the country has been deeply divided, the ANC has split and a new party, the Congress of the People (COPE) has emerged from its ranks; while various social forces have rallied in defence of the Constitution and the criminal justice system. The union movement has also begun to rupture in some quarters as COPE-aligned forces begin to build a rival union federation. Polokwane and Jacob Zuma's victory solicited a backlash from across civil society. Moreover, it cemented neo-Stalinist populism, neo-corporatism and the BEE agenda as a new basis for bourgeois nationalism and state capitalism. The Nzimande/Cronin faction is deeply entrenched in this, but is also greatly responsible for the deep divisions inside the Alliance structures and society.

The 2009 elections and the political suicide of the SACP

In the April 2009 elections the ANC led by Jacob Zuma won by less than a two-thirds majority. An ANC victory was predicted early on but this could not be taken for granted. While this was a very Americanised election in many ways, with crude caricatures of Obama-like political moves particularly with regard to courting the youth vote, this election held more uncertainty for the ANC than any other. For the first time it faced an electoral challenge from a political force that could appeal to all South Africans, but in particular its own black support base. Moreover, this was the first time the SACP was fighting this election not just as an ally but as a political grouping collapsed into and entrenched at the centre of the ANC. These realities threw up two important features around the 2009 election: first, the dynamics underpinning the ANC election victory and second the implications for the SACP.

Many ANC supporters and leaders believe the ANC wins elections because it has a divine right to rule South Africa. The ANC is the national liberator, the

ANC is the people, democracy belongs to the ANC and so on. Dangerous views. When one looks at the 2009 elections closely various dynamics helped propel the ANC to victory. These dynamics are increasingly becoming different for each election. First, as the custodian of nation building the ANC lost the trust of large sections of the population. The Zuma factor was seen as a threat to the future of the country and still is. However, a critical variable that managed perceptions for the ANC was the role of Nelson Mandela. He came out in support of his party the ANC and his endorsement reassured many. His moral authority compensated for Zuma's lack of it. Second, the role of money cannot be underestimated. The ANC spent approximately R200 million to win this election campaign. It outspent all other parties' with the Democratic Alliance, the official opposition spending about R10 million. Three sources of finance were crucial for the ANC: patronage networks linked to BEE, the passing of party funding legislation on the eve of national elections in provincial legislatures, and external sources particularly from Angola, Libya and China. If we look at the external sources these are not countries led by left-wing governments but are authoritarian state capitalist regimes. Moreover, there are important interests linked to the ANC's campaign financing. How these interests cement with and underpin the new Polokwane project of state capitalism will be interesting to observe.

The third dynamic that underpins the ANC victory is the role of Zulu nationalism. In all provinces of South Africa ANC electoral support declined in the 2009 elections, except KwaZulu-Natal. This is the home province of Jacob Zuma but also the general secretary of the SACP, Blade Nzimande. KwaZulu-Natal witnessed a massive shift of electoral support to the ANC. A 20% swing of close to about two million votes was required to break the political grip of the Inkatha Freedom Party (IFP), a reactionary and Zulu nationalist political force. As comrade Mazibuko Jara puts it in his analysis of this dynamic: 'the ANC had to become the new IFP' to win in this province. The fourth dynamic underpinning the ANC victory was its populist electoral promises. In the context of a deepening economic crisis, the ANC promised the most. Its election manifesto raised high expectations for increased social grants and social expenditure. Forecasts suggest an extra R40 billion would be required in the national fiscus to meet these promises in a context in which tax revenues are likely to decline as economic growth shrinks. Again, the ANC had to pander to material interests to secure support. Research done by the Human Sciences Research Council on electoral patterns in South Africa concludes that South Africans no longer vote based on party loyalty but on material interests.

Instead of the SACP contesting the 2009 elections the Nzimande/Cronin faction collapsed it into the ANC. These forces are represented in the national leadership structures of the ANC and are now in Cabinet positions in government. Communists are also in some provincial government positions. About 14% of elected representatives of the ANC in national and provincial government are from the SACP. There are two critical implications that flow this. First, with the general secretary, his deputy and other senior members of the politburo being placed in the national Cabinet the independence of the SACP has been lost. Its leaders in the national Cabinet are not there as representatives of the SACP but as ANC representatives and bound by the discipline of the ANC. Given the dominance of this faction in the SACP and the proprietary claims they have over the party they have even thrown out constitutional provisions that require the general secretary to be full time in the SACP, to suit their interests. The appropriate thing to do is for these leaders to resign from their leadership positions in the SACP.

Instead, they are bent on amending the Constitution to suit their interests by convening a special conference. Moreover, they are going to attempt to use formalism to suggest the SACP still has some independence in this configuration. They are talking about a protocol with the ANC. Even if such frameworks fall into place the underlying relationship between the ANC and SACP is one of unequal power. The SACP has not built an independent and alternative bloc of forces around it, but instead merely controls a few key affiliates of the trade union movement and believes it can bully its way through. Its base of power is narrow and vulnerable. The bottom line is that the SACP under the leadership of the Nzimande/Cronin faction have taken the SACP over the cliff; they have forced it to commit political suicide to suit their careerist ambitions. This is a betrayal of the working class and the poor.

The second implication of the 2009 elections for the SACP is that its surrender to bourgeois nationalism forces it into a reactionary politics. In the context of a deepening economic crisis and to ensure stability for state capitalism the SACP will attempt to contain and stage-manage mass struggles. It will increasingly attempt to defend bourgeois nationalism by presenting it as left wing. It will secure a few concessions for the working class in the context of state capitalism, but in the main the passive revolution will continue under Zuma but take a new form. During the election campaign and even after, the rhetoric from the SACP suggested the ANC was the champion of the working class and the poor. However, if we interrogate this and go beyond the left cover, what do we see? The ANC did not fight the elections campaign through a critique of capitalism, including neoliberalism, it did not have an anti-imperialist aspect to its campaign (actually Zuma the working-class hero was wooing investors and transnational capital), it took money from countries like China that have combined the worst of Western capitalism and Stalinised socialism, and most importantly the ANC did not put forward a socialist programme.

The reactionary role of the Nzimande/Cronin faction vis-à-vis the wider left is going to increase. Most importantly they are going to be the key enforcers who try to block a left re-alignment in South African politics. Being in bed with bourgeois nationalism gives neo-Stalinist populism no other choice but also places it in a weak position. Their containment inside the ANC has already begun under Zuma. Their own personal political ambitions are also going to force them to manage their presence carefully. They are surely looking at a post-Zuma scenario to ascend into key positions, more lucrative and prestigious than the junior Cabinet posts they have now. For the Nzimande/Cronin faction to get what they want and secure what they have, another bloody round of intra-ANC struggles will have to happen. These forces will have to capture the ANC and convert it into their vanguard. In the end, how far will their ambitions and appetite for power take them? Will other bourgeois nationalist forces also hungry for power let them have what they want? Will the Nzimande/Cronin faction tear the ANC apart to get what they want in the next few years? They have already done a great deal of damage to the national liberation struggle, including destroying the future of the SACP. In other parts of the world where such strategic divergences have occurred such as in India, the Communist Party split in the 1960s. Will the rank and file in the SACP allow themselves to be bluffed and manipulated once more from the top?

Keeping history open: The struggle for a democratic left project in South Africa

The logic of socialist renewal inside the SACP, if genuinely deepened and elaborated, could have placed the SACP at the cutting edge of the re-alignment of left politics in South Africa. It could have laid the basis for a post-Soviet, post-social democratic and post-national liberation project: a democratic left project. This has not happened. Instead, the organisation has been captured by a careerist faction that has killed inner-party democracy, abandoned socialist renewal and taken the SACP, including sections of the working class, down a state capitalist path; a dead end for socialist politics. Their dream of converting the ANC into a vanguard party of the working class is a fundamental strategic mistake with serious implications for the future of South Africa. In this context those of us who have been silenced and beaten back in the SACP for differing with the undemocratic practices of the leadership, for championing the need for the SACP not to squander its moral authority and the need to keep strategic options open for the working class and the poor beyond national liberation orthodoxies and neo-Stalinist populism, have to make hard choices.

The Nzimande/Cronin faction and their project of state capitalism does not represent a hegemonic left project and is not grounded in building the capacity of the working class and the poor to lead transformation from below. This is well documented in a book entitled: *Roots of Participatory Democracy: Democratic Communists in Kerala, India and South Africa*. The Nzimande/Cronin faction will continue to manipulate, instrumentalise and control mass forces from above to legitimate their careerist ambitions and provide cover to bourgeois nationalism. What is to be done to ensure the socialist project is no longer hijacked by opportunism? How do we confront the treachery and betrayal of the South African working class by the Nzimande/Cronin faction? This is a fundamental battle that has to be waged but I do not believe it should be prosecuted in a lumpen and Stalinist way. Means and ends are important as I have been arguing. I believe the most effective way of keeping strategic options open for the working class, advancing socialist renewal and building the capacity for left politics in post-apartheid South Africa requires the following:

Building ideological capacity: this means re-engaging the rank and file inside the SACP and the wider left about socialist renewal. The premise for this engagement is recognising that all mainstream working-class ideologies of the twentieth century are in crisis: Stalinised Marxism–Leninism, social democracy and national liberation. This does not mean revisionism is the answer. On the contrary, there is a much more fundamental question facing socialist renewal in the twenty-first century. That is the question of what do we abandon? Let me use orthodox or Stalinised Marxism–Leninism as an example. I believe this entire edifice, including its Trotskyist variant, should be thrown overboard. Without blinking an eye we should throw orthodox Marxism–Leninism into the dustbin of history. This includes abandoning core doctrines and practices such as vanguardism, socialism in one country, dictatorship of the proletariat, the cult of the personality and dialectical materialism.

Besides the ugly expression orthodox Marxism–Leninism has inside the SACP and contemporary South Africa, there are other crucial reasons why it should be abandoned to make way for democratic left and socialist renewal. Some of these reasons derive from the interviews contained in this book. First, this is an unthinking and frozen Marxism. The categories and doctrines of orthodox Marxism-Leninism are part of a finished historical materialism. This means it is a working-class ideology that is closed and disassociated from a rapidly changing world. It carries within it certainties based on an understanding of a world very different from our own. To put it sharply, a Marxism born in a feudal society at the beginning of the twentieth century is inappropriate for the twenty-first century. Hence, its dogmatic prescriptions for socialist change and politics do not provide answers to the contemporary world. Second, and because this a frozen Marxism, it is married to practices that have produced some of the worst horrors of the twentieth century. The violence within the imagination of this Marxism is profoundly against the genuine emancipation of the workers and the poor. Actually, its history is one of working-class oppression rather than emancipation. Third, this is a Marxism bereft of a democratic impulse, both in terms of the political organisations it spawns and the society it seeks to build. It is a Marxism of barrack socialism, in which the gun and the nuclear weapon impose change rather than the self-organisation of the working class and the poor. It is a Marxism of statist change rather than socialist pluralism and the deepening of democracy. It reproduces barbarism rather than ending it.

Alongside the question of deciding what has to be abandoned, socialist renewal requires a research agenda around new themes for South African Marxism. Such a research agenda should place contemporary dimensions of capitalism within a new theoretical and analytical frame of historical materialism. Some of the themes that could inform such a research agenda could include: critique of Marxist orthodoxies, dialectical method and critical theory, global capitalism and crisis, a new analysis of the South African social formation and its contradictions, a people's history of the South African struggle, learning from grassroots struggles, learning from non-Marxist anti-capitalist thought, and so on. This book on *New Frontiers for Socialism in the 21st Century* is a modest resource, alongside others, that can contribute to this task.

Towards a democratic ecosocialist programme: a programmatic politics is an essential ingredient for a new democratic left politics and it has to address the current contradictions of global capitalism. Moreover, a programme-centred politics is important in three other respects. First, such a programme-centred politics is required to anchor new Marxist and anti-capitalist perspectives around an ideological pole of attraction. It is about taking left politics beyond narrow social movement opposition and lobbying practices. It is about providing a new compass for socialist and left politics in South Africa. Second, such a programme has to be constituted through participatory and bottom-up engagements. It has to be defined through the voices of workers in factories and on farms, the unemployed in townships and informal settlements, women's movements, HIV/AIDS movements, gay and lesbian movements, environmental movements, religious movements and various other social forces. Ultimately a new political programme for socialist politics in South Africa has to emanate from the lived realities of exploitation, environmental injustice and oppression. It cannot be drawn up by an arrogant and self-proclaimed ideologue floating above the struggle. It has to be the product of a collective intellectual process rooted in struggles, so that it is owned by mass forces. A programme for a democratic left politics must be grounded and emanate from the actual experience of democracy and it should provide a school for building capacities for participatory democracy. A third and crucial reason for a programme-centred left politics, is that it fosters grassroots activism. It is about stimulating the unity of theory and practice and ensuring a democratic left politics provides solutions and articulates alternatives in actual struggles. In this sense, it is about inserting a critical left discourse into public life. Moreover, the unity of theory and practice around a programme-centred politics builds commitment and loyalty to collective ideas rather than to big men. It assists in overcoming the problem of the cult of the personality.

Building a democratic left historic bloc: various political forces are beginning to talk the language of ecological crisis. At the one extreme, capital believes greening the economy is another market opportunity. On the other side, state capitalists (sometimes referred to as SACP leaders) give a greenwash to another wave of state-led capitalist modernisation. South Africa needs a new political project, an alternative, that puts forward a democratic ecosocialist programme as the way forward for the country. Such a programme should demonstrate theoretically, empirically and concretely an alternative direction for the post-apartheid political economy. However, for such a programmatic alternative to become an option for society requires rooting it in society through struggles and popular engagements. It requires building consent in a bottom-up manner on the terrain of civil society for such an alternative. In this process a democratic left politics has to be the means to find convergences, develop shared perspectives and engender common understandings for this programmatic alternative. Such a process to accumulate new social forces should include mass movements, trade unions and the left intelligentsia around the imperative of taking forward a democratic ecosocialist solution for South Africa. This amounts to building a new democratic left historical bloc of forces with the capacity to lead society.

Deciding on a political instrument: the SACP does not belong to a faction. If the dominant faction continues to control the organisation and fails to resign from leadership positions (because of crossing over to government), continues in an undemocratic manner, and refuses to accept a plurality of currents in the leadership and alternative strategic viewpoints, then there are two possible options. These are not mutually exclusive in my view and are available to those who want to advance the project of socialist renewal in post-apartheid South Africa, keep strategic options open for the working class and build capacities for left politics: (i) the split that has already been imposed by the dominance of the Nzimande/Cronin faction should be formalised. Those of us that are forced to leave could re-found the SACP as the Democratic Communist Party of South Africa; and/or (ii) a new people's front is created based on the UDF of the 1980s, which unites converging left forces.

The UDF was a people's organisation and contributed to harnessing mass and popular power. It provided the institutional frame to bring together diverse ideological currents and social forces around resisting apartheid. The challenge would be to utilise the UDF or a new United Democratic Left Front to unite mass and popular forces around a new democratic eco-socialist programme. Crucial to such a political instrument is creation of an internal universe in which the values and practices of democratic left politics prevail. Moreover, such an instrument should not be vanguardist, electoralist or party-movement in its mould. It should be a movement of democratic left forces, including a newly constituted Democratic Communist Party of South Africa. Such a formation should aim to be a political form rooted in bottom-up practices. It should be about building grassroots capacity to advance and utilise logics of participatory democracy. Even if an electoral dimension has to emerge, such a dimension should be a mere tactic subordinate to building self-conscious mass power and advancing counter hegemonic generative alternatives from below.

International solidarity: is a crucial pillar and condition for advancing a new democratic left project in South Africa. From the interviews conducted for this book it is apparent that global left forces share certain common concerns and challenges. Most importantly, they want to journey with others who have come to the same frontier. The form of this renewed solidarity has become more defined through the WSF and other important intersection points for democratic left solidarity. Such forms of international solidarity are very different from taking the line from Beijing for instance. Building international support and extending international solidarity through some of these institutional platforms can only strengthen the advance of a new democratic left project in South Africa.

Limits facing a democratic left project

A new democratic left project is very much about a new way of engaging in left politics; in its essence this is about a new socialist politics. It is a politics grounded in values, self-aware about means and ends, serious about building bottom-up capacities, programme-centred activism and encourages self-conscious collective struggles (both oppositional and generative). To embark down a road to build such a new left politics in post-apartheid South Africa requires an honesty about the limits facing such a project. In my view there are three crucial limits or constraints facing such an initiative. The first relates to the 'wait and see' or 'sitting on the fence' left. These are progressives who want more from post-apartheid South Africa, who have critical perspectives on aspects of the transition, who dabble in left initiatives but who rationalise the failure to realign left forces by arguing the ambiguities of history and the national liberation project. In a sense there is belief in a false hope that the ANC-led Alliance will eventually deliver on its promises. This is despite the trajectory of embourgeoisement that has taken hold and the state capitalism coming to the fore. In a sense the mythologies of national liberation still have an emotive appeal. For the left intellectuals that hold this position the policy discourses and objectives of ANC-led Alliance conferences are still the guide to change. Formalism is more important than substance and actual practices.

The danger with this orientation is that it easily engenders an apologist discourse in the current conjuncture. This is an orientation that was advocated by the late Harold Wolpe, a leading South African Marxist, concerning the role of intellectuals in the national liberation struggle. Is this approach to defining the role of left intellectuals still relevant in post-apartheid South Africa? Should the objectives of state capitalism, and very possibly an authoritarian state capitalism, still be the objectives that guide left intellectual forces today in South Africa? Is a passive revolution that demobilises or manipulates mass initiative still a left project? The Wolpe position is an orthodoxy of the national liberation movement which has to be ruptured at a common sense level. Its lack of correspondence to the new realities in post-apartheid South Africa need to be challenged.

A second crucial limit facing a democratic left project relates to the deradicalisation of political consciousness in the ranks of the ANC-led Alliance and within society. This is a function of the absence of political education, electoralism and the emergence of new careerist leadership layers in the unions and ANC-led Alliance. Increasingly politics is defined by the party machine and hierarchies of the national liberation movement. Militant rhetoric, the line from the top, media spectacles, celebrity performances, the cult of the personality, stage-managed mass action and scandal is the stuff of contemporary South African politics. The media does not assist this but feeds into the sensationalism and hype. Some journalists even participate in public life as extensions of factions in the ANC-led Alliance and other political parties. Absent is rigorous analysis, alternative left interpretations and conceptions of politics beyond powerful individuals. A mindless militancy together with a crass liberalism permeates South African public life. For a new democratic left politics to take hold it has to rival these two monopolies that operate in public discourse. An alternative media has to be created and new pedagogies of the oppressed have to come to the fore from below. Alternative sources of information and spaces for thinking, understanding and interpreting the world have to be consciously created through public forums, the internet, independent film making, magazines, newsletters and other tools for mass empowerment. The contest of common sense is a big challenge and the war of position in civil society requires new tactics to create a new democratic left political culture.

A third and critical limit facing the emergence of a democratic left politics is the role of money in South African politics. Patronage, careerism, empowerment deals and corruption have become a big part of South African politics. Class mobility provides a powerful attraction even to the working class. This opens the way to co-option, division and deradicalisation. For a new democratic left politics to take root requires the hard slog of grassroots activism, sacrifice and a firm commitment to values. In short it requires a moral authority. There are many in South Africa who still believe that the ugliness of a racist and exploitative past can only be overcome with fundamental transformation in the present. The challenge is to politically organise such forces.

We are living through a time of barbarism. Global capitalism at the beginning of the twenty-first century has become increasingly moribund, obsolete and destructive. To confront this crisis requires a renewed socialist alternative. The hope of the left in the South African context was a renewed socialist project emanating from within the SACP. With the unbanning of the oldest communist party in Africa in 1990 my generation embraced this possibility with passion, commitment and hope. We placed ourselves at the frontier of evolving a democratic communist imagination and project for the twenty-first century. This book and the global journey we went on were an integral part of widening the horizons of renewal inside the SACP and the left more broadly in South Africa. This book was and is meant to be a modest contribution in the search for a renewed left politics and socialist project. We have offered this book as a resource for conversations, debates, popular education and further learning.

However, as we journeyed inside the SACP we were betrayed by the ambitions of a morally, politically and ideologically bankrupt leadership faction. This faction has abandoned the project of socialist renewal and has chosen a careerist path under the banner of a neo-Stalinist populism. Instead of the Afro-neoliberal Mbeki destroying the SACP, it has been the Nzimande/Cronin faction that have destroyed it and imposed their personal ambitions on the class struggle. The barbarism of their neo-Stalinist populism is merely one expression of the barbarism of our time. They represent a politics with no future except self-interest. Despite this betrayal of the workers and the poor, and the blocking function the Nzimande/Cronin faction will play in trying to prevent the emergence of new left project in South Africa, the struggle will and must continue. The left has made many compromises and has lost a lot of ground in post-apartheid South Africa. The way forward was not to reduce the SACP to a corpse and to surrender sections of the working class to bourgeois nationalism.

Instead, we need to reject shortcuts and build in a bottom-up and painstaking way a serious socialist alternative: a democratic left project. Such a democratic left project needs to be much more self-aware about means and ends, not trapped in the myths and orthodoxies of national liberation ideology and should be grounded in a post-national liberation politics drawing on a people's history of struggle against racial oppression and contemporary global capitalism. It is a left project for present and future post-apartheid generations. This might take a long time to achieve but personally this is a journey I have embarked on, even if I don't see the fruits in my lifetime. This is the most important lesson I take from the experiences, intellectual insights and contributions made by those interviewed in this book. An alternative to the barbarism of global capitalism is a civilisational alternative; it is a democratic ecosocialism.

New Frontiers for Socialism in the 21st Century: Conversations on a Global Journey. Johannesburg: COPAC, 2009.

We Need a Truly Transformative Democracy

WHO IS A DEMOCRAT TODAY? The simple answer would be most of us. It would seem street protesters in Greece, Brazil and Egypt as well as Barack Obama, Jacob Zuma and Julius Malema are all democrats. Is this really the case? The discourse on market democracy would want us to believe that this is so. The rationality of this standard of democracy works to extinguish distinctions, conceptual precision and, most importantly, the radical impulse of democracy. In South Africa, our public discourse on democracy works in the same way. There are three crucial voices that dominate our conversation and define South Africa's version of market democracy.

State discourse and corporate power

First, there is the state's version of market democracy. Despite South Africa's Constitution providing for a broadening of democracy beyond mere voting in elections to include participatory democracy, this broadening has not happened. At the same time, the technocratic managerialism driving the state has made it impervious to popular pressure from below. This partly explains the violent nature of grassroots protest actions; an unresponsive state creates antagonism. While the mineworkers of Marikana were engaged in a just struggle against mining capital and its allies, it was the state that violently brought a relative stability to this sector. Mining investors and owners were assured that risk to capital was not being compromised. Ultimately, electoral mandates are rendered meaningless as the entire economy is geared around the interests of market forces and globalised capital. The state's version of market democracy is about less democracy and more power to markets.

Second, the main political parties in South Africa share a common centre-right consensus on market democracy. The ANC-in-power and the DA-led opposition do not have fundamental differences on economic policy. The institutional political system is locked into a neoliberal ideological frame that is elitist and skewed in favour of a narrow set of ideas. Many of the values (possessive individualism, competition and greed), policy frameworks and legislative agendas emanating from this consensus have not worked to address inequality, unemployment or climate change. The National Development Plan (NDP), endorsed by our political parties, reproduces this consensus and does not take us down a path that can secure a democratic future for South Africa.

For instance, the NDP's commitment to climate change, the most serious challenge we face as a species, supports fracking, more mining rents and carbon trading. Simply put, it continues the path of the past two decades in which market rationality and corporate power prevail over democracy.

Liberal intelligentsia and failing market democracy

Third, we have the amplified voices of our liberal intelligentsia, who are constantly given the space and platform by South Africa's media to prescribe to us the virtues of market democracy. These voices come at the issue from different starting points but end in the same place. It is akin to listening to the same boring soundtrack, but remixed.

Ultimately, the concerns for democracy, such as its conditions of existence, its institutional underpinnings and power dynamics, assume that elections are the essence of democracy. This formulaic understanding of democracy furnishes us with a false guarantee about outcomes: if you just vote every five years, expect justice, policy change and transformation. This is meant to be the real meaning of democratic politics; a South African version of Americanised market democracy.

The tragedy of almost 20 years of South African democracy is not so much the so-called clichéd loss of our innocence, but rather the extent to which our democratic imagination and horizons have been limited in mainstream public discourse. South Africa is the exemplar of a failing market democracy. It is with this recognition in mind that democrats on the left in South Africa also need to be given a hearing in the interests of a maturing South African democracy. One such voice is the emerging Solidarity Economy Movement in South Africa.

Inventiveness

This movement (involving the unemployed, the renewing civic movements, small-scale farmers, children, youth, women's organisations, workers and progressive public intellectuals) hosted its second national conference recently, with an inventiveness and enthusiasm for democracy very different from market democracy.

It explicitly rejected the prescriptions of market democracy: less democracy instead of more, democracy equals the interests of markets and corporate power, and is merely about electoral contestation. Instead, the Solidarity Economy Movement embraces a constitutive understanding of power and democracy from below that includes participatory democracy (in the political and economic sphere), direct democracy through street politics (as in Greece, Brazil and Egypt) and the claiming of citizens' rights and freedoms.

Together this triad of popular democratic power is meant to deepen democracy and determine the shape of electoral democracy. In concrete terms, this form of transformative democracy seeks its expression through experimenting with participatory budgeting, a campaign for worker co-operatives and a campaign for food sovereignty.

Through embracing participatory budgeting, the emerging Solidarity Economy Movement is seeking to learn from international experience such as Porto Alegre in Brazil in the late 1980s (but diminished once Lula's Workers' Party was ensconced in power) and in Kerala, India, in the 1990s in which the decentralisation of financial resources enabled democratic planning. In the South African context, advancing participatory budgeting translates into some of the following: democratising ward committees (currently extensions of the ANC's patronage machine); holding government accountable for disaster management legislation to ensure informal settlements are protected from fires, flooding and other avoidable disasters; and more generally influencing how resources are used to create liveable spaces such as housing, libraries, parks, bicycle lanes and other public infrastructure.

Alternative

Through the campaign for worker co-operatives, the Solidarity Economy Movement seeks to provide an alternative for the unemployed, particularly the youth, in South Africa. The work provided in a worker co-operative is worker-owner-based work; that is, everyone has equal rights in decision-making, shares in profits and losses, and workers own the enterprises. This is different from a capital-managed firm, or a nationalised enterprise, with hierarchies of control and in which labour is merely treated as a factor of production to be exploited.

The campaign for food sovereignty is about connecting various movements in South Africa to reclaim the food system from large transnationalised agricultural corporations and ensure agro-ecological farming methods are used for food production. It is inspired by the largest peasant and small-scale farmer movement in the world, La Via Campesina, which seeks to ensure the right to food gives democratic control over the production, distribution and consumption of it back to communities and citizens.

In short, these initiatives of the Solidarity Economy Movement are about giving citizens the means to sustain life, develop capabilities, build transformative democratic power and institutionalise progressive values such as social justice, equality and ecological consciousness. It is through these marginalised voices that South African democracy is being democratised, remade and imbued with hope. These voices are helping us to understand that democrats in the streets in Brazil, Greece and Egypt (despite the complexity of the last) are about a different kind of democracy, a transformative democracy. This is fundamentally different from the market democracy on offer from Obama, Zuma and Malema's EFF.

Mail & Guardian, 6 September 2013.

'No!' Tells the ANC Enough is Enough

PICK UP ANY NEWSPAPER or tune into any radio broadcast and, before long, you are likely to hear discontent about the state of the nation and, in particular, the ANC. This is expressed through the militancy of strike action, campaigning outside government buildings, booing the powerful and community protest actions, ranging from tyre-burning to stone-throwing and even setting fire to government buildings. Increasingly, these expressions of discontent are coming from people who once (and some still do) identify with the ANC. This might seem a natural process in a political democracy in which citizens actively engage their parties. But this is no ordinary political party: the ANC is unique for its long and proud liberation struggle history, its once-visionary leaders and its commitment to a non-racial, non-sexist South Africa that sought economic transformation that benefited the majority of South Africans.

For those of us who were born into and wholly identified with the ANC, it is an enormous challenge to openly criticise the party. Many fear to do so, given the cronyism, factional control and closed ranks. But it is also liberating, necessary and in South Africa's best interest. Many who are sympathetic to the ANC have been unhappy with it but have felt powerless to do anything or say anything publicly.

A growing number of voters stay away from the polls, despite higher voter registration. The Vote No! – or Vukani (rise up) or Sidikiwe (we are fed up) – campaign aims to reverse this trend, to empower people to reclaim their vote to say: 'Enough is enough.' In doing this, the Vukani/Sidikiwe campaign has added a crucial dimension to our national conversation. The evolution and reception of the campaign allows us to gauge the state of various aspects of our constitutional democracy. At the campaign's heart is a simple but powerful proposition: vote in the national election but choose either to spoil your ballot (by writing 'No!' across it) or vote tactically for parties other than the ANC and Democratic Alliance.

The intention of the campaign is to raise voter awareness about political choice. It is not an NGO voter-education initiative. It is a serious, unprecedented political intervention by activists and citizens who fought against apartheid and who continue to contribute to strengthening our democracy. It is informed by deep concern that the degeneration of the ANC, as the dominant political party, is threatening the future of the country and democracy.

The abuse of power by the ANC – as reflected in widespread corruption, economic policies that deepen inequality and unemployment, failure to embark on a just transition to address climate change and attempts to roll back democratic rights (through the infamous Protection of State Information Act, the Traditional Authorities Bill and the tragic Marikana massacre) – suggests we are fast becoming a failing democracy.

Those who vote for the ANC are giving a mandate for more of the same and must take responsibility for this. More importantly, the only way this crisis of democracy can be addressed is if citizens shrug off their apathy (12.7 million eligible voters did not participate in the last election) and participate in the elections to challenge the ANC. Given the stakes, citizens must think carefully about how to use their vote. Our democracy is at a turning point; its future can only be secured if we mobilise collective power to say no to the abuse of power by the ANC.

The campaign's origins are not a top-down intervention. The main idea (spoiled ballots) came from the democracy from below initiative, made up mainly of young, grassroots activists inspired by the radical turn in youth politics, as in the Arab Spring, the Occupy movement and the militant unemployed people's movements rocking Spain and Latin America. Many such young people are searching for new ways of engaging in democratic politics, beyond political parties, from which they feel disconnected and alienated. Ronnie Kasrils and Nozizwe Madlala-Routledge are patrons of the Sidikiwe movement. The spoiled ballot idea was shared with Awethu!, a platform for social justice made up of grassroots NGOs and movements. Various Awethu! participating organisations endorse the initiative. The spoiled ballot idea was also shared with and endorsed by the DLF, in which various social movements and left groups converge. At a meeting with NUMSA, hundreds of shop stewards seized on the idea. Formally, NUMSA is sticking to its resolution not to support any political party but will engage with parties and groups.

All this affirms that, after 20 years of democracy, during which popular demobilisation took place, progressive civil society is experiencing an awakening. It is willing to fight to deepen democracy (both representative and participatory) and to push for direct democratic action. The Sidikiwe campaign has been viciously attacked by the government and the ANC-led Alliance leadership.

Senior Cabinet ministers have said it is treasonous. The ANC secretary general has attacked Kasrils and Madlala-Routledge personally; other Alliance components have denounced it in strong, sometimes vitriolic and inflammatory, language; confirming that this campaign challenges and bothers the ANC.

Twenty years of ANC rule has not produced a democratic culture of tolerance, respect for difference and a plurality of voices. It also shows that the ANC can't see that politics in our constitutional democracy does not begin and end with the ANC. The Constitution gives the Vote No! campaign the right to exist. The media are crucial in their ability to amplify debate and engender a democratic culture. Our campaign was planned for the eve of the elections to add dynamism to the debate, and the media have risen to the challenge. But some media have focused on individuals – a celebrity discourse. It's important for the media to speak, also, to people on the streets, to grassroots movements such as the UPM, workers in the winelands, mining-affected communities and striking platinum miners. The media should seek to widen the conversation. It must ensure our public sphere is not merely spectacle and elite performance. We need a media committed to democratising our public sphere so that voices from below give it greater meaning.

Many are engaging in the Vote No! debate, with different emphases on the proposition: a spoiled ballot or tactical voting. The vibrancy of the national conversation is the primary goal of the campaign. Many media editorials (such as the one in the *Mail & Guardian* last week) and commentators have come out in support of tactical voting. We agree that tactical voting has a greater material impact. The most powerful political statement is to vote for any party other than the ANC. But the Sidikiwe position has a nuance here: it challenges us to think carefully about what is on offer and what are the values, practices and policies of each party.

Twenty years of electoral competition and it would seem none of the centre-right opposition parties can assail the dominance of the ANC, despite lower voter turnout for the ANC in 2009 compared with 1994. This prompts the question: are the opposition parties really speaking to the aspirations and needs of South Africa's majority? Has the time arrived for a serious left-wing party?

The campaign does not seek to determine how South Africans vote. Many engaging in debate would prefer them to vote for any party other than the ANC, but it is important to balance the debate. For the first time in a national election, we have a campaign asking the Electoral Commission of South Africa (IEC) to count and publicise the 'no' votes, believing that the Constitution would defend the right of voters to register a protest vote, and that vote should be counted. It is likely that we shall see a spike in the number of spoiled ballots from its current average of about 200,000. Many of those disaffected by the ANC or not attracted to the opposition, and who might usually simply not vote, will consider it.

There are three reasons for this. The first is symbolic. A 'no' message conveys outrage at the ruling party and affirms the power of citizens' voices: it says our democracy and our future are more important than degenerate ANC rule. Second, it affirms the need for ethical standards (honesty, accountability, transparency and service to the people) in our politics, without which we will end up with an Americanised democracy riddled with hypocrisy, media hype and big business control. Third, it helps deepen democracy by citizens' actions, from below, and helps the growth of a movement that, even after the elections, can defend democracy against the abuse of power.

The world's largest democracy, India, has formalised the 'no' vote as a valid option, calling it 'none of the above'. If parties in South Africa are not helping to realise the aspirations of the excluded majority, we have the right to withdraw our consent for their rule. A spoiled ballot forces political parties to see that they can't take the needs and aspirations of the people for granted. The IEC should include it on ballots. In this election, citizens who do not want to vote for any of the parties must consider spoiling their ballot by writing 'no' across it. In the end, the real winner is democracy.

Mail & Guardian, 24 April 2014.

It's Up to Us to Make Sure Zuma Goes

THE NIGHTMARE OF THE Jacob Zuma presidency has its roots in the SACP bandwagon to displace the neoliberal Thabo Mbeki and affirm a supposed working-class hero at the helm of the state.

The SACP command centre spiked all strategic debate about contesting state power, tied trade union federation COSATU to its disastrous plans and narrated the Zuma Trojan horse as the victim of a conspiracy; and anyone providing principled opposition was victimised, humiliated and herded out of the SACP. Although senior leaders of the liberation struggle such as Ahmed Kathrada, Denis Goldberg and others did not speak out at the start of the Zumafication of South Africa, it is comforting that they refuse to defend the indefensible today. The country needs more stalwarts to stand up and say: Zuma must go.

The SACP in Gauteng (I was the party's provincial secretary at the time) challenged the morally and ideologically bankrupt politics of the SACP leadership. The party in Gauteng leaned towards the SACP contesting state power through mass politics to reclaim the strategic initiative for the left and working class at its 2005 Special Conference on State Power. If the SACP had resolved to contest power electorally then, South Africa would have been in a different place today; very likely with a more robust and mature democracy, including a serious left discourse in the mainstream of society. In the end the debate was killed and this path was not taken by the SACP.

I was formally expelled in 2009 for writing about the misguidedness of the Zuma path to socialism and the political suicide of the SACP. SACP-constructed populism brought together various elements: authoritarianism, ethnic chauvinism, patriarchy, an anti-constitutionalism, corruption and the cult of Zuma. This was not the making of a left shift by any stretch of the imagination, yet it was given a class belonging, draped in a radical rhetoric and positioned in the theatre of militant street politics. Unleashed on the country since Zuma's rape trial in 2005, this bandwagon swept through Polokwane and has marched through our democratic institutions with the imprimatur of the Zuma presidency.

What has this authoritarian populism produced? In simple terms a catalogue of impunity against the grain of national liberation history. This has worked in three ways. First, through the brazen acquisition of wealth at the expense of the people. The ANC cadre has evolved the idea of the liberation tax (alternatively known as BEE), which means we have struggled and therefore deserve to be rich. The people owe us – and we, as liberators, have to be paid back. Sacrifice, servant leadership and ethical commitment to the people is all but extinguished. The nefarious Gupta business empire, conspicuous accumulation by the Zuma family and many other scandalous schemes of wealth acquisition have created a moral gulf between the ANC and the people. This schism is most starkly expressed in the 2012 Marikana massacre of mineworkers, who were demanding a monthly wage of R12,500, and pervasive localised protest actions against corrupt and inept ANC councillors.

Second, the mythic and actual heroism of national liberation has been reduced to the political whip of skeletons in the closet, according to Bathabile Dlamini, president of the ANC Women's League. Corruption is rampant; therefore all ANC cadres are compromised and must display obeisance to Zuma. Put differently, we are closing ranks in the ANC because we are no different from Zuma and are as culpable as he is for looting.

Third, farcical apologia for failed leadership. Zuma has made numerous apologies – including to Malawi for his xenophobic barb about the state of its roads – and this has become the default mode to excuse the conduct of a deeply flawed president. After the Constitutional Court affirmed Zuma's unconstitutional conduct on the Nkandla issue, he apologised; again, merely to scapegoat legal advisers.

It is in this context that we hear important moral voices from stalwarts of the struggle such as Kathrada, Goldberg, Ronnie Kasrils, and others. They know and are affirming that Zuma and those standing with him are making and writing a history that undermines national liberation history. Zuma's ANC is producing a history against the people that places South Africa in a dangerous place. In itself, this recognition should move all generations of activists, inside and outside the ANC, to stand up and be counted against Zuma.

The second consequence of authoritarian populism is about imperilling the country. The SACP's Zuma bandwagon produced the likes of EFF leader Julius Malema, now referred to as a fascist in SACP propaganda, yet he is the progeny of their Zuma project. Authoritarian populism has become contemporary South African politics. In this cauldron we have seen the rise of a vulgarised black consciousness (even at universities), Africanism and more white racism. The diffusion of authoritarian populism as the measure of what it means to be political has put society on a collision course with our constitutional democracy. The valorisation of affect, the body, identity and violence (from Umshini Wami songs to burning art and buildings at universities) misses the larger picture of a democracy being hollowed out by globalised finance and an avaricious black and white elite.

For Zuma, a cult figure reinforced by the cloak of presidential authority, a divided country and a polity that operates more like him in the political sense, means he can do as he pleases and hence the manipulation of parliament, defiance of the public protector, the compromising of the NPA and now indifference to the real meaning of the Constitutional Court judgment against him.

At the people's assembly of the Zuma Must Go campaign in Soweto last week, citizens from different walks of life and from more than 70 organisations affirmed the limits of a Zumafied democracy. 'We will not be Zumafied!' was a constant refrain and we will not defeat Zuma by being like him. A people's line was drawn; a push-back plan through non-violent and disciplined political action was affirmed and a defence of constitutional democracy was unequivocally committed to. In the open and democratic conversation that ensued in Soweto, citizens placed Zuma on notice. Unlike the recall of former president Mbeki, which was an internal ANC-led Tripartite Alliance coup, the Zuma Must Go discourse is broader than the ANC and is about affirming citizens' power as the bedrock of our democracy. It is a real political test for the ANC: can it genuinely listen to and respect citizens' voices? The Zuma Must Go campaign seeks to send a message to all political elites that operating outside the Constitution has costs and will not be tolerated. Hence the boldness of the call: dissolve this parliament and have a snap election to address the undermining of parliament by ANC cronyism. The criminal racket set up to defend Zuma has defiled parliament and calls into question whether it embodies the will of the people. This is an open dare to the ANC, which has brazenly taken the people for granted throughout the Zuma saga. Moreover, the meme Zuma Must Go is an open act of defiance towards the ANC's attempt to silence this call inside the ANC and in society. It will haunt Zuma wherever he goes in public; it will find its way into important spaces and at key moments. From bumper stickers to pickets, from occupations to a social media barrage, the Zuma regime should expect his illegitimacy to be amplified. This is a message that will only go away when Zuma goes. This is also when Zapiro can remove the shower head.

Citizens gathered at the Soweto meeting also recognised that rolling mass action will be a powerful weapon of people's power in coming months. It was recognised that merely having a mass meeting, a rally or even a march was not sufficient to pull Zuma down. In coming months, expect actions on key national days such as 27 April, at the launch of the new labour federation, at a people's Drought Speak Out, #FoodPricesMustFall actions and at bread marches. This is about harnessing the symbolic power of the people to affirm that their suffering, hunger, voicelessness and marginalisation are all connected to Zuma being in power.

Of course, Zuma's ANC will call all of this an imperialist plot, or some other such mindless slander will be spewed out. Although we expect the shrinking number of the brave and principled in the ANC to defend our right to exist in a democracy, it is also important to recognise that the ANC lost its anti-imperialism a long time ago. A deeply globalised economy under ANC leadership for the past 21 years has merely shored up imperial power at the expense of the people. So, hopefully, the Zuma Must Go campaign will assist the ANC in realising how anti-people it has become. But, more importantly, we want this campaign to affirm that the future of South Africa's democracy belongs to each of its citizens. It is time we all took responsibility to ensure Zuma goes now – and that we do not let South Africa fall further.

Mail & Guardian, 21 April 2016.

Protests Mustn't Harm our Future

FACED WITH FAILING ECONOMIES and climate change, free education fights need better solutions than shutdowns and technocratic responses.

Watching students graduate is one of the most heartening experiences – more so when African students are capped and handed their degrees. The ululating affirms an unprecedented pride. Many of these students are the first in their families to have studied at university and received academic degrees. My generation in the 1980s fought for and contributed to this realisation. We did not burn our universities, even at the height of apartheid repression but appreciated that the privilege of education must be shared with all in the future.

Moreover, when we used the tactic of shutting down universities – for example to challenge the restriction of the UDF – we united all in the university community. We used this collective power to demonstrate, in a non-violent way, our opposition. Shutdown tactics would not have worked as an effective political tool if these conditions were not realised. A shutdown was merely a step towards strategic mass mobilisation and disciplined resistance in the streets: marching together with all against apartheid. When students receive their degrees, the journey to this accomplishment cannot be ignored. Many come from families that are distressed by low income, the effect of drought, precarious work, high unemployment, hunger (53% of South Africans are food insecure) and increasing service costs. These realities shape the aspirations of our students and lie at the root of demands for free, quality university education. This demand is a challenge to the post-apartheid political economy.

South Africa's transitional consensus has been undermined by failed globalisation and market-based policies. Wealth has been redistributed upward, moved offshore and captured by corrupt transactions. The boundary between the market and the state has been reset in favour of markets. With declining state support, public universities are being driven into the clutches of the market and forced to operate in an exclusionary way. The instability at universities is not going to go away, given the stakes for present and future generations. The damage done to universities during violent protests last year and this year now stands at more than R600 million. Academics cannot teach in such a context, and neither can we remain silent. We cannot teach in a securitised environment and be indifferent. Fear, entrenched positions and antagonism inhabit the world of the universities. Universities are at their limit and can be irreparably harmed. Achieving free, quality higher education in this context of destroyed universities is not a victory.

Students have a right to protest and the space to do so exists at universities, but every struggle has its limits and constraints. Struggles also have unintended consequences, such that the violence at universities will legitimise a destabilising mode of politics for all institutions in society. It could also provide licence to the further securitisation of state–society relations. The student protests have the potential to avoid these pitfalls and it is not too late to do things differently.

South Africa's economic crisis is further exacerbated by the onset of climate shocks such as drought, inducing increased food prices and hunger. Student protests are a symptom of these twin crises. In this context, current and future generations of students are best understood as the Anthropocene generation, living in a new age marked by struggle with deep inequalities and a climate-driven world in which conditions to sustain life are going to be challenged.

A new vision for South Africa has to start with these realities so we think boldly about a just transition based on alternatives such as basic income grants, public transport systems, the communing of resources, socially owned renewable energy, climate jobs, zero waste, food sovereignty pathways and solidarity economies. The student protests are prompting us to think about society in a different way. This means free, quality education has to be located in an effort to renew a social contract for South Africa, as part of the just transition to address the economic and climate crises.

We need a new CODESA (Convention for a Democratic South Africa) now, so all institutions take on the imperative of building capabilities to survive the climate crises. Free and quality university education has to be the building block for such a social contract and approach. This means South Africa's leaders are faced with an opportunity to renew nation building to confront some of the greatest challenges facing human societies. The student protests are not a threat but an opening for another path.

The South African state, including the Treasury, is failing to appreciate this imperative because of its technocratic approach. The announcement by the Minister of Higher Education, while respecting the autonomy of universities and making a crucial concession in getting the state to carry the cost of fee increases for 2017 for households earning less than R600,000 (up from R122,000 to include the missing middle), does not go far enough in addressing this imperative. His proposal reinforces the commercialisation of universities, locks students into a debt-based loan scheme and takes forward the ANC's fiscal populism of zero fee increases for some, but in a disingenuous way. It is far from where students are. The wrath of students could have been mitigated if it were clear that he was working tirelessly to secure state support to place universities firmly on a path towards decommodified education. The minister could, for example, have set the basis for converting the current student loan scheme into a merit-based bursary scheme, instead of adding the missing middle.

The minister could have made the case to business for an increase and a greater percentage of the training levy to be channeled to universities; this as part of a new social contract to position universities to build knowledge capabilities to lessen the effects of catastrophic climate change and for a sustainable green economy. This boost in subsidy could have been tied to bringing down the cost for the missing middle. At the same time, as an interim measure, universities could have considered increasing fees for those households with incomes above R600,000 to about 20% or more, given that universities are underpriced for the rich and in relation to their spend on private schools.

This is a version of the wealth tax that could have gone immediately into university budgets. Moreover, all graduates could have been given the choice of serving in a national climate jobs programme. All of this would have not delivered free education now for all, but would have moved the university system significantly in this direction and demonstrated a commitment to embed this logic institutionally.

Yes, the immediate response of the state to student demands could have been more transformative. Fixing conflict-ridden universities means addressing the crises of market-led politics in South Africa. Let's hope our policymakers, politicians and university administrators understand this. Privatising public higher education is a dead end and not viable. It is a time for a new policy direction and politics. Students have led a struggle that affirms universities as a public good. They need to struggle in a manner that gives universities and themselves a future. They are not the only ones who want free, quality university education.

Mail & Guardian, 7–13 October 2016.

Fees Protests: History Shows True Revolution Lies Not in Violence

THE CRISIS AT OUR universities cannot be solved through shows of strength by opposing sides, nor through an all-out crackdown on students by the state. We need an urgent national conversation.

After #FeesMustFall captured the national and global imagination in October last year, it plunged into a mode of violent politics. Non-violent pickets and occupations turned into riots and arson attacks at some universities. The cost, estimated at over R470 million, is a slap in the face for all South Africans. The anarchy of non-representative and unaccountable groups turned into a clash with the ethos of intellectual freedom and tolerance that characterises fundamental principles of universities.

An infectious copycat or mimetic politics, with a violent underbelly, has returned. Arson at the University of KwaZulu-Natal, tyre burning at others and battles with private security outside the Great Hall at the University of the Witwatersrand have brought back a siege mentality with deep suspicions and an aversion for dialogue. Teaching, exams and even potential jobs for university leavers are being disrupted. Poor students are bearing the brunt of this. Some have chosen to ignore this tension-filled reality in their populist fervour and glorification of student militancy, and celebrate violence as performative revolutionary practice in the cauldron of struggle.

In this context, there is no moral limit. But the threat facing our universities reflects a deeper challenge; it is an echo of a nation in crisis. Student rage largely stems from several lived realities. South Africa's post-apartheid generation faces a tightening labour market at one end and a highly competitive one in the upper segment. A free quality university education is crucial to give present and future generations life chances. It is one of the few mechanisms for class formation and mobility of an aspirant middle class. Yet this imperative is not being understood by the rulers of this society. The corruption, maladministration and waste of the ANC state has created a legitimacy deficit. Students perceive bail outs to corrupt, state-owned enterprises, megaspend on Nkandla, golden handshakes to useless bureaucrats, huge salaries for politicians and avaricious tenders as brazen acts of disregard for their aspirations. The ANC is seen to be a degenerate and unresponsive political force, and students are asking hard questions about ANC leaders and the party's role in the state.

The ANC and its degeneration have also given birth to authoritarian populism. Some in the student movement believe they carry the mantle of revolutionary emancipation. They are harbingers of revolution now. Yet, in modern human history not a single violent revolution has brought forth an emancipated society. This was the case even in Frantz Fanon's Algeria, an example students tend to venerate through a shallow reading.

In a recent survey of Wits academics by their union, the overwhelming majority support free quality education and some student leaders are beginning to understand the importance of solidarity with wider social forces. A recent interfaith prayer service at Wits, led by the student representative council (SRC), began to create such a climate.

State and university leadership have also failed to appreciate the importance of deep, ongoing democratic engagement with students. Minister of Higher Education Blade Nzimande's announcement, although positive in some respects, was a technocratic pronouncement. If it was a position based on consultation, vice-chancellors and SRC presidents should have been part of the announcement. University leaderships failed to announce clearly and in tandem what the minister's announcement meant for each institution. Now universities are overrun by hysteria. Although South Africa is struggling to build viable state institutions, public universities have mostly grown into successful institutions. This enormous achievement is under threat of being pushed back by more state irrationality, cutbacks in subsidies (for over two decades) and growing demands on universities. Wits vice-chancellor Adam Habib has suggested a fully state-funded university system will cost South Africa about R50 billion. This is far less than the arms deal, World Cup or the proposed nuclear programme. The conversation needs to shift to how this can happen sustainably.

Students, with progressive academics, supportive parents, sympathetic university leadership and other allies, need to come up with a strategic plan and visionary road map. Most importantly, students need to appreciate that they have made dramatic short-term gains, such as insourcing at Wits. These gains have to be claimed and non-violent tactics invented through democratic deliberation to secure more victories.

Sunday Times, 2 October 2016.

The EFF's Wrecking Ball Politics is Fascist Rather than Left

STUDENT POLITICS IS FRACTIOUS and complicated by its populist character; whoever steps in front leads the crowd. I came face to face with this reality twice in the past few months: first in a church at a University of the Witwatersrand peace meeting in October and, more recently, at the Higher Education Convention, co-hosted by the National Education Crisis Forum. The peace meeting was disrupted by the Economic Freedom Fighters (EFF). At the convention, students and workers wanted recognition for their struggles and the convention was one way to affirm that and ensure the powerful were listening. The convention ended in an EFF-led brawl and with students turning on each other. Months of organisation and preparation for an inclusive platform for constituency-based policy dialogue were destabilised.

The alternative to dialogue is too ghastly to contemplate: violent student protest and deepening state-led securitisation at universities and, more broadly, societal struggles. Universities will not survive in this context and South Africa's tenuous democracy will plunge further into crisis. Student formations are generally extensions of political formations. This complicates the dynamics in student politics and in #FeesMustFall protests. Who is really leading? The EFF is an interesting example in this regard, given its militaristic and hierarchical form of organisation. For the EFF, delegitimising the ANC at all costs means the worse things get, the better for the party in any social arena.

Deepening crisis through disruption is a political strategy. From parliament to universities, the EFFs' mode of often violent disruptive engagement is becoming central to its political practice and this is also diffusing as a societal norm. This means the EFF, in the context of the Higher Education Convention, was not willing to rise above its narrow partisan interests and place the interests of the country first. Solutions to take the country forward are not important but short-term political calculation to upstage the ANC state is all that matters; even in a context in which the main protagonist of social dialogue is not even the ANC state.

This is not oppositional politics but the politics of wrecking everything because collective societal solutions don't matter. It also means this short-term strategy will, intentionally and unintentionally, unleash forces that will also clash with the EFF down the road. It is breeding politics that will come back to harm it, assuming it is successful in growing in electoral terms. But perpetual violent disruption as a mode of politics also means politics bereft of an understanding of what is essential for a democracy to work. South Africa's transformative constitutionalism, like all modern democracies, requires all contending political forces to accept certain rights and procedural standards in the political game. A crucial assumption at work in this political framework is the idea that political difference is acceptable and should not become antagonistic. The EFF does not respect political difference and is antagonistic to all political forces that do not agree with it. It is not just unSouth African, as some have suggested, but is also deeply undemocratic.

Competitive political escalation for the EFF means: accept its way or face violence. Does this make the EFF fascist? Liberal journalists, some academics and even the SACP have declared the EFF fascist. The notion of fascism is a slippery concept to define. As an appellation it has multiple meanings, both historically and comparatively. Liberal scholars usually work with a typology of key characteristics to define fascism such as: charismatic leadership, racism, ultra-nationalism, paramilitarism, violence (actual or threatened), anti-parliamentarianism, anti-constitutionalism and anti-Semitism.

This is helpful to a degree, but runs into analytical problems given that context-specific conditions and dynamics shape fascist forces. In the first half of the twentieth century it was easy to discern national variations of either Italian fascism or Nazi totalitarianism. Today, fascism is mutating and manifesting in a complex matrix of national and global material conditions. It has arrived dressed in pinstriped suits or sometimes as a suicide bomber.

This brings us back to the question: Are those wearing red berets under the EFF banner fascists? Is the main contribution the EFF has made to South African politics merely to draw tauter the line between those for democratic transformation and those against? The EFF is a contradictory formation and on its current trajectory it is not a visionary nation builder, nor a programmatic force for change, nor a democratic political opposition. Although at some moments it looks good in relation to the kleptocratic Jacob Zuma regime, we should not assume that it is better.

The EFF expresses serious ambiguities in its ideological make-up: constitutional/anti-constitutional, Marxist-Leninist/stakeholder capitalist, male chauvinist/yet appealing to some women, decolonising/yet willing to accept support from white capital. The EFF, like historical fascism, draws its ideas from across the political spectrum. As a result, what it stands for in terms of values, beliefs and ideology is unclear. It makes it up as it goes through the theatre of national politics, expedient political manoeuvring and through its authoritarian populist inventiveness.

The EFF received just over a million votes in the previous elections. Does this mean that those who vote for it believe in its mercurial, shallow and makeshift belief system? Are these the citizens who buy into the spectacle of authoritarian populist politics? An electoral outcome is difficult to decipher. There are always different degrees of support for any political party. This ranges from hardcore support and sympathisers to swing voters. In the last election, the EFF certainly picked up a significant anti-ANC vote and it also found traction in sections of the black middle class and the unemployed poor.

The EFF could not build on this momentum of national support and win a local government election outright. Instead. it emerged from the elections as a coalition partner to the neoliberal Democratic Alliance in most big metros. Moreover, given its disposition to violent disruption and its inability to provide a way forward on national challenges, it is likely that its electoral support has peaked. The next national election will be telling and it will really be surprising if South Africans vote for a party that merely offers fiery rhetoric, intolerance and violence.

But this still leaves red on EFF T-shirts, berets and paraphernalia. What does this mean? For some the red dimension of EFF identity makes it left, coupled with a militant dose of rhetoric, such as evoking the big N word – nationalisation. Nationalisation has always been about state capitalism and nothing more. The EFF has successfully claimed a space to the left of the ANC and has projected itself as a left force, picking up on residual anti-establishment sentiment. Yet its antics in parliament of representing workers with overalls and hard hats smacks of hypocrisy. Whereas most workers earn less than R3000 a month, an EFF MP earns more than R1 million a year, or more than R80,000 a month. It pays to act exploited in the EFF script.

But the EFF should not believe that workers are not watching or are unaware of the social distance. Moreover, the EFF has not united left forces of the working class, the left intelligentsia or more generally left social movements. Nor has it provided a serious analysis of contemporary capitalism to guide its interventions. The EFF, in claiming to be left, has undermined the prospects of the left in South Africa. It is contributing to the defeat of the left. The EFF is not a left force by any stretch of the imagination despite its own declarations, the colour red in its identity and simplistic media representations of it as a left party. An EFF in power will not take South Africa to the left; it does not have what it takes. An EFF-led South Africa will probably mean most South Africans will think the Zuma days were wonderful.

There is no straight line from Malema to the United States' Donald Trump, to France's far-right Marine Le Pen or even the fundamentalist group al-Shabab. The EFF is not fascist in the twentieth-century sense, but certainly expresses elements of a twenty-first-century fascism in its role in South African politics. It is pioneering an original fascism in the South African context. As it fights the ANC and other progressive social forces violently, it is also delegitimising democratic processes and forms of dialogue. Unlike the ANC, the EFF claims to be left yet it is politically and ideologically certainly not left. Anti-capitalist ideology is meaningless in the EFF understanding of the world and thus it is not a serious left-orientated force. The interests it seeks to aggregate are disparate and not representative of the working class as a whole. Its disdain for hard-won democratic values, constitutional principles and practices makes it nothing less than an anti-democratic pariah.

South Africans need to choose carefully where they stand in relation to the EFF. The national dialogue to resolve the higher education crisis will continue in coming months, with or without the EFF. Student formations also have to reflect on their commitment to disciplined, inclusive and respectful democratic dialogue to find policy solutions.

Mail & Guardian, 4 April 2017.

Zuma's Cabinet Reshuffle Inaugurates South Africa's Zimbabwe Moment

HISTORIANS REVIEWING THE recent short span of history, the past 50 years, or even the *longue durée*, over 200 years, would agree that national liberation movements fit into a larger pattern of historical change that has not yielded a fundamental break with colonialism and, in the case of South Africa, with apartheid as well. The movements have brought more of the same, or even degeneration, to their societies. Southern Africa has a litany of examples but President Robert Mugabe's Zimbabwe is considered a classic case of revolution derailed by its own leadership.

President Jacob Zuma's recent Cabinet reshuffle has inaugurated our Zimbabwe moment. It has haunted our subconscious, but now it looms large on the national stage. The morbid signs have been there for a while as the looting and state capture has intensified. But the reshuffle has sunk the Zuma ship, hurtling it to the bottom of the ocean, with the ruin of all in sight. One would have expected the oldest national liberation movement in Africa, with its intergenerational experience and strong traditions, to have prevented a single individual from substituting for the nation, the state and the party. But, on the other hand, the Zuma bandwagon, with its origins in his rape trial more than 10 years ago, portended a constitutional and political crisis, particularly with his brand of patriarchal, ethnic and authoritarian populism and by engendering a vicious intolerance in the ranks of the ANC-led Tripartite Alliance.

Zuma's rise fitted in perfectly with the power concentrated in the presidency, both because of constitutional fiat and because of former president Thabo Mbeki's centralising approach. Zuma's control of the presidency and his factional hold on the ANC has given him the confidence to sink South Africa for his own selfish interests.

But is this the endgame for us all? Are we going to live through the destruction of our young democratic institutions and the rolling back of our rights? Are we condemned to live through more than three decades of kleptocratic takeover of the state and economy, as in Zimbabwe, and its eventual collapse? South Africa is not exceptional but it is also not Zimbabwe.

Many commentators have begun to suggest that Zuma has it all worked out strategically. This is an all-knowing and calculating strongman who will not be pushed back by any social force.

Pallo Jordan, one of the most brilliant intellectual minds in the ANC, said a few years ago that South Africa has a well-developed private sector and civil society, which distinguished it from Zimbabwe, and that these will serve as a bulwark against regression. There are also other features such as our geopolitical relations, the complexity of the interlocking political relationships in the ANC-led alliance and our robust intelligentsia.

Geopolitically, under Zuma South Africa has been isolating itself from the broader African context through a state practice that is increasingly xenophobic in managing refugees, migrants and immigrants. But a backlash is growing in the continent, which will limit how far Zuma can retreat into the old boys' club in Africa.

In the BRICS (Brazil, Russia, India, China, South Africa) bloc, we are a small player among mega-states that have been skewing our economic priorities. China is content with not overreaching or compromising its neo-mercantilist interests with South Africa. On the other hand, Russia has been gaining a global reputation as a mafia state, which is disposed to meddling even in Western democracies. This will have widespread implications for a Zuma regime in bed with Russia on nuclear energy, for example. It is very likely the entanglement will be about reducing the Zuma regime to a client state, further constraining the president's choices.

But, most crucial at this stage in terms of geopolitical relations is the unplugging of foreign investment. An exodus out of government bonds, equities, real estate and from the productive economy will be calamitous for an economy struggling to reboot. An economy in recession will mean lower revenue collection, continued high unemployment and limited economic room to manoeuvre. Fiscal populism in this context will not work but will merely bankrupt the state, deepening its legitimacy crisis.

The private sector, though enjoying immense structural power because of a globalised economy, has had a contradictory relationship with the post-apartheid state. It has not been able to lead the state and neither has the state been able to direct the sector's capital, despite huge concessions made to it.

Although black economic empowerment has deracialised parts of the economy, this has been a shallow process, involving politically connected elites. In the main, there is no direct control over the trillions of rands sitting on balance sheets, which could be invested; and this investment strike is likely to continue. A Zuma regime will drive more capital offshore either legally or illicitly, and a hollowing out of the economy will aggravate the regime's legitimacy.

South Africa's intelligentsia, professional and organic, are generally critical about the state of affairs. A whole genre of literature has proliferated in just over 20 years of ANC rule with titles such as: *Unmasked: Why the ANC Failed to Govern* (Khulu Mbatha), *Recovering Democracy in South Africa* (Raymond Suttner), *We Have Now Begun our Descent: How to Stop South Africa Losing its Way* (Justice Malala), *How Long Will South Africa Survive?* (R.W. Johnson) and *Turning Point: South Africa at a Crossroads* (Theuns Eloff), among others. Black and white intellectuals capture the zeitgeist of our times. But inter-subjective conversations about what we have become and where we are going have also captured the national imagination.

The ANC-led Tripartite Alliance has been both a strength and a constraint on the party. As a crystallisation of social forces across all classes, strata and popular forces, it has provided deep roots for the ANC. But its interlocking and overlapping relationships have also worked against the ANC. For instance, the undermining of trade union federation COSATU as an independent worker voice has led to enormous realignments, particularly in the wake of the Marikana massacres and the development of new trade unions, including the Association of Mineworkers and Construction Union (AMCU) and the new labour federation, the South African Federation of Trade Unions (SAFTU). Workers in COSATU clearly did not put their weight behind the ANC in the recent local government elections.

As for the SACP, it has moved from being a principled and strategic force of the left to being one of Zuma's staunchest allies, opening up a big space to the left of the ANC.

For the ANC more directly, the overlapping of membership with COSATU and the SACP also means a turn against Zuma could also mean a massive rupture inside the ANC. Although these forces are beginning to shrug off their loyalty to Zuma and are calling for him to step down, they are not going far enough to push back the web of kleptocratic rule, anchored in the conflation of the ANC and the state. Zuma might be pressured to go but the rot inside the ANC-state nexus is deep.

Finally, civil society, although not homogeneous or progressive in all quarters, has been the hotbed of progressive forces. Post-apartheid, South Africa has been through two cycles of resistance and has thrown up important movements such as the Treatment Action Campaign (TAC), the Landless People's Movement, the Anti-Privatisation Forum and now, more recently, the Right2Know Campaign, the SAFSC, the Inyanda National Land Movement, various NGOs and campaigns involved in defending constitutional rights, the #FeesMustFall movement and many more.

Former finance minister Pravin Gordhan was correct to state publicly that 'South Africa has a long history of mass mobilisation', and residues of these live on in civil society.

The world has also taught South Africa about non-violent civil resistance. From Mahatma Gandhi and Martin Luther King to Solidarity in Poland, the People's Power Movement in the Philippines, the unemployed and homeless in Europe, the Occupy movement in the United States and many others, they have given South Africans an appreciation of non-violent mass power as a strategy to transform society.

Since Ahmed Kathrada's funeral and the sharing of the letter he wrote calling for Zuma to resign, this message has been gaining widespread support across society. Memorial services for Kathrada, occupations outside the Treasury, shutdowns and marches, including to the Union Buildings, are now all coming to the fore in the best spirit of who we are in the spirit of Madiba and Kathrada.

Zuma has placed the ANC and the state on a collision course with society. His forces will play various moves but there will be mass counter moves in coming months, and very likely even into the general election in 2019, if he does not resign. The ANC is also likely to be destroyed by Zuma if it does not act against him now.

In many ways, although our Zimbabwe moment has arrived, we are also back in the 1980s, fighting a regime with the same moral and political outrage that won us our democracy. South Africa will not be Zimbabwe as long as we refuse to submit.

Mail & Guardian, 20 April 2017.

South Africa Must Resist Another Captured President, This Time by the Markets

THE ANC HAS MADE a dangerous habit of bringing post-apartheid South Africa to the brink of instability and the common ruin of all. The resignation of former President Jacob Zuma and his replacement by Cyril Ramaphosa was such a moment. It brought home the point that the over-concentration of power in the office of the president has clearly not worked. A rethink on president-centred politics and the threats it poses to the democracy are crucial for the post-Zuma period. South Africa needs to re-imagine democratic practice, leadership and how power works.

Some sections of South African society have reduced the Zuma problem to corruption. Dismantle Zuma's kleptocratic network, the argument goes, and all is solved. Zuma's demise and a few high-profile prosecutions will suffice.

But another view on the Zuma problem, and one with which I concur, suggests it is a problem of contending class projects inside the ANC. The neoliberal class project under Presidents Nelson Mandela and Thabo Mbeki saw South Africa integrated into global markets. It maintained stability through modest redistributive reforms. This project laid the basis for a new black middle class to emerge while systematically weakening labour and the left. But it surrendered the state (including the presidency) to transnational capital and the power of finance.

The Zuma project, on the other hand, advanced looting as the basis of accumulation and class formation. The extra-constitutional state that emerged deepened the macro-economic, institutional and legitimacy crisis of the ANC-led state. The left and labour, aligned with the ANC in the Tripartite Alliance, were co-opted and divided. Both these projects are entrenched in the ANC.

Now what? Messiah-centred presidential politics is extremely dangerous. This is particularly true in a country of extreme inequality and with a formal concentration of power in the office of the president. If politics is not represented, thought and acted beyond this, South Africa is going to repeat historical mistakes.

Since the ANC's December 2017 conference, the media, the banks and international institutions have been talking up a narrative of the 'Cyril effect'. Zuma's removal is attributed to this. In fact, the Cyril effect is a narrative of capture of South Africa's new president by transnational and financial capital. South Africa's democracy cannot afford another captured president beholden to credit rating agencies, currency fluctuations, investment flows and business perceptions. South Africa's democracy has to be grounded in the needs of its citizens and the mandates given by its Constitution.

The Cyril effect is hyperbole

The end of Zuma was in fact not because of the Cyril effect. In the main Zuma was removed by the people's effect which connected the dots of corruption, a mismanaged state and rapacious capitalism. This resistance was expressed over 15 years through various institutions and social forces. These included:

- battles inside the SACP against Zumafication but which led to expulsions;
- by feminists during Zuma's rape trial and subsequently through #RememberKhwezi;
- artists and cartoonists lampooning Zuma, including the shower heads;
- ongoing struggles in communities against corrupt officials;
- the Marikana massacre in 2012. This produced rage among workers and major realignments away from the ANC;
- the call by trade unions like NUMSA for Zuma's removal;
- the Vukani-Sidikiwe campaign during the 2014 elections which opened up a national debate on how citizens should vote;
- the rise of #ZumaMustGo Campaign. This was in response to the sacking of Nhlanhla Nene as finance minister in December 2015. The NUMSA-led United Front played a crucIal role in this;
- the #FeesMustFall movement. Students' demands included labour insourcing as well as quality, decommodified and decolonialised higher education;
- the 2016 local government elections. These were a harbinger of seismic political realignments against the ANC in key cities;
- the role of investigative and nonpartisan media in probing corruption scandals. And the publication of the Gupta-leaks as well as *A Simple Man* and *The President's Keepers*;
- the courageous role from 2010 onwards of then public protector Thuli Madonsela in drawing attention to ethics and legal violations by Zuma;
- court decisions affirming the judiciary's independence in relation to Zuma;

- Zuma's miscalculation in firing finance minister Pravin Gordhan, the rallying of activists and the rise of #SaveSouthAfrica. What followed were some of the largest post-apartheid protest marches;
- the powerful voice of liberation struggle veterans like Ahmed Kathrada and others who called for Zuma to resign.

The ANC's legitimacy crisis

As a result of all this activity the crisis of legitimacy in the ANC, and the ANC state, has deepened. This has placed immense pressure on the party to act. In this context, Ramaphosa is playing out his role out of necessity and to secure the ANC's electoral fortunes. For middle-class and rich South Africans Ramaphosa's state of the nation speech represented a return to normalcy, a democracy that works for a few. That's not to say that the new president didn't make some important announcements in his state of the nation address. This included his comments about state-owned enterprises, redistributive state programmes and anti-corruption mechanisms. Nevertheless, the speech struck chords that resonated with the return to normalcy narrative.

But South Africans can't repeat the mistake made in 1994 when progressive civil society demobilised. The people's effect has to continue to shape a post-Zuma democracy in the interests of all. The ANC has abused majority support and cannot be trusted with the future of South Africa. People's power has to be strengthened and continuously mobilised around strengthening democratic institutions, ending corruption, fundamental economic transformation and advancing systemic alternatives to the climate crisis.

The Conversation, 20 February 2018

Trump May be Gone, but Neofascism Remains Alive and Kicking in Mainstream American Society

AT LAST, THE DONALD Trump presidency has crash landed and he is out of the White House. Now, we can all start dealing with Trump trauma and shock. What did we live through over the past four years? This is a planetary question. It is a question we are all grappling with because the world is now capitalist on a global scale and America is the leading power making that world. Post the Cold War we were all conscripted to be Americans and the American Dream was declared the global dream. Even China bought into it through its own self-interested and authoritarian way. They became so good at it then even Trump baulked. He wanted it back and declared Make America Great Again.

While we do not physically live in America, through the global media we are front-row spectators gazing into it, watching the theatrics of its leaders while grappling with its presence in our everyday lives. The US has set the standards of so-called civilisation by asserting a set of universals – democracy, progress, competition, individualism and free enterprise. These universals are the props of a mythic America, standing tall at the vanguard of the free world, and which reveals itself through the iconic hamburger, unthinking patriotism, voting in elections, the veneration of a masculine gun culture, Hollywood movies and mass consumption.

This idealised liberal version of America and its material roots is what Trump remade. He could do this because he exploited one of the most fatal flaws of US democracy: the over-concentration of power in the US presidency and the cult-like aura that surrounds this political institution. This weakness exists despite the constitutional separation of powers and Trump ably demonstrated this. One individual controlling the world's most deadly nuclear arsenal, a powerful communications megaphone, commander of the military, imbued with a veto against Congress and extensive executive power, including for extra-judicial killing anywhere in the world, got busy wrecking everything since his election in 2016.

Rising to the top of the system

At times, with his racist utterances he looked like Hitler, and at other times, in his anti-democratic performances like Stalin. A Trumpian presidency also demonstrated how an anti-democratic, neo-fascist could use the weaknesses of a corporate-controlled market democracy to rise to the apex of the US political system. Money, exclusionary nationalism, a sympathetic right-wing media and an effective social media strategy easily secured entry into the White House. This is not unique to the US, but has become a feature of many market democracies in the global North and South.

The third wave of democratisation (1973 to the mid-2000s), based on American liberal universals, has been halting. As it plunges into crisis all over the world, it is giving rise to a second coming of fascism including in India (the largest democracy in the world) and Brazil (the largest democracy in Latin America). Inequalities have broken market democracies and ritual voting every few years for more of the same pro-business policies is breeding deadly divides across precarious societies. Covid-19 has only made this all worse.

Beyond mythic America and Dow Jones economic performance indicators is an extremely divided country. Since the 1970s, corporate America started pushing harder to end the US social contract that provided certain minimum social protections. Ronald Reagan's unleashing of corporate power, coded racism (referred to in the mainstream as Republican conservatism) and renewed Cold War competition paved the way for Bill Clinton to entrench the power of US corporate finance into every nook and cranny of US life. This also provided the institutional basis for global corporate finance, centred on the dollar and Wall Street, to shape deepening globalisation.

In this expansionist economic tide there were winners and losers. The winners are the super-wealthy plutocrats. In 1965, an average CEO salary was forty times as much as the average wage; today that number is more than 300 times as much. Today, the top 5% of households possess nearly 75% of the nation's wealth, while the bottom 60% of American households have lost wealth. Unionisation of the American workforce played a crucial redistributive role but this has declined from a high of more than 30% in the mid-1950s to fewer than 10% today. In this fragile society dramatic shocks easily reveal its underbelly. For instance, Hurricane Katrina in 2005 brought home vividly racial exclusion and wealth disparities in New Orleans. Moreover, the great financial crash of 2007–2009 exacerbated inequalities, as finance houses were bailed out and the precariat of American society lost homes and jobs. Barrack Obama and the Democratic Party did very little to change the direction of American society and deep social fault-lines widened.

Some context

The Trumpian response has to be located in this context. It was a right-wing challenge to the hypocrisy of liberal nationalism and internationalism. Trumpism was about revanchist nationalism, to regain lost ground for white Anglo-Saxon supremacy, while drawing from deep wells of anti-intellectualism and discontent within American society. He was the strong man in the White House, in the age of social media, who was going to build walls, persecute the children of immigrants, crank up Islamaphobia and crush protests in defence of black lives. In geopolitical terms he was also readjusting relations with trans-Atlantic allies and China to affirm a crude version of US transactional unilateralism, something which Democrats cloak in multilateralism.

Trump was doing all of this while keeping American capitalism going to keep plutocratic America happy. Tax cuts for the rich, Wall Street finance flowing, elite charter schools, enabling fossil fuel extraction, promoting climate denialism and asserting an anti-science approach to Covid-19. On the latter, Trump was demonstrating to the world a misguided libertarian individualism, rejecting mask wearing as more important than the common good. Trump was the unapologetic and arrogant white male capitalist political ruler. In the context of the Republican Party, despite a few individual noises and divergences, Trumpism resonated because it amplified what was inside the Republican Party.

The American dream in this narrative is about a plutocratic white America being able to do what it wants despite the formality of democracy. Trump confirmed this with his Cabinet appointments which included several billionaires, millionaires and centimillionaires. For Trump, wealth, privilege and power was even licence to invent reality as he saw fit. Thus, any divergence from his world view and interests were fake news. Trump ensured the plutocratic wealthy were no longer in the political shadows but now in the mainstream. This political reality essentially short-circuited the Washington beltway, with its patronage wheels greased by mega business lobbies to buy out policies and regulation. Wealthy plutocrats were now directly in charge and at the apex of the state. This in turn constituted corporate power as the definitive marker of whiteness and the market as freedom. About 74 million who voted for Trump believe the same and this makes neofascism a living political phenomena in the mainstream of American society, even if Trump disappears.

On 6 January, the storming of the Capitol was a desperate plutocratic move Trumpism played to affirm its anti-democratic credentials. This moment of infamy was very similar to scenes in many parts of the world as the crisis of market democracies worsened. In the American context it flipped the narrative of the Muslim fundamentalist terrorist as being the barbarian at the gates to homegrown white neofascism. At the same time, the American standard of democracy, with its hypocrisy, exclusions and limits was rendered visible. It ended a propagandistic myth of the perfect democracy cultivated since the end of World War 2, through the McCarthy red-baiting period, Cold War destabilisation of many countries and in the era of corporate led globalisation. The scary fact lurking in all of this is 139 Republican representatives (66% of the caucus in the House) and eight Republican senators voted to overturn the recent national election. Stealing the election was a consistent agenda that united Trump, the mob and the majority in the Republican Party. This was further affirmed when only a small minority (10 out of 211 Republican representatives) voted in favour of the second impeachment of Trump.

The Joe Biden-led Democratic Party is off to a good start to criminalise the mob violence but a narrow law and order approach is not going to solve the deep divides wrenching American society apart. Trumpian white supremacists and plutocratic elites can be securitised to ensure political management and oldstyle deal making can kick in to divide the Trumpian support base but this is not new in America. This has been happening to African Americans since the civil rights victories of the mid-1960s: incorporation for some, exclusion, securitisation and incarceration for the many. As a result, the real challenge of the racial divide was not addressed.

America needs a new nation-building project that addresses the deep roots of crisis. An immediate priority is ending Covid-19 devastation and policy failures. However, beyond the pandemic nothing short of a new constitution, electoral reform that removes corporate financial influence, including a break with the two-party system and the outdated electoral college, climate change economic policies that are transformative, progressive immigration policies, tight gun control laws, democratic regulation of social media corporations and international relations that respect societies that democratically choose not to be like America, could lay the basis for renewal. Biden's Democratic Party faces this historical test. If it fails in this task the world should expect further decay and social conflict in American society as it declines as a post-hegemonic power.

Sunday Times, 31 January 2021; republished in *The Bullet*, 7 February 2021.

South Africa is Turning on Itself
with Awande Buthelezi

THE MASS LOOTING OVER the past few days is not a sign of revolution in our streets and on television. Instead, this is the coming to life of South Africa's most scary nightmare: a society turning on itself in an orgy of large-scale public violence.

More than 25 years of ANC misrule placed us on this trajectory as it produced a crisis-ridden society through AIDs denialism, a consistently high structural unemployment rate (now at 42%), rampant corruption, instability in higher education, the Marikana massacre, a dysfunctional state, an inadequate pandemic response and now factional divisions fuelling societal conflict. These failures explain the misery of the African majority but have also set the stage for South African society to kill itself. Are we going to be victims or are we going to move beyond the nightmare of a degenerate national liberation politics? What we do now to stop the killing of our society will determine whether we have a post-ANC future.

We are both from KwaZulu-Natal, with roots and strong family ties in the province. Awande has family living in communities in which violence has been perpetrated by members of those communities against workplaces – malls, factories and shops – that employ members from those very same communities. This community-worker divide challenges any crude ethnicisation of the violence; such as Zulus against Ramaphosa's government. Vishwas has family in communities that have thrown up self-defence and armed protection units. From Indian neighbourhoods in the city of Pietermaritzburg, where Gandhi's statue stands, to Stanger, Phoenix and beyond, fear, racial tension and division separate groups of mainly African looters and Indian residents. Despite these volatile and dangerous fault-lines, this is not a race war and cannot be generalised into an African versus Indian conflict; though some insidious forces want it to become such.

When several trucks were burnt on the N3, after Zuma's incarceration, what was striking was how ineffective the KwaZulu-Natal political power structure was in stemming the escalation. Institutions of Zulu nationalism, such as the

IFP and Chief Mangosuthu Buthelezi, prime minister to the Zulu monarch, faded into the background; though the belated statement by the new Zulu monarch calling for an end to the violence must be acknowledged and welcomed. The premier of the province sat neutralised in a deeply divided ANC, the general secretary of the SACP, who hails from Dambuza in Pietermaritzburg, put out a meek statement against the violence. COSATU, which played a crucial role in community peace pacts in the early 1990s, vanished in the maelstrom of the moment.

What is emerging instead are local community leaders reaching out to each other across race and community divides. All are trying to secure a just peace and keep alive non-racial leadership. These are leaders who have been made by this crisis and will have to face a province in which destroyed shops, malls and factories are rebuilt and disrupted value chains cranked up again. These are the leaders who will have to deal with the food shortages. These are the leaders who will observe how middle classes of all races migrate out of the province as it becomes infamous as a paradise for looters. South Africa has to support this new leadership as it holds the line.

How do we analyse the violence? Zuma instigation is an obvious theory, but it breaks down in the unfolding chaos. The media optic was crude as it either collapsed everyone into a #FreeZuma protester or a looter. It is clear there are different social forces driving the looting including organised criminal elements, starving people (over 30 million live in food stress) and greedy opportunists (driving fancy cars and hauling away loot). Each of these elements requires a different strategy.

Zuma-linked instigators need to be tracked through social media network analysis of public statements inciting violence and arrested. Local crime intelligence needs to kick in and make the connection between existing crime networks and community hot-spots, even offering rewards for information leading to arrests. Opportunists need to be picked out and made to face the courts. The hungry should not be criminalised, but targeted for direct material support. The NPA needs to support the building of this evidence-based pipeline.

Instead, the Minister of Police is overplaying the narrative of violence against the state, the 12 major kingpins behind it all and has exaggerated his behind-the-scenes role to prevent worse mayhem. With thousands of jobs on the line, Bheki Cele's media spin wears thin. His current public narrative does not address mass-based looting. If the rule of law is to be affirmed, the violence has to be addressed in a precedent-setting way to prevent future recurrence. There has to be serious consequences. Only 12 kingpins going to jail is certainly not enough. All those responsible must be held to account. Smart frontline policing, working with communities and social constituencies, has to bring this tragic saga to a just end.

Several ghoulish characters have been revealed, each with a role in the killing of our society. Zuma is like Michael Jackson in *Thriller*, a master of the great disaster, at the forefront of the zombie hordes. He has played his endgame: you bring me down; I bring it all down. His remaking of thievery as legitimate and the crux of national liberation has not been lost on the hordes. Zuma lives in radical economic looting. However, social and political chaos cannot be controlled, even by the kingpin of the zombies. Even after the unthinking hordes wipe out everything, they are faced with the logic of this process; and they turn on each other.

President Ramaphosa, a shift-shaper, projects himself as a parody of Nelson Mandela, but with a failing strategy. His current government response to the pandemic has been uncaring. Food relief failed, social relief grants were dropped, austerity is biting into an embattled public service and he assumes a private sector that has failed to create decent jobs over several decades will do so now. Social conflict and desperation stalk the land because of his government's policy choices.

This is in contrast to US president Joe Biden, for instance, who recognised that to keep his society together massive cash transfers had to happen. Biden also recognised income inequality and disparities in wealth have to be challenged through progressive taxation.

Our shift-shaper gives a national address on the violence and hints at unemployment as a problem and offers nothing concrete. His government has arrogantly ignored calls from across progressive civil society for a non-means-tested basic income grant (BIG) and for the democratisation of food relief efforts by the Solidarity Fund and government departments, so communities are directly involved in building food sovereign systems.

Then there is the vampire of capital, feeding off the economic body of the imagined nation. In South Africa, 10% of income earners receive 65% of wealth. Moreover, wealth is also disproportionately owned, with 10% having about 80% of the wealth. Wealthy plutocrats believed that by donating to the Solidarity Fund their responsibility to society was over. In the midst of the pandemic, millions are being paid to CEOs as bonuses and through high salaries. Business organisations and people are not stepping up to say these salaries are no longer viable in such an unequal society. None are standing up to say we need greater taxation on the wealthy to ensure we have an inclusive democracy. The vampires need to understand the current moment in South Africa is also about the greedy choices they have made.

Racial divides cannot be allowed to escalate into crimes against humanity, genocide, war crimes or crimes of aggression. The underlying conditions of inequality and social desperation that intersected with the pandemic have to be addressed. More social explosions are likely but there is no need for a state of emergency or massive spending on excessive military deployment. Instead, resources must be channelled into immediate food relief, food sovereignty pathways and a universal basic grant (#UBIGNOW). The grant can be designed and implemented without increasing public debt, particularly if it is linked to progressive taxation.

Now is the time for bold, systemic solutions to improve the lives of the majority and continue our unfinished radical non-racial project. South Africa must move beyond ANC factionalism and failure.

Daily Maverick, 16 July 2021

International Mandela Day: Respondent to Keynote Address of President Cyril Ramaphosa, 18 July 2021

THANK YOU FOR THE INVITATION.

Admission: I am critical of the president, the government and the ruling ANC Alliance. I accepted this invitation to continue a critical, respectful and honest engagement on the challenges facing the country by reflecting on the legacy of Nelson Mandela.

1.

Acclaimed African scholar Mahmood Mamdani, who was expelled by Idi Amin together with other Asians in the early 1970s from Uganda because of his ethnic identity, but who is now back in the country after Ugandans turned against Amin's racist madness, has published a recent book entitled *Neither Settler Nor Native: The Making and Unmaking of Permanent Minorities* which is relevant to our engagement this evening.

Mamdani lauds the importance of the non-racial tradition in South Africa. More than most countries that experienced colonialism he argues that non-racialism in South Africa provides the intellectual and political foundations to build a truly decolonial society. In his view, it provides the basis for a refusal of the divisions of apartheid whether economic, cultural, or political, and he essentially, in my view, affirms the radical non-racial tradition as a basis for a decolonial identity

Now, Nelson Mandela did not invent the non-racial tradition but he was actually a product of it and he made a very powerful contribution to it on his own terms both theoretically and practically. The Mandela legacy is definitely part of the decolonial cannon. If we look at Mandela's ideological formation, he shifted from African nationalism to revolutionary nationalism and then to what I would call emancipatory humanism.

Emancipatory humanism is about an existential journey to confront the dehumanised subject; it is also about confronting the demons of racism in all of us. Mandela is one of the best examples of emancipatory humanism. We must appreciate he was human, he wasn't a god, he was not perfect but he is one of our best examples of humanising the self and advancing a decolonial self which is a very important contribution to our tradition of non-racialism. It is visible in how he embraced all races.

Non-racialism in South Africa exists at different levels. There's formal non-racialism, a core value of our constitutional order and enshrined in our Constitution. Then there is what I would call a historical inheritance of people's non-racialism based on a people's history of struggle. This lives in the everyday memory and fabric of our society. A people's non-racialism is what courses through our everyday life forcing us to confront our own racism and dehumanisation. However, there is a third level at which non-racialism exists in our society. This is the non-racialism claimed by the ANC-led Alliance, the proclaimed leader of society.

In the context of the crisis in South African society, the crisis of nation building and non-racial democracy, the ANC-led Alliance has to take stock of its commitment to non-racialism. From where I stand in society there's a gulf, there is a distance, between non-racialism and the ANC-led Alliance. It would seem that the ANC Alliance is more and more the harbinger of hatred, division, ethnicity, racism and all forms of polarisation in our society. As it continues to claim to lead society it seems more and more like a pariah, an anti-constitutional force and an anti-democratic force in our society. This moment calls for deep reflection in the ANC Alliance. When did it lose its commitment to non-racialism; when it started referring to non-African groups as minorities? When it continued racial classification in governance? Did it lose its non-racialism when it embraced market orthodoxy that has continued racialised accumulation? Did it lose its non-racialism in the moment of Zumafication ... a hard and difficult process has to be inaugurated.

2.

The decolonial Mandela is not just about radical non-racialism as decolonial scholar Sabelo Ndlovu Gatsheni shows us through his reading of Mandela's life and legacy. Mandela represents a challenge, an antithesis to the paradigm of war. The paradigm of war in Gatsheni's view is derived from imperial/colonial/apartheid hierarchies, classifications and divisions.

In the Rivonia trial Nelson Mandela said: 'I have cherished the ideal of a democratic and free society in which all persons live together in harmony and with equal opportunities. It is an ideal which I hope to live for and to achieve. But if needs be, it is an ideal for which I am prepared to die.' This quote is on the walls of the Constitutional Court as well.

What we see in Mandela's political life is a shift from the guerrilla fighter to the agent of the paradigm of peace, but without abandoning his principles and cherished beliefs. This, I believe, he would have advanced even if he had not received the Nobel Peace prize with De Klerk in 1993. Mandela's historical contribution was to advance the paradigm of peace: this is about democracy, human rights, racial reconciliation and what I have called an emancipatory humanism. It is this paradigm of peace that also clashed with Sani Abacha in Nigeria in the early 1990s when Mandela raised his voice in defense of Ken Saro-Wiwa and other activists. He stood up in defence of their human rights. Of course, many have argued that Mandela's commitment to human rights in international relations and global politics was naive but actually he has been trailblazing.

The architecture supporting and defending human rights has been evolving in our global power structure. The Rome Statute was adopted in 1998 which provides for the International Criminal Court. It provides for redress against crimes of genocide, crimes against humanity, war crimes or crimes of aggression. In the legal opinion that we have solicited over the past few days given the situation in the country, I've come here today to say to the president that South Africa must not withdraw from the Rome Statute. President Zuma did make moves in that regard.

I have also not come here today to demand that the president pursue the issue of crimes of genocide, crimes against humanity and crimes of aggression because South Africa over the past few days has narrowly averted an orchestrated race war. Recently, many communities were under siege particularly in KwaZulu-Natal, but the Indian community was under siege because of its Indian identity; it faced a racialised onslaught that could have led to genocidal violence in the context of extremely toxic social media. The state failed to protect and guarantee the constitutional rights of Indians in these communities. It also failed to guarantee the rights of African people. Many of these historically Indian communities became cauldrons of fear, suspicion and defensiveness. While the situation is volatile in some areas, some level of calm is returning in other parts of the province. We have stepped back from the brink.

I'm not going to remind this audience about the historic and heroic role of the Indian community in the struggle for national liberation. I really do not believe that it makes a difference or has any value any more. Maybe this is my cynicism but what's important is that what has happened over the past few days cannot happen again in a country that considers itself a modern, constitutional democracy.

I fully support the investigations into the murders in Phoenix. Those responsible for the killings must be held accountable. However, this is not enough. I would like to argue and propose that consideration be given to resourcing and giving a mandate to the South African Human Rights Commission (SAHRC) to pursue an inquiry into what happened in KwaZulu-Natal between African and Indian peoples. This has to be a mandate to pursue a just and a non-racial peacebuilding agenda. The HRC should go to all hot-spot communities now and start such a process of inquiry, of dialogue and make recommendations to parliament for a just and non-racial peace building agenda. This is consistent with the Mandela peace paradigm.

3.

There are several narratives swirling around this complex historical moment and events of the past few days. My own view is that the unfolding mass-scale violence we all witnessed was an expression of a deep social ecological crisis in our society.

Mr President, you preside over and lead an unviable and desperate society that has been in the making for the past two and a half decades of ANC rule. Sixty-five per cent of national income is in the hands of 10% of income earners, 80% of wealth is in the hands of 10% of the population. This is not a viable society; critical social science affirms there is a direct relationship between inequality, social polarisation and crisis. I do not have time to go into examples.

We have been a desperate society before Covid-19, deeply polarised around inequality fault-lines and this has worsened during Covid-19. It is time that we do not place the interests of business above society, it is time we do not place the elite interests of the ANC above society. Society has to come first, now!

President Joe Biden in his inaugural address used a framing of multiple crises facing American society. What the president was doing was evoking critical social science and based on that analysis he committed and has advanced a consistent agenda to build an inclusive society which even includes tackling wealth and income disparities.

South Africa is facing multiple crises: climate shocks (a drought that has lingered), the pandemic, economic crisis and a worsening crisis of democracy. Nelson Mandela faced a crisis-ridden society and what's clear from his paradigm of peace is that he was committed to addressing those crises through building and advancing an inclusive society. Here the Freedom Charter stands out, the RDP stands out; but crucial is the idea of people's power. In Nelson Mandela's *Long Walk to Freedom* the idea of street committees is really about deepening democracy and that's what we need to do today.

In this regard there are three important practical suggestions I'd like to make. The first relates to state failure regarding food relief in South Africa. Mr President, the mechanisms that you've used; the Solidarity Fund and the Department of Social Development have failed. The scale and the magnitude of the hunger crisis in South Africa is huge. We have about 30 million people in food stress. During level 5 lockdown we actually witnessed a trend of supermarkets being attacked and food trucks being hijacked. This was an indicator of levels of desperation, but what we also saw was communities filling the gap when they stepped up to meet their needs through soup kitchens, community gardens, informal trading networks, subsistence fishing and so on. The important point here is that we need to democratise the food relief effort in the context of the crisis. We engaged with the disaster management people through our National Food Crisis Forum and we realised that the Disaster Management Act provides for civil society to be part of the disaster management response; involving local government, civil society organisations, aid organisations and even business organisations who could all work together to address the humanitarian crisis. There is a legal basis for it and if you go this route, you'll be ensuring that solidarity in action comes to the fore between the state and society; you would be making the new social contract for South Africa.

The second idea is support for food sovereignty pathways to feed villages, communities, towns and cities. Our drought was a major climate shock in South Africa and in the midst of that drought we built the SAFSC. We have argued consistently on this platform that we need a new food system that is controlled by small-scale farmers and communities and consumers; that is deeply ecological; that is culturally appropriate and that is healthy. We've also seen now in the context of the violence the destruction of shopping malls; so South Africa cannot be dependent on current food value chains. The world we are going into is a world of multiple shocks and crises and demands that we advance people's food sovereignty. We even have a People's Food Sovereignty Act. We took this to parliament in 2018 but were ignored. Based on food sovereignty hub building work we have been busy with, and which contributed to strengthening some of the community responses to the crisis, we took a proposal to the Solidarity Fund last year, and if they had listened to and worked with us in partnership we would have fed ten million people and laid the basis to expand this in 2021. This was a missed opportunity.

The third idea that we have is the idea of a universal basic income grant. It was heartening to read in today's *Sunday Times* an editorial calling for it. But the *Sunday Times* is really amplifying a campaign that has been carried out across progressive civil society. It's imperative that we put this mechanism in place as a democratic systemic reform that can immediately transition our welfare system. Through our #UBIGNOW campaign we have done two bits of technical economic modelling.[1] It shows we can have a fiscally neutral #UBIGNOW and that it does not have to increase the debt to GDP ratio. We know that it can generate resources for the state, increased revenues through its multiplier and revenue-generating effects. We also know there are numerous financing options that the state could take up including progressive taxation. We have amplified a societal consensus through our campaigning and government needs to catch up.

We need a caring government.

Thank you

---

1   #UBIGNOW policy approach and proposals, available at https://www.safsc.org.za/wp-content/uploads/2021/02/UBIG_Policy-Approach-and-Proposals_FEB2021.pdf, #UBIGNOW Approach and Scenarios document, available at https://www.safsc.org.za/wp-content/uploads/2021/05/ADRS-Fiscally-Neutral-BIG-for-South-Africa-The-Bridge-May-2021.pdf.

Without a Serious Challenge From the Left, the Political Field in South Africa Could See the Emergence of an Extreme Right

THERE IS A SECOND COMING of fascism underway in the twenty-first century that cannot be understood through the conceptual apparatus of interwar twentieth-century fascism. While there is immense value in comparative perspectives on old and new fascism, to highlight continuities and discontinuities, the expression of new authoritarian and fascist forces also has to be studied in the context of a new matrix of historic socio-ecological conditions.

This volume in the Democratic Marxism series entitled *Destroying Democracy: Neoliberal Capitalism and the Rise of Authoritarian Politics* provides a taxonomy to situate the new authoritarian and, in some instances, full-blown neo-fascist forces advancing deliberate reactionary class-based ideological projects. The geographic scope of this analysis provides an optic to appreciate the political economy dynamics shaping the hard-right shift in the world order, in the vanguard of liberal democracy (the US), the largest democracy in the world (India), the largest democracy in Latin America (Brazil) and the most promising democracy in Africa (South Africa).

Crises of neoliberal capitalism and market democracy

Liberal theorists have declared the end of the third wave of democratisation from the early 1970s until the mid-2000s. Beyond this shared insight, Marxists and critical theorists have a very different explanation for the contemporary crisis of democracy. This volume highlights several important historical conditions that need to be taken into account in thinking about the shift to a new hard-right neoliberalism.

First, it is important to utilise a historical perspective to situate the new right and to understand its tendential orientation within moments of general capitalist crisis. The modern right wing has a history going back to the nineteenth century. In the twentieth century, it has been the face of counter-revolution to ward off any challenges to capitalism. Its authoritarian defence of the institutions and social relations of capitalism has spawned the Ku Klux Klan, Italian fascists, German Nazis and military dictatorships in the global South. Each of these reactionary social forces was also shaped by conjunctural and historically specific conditions. There are residues and resurgences of such extreme right-wing forces that we need to understand, but in terms of current realities. The alt-right in the US, for instance, is not the same as the Ku Klux Klan, but bringing the history of the Klan into view helps us appreciate what is new in the contemporary US context and how this is expressed by white nationalist Trumpian politics.

Second, the contemporary civilisational crisis of capitalism is caused by the unbridled financialisation and commodification of neoliberal capitalism on a global scale. The precariousness, inequality, social anomie and deeper systemic crises, such as the global climate breakdown, are happening in a context in which the global ruling classes are committed to defending and continuing the same rationalities of marketised rule. Understanding the specific class projects and crisis dynamics giving rise to the new right is crucial. For instance, market democracy has become both constitutionalised in the interests of transnationalising capital and incapable of being responsive to citizens' needs. More of the same has given rise to the new authoritarian and neo-fascist forces on the march.

Third, the left has been in retreat despite a few breakthroughs and important moments of resistance globally. Since the neoliberal class offensive of the 1980s, labour movements in both the global North and South have been dramatically weakened. The rise of the Workers Party in Brazil and the ANC in South Africa portended prospects for transformative change. However, these forces were primarily halted by the loss of nerve and commitment to deepening mass-based logics of democratisation. As a result, market democracies in both these societies have created the conditions for authoritarian shifts. Brazil has moved to the hard neoliberal right and South Africa's future is not certain, but can very likely end up in the same place. Without a serious challenge from the left, the political field is open for the new right to emerge.

Identity politics and neofascism

The new hard right clings to core tenets of financialised capitalism and its institutions, including globalised financial markets, international trade regimes, private property, corporate power and precarious labour markets. However, in this context, harnessing discontent has meant a revanchism through reactionary identity politics.

Neo-authoritarianism and fascism in the twenty-first century are deeply grounded in forms of exclusivist nationalism – from Britons who want their country back from the European Union, to right-wing Germans, Italians, Greeks and Poles, for instance, who want their countries expunged of refugees and migrants. White nationalism and supremacy are directly involved in exclusionary border regimes in the Euro-American world. Trump's US gave this shift greater momentum.

All of this connects with an ecofascism bent on reproducing a carbon-based capitalism through climate denialism or, in some instances, using the climate crisis to build walls around societies rather than deal with the root causes of the worsening climate crisis. In South Africa, the EFF wants a South Africa exclusively for Africans. Essentialised racial identities are at work in these nativist nationalisms.

At the same time, fundamentalist religion is also constitutive of reactionary identities. Charismatic Christians in Bolivia, Brazil and the US have converged with patriarchal white nationalists. Hindu fundamentalism (India), Islamism (Iran, Saudi Arabia, Afghanistan and Pakistan) and Zionism (Israel) are all advancing neo-fascist exclusionary class projects.

Identity politics, with its emphasis on the particular accentuation of difference, standing against subaltern universals (or shared principles of solidarity) and rejection of structural social relations like class, has fed directly into the rise of neofascism. This is not to argue against respecting cultural diversity, secularism and pluralism. However, the accentuation, weaponising and constitution of obscurantist identities, as part of hyper-exclusionary nationalisms, are both anti-democratic and central to the making of a new twenty-first century fascism and authoritarian politics.

Defending democracy by and for the people

In this volume, the chapters collectively and individually illustrate the varying ways in which neoliberal capitalism undermines democracy. Corporate control of politics has reached fever pitch and its destructive forces are undoing the very states that made its rise possible. With the rise of authoritarian politics and neo-fascist parties, there is new-fangled urgency.

Democracy must be reclaimed but also remade. Modern democracy has always been part of a people's history of struggle and grew up alongside capitalism. Democracy has given us the basic freedoms, rights and powers we have accumulated and enjoyed over the past few centuries. At the same time, democracy is always subject to contestation; it is never complete and never fully arrives given the nature of class and popular struggle.

Rising mass movements defending democracy, advancing climate justice and challenging financialised inequalities face the challenge of advancing systemic alternatives that amount to new class and popular projects that can provide a new direction to societies beyond the impasse of market democracies. A new left orientation of constituting power from below, through building democratic alternatives controlled by citizens, is crucial. This includes commoning, solidarity economies, food sovereignty, democratic planning and more.

At the same time, international solidarities are absolutely essential. The global civilisational crisis of capitalism requires a global response. A mass-based and institutionalised climate justice movement is crucial as part of a larger, new internationalism of the left that confronts the oppressions of the new authoritarianism and carbon-based ecofascism.

Rather than seeing the state, civil society and the economy as given, the balance of power among them must be scrutinised and analysed to push forward an expansion of democracy beyond market democracy. To reclaim a more expansive democracy, new state institutions must be created, ones that secure the public good and deepen the logic of democratisation from below. New forms of democratic political instruments need to be invented that enable citizens and movements to define political agendas and hold politicians accountable. A new generation of post-neoliberal, post-national liberation and post-social democratic left parties need to emerge on the world stage, deeply informed by the lessons of failed market democracies.

Moreover, left politicians must serve the publics that elect them and practise an ethics of accountability, transparency and enabling citizens' power. Government officials and public servants must be re-inspired and educated to serve the public. And most of all, states must once again regulate and advance democratic planning of the economy, such that corporate power is subordinated to the needs of human beings and nature.

Daily Maverick, 18 November 2021.

The Challenge of Left Renewal in the Context of Worsening Capitalist Crisis

The Left Project and Post-National Liberation Politics

POST-APARTHEID, WHAT ARE the dilemmas facing a left project in South Africa? This essay looks at the future of the left project. Like all twentieth century revolutions, our revolution concentrated within it multiple utopias. The Freedom Charter embodied a vision of post-apartheid capitalism either social democratic or revolutionary nationalist (strong state interventionist), as well as a vision of Sovietised socialism.

The pendulum and history

In the 1990s, these alternatives were overtaken by history. The Soviet Union collapsed while postcolonial Third World statism and social democracy were hegemonised by the global restructuring of capital. Although neoliberal capitalism has blatantly failed, it is not given that the pendulum will swing back to the old left project.

Joe Slovo inaugurated a process of Marxist renewal within the SACP. This came from above, came rather late and was a mere echo of various left critiques of Stalinised socialism. However, Slovo's authorisation of renewal inaugurated and informed attempts by the SACP to remake itself. The renewal was uneven and ultimately failed. It did not succeed in constructing an internal political life consistent with a vision of a post-Stalinist socialism. What has emerged is a resurgence of orthodoxy, bureaucratic centralism, populism and old-style vanguardism.

Re-finding the left compass

Renewing Marxism in the SACP could have taken the left project beyond national liberation politics and recast the compass of the left project around a new socialism relevant for the times. A re-Stalinised socialism in the SACP shares with nationalist statism and social democracy an elitist ideological and political conception: social transformation must happen from above, the people must be liberated from the outside, the line must come to the masses, and the people must be brought into history rather than make their own history. Such an approach is dangerous for democracy, and under current global and national conditions prone to failure.

The broad left in South Africa cannot immunise itself from global transformations on the left. The rising new global left is preoccupied with inventing alternatives to transform global capitalism. This global left represents a fourth historical wave of left politics, distinct from the First, Second, and Third Internationals. It is a left shaped by Marx's humanism and the many non-scientific utopian socialisms; it is grounded in a historical critique of Stalinised socialism and attempts to draw lessons from its failures. It is conscious of the technocratic statism and neoliberalisation of social democracy and postcolonial projects, in tune with various currents of anarchist socialism, radical feminism and ecosocialisms, and at the forefront of challenging the structural power of transnational capital. It is truly a celebration of dissidence and a challenge to the arrogant certainties of the old left projects.

This re-imagining of a self-aware left points to and resonates with the salvaging of an episodic, marginalised, fourth utopia in the Freedom Charter: people's power. It is only with the genuine re-finding of this premise that the left project in South Africa can remake itself for the twenty-first century.

The left project and permanent renewal

The starting points for renewing the left project are two important conceptions in Marxism: (i) in changing historical circumstances we are also changing ourselves, and (ii) the self-emancipating historical subject is at the centre of transformation. This breaks with a static politics and is essentially about permanent renewal. It is about a self-aware praxis grounded in a radical understanding of power relations which is more expansive and goes beyond the old state-centric understanding of power. The new left has to live the change it wants now and not wait for the heroic capture of state power; we have to build while we dream. Another defining aspect of the new left relates to its consistent efforts to create the conditions, spaces and momentum for the self-emancipating protagonist – the people/the citizenry – to extend its power over the economy, the state and the community. It is about fighting and departing from the logic of capital accumulation as we assert the logic of human need and the requirements of nature. For such a politics of permanent renewal and critical self-understanding to take root, the left in South Africa has to remake its politics in fundamental and profound ways. In this regard, some of the following dimensions of left-wing politics in post-apartheid South Africa have to be revisited:

1. The formation of a new left historical bloc for generative politics: if the left is to foster a politics of renewal then it has to stop defining itself in relation to the ANC. A new historical bloc of left forces has to be constituted that has a non-antagonistic relationship to the ANC. The new left has to work consciously with the people to concretely build their capacities for self-emancipation. This will certainly entail embracing some of the progressive reform initiated by the ANC on co-operatives, ward committees, people's housing and so on, but it will also mean giving content to these from below and even going beyond. It will also mean widening the agenda of generative politics to include building alternative media from below to empower with information, draw on organic knowledge and invent new pedagogies of the oppressed. In short, a new left historical bloc has to be invented that advances, embraces and co-exists with various emancipatory projects – some old, some new – while testing the limits of our democracy and widening its horizons.

2. Multiple oppressions under capitalism: a left engaged in a project of permanent renewal has to go beyond merely a class-based understanding of this oppression. We have to recognise multiple oppressions within capitalist social relations. These oppressions are a mainspring for struggles: around the environment; against racial, religious and gender-based discrimination; regarding violence perpetrated against women and children; cultural alienation; new imperialism and so on. In fighting these multiple oppressions, different social forces will come to the fore and at times have to lead society. A new left has to embrace and work with these social forces to challenge and transform capitalism.

3. Rethinking political organisation: in the vanguardist or mass party of the social democratic type there was a failure to build an internal political culture that brought the alternative to life in these institutions. Internal politics was not humanised but instrumentalised. This model of political organisation did not grow conscious cadres but rather produced functionaries. Such organisations were easily bureaucratised and captured by factions. A new type of political organisation has to be developed that speaks to the politics of permanent renewal. Political organisation has to be thought of in minimalist terms. This means that the centre of political life

has to be the people and not the party! If a new left political organisation is to emerge, then it has to embrace and co-exist with various emancipatory projects and this ironically has to be something like the UDF, our movement of movements. In such a political organisation mass membership is not the priority; but rather central to its functioning is the link with the people and the co-ordination of struggles against the multiple oppressions of capitalism. The affiliates (women's groups, community organisations, activist forums, social movements, NGOs in the not-for-profit sector, youth organisations, development projects, trade unions, co-operatives and so on) of such a formation should embody the struggles for emancipation from capitalism, while working with a common vision and a collectively defined programmatic orientation. Such a network form of political organisation is in practice a collective intellectual and, it would seem, the most effective model of a party-movement in motion from below.

4. Global solidarity: our failure to bring the global into the local is a glaring silence. We have not learnt lessons from the failures of the post-colonial left in Africa and have not really tried to understand the new global left. Today in the era of globalising capitalism, people's power more than ever before has to be globalised. In this regard the renewal of the South African left has to rise to the challenge of re-invigorating anti-apartheid global solidarity into post-apartheid solidarity for the transformation of South Africa, Africa and the global South.

Conclusion

This reflection is not intended to solve all the problems and challenges facing the anti-capitalist and pro-socialist left in South Africa. Although neoliberalism is in crisis, only concerted political initiative and struggle from the left can seriously turn the historical tide. We should also accept that the challenges for rebuilding and renewing the left project in South Africa can only be done in a new frame of politics; that is, a post-national liberation politics. This means defining an agenda for generative politics that is broad enough to incorporate progressive aspects of the ANC-led national liberation project, but more importantly advances a set of hegemonising initiatives that democratically wins over society to a left praxis.

More sharply, the left needs to claim its space in the post-apartheid context to ensure that our aspirations and hopes for change are not narrowed to the point where we remain jaded, and even worse, experience a complete loss of confidence in the alternatives we believe in. The time has come to take seriously a new left politics that is about a self-aware political practice, ensuring the people are genuinely at the centre of social transformation, and ultimately about permanent renewal. All the proposals and ideas shared here about this process of renewal are not fully elaborated, but are meant to provoke and invite a constructive debate. They are not dogmatic conclusions.

Amandla Magazine, pilot issue 2, October 2007.

There is a Democratic Left Response to the Global Crisis

OVER THE PAST FEW weeks many commentators have characterised the global crisis as a crisis of the global financial system. The interventions by leading governments in the developed centres to solve this crisis have been foregrounded in public discourse; in the main to manage public perception and ensure public confidence in the financial system does not evaporate.

Many of these interventions, ranging from bail-outs to nationalisation, have been presented as important solutions to save the global financial system. However, in themselves these solutions appear to have merit as confidence-building measures, but do not address what seems like an intractable financial crisis. Over the past few weeks, governments of the world have pledged about $3.2 trillion (with the US government merely pledging $700 billion) while the credit derivatives market, which is at the heart of this crisis, is estimated at $60 trillion dollars.

In all likelihood we are only seeing the tip of the proverbial iceberg in terms of the scale and depth of the crisis. If this unravelling spirals out of control in itself the crisis of the global financial system has the potential to end capitalism. Simply put, the end of financial intermediation means the juggernaut of accumulation collapses and capitalism dies.

Another stream of analysis has gone beyond a narrow problem-solving framework of trying to fix the global financial system. Such an analytical frame has connected the dots and points to a deeper structural crisis. What started out as a sub-prime housing market crash in the US is now a crisis that has reached into the real economy. Talk of recession and revisions in growth forecasts have all captured this trend. Moreover, the worst-case scenario predicted is that of another Great Depression and probably worse than that experienced in the first part of the twentieth century.

However, an old left response to such a scenario would frame the choices for humanity as: capitalism or Sovietised socialism. Echoes of the latter have come out of the ANC-led Alliance economic policy summit recently with neo-Stalinist populists advocating a planning commission, greater centralisation of decision-making around the presidency and a two-tier Cabinet system. In short, the old left response is bent on taking South Africa from a market-led development path under Mbeki to a state-led one under Zuma. In political economy terms this means introducing a state capitalism and probably in their misguided militancy unhinging South Africa from globalising processes; ultimately driving us into a fortress capitalism under the banner of national liberation.

However, a new left approach to the global crisis prompts us to think about a new hypothesis to explain what we are living through. This is a crisis of civilisation, more specifically a crisis of market civilisation. Such a market civilisation has been in the making for the past three decades and is an unrealisable market utopia. Such an insight and critique was first made by Karl Polanyi, one of twentieth century's most discerning economic historians, in his important book *The Great Transformation: The Political and Economic Origins of Our Time*. This text was published in 1944, coincidentally at the same time that the chief ideologue of free market capitalism, Friedrich Hayek, published his book *The Road to Serfdom*.

Polanyi cautioned against the irrationality of a market utopia and the danger it poses to human beings and nature by studying its role in causing World War 1, the rise of fascism, the first five-year plan under Stalin and the collapse in the interwar years. However, unlike Polanyi's time, the free-market utopia of today has been imposed on humanity through four key historical structures: (i) superpower dominance by the US after the Cold War; (ii) liberalisation and deepening integration of global production and financial structures; (iii) the reconstitution of states as internationalised competition states and (iv) a world view that privileges self-regulating markets and individualism, commonly known as neoliberalism. In the context of the civilisational crisis we are witnessing, it is unclear which of these props will be sacrificed to save capitalism. Various commentators, analysts and critical voices are beginning to hint at a post-neoliberal and post-US-dominated world order. This is increasingly chiming with talk within leading business magazines about a new capitalism.

However, change in a post-capitalist direction requires struggle and solutions from the new global democratic left. It actually requires an alternative on the scale of a civilisational alternative. Today the new global democratic left is not as back-footed as the old left was after the collapse of Eastern Europe. Elements of a civilisational alternative have begun to emerge within theoretical discourses and practical political projects. From within the WSF process to national struggles against neoliberalism as in Latin America, parts of Europe and India, various elements of a civilisational alternative are coming to the fore.

First, there is a need for a new global regulatory regime to manage trade and finance structures. Such a regime should not be built on the flawed Bretton Woods system and the WTO, but instead it requires new institutions in which power relations are such that all countries have an equal voice to determine the direction of global development.

Second, given the crisis of neoliberal hegemony and attempts by the US to remake the world in the image of Anglo-American capitalism, a new multipolar world order needs to be constituted around regional development blocs in which the needs of human beings and nature prevail.

Third, a new role for states is needed, based on a recognition that the role of states in national development is not about fixing market failures but that states have to embed markets through regulatory and institutional interventions in financial, labour and land markets at a minimum.

Fourth, national economies have to provide for a third space in which alternative forms of production and consumption can be organised through co-operatives, social enterprises and democratic collectives. This seems to be happening in Canada, Brazil, Venezuela, Argentina and Kerala, India.

Fifth, democracy has to be widened beyond narrow electoralism to ensure democratisation reaches into institutional practices of the state, parliament, mass mobilisation and participatory forms. In short, a new conception of democracy has to prevail in which all citizens can ensure capital is accountable and the people are empowered with the means to control power.

Unfortunately, in the South African context none of the political parties represent such a democratic left alternative. The old left, which snatched the liberation mantle at Polokwane, does not have the political imagination, vision nor alternatives.

Amandla Magazine 5–6, December 2008.

Occupying the Economy

WORKER STRUGGLES IN South Africa have entailed strikes, go-slows, pickets, sit-ins, and in the 1980s unions also utilised worker co-operatives in the context of retrenchments. However, the Mine-Line factory occupation on the West Rand (of Gauteng) is a new tactic on the frontline of worker struggles. It is a direct response to the job losses. South Africa's unemployment rate (over 25%) has inflicted a social crisis, which in other contexts have brought down governments. In Argentina in 2001, an unemployment rate of 20% contributed to bringing down four governments through mass pressure and gave rise to a factory occupation movement involving over 200 enterprises contributing close to 10% of GNP. These worker takeovers have recovered production levels to pre-crisis levels and have transformed property relations from below through worker co-operatives. This movement is gaining strength in the context of the current (2010) global capitalist crisis. The Mine-Line workers' occupation of their factory, a metal engineering and fabrication plant, holds out the potential for a similar movement to emerge in South Africa and for the renewal of worker control in labour politics.

A flawed insolvency process

The Mine-Line factory is located near Soweto, the largely black working-class township of Johannesburg. It employed 110 workers as part of its operations. As a niche manufacturer it produced valves, underground trains for mines, and other customised metal products. In August 2010 the Mine-Line factory experienced a tragedy. Three workers were killed when a boiler machine exploded. Threats to sue the company by the Metal and Electrical Workers Union of South Africa (MEWUSA) and the financial crisis precipitated by the owner led to a unilateral closure of the factory by the employer. According to the liquidator the employer created the financial crisis by borrowing R35 million from ABSA bank and then siphoned off R15 million from the business.

The unfair dismissal of the workers and a failure to pay death benefits to the families of the dead workers enraged the workers. In response the union brought in a liquidator to wind down the company and secure worker benefits (wage and non-wage). However, over the past few months the liquidator has sold off finished products and allowed the employer to remove machinery from the factory without consulting the union and the workers. This prejudicial action by the liquidator came to a head on Wednesday 20 October when Mine-Line workers gathered at their factory to demand an explanation from the liquidator about machinery and proceeds from finished products taken. With the liquidator failing to provide proper verification of assets taken and explanations for why asset stripping was taking place, the workers decided to secure their benefits and jobs by occupying the factory.

Implications

There are several important implications that highlight the wider significance of the Mine-Line factory occupation.

Challenging the responsiveness of the state

In the context of the global economic crisis the ANC-led government placed on the national agenda an initiative called 'Framework for South Africa's response to the international economic crisis'. This framework committed the state to support stressed sectors of the South African economy through financial support for turnaround strategies through the Industrial Development Corporation (IDC) and through training linked to layoff schemes. Engineering is a key sector prioritised in this framework and provides an opportunity for the retrenched Mine-Line workers. However, COPAC, assisting the Mine-Line workers to set up a worker co-operative, has verified that both the IDC stress fund and the training layoff scheme have not supported insolvent enterprises and have not come in to assist with worker takeovers of distressed enterprises. As it stands, the Mine-Line option to convert their factory into a worker co-operative is outside these frameworks. A stressed enterprise is different from one that has stopped production. However, the insolvency laws do provide for an option for the workers to buy out the company. This will require state support and a political struggle to ensure the state is responsive to the needs of the Mine-Line workers through the IDC and the training layoff scheme. It will be critical for these state support programmes to go beyond bailing out capital to support the needs of workers.

Shifting the property relations debate

Post-apartheid South Africa has not developed a transformative approach to property relations. Land reform has been mired in the muck of a market-driven approach, BEE has emphasised deracialising existing capitalist structures to engender a black elite, and the more recent debate on nationalisation has merely degenerated into another front for the factional battles inside the ANC. On the one hand, the SACP has rejected nationalisation of mines, calling it 'state capitalist', and on the other the ANC Youth League is arguing for nationalisation as a necessary and strategic intervention by the so-called developmental state. The Mine-Line Factory occupation takes us beyond the polemics of the ANC-led alliance and gives primacy to the voices of workers. Through debates and deliberations as part of the build up to the factory occupation two approaches have emerged to secure ownership of the factory as part of defending workers' jobs.

The first approach is partial socialisation which requires the state to step in and pay out creditors so that the machines are secured for the Mine-Line workers. The machines and the factory would then be run by the workers through a worker co-operative. State ownership combined with worker control has thus been mooted as one way forward.

A second approach is full socialisation in which the removed machinery is returned, the state pays out creditors their proportionate share as per the liquidation and provides working capital to the workers to re-start production through a worker co-operative. Eventually the worker co-operative reaches an agreement with the state and the assets are placed in the hands of the worker co-operative. Worker ownership and control prevails over the means of production. These transformed property relations, either partial or full socialisation, are the key to achieving the objectives of the factory occupation.

Advancing the solidarity economy movement from below

A BEE approach to co-operatives has not worked. A 2009 baseline study by the DTI confirms this. In 2009 the national Co-operative Registrar's office officially had 22,030 active co-operatives on its list, but the baseline study shows that only 2644 were operational, confirming a survival rate of 12% for the country. Moreover, state control of the emerging co-operative movement has undermined the transformative role co-operatives can play in structural transformation. To address this, a new grassroots transformative movement is emerging from below: a solidarity economy movement. This movement is not yet institutionalised;

but it is a loose activist network, currently advancing, member-driven, values-based and horizontal solidarity link between co-operatives and other socialised economic forms. The Mine-Line factory occupation and takeover to establish a worker co-operative joins various community-based worker co-operatives trying to build a solidarity economy movement from below among the unemployed. Many of these community-based worker co-operatives support the Mine-Line occupation. Moreover, if Mine-Line succeeds in inspiring a factory occupation movement this would be a crucial pillar to strengthen solidarity among the employed and unemployed as social relations are transformed through a solidarity economy movement.

A transformative option for trade union strategy

Trade unionism in post-apartheid South Africa has increasingly lost a commitment to worker control, both as a principle of internal union practice and as a strategy for transformation. Business unionism and democratic corporatist deal-making (through NEDLAC) have become the main preoccupations of mainstream unions. The current ANC government's call for an incomes policy negotiated through NEDLAC further widens the gulf between workplace trade unionism and union bureaucracy at the top. Generally union practice in the mainstream has not stemmed the tide of job losses. Instead, worsening unemployment rates are reflected in shrinking membership and declining member dues. The tactic of worker occupations to defend jobs and advance new socialised property relations brings back worker control to the centre of union politics. It gives unions and workers a new option to advance transformation from below beyond narrow wage-based collective bargaining. It also has the potential to build active civil and community solidarity with workers trying to defend their jobs and transform property relations from below.

Amandla Magazine 17–18, November/December 2010.

Reclaiming a Vision of Hope and a Life of Dignity

IN A SPEECH GIVEN at the first national conference of the Democratic Left, Vishwas Satgar sets out what it stands for, why it is needed and the role it will play in ensuring that 'a collective wisdom frames a new South African future'.

1. Introduction

1.1 After this historical conference, South Africa will not be the same. Over the next few days we will be broadening the horizons of our 17-year-old democracy. We will be adding a new term to the South African political lexicon: Democratic Left.

1.2 I want to talk about this new category but by trying to place into perspective where we are as a country and the world. I am hoping through this contribution South Africa and the world would be much clearer about what the Democratic Left stands for.

1.3 I want to start with a sharp and provocative question: how did Afro-neoliberalism steal the South African dream?

2. How did Afro-neoliberalism steal the South African dream?

2.1 In South Africa the struggle against racial and capitalist oppressions spawned a dream of a liberated South Africa. Such a dream was not just the words in a document called the Freedom Charter it was also the everyday longing of the oppressed majority for a life better than the irrationality of apartheid. It is these multiple yearnings for hope and for dignity that framed the South African post-apartheid dream. This South African dream has not been realised but has been stolen by an indigenised transnational neoliberalism, a neoliberalism with African characteristics. Such an Afro-neoliberalism has remade the accumulation model, state form, state–civil society relations and our international relations. It has imposed a re-imagined present on us. But how did Afro-neoliberalism steal the South African dream?

2.2 The short answer to the preceding question, which is both opportunistic and misleading, is that the glorious NDR was hijacked by a 1996 class project. This explanation, which has become common sense among the mainstream national liberation left, and which has been used to propel a neo-Stalinist populism to the centre of South African politics, does not tell us how the South African dream was stolen. It is inadequate to say the least. Neither was the South African dream stolen by a conspiracy or by the parasitic and corrupt elements in our society.

2.3 The South African dream of hope realised and human dignity was stolen from the people through a new form of class rule. It is a form of class rule that has globalised the South African economy on the terms of transnational capital, has reduced the state to a technical manager of the ubiquitous market and has reduced citizenship to a formal ritual of passive voting. This structural shift had an agent, a champion or more precisely a bloc of popular and class forces. Central to this has been the ANC-led alliance which has made the choices that have brought us to where we are. It has done this as the ruling force in South Africa today. It has chosen to rule South Africa in the interests of transnational capital and not in the interests of the people and ecological web that sustains life. This ANC-led Alliance must take full responsibility for the fear, the despair and deprivation still endured by the majority, particularly the workers and the poor. When millions remain unemployed, when inequality widens, when hunger stalks many households in the land, this is the product of ANC-led Alliance rule. This cannot be blamed on apartheid! Changing one ANC president for another, changing one ANC leader with another is not going to change this. Voting for the ANC at every election is not going to change this.

2.4 This theft of the South African dream has merely plunged South Africa deeper into crisis, a double conjunctural and structural crisis and a double squeeze on democracy.

3. *South Africa's double conjunctural and structural crisis: Afro-neoliberal dystopia and the global civilisational crisis*

3.1 Post-apartheid South Africa moved in a straight historical line from one of the most heinous, unjust and offensive social systems in the world called apartheid to Afro-neoliberalism. This is the big irony of national liberation. This great domestic conjunctural leap has been a great leap into dystopia. The deepening of the South African economy's immersion into global financial, production and trade structures through macro-economic adjustment has produced a country with one of the highest unemployment rates in the world, obscene inequality, a deepening ecological crisis and growing hunger. Post-apartheid neoliberal South Africa is in a conjunctural crisis in which a capitalist pattern of development is not able to meet the needs of the people and the ecological web of life. It is a South Africa that is not viable.

3.2 South Africa is not exceptional. Despite the specificity of Afro-neoliberalism, the world over has been locked into a neoliberal trajectory of development over the past few decades. This globalised expansion of capitalism on a global scale has placed finance capital in the driving seat of global restructuring. The analogue for this is what happened in the 1920s and 1930s sometimes referred to as the Great Depression.

Ironically, under conditions of the Great Depression the world witnessed the rise of fascism. Today the world is in the grip of neoliberal dogma and superpower imperialism. Actually, I would like to contend that transnational neoliberalism is the face of a new global fascism in which the rule of capital prevails on a planetary scale. Its own extremism is also engendering other extremes like religious fundamentalism, xenophobia and racism for instance.

3.3 However, besides transnational neoliberalism driving a global restructuring process in the interests of transnational capital it has also brought about a civilisational shift. It is about a civilisation of endless capitalist accumulation at the expense of human life, the ecological web of life and even democracy. In short, the crisis of transnational neoliberalism today due to the unravelling of global financial markets, which is a conjunctural crisis, is also a civilisational crisis. It is a civilisational crisis that could lead to the demise of planetary life in all its forms. This conjunctural and civilisational crisis has also added to the crisis of a globalised South Africa. A country which is tied into volatile global capitalist circuits of accumulation and which has made itself a willing node of reproducing capital and its exclusions. As a result, it has brought to our shores the loss of one million jobs. Trevor Manuel's macro-economic policy did not work! Afro-neoliberalism has not worked. This is South Africa's second crisis.

3.4 All indications globally suggest that through the G20, the Cancun Summit, the WEF and even the crisis response of the United States the global ruling class is not willing to define a world beyond capitalism and its total crisis. The solutions that go to the root of the global conjunctural and civilisational crisis are not on the agenda.

4. South Africa's double squeeze on democracy

4.1 Historical democracy has never been part of capitalism. There is no organic or pre-given link between democracy and capitalism. In fact, modern democracy grew out of popular struggles alongside the development of capitalism. This is the case in South Africa as well. Apartheid capitalism never gave us democracy; but instead the people (the workers and the poor) have struggled for it. It is a product of sacrifice, of human will and a passion for liberation from oppression. It is precious because it is essentially about rule by and for the people. It is not about rule by capital.

4.2 The neoliberalisation of South Africa over the past 17 years has not produced a democracy responsive to the needs of the people and the ecological web. The internal re-engineering of democracy has produced the first squeeze against democracy. First, the disembedding and deterritorialisation of the market has utopianised the market. It has made the market our present and our future. The trap and cage of the market master narrative is profoundly undemocratic. It has been propagated in our public sphere such that its values of greed, possessive individualism and competition are hegemonic. It has become naturalised in everyday South African life. The values of Afro-neoliberalism guide our everyday social choices and has produced a dog-eat-dog society. In this way it closes and it ends history at the same time. There is no alternative. Now human beings in South Africa and the world over love to fantasise, to dream and rearrange reality through hoping for more and for something better. Without this disposition an intrinsic part of what makes us human is killed. To dream of a better world and South Africa based on hope and dignity is a use value. It is outside capitalism. But the undemocratic and authoritarian nature of neoliberalism wants to take this away from us. It is narrowing democracy in a way that may not be visible but is actually terrifying.

4.3 Second, and part of the domestic squeeze against democracy, has been a narrowing of the boundaries of democracy and the meaning of citizenship. Our dream of a people's democracy has been shrunk from the triad of strong representative, associational and participatory democracy dynamically working together, to a form of weak representational democracy. Our politicians have become technocrats in this context merely to serve the market and ultimately the power of capital. Politicians must manage market democracy such that the juggernaut of accumulation is not constrained and growth is realised at all costs. This means a shallow performance or semblance of democracy is enough. The index of electoral voting is a measure of market democracy. A free and fair election with a high voter turnout is adequate to legitimate the rule of capital and give a formal meaning to citizenship: I am a voter. Actually, in this context we are not citizens but still subjects of capital!

4.4 The external squeeze on democracy emanates from the restructuring of the South African state. Besides globalising the economy, a globalised state has also reduced democratic space. This has happened through locking the South African state into a global power structure serving and reproducing the rule of transnational capital. The WTO, IMF, World Bank, G20, WEF, and the UN are all crucial to transnational policy making. These institutions are not there to serve global citizenship but to ensure global capitalism thrives. South Africa is a key player in all these institutions. Through its participation in this global power structure South Africa transmits a global consensus on what capital wants back into the domestic context. A weak representative democracy is literally a transmission belt of this global consensus.

5. *Redefining the category left: Authoritarian left versus democratic left*

5.1 Today's Conference of the Democratic Left (CDL) has a profound historical significance. It is a platform that is inaugurating the beginning of a left shift in South African politics. However, for the character of this shift to be understood we have to provide a distinctiveness to our identity as a Democratic Left. What are the *differentia specifica* or specific characteristics of who we are? What makes us a Democratic Left? This is an important question for this conference and process. I want to suggest that the best way to understand who we are is by distinguishing ourselves from the authoritarian national liberation left.

5.2 So then what are the specific characteristics of an authoritarian national liberation left? Simply there are three defining characteristics. First, the authoritarian national liberation left is implicated directly and indirectly, consciously or consciously, intentionally or unintentionally, in engendering the double crisis of South Africa and the double squeeze on South African democracy. It is a left not transforming capitalism, but trying to manage it even through sacrificing democracy. It is a left not willing to go beyond it. This has and will express itself either as neoliberal variants of state capitalism, social democracy or African capitalism. The Democratic Left on the other hand is seeking transformative alternatives to the double crisis of South Africa and is seeking to renew democracy as a weapon against capitalism. The Democratic Left is anti-capitalist.

5.3 Second, the authoritarian national liberation left is locked in a state-centric practice. Society must be engineered from above and through the state. The coercive apparatus of the state, its intervention capacity, must be harnessed to bring change to the people. The people are passive recipients of what is deemed in their best interests. The Democratic Left on the other hand is seeking to democratise and embed the state in civil society. It is about building the capacity of the people, particularly the working class and the poor from below, to lead societal change. It is about a relational understanding of the state in which the power of the people determines the power of the state.

5.4 The third defining characteristic of the Democratic Left is about our vision of hope and dignity for South Africa. Unlike the authoritarian national liberation left our vision is not technocratic or defined by an ideological vanguard. Our vision is people driven. This then speaks to how we construct a vision.

6. *Capitalism, the enemy of hope and dignity: Guidelines for reclaiming an anti-capitalist vision of hope and dignity*

6.1 The Freedom Charter once upon a time embodied a vision of hope and dignity for South Africa. In the light of South Africa's double crisis and double squeeze on democracy it is a hollow vision. This calls forth the need for a new South African vision of hope and dignity, a genuine anti-capitalist vision. For us as the Democratic Left it means a people-driven South African vision of hope and dignity that emerges from below. This implies a self-conscious practice guided by the following:

6.2 First, to develop a South African vision of hope and dignity necessitates an appreciation that history does not have a predetermined outcome. There are no certainties that capitalism will end up in a post-capitalist world. At the same time, this necessitates an appreciation of having a utopian orientation in our practice. It means being conscious of the passions, dreams and aspirations among the people that frame a vision of hope and dignity. It means taking seriously and being attentive to the expressions of people's utopian ambitions as expressed through various cultural forms like music, art, poetry, architecture, essays, stories and so on for a life world beyond capitalism.

6.3 Second, that a South African vision of hope and dignity, a utopian dimension to Democratic Left practice is born out of struggles and is therefore concrete. It has to be a vision forged on the frontlines and battlefronts against the multiple oppressions of capitalism. It is a vision that has to anticipate the making of another South Africa possible and necessary by articulating a grassroots appreciation of what it means to build a South Africa beyond and outside capitalism. It has to be a vision shaped and formed by the values, aspirations and alternative understandings that have emerged in grassroots struggles. All we can do is create the conditions for these voices to emerge from below to articulate this vision in a coherent way.

6.4 Third, and flowing from the preceding point, is that we do not have the answers and do not have a blueprint for the future. As a political process we will create the conditions for the social character of knowledge to prevail. We will learn from and with the people about the way forward beyond capitalism. The Mine-Line factory occupation is a clear example of this. Such a learning process will ensure a collective intellectual endeavour of equals prevails inside the CDL process. Workers, street traders, the unemployed, academics and so on will learn from each other and ensure a collective wisdom frames a new South African future.

Amandla!
Long live the Democratic Left!
Another South Africa is possible!
Forward to a people-driven vision of hope and dignity for South Africa!

Pambazuka News, 27 January 2011.

NUMSA Moment Leads Left Renewal

THE POSTCOLONIAL LEFT IN Africa has been savagely defeated over the past few decades. Southern Africa in particular was a Cold War battleground, with proxy wars and destabilisation.

The Cold War did not end, however, on the battlefields of Angola or with the signing of the Nkomati Accord; rather, it ended with the assassination of Chris Hani, general secretary of the SACP, on 10 April 1993. Hani's assassination drew to a close a dangerous era of global geopolitics and was meant to mark the defeat of South Africa's left and working class.

Two decades of ANC-led neoliberalisation, which has surrendered democracy, development and state formation to capital, consolidated the strategic defeat of the left and working class in South Africa. The NUMSA moment and process, led by South Africa's largest (more than 330,000 members) and most militant trade union, is all about confronting this strategic defeat. It is about a battle to determine the future of South Africa and reclaim the strategic initiative for the country's working class.

The stakes are high. There are intensifying attempts to destabilise NUMSA. This includes disciplining it within its federation, COSATU; squeezing it through the Department of Labour; the formation of a rival metalworkers' union by forces aligned to the ANC and SACP; and the assassination of three NUMSA shop stewards in KwaZulu-Natal on the eve of the NUMSA-convened symposium with left parties and movements, among other pressures.

The assassination of the NUMSA shop stewards is similar to the violence unleashed on workers in 2012 at Marikana. Such violence attempts to end democratic politics and crushes dissent. The undermining of the NUMSA initiative by the dominant political forces will determine whether we are becoming an authoritarian postcolonial African country, like Zimbabwe, or whether we have a future as a vibrant, plural and transformative democracy.

We are at a turning point: we face either the common ruin of all, or the maturation of our democracy. With Marikana, the economic and political consensus of the post-apartheid order, favouring capital, has been unhinged.

Madiba is gone and the phase of national reconciliation is past us, but we have achieved a commitment to a constitutional democracy grounded in egalitarian values, non-racialism, non-sexism and a broad conception of democracy.

At the same time, as the ANC unravels and loses its grip on power, it has to appreciate it will be held to account in the future for what it does in the present. The Arab Spring and the rise of a democratic left in Latin America have been part of the challenges to authoritarian neoliberal capitalism, and are instructive.

The maturation of South Africa's democracy requires open, democratic and fair contestation at all levels. Ideological contestation from the democratic left and right is authorised by South Africa's Constitution, so the emergence of NUMSA's left initiative has a legitimate, democratic right to exist.

NUMSA's right to pursue its decisions to break with the ANC-led Tripartite Alliance, withdraw electoral support for the ANC, build a united front and explore the formation of a workers' party or movement for socialism, derives from its appreciation of history and the role workers have played in the making of South Africa. When NUMSA looks into the past, it appreciates three historical developments as the basis for its political decisions:

- The Freedom Charter, the programmatic cornerstone of the ANC-led liberation movement, was embraced by workers but has not been realised. NUMSA believes in the national liberation commitments made in the charter: to build people's power, bring the state into transformation, including nationalisation, and the centrality of the principles of non-racialism and non-sexism. It refuses to accept apologia from the ANC about apartheid being determining of the present. Instead, NUMSA appreciates contingency in history, as expressed through the choices made by the ANC to abandon the Freedom Charter and embrace global capitalist restructuring and BEE over the past two decades. NUMSA is fully aware of the costs of this to workers and the African majority.
- NUMSA is aware of the militant role and tradition of shopfloor politics in the fight against apartheid. It is alive to the struggles of the vibrant shop stewards' movement, which it was part of, that confronted racism in the workplace, reached out to communities and built modern industrial unionism. The independence of the labour movement, its unifying role and the struggles it led, were necessary conditions for the end of apartheid. Hence NUMSA defends independent labour politics in COSATU and the need to ensure labour as a democratising force is not compromised.
- COSATU is one of the few labour movements in the world to develop a

capacity for strategic politics. In the 1990s, this expressed itself as a social-democratic agenda for labour: the RDP, the ANC-led alliance, and neo-corporatist bargaining, driven by class struggle, through the NEDLAC. NUMSA knows this strategy has been defeated, hence the need for a new initiative from the socialist labour left.

It is in this context that NUMSA hosted a symposium of left parties and movements to learn about left politics in the world today and to inform its political decision-making on a strategic way forward. It hosted the leading left forces in the world, either in power, in opposition or in resistance. The symposium included themes such as left understandings of capitalism's crises and limits, strategies of transformative resistance, and the nature of political forms. Consistent with NUMSA's tradition of worker control, these deliberations were a moment of intense political education for the union, the united front it is building and left forces generally.

The theme of the crises of capitalism was articulated by NUMSA itself in describing South Africa's post-apartheid political economy, but the dispossessions, inequality, ecological destruction, hollowing out of democracy and general crisis of contemporary capitalism were also brought to the fore in various presentations by international participants.

Essentially, the new global left is struggling against a neoliberal capitalism that is increasingly authoritarian and driven by a logic that will destroy all planetary life forms. This new left is resolute in defending democracy against corporate capture and ensuring it is utilised for transformation. This perspective stood out in the contributions from Latin America, the region in the world going furthest in breaking with neoliberal capitalism.

The jaded left debate in South Africa – reform versus revolution – was challenged by various strategies of transformative resistance as shared at the symposium:
- mass-driven participatory democracy (such as neighbourhood councils) to re-embed the state and secure national sovereignty as in Bolivia, Venezuela and Ecuador;
- advancing the solidarity economy and networks as in Brazil, Venezuela and Greece;
- food sovereignty, to ensure countries can feed themselves (Bolivia and Ecuador), and through the land struggles of the Landless Workers' Movement of Brazil;

- discourses on the rights of nature (Bolivia and Ecuador);
- nationalisation of key sectors of the economy;
- new forms of regionalisation, including a new vision of Europe, as articulated by Syrizia, the leading opposition party in Greece; and
- strengthening trade union independence and solidarity across borders through left forums (such as the Sao Paulo Forum and the Asian Left Conference), movement-to-movement links and regional left parties such as the Party of the European Left.

These all provide alternatives to the left of twentieth-century social democracy.

Over the past three decades, various labour movements have spawned workers' parties – examples are South Korea, Zimbabwe and Zambia. The NUMSA symposium scrutinised these experiences to understand the limits and lessons to be learned. A striking aspect here was recognition that communist vanguard parties have been eclipsed by new left political forms: electoral parties (Germany), party movements (Brazil), left fronts (Greece, Uruguay) and movements for socialism (Bolivia).

The NUMSA symposium is one of many crucial steps to unite South Africa's rather dogmatic and fragmented left. NUMSA and its allies are imagining a new socialism, with different premises, various historical reference points, new conceptions of strategy, and a serious rethink of political forms. It is leading a cutting-edge process of left renewal. Not only was it inspired by its international guests but also inspired them.

NUMSA is not building its process on individuals, like a Hugo Chávez, but on worker control, power and capacity. NUMSA is at the forefront of thinking about a new future for South Africa, in which workers play a central role, democracy is strengthened and transformation happens.

Mail & Guardian, 21 August 2014.

Between Crisis and Renewal: Where to for South Africa's Left?

IN OCTOBER 2015, South Africa was rocked by over two weeks (commencing on 14 October) of student protests. These protests shut down most universities, led to violent confrontations between police and students (most notably at parliament and with a march of thousands of students on the Union Buildings), and vocalised demands that President Zuma address the call for free higher education, insourcing and a moratorium on fee increases for 2016. Twenty-one years into post-apartheid democracy a new generation of university student activists openly rebelled against the ANC government's neoliberal fiscal cutbacks of public universities and reclaimed the importance of public goods. The use of mass mobilisation and social media, such as #FeesMustFall, led some commentators to suggest the Arab Spring moment had arrived in South Africa. Students themselves in their assemblies and messaging also discoursed in the language of revolution. This manifestation of resistance is far from over and cannot be isolated. It has to be located in the crisis of national liberation politics and renewal of a new South African left.

After World War 2, national liberation politics captured much of the left imagination. For the South African liberation movement, the 1980s were decisive years in which the internal and external movements consolidated their struggle against the apartheid state. The future seemed poised for a radical alternative. What is often not acknowledged, however, is that national liberation politics was actually exhausted by the 1980s (Amin, 1994: 105–148). The Bandung project's anti-colonial and revolutionary nationalisms came unhinged by their own internal limits and the shifting relations of imperial force. This crisis of national liberation politics existed alongside the collapse of the Soviet Union. Moreover, the neoliberalisation of social democracy forced the left into defensive struggles to protect gains achieved under Keynesian-welfare capitalism. Since 1980 global neoliberal restructuring completely remade the ideological and political landscape. The defeats endured by the left in this conjuncture added to the confusion of left politics and identity. Coupled with earlier horrors, strategic defeats and political shortcomings this further contributed to the left's discredited twentieth-century inheritance. In this context revolutionary nationalist, communist and social democrat are all anachronistic labels and meaningless slogans to the generation of youth rewriting history through their recent protests. In this article, I look at the crisis of the South African left and explore the possibilities for its renewal.

For even as the twentieth-century variants of left alternatives to capitalism have waned, we see new manifestations of resistance struggles. Global neoliberal restructuring has given rise to a new cycle of global resistance engendering a renewed global left imagination, new practices of strategic politics, alternative forms of mass power, the rethinking of our political instruments and an articulation of transformative systemic alternatives (Harnecker, 2015; Panitch et al., 2012). This cycle is punctuated by the social movements in Latin America, the institutional left experiences from the Workers Party in Brazil to Chavistas in Venezuela to Syriza in Greece, the Arab Spring, Occupy Wall Street and the transnational activism of global networks, movements and the WSF. In these experiences there have also been defeats, setbacks and challenges. But most important for the left is its new acknowledgement of the complexity of transformation and the growing sophistication of its sense of the diversity of contexts, the timing and democratic co-ordination of multiple confrontations – this instead of the mere mimicking of a one-size-fits-all model of change as a basis of resistance. In fact, taken together all these new experiences provide important reference points for building a vital anti-authoritarian new left in South Africa.

When South Africa secured its democratic transition in 1994, the South African national liberation left was largely shaped and influenced by the revolutionary nationalist, communist and social democratic traditions of the twentieth century, which provided it with a template, identity and grammar. At the same time, the liberation movement developed and translated these influences into a South African discourse shaped by local conditions. The ANC-SACP-COSATU Alliance both expressed and further evolved this ideological orientation: the ANC championed the national question and liberation for all South Africans from apartheid, the SACP evidenced a vanguardist and Sovietised imagination, and COSATU's populist worker-controlled socialism was heavily influenced by social democracy. The legacies of these conceptions of left politics continue to influence left movements in South Africa, even as many try to wrench themselves free. This challenge for contemporary left politics in South Africa is also explored in this article.

The crisis of the national liberation left in South Africa

Central to understanding the crisis of the national liberation left is the question of working-class hegemony. Many commentators and analysts work with a static conception of hegemony in which the South African political scene is reduced to the unassailable power of the ANC and a naturalised hegemony transcending all conjunctural shifts (Marais, 2011: 388–424). Linked to this is a failure to appreciate the necessary conditions for maintaining class hegemony and a tendency to read the ANC's continued electoral successes as an indicator of such class hegemony.

In fact, contrary to this understanding working-class hegemony of the post-apartheid order organised through the ANC-led Alliance was actually a short-lived affair. The ideological project of working-class leadership of society through national liberation vanguardism was dead by 1996, when the ANC adopted its homegrown strategy of financialised and globalised accumulation, the GEAR macro-economic strategy. The adoption of GEAR not only demonstrated the limits of a vanguardist politics in a world of globalising capitalism, but vitiated working-class agency. For the better part of the last two decades the working class has been increasingly squeezed by the imperatives of neoliberal accumulation: stagnating low wages, precariatisation, high and growing unemployment, poverty that disproportionately affects women, the Marikana massacre of mineworkers and now the destruction of COSATU by an ANC-SACP faction operating in the labour federation (Satgar and Southall, 2015). This is neither hegemonic working-class politics nor can it be defended as left politics. Rather this is about the co-option and undermining of working-class leadership of society to ensure the reproduction of a globalising capitalism and the rule of transnationalising capital through the ANC-led Alliance.

At the same time, corruption and the theft of public money by the ruling party and its deployees in the state have become widespread and systemic. The licence for corruption emanates from the top in the ruling ANC with the sitting president of the country and the ANC, Jacob Zuma, implicated in arms deal corruption, patronage relations to promote members of his family and more recently the R240 million Nkandla scandal in which a palatial rural home was built for him with taxpayer money. Zuma is merely emblematic, the face of a deeper crisis that accompanies corruption: the parasitic creation of a bureaucratic capitalist class with immense social distance from the masses. This disconnect is growing and expressed through violent and non-violent protest actions across civil society, including the recent student protests. In short, the crisis of state and ruling party legitimacy is deepening (McKinley, 2015).

Moreover, contrary to the national liberation myth in which the ANC is synonymous with the people, a people's history and understanding of South Africa's struggle suggests that all progressive South Africans (from all race groups) achieved democracy, whether through resisting pass laws, marrying across colour lines, living defiantly together in some mixed communities and struggling against apartheid through various movements. Resistance, both formal and informal, organised and unorganised, domestic and international – all these played a part in ending apartheid. At the same time, and contrary to the ANC's articulation of African nationalism, elements from all race groups also tried to defend and reproduce the apartheid system. Who were the liberators and who were the oppressors under apartheid is a complex issue as Dlamini (2014) powerfully demonstrates. At the same time, the ANC's embrace of erstwhile enemies such as the National Party, traditional leaders and former homeland leaders further undermines the ANC's proprietary claims over post-apartheid democracy and also reduces non-racialism to electoral expediency. Moreover, the ANC rules South Africa with such disregard for the complexities of how post-apartheid South Africa was made that through the hubris of power it is increasingly playing a role in weakening constitutional democracy and rolling back democratic gains that were fought for by all progressives, both South African and internationalist.

The ANC-led Alliance has also re-racialised and deepened patriarchal norms in South African society in hideous ways. The ANC-led Alliance's degeneration and its maldeveloped ideological template expressed through a claim to South African exceptionalism as the cornerstone of its theory of colonialism of a special type has meant that, in its very nationalism, the ANC Alliance's understanding of Africa in terms of the centrality of such nationalism has always contained the seeds of xenophobia. Today, in fact, the Alliance's narrow African nationalism not only turns against pan-Africanism but also is increasingly about sub-national exceptionalisms linked to old ethnic identities constructed around apartheid-era bantustans. There is a dangerous retribalising of ethnic identity at work in the ANC's nationalism (Jara, 2013: 272–276). This is further re-enforced by increased power given to traditional authorities and through land dispossessions happening in rural communities, this mainly in favour of extractive industries. Moreover, in such a context, women have had to struggle particularly strenuously to affirm their rights, power and agency as modern citizens (Claassens, 2015).

At a structural level, in short, both race and gender hierarchies have been remade but also reinforced in the context of a globalising capitalism. The racism and male domination of neoliberalism has its roots in a Eurocentric patriarchy that has been constructed over 500 years through militarist mercantilism, slavery, colonialism and imperialism. Indeed, the existence of global racism has never been part of the remit of analyses linked to the centrality of a NDR, this including national question debates within the ANC-led Alliance (Van Diepen, 1988). This also made it increasingly difficult for the ANC to appreciate how transnational neoliberalism has been tied into reproducing racialised patterns of global accumulation and masculinised imperial domination. It also means the historically specific globalising of both apartheid and male domination, as brought in from the outside, have been central to deracialising monopoly capital in the country as part of neoliberalisation. Thus, the commanding heights of South African capitalism are about transnationalising monopoly power, which, despite the freedom of post-apartheid democracy, is still white and male dominated.

South Africa's racialised income inequality bears testimony to this as it stands at the centre of explanations about the crisis of social reproduction in South African society (Forslund and Reddy, 2015). In this regard liberal historiography, with its argument that racism was not essential for capitalism, has been wrong. For the end of apartheid has not ended racialised and male-dominated accumulation; actually, with globalisation this has been deepened, both from within and from the outside. In this context, any such break with a racialising and masculinised neoliberalism has not happened despite the much-vaunted expectations created by the parasitic, ethnicised and sexist Zuma project that now dominates the ANC-led Alliance.

Hence, it is important to ask what is meant by left of national liberation politics today? From the perspective of working-class hegemony, what can we identify and defend from the more than 20 years of post-apartheid democracy? Is it not farcical to talk about the agency of a national liberation-centred left given what has actually happened in South Africa? Indeed, isn't it quite possible that the ANC-led national liberation movement has reached its historical terminus and the most it can evoke is a mythical and sentimental past as a means to justify the present. Yet this now clearly means that state power is increasingly instrumentalised merely to reproduce a South African order that meets only the needs of a few, especially those of the ANC's own heroic cadre of leaders and with the national interest now deemed to be synonymous with the patronage machine of the ANC (Southall, 2013). And yet, as inequality and poverty have grown, this has actually become ever more morally and politically indefensible: both illegitimate from the perspective of students wanting free higher education, for example, but also contrary to working-class hegemony.

The making of a new left from below

Almost three decades of neoliberalisation has enabled important resistance against racialised and gendered forms of commodification, dispossession, exploitation and ecological destruction. In the post-apartheid context this resistance has gone through two cycles. The first cycle (the late 1990s into the early 2000s) was marked by the emergence of the TAC, the Landless People's Movement and the Anti-Privatisation Forum, many of which are now moribund or trying to renew themselves (like the TAC). A second cycle has come to the fore, this marking the emergence of a much more discernible and variegated left. Beginning in 2007 (to the present) this has been punctuated by struggles for service delivery, building solidarity economies, the Right2Know, Equal Education, social justice, defence of constitutional freedoms, food sovereignty, rural democracy and rights for women, against extractivism, climate jobs, housing, the rights of lesbian, gay, bisexual, transgender and intersexed (LGBTI) people, the recent student protests demanding decolonisation, free education and insourcing of universities and struggles against corruption (including a Vote No campaign during the 2014 national elections). Nor is it merely a rebellion of the poor (Alexander, 2010) or a violent democracy (Von Holdt, 2013) as suggested by some sociological perspectives. For these reductive analyses mainly focus on service delivery struggles; and miss the broader range of struggles emerging in contemporary South African civil society and the polyvalent character of institutional agency and the various and diverse forms of resistance coming to the fore. In fact, while there may be different tactical repertoires and institutional bases taken by these struggles, their predominant thrust addresses systemic challenges, articulates transformative alternatives and mobilises popular power.

Moreover, three other factors have contributed to amplifying the recent cycle of resistance. First, the rise of Jacob Zuma in the ANC, culminating at the Polokwane conference in 2008, was a deeply polarising process inside the ANC-led Alliance and the country. Not only did the ANC experience its first split (with the break-away of many in the Mbeki faction to form COPE), but it also closed off strategic debate across all the Alliance's constituent formations.

In this context, critical voices challenging the Zumafication of the Alliance and society were vilified and declared dissidents (Satgar, 2009c: 294–316). Thus, in the end, the closing of the ranks around Zuma served to produce deep factions inside COSATU and purges in the SACP, culminating in the factionalising of the SACP and its further weakening through its co-option and collapse into the ANC. More positively, this reconfiguration of a Zumafied ANC-led Alliance has loosened loyalties to the Alliance among committed cadres, opened up space to the left of the ANC, and disaffected many once sympathetic to the ANC-led Alliance – all developments that have fed directly into the deepening cycle of resistance.

Second, since 2008 various grassroots activists involved in movements and campaigns, and coming out of the ANC-led Alliance, part of the independent Marxist left, the labour left and the Trotskyist left, began conversations about the global crises of capitalism and the national liberation project. The significance of this convergence cannot be understated as it is the first time that such a broad range of different traditions came together to work collectively. This gave rise to the formation and launch of the DLF in January 2011. The DLF was not formed as a political party but more as a space for solidarity, building capacity for resistance around transformative alternatives, developing analyses of the contemporary crises and advancing an anti-capitalist imagination beyond neoliberalised national liberation politics (DLF, 2011). It essentially functioned as a pole of attraction as part of a process of reclaiming lost ground. While the DLF did not realise all its objectives and has become much too centred around South Africa's Trotskyist left, it has played a crucial organising role to bring South Africa's very divided left into a common political space to begin crucial conversations. It provided a political home for some, supported important resistance to xenophobic violence, campaigned against the wasteful expenditure of the World Cup, and gave support to several grassroots community struggles, including worker committees involved in the platinum belt and the Marikana Campaign for Justice, and the Climate Jobs Campaign. True, the DLF is at a crossroads as grassroots social forces are being realigned around the NUMSA-led United Front, some aligning to the EFF) and as rising anti-systemic forces build their own capacities as part of the cycle of resistance. And yet the DLF has provided valuable lessons for left convergence. And it may still have an important contribution to make to strengthening the emerging alliance between community and worker struggles, as part of building the NUMSA-led United Front.

Third, the massacre of 36 platinum mine workers on 16 August 2012 did not mark just another militant moment in post-apartheid industrial relations or a mere expression of the securitisation of neoliberal politics. For this brutal massacre and historical event was in fact a truly conjunctural development, one that gave rise to a fundamental rupture in the working-class support base of the national liberation bloc of forces. The realignments flowing from this have given rise to an independent union in the platinum mining sector, the Association of Mineworkers and Construction Union (AMCU), taking away significant support from the ANC-aligned National Union of Mineworkers (NUM). In addition, Marikana has had significant ramifications for COSATU itself – contributing directly, for example, to the largest union in South Africa, NUMSA with over 340,000 members, withdrawing support for the ANC in the 2014 elections, leaving the ANC-led Alliance, and exploring the process of developing a United Front and a Movement for Socialism (NUMSA, 2014). Since NUMSA resolved on this direction at its 2013 special congress, it has convened a resistance assembly to learn about grassroots movements, campaigned against neoliberal policy proposals such as the youth wage subsidy and the national budget, hosted an international symposium with various left movements and parties from around the world, initiated a United Front building process, convened a conference on socialism and actively championed mass mobilisation against corruption. Today NUMSA, together with eight other unions, is also poised to lead the building of a new labour federation in South Africa after it was expelled, together with the general secretary Zwelinzima Vavi, from COSATU.

The horizon and challenges for post-national liberation left counter-hegemony

There is growing consensus that South Africa's national liberation project is exhausted, in part due to its profound capitulation to neoliberalisation. Put more starkly, such national liberation politics is, like most national liberation projects, not a way forward for the working class and national popular forces committed to transformation. Thus, while it was perhaps not inevitable for the national liberation project to end up where it has, it is in fact being eaten up by its own contradictions and limitations. Not that this, in itself, guarantees the emergence of a genuine left alternative. The EFF is a negative example in this regard. It is a product of the ANC and it has emerged by feeding off the ANC's weaknesses, particularly through it being anti-Zuma. In its practice, however, it is a self-styled vanguard, organised around the cult of the personality and a militarised internal hierarchy, and lumpen in its tactical interventions in everyday politics. The EFF gestures to the left of the ANC–led Alliance, but is afflicted with the same limitations and contradictions as the ANC. While it captures headlines for its disruptive and populist politics, it has not broken the mould of national liberation politics and has not captured the imagination of most South African youth, including those involved in the #RhodesMustFall movement, the students demanding free education (#FeesMustFall) and others involved in the various anti-systemic movements that are on the rise. The EFF is in its essence an electoral opposition, and would really be tested if it were ever to come to control state power even at a local government level. How different, we might well ask, would it actually be from the ANC if in power?

In short, for an effective and meaningful left to emerge as a serious contender it will have to provide an imagination and horizon of politics beyond the national liberation template and neoliberal capitalism. It will have to remake itself in fundamental ways in order to constitute a new balance of forces and a political project with broad mass appeal, while also advancing new transformative practices. It is too simplistic to believe that merely replacing one kind of vanguard with another or narrow electoral contestation will bring about a rupture with neoliberal capitalism. Similarly, evoking old formulas from the revolutionary nationalist, social democratic and Soviet experience is inadequate to the new conjuncture. A globalising capitalism, grounded in transnational circuits, harnessing new technologies and constituting new space-time dynamics has remade social relations in fundamental ways. Central in this regard is the weakening of the global and domestic working class, of course. Yet South Africa's post-national liberation left is itself in transition from crisis to renewal: still being made but with immense potential!

In fact, there are four formidable challenges confronting South Africa's left. But, in light of the advances that are now being made, they are not impossible to address. First, South African capitalism reflects a deep set of systemic crises that were not resolved by the national liberation project and have worsened in the context of neoliberal restructuring and deep financialised globalisation. A crucial challenge in this regard is the deglobalisation of finance to reverse the economic regression and financialised chaos that has taken place over the past three decades and to which South Africa's political economy is articulated. Contrary to Piketty (2014: 515–539), who visited South Africa in 2015, this requires more than just increased taxation on capital but also the introduction of exchange controls, new investment laws, structurally diversifying the financial system, the introduction of a universal BIG and democratic planning. Moreover, it requires a programmatic politics unifying various anti-systemic solutions emerging from the new cycle of resistance in the country such as free university education, insourcing, food sovereignty, climate jobs, Right2Know proposals, equal education, and so on.

Of course, this will have to be done in a manner that is deliberative and participatory and one that, in pursuit of genuine left convergence, respects the independence of social forces. But the conditions are ripe for this. Thus, if the NUMSA-led United Front appreciates that left convergence is more than merely connecting service delivery flashpoints, it could be central in facilitating such convergence around a common programmatic platform of resistance from below. Moreover, if rising anti-systemic movements appreciate the necessity of solidarity then a new mass politics is a real possibility. In this process of democratic convergence, a new class and national popular alliance of the organised working class, the precariat, the permanently unemployed, the landless, youth, students, sections of the progressive middle class and left intelligentsia could congeal. A new historical bloc and class project could potentially emerge articulating transformative alternatives for a post-neoliberal South Africa.

Second, the sectarianism of some sections of South Africa's left – rooted in their belief that they have historically always had the correct analysis, the monopoly on political truth and the only understanding of what revolutionary change is – will not assist left convergence. The historical inheritance of socialism was never about one transhistorical model. Instead, the historical inheritance of socialism is rich and varied. Socialism as an object of study is more than recovering blueprints and state-centric formulae but requires a deeper and more critical analysis of the Soviet experience (and its copies), of revolutionary nationalist experiences and of social democracy. Many on the South African left hold onto a romanticised understanding of the 1917 Russian Revolution or of the golden years of social democracy or merely crudely justify revolutionary nationalism.

More specifically, the African experience of revolutionary and transformative change does not even feature as a critical point of reference.

This entire inheritance of twentieth-century socialism has to be engaged with critically to appreciate what were the limitations, contradictions and excesses (Saul, 2013; Glaser, 2013). These critical reflections, conversations and engagements need to begin in earnest and as part of ongoing attempts to ensure a broad horizon and vision for transformative change, even as transformative systemic alternatives are being advanced in the present to address the new contradictions of a globalising capitalism. Ultimately a twenty-first century South African socialism should be shaped by its rigorous appreciation of historical socialism's limitations and the systemic alternatives required to overcome the new contradictions of globalising capitalism.

Third, the re-racialising dynamics of post-apartheid South Africa has affected class, gender, spatiality and ecology. Race still matters at every level of society and is important for a renewed left politics. In this regard, questions related to the non-racialism of mass politics and of the constitutional order cannot be surrendered to the ANC. Indeed, it is the ANC's own version of non-racialism that is itself in crisis, this further affirming the need to move beyond a singular conception of non-racialism as a political tradition. For it suggests instead the importance of affirming a plurality of non-racialisms: a diverse tradition of official and non-official, everyday non-racialisms. Moreover, non-racialism as an organising principle and a fresh critique of capitalism (connecting race, class and gender) are existential resources for reflecting on blackness, whiteness and their intersections with class and gender and developing the new imaginary and programmatic referent (a real Freedom Charter) that has to be rescued from a degenerate ANC-led Alliance.

In short, non-racialism must be regrounded in a new political economy analysis of a globalised social formation, one that evidences dangerous ecological contradictions, must be brought into dialogue with a resurgent Black Consciousness (BC) movement and must be the principled basis for confronting white and black privilege. In this regard, a non-racial approach to the climate crisis and the just transition is a crucial challenge for left politics in discovering a new horizon for itself. For the mere affirmation of blackness or whiteness actually becomes meaningless in the context of a scorched country and planet and ultimately the extinction of the human race. We need to find a renewed human solidarity to confront this challenge and to survive. In this regard, a true, hard-won non-racialism must be key to a struggle for systemic transformation as part of the just transition. But there remains much work to be done on this front.

Finally, a new left politics has to appreciate the need to build capacity for a new revolutionary politics, one more appropriately termed a new transformative politics. This is very much the horizon of the global left and many of the social forces championing systemic alternatives as part of the new cycle of resistance in South Africa. Transformative politics is very different from the technocratic managerialism of social democracy or coercive control of Sovietised Marxism or the patronage machine politics of revolutionary nationalism. In each of these frames of politics a vanguard was featured as a self-declared advanced layer and the custodian of history and change. Transformative politics now promises to turn its back on this elite understanding of agency, power and politics.

Instead, transformative politics is about prefiguring the future now through building systemic alternatives, evoking capacities for change from below, constituting new forms of mass power, rethinking the political instrument, extending and broadening democracy, reclaiming a transformed, genuinely popular, sovereignty and strengthening international solidarity. It is consistently anti-authoritarian and about democratically constituting a new working class-led counter-hegemony to sustain life. In South Africa the idea of a movement for socialism best embodies the logic of this politics, one within which a United Front of anti-systemic movements, an independent and worker-controlled trade union federation, and a mass left party are constituted. But it is not led by 'the party'. Instead, such a movement for socialism is grounded in collective leadership in all its structures, a democratically conceived and commonly agreed programme and a political division of labour in which a party is merely a tactical device in a mass transformative strategy. There is potential for this to be realised although whether this is what will actually happen remains an open question.

Review of African Political Economy, 2016.

PART II

DECOLONIAL CRITIQUE OF ECOCIDAL CAPITALISM

Perspectives on Ecocide

Marx and the International

KARL MARX WAS AN intrepid traveller in the European context in the mid-nineteenth century. Don't imagine the bearded one moving around with a roller suitcase, tourist guides and staying at fancy hotels. Marx, the red mole, travelled around a tumultuous Europe out of political choice but also because of the strong arm of ruling-class repression.

The frontiers of struggle and revolution were what kept Marx on the move. His seditious missives against aristocratic, religious and bourgeois classes and commitment to revolution earned him infamy amongst ruling classes in Europe. Marx was forced to leave various countries due to legal prohibitions issued by the Prussian Empire, the King of Belgium and the French authorities.

This article is not about Marx's biographical adventures and escapades, which in themselves reveal a great deal about his commitment to internationalism. Rather, this contribution is about how Marx thought about and acted the international. How was the international part of Marx's theory and practice? It is also about how Marx's ideas have travelled to South Africa through internationalism, and the contribution South African Marxism has made to anti-racism, including its support for building a powerful anti-apartheid movement. The third theme in this article is on the current conjuncture and necessity for a renewed internationalism. Finally, this article concludes with possible directions and challenges for twenty-first century internationalism.

Marx and the international

For some international relations thinkers, Marx's work does not have much to offer in terms of thinking and understanding the international.[1]

That is to say, because Marx's political and ideological formation happened in a post-Napoleonic era in transition from the Holy Alliance to the concert of Europe, which secured relative peace for a hundred years (1815–1914), the lived experience of Marx's world supposedly occluded an understanding of

---
1 Vendulka Kubalkova and Albert Cruickshank. 1989. *Marxism and International Relations*. Oxford: Oxford University Press.

international relations. This is based on a superficial reading of Marx's work and his praxis as a revolutionary. Anybody reading *The Communist Manifesto* and *Capital* would recognise the international character of capitalist expansion.

In the *Manifesto* it is the materiality of capitalism, the role of the bourgeoisie, class struggle and the historical agency of the working class that remakes the world. In *Capital* the self-expanding value of capital is crucial for its expansionary tendencies. Moreover, the original form of accumulating capital through primitive accumulation entailed a historical role for mercantile capitalism, in terms of slavery, conquest and trade within international relations. Some theorists also read Marx as furnishing his own understanding of imperialism and the importance for class solidarity in the imperial centres of capitalism and with anti-colonial struggles.[2]

Now, Marx was thinking and writing in the context of a Eurocentric milieu of the nineteenth-century. White supremacist thinking was also expressed in the Enlightenment, including Hegel's conception of world history, ethnographic accounts of the colonial, and the vaunting of scientific racism linked to nineteenth-century imperialism. Of course, we must be cautious in thinking with Marx, so we don't get infected by some of this distasteful racist thinking. But let us not make the mistake of reducing Marx to a racist or a Eurocentric thinker, as Edward Said does in Orientalism. Said is wrong. Marx was not a white supremacist. As several readings of Marx have pointed out there is a triple epistemological rupture with Eurocentricism in Marx's thought.[3]

The first relates to Marx's break with a linear conception of capitalist modernity and the idea that Western capitalism is the terminus of all non-Western societies. Informing this break is Marx's appreciation of the deleterious impacts of colonialism and his own active opposition to slavery.[4] Marx was a fervent abolitionist of slavery; he recognised how colonialism divided the working class, as in the case of Ireland; and regarding India he came to appreciate the complex relationship between the coloniser and

---

2   Lucia Pradella, 'Imperialism and capitalist development in Marx's *Capital*' *Historical Materialism* 21(2) 2013: 117–147.

3   In this regard see Gilbert Achcar. 2013. *Marxism, Orientalism, Cosmopolitanism*. Chicago: Haymarket Books; in which he deals with Marx's epistemological evolution. Also see Kevin B. Anderson. 2010. *Marx at the Margins: On Nationalism, Ethnicity and Non-Western Societies* for an excellent analysis of what I call the making of Marx's anti-racism.

4   See Robin Blackburn. 2011 *Marx and Lincoln: An Unfinished Revolution*. London: Verso Books. As this text confirms, Marx had a more radical position than Lincoln on the rights and freedoms of African Americans.

colonised, particularly the agency of the oppressed.[5]

His second break with Eurocentricism relates to Marx's appreciation that the Western transition from feudalism to capitalism could not be universalised. Initially, attempting to think Asia within this framework led to a realisation, as more evidence became available, that Asia has its own distinct social structures, which would shape its transition from pre-capitalist relations.

The third epistemological rupture relates to the transition beyond capitalism. In this regard a lot has been written on Marx's exchange with Vera Zasulich on the Russian road to socialism and rural social relations, in which he recognises the Russian commune (*mir*) as a potential part of the transition.[6] This affirming of a multilinear approach to socialism, through various pathways based on national histories, cultures and social practices, becomes even more apparent when reading Marx through his own understanding of ecological relations and the limits of productivism.

Universal working-class role

Marx's connection to international relations also emerges in his discussion of the universal role of the working class as the subject of history and as central to the revolutionary transformation from capitalism. Such a conception of the working class is present in the *Communist Manifesto*, and in the centrality he gives to the sale of labour power in his conception of the labour theory of value and his conception of exploitation in *Capital*.

At the same time, Marx lived out his commitment to the working-class and international struggle in various ways. These included his association with clandestine worker groups in France including the League of the Just (from 1843); his links with the Chartist movement in England (1845) and then again deepened through writings for the Chartist newspapers (1851–1862); his co-organising the Communist Correspondence Committee in Brussels (1846) to unite socialists and politically engaged workers in various countries; his joining the League of the Just on their invitation (1847) and assisting them to organise and develop an open revolutionary programme which resulted in them changing

---

[5] I agree with Pranav Jani in recognising that Marx developed a deeper appreciation of India beyond his descriptive commentary on the role of the bourgeoisie. See Jani. 2002. 'Karl Marx, Eurocentrism, and the 1857 revolt in British India' in *Marxism, Modernity and Postcolonial Studies* edited by Crystal Bartolovich and Neil Lazarus. Cambridge: Cambridge University Press.

[6] See Teodor Shanin. 1983. *Late Marx and the Russian Road: Marx and the Peripheries of Capitalism*. New York: Monthly Review Press.

their name to the Communist League, embracing the slogan 'Working Men of All Countries Unite' and adopting the Communist Manifesto (1848).

His education work amongst workers' groups included delivering lectures on political economy (published as Wage Labour and Capital). His support of the German Revolution of 1848 through publishing the *Neue Rheinische Zeitung* provided a platform to call for a unified German state, rally support for workers and peasants' struggles and support national liberation struggles in other countries. Between 1851 and 1862 Marx contributed journalistic articles to the New York *Daily Tribune* on various struggles, international affairs and political economy developments.

Finally, Marx's involvement in the creation of the International Working Men's Association (1864), the First International, enabled him to foreground various international developments, influence the creation of the Social Democratic Party in Germany, contest the destructive role of anarchists, and foreground the importance of the Paris Commune.

The encounter with South Africa

Marx the anti-racist found his way into the anti-colonial and anti-apartheid struggle in South Africa through various interlocutors in the late-nineteenth and early-twentieth centuries. This included the work of the socialist and anti-imperialist feminist Olive Schreiner, expatriate workers from Europe, the Communist Party of South Africa, Trotskyist groups, and revolutionary nationalists.

Marxism played a crucial role in developing the theoretical and analytical tools to understand the relationship between capitalism and racial oppression. Much later, women's oppression was added to the roster of oppression and the vast corpus of South African Marxism. Three influential theories – articulation of modes of production developed by Harold Wolpe, colonialism of a special type put forward by the South African Communist Party (SACP) and racial capitalism developed by Trotskyists such as Neville Alexander – all contributed to resistance in South Africa.

Each of these theories has a lineage that can be traced back to Marx. Wolpe's articulation of modes of production and the Trotskyist versions of racial capitalism draw from and innovate on Marx's historical materialism and conception of primitive accumulation as it relates to pre-capitalist relations in the transition to capitalism. The SACP's colonialism of a special type involved a structural class analysis of monopoly capitalism and a critique of a colonial social formation in which coloniser and colonised shared a common spatial reality. Again, these theoretical ideas connected back to Marx's understanding of class, racial oppression and his critique of colonialism. All the theories mentioned are not direct derivatives from Marx, but definitely elaborate aspects in his theory of capitalism, historical materialist framework and political writings.

Marx's abolitionist stance against slavery, for instance, was very similar to anti-apartheid activism. More precisely it was similar to the anti-apartheid movement that developed in various parts of the world, cutting across Cold War fault-lines, to rally resistance in streets, outside embassies, for sanctions, providing aid to national liberation movements and including battle grounds as in Angola.

The anti-apartheid movement made a crucial contribution to isolating the pariah Afrikaner nationalist regime, and to the end of apartheid. As an internationalist movement, the anti-apartheid movement was an important precursor to the more recent anti-globalisation movement-of-movements. Its experience, history and lessons for renewing a twenty-first-century internationalism is crucial.

Neoliberal crisis and resistance

Today's world has endured over three decades of neoliberalism, which has engendered a crisis-ridden global political economy. Financial liberalisation, conjoined to the inherent instability of globalised finance, has destabilised a number of economies in the global South.

Around 2007–2008 the global financial crisis finally reached the heartlands of capitalism. Instead of learning lessons from this general and systemic crisis, global ruling classes are still committed to financialised accumulation. Trump, like Obama, has not reined in finance. The crises of neoliberalism have not ended the neoliberal regime as a class project. Instead, the conjunctural crisis of neoliberalism, grounded in a systemic contradiction of worsening inequality, is now converging with other dangerous systemic contradictions like the climate crisis and the hollowing out of market democracies.

A new fascist menace is rising in the world. Religious fundamentalism, ethno-nationalism, racist border regimes, climate denialism and authoritarian approaches to globalised market economies are emerging. This ideological disposition is being expressed in various combinations, with different emphases, in Trump's White House, Brazil, India, Turkey, Russia and several countries in Europe.

The global left has not been able to resist hegemonic neoliberalism effectively. Today, neoliberalism is becoming neo-fascist-like in response to its own crises and domestic conditions. Global capitalism is experiencing a conjunctural and a set of systemic crises, yet resistance is episodic, defensive and even being pre-emptively crushed. This poses serious challenges for the renewal of twenty-first-century internationalism. National struggles are weaker and vulnerable without international solidarity.

Where to for internationalism?

The classical inheritance Marx has left us on the centrality of the international in left politics is something we should learn from critically, while being informed by contemporary conditions.

In the global cycles of resistance against the neoliberal class project, the WSF was a crucial space for convergence. WSF presented a critique of plutocratic class power – expressed through the elites' WEF – offering a self-reflexive space for the new global left, enabling solidarity-based sharing of anti-systemic perspectives, inciting a twenty-first-century emancipatory imagination, and provided a platform for confrontations with the IMF-World Bank-WTO and other globalising forces. However, the WSF did not become a strategic centre for the global left, nor did it develop a programmatic approach to global resistance. Institutionalising left power, in a democratic manner, has eluded the WSF. It just might be that the WSF has exhausted its historic role.

This question requires further debate and clarification among the global left. Samir Amin, the leading Marxist thinker from Africa, made it a central priority before his passing to call for a New International of Workers and Peoples.[7] Feeling strongly that the WSF had slowed down, Amin centred his call on the crisis-ridden nature of contemporary capitalism including ecological destruction, its soft totalitarianism which can easily become a hard totalitarianism, and the failure of existing left forces in national spaces, particularly the global North to resist contemporary imperialism.

His call for an inaugural meeting of a New International of Workers and Peoples was aimed at anti-capitalist activists, movements, parties, networks and unions from all continents. It envisaged a convergence that would build a democratic organisation and critically learn the lessons of historical

---

7   Samir Amin wrote up his analysis and argument, entitled 'It is imperative to reconstruct the International of Workers and Peoples' in 2017 and put out an email call on 24 June 2018 entitled 'Letter of intent for an inaugural meeting of the International of Workers and Peoples'.

internationalism. In short, based on his analysis of the autumn phase of capitalism, Samir Amin believed in the necessity of the peoples Spring informed by a socialist perspective. This is another possible way forward.

At the same time, various social forces on the ground are seeking to build transnational solidarities that can feed into a renewal of internationalism, from below, and through a new strategic politics. A number of examples stand out on the global terrain of struggle such as campaigning for food sovereignty pathways, inaugurated by La Via Campesina, through various national and continental alliances; climate jobs, energy sovereignty and just transition campaigning by unions and red-green alliances in various countries; transnational campaigning platforms for dismantling the power of transnational corporations and for national and global regulation. There are also global union struggles: the International Transport Workers Federation, effectively organising support for workers across national borders to take on the exploitative, low-cost Ryanair; indigenous peoples' resistance to carbon extraction, the destruction of ecosystems and more.

In this context, I firmly agree with Marx on the need for anti-capitalist internationalism but also with Samir Amin on the imperative of building a New International of Workers and Peoples in the twenty-first century, if we are to survive a rising ecofascist and ecocidal global capitalism. We rallied courageous human solidarity against apartheid and its imperial allies. We can do it again, from below and in a democratic manner, before it is too late.

Against the Current 197, November/December 2018.

Seven Theses on Radical Non-Racialism, the Climate Crisis and Deep, Just Transitions: From the National Question to the Ecocide Question

IT HAS BECOME COMMONPLACE, in the current conjuncture, to attack non-racialism and argue for new identities, African nationalism and the importance of BC. Moreover, within popular consciousness, despite non-racialism being a founding constitutional principle, there are banal and ahistorical conceptions of non-racialism at work merely reducing it to being colour blind, with no definitional content. This chapter takes issue with the onslaught against non-racialism and the increasing shallow, popular understandings of non-racialism. Radical non-racialism is defended in this intervention and an argument is made for its reaffirmation. This is different from the official non-racialism of the ANC, which has morphed into different inflections of state-centred nationalism during different phases in post-apartheid South Africa, to include rainbowism, Afro-neoliberalism and resource nationalism. Official non-racialism is in crisis in the context of the unravelling of ANC-led national liberation hegemony and the degeneration of the ANC itself.

The defence of radical non-racialism affirms a crucial principle and practice for prevailing anti-racism, in dialogue with some currents within contemporary BC, and as part of the renewal of left politics in South Africa. The argument made in this chapter is that official ANC non-racialism, tied to a contingent political-economy analysis and within the frame of the national question approach, is outdated, in crisis and discredited. It is dying with the ANC-led Alliance. At the same time, this chapter argues for replacing the national question with the ecocide question, in the context of the existential threat posed by the climate crisis to human and non-human life. The ecocide question is central to a post-national liberation, post-neoliberal and renewed left politics, as the basis for radical, non-racial nation building to sustain life. This perspective is set out in seven theses below.

Thesis 1

Radical non-racialism is central to a people's history of struggle and achieved a hegemonic location in the national liberation struggle against apartheid. Its challenge to racialised exploitation, white supremacy, gender oppression and oppressions in general, because of its deep humanist impulse, defined its radicalism.

Does non-racialism, as a political principle and practice, belong to the ANC? In the mythologised history of the ANC, in the construction of its post-apartheid hegemony and in its official practices as a ruling party, it would seem the ANC has proprietary claims on non-racialism.[1] As the party of national liberation and the dominant ruling party for over two decades, it has constructed and articulated post-apartheid nation-building nationalism, in which non-racialism has been a crucial ideological element. This has been part of its project to rule a capitalist South Africa and has impacted on its approach to economic transformation, state building, state–civil society relations and international relations. Various presidents of the ANC and the country have also imbued official non-racialism with particular discursive elements and practices. For instance, Nelson Mandela was the fulcrum of a rainbow nationalism; Thabo Mbeki harnessed rainbow nationalism for deep globalisation, BEE and the indigenising of neoliberalism as Afro-neoliberalism; and Jacob Zuma has brought in an element of resource nationalism linked to a corrupt transactional politics. The success of these nation-building efforts is a separate question; suffice to note that the ANC's articulation of official non-racialism is in crisis.

On the other hand, radical non-racialism as part of a people's history of struggle does not belong to the ANC.[2] Three defining moments of national liberation struggle in the twentieth century affirm radical non-racialism as an orientation in mass politics, as part of popular struggles and as belonging to the people. The first was the formulation and adoption of the Freedom Charter in 1955 at the Congress of the People, including its embrace of the idea that South Africa belongs to all who live in it, black and white. The initiative to formulate the Freedom Charter was not an initiative of the ANC exclusively but of the Congress Alliance, made up of the ANC, the South African Indian Congress, the South African Coloured People's Organisation and the South African

---

1   Frederikse (1990) argues for the official unbreakable thread of non-racialism as central to the ANC. See Everatt (2009) for a more complex history on the origins of non-racialism.

2   A people's history of struggle and radical non-racialism still has to be written in South Africa beyond the mythologies of the ANC's official non-racialism or bigman histories.

Congress of Democrats. Moreover, the process to formulate the content and ideas of the Freedom Charter gave primacy to grassroots dialogue, input and registering the voice of the people.[3] Essentially, the participation and input of the people is what gave the Congress of the People and the Freedom Charter its legitimacy. While the Freedom Charter became a programmatic basis of national liberation politics, it reflected the aspirations of the people, including the idea of an inclusive non-racial democracy and nationalism. This does not belong to the ANC.

The second crucial moment was the emergence of militant black trade unionism from 1973 onwards, propelled by the powerful Durban strikes. The rise of independent trade unions, their growth and eventual merger into COSATU in 1985 was crucial for affirming radical non-racialism within the organised working class in South Africa. COSATU embraced non-racialism and the Freedom Charter after serious internal debates. Various affiliates of COSATU also carried firm commitments to the principles of non-racialism and socialism.[4] COSATU did not belong to the ANC and was an independent, worker-controlled labour federation.

The third crucial moment was the resurgence of mass resistance against apartheid in the 1980s, spurred on by the student uprising of 1976. The mass movement that rose in the 1980s, under the banner of the UDF, brought together sport, cultural, faith-based, youth, women, student, union and civic organisations, as well as various other formations. These organisations were not controlled by the ANC, although there might have been ANC sympathisers, underground operatives and members in some of them. Moreover, some in the UDF leadership also openly affirmed the importance of the link to the ANC.[5] However, the embrace of the Freedom Charter by the UDF strengthened the impulse of mass, radical non-racialism. This impulse did not belong to the ANC.

But what is the content of radical non-racialism, a people's non-racialism? It

---

[3] See Suttner and Cronin (1986) for an important history of the Congress of the People campaign and how the Freedom Charter was put together through people's demands and ideas from below.

[4] The NUM adopted the Freedom Charter. The NUMSA, the most left-wing affiliate of COSATU, adopted the Freedom Charter as well as committing itself to developing a more explicit working-class programme (see Forrest, 2011: 418).

[5] See Seekings (2000) for an instrumentalist history of the UDF, in which the ANC made it all happen and was determining. This is another example of official non-racialism in the historiography of South Africa's struggle, which needs to be challenged through a people's history of liberation. Of course, this is not to argue that the ANC did not have influence but to over-exaggerate its role in history is propagandistic. It also takes away agency from the people and people's organisations.

has been first and foremost about solidarity and unity. It was about countering the racialised differences of apartheid by constituting strategic unity within and between race groups as concrete expressions of people's power, advancing a programmatic unity of all forces to overcome apartheid and the building of powerful people's organisations. The idea of people's power ('the people shall govern'), inscribed in the Freedom Charter, is about deep democracy and was central to Mandela's political thought in the 1950s.[6] This process of strategic unity was forged in different racialised spatial and sectoral contexts and went through various conjunctural phases since the 1940s. In organisations such as the Communist Party and the black trade union movement, non-racialism was taken further in terms of different races being part of the same organisation and playing a leadership role. The ANC, on the other hand, remained an African organisation into the 1960s, and non-African leadership was elected into its structures much later.

Second, radical non-racialism was deeply anti-capitalist. It married a critique of racial oppression to a critique of capitalism. The Freedom Charter, while a people's document, was also a product of its time in terms of its imagination and horizons. It was a document deeply imbued with a state-centric perspective, shaped by Soviet socialism, revolutionary nationalism and social democracy. As a people's document, the Freedom Charter was anti-capitalist. Moreover, the non-reductionist conception of racialised and gendered class understandings expressed itself in Communist Party thinking, in trade union organising and in mass organisations, such as the UDF, with principled commitments to working-class leadership. Class and race were linked in theory and in mass organisations against capitalism and its racialised structures.

The third aspect of radical non-racialism was that it was not anti-white but it was anti-white supremacy. Apartheid (1948–1994) was a white supremacist social order with a history going back to the early colonial encounter. Apartheid imbued whiteness with a racialised superiority against the subhuman non-white. It was a social order that brought together racialised economic relations with political and ideological relations to affirm white superiority through Afrikaner nationalism. The radical non-racial tradition embraced those whites who consciously stood against white supremacy and supported the national liberation struggle. In the Communist Party, in the trade union movement, in faith-based organisations and in the UDF, this was certainly the case.

---

6   This is the Mandela that has to be read and reclaimed for our contemporary period. See Mandela (1994), particularly the chapter entitled 'The struggle is my life'.

The fourth aspect of radical non-racialism was its recognition that race as a group attribute and racism as a form of discrimination had no scientific basis for its existence in social relations. This was not about being colour blind in a facile sense, but was grounded in a deep humanist and universalist commitment to see and live beyond colour, as part of the struggle for a new society. While apartheid constructed a racist society and organised society through racialised relations, which impacted on all South Africans, our individual and collective challenges were to overcome these racialised social relations and its consequences. Racism in South Africa stole the humanity of the oppressed but it also tried to install a socially engineered racist in all of us, to keep the people divided. The brutalised humanity and racist consciousness among the oppressed also had to be confronted. The radical non-racial principle was a crucial guide on this existential journey. Many biographies and autobiographies of radical non-racial activists tell this story and are important resources of existential phenomenology.[7]

In all four respects, radical non-racialism is still relevant in South Africa: as a basis for strategic unity and solidarity for democratic people's power, as an anti-capitalist critique and practice, as anti-white supremacy and as an existential guiding principle to achieve a humanised society and world. Radical non-racialism is crucial, now more than ever, for a new left politics grounded in addressing the ecocide question. This will be developed further below.

Thesis 2

Radical non-racialism shares important common ground with BC but also goes beyond it in significant ways to achieve a future South Africa beyond skin colour. The BC movement made an important contribution to the liberation struggle in the 1970s. Its most prominent intellectual leader, Steve Biko, as part of this movement, left behind a powerful legacy, which impacted on philosophy, culture, black feminism, psychology, community-empowerment practices, black theology and a critical engagement with liberalism.[8] BC still resonates in the present. A rough typology of post-apartheid BC suggests there are three articulations, each with different approaches to South Africa's future, and includes: (i) academic BC, (ii) populist BC and (iii) Africanist BC.

---

7 See Mandela (1994), Sisulu (2002), Kathrada (2004), Reddy (1991), Meer (2002), Bernstein (1999), Simons (2004) among others.

8 Mngxitama, Alexander and Gibson (2008) and Pityana et al. (1991). Both are important collections reflecting on the legacy and impact of BC.

Academic BC has produced some important interventions in our national conversation about continued racial oppression, the relevance of black identity and key solutions for the way forward for the country. Xolela Mangcu, for instance, argues, following Biko, for a joint culture among different groups of people, based on race-transcendent leadership and a public philosophy. He argues against the ANC's non-racial inequality (Mangcu, 2015). While Frantz Fanon would be uncomfortable with the essentialist underpinnings of both Biko's and Mangcu's understandings of culture, a joint culture premised on the lived experience of the people and born out of struggle to build a deeply democratic society shares common ground with radical non-racialism. Zimitri Erasmus posits a new humanism for South Africa. She suggests love as a political practice, which brings together friendship, imaginative co-creativity, care for the other and transformative politics as crucial for emancipation (Erasmus, 2017: 141). Erasmus's politically engaged humanism shares much ground with the existential journey central to the practice of radical non-racialism, which has been at the frontline of overcoming racial domination in South Africa. Radical non-racialism is a deeply political humanism that exists and does not have to be invented. It has to be further elaborated.

Populist BC is best expressed in student politics today. With the rise of #RhodesMustFall and subsequently #FeesMustFall in 2015, student politics quickly lost its radical non-racial character and became explicitly BC orientated. While this shift has its own explanations, it also had its own implications for student unity as the pain of the aspirant or already existing black middle-class child was exalted in performative ways. Moreover, two crucial intellectual ideas stand out: decolonising the university and intersectionality.[9] The populist version of decolonising the university would mean removing all white academics and all intellectual work by white academics. This is akin to a Pol Pot approach to the university, smacks of adventurous millenarianism and is deeply racist. On the other hand, decolonising the university, as an epistemological and decolonising project, shares important ground with radical non-racialism in terms of not being anti-white but resisting white supremacy in all its forms. Moreover, intersectionality, as an analytical category, is not new to radical non-racialism and its non-reductionist understandings of class, race and gender related to capitalism. Also, it just might be that radical non-racialism has a much richer analytical tradition around the challenge of simultaneous oppressions

---

9 See Chinguno et al. (2017), a compilation of reflections and analyses by students involved with Fallist politics and student protests at Wits University.

which is home-grown. Intersectionality, understood as a concept of political practice to build solidarities among workers, women, students and society, also shares ground with radical non-racialism in terms of advancing strategic solidarities. While there might be different language registers at work and discursive distance, radical non-racialism has come to appreciate this challenge in the course of decades of mass resistance against apartheid oppression and capitalism.

An Africanist BC is expressed through the resurgent Pan African Student Movement and the EFF, a breakaway political party from the ANC that is led by Julius Malema. These are political forces whose political practice is premised on generalised and essentialised understandings of race and racism. Their dialectic of change is simple: African versus the rest. With the crisis of the ANC's official non-racialism, these forces have been capitalising on this to argue that the entire non-racial tradition is irrelevant and they have been gaining important ground in some sections of society. As African nationalists, their future for South Africa is exclusionary, populist and based on a dangerous proclamation of racialised difference to advance revenge. It clashes directly with radical non-racialism.

Thesis 3

Radical non-racialism was defeated in the transition to democracy and displaced by rainbowism, an Afro-neoliberal approach to nation building and the authoritarian corruption of the Zuma regime. Radical non-racialism is not the same as rainbowism, liberal democracy or narrow black nationalism:

The ANC-led Alliance has disarticulated radical non-racialism since 1994.[10] This means that the official non-racialism of the ANC-led Alliance and state, at the level of ideological relations and articulation, has eviscerated it. The ideological framing of non-racial politics was remade and this occurred in the context of electoral politics, state policy making, shallow nation building and managing the globalisation of a capitalist economy. This means that national and class struggle, race and class, were not articulated in national liberation political practice against, with and beyond post-apartheid capitalism. The programmatic content of national liberation, as contained in the Freedom Charter, was abandoned. Instead, a deeply racist capitalist society was embraced as the means

---

10 Stuart Hall (1980), building on Gramsci, assists us to think about the contradictory, non-deterministic and contingent ways in which ideology operates. His method of articulation and how ideologies are constituted through various elements, linked to power and material conditions, is instructive.

to achieve national liberation. Non-racialism became about normalising the requirements of a globalising capitalism, including racialised labour processes, accumulation and new logics of commodification. The dialectic of working-class solidarity, mass power and radical non-racial unity was surrendered to the power of domestic and global capital. ANC-led Alliance ideological hegemony, through radical non-racialism, was remade against the interests of the historical subjects of liberation struggle, the oppressed black majority (African, coloured and Indian) and the working class.[11] This profound revision in the ideological imagination, articulation and practice of national liberation in the post-apartheid period has to be located in the following material and ideological conditions.

First, reconciliation, national unity and nation building were ideologically uncoupled from radical non-racialism. Instead, nationalism in post-apartheid South Africa became about a fuzzy rainbowism. We were a country in which racialised difference and oppression was dissolved in the hues and shades of a fictive and re-imagined rainbow nation. We were all the rainbow; the rainbow was us. To dissent from and resist was to stand against the beauty of who we all were as a rainbow nation. The TRC, the GNU, the Mandela factor, the role of sport, including the Rugby and Soccer World cups, were all marshalled to address the deep historical fault-lines of racial oppression, class exploitation and sexism. A country ravaged by dehumanisation was now meant to be living the rainbow dream, a new normalcy. The deep racial structures of formal apartheid were also dismantled to prop up this re-imagined nation. A progressive and new constitutionalism was crucial in this regard. Non-racialism was reduced to the celebration of racial diversity in the rainbow. We moved from apartheid racial classification to post-apartheid racial classification.

Second, the ANC-led Alliance and state, despite some intra-alliance quibbles, embraced another ideological element as part of post-apartheid national liberation: neoliberalism. Transnational neoliberalism was central to US-imperial hegemony and international relations over the past few decades. Not only did it seek to lock in the power of US financial markets across the globe, it also sought to remake the functions of the nation state to serve the market and weaken the power of labour. For the ANC's rainbowist nationalism, this meant the state and economy were to be deracialised but not fundamentally transformed through radical non-racialism. A deracialised state amounted to being an African state. This is not a capable, non-racial, nation-building state

---

11 I have covered this ground in other work, which I draw on for this part of the argument. See Satgar (2008, 2009b, 2012, 2014c, 2015c).

directing, disciplining and reallocating capital. It is not a state capable of leading a nationally determined and driven development project. Despite the rhetoric of constructing a developmental state, the post-apartheid state merely appeases African nationalism and for more than two decades has been about subordinating this state to the power of global finance. The state has been an Afro-neoliberal state, managing a deeply globalised and financialised economy. The ubiquitous market has squeezed and disciplined the state. With the Zuma project, the state has been squeezed through corruption and rent seeking. The formal authority of the state has been increasingly undermined and an informal, shadow state has emerged. Market-driven and financialised black economic empowerment has been supplemented by state-driven, transactional BEE. A new parasitic black capitalist class has been in the making in the nexus of the state-market-ruling party. All of this is consistent with a neoliberalised global capitalism that is deeply corrupt and driven by an accumulation logic centred on increasing inequality. In this context, black capital and white capital have become the champions of an ostensible non-racialism to ensure harmonious race relations and radical economic transformation in the rainbow nation. A society led by capital has become the linchpin of national liberation practice and ideology.

Third, radical non-racialism has also been supplanted by marrying nationalism to liberal constitutionalism. Ironically, the ANC-led alliance has always maintained that historically, the national liberation struggle has never been narrowly about civil and political rights. This was a struggle for fundamental transformation of the racist political economy. Despite this, South Africa's transformative constitutionalism has been reduced to a liberal constitutionalism articulated with national liberation ideology and its commitment to being a well-governed Afro-neoliberal state. An abstract citizenship has rendered all equal before the law; every South African is now the bearer of rights and a custodian of voting electoral power every five years. In the economy, every citizen is free to sell their labour power and harness the free market for wealth acquisition. This liberal fiction, imagined as part of the rainbow nation, stands in stark contrast to the lived experience of precariousness among workers, deep inequality, widespread hunger, high unemployment and extremely high costs to access the courts in South Africa.[12] South Africa's imagined liberal democracy works only for a minority; hence between electoral cycles there are widespread

---

12 According to Statistics South Africa (2017a), the unemployment rate was at 27.7% in 2017 and income inequality was at 0.68 (2017b), with sharp increases in income per capita inequality among whites and Indians. Both the unemployment rate and per capita income inequality are among the highest in the world.

social protests and increasingly violent civic struggles to gain recognition for the suffering in the everyday lives of the people. Shallow change, without fundamental transformation based on the Constitution, has made South Africa a dangerous rainbow nation with a minority inside the imagined liberal democracy and the black majority outside.

Fourth, the centrality of the working class and working-class leadership was also a pivotal element in national liberation ideology, nationalism and the politics of radical non-racialism. The rise of powerful black trade unions in the 1970s and the formation of COSATU in the mid-1980s gave a crucial organised expression to the working class in the South African national liberation struggle. The organised power of labour was also an important democratising force. Workers were actively engaged in their communities, as well as building popular organisation and constituting mass power prior to 1990. Today, in the context of the ANC-led Alliance, COSATU has been split, it has lost its strategic capacity to shape South African politics, unions have been bureaucratised and there is growing social distance between organised workers and society.[13] Moreover, the Afro-neoliberal accumulation regime has introduced racialised and gendered precariousness, apartheid-style labour relations persist on farms, fragmentation of unions has taken root and worker control in unions has been replaced by a growing business unionism linked to BEE. South Africa's working class has been defeated by African nationalism. The erasure and denial of radical non-racialism reinforces both white and black privilege for a minority. This is what the radical economic transformation agenda of the ANC really means.

Thesis 4

The ANC's embrace of deep globalisation, the unravelling of its hegemonic project and its populist call for radical economic transformation has unleashed new conjunctural racisms in South Africa, undermining the future of the country.

The roots of racism run deep in South Africa and the making of a racialised social order extends to the colonial encounter of dispossession, slavery, genocide, segregation, proletarianisation in the context of agricultural modernisation and industrialisation, and institutionalised apartheid. The racial structures of society have articulated with class and gender in different historical moments and conjunctures in the development of capitalism. Post-apartheid South

---

13 The crisis of COSATU is well documented in Satgar and Southall (2015) and Bezuidenhout and Tshoaedi (2017).

Africa inherited these racialised structures and relations of oppression. The ANC's embrace of Afro-neoliberalism and corrupt capitalist accumulation has unleashed both deracialising and re-racialising dynamics as part of the rainbow nation. Deracialisation has been led by market and transactional class forces producing a black capitalist class and a sizeable black middle class.[14] This is sometimes referred to as the 30% solution and has not laid the basis for a viable transformative democracy and social order.

Moreover, re-racialisation of social relations has also emerged in the context of the thin veneer of rainbowesque nation building evaporating as perceptions and insights into corruption at the heart of the ANC-led state have become more visible. The Zumafication of corruption has given licence to looting at various levels of the state and has grown grotesque since the ANC's vaunted Polokwane conference, which brought Zuma to power at the helm of the ANC and then the country. The Nkandla scandal, Gupta Leaks, revelations about state capture in the public protector's report, corrupt dealings in relation to mega-government spend, the compromising of criminal justice institutions together with failed service delivery have fed into the deepening legitimacy crisis of the Africanised state. All these realities have rolled back nation-building efforts and have fuelled racist tropes and stereotypes about the ANC state in everyday common sense. The ANC's commitment to non-racialism is now in question as it no longer represents the interests of society but the interests of corrupt factions seeking looting opportunities in processes of parasitic accumulation. The ANC's calls for radical economic transformation ring hollow, given how criminalised its politics has become and how the deep legitimacy crisis of the state re-racialises South Africa. Authoritarian populism will merely further divide the country.

At the same time, the land and agrarian challenge has not been addressed in South Africa, and this is an emotive issue given the historical injustices related to land dispossession. The ANC's approach to land reform has been modest and has actually not worked in several instances. On its current trajectory, the ANC would take at least another 40 years to achieve even its modest target of 30% land reform. The lack of a proper agrarian transformation strategy (except the use of liberalisation and marketisation since 1994), policy failure and a narrow productivist approach to agricultural development, through agri-business hubs and export-led agriculture, has again produced a class of small black farmers, connected to the dominant white-controlled and globalised agrarian economy while undermining the potential for more broad-

---

14 Southall (2016: 42) provides a crucial analysis of the new black middle class. He also looks at the size problem covered in the various studies that deal with this issue. The largest measurement suggests the new black middle class comprised 9.3 million in 2008.

based small black farmer development (Jara, 2014; Hall and Kepe, 2017). At the same time, the land question has become deeply racialised. White farmers still control 73% of agricultural land in South Africa.[15] They are insecure and fearful of the populist direction of the ANC. At a recent demonstration concerning murders of white farmers, called #BlackMonday, a reactive and reactionary Afrikaner chauvinism came to the fore. The old apartheid flag was raised in some quarters and the new South African flag was burnt. These were deeply inflammatory and provocative moves.

The African nationalist EFF, through their fiery leader, Malema, has an extremely populist approach to land reform. They have vaunted the Zimbabwe experience of land grabs and have also staged a few land occupations. Malema's EFF has a profoundly Africanist politics on the land question and he positioned himself as the voice of African nationalism against the Afrikaner chauvinism of #BlackMonday. He further racialised the national discourse, polarising the country even more. The land question has to be resolved but without a populist-engendered race war and in the context of failing corporate-controlled food systems. How the land question is dealt with can be an opportunity to build a new, resilient and food-sovereign system that advances radical non-racialism.

Another crucial expression of conjunctural racism is the rampant xenophobia in society. It is becoming increasingly incontrovertible that state practices and the state's policy approach to the migration regime are deeply xenophobic. This is contrary to the human rights framework of the country and the country's international relations commitments to the continent. State xenophobia has also contributed to divisions among the working class. Over the years, many of the violent flare-ups against non-South Africans have occurred in black working-class communities. These communities experience high levels of hunger and unemployment. The competition for economic opportunities is intense, given the crisis of social reproduction and the inability of the state to dynamise a labour-absorbing growth path. State xenophobia has certainly fuelled this situation. Moreover, working-class organisations such as unions, informal trader organisations, civic organisations and faith-based organisations have not done enough to build solidarities and support for migrants/immigrants in these communities. The once deeply solidaristic, radical non-racialism has again been further undermined by the crisis of national liberation ideology, state practice and the re-racialising dynamics of ANC leadership in South African society.

---

15 A land audit by Agri-SA suggests that white farmer ownership of agricultural land declined from 85.1% in 1994 to 73.3% in 2016. See J. de Lange, 'Who owns SA's land?' *City Press*, 29 October 2017: 8.

Thesis 5

The climate crisis threatens the existence of humans and non-human life forms. Eco-imperialism and capital, as a geological force, are driving the climate crisis in the context of the Anthropocene.

On a planetary scale, capitalism has undermined various natural cycles of the Earth's ecosystem. The assumption of endless capitalist accumulation, as part of fossil fuel and natural resource extractivism, globalised production patterns and wasteful mass consumerism has overshot various planetary limits. Resource peak, widespread pollution and ecological destruction are commonplace. The central contradiction in this context is the climate crisis (Satgar, 2018b). The climate crisis, involving the heating of the planet, poses the gravest threat to human and non-human life. We have crossed a 1°C increase in planetary temperature since the industrial revolution and are heading rapidly to overshoot 1.5°C in the next two decades or sooner. Many scientists also predict that we will cross the two-degree increase in planetary temperature in this century. These increases unleash dangerous feedback loops and extreme shifts in the Earth's ecosystem. There are already indicators of the awesome destruction and unbearable living conditions resulting from a heating planet. Hurricanes, droughts, heat waves, floods, rising sea levels threatening island states and low-lying areas, and freak extreme weather events are becoming the new normal. In this context, the conditions to sustain life on Planet Earth, including South Africa, are being undermined. To make sense of the human impact on the planet, scientists, particularly geologists, have declared that we have left behind almost 11,000 years of stable climatic conditions, known as the Holocene, and are now entering a new stage in planetary history known as the Anthropocene.

This means humans are a causal factor in shaping planetary conditions such as climate change. This is a scientific fact. On the face of it, this approach to the climate crisis makes sense. However, from the standpoint of Marxist ecology, the Anthropocene is really about imperial ecocide, that is the role of the US as the dominant imperial power refusing to let the world take the climate crisis seriously, given that a decarbonised civilisation requires fundamental systemic transformation, including going beyond capitalism, if we are to survive. In addition, capital as a geological force is responsible for global carbon extraction, for burning fossil fuels and driving global carbon-based accumulation, including production, consumption and everyday patterns of living that are carbon-centric, wasteful and destructive to planetary ecosystems. Capital as a geological force has for 150 years enlisted the role of rich industrialised countries in the global North, petro-states and carbon-addicted ruling classes.

Of late, industrialising countries such as China and India are also contributing, in aggregate, to global emission levels. Similarly, South Africa is a carbon-intensive economy and has extremely high levels of aggregate carbon emissions.[16] Global leadership has failed in multilateral institutions and at the state level. The UN Paris Agreement brings too little, too late, and has already been undermined by the Trump administration. Vulnerable island states are challenged by increasing sea levels and climate shocks, such as hurricanes. In 2017, hurricanes Harvey, Irma and Maria left a trail of destruction in their wake and extremely high costs for reconstruction. South Africa is a carbon-addicted society. Our economy is heavily invested in coal and the government has flirted with a nuclear deal that would bankrupt the state. South Africa's carbon capitalist forces are also driving a resource nationalism that would lead to fracking in parts of the country with fragile ecosystems and gas/oil exploration of our coastlines through Operation Phakisa. These extractive initiatives aim to yield complex hydrocarbons that will worsen the climate crisis and also involve extending and deepening the carbon-based minerals-energy complex. South Africa is a carbon criminal state seeking to make a few super wealthy, through carbon capitalism, while the rest of society bears the brunt of climate shocks. This is the terminus of the ANC-led Alliance approach to the National Democratic Revolution. It is not about sustaining life but about destroying it.

Thesis 6

The ANC-led Alliance approach and, more generally, the orthodox Marxist approaches to the national question are outdated in the context of the dangerous climate contradiction and the deepening planetary ecological crisis. The national question has to be replaced by the ecocide question.

The ANC-led South African state is a carbon criminal state and a failed climate crisis state. It is undermining the right to life of present generations and generational justice for future generations. South Africa's drought, since 2014, has been one of the worst in the history of the country. It has had dramatic impacts on food prices, hunger (14 million South Africans went to bed hungry before the drought), water systems and food production. Cape Town has experienced acute water stress and could become the first major urban conglomeration that might not be viable because of water shortages

---

16 EDGAR (2016) highlights that South Africa was 40th in the world in 2015 in terms of carbon emissions per capita and was 18th in global ranks in 2015 in terms of aggregate emissions.

linked to climate change. South Africa's drought is linked to the El Niño effect but also to a heating planet. Moreover, the Knysna fires of 2017, wave-surge flooding in the city of Durban and freak weather events (extreme downpours or cold spells during the onset of summer 2017) all portend a climate-driven South Africa and world. In this context, more droughts, flooding, heat waves and other extreme climate shocks should be expected. More climate shocks also mean more costs for society related to infrastructure, health, food and adaptation. A fiscally constrained state, due to mismanagement and corruption, is already a failed state.[17] With climate shocks, such a state will not survive. The South African state thus far has not been able to factor in the costs of these climate shocks and is failing to appreciate the death spiral of society due to climate change. Instead, the state is preoccupied with preventing the Eskom death spiral by trying to save South Africa's corrupt coal-driven electricity monopoly at the expense of society. This is all about return on investment in the context of bad policy decisions, state capture and a worsening climate crisis. South Africa should be leaving ESKOM behind as a stranded resource and transitioning to socially owned renewables at local government and community level.

The climate crisis is merely the expression of the deeper ecocidal logic of global capitalism. More sharply, the climate crisis reveals how capitalism, including post-apartheid capitalism, is incapable of solving the most serious existential threat faced by human and non-human life. Instead, capital, while it is causing the climate crisis, is also undermining the conditions that sustain life, leading to a sixth planetary extinction. This is the crux of the ecocide question. Yet the ANC-led Alliance in South Africa has embraced carbon-driven capitalist modernity, neoliberal globalisation and its ecocidal logic. The argument that more carbon-based energy or even nuclear power is required for industrial development is a false argument, given that there are cheaper renewable energy sources that can power the country at scale and meet its development needs. The national question in South Africa, as I have argued, has been resolved contra the interests of the workers, the poor and the majority. Class and race, in the ANC's non-racialism, has been about class formation for the few, as part of African nationalism. This has become the dominant agenda of national liberation. Such social forces are incapable of leading deep social change and transformation.

---

17 South Africa's debt to GDP ratio is increasing and is currently at about 56%. State-owned enterprises are highly indebted and if these institutions default, the entire fiscal system could be brought down. At the same time, looting of public resources is inducing tax fatigue and a massive leakage of public finance.

This prompts a serious question: why has the national question ideological approach to liberation ended up in such a degenerate, politically bankrupt and ecocidal place with a fundamental disregard for the most dangerous contradiction facing human and non-human life? Part of the answer relates to the kind of Marxism that has provided the intellectual scaffolding, template, imagination and tools to think through the national question and which has brought South Africa to this destructive turning point. South Africa's embrace of the national question approach to understanding racial oppression has its origins in Lenin's thesis on the right to self-determination, which was further elaborated by Stalin. It was imported into South Africa through the SACP (then called the Communist Party of South Africa, CPSA) and became central to ANC-led national liberation discourse to understand national oppression.[18] This framework evolved from the 1950s on, and became an analytical tool to understand class, race and capitalism as part of colonialism of a special type. The SACP's approach to understanding settler colonialism through positing and analysing colonialism of a special type, from its beginnings in modern economic relations through its vicissitudes of segregation and apartheid, became the hegemonic understanding of the national question in the ANC-led Alliance. It articulated a dualistic understanding of a coloniser/colonised society, in which the oppressor and oppressed shared a common territorial space. Similarly, Trotskyists evoked the political economy concept of racial capitalism.[19]

All the Marxist approaches to the national question in South Africa are marked by a deep productivism, which means that they did not bring into perspective the dimension of nature in historical materialism and in their understandings of South African capitalism. A crucial premise for these Marxisms was the idea of dominating nature, and even the envisaged socialist modernisation, with its state-centric relations of production, was about the march of the forces of production. Soviet modernisation was the answer, despite its extremely destructive ecological relations. Today, China has such an attraction as well with its growth-driven political economy. This is an

---

18 Mzala (1988) provides a useful account of the intellectual genealogy and itinerary of the national question approach. It should be noted that Marxism has also had other approaches to racism and colonialism.

19 Other Marxists utilised neo-Poulantzian structural analysis, racial Fordism and modes of production approaches. See two useful collections that capture the national question approach in South Africa: Van Diepen (1988) and more recently Webster and Pampallis (2017). What is striking about the latter collection is the complete absence of any recognition of the corporate-induced climate crisis and its ecocidal implications by the contributors.

anthropocentric and Promethean Marxism, marked by a fetish for ecocidal industrial development. Whether married to a first or a second stage of revolutionary change, these frameworks are deeply flawed from an ontological point of view.

In addition, the national question approach is based on an additive model of change. Thus, while a non-reductionist approach to class and race were the primary contradictions in the national liberation struggle, this was then extended to include the women's question and oppression. A hierarchy of oppressions was set up within the national liberation canon and this was mediated by the contingencies of the struggle within the NDR. However, this can easily degenerate into a static understanding of society such that the complexities, contradictions and dynamics of change in a social formation are not fully grasped. Looking at the Freedom Charter, the cornerstone programmatic basis of the ANC-led national liberation movement, and post-apartheid policy documents of the ANC, there is no ecological thrust in these documents that makes the connection between race, class, gender and ecological relations. National liberation thought has no conception of the ecological, even on the terms of its additive model of change. While climate determinism will register and will probably be added to the national question roster of contradictions, this will largely be an add-on that is reactive to a changing reality and not based on a deeper understanding of how it relates to the making of an ecocidal capitalism in South Africa. This will not be an effective basis to shift society and can easily be about green climate capitalism, a false solution.

Finally, South Africa's vanguardist national liberation forces (the ANC-led Alliance) are the real custodians of the national question, not the people. These forces are firmly entrenched in a carbon capitalist trajectory and the reproduction of South Africa's minerals-energy complex, revealing another fundamental weakness of the national question approach to the dangerous climate contradiction and ecocide. Theory and theoretical analysis, as the basis to guide revolutionary practice, cannot be the preserve of ideologues and vanguardist forces that proclaim to have the monopoly on the truth. Vanguards lose their way and are not the guarantor of revolutionary success, even for the resolution of the national question. History has repeatedly shown this to be the case, including in contemporary South Africa. Put differently, South Africa's vanguardist forces, such as the ANC and SACP, are historically exhausted, have failed and cannot be the basis to address the ecocide question. An alternative politics is required to address the ecocide question and challenge.

While the national question framework has had a decisive impact on the national liberation struggle, it is outdated, discredited and incapable of dealing with the life-threatening challenge of the climate crisis contradiction within global and South African capitalism. As it stands, the national question framework is married to carbon capitalism in South Africa and an avaricious resource nationalism in practice. It might take on elements of a green climate capitalism but this will not be enough. The national question framework is part of the problem. The climate crisis and more generally the ecocide question has to be the basis for a new emancipatory, deeply democratic and transformative politics. The time for the ecocide question is now.

Thesis 7

Securing a future and overcoming the ecocidal logic of capitalism lies in a democratic ecosocialist nation-building project. Such a project has to confront the climate crisis through deep, just transitions, grounded in radical non-racialism, mass transformative politics and the reclamation of our sovereignty to sustain life.

The ecocide question is the question of our time, for present and future generations and for human and non-human life forms. We cannot sustain life on Planet Earth, including South Africa, with runaway global warming and worsening ecological crises. This is not about catastrophism, ecofatalism or end of times millenarianism. The doomsday clock is ticking but there is still time to act. A fundamental shift in planetary consciousness is required to deal with and overcome the logic of capitalist ecocide. As I have argued, global leadership in multilateral institutions and in national states are not up to this task. Actually, they have failed. In this regard, crucial political imperatives have to be advanced and realised, noting that these imperatives are emerging from grassroots mass movements, radical intellectuals, progressive think tanks and activists engaged with the challenge of sustaining life.[20]

Scientific evidence produced by the UN, the National Aeronautics and Space Administration (NASA) and the World Meteorological Organization (WMO), geologists and earth scientists are compelling in enabling us to understand the scale, pace and current and prospective impacts of the climate crisis. Embracing the science of climate change and other ecological crises has to be the basis for understanding the ecocide question and has to be made understandable to all in the public sphere.

---

20 See also Satgar (2018b) for more in-depth engagement with democratic ecosocialist systemic alternatives, practices and pathways.

Planetary ecocide is about understanding how ecological relations have been racialised, classed, gendered and imbricated in various forms of oppressions. It has been central to supremacist whiteness and is about understanding the political economy of 500 years of destruction of human and non-human life in the making of capitalism's ecocidal logic. Genocides, slavery, species extinction, colonialism, industrial-scale violence, apartheid and human brutalisation are central to this history of the origins and making of capitalism. These relations can no longer be reified and ignored as part of capitalism's endless accumulation logic. Moreover, with climate change, there are and will be disproportionate impacts on workers, the poor, indigenous peoples, black lives, women peasant farmers and more generally the poorer and darker nations of the world. Capital's ecocidal logic is deeply racist and anti-life, more generally. Confronting planetary ecocide is also about confronting supremacist whiteness and advancing decolonisation as part of radical non-racialism.

Radical non-racialism has to be re-engaged as the basis for renewing and building mass people's power to confront capitalism's ecocidal logic. This means the anti-capitalism, anti-racism and anti-oppression thrusts of radical non-racialism have to be harnessed to unite social forces, build alliances (of workers, the landless, peasants, women's organisations, the permanently unemployed, radical intellectuals, students and middle classes) and advance movements to sustain life. These movements are already on the march at the frontlines of confronting carbon extractivism, land grabs, protecting the water, seed and forest commons, protesting against nuclear energy, fighting for decent work and more. Such movements are engaged in finding transformative and systemic alternatives to the contradictions of ecocidal capitalism in local, national, regional and global spheres. The imperative is to bring out the best of humanity, including human consciousness, solidarity and collective endeavour to scale up these alternatives and sustain life in South Africa and beyond.

Deep, just transitions and democratic ecosocialisms are the horizons and visionary concepts of anti-ecocide politics. The system-change logic of systemic alternatives, such as food sovereignty, the solidarity economy, climate jobs, indigenous knowledge systems, rights of nature, socially owned renewable energy, mass renewable energy, public transport, universal BIG, water commoning, democratic planning and more, are about deep, just transitions beyond capitalism, from within and outside. It is about harnessing deep democracy at the household, community, village, town, city and country level to constitute transformative power from below. At the same time, such deep democracy practices assist with reclaiming, re-embedding and transforming the state so that the people can govern. It is about affirming an ecocentric ethics in our relationship with human and non-human life, while meeting human needs. Simply, the democratic ecosocialism project is about ending the capitalist war with nature and affirming human life, black and white, as part of renewing nation building in South Africa.

Racism After Apartheid: Challenges for Marxism and Anti-Racism, Democratic Marxism series IV, edited by Vishwas Satgar. Johannesburg: Wits University Press, 2019.

The Coloniality of the Scientific Anthropocene: Towards Decolonial Futures of North–South Relations

Introduction

THE ANTHROPOCENE HAS become a master category in the natural sciences and is disrupting the social sciences. As a discursive intervention, it is transgressive and has brought to the fore the importance of Earth system science for understanding the human-induced rupture in the Earth system and at the same time has catapulted the revenge of nature into an anthropocentric field of social science enquiry. Although the Anthropocene has still not been officially recognised as a geological marker (as epoch, period or age) in the deep geological history of our planet, the clash of geological and human temporality is hard to escape as planetary heating intensifies. This planetary reality poses a challenge to all bodies of disciplinary thought in the academy. Moreover, the lived realities of climate shocks, expressed through weather extremes, mark an end to planetary conditions that enabled civilisations, cultures, philosophy, mathematics and everyday human life to thrive. This period of relatively stable climatic conditions has been known as the Holocene (the past 11,000 years). The Anthropocene portends a terrifying world in which uncertainty, risk and climate harm are the basis for existence. The stakes are high with a worsening climate crisis. One would have expected International Relations to be one of the disciplines seized with thinking through this global problem, which engulfs all planetary life and scales of living and threatens everything. The United Nations-led multilateral negotiations on the climate crisis began in 1992, almost three decades ago, yet only over the past few years has International Relations found its disciplinary voice and intersection with the Anthropocene discourse and the real-life challenges it poses to our societies. Even these contributions have been underwhelming in relation to those of other disciplines (Simangan, 2020: 213–214).

Mainstream and hegemonic disciplinary International Relations knowledge is implicated in reproducing coloniality. Coloniality is defined as the ongoing subalternity of the global South and the reproduction of relations of race, class, gender and ecological oppression in the context of the ecocidal destruction of planetary conditions that sustain life as part of an ecologically blind global modernity.[1] More sharply, hegemonic International Relations knowledge reproduces ways of living and power that do not appreciate ecological relations and how dominant structures and practices are destroying planetary ecosystems. The challenge facing International Relations is to decolonise. Its theories, images and assumptions are trapped in frames of understanding, power relations and politics that occlude an appreciation of the ontological challenges of the Anthropocene. Hence, the central argument of this article is that a decolonial approach to International Relations as an academic discipline is crucial. In this regard, this article sets out the importance and role of, and approaches to, a decolonised International Relations. Consequentially, it stakes out a decolonial International Relations as the basis to critically interrogate the Anthropocene.

The second focus of this article is to engage with the coloniality of the scientific Anthropocene. This is not about a rejection of science or the global ecological perspective this discourse encourages, but rather about critically interrogating the claim of the scientific Anthropocene that the undifferentiated Anthropos or human beings as a species are the geological force shaping our planet. This critique in the social sciences is not novel. However, this article goes further to situate the international relations envisaged by the scientific Anthropocene as implicated in coloniality, a matrix of power that reinforces oppressive North–South relations and relations of oppression. Put differently, a direct challenge is provided to the scientific Anthropocene by furnishing a critique of the coloniality it expresses in its conception of the international.

The third and final focus of this article deals with the possible futures of North–South relations in the Anthropocene. This is done through the decolonial International Relations perspective informing this article. Such a perspective seeks to address the limits of hegemonic International Relations academic knowledge and the international relations problems with the scientific Anthropocene. In this vein, this article argues that states in the global South, as

---

1 The Latin American school or approach to decoloniality locates coloniality/decoloniality within the 500-year span of colonial conquest and its ongoing matrix of power and struggle in different spheres of life, even in the midst of global capitalism. Although some approaches are more relational than others in understanding the matrix of power, the coloniality/decolonial option finds a variegated expression in other parts of the global South. The work of Mignolo and Walsh (2018) is important in this regard. Moreover, a regional epistemological approach to coloniality/decoloniality and its preoccupations is not necessarily the same as tackling the challenge from a disciplinary perspective such as International Relations and its failure to recognise ecological relations as part of actual lived international relations.

a geopolitical specification referring to countries outside of and dominated by the global North US-led bloc, are not and should not be passive actors in the context of Anthropocene international relations. Instead, this article argues that countries in the global South have a scientific, political, ethical and decolonial obligation to act in the interests of human and non-human life to remake the Anthropocene world order, as they face the greatest climate harm for a problem they did not cause. Moreover, this means that the necessity to act to ensure the preservation of a stable Earth system and their societies must also be guided by decolonised global ecological conceptions of International Relations by drawing on Southern thinkers. The future of North–South relations in the Anthropocene must be shaped by claims of sovereignty informed by decolonised Southern thought. In this regard, this article highlights the possible futures of North–South relations based on the central conceptual categories offered by the thought of Enrique Dussel (a liberation philosopher from Argentina/Mexico), Samir Amin (who was one of Africa's leading political economists) and Vandana Shiva (a leading ecologist and ecofeminist from India) on a decolonised global ecological approach to North–South relations. Each of these thinkers offers ways of rethinking International Relations that challenges the hegemonic orthodoxies of a West-centred International Relations discipline, which reproduces the subaltern status of the global South and ultimately condemns these societies to destruction.

Decolonial approaches to International Relations

In this article, I refer to mainstream International Relations theory as the hegemonic and mainstream canon. The genealogy of such theory is normally located immediately after World War 1 and has its moorings in the Western academy. In its formative years as an academic discipline, its main preoccupations have been the dynamics of imperialism and the problem of war (Ashworth, 2014: 95). After World War 2, International Relations was increasingly considered an American social science. Over the past few decades, there have been several paradigm debates but these have centred largely on the dominant approaches of realism, liberalism/pluralism and structuralism, epistemological concerns, and the philosophy of social science (critical realism). This hegemonic canon has been reproduced in textbooks, curricula and classrooms.

However, this has not stopped immanent critique and attempts to unsettle the myths of the International Relations discipline, its dominant assumptions and its limited theoretical horizons. For instance, Rosenberg

(1994) has provided an important critique of realist theory as a starting point to advance an alternative history of the international system. Linklater (2007) attempted to reconstruct International Relations theory around the problems of community, citizenship and harm. He concludes with a call for critical International Relations theory as a sociology of global morals with an emancipatory intent. Levine (2012) highlights the reifications in International Relations theory and makes the case for sustainably critical International Relations theory. However, although all these approaches seek to assail the hegemonic mainstream to pose new problematics and epistemological approaches, this has not decentred International Relations as a discipline. Alongside these attempts to open up International Relations has been the emergence of postcolonial and decolonial approaches. Both these approaches go back to the colonial/anti-colonial moment and struggles against racism, including Du Bois's colour line of the twentieth century, anti-colonial and anti-apartheid struggles, and various sources of anti-Eurocentric critical intellectual thought such as pioneering work of Enrique Dussel on the *Philosophy of Liberation* (1985),[2] Edward Said on *Orientalism* (1979) and Samir Amin on *Eurocentrism* (1989).

The postcolonial moment has offered new readings and hermeneutic approaches to the afterlives of the colonial. Heavily influenced by postmodern theorising, it has brought non-Western thought into International Relations to fill in silences.[3] However, the decolonial approach has proven to be much more compelling in its engagement with hegemonic International Relations theory and disciplinary preoccupations. It has consistently opened up space for new epistemological approaches to the international and has deeply probed the coloniality of the International Relations discipline. This critical intellectual practice has opened up space for a decolonial research agenda with different strands of critical knowledge production to shape a decolonial conception of the international. Moreover, decolonising International Relations is buttressed

---

2 Originally published in Spanish in 1977.

3 Postcolonial theory and approaches have their origins in cultural and literary studies. The term postcolonial itself has come under critical scrutiny and is also contested in those arenas: see Mishra and Hodge (2013) and McClintock (2013). Also, in those disciplinary fields, postmodern approaches to theory and methods of analysis have thrived. Decolonial approaches have a genealogy outside the academy in actual struggles against colonialism and ongoing forms of coloniality. Its critical resources have been brought into the academy as a crucial project for critical thinking. This is a crucial difference between postcolonial and decolonial approaches: see Mignolo (2010) for one interpretation of this distinction. Moreover, decolonial critical thinking projects, options and practices exist on a planetary scale to overcome ongoing Western imperial control.

by shifting and contingent real-world dynamics – student protests against coloniality and for decolonising knowledge and universities, the rise of indigenous resistance, the failures of capitalist modernity and deepening crises of neoliberalised capitalism – but mainly the worsening climate crisis.

However, let us return to the coloniality of International Relations as a discipline. Put more sharply, what is the coloniality of International Relations as a discipline? How have critical scholars answered this question? Different scholars have committed to decolonising International Relations by focusing on different aspects of coloniality, as claims, assumptions or silences, within the hegemonic mainstream.

This includes the following:

1. Critique of the ontological primacy given to imperial dominance and violence as a normative good. In this regard, mainstream hegemonic International Relations theory has naturalised the role of imperial power as the counter to a world in chaos or structurally necessary for world order to prevail. Imperial power and its violence are legitimated. Geopolitical asymmetries are also engendered between wealthy countries in the centres versus poorer countries in the peripheries (Jones, 2006; Saurin, 2006).
2. Questioning white supremacist thought, assumptions and epistemological Eurocentricism that frames Western-led global modernity as the standard for being developed, civilised and necessary to be conscripted to the imperial order. This linear telos is deeply imbricated in hegemonic International Relations theory and is critically appraised (Anievas et al., 2015; Halperin, 2006).
3. Calling into question the objectification of countries in the global South as failed states, badly governed and prone to big man politics. This has its roots in orientalist modes of thinking and generally produces racial stereotypes. But decolonial scholars have also pointed out that this has deeper roots in the colonial and imperial origins of international law and notions of sovereignty that have been transplanted into the postcolonial world and instrumentalised (Anghie, 2005; Grovogui, 1996; Pahuja, 2011).
4. Hegemonic International Relations epistemology justifies patterns of inequality and unequal ecological exchange. These are considered givens and necessary for world order. However, the deeper implications for race, gender, and class, including the ecological consequences, are not considered. Some of these dynamics have been called into question by decolonial scholars working within International Relations (Anievas et al., 2015; Jones, 2013).

5. There are universal claims made on behalf of the US-led West and which are supported by hegemonic International Relations. For Wallerstein (2006), these are claims about human rights and something called democracy, the superiority of Western civilisation in the context of the clash with the rest and scientific truths of the market. These universal claims, he argues, are actually particularist and are merely pan-European claims. Instead, he believes that this rhetoric of power must be overcome not only through critique but through the affirmation of universal universalism.
6. The erasure of knowledge of the subaltern. Can the non-Euro-American think? This is a central challenge of decolonial scholars to the coloniality of International Relations. This has led to creating space to bring non-Western thought into International Relations and to advance post-imperial conceptions of the international (Shilliam, 2011).

All of these epistemological approaches to decolonising International Relations critique the imperial genealogy and orientation of the International Relations discipline, provide critical conceptions of how the international and coloniality persist, and create space in the International Relations discipline to advance subaltern alternatives of the international. All of these approaches to decolonising International Relations inform how this article critically engages with the international relations of the scientific Anthropocene, particularly to interrogate its coloniality, and what this means for decolonial futures of North–South relations.

International Relations

In 2000, Paul Crutzen and Eugene Stoermer (both scientists) published a short article entitled 'The "Anthropocene"' in the *Global Change Newsletter*. In 2002, Crutzen published a follow-up article entitled 'The geology of mankind' in *Nature*. Both articles make the case for human-induced changes on our planet. Several geoecological markers such as carbon emissions, human population growth and biodiversity loss are cited as evidence of human impact on the planet. For Crutzen, this amounted to a geological shift and necessitated a discursive shift in how the geological history of the planet is understood. Humans were no longer living in the relatively stable climate of the Holocene but were now in a no-analogue state which he preferred to term a new geological epoch: the Anthropocene. Humans were a geological force shaping the planet and our futures as a species. This intervention sparked a flurry of debate and further scrutiny. One line of thinking problematised the originary moment of the Anthropocene. For Crutzen, it was in the 1800s because of the widespread use of the steam engine and coal. This position has been nuanced by other scientists who suggest a great acceleration after World War 2 and a discernible spike in emissions and other ecological effects (Steffen et al., 2015). The case of the Anthropocene as a new geological epoch, including to the International Commission on Stratigraphy responsible for recording the Earth's history, has continued to be made. However, despite this lack of official naming of a geological epoch, scientific Anthropocene discourse has shaped global change research agendas, Earth system science (including work on planetary boundaries), the Intergovernmental Panel on Climate Change (IPCC) scientific reporting, and even the social sciences.

For international relations and politics, global climate negotiations are now framed using the language of Anthropogenic effects (Satgar, 2018a: 51). In 2007, the fourth IPCC report unequivocally affirmed that 'human induced climate change' is a scientific fact and hence that humans are responsible for climate change. Moreover, in the fifth IPCC report, the idea of Anthropogenic effects runs throughout its framing discourse. In the fifth IPCC report, there is an invented terminology at work which refers to 'human influence on the climate system', 'Anthropogenic greenhouse gas emissions', 'Anthropogenic forcings', 'total human induced warming', 'population growth' and so on. In effect, the main causal factor, in both scientific and technocratic terms, is all of humanity, including population growth. This means that the international is equated to the agency of every human on the planet. The global political economy of the planet, its power structure (institutions, ideas and capacities) and social forces do not feature in such a discourse. In other words, even hegemonic International Relations, both as a discipline and as actual power dynamics, is not considered relevant to explain and understand the Anthropocene. However, although this clash with the discipline of International Relations is important to keep in view, the international relations of the scientific Anthropocene is seriously flawed from a decolonial perspective.

More sharply, if the scientific Anthropocene informs actual international relations and politics, then it reinforces coloniality. How does this happen? First, human beings are advanced as the explanadum (the thing to be explained) and explanation of the climate crisis. This is inadequate and unacceptable from the standpoint of critical global political economy/ecology underpinning decolonial International Relations. Such a human-centred explanation completely occludes the power of imperialism over the past 150 years and how it has maintained and reproduced a fossil fuel-based global political economy. The nexus of relations between fossil fuel corporations and imperial power has been symbiotic. Carroll (2020: 30–57) points out in periodising imperialism – from the Pax Britannia of the mid- to late-nineteenth century, classic imperialism up to 1945, thereafter the Pax Americana until the 1970s, and now neoliberal global governance – how fossil fuel corporations and imperial power have worked together to lock in carbon capitalism. More recently, the US, under both Obama and Trump, accelerated fossil fuel extraction through fracking such that the US has become a crucial geopolitical player in controlling and influencing the global oil supply.

Second, although modernity is problematised in terms of the great acceleration, from the 1950s onwards, within scientific Anthropocene discourse, its imbrication in reproducing coloniality is completely ignored. The racialised and gendered ecologies of capitalism to achieve this acceleration are not explicated. Global nature as a site of extraction, dispossession, violence and commodification are not considered part of the explanatory frame. In short, critical global political ecology and specifically the process of global unequal ecological exchange (Hornborg, 2013) and the imperial mode of living of the global North (Brand and Wissen, 2021) with its huge per capita consumption footprints are not brought into view. This means that the ecological debt owed by the global North to the South is unimportant but rather we are all co-responsible for the great acceleration on Planet Earth that is leading to our extinction.

Third, with regard to emissions inequality, it is patently clear that the wealthy are responsible for carbon emissions in countries in the global North and South. This comes to the fore in a study by Oxfam International (2020), authored by Tim Gore, covering emissions from 1990 to 2015, during which time the total or cumulative emissions added to the atmosphere doubled.[4] The central question of this study is 'Who is responsible?' Some of the main conclusions are telling:

- The richest 10% of the world's population (c. 630 million people) were responsible for 52% of the cumulative carbon emissions – depleting the global carbon budget by nearly a third (31% in those 25 years alone;
- The poorest 50% (c. 3.1 billion people) were responsible for just 7% of cumulative emissions and used just 4% of the available carbon budget;
- The richest 1% (c. 63 million people) alone were responsible for 15% of cumulative emissions and 9% of the carbon budget – twice as much as the

---

4   https://oxfamilibrary.openrepository.com/bitstream/handle/10546/621052/mb-confronting-carbon- inequality-210920-en.pdf.

poorest half of the world's population;
- The richest 5% (c. 315 million people) were responsible for over a third (37%) of the total growth in emissions, while the total growth in emissions of the richest 1% was three times that of the poorest 50%.

In Africa (responsible for 3% of cumulative emissions between 1990 and 2015), the research results highlight that the top 10% (the wealthy) accounted for 64% of cumulative emissions, the middle 40% accounted for 31% of cumulative emissions, and the bottom 50% accounted for 4% of cumulative emissions. So, in this decade, if the carbon emissions planetary boundary is overshot beyond 1.5°C, who is really responsible? It cannot be all of humanity and certainly cannot be the poorest people and countries on the African continent. They do not have the per capita emissions, let alone the histories of carbon extraction and use, that make them culpable. This further reveals the coloniality of the scientific Anthropocene discourse.

Fourth, the human-centred explanation at the heart of the scientific Anthropocene is a dangerous liberal universal. It is dangerous because it suggests that we are all equally causing the climate crisis but also equally responsible. This is a false universal given how power works in the imperial-dominated world of uneven carbon capitalism. Individuals will never match the structural power of carbon corporations, finance houses or states with locked-in vested interests. Such a universal is also ahistorical in the sense of failing to understand how different historical forms of coloniality have persisted over the past 500 years and ensured the domination of the subaltern (Quijano, 2013). So, humanity is differentiated in its lived experience and dehumanisation it has had to endure because of the persistence of coloniality. Hence, the human-centred approach of the scientific Anthropocene is upended by this existential history of coloniality.

Fifth, the scientific Anthropocene confirms its coloniality in how it fails to appreciate the importance of subaltern resistance in the making of our contemporary world. Put differently, the Holocene world, at least over the past 500 years of Western planetary expansion, was marked by subaltern resistance against imperial ecocide, genocide, wars, coloniality/modernity, the Nazi Holocaust and apartheid; and for a decolonial world. In the two cycles (2004 until 2010 and then again from 2016 to 2020) of global climate justice resistance over the past two decades, it was the Bolivian state supported by indigenous people's movements that gave the world the Cochabamba Declaration of 2010; the Standing Rock resistance in the US that was at the frontlines of gridlocking fossil fuel extraction; the indigenous peoples of the Amazon are sacrificing their lives to save the Amazon; and grassroots movements in South Africa have now placed a Climate Justice Charter on the agenda of their national parliament as the basis to advance a deep, just transition, centred on race, class, and gender emancipation. Despite this, Crutzen believes the future is about an anthropocentric modernity, grounded in an instrumental reason, and ultimately coloniality:

> A daunting task lies ahead for scientists and engineers to guide society towards environmentally sustainable management during the era of the Anthropocene. This will require appropriate human behaviour at all scales, and may well involve internationally accepted, large scale geo-engineering projects, for instance to 'optimize' climate (2002: 23).

From the standpoint of decolonial International Relations, the discursive framing of the Anthropocene is regressive. It lacks a clear ontology grounded in critical global political economy/ecology and a clear opposition to coloniality. Hence, it has not been an effective discourse to address the underlying systemic and agential causes of the worsening climate crisis and its racial, gendered, class and geopolitical implications. This does not mean that the science of the Anthropocene or the category has to be jettisoned. Rather, there is a need to reframe the Anthropocene within a decolonial approach to international relations. This is elaborated in relation to the futures of North–South relations in the Anthropocene.

Decolonial perspectives on the futures of North–South relations in the Anthropocene

The planetary temperature increase exceeded 1°C in 2015, since prior to the Industrial Revolution, resulting in calamitous climate shocks being experienced across the world. For the global South, shocking realities have become headline news: the severest cyclonic activity recorded over two decades in southern Africa with the impacts of cyclones Idai and Kenneth, South Africa experiencing the worst drought in its history, one-third of Bangladesh being flooded, and the Amazon experiencing severe droughts, accompanied by wild fires and scorched-earth burns by loggers, ranchers and illegal miners. The vectors of change in this context ramify into the interstate system, the global economy and ultimately international relations. If this reality is not mitigated and business-as-usual trajectories continue, the Anthropocene will be equivalent to the extinction story of the human species. For centuries, the global South has been bearing the brunt of the coloniality of Holocene international relations and now Anthropocene international relations; hence, the struggle for climate justice and for reparations for ecological debt is crucial. However, although these claims must continue to feature as part of decolonial international relations, it is crucial for these countries to break new ground to protect their societies from worsening climate harms. In this context, they must also rise to the challenge of leading the world to secure a stable Earth system. This means that the agency of countries and peoples in the global South must be at the forefront of constructing a decolonial Anthropocene world order. Such a world order must secure a future of all life forms – human and non-human – and should be inspired by decolonial thinking in the global South.

To help us think about the possibilities of decolonial North–South futures, this article draws on key ideas developed by three thinkers in the global South: Enrique Dussel, Samir Amin and Vandana Shiva. These thinkers have several common premises. First, each thinker is anti-Eurocentric. They do not envisage a future based on the template of Euro-America and they reject Western supremacy. Second, they are all post-imperial thinkers. They do not accept the ontological primacy of imperial domination as the basis for ordering the world and they actually believe it must be resisted. Third, all are committed to a normative intellectual and political project of a more humanised and ecological existence. Fourth, all have been politically engaged for large parts of their lives and have intellectually contributed in pathbreaking ways to critical thought. Each thinker has written over 20 books and their intellectual corpus is vast. What follows is a modest engagement to think with key ideas advanced by these thinkers about possibilities for decolonial North–South futures in the context of a decolonising Anthropocene.

Enrique Dussel: Ethics of liberation and transmodern pluriversality

Enrique Dussel (born 24 December 1934) contributed to the development of liberation theology, liberation philosophy and decolonial research in Latin America. As a trained philosopher, he was pathbreaking in his generation. Three themes were entangled in his intellectual itinerary: religion, the history of Latin America and the philosophy of liberation. Dussel experienced the explosive 1960s while studying in Europe. In Argentina, he was persecuted by authoritarian forces in the early 1970s and he fled into political exile in Mexico just before the military dictatorship (1976–1983) took power in Argentina. Dussel also experienced the pink tide of new movements and left forces in Latin America over the past two decades.

In developing a philosophy of liberation, Dussel struggled with the colonial history of Latin America, including the geopolitics of knowledge. In his *Philosophy of Liberation*, first published in Spanish in 1977, the opening chapter is on geopolitics and philosophy. In this he provides a scathing critique of the reception of philosophy from the imperial centres and how it is implicated in the reproduction of colonial oppression and war. This is a powerful decolonial move. Dussel goes further in this journey to develop a crucial conceptual approach to the philosophy of liberation. The concept of totality is crucial in this framework and to move beyond phenomenology. Dussel defines it as follows:

> Every world is a totality. Totality indicates the horizon of horizons. It is not strange that a Kant or Wittgenstein could say that the world can be neither an object nor a fact. It is evidently the horizon within which all beings (which can be objects or facts) find their meaning. The world is the fundamental totality; it is the totality of totalities (2003 [1977]: 22–23).

However, in this world, Dussel recognises an exteriority or alterity of where the other exists. In this sense, the totality is not closed and in the exteriority of the system the history of the people reveals itself as a collective history. For Dussel to affirm the exteriority of the oppressed is to affirm their history and liberation. The praxis of liberation that guides the oppressed is relational; it is about social and natural relations and the connectedness of these relations within the totality. For Dussel this means:

> When I speak of praxis (person-to-person relationship) I include also in this case poiesis (person-to-nature relationship). Liberating action that directs itself to others (brother or sister, woman or man, child) is simultaneous with work in their favor. There is no liberation without economics, without humanized technology, without planning, and without beginning with a historical formation. Because of this, the praxis of liberation (a practical poiesis or a poetic praxis) is the act itself by which the horizon of the system is crossed over and one really penetrates into the exteriority through which the new order is constructed, a new, more just social formation (2003 [1977]: 63).

The ethics of liberation guiding such a praxis is elaborated by Dussel in his *Ethics of Liberation: In the Age of Globalization and Exclusion*. Translated into English in 2013, this 689-page text provides an in-depth study of ethics. It builds on his analectic method to transition from naive involvement in the world to ethical consciousness. At the same time, Dussel elaborates three crucial ethical principles to guide a praxis of liberation: (i) the material principle, which relates to production and reproduction of human life in community and in harmony with ecosystems; (ii) the formal principle, which is about inclusive, democratic and deliberative procedures involving all those impacted by a particular decision; and (iii) the feasibility principle, which is informed by the conditions we find ourselves in and which must be informed by the prior two principles such that the outcomes are achievable.

In addition to Dussel's ethics of liberation derived from a decolonised philosophy, his work took him in the direction of rethinking the history of Latin America from a decolonial perspective. In this regard, his book *The Invention of the Americas: Eclipse of 'the Other' and the Myth of Modernity* (1995) provides a critique of a Eurocentric account of history and the philosophy of history. In this regard, he also problematises modernity, both its early Christian variant and later its Enlightenment version.[5] This lays the basis for his call for a transmodern pluri-versality in which subaltern knowledge is retrieved, there is dialogue to achieve understanding, modernisation and its obsession with technological and instrumental rationality are called into question, and all of this is grounded in an ethics and philosophy of liberation. Brought to the fore in the context of rising indigenous movements, the emergence of the decolonial option research agenda, and the worsening crisis of modernity, the ethics of liberation and transmodern pluri-versality argued for by Dussel is certainly part of lived experience and will shape decolonial futures of North–South relations.

Samir Amin: Delinking and a polycentric world

Samir Amin (3 September 1931–12 August 2018) was a Marxist economist who made a pioneering contribution to dependency theory, played a crucial

---

5 In Dussel's 2013 work (437), there are two paradigms of modernity: (i) Eurocentric modernity because of some kind of inherent technological superiority (accumulated during the Middle Ages) of Europe which informs its expansion and conquest of other cultures and (ii) a global paradigm of modernity that emerged after Europe's encounter with America in 1492 and which gave it certain comparative advantages and then from the eighteenth century onwards when Europe eclipses the high Asiatic cultures.

role in developing world systems thinking (even before Immanuel Wallerstein) and introduced the critical analytic term Eurocentricism. Amin was born and educated in Egypt. His life's journey intersected with the rise of Arab nationalism and later with the left turn in postcolonial Africa, including the rise of African socialism and scientific socialism, neocolonial control of newly independent African countries, the defeat of Third World Bandung revolutionary nationalism and pan-Africanism in the context of the Cold War and structural adjustment, and the making of a globalised Africa. Amin lived through these moments, studied them, and intellectually engaged with them.

In *Eurocentricism*, Amin makes this critical observation:

The Westernization of the world would impose on everyone the adoption of the recipes for European superiority: free enterprise and the market, secularism and pluralist electoral democracy. It should be noted that this prescription assumes the superiority of the capitalist system, as well as this system's capacity to respond, if not to every possible challenge in the realm of the absolute, at least to all the potential demands on the conceivable horizon on the future (1989: 108).

This conceit at the heart of Eurocentricism is what Amin challenged in his intellectual itinerary and brought him to argue for the delinking of countries of the periphery from the permanent adjustment to the terms of countries in the centres led by the US-aligned triad (Europe and Japan). Delinking for Amin (1990) was not about autarky but about a national popular project that gave priority to the needs of peoples as opposed to externalising economies to meet the needs of transnational capital.[6] He envisaged that this strategic concept would guide the articulation of countries in the periphery with the global North and internally would be shaped by statist, capitalist and socialist tendencies over a long period of time. It was a form of autocentric development, largely endogenous, and affirmed the sovereignty of a particular country.

The concept of delinking has to be located in Amin's attempts to understand the underdevelopment of the global South. This goes back to his PhD dissertation (published in 1970 as *Accumulation on a World Scale: A Critique of the Theory of Underdevelopment*), which in the 1950s focused on the mechanisms causing the underdevelopment of the global South. Already in his dissertation,

---

6 Ndlovu-Gatsheni (2021) provides a crucial overview of Samir Amin's epistemological contribution to decolonisation and democratic Marxism while highlighting the importance of Amin's critique of mainstream economics and his case for delinking and internationalism.

he recognised that countries in the global South had to skew their economies on the terms of the global North. This research focus continued in the 1960s and 1970s as he worked for the United Nations (UN). He wrote several studies on various African countries and their challenges to integrate into the global economy. He also engaged in a serious debate with dependency thinkers and theorists coming to the fore in Latin America. However, Amin also applied his analytical powers to understand the world system and came to appreciate the logic of polarisation inherent in the world system. In this track, Amin's analysis of contemporary globalisation presciently recognised greater chaos under US-led hegemony and a new phase of global monopoly capitalism such that the global North would not concede space for the South.[7] In other words, catch-up modernisation, development and adjustment where all a mirage. This added to his case for delinking, which he refined to include delinking of regional blocs and as a crucial basis to achieve food sovereignty in national contexts. The latter addition to delinking prompted a rethinking of the agrarian question and the ecological substratum of societies.

At the same time, for delinking to advance it was necessary to achieve a polycentric world in which power was distributed away from a single hegemon. This required a rigorous understanding of US hegemony and its limits. Amin's analysis of imperialism was extremely original in this regard. Unlike Lenin, who understood imperialism as merely a structural reality in the context of monopoly capitalism, Amin understood that imperialism was present during mercantile capitalism, competitive capitalism in the 1800s, monopoly capitalism and (since the 1980s) the global monopoly phase of capitalism. In this context, Amin (2006) understood that Europe needed to play a decisive role in ensuring that the geopolitical reconfiguration of the post-Cold War world opened up prospects for an alignment from London-Berlin-Moscow. This was not realised with the European Union (EU) but Amin did not allow his strategic perspective to be thwarted by this setback. In the latter part of his life, appreciating the defeat of Bandung revolutionary nationalism, pan-Africanism, and the limits of the WSF process, he increasingly turned to the task of renewing internationalism. Just before his passing, he made the call for a Fifth International of Peoples and Workers (Amin, 2020). This process is under way and can serve as the basis to achieve delinking and a polycentric world. However, even if a new global movement of mass forces does not emerge in the twenty-first century, the world

---

7   See Samir Amin's *Empire of Chaos* (1992), in which he sets his world systems analysis highlighting the dangers of structural chaos due to US leadership. This analysis is very apposite to our contemporary context. In *Capitalism in the Age of Globalisation* (1996), he provides an analysis of the new phase of global monopoly capitalism and its implications for the global South.

of climate chaos, worsening systemic crises, rising ecofascism and coloniality in the Anthropocene necessitate a decolonial future for North–South relations. Amin's concepts of delinking and a polycentric world will continue to flicker in the background in this context and will certainly incite the imagination of transformative forces in the global South wanting a different future.

Vandana Shiva: Ecofeminism, the commons and Earth democracy

Vandana Shiva (born 5 November 1952) is a world-renowned ecofeminist, food sovereignty activist, one of India's foremost ecological thinkers and an anti-globalisation advocate. Trained as a physicist, she dedicated her professional life to elaborating a people's science and approach to technology and ecology. She has been given numerous awards, including the Right Livelihood Award (1993), which is considered the alternative to the Nobel Peace Prize. Shiva lived in the context of India's postcolonial Nehruvian socialism, the criminalisation of Indian politics, its authoritarian turn under Indira Gandhi, and the shift towards a financialised and globalised India and world. In her political thought, the importance of women as farmers, guardians of biodiversity, and agents of socio-ecological reproduction emerged very early on, particularly in the 1980s, with the publication of her first book, *Staying Alive: Women, Ecology and Development* (2016, originally published in 1988). Her ecofeminist critique of reductionist science, corporate-controlled globalised agriculture, and India's green revolution all affirm the importance of biodiverse, small-scale, localised and women-controlled agriculture.[8] This is at the heart of her ecofeminism, which grew out of the defence of women farmers as bearers of tacit knowledge and ecological science and as essential for food sovereignty. The links to the critique of white male-dominated agriculture, science and patriarchy, going back to the Enlightenment, are elaborated in two other books which contributed to the articulation of ecofeminism as a new feminism.[9] As Ariel Salleh notes in the foreword to *Ecofeminism* about one of the key conceptual contributions of this text: 'Mies and Shiva paint a sharp contrast between social decay of passive consumerism and the social vitality of skilful, self-sufficient and autonomous livelihood economies: subsistence.'

---

8   See Vandana Shiva's (2016 [1988]) *The Violence of the Green Revolution: Third World Agriculture, Ecology and Politics*, in which she provides a critique of the myths of the much-vaunted green revolution.

9   See *Ecofeminism* (1993), co-authored with Maria Mies, and *Biopolitics: A Feminist and Ecological Reader on Biotechnology* (1995), co-edited with Ingunn Moser, in which ecofeminism as a new feminism is brought into global intellectual discourse.

The concept of subsistence is crucial both for the political agenda of ecofeminism and for the second crucial concept that grounds it, namely the commons. Shiva's activism, particularly her commitment to seed and food sovereignty, took her into major battles against the WTO's intellectual property regime and attempts at what Shiva called biopiracy, the patenting of life. In this context and as part of the organisations she worked with, including international networks, she pushed back against the patenting of India's biodiversity and took on leading agro-industrial corporations based in the global North. She fought against various enclosures of the commons of biodiversity, including against the attempt by the Grace Company to patent India's neem tree and against attempts by RiceTec Inc. to patent basmati rice. She also rallied international support against global biotech companies and their use of genetically modified organisms. Shiva's book *Reclaiming the Commons: Biodiversity, Indigenous Knowledge and the Rights of Mother Earth*, first published in 1997, was used widely in national and international debates on biodiversity and intellectual property rights. In the 2020 reissue of this book, Shiva writes a new introduction about her 30-year journey to defend the commons by standing up to biopiracy and intellectual property regimes. This sums up her position on the importance of the commons: 'This book is about the common creativity of the earth, her biodiversity, and people's knowledge. It is also about the scientific, legal, political and cultural struggle to defend the sovereignty of biodiversity, indigenous cultures and national systems' (2020: 7).

Another crucial concept that helps us think about possible decolonial futures of North–South relations is Shiva's idea of Earth democracy. It is literally about defending the commons – land/soil, water, biodiversity, public life and the Earth system – on a planetary scale. In her words:

> The rhetoric of the 'ownership society' hides the anti-life philosophy of those who, while mounting prolife slogans, seek to own, control and monopolize all of the earth's gifts and all of human creativity. The enclosures of the commons that started in England created millions of disposable people. While these first enclosures stole only land, today all aspects of life are being enclosed – knowledge, culture, water, biodiversity and public services such as health and education. Commons are the highest expression of economic democracy (2020: 3).

For Shiva, this means extending democracy to every part of our lifeworld – biodiversity, food, water, finance and more – to ensure that Earth democracy can flourish. She sees this also as a movement championed from below. In the context of a decolonial Anthropocene, Shiva's approach to a subsistence-based ecofeminism, the centrality of the commons, and more generally Earth democracy stand in direct opposition to the coloniality of the existing corporate-controlled, imperial and ecocidal world. If these ideas prevail in everyday planetary struggles, the future of North–South relations will be about ending the destruction of biodiversity, phasing out fossil fuels, deglobalising corporate-controlled agriculture, democratising our lifeworld to enhance life-enabling commons systems, and ensuring that grassroots women's power shapes our socio-ecological systems. In short, Shiva's decolonial future for North–South relations is truly about sustaining life.

Conclusion

This article poses a triple challenge. First, to the coloniality of International Relations as a discipline. It highlights the ways in which critical decolonial scholars have disrupted such discursive scaffolding in the discipline. Moreover, it draws on such decolonial approaches to international relations to critically interrogate the notion of the Anthropocene. This is the second challenge advanced in this article. The articulation of the international within the framework of the scientific Anthropocene clashes with International Relations as a discipline but also perpetuates coloniality in its conception of the international. This article argues against this coloniality and its deleterious role in understanding the worsening climate crisis. However, instead of jettisoning the science and the Anthropocene category, this article regrounds the Anthropocene as a decolonial Anthropocene by thinking through possible futures for North–South relations. This is the third challenge posed by this article. To take the latter challenge forward, decolonial Anthropocene thinking happens by thinking with anti-Eurocentric, post-imperialist, ecological and politically engaged Southern thinkers. Key concepts of their thought that could shape decolonial North-South futures are brought to the fore. The world that humans inhabit is fast heading towards irreversible change and disastrous consequences for our species and other non-human life forms. The time to end jaded and unworkable paradigms of thinking, including in International Relations, has arrived. Decolonial epistemology and thought are crucial ways forward for all of us.

Oxford Encyclopaedia of International Studies, 2022.

Crises, Socio-Ecological Reproduction and Intersectionality: Challenges for Emancipatory Feminism

Introduction

SOCIAL REPRODUCTION THEORY (SRT) made its return in the early 2000s and is now part of a fourth wave of feminism. SRT no longer faces marketisation of lifeworlds, but after four decades it faces the devastating and accentuated consequences of such a process. Despite stark gendered and racialised class inequalities, the economising of everything has continued unabated. Remaking the world in the image of the US and transnationalising capital has been a process of disruptive and patriarchal social engineering, in the global North and South. China as a hub of cheap labour has also played its part in this process of deep globalisation and restructuring. Every scale and level of globalising accumulation has brought precariousness, new enclosures, ecosystem collapse, climate shocks, lumpen ruling-class formation and state contraction. Subaltern women have not been winners in this process, and even less so in the Covid-19 conjuncture. As peasants, urban and rural working classes and as the permanently poor unemployed, life has been tenuous. A patriarchal global division of labour has meant a global outside has been created where many of these women exist as unrecognised and disconnected from wage-earning circuits yet they carry the burden of social reproduction.

At the same time, capitalism is in the throes of a civilisational crisis. Despite its own internally constructed dynamics of overaccumulation, capitalism's ecocidal logic is destroying the ecological substratum of life (human and non-human) on Earth. Turbo boosted by finance and the creation of a global economy, the ecologies of capital have reached their limits. Soils are seriously depleted; biodiversity loss is rapid; non-human species extinction is accelerating; the biochemistry of the planet is changing due to overuse of toxic chemicals (nitrogen and phosphates in globalised agriculture are a good example); oceans are polluted (including through micro-plastics); and skyrocketing emissions (despite the Covid-19 pause) are reshaping the planetary geography, with zones of unliveability, for instance, becoming more pronounced. Ecofeminist analyses, strategic politics and movement building have been confronting these realities for a while. Yet mainstream feminism has not taken these issues on board. Instead, there has been a preoccupation in the mainstream with theorising and clarifying intersectional analysis, identity differences and the strategic implications of such modes of analysis.

This chapter seeks to engage sympathetically but critically with dominant Marxist approaches to SRT, to affirm strengths but to also explicate areas that need further development. It is argued that dominant Marxist approaches to SRT have the potential theoretically to also explain the contemporary crises of capitalism. In other words, SRT can also be applied to explain the general and historically specific crises of contemporary capitalism. Up to now, within its remit have been powerful theoretical arguments and analyses about how subaltern women's exploitation and oppression is structurally implicated in financialised capitalism and its reproductive regime. However, these perspectives do not grapple with the multidimensional crises of capitalism. Moreover, the ecological dimension of SRT has to be strengthened. Drawing on Marx's ecology and ecofeminism, SRT can provide an ecological approach to social reproduction but as socio-ecological reproduction theory (SERT). It needs to be greened. In terms of resistance, sharp debates have emerged between Marxist/socialist feminists championing SRT and intersectional feminists. The position argued in this chapter is that SRT (and SERT) also can work with some currents within intersectional feminism while recognising its limits. The chapter concludes with the relationship between SERT and a rising emancipatory feminism, while highlighting the challenges such a feminism faces.

Dominant approaches to social reproduction theory and analysis

SRT began to make its appearance again in the early 2000s as financialised restructuring further intensified the remaking of the welfare state in the global North. Several important contributions led by Marxist and socialist feminists highlighted precarity in the realm of production, the roll-back of social welfare, a new politics of the family and how class, race and gender articulate in the financialised reproductive regime. It also became clear that gains made by second-wave feminism in the 1960s–1980s were now in jeopardy. The space for transforming gender relations within capitalism was closing as inequalities widened and precarity defined social life. In this context, the postmodern current within third-wave feminism with its emphasis on cultural identities and difference, as well as its disavowal of macro-social analysis and its vaunting of the end of metanarratives, could not explain these new material realities. Married to liberal feminism, it became part of the problem and reached its limits. The neoliberal conjuncture required feminism to restore capitalism as central to its analysis to explain how a few women advanced at the expense of the many, as well as the emergence of a universal condition of precarity in life making. More nuanced readings of Marx's and Engels' work on gender and the family, as well as anti-racism, together with the republication of Lise Vogel's *Marxism and the Oppression of Women: Towards a Unitary Theory* (2013), shed a whole new light on the relationship between Marx's Marxism and oppression, including women's oppression.[1] Simple caricatures, such as the subject of history in Marx's writings, the white male factory worker, proved to have been mere misrepresentation.

Today SRT is gaining ground in the academy and in everyday feminist struggles. There is a flourishing of SRT contributions.[2] For the purposes of this chapter, I will focus on just two leading theorists and the contributions they have made that are shaping the frontiers of SRT development. The point of departure in this regard is the contribution of Lise Vogel's text, first published in 1983. It emerged in a context in which second-wave socialist feminism was exhausted and she made an attempt to grapple with some of its limits. In particular, it made two important contributions that provide a bridge to contemporary SRT, which is being developed further. First, Vogel's intervention dispelled the idea of a singular cause for women's oppression. It displaced the white working-class household and unpaid labour at the centre of second-wave socialist feminist theory, thus challenging the dualistic emphases on patriarchy and capitalism, on the one hand; and on the other, class reductionism. Hence the sub-title of her book: *Towards a Unitary Theory*. Second, her approach provided a structural and material conception of women's oppression. It was situated within the contradictory relationship between reproductive labour and processes of capital accumulation. Various oppressive sites, mechanisms and social relations were imbricated in this contradictory dynamic but required concrete historical and empirical study. Such studies were necessary to show

---

1   In this regard Anderson's *Marx at the Margins: On Nationalism, Ethnicity and Non-Western Societies* (2010), Brown's *Marx on Gender and the Family* (2012), Achar's *Marxism, Orientalism, Cosmopolitanism* (2013) and Mojab's *Marxism and Feminism* (2015) are apposite.

2   See Arruzza (2013), Bhattacharya (2017a), Ferguson (2020) and Fakier et al. (2020). In the South African context, see Fakier and Cock (2009) and Mosoetsa (2011).

how reproduction of the working class was necessary for capital while at the same time capital denigrated and devalued lifemaking.

Tithi Bhattacharya (2017b) builds on the framework and lineage of Vogel's work. Her contribution recentres the centrality of the working class and its formation utilising SRT. At an abstract level, her starting point is classical Marxism, affirming the working class, living human beings in all their variegated aspects, as the source of value. At the same time, beyond juridical equality, coercion and domination define the labour-capital social relation. From here, and following SRT theorists like Vogel, she shows how labour power or capacity to labour is a commodity within capitalism, but how it is reproduced is not adequately dealt with in Marx. While recognising that women carry a disproportionate burden under capitalism, including in the household, for the biological reproduction of the worker, which includes care labour, the kinship family is not the only site of reproduction in the broader circuits of reproduction. In these circuits public education, healthcare, leisure facilities, pensions, elderly support, slavery and immigration are ways in which the working class is reproduced. Mediating this would be race, nationality and gender relations.

At another level of abstraction, following Marx, Bhattacharya affirms that production and reproduction are part of a whole. The moment of value creation and the moment of creating the working class are part of a larger process of the social reproduction of capitalism. In this whole of extended reproduction, however, the capital-labour relationship is predicated on: (i) the necessity for the worker to enter this relationship to meet needs due to separation from the means of production, and (ii) the fact that the worker enters the wage relation to meet subsistence needs. Drawing on the work of Michael Lebowitz, she demonstrates how the standard of necessity is not given but subject to class struggle. With increased productivity capitalists seek to drive down wages while workers seek to increase wages. Moreover, there are two moments of production: labour power is a means to satisfy the need for surplus value by capital while for workers this is about satisfying the goal of self-development. But this is a contradictory process with capital wanting greater surplus value, which prompts the creation of new needs for the working class and the production of new commodities. Ultimately, there is a second circuit for the reproduction of labour, while integral to capital's own circuit of reproduction, but this is not theorised by Marx. The production and reproduction of the labour power circuit is about a process of the worker's self-transformation as part of meeting social needs. This has implications for social reproduction as a framework for strategic working-class politics, including an expansive conception of the working class and broader struggles related to the social reproduction of labour power.

Nancy Fraser (2017) is one of the most original and innovative Marxist-feminist theorists today. Her contribution to social reproduction theory expands on Vogel's contribution in several pathbreaking ways. Her starting point is recognising that care labour is both material and affective but without it, society cannot be reproduced: there can be no culture, economy or political organisation. The crisis of care is part of a larger crisis of social reproduction of society and a general crisis of capitalism. The social reproduction strand of the crisis is directly imbricated in the general crisis but has to be grasped together with the other structural contradictions. Theoretically, the social-reproductive contradiction of financialised capitalism exists because social reproduction is necessary for capitalist accumulation, but endless accumulation threatens to undermine the reproductive processes and capacities that capital and society need. This contradiction sits at the interconnection between production and reproduction; it is not intra-production and neither is it intra-domestic. As the logic of capitalism destabilises social reproduction, it also undermines long-term accumulation. Every capitalist society harbours a deep-seated systemic tendency towards a crisis of social reproduction. The background condition of social reproduction, together with nature and politics are crucial for capitalism to exist. This also means capitalism cannot be understood in a narrow economistic way but has to be understood in a broader sense as it relates also to its non-economic background conditions.

Fraser provides a concrete and rich historicisation of how waged labour and unwaged care labour (in its expanded sense and not exclusively in the family), or reproduction-production regimes, span nineteenth-century liberal competitive capitalism, post-World War 2, state-managed capitalism and, more recently, financialised capitalism. She explores the social reproduction contradiction (both in the centres and in the peripheries), its crisis tendencies and ruling-class responses to the making of the gender order. In this historical tracing, Fraser pinpoints how the realm of social reproduction was constituted and gender relations institutionalised: factory legislation and a bourgeoisie imaginary of domesticity shaped the liberal production-reproduction regime; public investments in social goods, mass consumption and a compromise between marketisation and social protection shaped the gender order of state-managed capitalism; and low-wage employment, corporate and state divestment from social welfare and privatised reproductive care (buttressing the mobility of professional middle-class women) and debt marked the financialised capitalist gender order. It is in this context that there has been an upsurge of boundary struggles, intertwined with class struggles, but related to production/social reproduction. Moreover, she argues, a triad of forces – marketisation, social protection and emancipation – are contending in these boundary struggles. Ultimately, she hopes social protection and emancipation triumph and determine how the boundaries between production/reproduction and capitalism/society are set.

Both Bhattacharya and Fraser provide important structural perspectives on gender and, more generally, oppression. Like Vogel, they do not treat social reproduction as an add-on or sideshow but demonstrate how it is central to the reproduction of the working class, gender orders, production and society. The social relations entwined in this include class, gender, race and imperialism. At the same time, within these theoretical apparatuses there is space for agential and strategic politics. Bhattacharya's call for a more expansive conception of the working class and the need for struggles related to the reproduction of the working class provide for a wider political field of struggle, ranging from food and water to a universal basic income, for instance. Fraser's conceptual approach to boundary struggles, linked to class struggles, is extremely novel and holds out potentials for a trans-feminist politics within this framework. These are crucial strengths for Marxist SRT. However, there are three areas that require systematic development and clarification to further enrich the role these approaches to SRT can play in relation to emancipatory feminism. The first relates to nuancing SRT understandings of the contemporary civilisational crisis of capitalism; the second relates to ecology and SRT; and the third is about SRT/SERT, intersectionality and the relationship to intersectional feminism. What follows are contributions to enrich and rethink certain areas of SRT; three areas of rethinking contemporary social reproduction theory and analyses.

Everything in crisis

As part of the return of SRT, Isabel Bakker penned an essay on the critical questions that such a research agenda needs to ask. She prioritised three areas: (i) reproduction for what and for whom?; (ii) for what purposes and what consequences?; and (iii) what are the alternatives to dominant practices that are transforming social reproduction and what prospects do they hold for greater empowerment and democracy?' (2007: 553–554). These research questions were penned before the financial crisis of 2007–2009; the worsening ecological crises, including the climate crisis with a 1°C overshoot of planetary temperature since before the Industrial Revolution in 2015 and its attendant climate shocks; alarming reports on biodiversity loss; at least four major food system crises since 2006–2007; and the Covid-19 pandemic, as well as the crisis of liberal democracy due to the privileging of the sovereignty of capital over states and publics. These are interconnected, cascading and ramifying systemic contradictions through global capitalism. It is in this context that the neoliberal class project has entered a conjuncture of crisis marked by the rise of extreme right, neofascist and authoritarian forces in the largest democracies (India, Brazil and the US) in the world[3] (Williams and Satgar, 2021), Biden's neo-Keynesian push back against financialisation through massive spending bills, Putin's invasion of Ukraine and Xi's commitment to share the gains of globalisation through prosperity for all.

Today SRT has to grapple with the manifold crises of capitalism and how these relate to social reproduction in the domestic realm and more generally at the level of society and global capitalism. Bhattacharya's contribution to SRT does not deal explicitly with the crises of capitalism. Although there is potential in her approach to connect these systemic and conjunctural crisis dynamics to thinking through the crisis of the reproduction of the working class, this requires a shift to a different level of analysis, closer to concrete history. Fraser, on the other hand, has a firm theoretical and analytical grasp of the social reproduction contradiction and how it operates as a systemic crisis tendency within financialised capitalism. However, there are two issues that require greater nuance and development. First, it is necessary to be a bit more historically specific about the general crisis of contemporary capitalism. Capitalism has been through three major crises: in the late nineteenth century, with the Great Depression and during the early 1970s. We are now living the fourth major crisis of capitalism since *c.* 2007 to the present (Satgar, 2015a). Second, each crisis has its own systemic and conjunctural crisis tendencies that have to be explicated. In this regard Fraser's work on SRT has to be integrated with other work she has done on climate and the legitimacy crisis of financialised capitalism (Fraser, 2015; 2021). Put differently, the structural divides of production/reproduction, nature/society and economy/politics and the attendant background conditions she identifies have to be brought together into an analysis of the total systemic and conjunctural crises of financialised capitalism. More than any other Marxist-feminist theorist she

---

3   For the first time since the end of the World War 2, there are now neofascist parties in the German and Swedish parliaments and several right-wing parties rising in other parts of Europe.

has the conceptual and analytical resources to achieve this scale of analysis of the general crisis of social reproduction (or socio-ecological reproduction) of capitalist civilisation. More generally, SRT theorists also have to grapple with the crisis of everything; crisis as crises, in the plural.

Ecology and social reproduction

The re-reading of Marx in the recent period to bring out his conception of natural relations has led to the development of a Marxist ecology understanding. While Marx is not vaunted as the founder of modern ecology, a post-productivist Marx has been discovered. This has brought to the fore both crucial ecological premises underpinning his thought and a revisiting of his conception of being human (Satgar, 2022). Marx has four crucial ecological premises to his thought: (i) humans are dependent on nature and this is a starting point for historical materialist analysis; (ii) human beings are part of nature; (iii) nature is a source of wealth together with labour; and (iv) human impacts and the limits of nature are of concern. From this standpoint of Marx's ecology, humans are not merely social beings but are actually socio-ecological beings. This implies that SRT is actually about SERT.

Several ecofeminists, particularly ecofeminist socialists, have developed these aspects of Marx's thought and have also gone beyond. Ecofeminist political economy starts from the premise that the capitalist patriarchal system externalises the costs of gendered care labour and damage to nature. However, making the link between social reproduction (the exploitation of women) and natural relations has entailed various theoretical innovations, which in different ways affirm the existence of socio-ecological reproduction. Maria Mies and Vandana Shiva (2014: 70–90), in their classic *Ecofeminism*, show how development and growth impact negatively on women, children and nature and actually continue a colonial form of enclosure and extraction. More growth and development have meant crises of socio-ecological reproduction. Ariel Salleh (1994) explored how the nature-women-labour nexus is the primary contradiction of capitalism, while James O'Connor (1996) argued for the second contradiction of capitalism, which refers to the structural conditions within which the production process exists, that is, reproduction and the natural environment. With the intensifying ecocidal (mass destruction of human and non-human life) logic of contemporary capitalism as part of the fourth crisis of capitalism, conceptualising the crisis of socio-ecological reproduction at different scales and in different locales has become absolutely essential. It provides a crucial theoretical and analytical resource, informed by Marxist ecology and ecosocialist feminism, as SERT for emancipatory feminism. SERT provides a direct challenge to Bhattacharya's approach to SRT through its appreciation of the deeper, embodied materiality of reproducing labour as part of natural relations. For Fraser, there is space to bring in an alternative historicising of socio-ecological reproduction regimes under liberal, state monopoly and financialised capitalism.

Intersectionality and SRT/SERT

Intersectional feminism has come to the fore through black American feminism. It derives from a particular context but has travelled and gained ground in different parts of the world. For Marxist feminists such as Delia Aguilar, intersectionality represents the deradicalisation of feminism and is complicit in the 'conservatism' of the historical period. 'Put more sharply, the reformulations of intersectionality by feminists today merely reflect the corporatisation of the academy and its increasing subservience to a neoliberal global regime' (Aguilar, 2015: 203). However, what Aguilar misses is that intersectional feminism is not homogeneous; it includes various currents, ranging from postmodern identity/difference intersectional feminists to liberal/neoliberal market pluralists to anti-capitalist intersectional feminists. A sharp debate has raged in the academy and in activist circuits about the differences between Marxist feminists and intersectional feminists (Bohrer, 2022). On the one hand, Marxist feminists have been accused of class reductionism (thus occluding other relations of oppression such as sexism, racism and heteronormativity), attempting to universalise the experience of the white working-class/middle-class family (particularly Marxist-inspired second-wave socialist feminism) and utilising binary or dualistic structures such as patriarchy and capitalism. On the other hand, some Marxist feminists have hit back against intersectional oppression gymnastics and its own hierarchies, its ontological atomism, including individualising oppression and identities and a lack of appreciation for the distinctiveness of class.

This chapter approaches intersectional feminism, following David McNally (2017: 313), in the spirit of a 'dialectically revitalised social reproduction theory – one that rises to the critical challenges posed by intersectional analysis.' At the same time, it means recognising that Marx himself, through his own revolutionary humanism, went beyond abstract and general conceptions of the working class and embraced class (including the peasantry), gender, race and an appreciation of the deleterious consequences of colonialism (Anderson, 2020). Marx had his own intersectional approach to the capitalism of his time. At the same time, several intersectional feminists do not reject the relationship between oppressions and capitalism. The Combahee River Collective, Angela Davis and ecosocialist feminists such as Maria Mies, Vandana Shiva and Ariel Salleh are good examples. This is important common ground and has implications for where oppressions are located within SRT/SERT.

Both Bhattacharya and Fraser provide single-systems frameworks in which women are not homogenised or essentialised; class, race and gender relations of oppression all matter. Similarly, with SERT there is an additional emphasis on ecological relations of oppression. In a sense they have taken on board many of the criticisms of intersectional feminists. For Bhattacharya a host of relations of oppression inform and shape the reproduction of the working class across a variegated set of mechanisms and sites. Moreover, in her expansive conception of the working class and strategic struggles for the reproduction of the working class, various intersectional possibilities exist. Similarly, for Fraser reproductive regimes have been shaped by various relations of oppression, including the role of colonialism, imperialism and financialised debt. In addition, in her conception of boundary struggles, intersectional possibilities abound. However, both Bhattacharya and Fraser work in a Marxist-feminist register and have not explicitly evoked intersectionality but affirm the relationship between oppressions and capitalism. SERT certainly occupies the same ground, but embraces an intersectionality approach that recognises the link between capitalism and oppression. A dialectical embrace of intersectional feminism recognises its limits but converges on common ground.

The crises of socio-ecological reproduction and challenges for emancipatory feminism

For struggles today, SERT theory is crucial in order to centre women's anti-oppression struggles – but as anti-capitalist struggles. In some parts of the world this is articulated as feminism of the 99% or popular feminism as part of a fourth wave of feminism. In this volume we refer to this feminism as emancipatory feminism. Emancipatory feminism (Marxist, socialist, ecofeminist and indigenous) has immense transformative potentials. Grounded in SERT and an analysis of the crises of global socio-ecological reproduction, it is strategically positioned at the frontlines of the civilisational and conjunctural flashpoints of contemporary capitalism. Moreover, harnessing SERT as a single-systems framework centring various relations of oppression – class, race, gender and ecological relations – brings intersectionality into resistance against an ecocidal capitalism.

However, these potentials could be stymied if three important challenges are not dealt with. First, while emancipatory feminism has a broader remit to understand oppression, neoliberal politics has also tamed publics, such that crowd-sourced, single-issue politics and social media constructed narratives define politics. Even with huge demonstrations in streets, such a politics is extremely limited and faces power structures increasingly impervious to such pressures. In other words, marketised rationalities have priced this in and governments that privilege the sovereignty of capital perform attentiveness but have no intention of taking this further into transformative agendas. The defeat of the organised working class, in the global North and South, has placed subaltern forces on a defensive footing with an orientation around point of production issues. Economism and narrow, single-issue politics dominate unions. This has to be surpassed and trans-working-class politics has to emerge. Similarly, women's politics has to become trans-feminist and environmental politics has to reach for trans-environmentalism. Intersecting crises make this absolutely essential to build a broader convergence of social forces. Emancipatory feminism can both engender a politics beyond a narrow issue-centred focus and unite these forces. This is a challenge it has yet to overcome in practice.

Second, and as corollary to the previous point, Donald Trump's ascendance into the White House upended even liberal feminism. He mainstreamed a crass capitalist patriarchy, objectifying women as sexual objects and brought an angry white male machismo to the fore. While the worldwide Women's March on 21 January 2017 – a day after his inauguration – attempted to push back the Trumpian effect, it globalised and emboldened right-wing politicians committed to capitalist patriarchy. In countries such as Brazil, Hungary, the UK and the Philippines, this has expressed itself sharply as part of new right-wing political projects. Illiberal, socially conservative and authoritarian politicians, such as Trump, came to power through the ballot box; products of decades of neoliberal rule but now showing the full-blown anti-democratic face of the neoliberal class project. These political projects are remaking gender orders and power relations, with grassroots subaltern women on the receiving end. In the US, its highest court – given its conservative composition – has reversed the right to abortion, pushing back a crucial gain of second-wave feminism. More generally, the authoritarian neoliberal right wing is positioning states and their coercive capacities to advance greater law and order control, build hi-tec surveillance border wall regimes and increase the incarceration of blacks, migrants and refugees. With the worsening climate crisis and the limits to adaptation, millions are going to be on the move on the planet (IPCC, 2022). This has already begun, with women and children facing these challenges in different parts of the global South. In this context, exclusionary nationalisms need to be confronted head on with counter-hegemonic political projects capable of leading society through accelerating and deepening the just transition. This is a crucial challenge for emancipatory feminism.

Third, and building on the previous point, emancipatory feminism has the intellectual resources to advance a deep, as opposed to a shallow, anti-capitalism. In this regard, systemic alternatives to the global crisis of socio-ecological reproduction demand nothing less than a post-carbon capitalist society. Within strands of ecological Marxism, ecological socialist feminism and indigenous feminism, conceptions of the commons, subsistence economies, democratic planning, alternative provisioning, ethical engagements with the technosphere, care labour, decolonial knowledge and democratising the state furnish the basis for a democratic ecosocialist project. In this volume several chapters articulate such democratic systemic reforms, based on constitutive forms of power from below, as crucial for the deep, just transition. WoMin African Alliance on the continent is re-imagining a transformative and ecofeminist approach to a renewed pan-Africanism. Important lessons can be learned from Rojava about the transformative role of indigenous feminism in advancing an emancipatory project. In South Africa, resistance to carbon capitalism and worsening climate shocks have thrown up numerous fronts of struggle: against coal pollution and against further extraction, including coal, offshore extraction and fracking for gas and oil; food sovereignty campaigning; reclaiming the water commons in the context of drought; and the Climate Justice Charter process, now supported by over 260 organisations (Satgar and Cock, 2022). These are democratic ecosocialist forces with potential to coalesce around a political project with answers to the intersecting crises of socio-ecological reproduction. The challenge is to advance consciously in this direction, with emancipatory feminism anchoring this political leap.

Emancipatory Feminism in the Time of Covid-19: Transformative Resistance and Social Reproduction, edited by Vishwas Satgar and Ruth Ntlokotse. Johannesburg: Wits University Press, 2023.

PART III

BUILDING MASS RESISTANCE TO CLIMATE INJUSTICE

*For People and Worker-Driven
Climate Politics*

The World Social Forum and the Battle for COP17

IN A WORLD PLUNGED EVER deeper into an uncivilised global capitalist condition, the WSF is a crucial beacon of hope. At its recent gathering in Senegal, the news of the unfolding democratic revolutions in Tunisia and Egypt electrified the spirit of optimism pervading the multiple axes of deliberation. The geometry of left politics was redrawn from Latin America to North Africa and the Arab world. The expressions of people's power in these revolutions defied inherited formulaic understandings of twentieth-century revolutions. Instead of vanguards and armed uprisings, these revolutions organised without organisation through social media and the unstoppable mass surge of discontent. Egypt and Tunisia also fired an imagination for more: could people's power be harnessed to end the tenuous grip of neoliberal ideology on a world scale? Could the struggles in Latin America, the Maghreb, the Arab world, global climate change negotiations and beyond be connected to frame a new horizon for global transformation?

However, while this renewed confidence in popular resistance struck a militant chord, the sharp edge of debates on climate change revealed serious limits to WSF politics and the difficulties ahead for a genuine climate change solution at the United Nations Framework Convention on Climate Change Conference of Parties (COP17) in Durban. This came through as hard lessons were drawn from the recent Copenhagen and Cancun climate negotiations. Progressive civil society was divided at Cancun. NGO technocrats, donor-driven agendas, big egos, celebrity intellectuals and hard-lined social movement agendas prevented a common voice and united agenda to prevail outside the negotiations in the streets.

Such a rainbow-like plurality prevailed in the deliberations at the WSF and was consistent with its long-established ethos. However, as the week unfolded, it was the climate justice current that took the initiative to be self-critical and address the weaknesses of progressive civil society. This was laudable and the 'Basis of unity' document it tried to shape in the closing hours of the WSF is a step in the right direction, but is extremely constrained by crucial weaknesses of the WSF.

First, the national and regional forums of the WSF are uneven but generally weak or non-existent. The follow through required to keep focus and momentum on the 'Basis of unity' document is going to be difficult to sustain. Second, the WSF has not evolved to a point where it can co-ordinate in a democratic manner a platform of actions at transnational and national levels. It is a great space to philosophise about actions to change the world, globalise critique, share experiences and form links but it lacks a strategic edge.

This does not mean the WSF has to become a new programme-centred Fifth International. But given the systemic and conjunctural crisis of capitalism, it needs to find its place also at key battlefronts so that progressive humanity speaks with one voice about alternatives. The climate change negotiations are one such front where hope is taking a battering. Pluralism as strength can only be meaningful if the WSF confronts this weakness and evolves in a direction that gives it a new strategic edge.

Moreover, for some activists operating at a transnational level, the defeat at Cancun meant intensifying further transnational engagements. Strategy was suddenly reduced to a straight line: Copenhagen, Cancun, Durban (COP17), Rio+20 and beyond. Given the institutional weaknesses of the WSF it easily lends itself to reduction to a moment in an ongoing transnational circuit. However, this approach did not provide pause for serious reflection on the state of climate change negotiations and more importantly why Bolivia was alone in the world in its opposition to the Cancun summit outcomes. A serious and ethical conversation of honest assessment, above petty nationalisms and narrow agendas, reveals a climate change process that is increasingly being led by an agenda that favours utilising the ecological crisis as a new outlet and fix for capitalist accumulation. Within the Cancun framework carbon trading, geo-engineering and adaptation are just some of the elements of a new green neoliberalism. The future of the delicate ecological web will be determined by financial returns, speculation and risky technologies. For the World Bank, finance and investment in climate change are the new horizon for green capitalism, a dangerous and false solution.

In this context, Bolivia's argument around climate debt, rights of nature and opposition to grand market and techno fixes is on a terrain, inside the negotiations, in which governments – including South Africa – have surrendered to the climate agenda of transnational capital. Moreover, transnational capital has brought the inside out. In other words, it has been able to contest and exacerbate splits among civil society on the streets by supporting some in civil society propagating the green capitalist myth and who are lining up outside the negotiations to show active support. This further illustrates the inability of anti-capitalist civil society to advance an effective counter-hegemonic politics in support of Bolivia on the streets.

Finally, Bolivia is alone because anti-capitalist civil society has not been able to link the transnational in a manner that strengthens a national bloc of anti-capitalist forces. The national terrain has been surrendered for the glitz and jet-set lifestyle of the transnational climate change negotiating treadmill, including the occasional meeting points of the WSF. The painstaking task of local grassroots movement and anti-capitalist bloc building is not happening in most places around the world. Without this national power to hold governments to account and to contest state power, the climate negotiations at all levels of the world will be stacked in favour of capital. Thus, demonstrations outside the COP17 negotiations are not going to be sufficient in themselves to open the space for alternatives inside the negotiations.

These are strategic weaknesses that global anti-capitalist civil society has to confront as part of the build-up to COP17 in South Africa. More importantly, as articulated in the main organising assembly for COP17 at the WSF, the build-up to COP17 has to harness global public opinion around the alternatives represented by Bolivia and anti-capitalist civil society. The role of global public opinion, of over six billion humans on the planet, is crucial to democratise the climate change negotiations.

Currently, the UN has a democracy deficit. It is actually not the embodiment of global democracy; and the liberal internationalism through which it claims its legitimacy is in crisis due to the weakening of national liberal democracies in the context of global capitalist restructuring. Most states sitting at the climate change negotiations table are there due to weaknesses in national democracies. In most instances, representative democracy has been hollowed out as states have been transnationalised as part of reproducing the rule of transnational capital.

What's more, anti-capitalist civil society does not represent global public opinion on the streets. It needs to harness through a global internet referendum, involving national movements and activist networks, support for the Bolivian alternative to the Cancun green neoliberal consensus. The build up to COP17 and beyond has to pave the way for global public opinion to march alongside the progressive sections of humanity on the streets at the negotiations.

Moreover, for the South African anti-capitalist left, COP17 represents a focal point to expose the alignments of the South African government to green neoliberal capitalism in the climate change negotiations and in its approach to national development. Its increasing spend and commitment to coal-fired power stations, nuclear energy, fossil fuel-based agriculture, mining, industrial and urban development have to be critiqued as part of the build up to COP17. Such a critique has to also be globalised through street politics at COP17.

More importantly, the build up to COP17 provides an opportunity to present the Bolivian alternative and more specifically democratic ecosocialist alternatives to the South African public. The critical question in this regard relates to the role of the Congress of South African Trade Unions (COSATU). Will it be part of the inside-out strategy of the Zuma government to divide anti-capitalist civil society converging on Durban or will it align genuinely with anti-capitalist civil society?

Pambazuka News, 17 February 2011.

The Climate is Ripe for Social Change

IN A SURPRISING DEPARTURE from the corporate-controlled narrative on climate change, on 30 November 2015, during the build-up to the recent UN COP20 climate summit in Lima, the *New York Times* ran a front-page story in which climate experts warned that

> it now may be impossible to prevent the temperature of the planet's atmosphere from rising by 3.6°F. According to a large body of scientific research, that is the tipping point at which the world will be locked into a near-term future of drought, food and water shortages, melting ice sheets, shrinking glaciers, rising sea levels and widespread flooding – events that could harm the world's population and economy.

This surprising coverage went on to say a rising rate of emissions has left us with two future possibilities: an unpleasant world of climate crisis, chaos and disruption; or a world with a global deal that ensures the planet is habitable. Either way, the future we are facing is grim.

But for climate justice activists gathered in the people's space and on the streets in Lima, two decades of failing to reach a global deal required a different approach; a bold rejection of the pro-market and false solutions of the UN COP process such as carbon trading, the clean development mechanism (CDM), finance solutions that fail to acknowledge the climate debt of rich Northern nations and the commodification of forest land through the infamous REDD+ (reducing emissions from deforestation and forest degradation) scheme.

Activists have called for urgent action to advance transformative alternatives for system change as part of the people-driven just transition. The position of 'no to false solutions but system change now' has to be explained to appreciate why this is the necessary way forward to secure human and non-human life.

The real geological force

In 2000, Paul Crutzen, a Nobel prize-winning atmospheric chemist, introduced the term the Anthropocene Age. He theorised about an unprecedented human effect on our planet's life systems, equal in force and impact to a great geological event.

But his notion of the human as a geological force fails to appreciate how power works in class-based capitalist societies. Put simply, Crutzen has failed to appreciate it is not humans in general but capital that is the real geological force destroying planetary life. Driven by the need to make short-term profits, capital, through its organisation of production, distribution, consumption and social life, has overshot planetary limits, undermined natural cycles and now threatens human beings with extinction by means of climate change. Capital, in this context, has become a geological force capable of ending human and non-human life. It is wired into a systemic logic of ecocide and is incapable of solving the climate crisis.

Moreover, over the past three decades of transnational techno-financial capitalism, our world has come to move at a dizzying speed. Social life, history and change have dramatically accelerated. This includes the superspeeds of nanotechnologies, fast food and hyper-mobile globalised financial flows. At the heart of this is an addiction to growth, premised on the assumption of unlimited accumulation. Capitalist modernity, with its mastery of science and technology, has convinced capital that it is the conqueror of nature as well as its master. As a master, it seeks to reduce nature to a commodity, while ending an alternative conception of nature: nature as a commons.

This commodifying illusion informs the market-based techno-fixes of capital, such as carbon trading, which operate with the idea of no limits to capital. But the world is facing finite resources, over-consumption by a few and widespread pollution of rivers, land, forests, oceans and the biosphere. Hence, with capital prevailing over the UN climate process, we are heading for the fast death of our future.

The planet is heating up, fast

Finally, with the current trajectory of an increasing rate of carbon emissions, carbon concentration (over 400 parts per million) and a rapidly heating planet, climate justice movements are thinking hard about securing our common future. In this regard, they seek to counter two possible futures we face.

First, in various Pentagon research reports, well documented by Christian Parenti in his book *Tropic of Chaos: Climate Change and the New Geography of Violence*, the Pentagon envisages a world of climate-induced chaos. Thus, it seeks to use its awesome military power to discipline the zones of chaos while protecting lifeboat America. This is the ultimate fascist solution.

Second, a view of our future, as argued by Rebecca Sonlit in her book, *A Paradise Built in Hell: The Extraordinary Communities That Arise in Disaster*, recognises a pattern of human purpose and civic virtue coming to the fore in the context of disasters such as the great San Francisco earthquake and Hurricane Katrina. Her book assumes the Manichean make-up of human nature, with its disposition for both evil and good, but she documents a pattern in which altruism and mutual aid is manifest when disasters happen. Such a view celebrates the human spirit as a way to confront the adversity of the future and is generally a progressive response, but it tends to work with an implicit fatalism and falls short in terms of grappling with the agency required for system change now.

The rights-of-nature alternative

Instead, I would argue, a system-change perspective is grounded in appreciating that the pattern of history informing our future derives from the twentieth century. Essentially, it was marked by a contest between two sets of social forces championing contrary principles: on one side, social forces championing competition; and on the other, social forces championing solidarity.

It is this pattern of struggle and its understanding of human nature as socially determined that best equips us to confront and secure the future now. It is this perspective that also enables us to champion system change alternatives in the present.

An important example in this regard is the rights-of-nature alternative. Its power as a transformative alternative was demonstrated in Lima in a sitting of the International Tribunal in Defence of the Rights of Nature. The tribunal brought forth great creativity on the part of activists to demonstrate the power of this alternative.

Factual testimony, rhetorical inventiveness, valorising culture and evoking lost histories became crucial activist strategies to expose how capital is destroying rainforests, ancestral lands, water systems and communities, as it scrambles for fossil fuels and minerals with predatory extractivism.

Fracking in the US, now standing at 800,000 gas and oil wells, stood out as the source of 'fraccidents' such as earthquakes, pollution of water resources, as well as a second wave of genocidal violence against native Americans. Besides testimony, activists also highlighted how the rights of nature are an effective transformative discourse, providing a recourse to challenge such destructive practices, if enshrined in national laws or sub-national regulations. In seven states in the US, fracking is now banned. In short, the rights-of-nature alternative places a limit on capital's avaricious pillaging.

In addition to the rights of nature, other alternatives such as food sovereignty, solidarity economy, rights-based carbon budgets, climate jobs, socially owned renewables and affordable public transport are all adding up to a paradigm counter to capitalist modernity, redefining a relationship between humans and nature, and advancing a logic of systemic change. As part of a just transition, such alternatives seek a society based on solidarity to sustain all forms of life.

South Africa's just transition

In South Africa, the time for the just transition has arrived so that we can all survive climate change. As a response to the climate crisis, it affords us an opportunity to address the failings of South Africa's transition to democracy: inequality, unemployment, hunger, white privilege, ecological destruction and dispossession. It affords us an opportunity to build a South Africa that belongs to all who live in it, black and white, such that the wealthy pay the price for this achievement and we realise Nelson Mandela's dream.

Although the ANC state has a declaratory commitment to green growth, green jobs and even a notion of the just transition in the NDP, this is empty policy speak. There is also an add-on to carbon markets, renewed extractivism (including fracking), fossil fuel and nuclear energy sources, corporate-controlled renewables, export-led agriculture and de-industrialisation of transport and renewables manufacturing.

Essentially, the ANC state has surrendered to market-centred green neoliberalism and the logic of ecocide. It has shown itself incapable of leading a transformative just transition. Instead, this has to be led from below by forces such as the United Front (led by NUMSA), the emerging Food Sovereignty Alliance, the Solidarity Economy Movement, community-mining networks and rural movements. Such forces need to champion a people's CODESA on the climate crisis and a just transition before it is too late.

Mail & Guardian, 17 December 2014.

Worsening Climate Crisis and the Challenge of Red-Green Alliances for Labour: Introducing the Climate Justice Charter Alternative in South Africa

Introduction

THE CLIMATE CRISIS IS no longer a question of scientific or academic concern. Since 1992, the UN has attempted to involve the governments of the world in a process to solve this problem. The leading climate scientists, through the IPCC, have informed these deliberations with cutting-edge climate science and have drawn attention to the seriousness of planetary heating. Yet, the climate crisis has accelerated and is now a lived reality across the planet through extreme weather shocks such as floods, droughts, wild fires, hurricanes and heatwaves. The global power structure and carbon-addicted ruling classes are failing to address these challenges and dangerous feedback loops related to a receding Artic ice sheet releasing methane (one of the deadliest greenhouse gases) or increasing carbon saturation in the oceans or the destruction of carbon absorbing rainforests like the Amazon place us all on a path to species extinction.

For countries in the global South, these climate realities and the grip of imperial control entrench a crisis mode of socio-ecological reproduction. Neoliberal restructuring and adjustment to global capitalism, for a period of over three decades, has produced lumpen ruling classes and externalised extractivist enclaves and regimes, due to which life in Latin America, Africa and Asia has been dispossessed. Race, class and gender within these darker nations have been articulated along these fault-lines causing deep human suffering and ecological destruction. The only counter to these challenges is the reconstitution of politics from below by mass subaltern power. Climate justice politics, with its emphasis on confronting and preventing harm to the most vulnerable is central to the building of alliances between organised labour and other victims of the crises of socio-ecological reproduction. This means climate justice provides the gravitational pull for red-green alliances towards solidarity and ecological justice, thereby defining the politics of our time. Unions have consistently argued for a just transition politics to confront the climate crisis challenge (Morena et al., 2020). Broader alliances for climate justice have called for systems change, not climate change.

This article discusses how these two forces are converging in South Africa around the Climate Justice Charter (CJC) process. It is an introduction to situate alternatives emerging in the South African context to develop a mass-based climate justice movement that brings together trade unions, environmental and social justice movements, youth, faith-based organisations, the media, academics and climate scientists. The CJC is the first of its kind in the world and is emerging from South Africa, a country that is the twelfth highest emitter of carbon and the leading emitter on the African continent, and a region that has been declared a climate hot-spot by the world's climate scientists (Fripp, 2014). This means that with further heating southern Africa will be facing a catastrophic future. This also necessitates a people-driven just transition from below to advance systemic transformation of a fossil fuel-addicted South Africa. Neither labour on its own nor climate justice forces can lead this struggle or deal with the related challenges. Alliance building for a new transformative politics from below is crucial. The CJC process is one approach to this challenge, based on the convergence of struggles and the building of an ideological coherence for a deep, just transition and a post-carbon society.

The failure of the UN climate framework

Despite over 25 years of global engagements through the United Nations Framework Convention on Climate Change (UNFCCC), the world is far from resolving the climate crisis. The Paris Agreement (2015) has proven to be a flawed framework. The principle of voluntary national commitments has already been abandoned by Donald Trump's administration, thereby affirming that the US, with the highest historical carbon and per capita emissions in the world, has never been committed to resolving the climate crisis. Despite sub-national policy shifts against Trump's pro-carbon administration, this has not stopped the dominance of carbon interests in the US national energy mix and in the US military. In short, the Paris climate agreement is held hostage to national political dynamics and as right-wing shifts occur in national democratic spaces, from Brazil, India, the UK and Australia, carbon-ruling classes are strengthened by the stand of the Trump administration. This offensive by carbon capital is also reflected in the global energy mix, in which coal is still dominant. Global coal use has continued to increase, largely due to electricity demand in China, India and other parts of South and South-East Asia.[1]

Moreover, a global political economy, driven by global competition, is prompting industrialised countries to make policy choices based on national interests. China, now the largest carbon emitter in aggregate in the world, despite its renewable energy industries, is still accelerating the development of coal energy projects. Currently, China plans to have 226.2 gigawatts (GW) of coal energy, the highest in the world and which is 40% of the world's total planned power plants. At the same time, the UN COP process has been bogged down by its attempts to put in place financialised solutions to address the climate crisis. The last round of engagements at the Madrid COP, in December 2019, focused on the trading rules for carbon markets. Treating the global biosphere as natural capital that can be traded is a wrong-headed idea that has not worked and will not work (Bond et al., 2009). The idea of carbon markets has been around since the Kyoto Protocol and has not brought down global emissions. Climate justice critiques have highlighted how such mechanisms lead to the colonisation of the biosphere in the global South, reinforces racialised and gendered injustices and simply don't address the systemic roots of the problem (Satgar, 2018). Moreover, carbon emissions have been going up since 2017 and are estimated to be at 43.1 billion metric tonnes by the end of 2019, breaking another record (Harvey et al., 2019).

In this context, it is crucial to have national breakthroughs around deep, just transitions that inspire the world and provide examples of social tipping points around the urgency of the climate crisis. In the US, the UK and Germany (all major carbon emitters), there is a sea change in public opinion regarding the urgency of addressing the climate crisis. Such social tipping points challenge over 20 years of failed UN-climate negotiations. A combination of factors from climate shocks in everyday life, climate justice activism, the rise of the children's #FridaysForFuture and media mainstreaming of climate news are all coming together. In some countries, the notion of the Green New Deal, green economies, declaring climate emergencies and setting net-zero emissions targets have become crucial in defining climate crisis political discourse. However, while these are important green shifts this has not translated into active political projects reshaping trajectories for rapid and deep decarbonisation pathways. More fundamental transformative

---

1   www.iea.org/reports/world-energy-outlook-2019/coal.

political convergences have still to congeal in societies to ensure such deep, just transitions of socio-ecological transformation are led from below. In the African and particularly the South African context, this makes the CJC process and its emphasis on constituting red-green alliances crucial.

The Southern Africa climate hot-spot and worsening climate crisis

The world crossed the 1°C increase threshold since before the Industrial Revolution in 2015. The operating parameters of climate Earth have changed fundamentally since this overshoot. Climate science from the IPCC is very clear that with further heating, extreme weather events would become part of the new normal. In particular, southern Africa has been deemed a climate hot-spot. According to some of South Africa's leading climate scientists a hot-spot is not only determined by climatological conditions but also the lack of socio-ecological systems to address climate shocks (Scholes et al., 2020). So, a region heating at twice the global average is now on a trajectory to experience 3°C, when the global heating average overshoots 1.5°C in the next few years. This means with increased heating, water stresses will increase through more intense multi-year droughts, heatwaves will get more frequent and intense, while food systems will be pushed towards collapse. Southern African states are not prepared to deal with this. In the course of 2019, drought has continued in the region with at least 45 million having to face food shortages (World Vision, 2019). Cyclones that hit the region have devastated parts of Mozambique, Zimbabwe and Malawi, impacting negatively on 2.2 million people.

In South Africa, besides a worsening drought threatening both urban and rural areas, tornadoes have hit parts of KwaZulu-Natal, flooding also affected parts of the same province in April of 2019 and heatwaves have also been registered in different parts of the interior. Both commercial and small-scale farmers have been hit hard in this context, exposing the vulnerabilities of a globalised, fossil fuel and industrial-based food system, controlled by monopolies. The South African state only declared a national disaster in early 2018, almost four years into the drought and after devastating impacts. Moreover, its response has been dismal.

Climate breakdown has registered also on a planetary scale. All regions on Planet Earth have been impacted by extreme weather shocks in the course of 2019. Droughts, floods, heatwaves and fires have impacted different countries.

It is estimated that about seven of these events have cost about $10 billion each (Harvey, 2019). For poor countries this is catastrophic. In this context, pushing for a deep, just transition, which ensures the needs of the most vulnerable and those least responsible is addressed, is absolutely necessary. For South Africa, it means addressing legacies of racialised and gendered inequality together with the injustices of worsening climate crisis. The CJC is about confronting these realities.

The Climate Justice Charter process and alliance building with labour

The CJC process has its roots in six years of campaigning through the SAFSC and was initiated by the leading role of the Co-operative and Policy Alternative Centre, a vibrant alliance partner and co-founder of the SAFSC, in the midst of one of the worst climate induced droughts (2014 until the present) in the history of the country. The CJC germinated in various confrontations with carbon capital and its allies:

- Food corporations pushing up food prices, which was challenged through a hunger tribunal involving the SA Human Rights Commission, speak-outs on drought and a national bread march involving trade unions;
- Protest action outside the JSE against food profiteering during South Africa's drought;
- Development of a People's Food Sovereignty Act for South Africa (2017–2018) which was shared with South Africa's parliament and seven government departments;
- Protest actions at SASOL (the second highest carbon emitter in South Africa) headquarters, through a human chain, and at their annual general meeting;
- Protesting at media institutions with demands that climate crisis news be mainstreamed, including attempting to occupy the leading newspaper office (*Sunday Times*), the National Editors Forum and the Press Ombud.

Moreover, in 2019, deep dialogues with various constituencies from drought-affected communities, the media, labour, social justice, environmental justice, youth/children and faith leaders, unpacked ideas, alternatives and concerns regarding the deep, just transition. Think pieces from leading activists were also solicited and a draft of the CJC was launched at a conference in November

2019, which was then placed online for further inputs and thereafter, an online assembly on 16 June 2020, led by leading youth and child activists, secured final public input, despite Covid-19. The final version of the CJC was launched on 28 August 2020 at an online assembly led by leading ecofeminists in South Africa. Essentially, the CJC comes from a process of collective struggle and intellectual engagements.

As a campaigning platform, the SAFSC is a loose alliance of organisations from the agrarian sector, climate justice, food justice and solidarity economy movements. Following a successful national dialogue in 2014, the SAFSC was launched in 2015 to address the systemic crises of South Africa's corporate-controlled food system (Satgar and Cherry, 2019). Inspired by La Via Campesina, which put forward the idea of food sovereignty in 1996, the SAFSC has consistently translated and given substance to a South African approach to food sovereignty. Through its hunger tribunal, drought speak-outs, bread marches, food sovereignty festivals, water sovereignty dialogues and activist schools, it has developed a climate justice perspective on food sovereignty, seeds, water commoning, land use, agro-ecological transformation and solidarity economy.[2] In Gramscian terms, it has embarked on the long march through civil society to connect hunger, water stress, food price increases, drought and the worsening climate crisis; it has been taking the leap to develop a mass climate justice politics centred on ending hunger, thirst, pollution and climate harm. These lived realities of ecological crisis have provided the basis for a politics of positive solidarity, led by the most oppressed who have been impacted unjustly. The SAFSC has developed a transformative conception of activism which is neither merely about symbolic disruption to raise awareness nor just about tactical disruption of failing industrial food circuits but also includes strategic disruption to advance systemic pathways for a post-carbon food sovereignty system in villages, towns and cities, while locating this in an overall climate justice project, as expressed through the CJC.

The SAFSC is part of a second cycle (2007–2019) of resistance in post-apartheid South Africa, that has consistently confronted the deleterious impacts of racialised, gendered and ecological disasters of neoliberal capitalism. In its formation as a national campaigning platform, it involved just over 60 organisations (community organisations, movements and NGOs). This has grown at different moments of campaigning. In the midst of Covid-19, 110 organisations have endorsed its food sovereignty strategic response to hunger,

---

2 See www.safsc.org.za

125 water-stressed communities collaborated with its national platform and the SAFSC has rallied support for 388 food-stressed communities.[3] As a national platform, all partners share information as part of a food sovereignty commons, those partners wanting to co-ordinate campaign activities rally support on the platform with the resources they have and, most importantly, local food sovereignty pathways are engendering local alliances. The latter is the epicentre for systemic pathway building of food sovereignty and other transformative system change alternatives.

The SAFSC does not have formal and institutionalised leadership, but rather it is a space for transformative activist convergence. In all its activities, it has attempted to enable convergences with progressive social forces. Trade unions and unionists have been consistently reached out to and are being involved in its various campaigning activities. At this intersection, it has attempted to forge a red-green alliance in which there is a recognition that red has to be green and green has to be red. More sharply, social justice is about climate justice and climate justice is about social justice. Taking this further has been the CJC process led by the COPAC, a co-founder and active alliance partner of the SAFSC, together with wider SAFSC forces. In this process, convening a dedicated dialogue with labour has been crucial. This involved reaching out to all the leading trade union federations in South Africa and creating a convened space of trust and respectful engagement on the modalities of the just transition. The following crucial themes emerged from the dedicated CJC roundtable dialogue:[4]

- Trade unions and the just transition: While union federations in South Africa have grappled with the idea of just transition and started to translate it in the South African context, this has not been deepened within unions through education; adequate capacity has not been built to take forward union resolutions; there has been a disconnect between struggles against inequality and the climate crisis; despite alternatives being available like climate jobs, this has not been integrated into union campaigns; and, most importantly, unionists raised serious concerns about the state response towards the just transition including prioritising the needs of workers, as well as the state's ongoing commitments to a carbon-based economy. In this regard, the state energy parastatal ESKOM featured in the conversation.

---

3   See SAFSC Covid19 interventions and press releases documenting this work at www.safsc.org.za/category/media2/

4   The round table dialogue with South African trade unions was convened on 19 August 2019 in Johannesburg.

It is highly indebted at almost R500 billion and has various institutional challenges including corruption, poor management, lack of planning capacity and poor project management capacity, leading to major cost over runs for its energy projects (including one of the largest coal-fired power stations in the world). A just transition plan for transitioning ESKOM and SASOL, two of the largest carbon emitters, was understood as crucial but which had to place the interests of workers and communities at the front and centre. Ultimately, the dynamics of a neo-corporatist dialogue with the state was called into question as the basis to pursue a deep, just transition;

- The CJC and alliance building: The CJC was understood as crucial to raise awareness, marry daily struggles with climate justice, provide an opportunity to unite unions, assist shifting of mining unions locked into coal, facilitate a common rallying point and also support struggles towards the fulfilment of people's basic needs. In short, the CJC was understood as crucial for strategic convergence, movement building in mass struggle and provision of labour with a common agenda to advance the deep, just transition. A mass politics involving labour and progressive social forces enabled a shift in approach to deep, just transition;
- Advancing systemic transformation through the CJC: Unions wanted a deep, just transition and not a shallow one. This included addressing workers' control of pension funds as a lever to impact on the direction of the deep, just transition, socially owned energy systems, including the municipalised renewable energy, advancing worker co-operatives, climate jobs, rethinking industrial policy, democratising the media and giving consideration to a BIG.

Challenges

The CJC was adopted at an online assembly during Covid-19 on 28 August 2020. Its introduction calls for climate justice now, while the rest of the text sets out goals, principles for deep, just transitions and systemic alternatives; elaborates a conception of a people-led climate justice state; and finally calls for a climate justice deal not only in South Africa but also between Africa and the global North. On 16 October, the CJC will be taken to South Africa's parliament, together with a climate science document prepared by some of South Africa's leading climate scientists. The rallying slogan for this moment of engagement is 'End hunger, thirst, pollution and climate harm'. Moreover, all political parties in parliament will be invited to a debate on their commitments to seriously address the climate crisis. Climate justice forces gathering in this engagement will also demand the CJC be adopted in accordance with provisions in South Africa's Constitution.

However, four crucial challenges stand out in this process:

- First, uniting forces will not entail just a convergence on the CJC but also active relationship building in the context of ongoing struggles against carbon capital. In this regard, NGOs seeking environmental justice will have to go beyond narrow issue-centred and lobbying politics. Moreover, labour unions would have to overcome the degeneration tendencies that have come to the fore among them. A more proactive, strategic and transformative trade unionism has to confront tendencies towards defensiveness, business unionism and neo-corporatist co-option into green wash discourses. Building a consensus on rolling mass action to #gridlockcarbon through various forms of disruption has been central to the CJC process. This programme will test all forces, including labour.

- Second, the process of movement building is central to the CJC process and is about moving beyond climate justice politics which has been centred on activist groups and NGOs. Crowd politics as an expression of mediatised populism has also become a crucial challenge. A successful climate justice movement has to be well grounded in the basics of transformative grassroots organising. There are no short cuts. This would entail building a networked, education-centred and organised grassroots movement that builds mass capacities, is constitutive of power from below and leads the just transition. Systemic alternative building, such as deep, just transition plans, food sovereignty pathways, socially owned renewable energy, commoning and community-led natural climate solutions, would not have to wait for state power to be harnessed.

- Third, the media has to be consistently engaged to mainstream climate news, report on climate justice alternatives and ensure that public discourse is empowered. Currently, the majority of South Africans do not understand the science of climate change and its implications for their lives. The media's role in empowering public discourse cannot be underestimated. In the European context, for example, this has made a crucial difference. A climate-literate society will also assist in building a mass-based climate justice movement.

- Fourth, the response of the state to the CJC is going to be crucial. In October 2018, when the IPCC issued what has commonly been called its

1.5°C report, the SAFSC issued an open call to the South African president, endorsed by over 60 organisations and trade unions, for an emergency sitting of parliament to be convened to deliberate on this report and its implications for South Africa's climate policies and just transition (SAFSC, 2018b). The president ignored this call. The CJC is also a response to the failed climate crisis leadership of the ANC-led state in South Africa. Section 234 of the South African Constitution provides for charters to be adopted to compliment it. Demanding the CJC be adopted by South Africa's parliament will present both a legal and political challenge to South Africa's carbon-addicted ruling classes. It will define a crucial turning point for the deep, just transition. If the CJC is rejected, it will expose the lie at the heart of South Africa's political system on the urgency to address the climate crisis. On the other hand, if the CJC is adopted, it will not hold back the climate justice struggle but reposition the state to be society-led.

Your feedback on the people's CJC is welcome. I hope it serves as a resource in your own struggles and is taken further, developed and innovated upon in your own contexts. We are running out of time and large-scale systemic transformation is absolutely essential to give human and non-human life a chance of survival. The red-green alliance is imperative for this to succeed.

International Centre for Development and Decent Work, Working paper 31, 2020.

The Geopolitics of Vaccine Apartheid

On 22 April, Earth Day, US President Joe Biden convened a summit on the climate crisis with the heads of several important countries. While this was an attempt to bring the US back into the climate crisis multilateral game and to lead from the front on a global challenge, the hypocrisy of this move was not lost on the global public. At the time of the convening of this summit, 223.6 million vaccine doses covering 35.2% of the US population were rolled out. Whereas in contrast, Nigeria with a population of 201 million had only 1.2 million people vaccinated. The Biden administration cannot be asking the world to act collectively on the climate crisis when it is failing to ensure vaccine intellectual property is made available to countries in the global South.

The US is not alone in prioritising its own population for vaccines and defending profit making by pharmaceutical companies. The UK has also stockpiled 400 million vaccines, six doses for nearly each person living there, with a population of 67.61 million. Together with the US the UK also refuses to accept the need for a trade-related aspects of intellectual property (TRIPS) waiver in the WTO to ensure vaccine intellectual property and knowhow is transferred to countries in the global South to boost manufacturing for safe and effective vaccines for all. Leading Western countries are essentially turning their back on a just and global problem-solving approach to a common challenge.

For Russia and China, the Covid-19 crisis is being used to boost political legitimacy through their vaccine diplomacy efforts. They also are not willing to share intellectual property with the global South and neither have they publicly committed to make their vaccines open source. In the African context, China has pushed its Sinopharm vaccine on to the agenda with several African countries. However, up to this moment not a single African country has a serious vaccine rollout campaign. At the end of December 2020, Oxfam estimated that 70 poor countries will only be able to vaccinate one in ten inhabitants in 2021. In Africa 25% of vaccine supply will be covered by COVAX, 11% by the African Union while the vast majority of 64% will not have vaccinations in 2021. This is vaccine apartheid with Africa reflecting the moral and political crisis of such disparities.

At the same time, leading pharmaceutical companies are warning the US administration that overriding patents will handover sensitive mRNA technology to Russia and China. This argument merely entrenches geopolitical game playing to protect the profits of pharmaceutical corporations. Moreover, if the US is committed to a just recovery from Covid-19 for the entire world, it has to take the TRIPS waiver seriously in the WTO. Thus far Biden's top trade official, Katherine Tai, has signalled strongly to pharmaceutical companies and the WTO that their top priority is saving lives and that the US was serious about boosting production and equitable distribution of vaccines. However, this rhetoric has not translated into the TRIPS waiver actually being secured.

It is in this context that the victories of the HIV/AIDS struggles in achieving a TRIPS waiver are crucial for progressive civil society. Activists and movements in India, Brazil and South Africa achieved such a breakthrough in the context of the HIV/AIDS struggle for generics of essential HIV/AIDS drugs to be produced. This resonates with the many initiatives calling for vaccine justice: calls for a #PeoplesVaccine, calls by former political leaders and Nobel laureates for the US to scrap intellectual property on Covid-19 vaccines, Bernie Sanders' support for a global petition with over 2 million signatures calling for a TRIPS waiver, and initiatives by Africans themselves.

On 14 March 2021, global union federations, leading transnational movements like La Via Campesina, African movements such as WoMin, the African Food Sovereignty Alliance, and all progressive civil society forces in South Africa convened a Global Assembly (Stand with Africa/Safe and Effective Vaccines for All/Healthcare and Frontline Workers of the World Unite). This assembly affirmed the need for global solidarity to achieve a safe and effective #PeoplesVaccine. The tenor was that the world must rally to Africa's support, for us all to ensure public healthcare is central to a just recovery from the pandemic and to build an internationalist approach based on the ethics of care of health and other frontline workers. This was based on the conviction that we form a human community and share a common global challenge and therefore need to unite. This struggle needs to be intensified across borders, in our communities, in our workplaces and in our movements. The outcomes from this Global Assembly have been shared with the leaders of the rich countries, WHO and the WTO. The last organisation has responded recognising the call of the Global Assembly. It has also confirmed that high-level engagements are happening in the WTO on the need for a TRIPS waiver for Covid-19 vaccines. However, this decision has still not been made and therefore the struggle continues.

People's power is clearly the only way to overcome the geopolitics of vaccine apartheid. It was the same in the struggle against apartheid in South Africa: mass resistance and international solidarity worked effectively together. If we succeed in overcoming vaccine apartheid many lives will be saved and the end of the pandemic will be a reality for all. Moreover, a defeat for big pharmaceutical companies also provides momentum to deepen transformative global solutions for the worsening climate crisis. There will be momentum to shift the world to choose Earth, not carbon capitalism. Trade unions have to be at the frontline of the struggle for a safe and effective #PeoplesVaccine but also for climate justice. This challenge and opportunity lies before us all.

Rosa Luxemburg Foundation blog post, 6 May 2021.

*Raising the Alarm Louder
Against Climate Injustice*

Light a Fire Under SA's Climate Policy

MOST SOUTH AFRICANS don't appreciate that we are living in a new world, shaped — and increasingly determined — by a heating planet.

In 2015, when the WMO declared a 1°C increase in planetary temperature since the Industrial Revolution, it acknowledges that the planetary conditions that sustain life had been fundamentally changed. For geologists meeting in South Africa on 29 August 2017, and responsible for documenting the Earth's history, a sober scientific conclusion was reached. We are now living in a new geological epoch, the Anthropocene. This means humans as a geological force are shaping the Earth's systems and planetary conditions that determine life.

The Anthropocene is a geological, historical and climatic marker that confirms we have broken with a relatively stable climatic condition known as the Holocene, which lasted about 11,700 years. How we produce, consume and organise social life affects the Earth's systems. Carbon emissions from burning oil, coal and gas are contributing to global warming.

A planet that heats by three, four or five degrees will make human life almost impossible. If we do not act now, we are likely to breach two degrees in this century. As our planet heats, complex feedback loops such as methane release from melting in the polar zones, carbon saturation in oceans and even destruction of rainforests will feed into global warming. There is no time to spare if we want to create the conditions, institutions and practices that will sustain South Africa into the future. We also cannot hide behind false dichotomies of jobs and development versus the environment.

The longer we postpone the urgency of climate change the more costly and catastrophic it becomes. There are currently 20 vulnerable countries, mainly island states, with 700-million people who do not have the capabilities to deal with the climate shocks induced by a 1°C increase, including the rise in the sea level. Many of these countries will have to be abandoned and climate refugees will increase. Some estimates say Hurricane Harvey, which crashed into the US mainland last year, cost the country $180 billion. Together with hurricanes Irma and Sandy, these are now in the top five most costly hurricanes in US history. The US also experienced severe wildfires also linked to drier climatic conditions.

The Syrian conflict is also considered a climate war – one of the worst droughts in Syria's history (which fell between 2006 and 2011) caused the failure of most of Syria's agriculture and the migration of 1.5 million Syrians to urban areas. Although the conflict is complex, climate change as a contributing factor cannot be ignored.

The cost of South Africa's drought has not been calculated and we are not coming to terms with what we are dealing with. Most politicians and policy-makers use the language of a natural disaster, which suggests this is a freak event of nature – a transient problem and the concomitant response is disaster relief. This mode of thinking betrays a serious crisis of leadership and the makings of climate crisis in South Africa. The drought that has ravaged rural South Africa since 2014, and which is now threatening big metropolitan areas such as Cape Town, Nelson Mandela Bay and Durban, has to be a defining moment. The Cape Town water crisis portends the problems we face if we want to construct a climate emergency state that can support a citizen-led transition that affirms climate justice. The poor and working-class citizens of Cape Town have endured three levels of climate injustice and, if this repeats itself, climate conflict will tear South Africa apart.

First, inequality and geographies are racialised in Cape Town. A day zero approach, with its emphasis on disciplinary demand management and fear, squeezed households and neighbourhoods already dealing with water insecurity. Water management devices and punitive tariffs shifted the burden and cost to poor communities, whereas agriculture and business were let off the hook.

More generally, farming in South Africa controls 62% of our water resources. Because of irrigation-fed agriculture, including in the Western Cape, we are exporting our water as we export food. This approach to water and food systems contributes to climate injustice and is not viable in a climate-driven world.

Second, the state at all three levels has failed, thus passing the burden on to the most vulnerable. The city of Cape Town and the Western Cape did not have a sustainable water management strategy in place, despite numerous warnings and the science of climate change already forewarning drier conditions in the Cape.

The national government has been incompetent and in disarray, confirmed by the revelations of mismanagement coming to the fore regarding the failed leadership of the former water and sanitation minister, Nomvula Mokonyane. Moreover, parliament has been slow to respond, declaring a national disaster only recently. At the same time, activists and civic organisations have developed compelling critiques of the state's responses and have also developed systemic solutions. Many of the water crisis organisations in Cape Town justifiably reject desalination as an expensive techno fix, with serious negative environmental effects. Instead, they are calling for water leaks to be plugged, water to be harvested from water channels leading to the ocean, the protection of agro-ecological farming communities such as the Philippi horticultural area, the integration of ground water into the water system in a sustainable manner, incorporation of farmer-controlled dams into the water system. and reuse of water among other just solutions. A discourse on water and food sovereignty is emerging from below but is not finding policy traction in the state.

The third injustice experienced relates to an ANC government committed to a fossil fuel energy path (as entrenched in the integrated resource plan, IRP). This can be seen in President Cyril Ramaphosa's ambition to see mining as a sunrise industry – which includes more coal, fracking and offshore extraction – and an NDP that affirms the importance of resource nationalism. The carbon criminality of the ANC government is not exceptional and includes the US, Russia, China, India and other petro-states.

Essentially, ruling elites have chosen more carbon emissions and hence a climate-driven world with devastating consequences for the poor, working class and marginal. This exists alongside imperial designs to police zones of climate chaos and to keep the world enthralled by symbolic gestures such as the Paris Agreement, which provides too little, too late. Cape Town registers the disproportionate effects and climate injustices of carbon criminality.

We are in a no-analogue situation and as uncharted territory for the human race we have to develop a new paradigm to sustain life in response to the climate crisis. This has to reflect how we think about decarbonising our society and building new ecocentric systems (water, energy, food, living, governance) to manage climate shocks.

South Africa is one of the most unequal countries in the world. Climate change and shocks will deepen racial, gender and class inequalities, yet at the same time it affords us the opportunity to address these challenges and build for the future. The climate crisis does not have to be about catastrophism or end-of-times millenarianism. The ecocidal destruction of the conditions that sustain life can be confronted with radical non-racialism and a new direction for the nation-building project that unites us all.

South Africa can be a beacon to the world again. As a climate-justice state it can embrace a deep and just transition, an idea championed by trade unions and consider democratic systemic reforms already emerging such as food, seed and water sovereignty, climate jobs, zero waste, the rights of nature, socially owned renewable energy, solidarity economies, a substantive BIG and democratic planning, among others.

As in the struggle against HIV, the world could not stop us from producing the generic drugs we required to sustain lives. Trump's US cannot stand in the way of us confronting the existential threats of climate change. In this context, climate crisis international relations require us to build support for a climate-justice agenda in our continent, the inter-state system and isolating those countries that are carbon criminals. This might even include climate justice sanctions against some states.

Global leadership has failed over the past 20 years to tackle the climate crisis. South Africa, post-Zuma, can show a different way for humanity and other life forms we share this beautiful planet with. It is not too late to advance a deep and just transition for South Africa, as the central thrust of a new ecocentric NDP.

Mail & Guardian, 18 April 2018.

South Africa's Carbon Democracy is Going Over the Cliff

THE PAST FEW WEEKS have revealed palace wars: public protector against Pravin Gordhan; public protector against President Cyril Ramaphosa; more of the red berets' undemocratic moves in parliament and then former president Jacob Zuma going for broke with his toxic tales at the Zondo Commission.

All of this political theatre has become high drama in our political discourse. The liberal commentariat amplifies the narrative by framing the script with simple binaries: constitutionalists versus looters, democrats versus authoritarians. All of this correlating with good versus evil and all one has to do is choose the good saviours. While our political world shrinks and becomes inward-looking, the UN has drawn attention to the fact that the world is experiencing one climate disaster every week. This includes floods, heatwaves, droughts, cyclones and other extreme weather events.

Another optic to explain developments in contemporary South Africa is to think beyond the binaries. We are living through and observing the second transition in our market-driven carbon democracy. This transition is about the terminal decline of ANC-led national liberation politics and nationalism; it is exhausted. Its greatest achievement has been to engender the forces that will destroy it and possibly our constitutional democratic order.

For the past two decades, we have been fed a regular diet of how virtuous the middle class is by an Afro-neoliberal common sense. The ANC-led Alliance succeeded in creating almost nine million new African members of the middle class. This social class is marked by an Americanised consciousness which includes an obsession with acquisition, possessive individualism, a technology fetish, nihilistic celebrity culture and a carbon-centric way of life. As conscripts of a globalised American way of life, wanting to be more American than actual Americans, this middle class is also debt-ridden and precarious. At the same time, it has not been a bulwark against the degeneration of South Africa's democracy and its capture. In the largest democracies in the global South, India and Brazil, sizeable parts of the Americanised middle class have delivered their democracies to anti-democratic forces through the ballot box. The new post-apartheid middle class is centrally implicated in the degeneration of South Africa's democracy. To understand this, we have to understand how the ANC-led Alliance turned its back on the working class and the poor.

This is also the story of how South Africa has received and internalised neoliberal reason: a world order project to remake the global political economy in the image of the US and transnational capital. South Africa's national liberation movement is one of the oldest on the African continent and in the world. It was also a revolutionary movement. Moreover, the ANC was also a movement vaunted and celebrated given how repulsive, racist and brutal apartheid was. We imbued it with mythical virtues and gave it an over-inflated place in our national imagination.

Given the convergence of diverse ideological forces in its midst the ANC is also contradictory, facing limits and objectively constrained by the contingencies of power relations. At the same time, it made political choices that shaped the direction of nation-building and post-apartheid democracy. Many of these choices related to economic policy went beyond the necessities of stabilising a debt- and crisis-ridden post-apartheid economy and became entrenched in state policy for over two decades.

This became part of national liberation common sense and was championed by an Afro-neoliberal fraction of the national liberation bloc. This fraction included successive ministers of finance, technocrats in the Department of Finance, the new middle class in the state, financialised sections of emergent black capital, finance capital, transnational capital and various international institutions. The translation of neoliberalism into South Africa, by this fraction, entailed giving it a South African idiom, coding it in national liberation discourse but most importantly ensuring a measure of trickle-down (through social grants, for example) while encouraging recognition of tribal authorities, LGBTQ+, affirming a liberal feminism that is about representation in male-centred hierarchies, and allowing Mandelaesque rainbowism to refract social antagonism.

This homegrown Afro-neoliberalism is grounded in two forms of reason: a de-democratising commitment against society (Thatcherite influenced) and hard-boiled pragmatic calculations (Reaganite influenced) to ensure what works for the market, first and foremost, will ostensibly work for society. The Afro-neoliberal class project maintained the strategic initiative for over two decades, which entailed locking South Africa into deep globalisation through entrenching the power of global finance in the economy, shrinking manufacturing, encouraging further reproduction of the carbon-based minerals-energy complex such that platinum and coal became major exports and ensured that South African agricultural exports continued under further monopolisation of the sector. While this class project spawned a broader and racially diverse middle class, it failed in terms of unemployment, inequality, hunger and ecological devastation. It has been central in creating a crisis of socio-ecological reproduction for which workers and the poor have had to pay the price.

Moreover, Afro-neoliberalism also failed politically and this is what defines South Africa's second transition. Those at the centre of this project have to take responsibility for where South Africa's thin and fragile market-centred carbon democracy has come to. Afro-neoliberalism spawned three counter projects from within the national liberation bloc and all are led by aspirant or new middle-class forces. These forces are infused with the impulses of a desperate and crisis-ridden society.

First, Zuma's kleptocratic project has entailed criminalising the state to engender a transactional middle class. The ersatz scream of 'radical economic transformation' is from one fraction of the national liberation bloc wanting rapid class mobility. Second, the emergence of the EFF reflects the first significant rupture in the national liberation bloc. Malema and his red berets strut through our democracy with a patina of radicalism but this game is really about Malema's nose for weaknesses in our body politic which he can exploit to his advantage. The degenerate and neo-fascist logic at work will undermine every democratic gain achieved by workers and the poor, so this opportunistic and anti-democratic force can achieve power.

Third, Irvin Jim's Socialist and Revolutionary Workers Party, is the second significant rupture in the national liberation bloc, although it still has to be seriously tested politically. It is led by well-paid, middle-class union functionaries, who are building a caricature of the SACP, but grounded in sectarian dogma harking back to a Stalinised dystopia in which some are more equal than others and state terror is the means for social engineering.

These forces are not anachronistic and have the potential to fracture the ANC-led Alliance but also destroy the foundations of South Africa's constitutional order. To continue an Afro-neoliberal class project is to strengthen these forces. Cyril Ramaphosa's economic thinking has not displayed a fundamental break with Afro-neoliberalism. His fixation on FDI, as the basis of growth and development, completely occludes the socio-ecological crisis that is the result of such thinking.

A good example of this is how the business press has been cheering on the potential takeover of Pioneer Foods by a US investor as a realisation of Ramaphosa's dream for investment-led growth. In the context of climate shocks, volatility in globalised food markets and the recent collapse of South Africa's food system in the drought such investment is certainly not in the national interest. Also, the brazen intention by his government to break up ESKOM without a national debate and a clear plan to ensure a just transition for workers and society is a flashpoint that is also gridlocking South Africa's socially owned renewable energy transition. Again, the Afro-neoliberal class project expressing the power of credit rating agencies, investors and international institutions like the World Bank is a recipe for major social conflict.

In a climate-driven world, building blocks for society such as food, water and energy have to be ringfenced as strategic and even anchored around democratic public utilities and other socialised institutional forms. However, these issues do not feature in the Afro-neoliberal reasoning at work in Ramaphosa's class project. Hence a weak carbon democracy, anchored in explosive socio-ecological conditions, is being led down a self-destructive path. In short, Afro-neoliberalism, which has been at the heart of ANC rule, through its own anti-democratic practices which privilege the sovereignty of capital, has spawned a state of political disorder which defines South Africa's second transition.

Political disorder and the uncertainties of South Africa's future are compounded by the dynamics of intensifying climate chaos. The ANC electoral manifesto does not have anything serious to say about the worsening climate crisis, the lessons to be learned from the drought and the deep, just transition required now. Instead, it flaunts commitments to twentieth-century-style industrial development, a declaratory developmental state and resource nationalism. The ANC is willing to bury its head in the sand regarding the worsening climate crisis and premise its choices for the country on the false dichotomy of carbon development as opposed to addressing a mere environmental problem. This means the ANC simply does not care if more people die from drought, heatwaves, floods and other extreme climate impacts induced by global heating. It does not appreciate the challenge of socio-ecological collapse as an imminent possibility with the worsening climate crisis.

In this context, Barbara Creecy, Minister for Forestry, Fisheries and

Environment, does not have a strong mandate from the ANC to advance ambitious climate crisis policy. She is also leading a department that has consistently failed to hold accountable those responsible for carbon and broader toxic air pollution in our society. According to the World Bank, 20,000 people die annually from air pollution. Given that this minister was part of the Gauteng government responsible for the Life Esidemeni tragedy she needs to appreciate that one more death from air pollution because of ineffective regulation is unacceptable. Gwede Mantashe, Minister of Mineral Resources and Energy, is clearly hell-bent on driving the resource nationalism of the ANC, with more carbon extraction as the big game-changer.

Besides having ESKOM (number 29 on the list of 100 major carbon polluters in the world) and SASOL (number 45) within his portfolio, his pronouncements about the Total gas find, his opposition to the Xolobeni judgment against extractivism, and his commitment to the dubious idea of clean coal place him on a collision course with present and future generations. He and the ANC are imposing a death sentence on all life forms through support for carbon interests and the reproduction of this weak carbon democracy. It is not the first time Mantashe is on the wrong side of history. His boisterous support for Zuma was the first.

This time, he and the Afro-neoliberal project of the Ramaphosa regime will have to face the street rage of climate justice forces, led by children and other progressive social forces, rising in the country against human and non-human extinction. Hope born from such rage emerges at a social-ecological breaking point and has been unstoppable in history. Mantashe the communist dialectician should know this and heed the warning, because this time he will lose.

Daily Maverick, 24 July 2019.

Covid-19, the Climate Crisis and Lockdown: An Opportunity to End the War with Nature

COVID-19 HAS PUSHED an already weak and crisis-ridden global economy over the edge. Massive value has been erased from crashing stock market prices. Many commentators are talking about the return of economic conditions similar to the great financial crash of 2007–2009. The most powerful countries in the world from China to the US have ground to a halt.

This pathogen, possibly from delicate creatures like a pangolin or a bat, has engendered the worst global pandemic since the flu of 1918–1920 that killed 100 million people. Death rates are going up globally. Right-wing nationalists in Europe and the US have been confused as this virus has jumped racist border regimes and infected all populations. Citizens are no longer concerned about their racist messages, but rather about how to survive.

Governments all across the world are seized with the challenge of protecting their populations, at least that is what it seems like given the people-centred rhetoric. The geopolitics of Covid-19, engulfing the entire globalised world in its rapid spread, is also a shot across the bow of carbon capitalism. Elite consumption of exotic animals, at high prices, in Wuhan, China unleashed the swift and lethal revenge of nature.

This does not mean that this is a Chinese virus as the racist Donald Trump has suggested. We are all susceptible and are trying to live through the fear, paralysis and risks brought by this pandemic. Overnight, jobs have disappeared, pay cheques have shrunk, loved ones are in critical health situations fighting for their lives and hunger is knocking on the door of many. Healthcare systems, weakened and commodified through decades of marketisation, have or will be overwhelmed.

Yet the very same elites that caused the problem are not carrying the burden of the consequences of their actions. For climate justice politics, these injustices are not new. Elite use and consumption of fossil fuels is linked directly to extreme weather shocks such as heatwaves, droughts, floods and cyclones, for instance, which impact those most vulnerable the hardest. Yet there is no consequence for those responsible and the fossil fuel industry, carbon-addicted states, and the wealthy carbon-based consumers continue as though climate science does not exist.

Black swan event, or worsening systemic crisis

In the business world, Covid-19 tends to be reduced to a black swan event; a sudden or unforeseen happening, with great consequence and rationalised after the fact. The idea was initially popularised by Nassim Nicholas Taleb's five volumes on uncertainty including the famous black swan, which has been described as one of the most famous books since World War 2. While in his work, the concept has a richer philosophical grounding, it has become part of everyday risk management discourse. Business risk analyses missed the likelihood of a Covid-19 pandemic and it certainly was not a concern. Its occurrence, however, cannot be explained as a black swan event.

From an ecological Marxist perspective, it has to do with the contradictory relationship between natural and social relations, has a historical genealogy within how ecocidal capitalism works and can be causally attributed. Simply, for Covid-19 this means it's a dangerous problem that is engendered by capitalism's persistent domination of nature.

It spread from a wet market involving organised crime syndicates, linked to shadowy global poaching and smuggling networks that steal wild creatures from their habitats and place them on elite menus. Avaricious Chinese capitalism, with its appetite for resources and capturing markets, like the West, understands nature as a site of extracting value; nature must serve the juggernaut of accumulation. South Africans are now familiar with the appetites and reach of this capitalism due to the annihilation of our rhino population merely for their horns. Wet markets also exist in other parts of South and East Asia, and have not been restricted, leaving open the possibilities of new waves of pandemics.

For many years, epidemiologists and environmentalists have been concerned about the public health consequences of such markets, given that animal to human transmission of deadly viruses is a known fact and has been implicated in avian flu (from birds), MERS (from camels) and ebola (monkeys), for instance. These animals are also traumatised and kept in unsafe conditions.

In Brazil, Jair Bolsonaro has unleashed land grabs in the Amazon – one of the most biodiverse habitats on Planet Earth. Industrial farming, mining, logging and wild animal poaching are ending the natural protective barriers between human society and ecosystems, heightening the risks of pathogens spreading, but in this case also contributing to climate change, given the role the Amazon plays in a planetary ecosystem to sequester carbon.

Climate scientists have already warned humanity that further warming of the Arctic, for instance, will not only release deadly greenhouse gases such as methane, but also pathogens that have been frozen into ice sheets. Like Covid-19, the worsening climate crisis and its global shocks are not black swan events, but dangerous systemic crisis tendencies produced by a hard-wired logic based on the duality of capitalism versus nature. Science has provided us with understandings and warnings, and yet the global capitalist system persists in driving us towards harm and destruction.

Carbon capitalism and imposed collective suicide

A world led by those who place profit above human and non-human life, is placing us all in jeopardy. We are not given a choice as the ecocidal logic of global capitalism destroys the conditions that sustain life. Our planetary commons – biosphere, oceans, forests, land and water sources – are all being commodified and destroyed to make a few wealthy. On a planetary scale, we are living through an imposed collective suicide. As neoliberalism becomes authoritarian and mutates into the second coming of fascism to defend the wealth of the few, it is revealing a simple fact: It's not learning lessons about the harm it is inflicting. Instead, it wants to defend at all costs a life-destroying system.

Karl Polanyi in the social science classic, *The Great Transformation* (1944), drew attention to such elite behaviour when the ship is sinking. In the late nineteenth century, based on marketisation through the Gold Standard, the world was driven into World War 1. Lessons were not learned and the world was again locked into Gold Standard marketisation in the 1920s, and this gave rise also to fascism and World War 2.

This time, we are all dealing with the failure of capitalism's conquest of nature through treating it as capital through financialisation. The science on biodiversity loss, climate and water, for instance, are all unequivocal that we are breaching limits and surpassing boundaries that endanger everything. At the same time, the raw and infinite power of nature is gathering pace. The present generation of young people understand the dangers of this very well. One of my former students, an extremely intelligent and sensitive young person, placed this public post on his Facebook page in the midst of the Covid-19 outbreak:

Tonight, for the first time in a long time, I cried. I felt everything inside of me: the depth and immensity of my pain, my sorrow, my grief, my lament, my worry, my confusion, my longing, my despair – I felt it all and wept, wept for the sadness I've kept hidden so long, wept for the loved ones I miss so dearly, wept for the suffering and uncertainty of the world, wept for reasons I don't even understand.

Many of us weep for the collective suicide we are living through. This is not about victimhood, but about understanding the depth of crisis and the urgency to overcome this universal challenge of our extinction. It is a conscious knowing rooted in deep wells of pain, anxiety and existential suffering growing in prevalence among the young because of the collective suicide being imposed by financialised carbon capitalism. Greta Thunberg and many of the young climate activists in South Africa such as Raeesah Noor Mohamed, Nosintu Mcimeli, William Shoki, Awande Buthelezi, Jane Cherry and Courtney Morgan, to name a few, understand this. They carry their pain, their understanding of injustice as they protest.

But is the present resistance enough? The cry of the 1°C movements – Sunrise Movement, Extinction Rebellion, #FridaysForFuture and the CJC process in South Africa – are all coming up against power structures and ruling classes not willing to break with the imposed collective suicide of financialised ecocidal carbon capitalism. Yet in the context of Covid-19, not only are global populations shocked, but it has rocked, assailed and unhinged the very same power structure standing in the way of addressing the climate crisis. Covid-19 is forcing, even reluctantly, ruling classes to try to act with concern for life.

Lockdown and the ANC's epidemiological neoliberalism

Covid-19 has thrown us into a state of exception. From a climate justice perspective, this is a dress rehearsal for a world that breaches 2 and 3°C in which climate shocks on a global scale imperil life-supporting socio-ecological systems such as food, water and health systems through unbearable temperatures. Waking up then is too late.

This is the underlying premise of climate justice activism, given that climate science is telling us what is arriving with business as usual or low mitigation trajectories. With the Covid-19 crisis, our governments seem to be suddenly realising markets and corporations are not more important than human life. Is this the case?

The disaster capitalism of Covid-19, as Naomi Klein reminds us, brings forth profit-making opportunities even from the suffering of the people. Trump is leading the way. His first crucial move was to build up fossil fuel reserves thus keeping oil prices bolstered, then he unleashed the privatised healthcare system and is now keeping pharmaceutical companies free to manipulate the prices of essential medical equipment instead of repurposing production through the Defense Production Act. However, this is not the end of the story and struggles inside US society will certainly determine if Trump's epidemiological neoliberalism will triumph or not.

In South Africa, we have been witness to a sea change from kleptocratic state and neoliberal austerity policies (including cutting billions of rands from health spending), announced by Minister of Finance Tito Mboweni, to cross-subsidise corrupted and failing parastatals, to the war on Covid-19. The country is going into this government-declared war with a dualistic healthcare system, with the vast majority dependent on a public healthcare system gutted by corruption, mismanagement and austerity. This healthcare system, with these specific features, is what is going to be overwhelmed not just by Covid-19, but by over two decades of ANC misrule. The lockdown of South Africa has to be understood in this context.

Put more sharply, the warped rationalities of commodified healthcare for a few and failing healthcare for the many is clearly the frontline the government is trying to avoid in the country's Covid-19 response. For most South Africans, in a state of shock and panic, this lockdown crash-landing of the economy on the wretched lives of a precarious working class and poor seems like the best response. Of course, this shock therapy has been administered repeatedly since neoliberal strictures informed the first democratic budget in 1994 and the macro-economic shift of 1996, kleptocratic neoliberalism of the Jacob Zuma project and now the new epidemiological neoliberalism of the ANC. In this context, the so-called China success story of shutting down Wuhan peppers government-speak.

But the other epidemiological success story of South Korea is not referenced. South Korea did not lock down its economy, but put the emphasis on: (i) intervening fast through test kits produced on a mass scale domestically (100,000 a day); (ii) test early, often and safely (it has conducted over 300,000 tests), such that detection happens quickly; (iii) contact tracing, isolation and surveillance, which has used smart apps, mass messaging and has prevented an overload on the healthcare system; and (iv) enlist the public's help. While not perfect and easily replicable, it's nonetheless an important alternative to lockdown.

South Africa's lockdown has not been preceded by mass testing despite the two-month lead time the South African government had since the outbreak in China. Even as the country goes into lockdown, the costs of tests are prohibitive, there has been no clear communication about international partnerships to get testing going on a mass scale, there is no clear messaging on testing details and grassroots civil society has not been mobilised, despite its enthusiasm to rise to the challenge. Instead, the lockdown has shifted the focus to managing economic chaos, mitigation measures and privatised charity through a solidarity fund. Deep anxiety, fear and insecurity is running through society. South Africa is going into the lockdown as one of the most unequal countries in the world.

The crisis of socio-ecological reproduction is deep as expressed through high levels of structural unemployment, intra-African income inequality, hunger and water inequalities (54% of South African households do not have access to clean water through a tap in their homes). Lockdown means South Africa's precarious working class and poor are now responsible for solving the Covid-19 problem because they carry the burden. Lockdown is meant to save their lives while worsening their already wretched life worlds. Hence the ANC government is off the hook with this cunning move of epidemiological neoliberalism while taking Covid-19 disaster capitalism to a new level.

Ending the war with nature

Covid-19 is an expression of contradictory natural relations. On the one hand, it is devouring the most vulnerable in our society and, on the other hand, it is prompting humanity to slow down collective climate suicide. Carbon emission data is certainly going to register deep drops since the onset of Covid-19, with airlines, shipping, cars and other carbon-emitting technologies brought to a halt.

Covid-19 has achieved what almost three decades of UN multilateral negotiations have failed to achieve. If governments can take the Covid-19 emergency seriously, they can take the climate crisis seriously. The UN climate meeting in Glasgow this year has to open with lessons learned from Covid-19 to address the global climate emergency. In this context, South Africa will have to tell its story to the global public. However, there is a lot the South African government should consider as this pandemic unfolds, including its war on Covid-19 approach.

South Africa's government declared Covid-19 a disaster in terms of the Disaster Management Act. It has unleashed an important co-ordination capacity in the state, preventative regulations, is disseminating information, has imposed a 21-day lockdown and introduced economic mitigation measures. The command structure is led by the president. The Disaster Management Act was not kicked into gear during the worst drought in South Africa's history (2014 until now), which ravaged numerous communities, collapsed part of the globalised food system and pushed up food prices. Many communities still have acute water needs and are being challenged to maintain basic hygiene. As Covid-19 transmission spreads, water-stressed communities are going to be hotspots as these are poor communities and very likely also to have many with compromised immune systems. If the drought was handled properly by the ANC government, water issues would not have been a problem now.

Moreover, if the ANC government did not get caught up in the tides of populism around the land question and listened to the SAFSC, including taking seriously their People's Food Sovereignty Act handed over to parliament, we would be sitting in the midst of Covid-19 with more communities, villages, towns and cities having localised agro-ecological food sovereignty pathways to cope with the current situation. Instead, we are living the drama of a war-centred crisis management approach. The war approach to Covid-19 is limited in three respects and holds out dangers for how leadership is practised now and the capacities built in this defining moment. First, war works with a simple logic. There's an enemy, militarise (build war-making capabilities), mobilise society in the effort and deploy this to destroy the enemy. It is a reductionist way of thinking; it is not a systems view of the world.

Covid-19 is manifesting in our midst together with other systemic crises, such as economic crises and climate crises. Financialised capitalism has produced an unstable global economy and grotesque inequalities. It has not worked. The climate crisis is worsening with a lack of will to phase out fossil fuels and decarbonise. We are facing a 1.5°C increase in planetary temperature most likely in the next five years, accompanied by intensifying climate shocks. These crises are interconnected, cascade into each other and push our socio-ecological orders towards collapse. A war mentality does not appreciate the interconnectedness of all of this.

Put differently, even if Covid-19 is addressed with war-like precision and the epidemiological curve flattens globally and in South Africa, we are not returning to a new normal. We are returning to a world in permanent crisis; a new abnormal. Hence, how we address Covid-19 and reconstruction after it, must lock in democratic systemic reforms that cushion us from more crises.

South Africa will need an eco-justice stimulus package to tackle the impacts of Covid-19, the economic crisis and worsening climate crisis. South Africa's climate justice charter is a crucial point of departure in this regard.

Second, a war approach to Covid-19 is based on dangerous philosophical foundations. It continues the anthropocentric conquest of nature, central to capitalist thinking. Killing Covid-19 in this frame is about us being the dominant species. We demonstrate to the forces of nature our superiority. This is really a conceit which fails to understand that nature has been and will always be more powerful than us.

Moreover, we are extremely dependent on nature as a species to ensure our reproduction. With Covid-19, we are really trying to mitigate the revenge blow from nature. It's a moment to be humble and realise our finitude in a wondrous and infinite natural order. We are just one little part of a vast and delicate web of life. Ending Covid-19 should be about ending the war with nature. This includes ending wet markets for exotic animals, ending globalised industrial agriculture and rapidly phasing out fossil fuels.

Third, the war on Covid-19 keeps us bound up in an ethical knot and derives from deeply oppressive ways of thinking. Violence whether colonial, imperial, patriarchal, racist or ecocidal is not what the world needs. Modern industrial scale violence that is calculated, instrumental in its reason and deadly is breeding a fast violence from nature. A violence we cannot match. Everyday violence of poverty and structural inequality has to be addressed as we come out of this pandemic moment.

Complex and holistic systems thinking, grounded in an ethics of care rather than war has to prevail. Put differently, if Covid-19 helps jettison the Thatcherite neoliberal subject – competitive, greedy and possessive individual – for a more humane state of being and solidarity-based society, it would have produced our strongest defence against a crisis-ridden world. It would also have affirmed an ethics of care for our natural relations that nurture us, feed us and enable us to have life.

Daily Maverick, 25 March 2020.

Where Have all the Flowers Gone?: A Final Climate Crisis Warning

THE BIEDOUW VALLEY IS one of many spectacular wildflower hotspots in South Africa at this time of year. Rolling valleys, veld and mountains of breathtaking colour await intrepid travellers visiting the West Coast and Cederberg. Flowers are central to how humans imagine and experience nature.

In Germany during Covid-19 restrictions, florists were allowed to stay open so that loved ones could share flowers and homes could have flowers to brighten otherwise dark times. For the artist Van Gogh, the feral and mesmerising beauty of flowers, including sunflowers, was captured through his pathbreaking use of deep layers of colour. These iconic images evoke deep wells of emotion to this day.

As South Africans, we are aware that nature's sublime beauty stretches from the heights of Table Mountain in the south, to the undulating landscapes of the Kruger Park in the north and the two oceans that hug our coastlines. We are a country endowed with a natural diversity that is unique on Earth. Our ecosystems are home to all forms of life: from snoek, sardines, the rare sighting of the blue whale, the big five, rivers, forests, blue cranes and a unique floral kingdom. We have built a country on these precious and fragile ecological foundations. Yet, we are failing to appreciate that all of this is enmeshed in a delicate web of life, connected directly to the maintenance of a stable climate.

In 2015, the planet we consider our home changed dramatically. Climate science recorded a 1°C increase in planetary temperature since the First Industrial Revolution. The extraction and continued use of coal, oil and gas pushed Earth's thermometer to a place it has not been for the past 11,000 years. The climate our grandparents and parents grew up with and thrived in is being lost. Thirty years of climate science have warned us that a fossil fuel-addicted world will heat our planet and induce extreme weather shocks, and the time to address this crisis is limited. This was affirmed in 2018 when the world's leading climate scientists loudly sounded the alarm bell in the IPCC 1.5°C report shared with the world. This was our final warning about the urgency of the climate crisis. The next UN climate summit, postponed to next year in

Glasgow, will not tell us anything new, except that climate shocks are getting worse and how close we are to the edge of runaway climate chaos with its complex feedback loops.

Climate reality is catching up with everyday lived experience. Polls in the US show that a significant number of Americans are now deeply concerned about climate issues, which manifest in wildfires, flooding, hurricanes, heatwaves and sea level rise. Joe Biden's Green New Deal commitments are a direct challenge to Donald Trump's climate science denialism and utterances about it being a Chinese hoax.

In the midst of Covid-19, the world has also come to appreciate the disproportionate impacts of a global catastrophe in relation to race, gender and class. An unequal world means more harm for those without economic means. Moreover, the unemployed and low-income earners do not have lifestyles of air travel, resource-intensive consumption and high levels of carbon emissions that cause damage to the Earth system. Planet Earth is reacting to the life-destroying system that benefits a few with a power we cannot match.

An era of pandemics has also been announced by scientists, directly linked to further global heating and the destruction of ecosystems that keep zoonotic pathogens safely away from humans. This calls for a pause in the human journey and for our societies to think deeply about our choices. To continue with the assumption that dominating nature, even through green growth, and harnessing technology will save us is deeply flawed. Despite our power to re-engineer the genome, make hyper-intelligent machines and design nanotechnologies, this imagination of progress and productivism is deeply implicated in the prospect of our extinction.

In five years' time, if the planetary temperature rise overshoots 1.5°C, southern Africa and South Africa, heating by twice the global average, will be a dangerously hotter region and this will threaten everything. According to the consensus climate science we have in South Africa, our carbon-emitting industrial farming system from farm to table will face livestock and crop systems collapse. We will also experience multi-year droughts and more extreme climate-related shocks. South Africa's climate science is not an allegory, but is an echo of the final warning to all of us about a worsening climate-driven future.

We need new thinking informed by the urgency of climate science and complex systems thinking to remake everything to survive multiple crises affecting our societies. Such thinking is embodied in the CJC launched on 28

August by the SAFSC, COPAC and various allies in progressive civil society. This charter emerges from six years of campaigning during the worst drought experienced in South Africa and is a historic step, not only to affirm democratic, just and people-driven systemic alternatives to mitigate and adapt South Africa, but it also calls for a paradigm shift to emancipatory ecology that can ensure present and future generations have a chance of surviving.

An emancipatory ecology standpoint asks the deeper questions about the systemic lock-ins driving us towards an unliveable world and its implications for the most vulnerable, who are least responsible for climate change. These lock-ins include:

- Continued fossil fuel extraction, including complex hydrocarbons through fracking, tar sands and offshore extraction buttressed by financial investment, regulation, policy, corporate interests and in the global North, imperial power. South Africa's extension of its minerals-energy complex to the oceans is a good example of this lock-in;
- Using carbon-based energy systems and technologies in the airline, shipping, automotive, industrial agriculture, manufacturing, cement and digital sector. Phasing out fossil fuels in these industries requires more than a carbon tax in the context of the climate emergency and an understanding of how carbonisation is entrenched in these sectors and how some of these technologies such as cement or mono-industrial farming do not have a place in a post-carbon world;
- Mass consumption based on carbon-based, resource-intensive ways of living and excessive waste. In unequal societies, the wealthy have the largest carbon- and resource-intensive footprints. South Africa is no exception and this has to be tackled directly. A wealth tax or an ecological debt tax are just some of the measures that need to be considered; and
- Global heating due to historical and continuing greenhouse gas emissions from fossil fuel-driven societies. As the 12th highest emitter of carbon emissions in the world and one of the frontrunners on the continent, South Africa has to break its addiction to coal-driven energy now. It cannot unite African governments, let alone demand reparations from the global North for historical climate debts with its continued coal dependence. Moreover, important system-change transformations are necessary to ensure our society can endure extreme climate shocks.

The CJC seeks to confront and displace these lock-ins that are driving a rupture in our stable Earth system, while engendering a social practice of transformative systems regeneration as part of a deep, just transition. This relates to food, water, work, energy, transport, housing, a public climate insurance fund, a people-led disaster management system and much more that is essential to producing a caring society. The democratic systemic reforms envisaged will meet our social needs, prevent socio-ecological collapse and end the damage to our Earth system. If human beings do not make the shift to an Earth-centred conception of being human, recognising we are just one small part of a larger life-giving system, we will not survive.

On 16 October, during a national day of action calling for an end to hunger, thirst, pollution (including climate harm), the CJC and a climate science future document, prepared by some of South Africa's leading climate scientists, will be handed over to the speaker of parliament and all leaders of political parties. As concerned citizens we will be claiming the right of section 234 of the Constitution, which provides for charters to be adopted to strengthen the Constitution, and thus will demand parliament adopts the CJC.

The scientific warnings have been trumpeted loud and clear; we do not have a second chance to address the worsening climate crisis given the time wasted on green tinkering, false solutions and climate concern rhetoric. In addressing this dangerous challenge in a transformative manner, we can be certain of one simple truth: our collective failure to act systemically now means greater harm for all and future generations.

All living in South Africa need to embrace the climate problem and its systemic solutions as part of the new mass-based climate justice politics inaugurated by the CJC. In five years' time it will be too late and in 10 years' time certainly catastrophic if we do not rise to this challenge. Now is the time for united action, at every level of society, to advance deep, just transitions where we live and work. If you listen with your conscience and heart, the screams of pain of future generations born in a world of intolerable heat can be heard. But it does not have to be like this.

Daily Maverick, 7 September 2020.

Party Politicians Fiddle about with Climate Change while SA Burns

ANYONE STANDING ON THE banks of the overflowing Theewaterskloof dam, the largest in the Western Cape, could be excused for scoffing at any assertion that South Africa is on fire. With the dam 99% full, such an observer can also be excused for forgetting about the day zero challenge that engulfed Cape Town in 2018.

Welcome to the complexity of the climate crisis. According to climate science, South Africa is burning; one of ten hotspots in the world, it is heating up twice as fast as the global average. Johannesburg's recent heat wave, in the early days of summer, brought temperatures perilously close to 35°C – the point at which the human body can easily be overcome and perish. Those with access to water, air conditioning and living spaces do better, but many do not have such luxuries and endure climate injustice. This normalised inequality has been exacerbated during the Covid-19 pandemic.

Climate science has warned about the risks that further heating will bring to South Africa. In simple terms, it is telling us that increased use of oil, gas and coal means tomorrow is born in fire. In this decade, a 1.5°C planetary overshoot is very likely, which means South Africa will be 3°C hotter. At such temperatures, globalised commercial agriculture will break down and multi-year droughts will be a regular occurrence. Extreme weather shocks are also likely. Our ecosystems will be further stressed and our socio-ecological order will be pushed decisively in the direction of collapse. This is not science fiction or alarmist fear-mongering. These challenges are set out in a document prepared by some of South Africa's leading climate scientists and shared with parliament on 16 October, World Food Day.

The online assembly with parliament also shared the world's first CJC, demanding that it be adopted by South Africa. The charter comes out of six years of campaigning, during the worst drought in the country's history, led by the SAFSC. It was shaped by constituency dialogues and public input over a two-year period.

Why did civil society rally widely before the handover of these documents to parliament, under the banner of ending hunger, thirst, pollution and climate harm? Why did 220 organisations endorse the charter, including trade unions, informal traders, schools, social justice organisations, environmental organisations and leading political foundations like the Mandela, Gandhi and Kathrada foundations? Because we are dealing with a serious challenge, which everybody needs to own. But our political leaders are not taking it seriously. With the prospect of our extinction as a species on the planetary agenda, it is rational to assume that every person who considers themselves a leader in society – particularly every political party – will be seized with this issue. You would expect climate crisis news to be mainstreamed in the media. You would expect every policy agenda to mainstream it as a problem to be solved. Unfortunately, this is not the case.

South Africa is the 11th-highest emitter of carbon emissions in the world. Our coal addiction is criminal. Successive ANC governments have continued to reproduce the carbon-based minerals energy complex. Under the Ramaphosa government, including in his economic recovery plan, more mining is promoted, globalised agriculture is supported and he has fast-tracked the extraction of oil and gas. This is an anti-climate justice and anti-climate science government. At the same time, none of our political parties in parliament has a serious agenda to tackle the crisis. This was evident when the top four parties in parliament (the ANC, DA, EFF and Freedom Front Plus) declined an invitation to debate the urgency of the climate crisis at the recent online assembly. The three parties that did participate displayed extremely lacklustre conceptions of climate issues. Are these professional politicians really serious about the concerns of citizens?

When the world overshot a 1°C rise in temperature in 2015, a second cycle of global climate justice activism exploded onto the world stage, led by indigenous peoples' struggles at Standing Rock in the US, followed by Extinction Rebellion and then Greta Thunberg's #FridaysForFuture movement. These movements have raised awareness about the worsening climate crisis, but governments have continued to lack the commitment to decarbonise. At the same time, the SAFSC started its long march to connect hunger, food price increases, drought and climate crisis. In the hurly-burly of this activism the CJC was germinated. Like the Freedom Charter, it is premised on the need to give voice to the desires, visions and systemic alternatives that ordinary people want for a deep, just transition to survive a worsening climate crisis. It also calls for South Africa to lead a climate justice agenda in Africa.

After the nuclear arms race of the twentieth century brought the world to the edge of extinction, South Africa's new democratic government boosted its moral authority by destroying all nuclear weapons. This gave Mandela's government a stature unrivalled in the global North and South. Similarly, the CJC calls on South Africa to lead decarbonisation, to provide an inspiring example to the world and to lead a climate justice deal for Africa, including an end fossil fuel treaty in the UN system. The world needs such an example before irreversible climate change is locked in. The CJC movement born in this process will not settle for anything less.

In a year's time, on 16 October 2021, the CJC movement will return to parliament to confirm that the charter has been adopted. If South Africa's parliamentary parties do not rise to this challenge, all legal and democratic options will be pursued to advance a climate justice future for South Africa.

Sunday Times, 1 November 2020.

South Africa, the Climate Pariah, Needs to Change its Ways

A RECENT REPORT BY the IPCC confirmed that extreme weather and climate shocks have arrived, increasing threefold since the 1980s. For many societies, climate risks have already contributed to collapsing food systems. Some of the countries on this tragic list include: Zimbabwe (2015–2016 El Niño-induced drought), Ethiopia (El Niño-induced drought and now the Tigray region impacted by war, locusts and a prolonged drought), Puerto Rico (devastated by Hurricane Maria in 2017 with 80% of its agricultural yield wiped out), southern Madagascar (in famine after several years of drought) and Honduras (a four-year drought, two hurricanes and flooding, which resulted in the collapse of its food systems). In Mozambique at least 500,000 people had to receive emergency food aid or face starvation after cyclones in 2019. Mozambique is also facing drought in the southern part of the country.

South Africa's drought since 2014 was one of the worst in the history of the country. However, though agricultural sectors collapsed, the country was spared a climate famine this time, despite 14 million going to bed hungry, increased food prices and stressed subsistence production due to water problems. The failures of the ANC state to comprehend this reality and ensure our water systems are repurposed is apparent in the local government elections, with water needs a major concern in several communities.

The ANC state is far from being ready to face climate-induced weather extremes. Climate policy shifts in South Africa are not happening as part of a national strategy to place the country on a climate emergency footing but are rather taking place due to increasing climate justice pressure from below, the imperative of meeting formal international commitments, and the increased momentum in climate geopolitics.

The recent announcement by SASOL that it will cut emissions by 30% by 2030, divest from coal and shift to gas is significant. For climate justice activists, this shift came from making public research on SASOL's carbon criminality, forming a human chain around SASOL in 2019, challenging the leadership to engage on climate science, marching on its AGM, and putting stiff pressure on the inside through shareholder activism. And SASOL's climate commitments are still not ambitious enough, or guided by a just transition plan that secures workers and communities. This is the same with ESKOM. Yet the government holds this up as part of its commitments to a deep, just transition. The government's announcement of a commitment to cut carbon emissions is also a necessary shift as per commitments to the Paris Agreement. It is about optics.

The assumption in all of this is that transition risks matter, not human life. South Africa will lose out on green finance and access to markets. This conservative market rationality fails to appreciate that South Africa has been a climate pariah. It is the largest African emitter of carbon and owes the world a climate debt. It is not a moment of securing opportunities but rather about leading by example, morally and politically.

Last month two important UN conferences provided a global platform to test commitments to the climate emergency. The UN General Assembly, building up to the COP26 summit in Glasgow, gave us a glimpse of climate geopolitics. US President Joe Biden signalled strongly that he is working on more ambitious financial contributions to the Green Climate Fund. China has signalled an end to investments in coal-fired power stations in other parts of the world. The EU and the US are working on an ambitious plan to reduce methane emissions by 2030. However, while the US, China and Europe seem to be co-operating on climate, the overall picture is still not hopeful for Glasgow. As it stands, South Africa and other big emitters have not put forward ambitious enough climate pledges.

The second important UN summit was on food systems. Climate concerns were centre stage, but this conference was hijacked by corporate interests wanting to further entrench corporate fixes to the food crisis such as mono-industrial plant-based diets, nutritional fortification of food, and enhanced food aid. The summit failed to address the needs of small-scale farmers who are crucial to feeding the world. A parallel conference on food systems for people supported by global movements affirmed the importance of feeding countries through food sovereignty, agro-ecology and small-scale farming. South Africa's government believes in many of the false technofixes of the UN Food Summit and is committed to a water-intensive and export-led industrial agriculture system, in a context in which the world is moving closer to more widespread climate famines.

By now a South African state committed to addressing the climate crisis should have adopted the CJC, had a new deep, just transition national development plan in place, unpacked a new macro-economic approach consistent with advancing a climate emergency social contract, and worked closely with the African Union (AU) to secure a climate justice deal and treaty to phase out fossil fuel in the forthcoming UN climate summit. Most important, the ANC state should have ended the incoherence about climate policy by ensuring Gwede Mantashe and Barbara Creecy are part of the mainstreaming of a deep, just transition agenda guiding every policy and level of government. Instead, the Minister of Mineral Resources and Energy has outdated ideas about clean coal, Karpowerships and even nuclear power. The Minister of Forestry, Fisheries and the Environment is merely marching in lock-step with the climate needs of business and the imperative of leveraging international climate resources. She believes the just transition is merely about renewable energy and shallow adaptation. South Africa's growing climate-aware public and the world see this incoherence and lack of ambition. With the current crisis of leadership, every effort will have to be made to ensure the 2024 national election is a climate justice election to secure South Africa's future.

Sunday Times, 3 October 2021.

An Open Letter to Hosken Consolidated Investments and Minister Gwede Mantashe: A Beginner's Guide to Poppycock
with Janet Solomon

HOSKEN CONSOLIDATED INVESTMENTS (HCI) CEO Johnny Copelyn declared the criticism of seismic surveys to be poppycock in an interview with *Cape Talk*, subsequently carried by *Business Day* under the headline 'HCI board blasts criticism of seismic surveys as "poppycock"'.[1] Fortunately, this assertion has nothing to do with male genitalia and its size. In this case, Johnny's being bigger than everyone else's and thus the alpha white-male-knows-what's-best-of-all-of-us kind of posing. Thank you, Johnny, for steering clear of the cock fight!

Nonetheless, this discursive rant has set the tone for how the HCI board's letter[2] published in the *Daily Maverick* opposing resistance to seismic surveys has been received. Something is stirring in the command centres of HCI, a certain executive arousal, probably based on a realisation that the mass resistance to their interests in offshore oil and gas extraction is not about to disappear any time soon. Instead, it is the beginning of what they should expect in this life and death struggle to prevent climate breakdown.

The etymology of the term poppycock goes back to Dutch usage, *pappekak* or soft dung. In the course of its linguistic journey into the white supremacist colonial imaginary, it became part of conquering white reason. To be reduced to animal excrement was the worst thing in the colonial imaginary based on the hierarchy of white male supremacy over women, native peoples and non-human nature (animals, plants and ecosystems). To be poppycock or express poppycock meant that you were at the bottom of the pile: bullshit, valueless, idiotic, insignificant and ultimately devoid of voice. The online *Cambridge Dictionary* defines the term to mean old-fashioned

---

1   https://www.businesslive.co.za/bd/national/2022-01-24-hci-board-blasts-criticism-of-seismic-surveys-as-poppycock/.

2   https://www.dailymaverick.co.za/article/2022-01-23-seismic-surveys-south-africa-cannot-afford-the-luxury-of-refusing-to-develop-valuable-resources-on-which-it-sits/.

disapproving. It's clear Johnny has a penchant for old-fashioned English language usage. Smarter vocabulary could have been: bunk or garbage.

Anyway, we get the message: we are worse than animal scat. Of course, HCI is not the same as the Dutch East India Company or the British East India Company but there is certainly a continuity in its colonial ecological philosophy as expressed in its diction. It is stuck in a simplistic conception of the human–nature relationship: capitalist business is now at the apex of the human–nature hierarchy. It will determine what will happen to human and non-human life, even through its vaunted green investments. We beg to differ and will tell you why.

Pragmatic opportunism and faux development

Another revealing aspect of the HCI world view contained in its *Daily Maverick* letter is the assumption that its business interests, particularly oil and gas extraction, converge with the national interest; its investments in oil and gas will give South Africa economic autonomy, enable an orderly energy transition but most importantly this represents hard-headed realist thinking.

But is it really that? There are echoes of this position in the derisive statements made by Minister Gwede Mantashe against resistance to seismic surveys and fossil fuel extraction. Mantashe, in his defence of coal, gas (including the master plan) and oil has even suggested those who resist further extraction are anti-development and want to maintain apartheid and colonialism of a special type. Let's be clear, this is pragmatic opportunism, which draws selectively on knowledge to make its argument seem convincing. Pragmatism is also a fix-it philosophy, claiming to be above isms and practical about problems. This is a delusion given that solutions to economic problems are expressive of class interests.

For instance, HCI suggests it is merely working with government energy planning and trying to find a fit. HCI's investments in coal and interests in offshore oil and gas do more than work with government priorities, but actually ensure a dangerous carbon lock-in for the country. Energy planning, policy and HCI investment have become symbiotic and entrenched in reproducing the carbon-based minerals-energy complex, while the climate crisis worsens. The national interest becomes HCI interest and vice-versa.

This is not benign. The state's skewing of the IRP towards coal (44.6%) and gas (15.7%) by 2030 expresses these vested carbon-capitalist class interests. Simply, there are profits to be made by such extractivism and not some concern for an orderly energy transition. The counter-factual shows this up even more starkly. If tomorrow the state lifted the ceiling on wind, the country could meet its energy needs eight times over through offshore wind power, according to a recent study done by Stellenbosch University. According to the International Renewable Energy Agency,[3] the costs of renewable energy systems and unit costs of renewable energy generation have come down dramatically in comparison to fossil fuels such as coal.

Brown et al.[4] have shown the feasibility and economic viability of a 100% renewable electricity system for South Africa, meeting the energy needs of all citizens at all times is cost-competitive with fossil fuel-based systems, even before externalities such as global warming, water usage and environmental pollution are taken into account. They have established that this renewable system requires no re-invention of the power system; rather only a 'directed evolution of the current system is required to guarantee affordability, reliability and sustainability'. In far less than the six years before Total's offshore Brulpadda well comes online, there could be sufficient renewable electricity generation and storage technology to convert entirely to renewables.

So why is there a ceiling on renewable energy in the national energy mix? Who benefits from this failure to exploit limitless wind and sunshine? Certainly, the time has come for an orderly energy transition driven by the technical and economic advantages offered by renewable energy, including socially owned renewable energy in households, communities and local government.

Mantashe is also hiding behind a pragmatic opportunism, both as energy minister and chair of the ANC. He understands South Africa's mineral reserves are worth about R147.91 trillion and significantly half of this value is in coal. Defending coal is crucial for greasing the wheels of political support from the NUM, for the ANC and business aligned to the ANC invested in coal. In the case of labour, he is exploiting the failure of the ANC state to provide a serious just transition plan to the country (a point we shall return to below). His fervour for defending offshore oil and gas extraction is also probably linked to ensuring Shell, a partner of Thebe Investment (which owns 28% of Shell's downstream business), ultimately benefits the ANC. In news reports over the past two months it has been revealed that Batho Batho Trust, which owns 46% of Thebe gave a R15 million loan to the ANC to deal with its various financial problems. The logic is simple: Shell secures its interests in oil

---

3   https://www.irena.org/publications/2020/Jun/Renewable-Power-Costs-in-2019.
4   https://www.sciencedirect.com/science/article/pii/S1364032118303307.

and gas, Thebe benefits, Batho Batho Trust gains and ultimately ANC interests are realised. So, who is really pursuing the national interest and development in this context?

Moreover, according to the Alternative Information and Development Centre's climate jobs research, if socially owned renewable energy is scaled up, 250,000 climate jobs can be created in electricity and renewable energy alone, way more than what exists in coal mining. Current estimates sit at about 113,000 coal jobs in South Africa.[5] This also stands in contrast to oil and gas jobs, with international research affirming fewer, more technical jobs, are created in offshore oil and gas than projected. But Mantashe's rant about resistance to oil and gas entrenches colonialism of a special type rather than development, deserves a special type of response. The ANC has ruled South Africa for over 25 years and the economic crisis we are living through is simply a matter of its own doing: a horrendous 46% unemployment rate, in the midst of Covid-19; African women, among women more generally, continue to be the most vulnerable with a 41% unemployment rate; about 30 million food insecure; 10% of income earners receive 65% of national income; and 80% of wealth is in the hands of 10% of the population.

Then there is the staggering scale of corruption with billions looted from parastatals, state departments and local government. A crucial consequence in this regard is the theft of the future of millions of desperate and unemployed youth in South Africa. So, who has really been reinforcing and reproducing colonialism of a special type? Mantashe's disingenuous declarations need to be measured against the record of the ANC in power. He stands for a faux development that benefits him and his insider ANC cronies, certainly not the country. HCI is clearly on this bandwagon.

Licence over the whale

So why bother demonising small-scale fisherfolk and a few hundred thousand ocean activists? Zuma-era Operation Phakisa offshore oil and gas stream's founding documents highlighted the greatest threat to commodifying the ocean commons as social opposition to it. Offshore Phakisa (hurry up) has accelerated seismic survey since public pushback began to heat up after the Schlumberger survey of 2016 saw the highest recorded animal stranding numbers[6] along the

---

5   https://www.pwc.co.za/en/assets/pdf/what-a-just-transition-means-for-jobs-in-south-africa.pdf.
6   https://www.academia.edu/33381566/Annual_KZN_Stranding_report_2016_HighRes_pdf.

east coast, including KwaZulul-Natal's first mass stranding. A number of these strandings were unusual – a dolphin with its top and bottom jaw broken outwards and a deep-water Cuvier's beaked whale had washed up with its innards in its mouth, likely having suffered barotrauma (the bends). Fisherfolk, scientists, activists, sea users and journalists sensed foul play.

This seismic survey had been extended into the whale migration season, without the requisite public participation. Yes, there's a pattern here. The lubrication of the entry of oil majors onto South Africa's coastline for Zuma's offshore oil and gas development programme involved certain reversals in environmental regulation, since environmental authorisation for seismic survey reconnaissance is onerous.

Dropping protective legislation simultaneous to the launch of offshore Phakisa in 2014 was an attempt to remove barriers to extending the minerals-energy complex to oceans. That these animals were perceived to be acceptable collateral damage struck a chord with the South Durban community, who live with the real-life impacts of toxic air pollution from two of the country's biggest oil refineries. An Oceans Not Oil, a citizen-led marine environmental justice coalition, supported by academia and scientists, was formed.

HCI and Copelyn's elaborate discourses of denial construct an alternate reality that doesn't involve violent aftermaths to their dealings. Copelyn is practising an appeal to ignorance – that the claim of irreparable harm caused by seismic surveys is false because it has not yet been proved true. It is more convenient to ignore the science[7] and fantasise that an array of 32 airguns detonating sound[8] and pressure waves so powerful as to find gas reserves 40 kilometres below the seabed 8640 times a day in an acoustic watery home is without consequence.

At an Inquiry into Media Credibility and Ethics, the South African National Editors Forum found that Copelyn's eNCA news channel (owned by HCI) failed to disclose a conflict of interest when reporting on Shell/Impact Oil and Gas Ltd's Wild Coast seismic blasting, in which it has a material interest in success. HCI are the largest shareholder of Impact Oil and Gas, which sold a 50% working interest and operatorship of their Transkei and Algoa (Wild Coast) licence to Shell. HCI's letter to the editor cum advertorial forgot to mention that too.

That indigenous people's intangible heritage, social consensus and marine

---

7   https://oceansnotoil.org/environmental-impacts/.

8   https://oceansnotoil.org/seismic-surveys/.

science might have begun to pull the rug from Impact Oil and Gas's empire building, shifting its sovereign claim from acreage to meaningless lines on the blank blue of the petroleum exploration and production activities map, must be a worry to a man used to dictating the narrative.

Living ocean or oil?

Pipe dream gas-for-development is not reparative economics. Playing itself out in Mozambique currently is the recurring syndrome of the resource curse effect: increased indebtedness, corruption and instability which frequently follow major oil and gas resource finds, before extraction, during and post-production. E3G, an independent European climate change think tank, has found that on average Mozambicans are poorer than they were a decade ago with 90% under the international poverty line.[9] Cabo Delgado, where the gas projects are based and site of an ongoing violent conflict, has been hit the worst: household spending has dropped by 38% in the last five years.

The accelerating effects of CO_2 absorption by the oceans are manifesting themselves clearly now, so delusional forging ahead with 30 new offshore wells by 2030 shows cowboy risk tolerance. The IPCC in its 'Special report on the ocean and cryosphere in a changing climate'[10] lists ocean deoxygenation and ocean acidification as irreversible for centuries to come and makes achieving the 1.5°C target more difficult.[11] These dual stressors are profoundly altering ecosystems – globally 40% of coral species have died and local fisheries[12] have become vulnerable, to name only the obvious.

Once rare, extreme events are likely to occur in southern Africa now every year due to sea-level rise and increased storm intensity. In 2019 two cyclones, within the same season, battered southern Africa, killing over a thousand people and leaving over 2.5 million people in need of humanitarian aid. At the time of writing, there are also devastating tropical storm impacts and cyclone build-up happening on the oceans near Madagascar and Mozambique.

---

9   https://www.e3g.org/publications/the-failure-of-gas-for-development-mozambique-case-study/.

10 https://www.ipcc.ch/srocc/chapter/chapter-6/.

11 https://www.carbonbrief.org/analysis-major-update-to-ocean-heat-record-could-shrink-1-5c-carbon-budget.

12 https://wwfsassi.co.za/climate-change-impacts-on-south-africas-small-scale-fishers-and-popular-linefish-species/.

Bread and increasing systemic risk of fossil fuel extraction

In 2016, a bread march through the streets of Johannesburg led by the SAFSC, trade unions and community organisations made the connection between one of the worst droughts in the history of the country, high food prices and the worsening climate crisis. Hunger was being exacerbated by this climate shock. In 2018 the SAFSC, together with over 60 organisations, called on the South African president to convene an urgent sitting of parliament to debate the alarming 1.5°C IPCC report on the need to cut carbon emissions by half by 2030. The SAFSC and allies wanted parliament to mainstream the urgency of this challenge into government policy, but this went unheeded.

Hence, in solidarity with drought-affected communities and progressive sectors of society (including trade unions), the SAFSC went on to pioneer the development of a CJC for South Africa. The charter was handed over to parliament on World Food Day in October 2020, with the demand it be adopted as per section 234 of the South African Constitution which provides for the adoption of charters. Underlying the creation and championing of the CJC was a deep concern for the urgency of climate science and the dangers it highlighted for the future of South Africa.

According to leading South African climate scientists[13] working with the IPCC, South Africa is one of 10 climate hot-spots in the world and is heating at twice the global average. An overshoot of 1.5°C over the next decade would mean we are at 3°C warming. The existential risk this poses to life in the country cannot be underestimated and has to be acted on now, not in 2050. This urgency is underlined by the recent IPCC report entitled 'Physical science basis of climate change,'[14] which went into the recent Glasgow COP summit, affirming that extreme weather events (floods, droughts, heatwaves, cyclones) are our new reality and scientific attribution is clear.

This simply means if HCI gets its way with offshore oil and gas extraction and Mantashe continues to support the use of coal, oil and gas in the national energy mix, South Africa is headed for more extreme climate shocks, with disproportionate impacts on workers and poor families, and with an escalating price tag.

The recent drought (2014–2021) cost the Western Cape economy R5 billion and at a national level, the government had to bail out the Land Bank to the tune of R7 billion, mainly because of defaulting farmer loans due to the drought.

---

13 https://emancipatoryfutures.co.za/future.

14 https://www.ipcc.ch/report/ar6/wg1/.

Flooding in KwaZulu-Natal in 2019 was estimated at R1 billion and this year between December and January at R3.3 billion.

South Africa's ballooning public debt will increase with more climate shocks. From this perspective, Mantashe and HCI will bankrupt South Africa as they push for coal, oil and gas extraction which contributes to global warming and, in turn, feeds back as costly and dangerous climate shocks. More coal, oil and gas is literally about making the climate crisis a systemic risk and is against thinking climate economics and the future of South Africa. It is tantamount to unlawful endangerment and has to be stopped now.

Climate injustice, workers and peoples of South Africa

When day zero impacted Cape Town, the disproportionate impacts were on poor and working-class households, many being women workers in the textile industry in which SACTWU organises. They had to queue up to access water from public springs and faced punitive prices for water supplied by the municipality, increasing their care burdens.

When the drought made itself felt deep in the Eastern Cape, where many mineworkers come from, climate injustice was registering as hunger. When cyclones Idai and Kenneth pummelled Mozambique, Zimbabwe and Malawi, this also impacted the lives of migrant miners and other workers. HCI and Mantashe's drive for more coal, gas and oil extraction simply means more suffering, more climate shocks for the members of SACTWU, NUM, their families, communities and the working class in general.

The trade union movement in South Africa is waking up to the urgencies of the climate crisis. COSATU is working on a just transition blueprint. In a survey done by NALEDI, the overwhelming number of workers surveyed in COSATU support the CJC. The Federation of Unions of South Africa (FEDUSA) has developed a position on the just transition, the South African Federation of Trade Unions (SAFTU) is deeply committed to such and even Solidarity is engaging on these issues.

All these unions shaped and informed the making of the CJC. How unions champion the phase out of fossil fuels, the energy transition and systemic transformation required to decarbonise and build adaptive systems will impact the future of all in South Africa. The trade union movement has been bedevilled by the narrow interests of trade union investment companies and corruption, but the lived experiences of members in the context of intensifying climate harm is certainly going to force them to rise to the challenge of accelerating and deepening the just transition.

The #OceansNotOil Campaign and the CJC movement stand in solidarity and encourage unions to step up and lead society now. In this regard, the positions of Gwede Mantashe and HCI need to be tackled head on by workers who stand to lose the most.

What do we want for South Africa?

Weighing up the systemic risks of further coal, oil and gas extractions as they relate to the climate crisis shows that it will increase climate harms, economic costs, injustice and will undermine the immediate realisation of viable alternatives. This simply means there is no case for further coal, gas and oil extraction in South Africa; it is a climate curse. Mantashe and HCI have a narrow, self-seeking agenda that is at odds with the national interest. South Africa has used coal for more than 100 years and it owes the world a climate debt. It needs to act responsibly in this regard. At least 100 million Africans will be forced to be climate refugees in the coming decades. South Africa cannot be a carbon pariah in this context.

Instead, we need to be leading by example through renewing radical pan-Africanism to demonstrate how to accelerate and deepen the just transition now. The South African state is lagging behind and should have had a just transition plan in place that goes beyond climate modernisation (with its emphasis on money, markets, technology and more growth), and shallow tinkering. Merely declaring 'net-zero by 2050' is unambitious and delays decisive transformative action.

Rather, it should be taking its cue from the CJC pluri-vision to place the country on climate emergency footing now and enable transformative systemic change to be led from below. The charter is a compass of the many rising to advance climate justice, a thread of hope that reaches into the frontlines of struggles that are defending our oceans, biodiversity and lifemaking more generally.

Moreover, the translation of the charter into policies such as a climate justice deal for South Africa will demonstrate that legacies of exploitation, dispossession, oppression and racial exclusion must be addressed as part of the deep, just transition. A new society based on ending hunger through food sovereignty, socially owned renewable energy, democratising the water commons, a universal basic income, zero waste, climate jobs, ecomobility anchored by clean energy public transport systems, democratic planning, ecohousing and transition towns, ecological taxes on the rich, effective knowledge systems to assist with survival and the development of social innovation, a responsive and effective public healthcare system, natural climate solutions and a climate justice state are crucial to ensure we do not face societal collapse from worsening climate shocks.

These emancipatory ecologies, feminist and socialist commons alternatives are championed by various movements in South Africa. Maybe rather than environmentalist phobia and polarising rants, Mantashe and HCI should rather engage with these ideas so their loved ones also stand a chance of surviving in a world of worsening climate chaos.

Daily Maverick, 19 October 2021.

US, Russia and Ukraine: The death trap beyond the new Cold War and World War 3

Vladimir Putin's regime, unlike Franco, Mussolini or Hitler, has a formidable nuclear arsenal. In this context, the contemporary world stands on the brink, facing extinction either through nuclear holocaust emanating from battlefields in Ukraine or worsening the climate crisis, while in our everyday lives prices for food and fossil fuels are skyrocketing.

Precariousness, uncertainty and complex risk have become the lived reality of deep globalisation in which markets for finance, energy, food and production have been integrated. The fragility of this global economy was exposed in the Great Financial Crisis (*c.* 2007–2009) from which the world economy has not recovered, by the ongoing Covid-19 pandemic, and now by the Russian invasion of Ukraine. These realities cannot be understood through simple memes, propagandistic binaries or abstract security concepts.

The stakes are high

A global historical process has brought us to where we are, a political project to remake the world in the image of the US after the end of the Cold War. This project has failed after four decades and is driving all of us deeper into a death trap. Yet the leadership of the US and its allies continue to repeat the same mistakes. If we do not grasp this premise as the basis to understand the world disorder, we are also not going to escape this madness. Moreover, we are not going to be able to think through – or find a way out of – this crisis and will remain hostage to a paradigm of war shared by the US, the EU, Russia and China.

Using a more nuanced and critical geostrategic reading of the US, the Russian invasion of Ukraine and its wider implications will illustrate the point. Many security strategists and media commentators, mainly in the West, characterise the invasion of Ukraine as the inauguration of World War 3 or a new Cold War. This framing defines international politics by setting up two opposing sides with distinct ideological orientations: the liberal West versus the authoritarian Russian Federation and China.

This narrative has immense commonsense appeal but does not correspond to reality. US democracy sits on the same authoritarian spectrum as Russia and China. It is a failed market democracy, best designated as a plutocracy in which it has given overwhelming power to corporations over citizens. The Republican Party is also the harbinger of a minority project based on supremacist white nationalism, including voter suppression laws in several states. US democracy looks more like a racist banana republic than a shining example of democratic rights and freedoms. Moreover, the binary geopolitical frame is dangerous because it reinforces a paradigm of war which serves the interests of countries with big military-industrial-security complexes and as a result believes war is necessary to order international relations.

Philosophically, this rests on simplistic and static conceptions of human nature as inherently about violence. Both world wars in the twentieth century led to immense loss of life, about 80 million people, and scorched ecosystems. While the US likes to believe it won the Cold War through outspending the former USSR in an arms race, the fact of the matter is that Mikhail Gorbachev and his party realised – after decades of building nuclear arsenals, chemical and biological weapons – that the geopolitics of the Cold War was a dead end for humanity.

Nobody wins if we all self-exterminate

By the 1960s, both sides had nuclear weapons that could vaporise cities the size of Cape Town and Johannesburg. No matter what military doctrine and narrative was used to justify nuclear weapons, these technologies of mass annihilation were never about deterrence, but essentially about first strike extermination of millions of human beings.

About 40 recorded nuclear incidents occurred during the 45-year Cold War, including planes and submarines armed with nuclear warheads ending up in accidents. Our world could have ended during the Cold War because none of the safeguards really worked. A whole generation alive on our planet today does not understand this threat.

Most people also do not appreciate that nuclear war fighting has become ingrained in how the US understands its superiority in the world. After the Cold War, instead of embracing Gorbachev's invitation to secure a nuclear weapons-free world, the US leadership did the opposite. It failed to sign on to the Nuclear Test Ban Treaty and take seriously nuclear arms reduction and reductions in strategic ballistic missiles. Instead, it steamed ahead with the wrongheaded assumption that nuclear capability, both strategic and tactical, was necessary to complement conventional military capabilities.

In the 1990s, Russia's military budget collapsed and its nuclear arsenal was put into storage. However, other nuclear powers such as Britain, France and China followed the US lead. Putin jumped on this bandwagon once ensconced in the Kremlin, propped up by criminalised petro-capitalism (aided by US corporations), as NATO expanded east and his revanchist ultranationalist dreams of territorial empire took shape.

The world has to ask: why has the US not thrown up a Gorbachev? Why is the US, which has had the power to lead by example, not actively worked to prevent nuclear proliferation after the end of the Cold War? Where is the American leader who can ensure Israel, India, Pakistan, North Korea and all other nuclear powers terminate their nuclear arsenals and ambitions by showing the US will do the same for world peace? Militarist expansionism has its roots deep in US history going back to early frontier expansion and genocidal violence against native Americans. In the nineteenth century, this was married to the notion of manifest destiny which is about a divine right to expand the territorial boundaries of the country.

Hence, throughout its modern history the US has had a selective respect for international law, including the UN Charter. This was demonstrated starkly during the Cold War, when US-trained militaries in the infamous School of the Americas overthrew democratically elected governments in Latin America. In the so-called US backyard and beyond, about 10 million people were killed during hot wars in the global South. For Noam Chomsky, such forms of US interventionism were tantamount to fascism and up until now there has been no reckoning. In the aftermath of the Cold War, the US continues to furnish this example of hypocrisy to the world through violations of human rights, illegal invasions and extrajudicial killings during its war on terror. Putin is a good student of US hypocrisy and is putting it to the test in his own maniacal way. Some misread Putin and his denazification rhetoric as a progressive anti-imperialism.

In the post-Cold War world, based on a complex weave of fragile economic integration, the US also trailblazed with a new form of global warfare, adding to its nuclear, chemical and biological weapons capability. This is made up of three elements: (i) full-spectrum dominance (including air, land, sea, space and the cybersphere); (ii) hybridising full-spectrum warfare in combination with economic, extrajudicial actions, embedded journalism and even multilateral relations; and (iii) projecting global reach.

Producing copycats like the Putin regime

This war machine and national security orientation nonetheless has a contradictory relationship with its ambitions for global economic integration. Global war constantly disrupts economic circuits and introduces instability into the global economy. The first Gulf War had implications for oil supplies; the failed war on terror created risk all over the world; and US involvement in Syria added to the tragic refugee crisis (which did not receive the same commitment to humanitarian aid as Ukraine but instead exclusionary border regimes were utilised by European countries).

Current sanctions against Russia, including oil and gas bans by the US and UK, led to a spike in global oil and gas prices and triggered a food and fertiliser export ban from Putin causing a price spike and global food shock.

The logic of global war within US national security thinking has explicitly been about a collision with declared rivals such as Russia and China, ensnaring them in a spiral of escalation including defensive and dangerous pre-emptive moves. Both Trump and Biden's national security thinking fit this template. Even if Putin withdraws from Ukraine, the US is certainly on a warpath with China. Does the American public want this? Will the US plutocratic rulers democratise US foreign policy, including having a national referendum on such an issue? Does the world want this kind of explicit warmongering which threatens everything? The decline of the US and its inability to think beyond the global war paradigm was also on full display before and after Putin's recent invasion of Ukraine.

The faltering Minsk agreements, after Russia's invasion of Crimea in 2014, and the amassing of a sizeable number of Russian troops on the Ukrainian border over the past few months should have given the US and its EU ally pause to secure a lasting peace. Instead, aid packages have kicked into gear mainly to militarise the conflict. Both the US and EU have escalated the conflict with increasing military resourcing and thus have reduced Ukraine to a military proxy of the US-EU-NATO alliance.

Failure by the EU

The EU in particular has failed spectacularly to incorporate Russia into a pan-European project and break out of the shadows of US power. After the Cold War, a London-Paris-Berlin-Moscow project was a distinct possibility. Again, embracing the peace opening inaugurated by Gorbachev was dismissed. Instead, selective geostrategic relations were maintained with Russia for commodities and for laundering dirty oligarchic finance, mainly through London. Germany and the EU are now remilitarising and embracing the US global war paradigm. Together with Brexit, rising ultranationalism, deepening economic crisis and worsening climate shocks, the EU project faces serious challenges.

With growing signs of shifting towards robotised warfare (including drones, roboticised guard dogs on the US border and the robot soldier) the US is laying the basis to take the world into endless global warfare. The US military has one of the largest carbon footprints in the world; some studies show it has a carbon footprint larger than Portugal or Denmark. Biden's administration has just secured a bipartisan military budget worth close to $800 billion while at the same time only allocating $100 billion to assist poor countries with the climate crisis – a problem it has played a major part in creating. At the same time, in the midst of the conflict with Russia it has called on US shale oil and gas producers to increase supply, as well as Saudi Arabia and Venezuela to also meet global supply needs. The EU is also faltering in terms of using this moment to break its dependence on fossil fuels.

Recent studies show the world will only cut emissions by 9% rather than half by the end of the decade, which means the world risks overshooting the 1.5°C target, while the IPCC in its recent report entitled *Climate Impacts, Adaptation and Vulnerability* says over three billion people are now vulnerable to current levels of planetary heating.

An American failure

The Cold War wasted the talents and skills of two generations. The world cannot afford to repeat this mistake. All scholarly security thinking today highlights the climate crisis as the primary complex threat facing the world; the entire world needs to be seized with this challenge. The US is brazenly failing to take responsibility for its contribution to the worsening climate crisis and rather has become a threat multiplier in both military and climate terms to the world.

Is it time for climate justice sanctions against the US and those like it? Russia, China and the EU are no different if they remain within the US death trap. All these geopolitical competitors certainly do not represent the interests of the greatest superpower on Planet Earth: the human species. Even with a ceasefire between Russia and Ukraine based on commitments not to join NATO and security guarantees, the situation in Eastern Europe is going to be tenuous; there will be no lasting peace.

Hence, at minimum, anti-war politics today has to stand for a nuclear-free Europe and world (already billions of people in Africa, Latin America and parts of Asia are in nuclear-free zones); a renewed social rather than a market-centred pan-European project embracing both Ukraine and Russia; an end to NATO; the termination of war machines driving endless global war in Ukraine, Palestine, Yemen and elsewhere; extending support to all refugees on the planet, including enhancing humanitarian aid to Ukraine through cancelling all foreign debts; and an end to the war with nature, particularly the climate crisis, by immediately phasing out fossil fuels and going beyond a politics of nationalism to embrace a politics of human and non-human solidarity. It's time for collective human power to prevail over those who threaten all of us before it is too late.

The South African government, in its neutrality stance, is far from these concerns and is stuck in outdated geostrategic and security thinking. It needs to use the termination of the apartheid nuclear arsenal and chemical and biological warfare programme to echo the imperatives of contemporary anti-war politics on the global stage: in the AU, the UN, BRICS and in engagements with the US, EU and Ukraine.

Daily Maverick, 22 March 2022.

The ANC Needs a Wake-Up Call on the Urgency of the Climate Crisis

HUMAN LIFE ON PLANET Earth has faced three natural threats to its existence: catastrophic volcanic eruptions, a huge extraterrestrial object like an asteroid crashing, and the end of the Sun. None of these pose any immediate danger. This means it is up to us to make the best of our world while acting as stewards of this fragile web of life. Yet, with the levels of investment in fossil fuels and the increase in greenhouse gases, the human species faces the prospect of self-extinction this century. At a painful historic moment, without decisive action as called for by the UN in this decade, irreversible geophysical changes, together with extreme heat, will make Earth unliveable. Somewhere the last source of drinkable water will run dry, the oceans will boil, humans will cook and ecosystems will perish. Planet Earth would be post-human. Beyond the arcane language of climate science this is what we are facing.

If this happens, modern humans, bipedal, upright, with bigger brains and about 200,000 years old, on a 4.5 billion-year-old planet would have taken about 150 years of using oil, coal and gas to wipe out themselves and many other species. They would have ended the human journey. Those propelling us in this direction are deciding if our loved ones live or die, whether our children have a future, enjoy the gift of life, have a stable environment and can revel in the wonder of one of the most beautiful planets in the solar system. Those investing in more oil, coal and gas, thereby creating a global gas chamber to exterminate life, are determining the fate of humans and non-human species through their control of power and despite urgent climate science warnings. In pursuit of their greed, they are compromising all of our futures. There is no other way to say this.

Assuming you are a caring and thoughtful politician and serious about your duty to serve society, this worst-case scenario should keep you up at night. As citizens in a modern constitutional democracy, we can assume our government has thought this problem through, has clear answers and is making things happen to secure our common futures. The extinction of the human species together with other life forms is not a trivial matter. In a democracy it is a complex problem we all have to be empowered to deal with, and have a say in how we solve. This becomes even more urgent when the climate crisis is not a distant problem.

With the failure of political leadership for almost 25 years in the UN-COP climate negotiations, the increase in average global temperature from pre-industrial levels overshot 1°C in 2015. This was a major shift in the Earth system, such that we are now living on a new planet racked by climate-driven weather extremes, intensifying and more frequent flash floods, heatwaves, droughts (even flash droughts), cyclones, tornadoes and extreme cold spells. Climate change is already beginning to overwhelm everyday and seasonal weather patterns. UN climate science attribution is clear about this. Unfortunately, most humans do not understand this and have not been empowered to do so by their governments. The South African government has not seriously informed the public about this threat, nor does it have a valid reason for failing to act on these risks to our society.

It has been a party to the climate negotiations for almost three decades, it hosted the COP17 summit in 2011 in Durban, it is a signatory to the Paris Agreement of 2015, it is a participant in the scientific work of the IPCC, it is part of a global cities climate network and it is obliged to act on our constitutional right to a healthy and pollution-free environment. So, taxpayers can reasonably expect that by now South Africa should be a shining example of a just transition, adaptation strategies – including in the eThekwini Metropolitan Municipality – and even of accelerated decarbonisation. After all, as taxpayers we have paid for all this expensive and carbon-burning theatre.

Instead, South Africa has experienced several climate weather extremes since 2015, including the worst drought in its history, tornadoes, flash flooding (in 2017, 2019 and late 2021 in KwaZulu-Natal), landslides and wildfires, and the state has not acted to prepare and protect society. The ANC government has not learnt any lessons from these extremes. South Africa does not have a national extreme weather warning system, the disaster management system is not people-driven and fully capacitated; instead civil society has to constantly fill in gaps. There is no national public climate insurance scheme or national firefighting service; and local government planning has not adjusted to actively protect the most vulnerable. For instance, it has failed to ensure informal settlements are out of harm's way and that residents are fast-tracked into formal housing based on ecohousing standards. In terms of future emissions, President Cyril Ramaphosa touts offshore oil and gas as a game-changer for

South Africa and he runs a government with a coal-heavy energy mix. His government is actively ensuring South Africa contributes to a 1.5°C overshoot globally, which would place South Africa and southern Africa at 3°C. At these temperatures and higher we have to understand climate risk will be at a scale and magnitude that most societies cannot handle.

Pummelled by droughts, flash floods and other disasters, with food systems collapsing and water supplies constrained, South Africa, a failing economy and weak state riddled with corruption, is facing full-blown collapse. The tragic floods in KwaZulu-Natal (and parts of the Eastern Cape) and our recent drought (2014–2021) are glimpses of what's coming.

If our government was committed to its international climate obligations, concerned for its citizens and serious about the constitution, and it listened to the calls of climate justice movements, it should have placed the country on a climate-emergency footing a long time ago. The tragic loss of more than 400 lives during this month's floods could have been prevented. For the reasons stated, the president, his Cabinet, the premier of KwaZulu-Natal, the mayor of eThekwini and the deputy head of the climate commission, Valli Moosa, have been charged by the CJC movement with culpable homicide.

This simply refers to the killing of a human being through illegal and negligent action. The ANC government has given us AIDS denialism; the Marikana massacre; #LifeEsidemeni; corruption-related violence (including the July 2021 riots); structural violence against women and children linked to inequality; rampant corruption; and now a major climate disaster. The ANC has placed us all on a rollercoaster of endless disaster. It certainly cannot be trusted with securing our climate future. As long as it wants to lead our democracy, we must hold it accountable for its failings. If not, we are as complicit as it in destroying everything. The powerful in our country responsible for preventing the worsening climate crisis and taking measures to protect society have now been given legal notice to be accountable.

Sunday Times, 24 April 2022.

PART IV

FOR A DEMOCRATIC ECOSOCIALIST SOUTH AFRICA AND WORLD

Democratic Ecosocialism through Democratic Systemic Reforms

The Climate Crisis and Systemic Alternatives

CLIMATE CHANGE IS THE most serious challenge we face as a species. Despite numerous warnings – scientific studies, UN declarations, books, movies, progressive media reporting – global leadership has failed humanity. After more than 20 years of multilateral negotiations, we have not developed the solutions to solve the climate crisis decisively. Instead, we have continued emitting pollutants and intensively using fossil fuels and, as a result, have been recording the hottest years on the planet. The last two decades in the fight against the climate crisis have merely confirmed, at a common sense level, an Anthropocene-centred theory: as a geological force, we humans are heating the planet. A heating planet, induced by human action, unhinges all our certainties and places everything in jeopardy. It challenges our fixation with growth economics, catch-up development and every conception of modern progress that has incited our imaginations. Most fundamentally, it prompts us to ask: has globalised capitalism lost its progressiveness? Is today's fossil fuel-driven, hi-tech, scientific, financialised and post-Fordist industrial world leading humanity down a path of ecocidal destruction? How do we survive the climate crisis?

These are the central questions that deal with one dimension of the systemic crises of accumulation related to contemporary capitalism. Without falling into the trap of catastrophism, end-of-times millenarianism or apolitical acquiescence, the climate crisis should be treated as an emergency, demanding transformative politics and systemic reforms to remake how we produce, consume, finance and organise social life – it calls for civilisational transformation.

Marxism in the twentieth century as ruling ideology, mostly as Marxism–Leninism, privileged Promethean growth, vanguardist authoritarianism and catch-up industrialisation, and at the same time has been ruinous to the environment. Another view articulates a Marxism that is post-productivist, resituates nature at the centre of Marxism, confronts the patriarchal and racist oppressions inherent to capitalism, challenges contemporary imperialism, and appreciates the need to think and act democratically. In this journey, Marxism is shaped by its own self-reflexivity, by contemporary anti-capitalism and the challenge of confronting the climate contradiction. It is tested as an intellectual resource to be open and serve as the basis for a new future: a democratic ecosocialist world and South Africa.

The climate crisis as a systemic crisis of capitalist accumulation

In 1988, NASA scientist James Hansen drew attention to the heating of the Earth's temperature, otherwise known as the greenhouse effect or climate change (*Washington Post*, 3 August 2012). Yet the US refused to adopt the Kyoto Protocol, which locked in 'common but differentiated responsibilities' (Art. 3.1) for industrial countries (even this did not go far enough). Instead, the US has worked systematically to scuttle the Kyoto Protocol. Hansen, writing in the 13 July 2006 issue of the *New York Review of Books*, cautioned that the world has a decade to alter the trajectory of greenhouse gas (GHG) emissions or face irreversible changes which will bring disastrous consequences. Since this plea was made, another decade has been lost and today geologists and climate scientists are talking about a new world of unpredictable and no-analogue climatic conditions: the Anthropocene. Put simply, we are entering a world in which humans have altered planetary conditions, including our climate, breaking a 10,000-year pattern of relatively stable climate known as the Holocene.

For many, the climate crisis is a complex scientific problem. At one level it is, and it is very different from daily or seasonal variability in weather. The science of climate change has confirmed, with the measurement of GHGs and in the language of the UNFCCC, that 'human induced climate change' is happening (IPCC, 2014: 48). In 2015, we broke the halfway mark towards catastrophic climate change. This was confirmed by the WMO, which broadcast to the world that planetary temperatures had reached a 1°C increase higher than the period prior to the Industrial Revolution.[1] We have concentrated carbon, at over 400 parts per million, taking us rapidly closer to a 2°C increase in planetary temperature.[2] With this shift, extreme weather events such as droughts, hurricanes, heatwaves, drier conditions enabling fires and floods are becoming more commonplace. Sea levels are also rising, placing many low-lying communities, populous coastal cities and island states in

---

1   See   http://www.independent.co.uk/environment/climate-change/climate-changeglobal-average-temperatures-break-through-1c-increase-on-pre-industrial-levelsfor-a6727361.html (accessed 17 August 2017).

2   See   https://www.carbonbrief.org/how-scientists-predicted-co2-would-breach400pm-2016 (accessed 17 August 2017).

jeopardy. Moreover, climate change on this scale within the Earth system is not expected to unfold in a linear way. Instead, it can potentially happen abruptly or through feedback loops, further accelerating runaway climate change. For example, methane release from the Arctic ice sheet, carbon saturation in our oceans and the destruction of rainforests all feed into the climate change crisis. As we fail to address the climate crisis, it becomes more complex and more costly.

The much-vaunted UN climate negotiations, particularly the Conference of the Parties in Paris during December 2015 (COP21), promised to confirm a clear purpose and political will to ensure we overcome the climate crisis. The Paris Agreement makes a call for urgent action to prevent a 2°C increase in planetary temperature, with an emphasis on efforts to keep temperature increases below 1.5°C, at pre-industrial levels (UNFCCC, 2015). Despite the promises, these targets will not be realised. As things stand, most voluntary national commitments will lead to an overshoot of 2°C. The most up-to-date analysis of national pledges suggests that these are consistent with a temperature rise of 2.6–3.1°C above pre-industrial levels (Darby, 2016). Moreover, while this agreement came into force on 4 November 2016 it will only build momentum from 2020 onwards, thus losing another four years in the context of two decades of failed action. It is also expected, given the current emission rate and trajectory, that 1.5°C will be breached sooner than expected. In a recent study it was confirmed, 'The window for limiting warming to below 1.5°C with high probability and without temporarily exceeding that level already seems to have closed' (Rogelj et al., 2016: 631).

The 2°C threshold discussed in the Paris Agreement is far from being a protective barrier. Instead, it is a dangerous threshold taking the human world to the brink. Studies on tipping points (like the Arctic becoming ice free or major retreats in glaciers in the Himalayas) show that 18 out of 37 abrupt changes will happen by a 2°C change or less (Drijfhout, 2015). Put more bluntly, a 2°C increase in planetary temperature is extremely dangerous. For vulnerable nations, contributing less than 2% of current global GHG emissions, a 2°C target is nothing short of catastrophic.[3] With the current increase in global temperature, major consequences beyond their capabilities have already come to the fore for the most vulnerable 20 countries in the world, representing 700 million people and including poor, arid, landlocked, mountainous and small island states from Africa, Asia, the Caribbean, Latin America and the Pacific. These experiences

---

3   The Vulnerable 20 (V20) group of countries was inaugurated on 8 October 2015 in Lima, Peru.

provide us with a window into the future. According to the Vulnerable 20 (or V20), this is what they are already facing:[4]

- an average of more than 50,000 deaths per year since 2010, a number expected to increase exponentially by 2030;
- escalating annual losses of at least 2.5% of their GDP potential per year, estimated at $45 billion since 2010, a number expected to increase to close to $400 billion in the next twenty years;
- more than half the economic impact of climate change by 2030 and over 80% of its health impact for V20 and other low-emitting developing countries;
- a doubling in the number of extremely hot days and hot nights in the last fifty years as the planet has warmed appreciably;
- countless extreme events, which include typhoons with wind speeds that are around 10% stronger than they were in the 1970s, translating into more than a 30% increase in destructiveness;
- sea-level rise that will partially or completely submerge the island nations of Kiribati, Maldives and Tuvalu, displacing at least 500,000 people;
- the displacement of up to 40 million people due to the inundation of low-elevation land resulting from climate change-driven sea-level rise;
- the threat of increasingly devastating and more frequent disasters, such as storms, flooding and drought.

This leads us to ask: what is the Paris Agreement really all about? What are its limits and contradictions? How does its political economy work against us solving the biggest problem facing the human race?

First, the Paris Agreement abandons the Kyoto Protocol commitment to 'common but differentiated responsibilities' despite formally declaring its commitments to the protocol. The Kyoto Protocol explicitly placed a greater burden on rich industrialised countries. The Paris Agreement, by contrast, provides for voluntary and nationally determined commitments, which should not be confused with nationally binding and regulated commitments. Yet there are historical and contemporary inequalities regarding carbon emissions. Some of the rich industrialised countries of the global North have been polluting since the advent of the Industrial Revolution, in the context of uneven processes of capitalist development and imperial international relations. These countries

---

[4] See founding communiqué of V20 at http://climateandcapitalism.com/2015/10/11/most-vulnerable-nations-form-climate-action-coalition/ (accessed 17 August 2017).

carry a climate debt. However, climate debt and climate reparations do not feature in the Paris Agreement. Instead, there is a paltry commitment of $100 billion from developed countries for mitigation and adaptation, which pales in comparison to the finance injected into the crisis-prone financial system.

What this means is that those who have created (and continue to create) the problem, are off the hook. Without regulated commitments for reductions in GHG emissions based on historical climate debt, this inequality will not be addressed and emerging polluters, like China, will only commit to and act on what suits their interests. Moreover, the argument of industrialising countries for industrial development space cannot be addressed in the interests of the planet and all of humanity unless industrialised countries address the historic climate debt and aggressively lead the cutback in emissions through regulation. The Paris Agreement fails to do this, which means it is a business-as-usual trajectory for globalised and fossil fuel-driven industrial development, including global shipping and airplane emissions. Transportation emissions are not even mentioned in the Paris Agreement. In short, the Agreement has turned its back on common but differentiated responsibilities. A tenuous voluntary pledge system, favoured by the US, one of the leading carbon emitters, has been entrenched despite the world running out of time.

Second, the carbon space (or budget) in the Paris Agreement for developed and developing countries is left to each country to manage, in a global political economy in which competition rules. No country in this globalised race is going to surrender any advantages to address the climate crisis unless there are reciprocal and harmonised commitments. At the same time, if the pledge and review system falters, with some countries doing more than others, this is likely to cause consternation against free riders, which could undermine the mechanism. In the context of economic stagnation, corporate capture of political systems and the entrenched power of fossil fuel interests, the Paris Agreement is already being bypassed to ensure profit rates are protected and global accumulation is maintained. The geopolitics of domestic interests will constantly threaten and push back the pledge and review mechanism.

For instance, despite Barack Obama's rhetoric in praising this agreement, the US ruling class did not support him. Instead, their approach was to keep the globalised capitalist system going on a business-as-usual path despite the climate crisis.[5] Donald Trump, on the other hand, has given the go-ahead to

---

5   Obama has not even been able to secure legislation in the US Congress to support his diplomacy in the UN climate negotiations process.

expand fossil fuel pipeline development (the Dakota Access and Keystone XL), rolled back Obama's modest clean power plan, weakened the Environmental Protection Agency and withdrawn the US from the Paris Agreement. Ironically, the Paris Agreement was not even a legally binding agreement and gave the US room to bring whatever it wanted into the multilateral process. With climate change denialism back on the agenda in the US, and the world's climate being pushed into greater corporate-induced chaos, the US under Trump will seek to protect lifeboat America at all costs. As a result, a more securitised response is likely to come to the fore, from both the US and other wealthy countries. The only way to challenge this is if the geopolitics of international trade, finance and development is redefined. A climate-driven world cannot be held hostage by the whims of the US-led bloc. If we are to save life on Earth, neoliberalised global accumulation and the current policies of globally competitive capitalist development have to be abandoned. Given the climate emergency, a new political economy has to emerge to replace global competition. This requires just transitions (discussed below) at various scales and tempos to deal with the disproportionate impacts of the climate crisis on vulnerable, poor societies, the working classes and peasantries, who are already bearing the brunt of a highly unequal world. The Paris Agreement is not up to this task and is not moving the world in this direction. With Trump, supported by fossil capital and finance, the Paris Agreement is going to be a symbolic rallying point for only some countries. In fact, the crisis of climate multilateralism has become worse and reflects a crisis of global leadership.

Third, and rather obvious, the Paris Agreement reflects a balance of forces in favour of greening capitalism. This illusion comes through the false solutions embedded in the agreement, which include carbon trading, re-forestation and preventing forest degradation and offset mechanisms (UNFCCC, 2015). These solutions have been part of multilateral negotiations for the past two decades and have not worked in their implementation. Carbon trading is a clear example in this regard (Bond, 2012). As we run out of time, techno-fixes become more appealing than system change. So, contrary to Anthropocene theory, which suggests that we are all responsible for the climate crisis, it is actually the capitalist system and its class champions that are responsible for the climate crisis. A system that has produced a systemic problem cannot solve the problem, given that this is a carbon-based capitalist civilisation. Nothing short of the fundamental decarbonisation of production, consumption, finance and every life world on this planet will save human and non-human nature. The

Paris Agreement falls short of this imperative.

Fourth, it has become increasingly clear through numerous studies that if we extract more fossil fuels, we are going to breach 2°C of planetary heating. In the most recent study done on this and cited by Bill McKibben (2016), the conclusion is simple: keeping temperature increases below 2°C requires zero extraction of fossil fuels. We have reached the limits of drilling, digging and extracting if we want to survive. More shocking is the silence of the Paris Agreement about carbon corporations and the need to restrict their activities, even as a minimum gesture to incite hope and encourage a global shift away from fossil fuels. What is patently clear is that the agreement has not addressed the most immediate and obvious driver of climate change. Instead, by failing to spotlight carbon corporations (oil, gas, coal) it has given warrant for more deadly emissions. Fracking, tar sands, deep-water drilling and other new frontiers of complex hydrocarbons are all expanding. Trump and his class allies have given further momentum to this. This business-as-usual approach is the face of ecofascism and imperial ecocide. It is the biggest failing of the Paris Agreement, as it does not address the major obstacle to renewable energy systems and a transformative just transition.

The world is facing a perilous future, with a 1°C increase in temperatures since before the Industrial Revolution already providing signs of what the no-analogue world will bring. A hotter planet means the conditions to sustain human and non-human life will become ever more difficult. Global ruling classes have failed humanity and all life on the planet. We have a stark choice: end capitalism or perish. It is in this context that the rising climate justice movement is crucial, together with its potential to unite red-green forces,[6] advance deep, just transitions and build systemic alternatives from below. Building this movement is our only hope for the future. The climate justice movement will not guarantee our survival but will certainly lessen the catastrophic consequences of climate change and harness the best of human solidarity to sustain life.

Climate justice, system change and the just transition

The climate justice movement is part of a new cycle of global resistance seeking to push back neoliberal globalisation while advancing systemic alternatives.

---

6 The red-green alliance or forces refers to the strategic and programmatic unity of labour-centred movements (such as trade unions, think tanks, labour networks, parties) and ecological justice forces (including climate justice, water justice, food sovereignty) to advance deep, just transitions to achieve systemic transformation.

Four important conditions facilitated its emergence.[7] First was the failure of a reform agenda through the Climate Action Network inside UN climate processes. More ground was being conceded by progressive civil society until 2007, in Bali, when a breakaway was formalised through the call for 'climate action now!' (Bond, 2012). Second was the increasing shift in the balance of forces within the climate negotiations favouring green neoliberal and capitalist solutions. The greenwash of UN climate summits prompted the need to develop an alternative vision, practice and politics around systemic alternatives (Angus, 2010; Bassey, 2012; Tokar, 2010). The attempt by Bolivia in 2010, at the Cochabamba summit, highlighted the fact that only one state in the interstate system was willing to champion a more radical climate justice politics inside the UN climate negotiations. This attempt by Bolivia also came short, due to the contradictions within Bolivia, such as its own petro economy, as well as the dynamics of the power structure within UN negotiations. Increasingly, for climate justice activists UN climate summits became more about the outside – the theatre of street politics and platforms for people's systemic alternatives. An alternative narrative of climate justice was being globalised from below.

Third, as climate shocks began to emerge as part of planetary lived experience, common sense began crystallising as good sense. Hurricanes like Katrina and Sandy, California's mega drought, El Niño-induced droughts with longer duration and typhoons Haiyan and Haima battering the Philippines have all brought home the need to build from below. Fourth, the continued expansion of fossil fuel extraction, in the midst of the climate crisis, has also engendered some of the most radical activism by African women in the Niger Delta and among native Americans and other grassroots communities at the frontline of carbon corporations' regimes of extraction and dispossession (Bassey, 2012; Klein, 2014). Calls to keep 'oil in the ground, coal in the hole' have begun resonating on a global scale. Battle lines are being drawn all over the world against UN false solutions, carbon corporations and states promoting fossil economies. At the same time, systemic alternatives are coming to the fore such as food sovereignty, climate jobs, public transport, socially owned renewable energy, basic income grants, rights of nature, 'living well', ubuntu, commoning (of water, land, cyberspace), zero waste, solidarity economies and many more systemic alternatives.

---

7   There is a vast literature containing documents from the climate justice movement amplifying voices from within it that have made the case for mobilising mass power to deal with the climate crisis. See Angus (2010), Tokar (2010), Wall (2010), Bassey (2012), Bond (2012) and Klein (2014).

The challenge of system change is key for survival. Climate justice politics foregrounds this. The most crucial idea in this regard is the notion of the just transition as articulated by trade unions. Central to this notion is recognition of both the slow but immediate and long-term violence associated with the climate crisis as it impacts on the lives of the poor, the working class, the peasantry and the vulnerable. This is disproportionate and disparate, within rich countries as well. Climate shocks are induced by the capitalist system and have become internal to the dynamics of capitalism, but this does not mean the working class and poor have to bear the brunt and cost of the climate crisis. The notion of the just transition affirms the importance of transforming our societies now, but in a manner that privileges the interests of the majority as opposed to the 1%. Moreover, as Jacklyn Cock cautions, for this to happen such transitions have to be more than shallow changes. This means that system change of everything is crucial to sustain life. It is in this context that it is necessary to bring to the fore key systemic alternatives that would inform a transformative just transition and the building of a democratic ecosocialist South Africa, and world, from below.

At the same time, there are limits and challenges faced by climate justice politics in achieving a transformative just transition. In this regard there are the following:

- Confronting the challenge of building viable and sustainable societies as part of the just transition: While the transformative politics and systemic alternatives of climate justice politics are not abstract or utopian blueprints, there is a need for a concrete vision of another world and society beyond capitalism. Drawing on the rich and emancipatory traditions of socialism together with contemporary anti-capitalism is crucial for constructing this vision.
- Connecting grassroots, frontline struggles to national, regional and global struggles: Geographical scale and critical mass are challenges to push back fossil fuel capitalism while creating the space for systemic alternatives. These have to unleash an alternative logic, build new values-based institutions and enable momentum for democratic transformation through systemic reforms.
- Building red-green alliances is crucial and means system change and transformative politics have to enable red to become green and green more red. The working-class and green movements have to converge. It is imperative to forge these alliances in practice around common analyses, campaigns and building systemic alternatives.

- Fostering and promoting transformative just transitions as a credible imperative embracing systemic change is key. This raises questions about state power and how climate justice activism should transform and re-embed the state as it builds from below.
- It is with regard to these challenges that this volume orientates its contribution around systemic alternatives and transformative just transitions, particularly in relation to democratic ecosocialist alternatives.

From socialism to democratic ecosocialism

Marxist-inspired socialism in the twentieth century has been discredited, whether as social democracy, Marxist-Leninist-Maoist regimes, or as revolutionary nationalist projects. With the deepening crisis of contemporary capitalism, some argue that these historical failures were tainted, including by Western propaganda. According to this argument, what is required is a reaffirmation and retrieval. There is a need for a better version of the same, and maybe with better leaders, outcomes will be different. Such positions lend themselves to voluntarist readings of history, of both internal and external conditions that contributed to failure, and are rather dogmatic. Moreover, such approaches fail to see problems with Marxist theory implicated in these historical experiences of socialism, the limits to forms of struggle waged, the contradictions of contemporary globalised capitalism and are closed to the new anti-systemic politics emerging among new anti-capitalist movements and forces. A dogmatic approach to the history of socialism will not assist the renewal of socialism.

This dogma can be confronted by looking at the failures of twentieth-century socialism through the critique, theoretical development and practical horizons of democratic ecosocialism. In this regard, there are five crucial historical moments and approaches to the development of contemporary democratic ecosocialist analysis and struggle.[8] These moments span the latter half of the twentieth century and include the present. Such moments and approaches can be delineated as follows: (i) a Marxist ecology critique of actually existing socialism; (ii) greening Marxism through ecology; (iii) re-finding a complex ecology in classical Marxism; (iv) utilising a historical materialist ecology and theory of capitalist crisis to engage with current environmental problems; and

---

8   Foster and Clark (2016) suggest there are only three moments to the development of ecosocialist analysis: greening Marxism, retrieving and defending Marx's ecology, and thinking about ecological problems through Marxist ecology. I disagree and set out a different mapping.

(v) the rise of ecosocialist forces in the world championing systemic alternatives. Each of these is unpacked below. All these approaches to ecosocialist analysis and struggle, despite tensions and unresolved positions in some instances, can be embraced.

The first moment and approach to democratic ecosocialism derives from the experience of actually existing socialism.[9] These are dissident voices that have challenged the productivism of the former Soviet Bloc and contemporary China while arguing for ecological transformation. Two crucial examples stand out. Rudolf Bahro's *The Alternative in Eastern Europe*, published in 1978, provides a devastating critique of the making of industrial despotism and the deep alienation central to the anatomy of party-controlled state socialism. Moreover, he argues for a remaking of the division of labour through greater worker self-determination, greater democracy and a cultural revolution. Bahro wanted existing socialism to become a truly emancipated civilisation of free producers. With the publication of his book, he was jailed and declared a spy. He was only released by the East German regime after an international outcry. In West Germany he went on to become one of the leading voices of the German Greens but was later disaffected by its narrow electoralism and convergence with the Social Democratic Party.[10] With regard to China, one of the most incisive Marxist ecology critiques is Minqi Li's *China and the 21st Century Crisis* (2016). Li points to the class and ecological contradictions central to China's capitalism. He argues powerfully for understanding the climate crisis and oil peak as central to the unsustainability of Chinese capitalism. Ultimately, he suggests a transition is necessary which has to grapple with the challenges of reform, revolution or collapse.

The greening of Marxism, which is the second moment and approach to democratic ecosocialism, develops largely out of ecological critiques of productivist Marxism, with its emphasis on socialist modernisation and industrial accumulation. Some critiques have gone as far as suggesting that the origins of productivism lie with Marx. This is because, it is claimed, Marx did not have an adequate understanding of nature, venerated the development of the forces of production, was blind to ecological limits, was anthropocentric and promoted an industrial vision of a post-capitalist society based on abundance.[11] Moreover, it is argued that as a result, the Soviet Union

---

9   Also note Sarkar's (1999) critique of existing socialism and capitalism.

10 Two other of Bahro's important books crucial to the development of ecosocialist thought are *Socialism and Survival* (1982) and *Building the Green Movement* (1986).

11 The edited collection by Ted Benton (1996) best captures this approach. Prominent in this

(and now China) encapsulated the worst kind of productivist Marxism. Many of Marx's ostensible theses are considered the problem within historical Marxism and therefore Marxism is inadequate to deal with the ecological challenges of our time. Instead, Marxism has to be brought into ecology. The greening of Marxism entails taking on board the concerns of ecology, including the intrinsic value of nature, the Malthusian population challenge, the dangers of science and technology, and planetary ecological limits. Thus, Marxism has to become an ecological Marxism.[12]

The third moment and approach to developing democratic ecosocialism is by Marxists who have not accepted the critique of Marx by ecological Marxists. Instead, such Marxist ecologists have re-read Marx to find the lost ecological dimension in his work. This spans various Marxist thinkers, each with a different emphasis in their reading of Marx's ecology. For instance, Paul Burkett (2014) refutes claims about Marx's thought being productivist with three arguments. First, Marx always understood human wealth as having a nature component, not just labour. Second, Marx always understood that human production, under any social system, would be constrained by natural and ecological laws. Third, Marx was very aware of the wastefulness inherent in capitalism's development of the productive forces and its destructiveness. Burkett salvages a Marxist ecology by recognising the importance of nature to Marx's historical materialism, value-form analysis of capitalism and the importance of nature in the struggle for an alternative society. John Bellamy Foster (2000) adds to this by bringing out an ecological dimension in many of the neglected aspects of Marx's thought. He draws on Marx's writing on philosophical naturalism, evolutionary theory, capitalist agriculture and soil theory. Foster's reading provides us with a conception of the metabolic rift central to Marx, which is about the separation of the human being from nature, including the divide between town and country. He demonstrates a powerful ecological sensibility in Marx.

The fourth moment and approach to democratic ecosocialism builds on Marxist ecology. It recognises that a complex historical materialist ecology, a theory of capitalism related to ecological crisis and a new democratic conception of anti-capitalist agency, has a great deal to offer in terms of an analysis of ecological contradictions. Such contradictions include: extinction of species

---

approach is James O'Connor's second contradiction in capitalism which suggests that capitalism undermines the natural conditions of its existence.

12 The marriage of ecology and Marxism has not been without tension. See Pepper (1993) and Kovel (2003) for critiques of the limits of deep ecology.

through loss of biodiversity; acid rain; destruction of the ozone layer; desertification; pollution of oceans; contamination of lakes, rivers and streams; dispossession of people's land; overfishing; hazardous working conditions; incineration of waste; famines and breaching all planetary ecological limits; with climate change being one of the biggest challenges. David Layfield (2008) dedicates an entire text to showing how this all fits together from the standpoint of the intersection of Marxism and ecology, while activists like Nimmo Bassey (2012) and Naomi Klein (2014) demonstrate how the climate crisis is not only driven by a capitalist political economy, but is also about a new resistance that is rising at the frontlines of preventing extraction of fossil fuels and also in the context of climate justice struggles.

The fifth moment and approach to democratic ecosocialism is informed by the agency of the climate justice movement and a host of other anti-systemic forces that are rising to advance systemic alternatives.[13] The slogan 'System change, not climate change' best captures the democratic ecosocialist orientation of these movements. These movements and their organic intellectuals are fighting against carbon corporations expanding into tar sands, fracking and offshore drilling. Their systemic alternatives are informed by indigenous cultures, cosmologies and rights-based discourses. The dialogue with Marxism and how class, race, gender and ecology interact is also part of this ferment. These organic discourses are shaping the frontiers of democratic ecosocialism as well. For example, rights of nature tribunals have been convened as part of the people's spaces alongside UN climate summits. Crucial is how the dispossession of indigenous people's rights to land, water and life has been connected to fighting corporations and capitalism.[14]

Moreover, there are movements fighting against the dispossession of the peasantry, mainly women, who produce almost 70% of the world's food (Shiva, 2015: 16), and who are taking a stand against transnational food corporations and their regimes of dispossession through food sovereignty politics. La Via Campesina, with over 200 million members and a myriad of food sovereignty alliances in different countries and regions, has been crucial in advancing this systemic alternative. Food sovereignty perspectives and ecofeminists recognise that globalised industrial food systems are responsible for 25% of the world's carbon dioxide emissions, 60% of methane gas emissions and 80% of nitrous oxide emissions, all deadly GHGs (Shiva, 2015: 54). It is not surprising that

---

13 See Wall (2010) for a mapping of these forces. Also see Angus (2010) for a great collection of documents written by ecosocialists within the climate justice movement.

14 V. Satgar, 'The climate is ripe for social change'. *Mail & Guardian*, 17 December 2014.

there is a growing call for food sovereignty pathways based on the science of agro-ecology and the democratic building of grassroots movements.

Today, the five moments and approaches to democratic ecosocialism confirm its arrival and importance. The meaning of socialism (and to be a socialist) today is fundamentally about being democratic ecosocialist in identity and in ideological representation. Merely referring to socialism or representing one's self as socialist equates to a failed commitment to democracy as people's power, as evidenced in the twentieth century, and also equates to productivist socialism which cannot be realised on a scorched planet and, more fundamentally, will only contribute to such a disaster. Instead, a renewed democratic ecosocialism faces squarely the challenge to save human and non-human nature from capitalism's ecocidal logic through a radical practice and conception of democracy as people's power, mediated by an ethics to sustain life.

This of course does not mean that race and gender are unimportant to the identity of a democratic ecosocialist. In all the democratic ecosocialist struggles emerging today, whether through resistance on indigenous land against fracking or oil extraction, struggles against dispossession of women peasant farmers, or neo-Marxist political economy analysis of ecological problems, race and gender are integral (Bond, 2012; Klein, 2014). A democratic ecosocialist is feminist and anti-racist. At the same time, the conceptual remit of a renewed socialism prompts us to think more analytically and conceptually about democratic ecosocialism. To assist us we draw on Raymond Williams, a Marxist cultural theorist, particularly his book *Keywords* (1983).

In *Keywords*, Williams derives the origins of the word democracy from the Greek word *demokratia* with its emphasis on *demos* (the people) and *kratos* (rule) – in other words, rule by the people. However, he is aware of its various definitions and usages and cautions us against its appropriations both by the liberal and socialist traditions. Central to the development of the term democracy was the idea of class rule, or sometimes rule by the multitude. From the latter part of the nineteenth century, it was adopted in political language and used in modern party politics. Liberals tended to focus on representative democracy and qualifying the meaning of the people to certain groups, such as freemen, wisemen, white men and owners of property. Socialists tended to emphasise democracy as meaning popular power and a state in which the interests of the majority were central and were exercised and controlled by the majority. However, Williams (1983: 97) cautions that in practice both liberal and twentieth-century socialist people's democracies undermined people's power. Representation was manipulated and popular power was reduced to bureaucracy or oligarchy. In the twenty-first-century renewal of socialism, democracy is about a radical practice, various institutional forms, conditions that protect both negative and positive freedoms and an ethics to sustain life. It is about democratic movements, direct citizen action, participatory forms, representative processes, rights and deliberated ethical choices. People's power is affirmed in all these ways to ensure that political and administrative state structures are also democratised.

Williams (1983) confirms that the word ecology first came into usage in the 1870s through the work of a German zoologist, Ernst Haeckel. Haeckel's conception mainly focused on the habitat of plants and animals and on their relationship with each other. Ecology in the twentieth century was briefly overshadowed by environmentalism, particularly in the mid-1950s, to express concern with conservation and for measures against pollution. However, ecology further extends its meaning to include human relationships with the physical world. Today, ecology situates human beings as an integral part of nature and within planetary ecosystems. It grapples with human beings' coeval relation to and co-creation of nature. In the twenty-first century, ecology has also become integral to the prefix eco- within democratic ecosocialism.

The words socialist and socialism really get established in modern usage in the 1860s, alongside co-operative, mutualist, associationist and collectivist (Williams, 1983: 288). Different traditions used the word socialism to refer either, like Marxists, to a transitional society between capitalism and communism or, like Fabian socialists, to an understanding of socialism as the logical development of liberal society to achieve the economic side of the liberal ideal. In the twentieth century, communist parties formed out of the Russian Revolution maintained a commitment to socialism but tried to distinguish their socialism from that of social democratic parties. Revolutionary nationalists also devised variants of socialism such as African socialism or Nehruvian socialism. Today socialists are championing struggles against exploitation, commodification, dispossession, oppression (racial, gender, sexual) and for greater democracy in government and the workplace. At the same time, property relations are being rethought to include various forms of the commons (land, seeds, water, knowledge) and socialised property (such as worker co-operatives, municipal ownership involving communities and workers and community trusts) while recognising the importance of democratised public ownership. Moreover, democratic planning of food systems, energy and resources (like participatory budgeting) are also being attempted in practice and are part of the just transition to sustain life. Socialism in the twenty-first century is no longer the preserve of vanguard parties but is emerging as part of anti-systemic movements, grassroots networks, progressive think tanks and democratic political instruments wanting transformative change. Conjoined to radical democracy, it is also about ethical values informing individual and collective choices to save life – both human and non-human.

Ultimately, bringing these keywords together means socialism in the twenty-first century is democratic ecosocialism. It is a living socialism in a historical process of realisation, and is informed by the five moments and approaches to democratic ecosocialist analysis and struggle mentioned above.

Chapter in *The Climate Crisis: South African and Global Democratic Ecosocialist Alternatives*, volume III in Democratic Marxism series, edited by Vishwas Satgar. Johannesburg: Wits University Press, 2018.

Climate Ecocide and Democratic Ecosocialism in South Africa

THE END OF THE HUMAN race is a very real prospect in the context of climate change and ultimately a heating world. Global warming at increases of 3, 4 or 5°C means Planet Earth will no longer be habitable for human and most non-human life. There is scientific evidence that this has happened to other planets like Venus but was caused through natural processes. Our end is not inevitable and neither can it be prevented by false solutions. As a scientific process, climate change is the result of the sun's rays (energy flows) being trapped in the Earth's atmosphere by greenhouse gases (such as carbon and methane). This is creating a heating planet. This article engages with this challenge from a climate justice perspective.

The making of climate ecocide

There is a history as to why Earth is heating. For the past 150 years capitalist societies have been at the forefront of extracting, burning and emitting carbon through coal, oil and gas. Over the past 50 years there has been a golden spike and what climate scientists call the hockey curve feature of carbon emissions. This means that there has been a consistent and intensive increase in carbon emissions. The scientific consensus is simple: human beings are a geological force shaping the planetary conditions that sustain life. We are causing climate change. This is now known as the age of the Anthropocene.

While we can accept at a general level such a scientific conclusion, it is misleading in terms of the actual political economy of carbon emissions and carbon capitalism. For the past 150 years of emissions the industrialised countries of the global North carry a climate debt as the main contributors to carbon emissions. In addition, about seven oil companies (Shell, BP, Exon, Saudi Aramco and others) have also profited from extracting and supplying fossil fuels. Various countries are also part of extracting and burning oil, gas and coal. These carbon corporations and states constitute carbon capital which is a key contributor to climate change.

The US has the largest per capita carbon footprint on Earth. Today, through fracking and support from Obama and Trump, the US is the leading fossil fuel producer in the world. The US imperial state is preventing the world from addressing the climate crisis in any meaningful way. This has been happening for more than two decades, under every US president, and this has meant the UN-led process to secure a climate deal has never been successful. The Paris Agreement (2015) is a failed solution, with a weak pledge and review mechanism, married to green capitalist solutions that have not worked and will not work.

The capitalist Anthropocene reveals that rich industrialised countries, carbon capital (including in the global South like South Africa), the US imperial state and the lack of a climate justice agenda within the UN multilateral system are the vanguard destroying the conditions that sustain life of human and non-human nature. Climate ecocide, the destruction of all of us through climate change, is being led by these forces.

South Africa's carbon capitalism

South Africa is one of the most unequal countries in the world according to any measure. Ironically, this is a conclusion of the World Bank in its recent 2018 report. The Southern Africa Labour and Development Research Unit (SALDRU) has made these observations since 2014. Its research has shown that the top 10% gets two-thirds of South Africa's income. Half of all South Africans are chronically poor, living in households with a per capita income of R1149 or less per month.

With South Africa's drought, our first major climate shock, these inequalities have been made worse through high food prices, for instance. In addition, new climate inequalities have been created through the privatisation of water. The working class, unemployed and poor have borne the brunt of the drought. Alongside racialised and gendered super exploitation, high unemployment and increasing poverty, South Africa is a carbon intensive economy, based largely on coal. It is the 14th highest emitter of carbon emissions in the world, and despite energy inequality has a per capita carbon footprint higher than China, India or Brazil.

Carbon capitalism was the bedrock of apartheid and has been part of ANC hegemony, and then dominance, in the post-apartheid period. With the climate crisis, South Africa is a carbon criminal state, contributing to the greenhouse effect and the extinction of the human species and other life forms. It is an ecocidal capitalism, destroying the conditions that sustain life.

Limits of historical socialist alternatives: A Marxist ecology critique

South Africa has had a diverse socialist imagination which has included Sovietised socialism (even Trotsky's minimum programme), revolutionary nationalism and social democracy. The ANC Alliance is shaped by all three versions of twentieth-century socialism. These socialisms have not come to the fore in South Africa in the post-apartheid period. But they lurk in the national liberation imagination. They have been theorised in a manner that grounds them in particular assumptions about nature and historical experience of these socialisms.

From a Marxist ecology perspective these socialisms have the following problems:

- A blindness to the fact that Marx was an original systems thinker, who connected human social relations with nature. Marx understood that the labour process mediated the relationship with nature. Further, the human-nature relationship underpinned a metabolic relationship with nature as a whole. This means that the more capitalism undermined natural cycles and ecosystems, the more the antagonism with nature deepened.
- An absence of thinking about value creation as grounded in both nature and labour. While labour was priced in, all these socialisms externalised the costs of nature in the production process. So, pollution, climate change, species extinction, ecosystem destruction, for example, are not taken into account in production organisation. Nature must be conquered.
- These socialisms are all productivist. They copied capitalism's obsession with growth. This meant that accumulation and wealth creation were based on the assumption of endless resources. There were no ecological constraints.
- All these socialisms are obsessed with technology as progress. But technology is not neutral. It is embedded in class relations. For corporations, science and research are about profit making. So, unleashing the forces of production will not necessarily meet the needs of society and, worse, will have destructive consequences for nature. Genetic engineering of seeds is a good example of this.

Beyond fatalism: The struggle for a democratic ecosocialist South Africa

South Africa's historical socialist alternatives are limited and inappropriate for the struggle to address ecological crises and, particularly, the dangerous contradiction of climate crisis. Moreover, the dominant carbon capitalism is the real challenge. Many believe that carbon capitalism is too big a problem to solve and hence either accept the end of the human race or a catastrophic future. We are at the end of times. This is a fatalism that legitimises the madness and irrationality of carbon capitalism. It undermines any kind of mass working class-led response and is also blind to the science. Such resignation is deeply reactionary.

We have a rapidly heating world, with 12 years left to prevent catastrophic climate change and an overshoot of 1.5°C. According to the IPCC global warming 1.5°C report, massive reductions need to be implemented, much before 2030. At least 40% of reductions must happen at 2010 levels before 2030. By 2050, net zero emissions must be reached. In this context we have to be clear about the dynamics, logic and character of contemporary carbon capitalism.

Carbon capitalism produces class, racialised and gendered inequality. But it also produces climate inequality and ecocidal destruction of human and non-human life forms. Carbon capitalism is anti-life. In this context, democratic ecosocialism is central to the demand: 'System change, not climate change'. It recognises that democracy (rights, freedoms, procedures and institutional forms) is about a people's history of struggle against capitalism and oppression; ecology, or the human relationship with nature, is essential for our survival and socialism is necessary to achieve the end of exploitation, racism and gender oppression and ensure the rational organisation of society to meet human needs.

Democratic ecosocialism: Challenges and tasks for deep, just transitions

There are no stages in this struggle to secure human and non-human life. We need to break with the anti-life and climate ecocide logic of carbon capitalism now. The first challenge in this regard is to overcome old modes of politics and thinking. This means reformist pragmatism or revolutionary maximalism is not what the historical moment demands.

We are in an uncharted moment in human history which requires a response that brings to the fore what is necessary to sustain life as part of the deep, just transition, an idea articulated by trade unions. We need a transformative politics that constitutes power from below, transforms the state into a climate emergency state, builds new systems to sustain life and advances just transitions in every living space so workers and the poor don't bear the brunt of climate change. The second challenge is to recognise there are two fronts of the climate justice struggle: (i) decarbonisation across society – from extraction, production, consumption, finance, living spaces and the state; and (ii) the proactive emergency responses to climate shocks – when communities are devastated by fires, flooding, drought, heatwaves and sea level rise.

These challenges affirm the organic and immediate tasks facing democratic ecosocialists today. Democratic ecosocialists have three crucial tasks as part of the deep, just transition:

- First, building a transformative climate justice movement – a red-green alliance that can lead society. This means environmentalists have to become socialists and socialists have to become environmentalists to ensure fundamental transformation of capitalism. A new post-carbon bloc of counter-hegemonic red-green alliances led by the working class has to crystalise. This is already happening.
- Second, a programmatic approach to democratic systemic reform including decarbonisation; democratic planning; food, seed and water sovereignty; socially owned renewable energy; climate jobs; zero waste; mass clean energy public transport; solidarity economies; a substantive BIG that has to be scaled up now as part of deep, just transitions. The CJC process under way is crucial in this regard.
- Third, democratic ecosocialists have to advance a vision and conception of the climate emergency state that is deeply democratic and which builds the relevant capacities to decarbonise and have functional and responsive emergency services and constructs through democratic planning the new systems to sustain life.

Amandla 61/62, 2018.

Why Ecosocialism: For a Red-Green Future

MICHAEL LÖWY'S ESSAY on ecosocialism has stimulated an interesting array of critiques from feminists, democrats, eco-capitalists and more in this exchange. This is an exciting debate and, I would argue, a necessary one to ensure the twenty-first-century return of socialism is not grounded in abstract certainties, dogmatic formulas and intellectual vanguardism. From the African context, particularly South Africa, after two decades of disastrous post-apartheid financialisation and unleashing of unbridled markets, we are facing realities that even the World Bank is confounded by in its recent 2018 report. The World Bank suggests that, by any metric, we are one of the most unequal countries in the world. SALDRU has made these observations since 2014. Its research has shown that the top 10% gets two-thirds of South Africa's income, while half of all South Africans are chronically poor, living in households with a per capita income of R1149 or less per month.

Beside such hideous inequalities, South Africa has a structurally contracting economy and a carbon intensity per capita surpassing that of China, India and Brazil. Its democracy has been dramatically weakened by the power that credit rating agencies wield, the grip of monetarist policy that merely privileges globalised interests and systemic levels of corruption, which most political elites have surrendered to, as part of the normalcy of a market democracy. Our current drought is the worst in the history of the country and is certainly our first climate shock. Pre-existing inequalities are supplemented by new climate inequalities such as increases in food prices, water privatisation and so on. South Africa is a poster nation for a 3-4°C increase in planetary temperature. Of course, it is not alone alongside other OECD countries, including the US, which has eclipsed Saudi Arabia and Russia in fossil fuel extraction, due to the fracking boom and Trump's carbon capitalism.

South Africa and its carbon democracy do not have a future with more of the same marketised approach, even in a lightly renovated form, as suggested by economists such as Dani Rodrik. So, we are sitting with an NDP (neoliberal, financialised and marketised) that is meant to guide our development until 2030. This plan includes more exports of primary commodities like minerals and agriculture, reproducing our coal-driven minerals-energy complex and a globalised food system while 14 million go hungry every day. Carbon emission scenarios are based on science that is already outdated due to the latest IPCC report, and renewable energy is locked into a ceiling of 20,000 megawatts by 2030 to ensure that the World Bank can recover its loan finance (plus interest) for some of the biggest coal-fired power stations in the world.

South Africa's NDP is not about democratic planning as envisaged by Löwy. Instead, it is a technocratic ideological device that even fails at class compromise. It speaks to global markets and institutions that merely want to see a disciplined subject, a good governed African state that marches in tune with the strictures of the IMF, World Bank, WTO, and the global power structure that manages a globalised capitalism and is not willing to learn lessons from history. Karl Polanyi's historical sequence, highlighted in *The Great Transformation*, of marketised capitalism in the late nineteenth century which led to the collapse of the international system and World War 1, then again, unleashed with the return to the Gold Standard and which ultimately led to World War 2, does not inform the economics departments or institutions in Europe or the US. After the crash *c.*2007–2009, we are returning to more of the same, more disembedded markets!

In this context, capitalism has clearly not learned lessons from its past, including the hollowing out of democracy it has engendered and its current failures. A democracy that privileges the sovereignty of capital over the state and society is not a democracy. It is a market democracy based on the tyranny of the modern corporation. The demos reduced to a political market with limited ideological choices is not a democracy. In this context, is the US taking us into World War 3 as it tries to reassert its dominance after the recent and ongoing crisis? A naturalised hegemony of capitalism is as dangerous as an unreflective socialism.

Capitalism carries the burden of its horrors, limits and failures. So does socialism. It does not help the debate to be one-sided on these issues. For socialism, there are two issues in this rich history which ecosocialists cannot run away from and which has been foregrounded in this exchange. Democracy as rule by, with and for the demos is absolutely necessary. Moreover, markets as embedded, regulated, values-based and socialised institutions are also absolutely necessary. Radical democracy and markets will have to find a place alongside democratic planning in variegated contexts and through the struggles that are emerging in different societies to prevent the ecocidal extinction of all of us. These institutions cannot be blueprinted, designed or prescribed, but will emerge as struggles develop to advance democratic systemic reforms to achieve democratic ecosocialisms (plural) in the twenty-first century. Food sovereignty, solidarity economy, climate jobs, socially owned renewable energy, zero waste and water commoning are just some of the democratic systemic reforms envisaged by current movements at the frontlines of climate justice. They embody radical democracy, socialised markets and democratic planning as crucial aspects of the logic of these democratic systemic reforms. Moreover, anti-racism and women's emancipation are central to the imaginary of these decolonising and transformative alternatives. Many of these democratic systemic reforms feature in a volume I recently edited entitled *Climate Crisis: Democratic Ecosocialism in South Africa and the World*.[1]

Finally, socialism was diverse in the twentieth century – social democracy, Sovietised socialism (and its copies) and revolutionary nationalism (Nyerere's African socialism, Nehruvian socialism in India, and so on). In the global South in reflecting on our legacies of socialism, we also have to take stock of the paths not taken, which also feed into the constitution of the democratic ecosocialist imagination in the twenty-first century. In this regard, various examples stand out, such as Minqi Li's critique of China's socio-ecological limits and the transformations required. Another example is Gandhi's critique of Western modernity, commitment to village-based democracy and stewardship of the commons, and his bioethic of living slowly and minimally which did not triumph against Nehru's productivist and nationalist socialism. Add to this the historical critique by indigenous communities of forced modernisation (including productivist socialisms), its dangers, and the need for the validation of indigenous ecologies. Democratic ecosocialism is not merely an intellectual debate; it is central to the practice, struggles and visions of movements struggling to overcome the ecofascist logic of carbon capitalism. Moreover, in the twenty-first century, the horizons and imaginary of democratic ecosocialism certainly do not belong exclusively to Marxist ecologists, including myself.

Contribution to *Great Transition Initiative Roundtable: Do Red and Green Mix?*, December 2018.

---

1 http://www.oapen.org/search?identifier=1000474

Marx, the Commons and Democratic Ecosocialism

Introduction

HUMAN AND NON-HUMAN life face a perilous existential crisis. Covid-19 has been merely one of many crises bringing into focus the society–nature relationship. In this regard, the notion of the commons is apposite as a social scientific category, part of transdisciplinary thinking and as part of lived planetary experience. How we think and engage the commons from a radical and critical perspective also means reckoning with Marx. However, Marx's thought has been layered by interpretations by his followers and the historical experiences of socialism. With the global defeat of the left and over three decades of relentless commodification, precarity, inequality and environmental destruction, re-finding Marx's own thought has become crucial. Marx is not surpassed as providing one of the most trenchant, systematic and compelling critiques of capitalism. However, with ecological crises – pollution, global warming, extractivism, species extinction and resource constraints – looming large, the relevance of Marx's thought to these challenges has become a terrain of intellectual combat but also of renewal. At stake has been Marx's conception of ecology. Central to the perspective of this chapter is a reading of Marx as a thinker on the commons. This is not to argue that Marx was the first thinker on the commons. Instead, it is suggested that Marx had a conception of the commons that was central to his philosophical outlook, that his critique of capitalism was also a critique of the destruction of the commons, and this has implications for how we think about ecosocialism. It just might be that Marx had a richer understanding of the commons than assumed and which provides the basis for a theory of the commons.

This chapter has four objectives. First, to highlight the extent of the ecocidal destruction of the commons. The large-scale loss of human and non-human life is immense since the advent of proto-capitalism, about 500 years ago. Enclosures of the commons have been central to this process in the global North and South. However, this has been about more than expropriation and the transformation of life-enabling systems into private property. Such a process has also been about obliterating the conditions that sustain life. Private capitalist property is anti-ecological. Today we are living through the last great dispossession of the natural commons, including the Earth system, as capital seeks to reduce all of nature to natural capital. This foreground assists in thinking with Marx about the significance of the commons. However, this is not as straightforward as it seems because Marx's thought is contradictory and has lent itself to being anthropocentric and anti-ecological. Thus, the second objective of this chapter is to highlight how the Promethean Marx came about. This has to do with the canonisation of scientific socialism as productivist socialism and the neglect of the naturalist basis of Marx's thought. It is argued that this is the Marx and Marxism that has to be rejected in the twenty-first century. This casts a long shadow which hinders an ecological appreciation of Marx.

The third objective of this chapter is to highlight the central role of commons thinking in Marx's work. This is not about a search for a definition of the commons but rather an attempt to re-read aspects of Marx's work to identify space for the commons in his thought. Such a reading spans three critical areas: (i) the ecological premises of Marx's thought; (ii) key categories in his critique of capitalism, which can be extended into emancipatory ecological critique and serve as a basis for the defence of the commons; and (iii) a reading of his approach to non-capitalist societies, to the commons and to commoning as a practice of reproducing the commons. This reading of Marx is also about establishing whether there is potential in Marx's thought for a theory of the commons, a Marxist ecological theory of the commons. The fourth objective of this chapter is to think through the implications of Marx's approach to the commons for contemporary class and anti-oppression struggles, particularly climate justice struggles. Climate change brings the question of the natural commons front and centre. Carbon capitalism's use of fossil fuels has ruptured the Earth system and imperils all life. How this is engaged with as part of elaborating a democratic ecosocialist project in South Africa is elaborated; as part of assessing the proximity of Marx's approach to the commons in contemporary struggles to defend the commons.

The last great dispossession of the commons

According to De Angelis (2019: 124) the commons refers to 'social systems formed by three basic interconnected elements: 1) a commonwealth, that is, a set of resources held in common and governed by 2) a community of commoners who also 3) engage in the praxis of commoning, or doing in common, which reproduces their lives in common and that of their commonwealth'. While this definition of the commons is extremely useful, it lacks a systems understanding of what it classifies as resources. The concept of resources is laden with instrumentalist reason and a reductionist approach to nature as a thing. Instead, the historical experience of the commons has been about life-enabling socio-ecological systems, entangling human and non-human relations, ranging from land (including soils), water (oceans and freshwater systems), biodiversity (including plants, insects, trees and animals), labour, energy and more recently the cybersphere and the Earth system. The commons have been about defending and reproducing life. With the emergence of capitalism, and its transition from feudalism to capitalism, numerous enclosures were imposed which reduced the commons to private property relations and subsumed such systems as part of capitalist accumulation. Karl Polanyi in *The Great Transformation* (1944) provides important insights into how land and labour were transformed into fictitious commodities through enclosures. Colonial expansion further extended enclosures into dominated peripheries. In this regard Rosa Luxemburg's classic text, *The Accumulation of Capital: A Contribution to the Economic Theory of Imperialism* (2002) highlights how the expansion of capital from the centres to the non-capitalist peripheries is premised on the destruction of the natural economy. As life-enabling systems the commons supported pre-capitalist forms of life, culture and interstitial processes of socio-ecological reproduction.

Over the past 150 years of carbon capitalism and imperialism, the ecocidal logic of industrial capitalism and its dominated peripheries have continued to impact negatively on the commons. From the middle of the twentieth century earth scientists refer to this process as the great acceleration which has increased the enclosures of life-enabling systems (Steffen et al., 2015: 849–853). Industrial-scale capitalist societies increased growth, car use, fast food, tourism and other resource-intensive practices. This pattern of industrial-scale dispossession has fuelled the expansion of carbon capitalism and together with the most recent wave of globalisation (late 1970s to the present), based on intensifying the conversion of nature into private property, there have been ecocidal consequences on life-enabling socio-ecological systems. Several studies confirm this including the most recent report by the International Panel of Bio-diversity and Eco-system Services. The key highlights of this study underline the following:[1]

---

1   See https://www.ipbes.net/news/Media-Release-Global-Assessment.

- Three-quarters of the land-based environment and about 66% of the marine environment have been significantly altered by human actions. On average these trends have been less severe or avoided in areas held or managed by indigenous peoples and local communities.
- More than a third of the world's land surface and nearly 75% of freshwater resources are now devoted to crop or livestock production.
- The value of agricultural crop production has increased by about 300% since 1970, raw timber harvest has risen by 45% and approximately 60 billion tonnes of renewable and non-renewable resources are now extracted globally every year; having nearly doubled since 1980.
- Land degradation has reduced the productivity of 23% of the global land surface, up to $577 billion in annual global crops are at risk from pollinator loss and 100–300 million people are at increased risk of floods and hurricanes because of loss of coastal habitats and protection.
- In 2015, 33% of marine fish stocks were being harvested at unsustainable levels; 60% were maximally sustainably fished, with just 7% harvested at levels lower than what can be sustainably fished.
- Urban areas have more than doubled since 1992.
- Plastic pollution has increased tenfold since 1980, 300–400 million tonnes of heavy metals, solvents, toxic sludge and other wastes from industrial facilities are dumped annually into the world's waters, and fertilisers entering coastal ecosystems have produced more than 400 ocean dead zones, totalling more than 245,000 km^2 (591–595), a combined area greater than that of the UK.

In this context, the recent United Nations Environmental Programme report is appropriately entitled *Making Peace with Nature* (2021).[2] However, the pattern of dispossession and ecocide (the large-scale destruction of human and non-human nature) underpinning these realities has to be understood as the last great dispossession of the commons. This antagonism with nature threatens everything. Land use patterns, topsoil depletion, water privatisation, biodiversity loss, oil peak, precariatised labour, increasing corporate and state control of the cyber commons and the rupture in the Earth system due to worsening corporate induced planetary heating are where the battle lines of the last great dispossession of the commons are being drawn. The commons has been part of the ecological sub-stratum of capitalism enabling socio-ecological

---

2   Full report available at https://www.unep.org/resources/making-peace-nature.

reproduction of countries and planetary civilisation. Commoning practices and patterns have emerged to resist such ecocidal practices and even opt out of capitalist logics, informed by socio-ecological and cultural contexts. These counter-hegemonic practices include indigenous peoples' defence of forests, water, land and food sovereignty, democratically owned public goods, socially owned renewable energy, climate justice approaches to deep, just transitions and cyber commoning (peer-to peer learning, Wikipedia, open-source systems). It is in this context we have to ask the question: what does Marx's thought offer radical social theory and praxis today? Given how high the ecological stakes are, including for the future of human and non-human life, is Marx's Marxism up to the challenge of overcoming ecological catastrophe and informing a more emancipatory historical trajectory based on the commons and the practice of commoning?

Marx the Promethean?

The anti-ecological Marx, or Marx the Promethean, is a powerful critique of Marx's Marxism. Such a critique resides within and outside Marxism. There is a lot to wrestle with in these critical engagements and in trying to situate Marx in relation to commons. These critiques speak to an imaginary in dominant streams of Marxism that emerged in the twentieth century and which still has a powerful hold on the left imagination. In summary, Marx is considered a Promethean for the following reasons: (i) belief in the linear development of industrial capitalism and its technologies as the basis for progress. His theory of historical materialism also gave primacy to economic reductionism and ultimately the forces of production; (ii) he disagreed with Malthus on the universality of population growth as providing limits to capitalism. While Marx was correct in this position, he tended to foreground intentional and agentic human action as the basis to overcome such socially constituted limits.[3] Ultimately capitalist or socialist modernisation did not face any natural limits; (iii) this relates to Marx wanting human domination over nature as a measure of self-realisation and ultimately a rational organising of production as the means to ensure needs are met. It is a view that Marx is

---

3 Engels articulated this conception of rationally organising society to overcome natural limits also in his *Outlines of a Critique of Political Economy* (1959 [1843]). He believed that the 'productive power at mankind's disposal is immeasurable. The productivity of the soil can be increased ad infinitum by the application of capital, labour and science ... Capital increases daily; labour power grows with population; and day by day science increasingly makes the forces of nature subject to man.'

essentially anthropocentric, and nature is an object to be exploited by humans. Marx's corpus is vast, unfinished, contradictory and there is evidence in his work that these positions exist and lend support to these critiques. Moreover, several other crucial factors entrenched this strand of productivist Marxism. In the twentieth century, actually existing socialist societies, social democratic societies and revolutionary nationalist ones were shaped by this approach and reading of Marxism. Stalin's forced march industrialisation (despite being informed by Engels' approach to dialectic materialism as applying to nature), China's post-Mao embrace of market reforms, technocratic managerialism in welfare states and corrupt nationalist ruling classes in the global South all contributed negative environmental impacts. Chernobyl was the world's worst nuclear disaster, pollution in Chinese cities is beyond basic standards of clean air quality, most Western welfare states were carbon democracies with extensive human consumption footprints and most peripheral ruling classes have opened their economies to extractivist practices and mono-industrial farming systems. In a sense proving the anti-ecological thrust of growth obsessed industrial and productivist Marxism.

In the Western Marxist tradition, there was a backlash to Engels' version of dialectical materialism as applicable to both nature and society; the dialectics of nature were considered anachronistic (Foster, 2008). However, this rejection went even further and even rejected the naturalist aspect of Marx's thinking. As a result, and despite the critical approach to Marx, Marx's ecology was not part of Western Marxist theorising for most of the twentieth century. The rise of modern environmentalism further entrenched the green critique of Marx and Marxism in general. Marx's ontology of work, commitments to linear industrial progress and anthropocentric intellectual orientation were all regarded as anti-ecological. The bogey of the Promethean Marx was born. Finally, many of Marx's crucial writings and works were not published when these productivist strands of Marxism took root. Marx's *Economic and Philosophical Notebooks* (1932), the *Grundrisse* (1939), *Ethnological Notebooks* (1974) and his *Scientific and Natural Notebooks* (part of the Marx-Engels-Gesamtausgabe or MEGA project in the making for several decades in the twentieth century) were all published much later and only engaged with after these projects were shaping the imaginary of many on the planet.

Towards a Marxist ecological theory of the commons

Marx is not perfect, and neither is there a true Marx that has all the answers.

Marx's development as a radical thinker evolved and he was constantly attempting to think with the intellectual raw materials of his time to ground his historical materialist method and critique of capitalism. Thus, when thinking about Marx's work as a whole, the Promethean Marx is contradicted by an ecological Marx, with a strong naturalist basis to his thinking. Such a Marx was always present but becomes pronounced at different moments in his corpus. The ecological Marx expands the political economy critique of capitalism to an emancipatory ecology critique and as the basis for defending the commons. Such a critique is also a decolonial critique, recognising that colonialism had deleterious consequences and Euro-America is not the universal civilisational standard we all have to inhabit to achieve socialism. What follows is an attempt to foreground Marx's ecology as the basis to develop a Marxist theory of the commons. Three tasks are performed: (i) highlighting the ecological premises of Marx's Marxism; (ii) foregrounding several categories in Marx's thought that provide resources of emancipatory ecological critique of capitalism and the defence of the commons; and (iii) providing an interpretation of Marx on the transition beyond capitalism that emphasises the commons and commoning.

The ecological premises of Marx's Marxism

Callenbach provides a useful definition and insight into what ecology is all about. He says:

> Actually, the science of ecology studies all interactions among living beings and their environment, whether we humans are involved or not. Air and even some rocks that function as parts of life's cycles are included too. Ecology is a study of patterns, networks, balances and cycles rather than the straightforward causes and effects studied in physics and chemistry. The goal of ecology is to understand the functioning of whole living systems, not simply to break them down into component parts of analysis (1999: 34).

While Marx did not invent modern ecology, there are important ecological premises to his thought. Moreover, Marx was also a pioneering systems thinker in how he understood the totality of capitalism, including nature. The re-reading and retrieval of the ecological premises of Marx's thought has produced a rich body of work. Since the end of the 1990s up to the present there has been a revisiting of the classical foundations of Marx's thought and an attempt to reconstruct Marx's Marxism from the standpoint of Marx's conception of ecology. This has been about reading Marx afresh, informed by the full corpus of his work, while clearly specifying where and how the thread of nature features in his thought. This research agenda has come a long way and has been extremely fruitful in bringing to light Marx's ecology.[4]

Deriving from this Marxist ecological reconstruction are four crucial ecological premises in Marx's thought that place Marx on the terrain of understanding the commons as life-enabling socio-ecological systems. The first ecological premise in Marx's thought recognises that humans are dependent on nature. This is a theme central to the basis for the elaboration of historical materialism in the *German Ideology*. In this regard, it is stated as follows:

> The first premise of all human history is, of course, the existence of living human individuals. Thus, the first fact to be established is the physical organisation of these individuals and their consequent relation to the rest of nature. Of course, we cannot here go either into the actual physical nature of man, or into the natural conditions in which man finds himself – geological, oro-hydrological, climatic and so on (Marx and Engels, 1998: 37).

The point about this premise is that the dependence of humans on nature is an empirical reality that needs to be studied and confirmed; there is a natural history bound up with a human history. While modes of production and divisions of labour become more complex, it does not mean that the natural conditions of production and the dependence on nature disappear. A second crucial ecological premise in Marx's thought relates to humans being part of nature. In the more Hegelian-inspired *Economic and Philosophical Manuscripts* Marx states:

> Nature is man's inorganic body – nature, that is, insofar as it is not itself human body. Man lives on nature – means that nature is his body, with which he must remain in continuous interchange if he is not to die. That man's physical and spiritual life is linked to nature means simply that nature is linked to itself, for man is a part of nature (Marx, 1981: 67).

---

[4] Such works include Bellamy Foster, *Marx's Ecology-Materialism and Nature* (2000), Paul Burkett, *Marxism and Ecological Economics: Toward a Red-Green Political Economy* (2006) and *Marx and Nature: A Red and Green Perspective* (2014); and more recently Kohei Saito, *Karl Marx's Ecosocialism: Capital, Nature, and the Unfinished Critique of Political Economy* (2017).

As part of nature and in a dependent, symbiotic relationship with nature, the human is more than just a social being but a socio-ecological being. The socio-ecological nature of the human is also contingent and historical. This links also to a third ecological premise in Marx which recognises nature is also as a source of wealth together with labour. In *Capital* (1976, 1981), Marx's labour-centred ontology is further elaborated with an emphasis on the labour theory of value, which is crucial to demonstrate exploitation through the extraction of surplus value. However, within productivist and anthropocentric Marxism this occludes any relationship with nature. All the ecological premises of Marx's thought are thrown out of the window. However, Marx reminds the German working class about the wealth creation role of labour and nature in his *Critique of the Gotha Program*. He states: 'Labour is not the source of all wealth. Nature is just as much the source of use values (and it is surely of such that material wealth consists!) as labour, which itself is only the manifestation of a force of nature, human labour power' (Marx, 1996: 8).

The final ecological premise of Marx's thought relates to human impacts on nature and limits. In Saito's (2017) ecological reading of Marx, particularly the *Scientific and Natural Notebooks*, he provides extremely novel insights about Marx's deep concerns with impacts of capitalist agriculture on nature and deforestation. Marx was concerned with depletion of the fertility of soils, the robbery from the soil, and extensive destruction of forests. Marx began to acknowledge and recognise natural limits to capitalist accumulation. This was also central to his conception of the metabolic rift with nature, involving the flow of energy and matter but mediated by labour relations, which has been elaborated into metabolic rift theory by John Bellamy Foster and others.

Marx's critique of capitalism and the defence of the commons

With Marx having solid ecological premises to his Marxism, his political economy critique of capitalism can be situated and shifted towards emancipatory ecological critique of capitalism. Such critique recognises natural and social relations are contradictory and mutually constitutive on a planetary scale, but are nonetheless constrained by our dependence on nature, our imbrication in nature and the limits of nature. A society, a capitalist system, built on the endless and total destruction of nature, will not survive. In this regard, four important categories in Marx's critique of capitalism provides a bridge to such an emancipatory ecological critique and most importantly to locating the commons, both its enclosure/destruction and life-enabling role, as central to how we understand capitalism.

The first category is primitive accumulation. While Marx observed the process of primitive accumulation firsthand as a young journalist, when he wrote about the theft of woods, this was not understood as part of the larger process of the making of capitalism. Yet as Linebaugh (2014: 43–62) points out, Marx's writings (five articles) in 1842–1843 for the *Rheinische Zeitung*, were related to a particular phase of development of capitalism in Germany but also the struggles around agrarian relations. More specifically, it would seem these writings and actual insights of the class struggle, related to peasants stealing wood from forests, where also about a shift from an inadequate study of crime to the study of political economy. In *Capital*, Marx provides a detailed analysis of how enclosures of the commons were established, in different phases, to separate the peasantry from the means of production in Britain. Moreover, in part 8 of *Capital*, Marx explores primitive accumulation as forming the basis for the origins of capitalism and providing the preconditions for the development of this mode of production. Central to this study is an analysis of colonialism that highlights the role of slavery, racism, brute force and the appropriation of land. However, while Marx is trying to situate the making of capitalism in the peripheries, he is also showing how a racialised colonial subjectivity, the making of wage labour and land enclosures are crucial in this process. Primitive accumulation as a category central to the critique of capitalism then and now assists with the emancipatory ecology critique of capitalism to highlight the mass-scale destruction of human and non-human nature; that is, ecocide. Thus, a more appropriate phrasing and appreciation of these contemporary processes would be accumulation through ecocide.

The second crucial category is alienation. This is central to Marx's critique of capitalism both in the *Economic and Philosophical Manuscripts* and *Capital*. For Marx alienation is centred on four aspects for labour: (i) from the products of labour, which refers to labour being part of the product produced resulting in objectification and then such products being separated from the worker; (ii) in the division of labour the worker is a commodity, their labour is external to themselves, it is forced and is dehumanising; (iii) as species being alienated from nature and herself. The universal human is now reduced to utilising her individual self to ensure her physical existence; and (iv) estrangement from human to human. Marx's conception of alienation has a strong hint of anthropocentricism, in parts, in how he understands the superiority of humans to animals. However, read and interpreted from the standpoint of the ecological premises to his thought, the human as a manifestation of nature engaged in exploitative work and separated from natural relations is in a state of alienation. Capitalism ensures the alienated human is not part of the natural commons. But underlying this labour-centred ontology and conception of alienation is the role of property relations. It is the creation of labour as property, and through labour the creation of property, Marx places at the heart of alienation. Workers and ultimately humanity-in-nature are part of the struggle for de-alienation at the point of production. More concretely, this means traditions of worker control and resistance have to embrace an emancipatory ecological consciousness and ultimately a crucial role for the commons. Put more sharply, an ecologically conscious working class and subaltern should be at the frontlines of defending and advancing the commons to ensure de-alienation.

The third category that emancipatory ecology can draw on from Marx's political economy is the notion of use value to both deepen the critique of capitalism and defend the commons. In *Capital*, labour and nature are use values, to meet human need. However, with capitalism labour and nature are commodified; labour sells labour power for a wage, nature such as land produces rent. Labour as a commodity is exploited and generates surplus value; the worker is constantly forced to supersede necessary labour time (the wage) and ensure an increasing role for surplus labour time (unpaid labour). At the same time, capital uses the use value of labour and nature to produce more commodities as exchange values. Commodities as exchange values also have use value to them, but mediated by labour and the labour process, produce surplus value for capital. For emancipatory ecology, the defence of the natural commons, including labour, is about defending use values. This is central to class and anti-oppression struggles.

The fourth crucial category is social reproduction, both in its broad social sense and as it relates to the abode of the household and care labour. Production and social reproduction are two sides of the same coin in how life and society is reproduced. Marx in *Capital* understood that the socially necessary labour time was also about reproducing the worker and her dependents. Exploited, low-wage and precariatised workers thus struggle to reproduce themselves and their families. However, it was Marxist feminists in the 1960s and 1970s who went further than this and recognised women's care labour as a use value, was unpaid but was also not inherently gendered (see Vogel, 2013 and Gottfried, 2015). Today social reproduction theory is making a return and Marxist feminist theorising is locating the production/reproduction contradiction within periodised regimes of reproduction. Nancy Fraser's (2017) work on reproductive regimes from (i) liberal capitalism; (ii) state-managed capitalism and (iii) financialised capitalism provides a framing to bring in the commons and the ecological premises of Marx's Marxism. Put more sharply, socio-ecological human beings have been organised into socio-ecological regimes of reproduction. How these regimes destroy the commons and oppress women are crucial for analysis and ongoing struggles.

Non-capitalist societies, the commons and commoning

In the *Communist Manifesto* (Marx and Engels, 2002) there are two problems that loom large in Marx's thought. First, there is a strong Eurocentric message about the progressiveness of capital and capitalism, ending primitive societies. Moreover, the world historic advance of capital produces its grave digger, the working class, in its wake. This is an epistemological Eurocentrism which continues in Marx's thought into the mid-1850s. However, according to Anderson (2010), there is an epistemological rupture in Marx who leaves behind this Eurocentric moment; Marx moves beyond linearity in his understanding of history. This requires Marx to break with a Hegelianised and theological understanding of world history; moreover, recognition that non-capitalist societies have their own histories, differentiated ownership systems and hence their own modalities for the transition beyond pre-capitalism. The West's transition from feudalism to capitalism was not a universal process. Finally, instead of colonialism and the world market bringing about progress and the development of the forces of production it had deleterious consequences. Besides his insights in *Capital* about the brutality and racialised basis of primitive accumulation, Marx's writing on race, ethnicity, class and colonialism in relation to slavery in America and British colonial control of Ireland are apposite. This is the decolonial Marx recognising that history was much more contingent, open and subject to multilinearity with variegated processes of transition from feudalism to capitalism and from capitalism and beyond. This becomes even more stark in his political writings after the *Communist Manifesto*, and which also have profound implications for how we think about the commons and commoning in non-capitalist societies.

However, to appreciate the shift to multilinearity we have to return to the second problem raised by the *Communist Manifesto* in Marx's thought. This relates to the issue of abolishing bourgeoisie property. The part of the manifesto dealing with measures to be taken by the working class and communists is explicitly state centric. An instrumentalised conception of the state is at work and a working class-led state merely has to wield the instrumental power of the state and take over key forms of bourgeoisie property. Centralised state control is needed to be exercised over key instruments of production such as credit, communication, transport and factories. However, informed by his non-Eurocentric approach to history, Marx departs from this state-centric approach to property relations, and which converges more with affirming a role for the commons and commoning in advancing beyond capitalism. This comes through in his support for co-operatives in his inaugural address to the First International, support for the Russian commune in his exchange with Vera Zasulitch and in the preface to the Russian edition of the *Communist Manifesto*, embrace of the Paris Commune as a new form of organising working-class power (also through co-operatives) in the *Civil War in France* and firm support in the *Critique of the Gotha Program* for the common or socialised ownership of the means of production. In short, while Marx did not blueprint a post-capitalist society, he recognised free and associated labour came into existence through collective inherited property forms, socialised interstitial property forms and more decentred and participatory forms of democracy as crucial for a post-capitalist society.

These are all institutional forms consistent with the commons and commoning to ensure life-enabling systems bring about all rounded human development. However, this thread in Marx's thought is a consistent one and goes back to his search for an antidote to the alienation and estrangement that comes with private property relations. In the 1844 *Philosophical and Economic Manuscripts*, he resolves this problem, in general terms, in this way:

> This material, immediately perceptible private property is the material perceptible expression of estranged human life. Its movement – production and consumption – is the perceptible revelation of the movement of all production up till now i.e. the realisation or the reality of man. Religion, family, state, law, morality, science, art, etc. are only particular modes of production, and fall under its general law. The positive transcendence of private property as the appropriation of human life, is therefore the positive transcendence of all estrangement – that is to say, the return of man from religion, family, state etc., to his human, i.e., social, existence (1981: 91).

The deep, just transition and democratic ecosocialism

The ecological side of Marx's thought is certainly anti-Promethean. The ecological premises of his thought, his critique of capitalism as emancipatory ecological critique and his understanding of non-capitalist modes of existence as part of the transition beyond capitalism are consistent with affirming the commons and commoning practices. Today in the contemporary world, socialism is being rethought from the standpoint of an ecological Marx, lessons learned from the mistakes of historical and state-centric productivist socialisms and at the frontlines of struggles to defend the commons. One of the most important struggles in this regard is the climate justice struggle, which is entering a third cycle of resistance in the midst of Covid-19. Climate justice forces are intensifying the struggle to give definition and content to the notion of the deep, systemic and just transition. More sharply, 'system change, not climate change'.

While capital is increasingly waking up to the realities of a worsening climate crisis, the hegemonic influence of carbon capital over the multilateral climate negotiations, during the past three decades, has brought the world to the brink of irreversible disaster. In 2018, climate scientists raised the alarm bell the loudest with the 1.5°C IPCC report which argues we have the current decade to prevent a 1.5°C planetary overshoot. The world is now at 417 parts per million (ppm) carbon concentration. According to Earth scientists we are in a danger zone far from the safe boundary of 350ppm, in which several dangerous tipping points and feedback loops can kick in.[5] This carbon capitalist rupturing in the Earth system is propelling the planet towards a hot house Earth, which will make it unliveable. Our planetary commons, including the Earth system, is being turned against human and non-human life. The last great dispossession of the natural commons threatens everything.

In this life and death struggle, the defence of the natural commons takes on a salience and meaning that brings it to the fore in climate justice struggles on a planetary scale. The deep, just and systemic transition is nothing short of realising a democratic ecosocialist project to preserve human and non-human life. In the South African context this is expressed in the struggle to advance a CJC.[6] There are four striking aspects about the charter that affirm its democratic ecosocialist orientation. First, it envisages a decolonial approach

---

5   These insights are contained in an interview with earth scientist, Will Steffen, available here: https://www.tandfonline.com/doi/full/10.1080/14747731.2021.1940070.

6   The CJC is endorsed by over 260 organisations and is available here: https://www.safsc.org.za/climate-justice-charter/.

to knowledge and to resisting capitalism. It explicitly rejects capitalist ideologic underpinnings of productivism, extractivism and technotopia. Instead, it affirms a critical embrace of knowledge (including earth science, global emancipatory ecology and indigenous knowledge), local history and culture as the basis to inform a delinking approach to the deep, just transition. In other words, the charter affirms the importance of multilinear approaches to transition beyond capitalism and it is certainly not about reproducing the Euro-American standard of civilisation.

Second, it contains 14 systemic alternatives (including democratic just transition plans, food sovereignty, solidarity economy, socially owned renewable energy, water commoning, zero waste and natural climate solutions) which are all about democratising life-enabling systems. In other words, it affirms ecocentric modes of living that place the commons and commoning central to the deep, just transition. Third, it is premised on a constitutive understanding of power. Power is organised, made and institutionalised from below. Thus, the charter envisages democratic systemic reforms prefigured in local spaces but scaled up and pursued beyond. In other words, the working class (urban and rural), grassroots women and the most vulnerable must lead deep, just transitions and ensure systemic alternatives are deepened over time through mass power. Fourth, this in turn ensures the South African state is remade as a climate justice state, and is people driven to create enabling conditions for democratic systemic reforms, to build new capabilities, to redirect resources and to renew radical pan-Africanism. The charter does not envisage a state-centric transition beyond carbon capitalism.

Conclusion

Marx's Marxism is a crucial resource in the twenty-first century to confront the last great dispossession of the commons and the ecocidal logic of carbon capitalism. Marx has crucial ecological underpinnings to his thought that embraces the commons. Moreover, his political economy critique of capitalism provides crucial resources of critique for an emancipatory ecology that stands in defence of the commons, as part of frontline struggles. These categories also assist with studying the commons and elaborating its significance as part of the transition beyond capitalism. In this regard the decolonial Marx (or non-Eurocentric) and ecological Marx meet. The commons and commoning are certainly part of a multilinear and context-specific approach to the transition beyond capitalism. Such an approach challenges narrow, state-centric conceptions of socialism but also enriches how the deep, just transition to democratic ecosocialism can come about from below.

In South Africa this is certainly what the CJC is all about. Rooted in a context in which a history of race, class and gender oppression looms large and which has continued under a black majority government, systems transformation and redistribution are conjoined, as the climate crisis is addressed. This simply means inequality, unemployment and all other socio-ecological reproduction contradictions have to be addressed in a manner that also socialises property relations, at a higher level, through the commons and commoning. This brings us on to intellectual ground occupied by the ecological and the non-Eurocentric Marx.

Far from being implicated in the last great dispossession of the commons, Marx stands against it and provides resources to develop a Marxist theory of the commons. It is up to us to clarify this and assert it. This chapter makes a start and a contribution in this regard. From here, we must continue deepening how twenty-first-century Marxists think and act as commoners in the struggle to defend life enabling commons systems.

Chapter in D. Fasenfest (ed.) *Marx Matters*. Leiden: Brill, 2022.

End Ecocidal Capitalism or Exterminate Life on Planet Earth: A South African Contribution to Ecosocialist Strategy

Introduction

GLOBALISED CARBON CAPITALISM is like a snake eating its own tail, self-inflicting wounds. This is not new in the history of capitalism. Between 1870 and 1914, capitalism was also plagued by a general crisis, contributing to imperial conflict and the World War 1, which claimed the lives of 10 million people. Rosa Luxemburg wrote her classic *Accumulation of Capital*, published a year before the war, in this context. She observed that:

> The more ruthlessly capital sets about the destruction of non-capitalist strata at home and in the outside world, the more it lowers the standard of living for the workers as a whole, the greater also is the change in the day-to-day history of capital. It becomes a string of political and social disasters and convulsions, and under these conditions, punctuated by periodic economic catastrophes and crises, accumulation can go on no longer. But even before this natural economic impasse of capital's own creating is properly reached it becomes a necessity for the international working class to revolt against capital (1951: 466–67).

From a Marxist ecological perspective, the catastrophes Luxemburg refers to here, resulting from the destruction of natural economies and non-capitalist strata, can be seen as referring not only to the economic convulsion brought on by capital, but also to its ecocidal logic. This is associated with enclosures in the centres and peripheries, large-scale destruction of human and non-human life, and expropriation resulting in ecocide. War is merely one form and moment of extending this logic of deep systemic crisis. In such conjunctures, strategic working-class and anti-oppression politics must come to the fore in order to leverage the crisis against capitalism. However, this kind of conscious strategic politics is not always given or inevitable; sometimes, the crisis of capitalism is also the crisis of the historical social forces meant to resist it.

Today, capitalism is facing the fourth general crisis (roughly from 2007 to the present) in its history. This is a crisis of socio-economic and ecological production on a world scale. It is a product of the restructuring of the global political economy through the neoliberal class project (starting around 1980), its implementation and lock-ins through structural adjustment and austerity, punctuated by currency collapses, ballooning private and public debt, overheating of housing markets, economic collapses and widespread precarity. Neoliberal logic intensified surplus value extraction through the contraction of welfare regimes, de-industrialisation, precarious labour market regimes, and a global labour arbitrage based on low unit-labour cost manufacturing in China and much of the global South, promoting universal commodification including nature itself. In this context, global rivalries have been intensifying between a declining US hegemon and geopolitical contenders, with the recent proxy war in Ukraine between the United States/NATO and Russia portending the intensification of militarised geopolitical competition. Despite the ideological varieties of neoliberalism, in different national and regional contexts, the current realities we live is its world-making essence.

In the four decades of its existence, neoliberalism has also accentuated deep systemic crisis tendencies, emanating from production/reproduction, nature/society, and economy/state divides. These have propelled monopoly finance capital into a phase of authoritarian neoliberalism: thin market democracies entrenching the power of transnationalising propertied classes from the US and Brazil to South Africa and India. A global ecofascist project, plunging the world into chaos and accentuating the ecocidal logic of global carbon capitalism, has arrived, threatening everything (Satgar, 2021).

In this context, democratic ecosocialist strategy has to proceed from the urgent premise that we must end ecocidal capitalism or face the end of life on Earth. This imperative is what distinguishes the fourth general crisis of capitalism from all previous crises. It is a poly-crisis, or multilevel total crisis, that cannot be managed with shallow reformism and technological fixes, at least not if human and non-human life are to survive. Moreover, democratic ecosocialist strategy has to come to terms with the complex global political field it has to contest, particularly the underlying conditions generating and maintaining an ecofascist class project. Along with this are the self-induced disruptions of global carbon capitalism, plus the spaces this provides for strategic advance and agential challenges, enabling a counter-hegemonic project on national and global scales.

To explicate these areas of strategic analysis, first we must situate the victory of carbon capital's lock-in of fossil fuels, which has been deeply embedded in global climate politics, providing a crucial element of ecofascist class politics. Second, we must analyse how the 2021 UN Climate Change Conference in Glasgow (COP26) ensured the continuity of the ecofascist project. Third, contemporary global carbon capitalism has unravelled as a challenge and limit to the advance of the ecofascist project.[1] Fourth, insights into democratic ecosocialist strategy and the climate justice project in South Africa can serve as examples of how to respond to the larger ecofascist conjuncture. The politics of defending the commons and advancing democratic systemic reforms must be highlighted to accelerate and deepen a just transition. Finally, I conclude with challenges to planetise the movement to end ecocidal capitalism and defeat the ecofascist class project.

Carbon capital's victory and the lock-in of fossil fuels

The increasing use of oil, coal and gas is exacerbating the climate ecological rift and creating a global gas chamber capable of wiping out human and non-human life. Despite this dangerous prospect, the US hegemon, the largest historical carbon emitter, and the UN multilateral processes have not put the work on track to solve the climate crisis. With almost three decades of climate science, multilateral negotiations and everyday climate shocks – together with a 1.1°C temperature increase since before the Industrial Revolution – fossil fuels still dominate the global political economy. In 2021, the International Energy Agency (IEA) declared that no new oil, coal and gas investments could take place if net zero is to be reached by 2050. However, so far, carbon-addicted states and corporations have not been adhering to this. At the same time, we have to ask: Why did the US, the UN, climate change conferences, and the IEA not declare this in the 1990s or early 2000s? The simple answer is that carbon capital won and entrenched the use of fossil fuels, despite the scientific urgency to reduce carbon emissions and the worsening climate crisis.

Three crucial political-economic conditions gave rise to this. First, there is the power of the carbon capitalist lobby in the Beltway in Washington DC. Since James Hansen drew attention to the urgencies in climate science in 1988,

---

1 In this article, I use democratic ecosocialist forces and climate justice forces.

Exxon, together with the American Petroleum Institute, National Association of Manufacturers, US Chamber of Commerce and 13 other industry associations went on the offensive (Rich 2019: 182–183). The Global Climate Coalition unleashed a public relations exercise that gridlocked the Beltway and sowed confusion in the US public and among global ruling classes. Climate science denialism, discrediting climate science and scientists, strategic lobbying and dishonest marketing all went into overdrive, even affecting the UN climate change negotiations. The IPCC, despite insisting on reducing carbon emissions, failed to place sufficient emphasis on the rapid phase out of fossil fuels in the global economy, allowing the idea of carbon credits, technological schemes with respect to carbon capture and sequestration, and negative carbon emissions to subvert the process. Meanwhile, the US public was kept in the dark about the urgent findings of climate science, with the captured political leadership in Washington overtly supporting fossil fuel interests. The Global Climate Coalition, for example, declared that it had won and was disbanded by 2002. Contemporary resistance to complex hydrocarbon extraction has been occurring in this context of the perpetuation of business-as-usual fossil fuel production. Blockadia and even divestment have been unable to stop the fossil fuel juggernaut.

Second, given that the US has been dominated by carbon capital, which is closely tied to ruling financial interests, it has failed to provide decisive leadership in the UN multilateral processes, from the Kyoto Protocol to the Paris Agreement. US presidents have consistently maintained that the American way of life is not up for negotiation and there can be no binding regulatory commitments, despite the deadly consequences of carbon emissions. This failure of imperial leadership emboldened a call for catch-up carbon development in the global South and ensured fossil fuel spigots remained open over the past twenty years to meet the needs of China, India and other G20 countries. At the same time, the billions for a just transition promised to countries that did not cause the climate crisis have not materialised. This has ensured that countries in the global South, including fossil fuel resource economies, have remained trapped in resource extraction. The winner in this context has been carbon capital.

Third, despite the fanfare, backslapping and public relations projection of a great success, after the Paris Agreement was put in place, a ruling-class ecofascist project has congealed and is shaping climate politics. This is made up of two dominant ideological currents: (i) centre-right neoliberals who hide behind the failed UN climate negotiation process and now the Paris Agreement.

Their rhetoric is all about market-led just transitions, technological fixes (carbon capture and storage, a not-always-green push for hydrogen, electric vehicles and geoengineering), and finance (carbon offsets, trading and taxes). Yet, in practice, these leaders and their countries have not been shining examples of decarbonisation – quite the opposite. The use of fossil fuels and climate modernisation is the name of the game, with the assumption of a linear and gradual process of change by 2050. They claim that the climate emergency can be managed from above and are sending mixed signals to the people to placate concerns, while actually trying to manage elite risk; (ii) hard-right neoliberals have accepted globalised accumulation and embraced exclusionary and racist nationalisms, and are ambivalent about climate science and its urgent messages. Where there has been a rejection of climate science, racist neo-Malthusian attitudes have emerged to buttress carceral border regimes.

COP26 and the continuity of the ecofascist project

The COP26 climate negotiations in November 2021 happened in the context of Covid-19 ravaging our societies, a powerful expression of the revenge of nature. In many ways, it serves as a prelude to the greater pain awaiting our societies as the climate crisis worsens. Despite this, world leaders and carbon ruling classes came up short in their commitments. According to Columbia University's Center on Global Energy Policy, after assessing nationally determined commitments, the world was only on track to cut emissions by 9% by 2030, far short of the necessary cutting of emissions by about half.[2] Only 14 countries have signed the net-zero goal into law. It would seem as if will and commitment is faltering at a policy-implementation level. The Joe Biden administration, while promising a renewable energy revolution, has released massive amounts of petroleum from US reserves and placed pressure on fracking businesses to meet supply-side shortfalls. US coal use is also on the rise. This has been induced by high oil prices and the bans imposed on Russia in response to the Ukraine war. According to the US government itself, US crude production is anticipated to climb to new heights under Biden.[3] Other examples of ongoing carbon criminality include Justin Trudeau's administration in Canada, which is delaying delivery of

---

2 James Glynn et al., 'Tallying updated NDCs to gauge emissions reductions in 2030 and progress toward net zero'. Center on Global Energy Policy at Columbia University SIPA, 16 March 2022, https://www.energypolicy.columbia.edu/research/report/tallying-updated-ndcs-gauge-emissions-reductions-2030-and-progress-toward-net-zero.

3 See Derek Brower, 'Big oil has nothing to complain about under Joe Biden'. *Financial Times*, 1 April 2022, https://www.ft.com/content/3fe7d626-7e3e-4cb9-bce5-6798c50c47e8.

a promised cap on emissions from the fossil fuel sector, insisting there is no need to curb production.[4] In South Africa, the Cyril Ramaphosa regime, one of the most carbon-intensive economies even in the BRICS countries, is still obsessed with a coal-heavy energy mix (at least up until 2030) and is currently pursuing offshore oil and gas extraction, gas-based Karpowerships (to meet supply-side challenges), nuclear power and fracking. Centre-right neoliberals are becoming indistinguishable from hard-right neoliberals, as ecofascism marches on.

Despite all the fanfare at COP26 about finance capital pulling the plug on fossil fuel investments, this is far from what is happening in reality. Despite its declared intentions, the Glasgow Financial Alliance for Net Zero, which includes the Net Zero Banking Alliance launched in April 2021, has funded huge transactions that go against the net-zero target, with dire implications for carbon lock-ins for coming decades. This includes $10 billion to Saudi Aramco (Citi, JPMorgan Chase) and $1.5 billion to Abu Dhabi National Oil Co. (Citi) in May 2021; $12.5 billion to QatarEnergy (Citi, JPMorgan Chase, Bank of America, Goldman Sachs) in June 2021; and $10 billion to ExxonMobil (Citi, JPMorgan Chase, Bank of America, Morgan Stanley) in August 2021.[5] In the 13th annual report *Banking on Climate Chaos*, the following critical observation is made: in the six years since the Paris Agreement was adopted, the world's 60 largest private banks financed fossil fuels with $4.6 trillion, with $742 billion in 2021 alone. In 2021 fossil fuel financing numbers remained above 2016 levels, when the Paris Agreement was signed. Of particular significance is the revelation that the 60 banks profiled in the report funnelled $185.5 billion just last year into the 100 companies doing the most to expand the fossil fuel sector.[6]

Maturing contradictions and capitalism's systemic disruptions

The current debate among the global capitalist intelligentsia revolves around the end of globalisation and the fragmentation of the neoliberal economic order.

---

4   Joe Lo, Cloé Farand and Isabelle Gerretsen, 'Canadian government ducks fight with oil and gas industry'. *Climate Home News*, 31 March 2022, https://www.climatechangenews.com/2022/03/31/canadian-government-ducks-fight-with-oil-and-gas-industry/.

5   'Bankers lie about fossil fuel finance'. *Climate and Capitalism*, 31 March 2022, https://climateandcapitalism.com/2022/03/31/bankers-lie-about-fossil-fuel-finance/?utm_source=rss&utm_medium=rss&utm_campaign=bankers-lie-about-fossil-fuel-finance.

6   'Banking on climate chaos' in *Fossil Fuel Finance Report 2022* (Rainforest Action Network, BankTrack, Indigenous Environmental Network, Oil Change International, Reclaim Finance, Sierra Club and Urgewald, 2022), https://www.bankingonclimatechaos.org/.

Dani Rodrick in 2016 was already cautioning ruling classes 'not to fret' about deglobalisation as what was required was an adjustment from deep globalisation. A more moderated globalisation, the argument went, was on the table with imbalances being adjusted and greater government responsibility coming to the fore.[7] Since then, various important developments have emerged to challenge liberalised trading systems. Donald Trump's big push to decouple the US economy from China, the impact of the Covid-19 pandemic on supply chains (including vaccine apartheid), Brexit, ongoing technological rivalry between the US and China, and the Russian offensive in Ukraine have contributed to upending all illusions about energy dependence. All the assumptions of open intellectual property and free-market trading systems have been shattered as governments rethink degrees of integration and globalisation, and how to manage systemic risk. The space this opens for exiting imperial disciplining and accelerating deep, just transitions cannot be underestimated.

Nevertheless, the remaking of global trading systems is merely the surface expression of the deeper systemic crisis tendencies shaping and limiting the globalised logic of the ecofascist class project. Financialised inequality and structural unemployment, further entrenching class, race and gender divides in society, are exacerbating the crisis of social reproduction in households and beyond. According to recent reports on executive pay packages, the trend of concentrating wealth at the top has continued, despite the suffering inflicted by Covid-19 on societies, with 280 of the 500 S&P companies that have reported figures this year highlighting that the median pay for CEOs in the largest capitalised firms on US stock exchanges has jumped to a record $14.2 million for 2021, up from $13.5 million in 2020.[8] Moreover, the median CEO to worker pay ratio has shot up to 245 for 2021 from 192 for 2020, an extremely large year-over-year increase. Women globally are in the lowest paid work, with 75% of women in developing regions in the informal economy, and about 600 million in the most insecure and precarious forms of work. Women do twice as much unpaid care work (with annual estimates at $10.8 trillion) and work longer days than men on average (when both paid and unpaid work is counted).[9]

In South Africa, structural unemployment has been above 20% since the

---

7   Dani Rodrik, 'There is no need to fret about deglobalisation'. *Financial Times*, 4 October 2016, https://www.ft.com/content/d9a28a08-895c-11e6-8cb7-7eada1d123b1.

8   'US executives reap record pay as historic income gap with staff widens'. *Financial Times*, 3 April 2002, https://www.ft.com/content/f02787c1-35a8-41c4-8099-395109e49b4f.

9   'Why the majority of the world's poor are women', Oxfam, https://www.oxfam.org/en/why-majority-worlds-poor-are-women.

1970s. Today, its highly globalised and financialised economy has an unemployment rate of 35.3% and the highest Gini coefficient (63) in the world, with 71% of the wealth owned by 10% of the population. In this context, unviable societies and the failure of trickle-down economics are also engendering new forms of resistance to tackle class, race and gender oppression. These forms of resistance can either be captured by exclusionary nationalisms or can be mobilised in a transformative direction.

The ecological rifts of capitalism are manifold. Biological disasters such as Covid-19 are certainly going to increase as natural habitats are destroyed. Biological warfare (involving laboratories experimenting with dangerous pathogens) and climate change will contribute to the proliferation of more pathogens, while ecofascist anti-science positions create more vulnerable populations. The enabling conditions for more zoonotic diseases are ripe. This means more disruptions, and these pandemic threats make it essential for public health systems to be strengthened and repurposed to also face the challenges of the worsening climate crisis. Water peak is another major ecological rift being exacerbated by wasteful water use: agriculture accounts for 70% of global water withdrawals, including the use of irrigation systems. Meanwhile, pollution from mining, mismanagement of water commons and climate impacts on the hydrological cycle through floods and droughts (currently such catastrophes have tripled from 97 per annum during the 1980s to an annual average of 309 between 2010 and 2019) are threats.[10] According to one estimate, water scarcity could impact global GDP by up to 14% in 2050, with the Middle East being one of the most affected regions. In this context, tighter water regulations on use and re-use, as well as democratic planning and management of the water commons, will be necessary to limit the power of corporations to appropriate and wastefully utilise scarce water resources.

The climate ecological rift is the most dangerous and intersects with other systemic crisis tendencies. As more coal, oil and gas are extracted, global heating and ultimately more intense climate extremes (droughts, coldwaves, floods, heatwaves, cyclones/hurricanes and tornadoes) register as shocks. Scientific attribution is clear on this planetary shift. In 2021, the US experienced 20 separate billion-dollar weather and climate disasters (including a coldwave event, wildfires, floods, tornadoes, tropical cyclones, and severe weather events), totaling about $145 billion (slightly cheaper than climate shocks in 2005 and

---

10 Li Yuan, 'Scientists warn of widespread drought in the 21st century'. Phys.org, 28 January 2022, https://phys.org/news/2022-01-scientists-widespread-drought-21st-century.html.

2017).¹¹ Madagascar, on top of a major drought in 2021 that left one million people in food stress, had to deal with four tropical cyclones (Emnati, Dumako, Batsirai and Ana) in early 2022, which destroyed about 90% of agricultural crops in some areas and affected many people.¹² These shocks are examples of climate injustices perpetuated by the ongoing emissions from using and burning fossil fuels. The most recent report from the IPCC Working Group III on Mitigation underlines the importance of urgently phasing out fossil fuels, including preventing new investments over the next three years (Intergovernmental Panel on Climate Change, 2022). Yet, from the preceding analysis on ecofascism, carbon investments and lock-ins continue.

The liberal democracies, as thin market democracies entrenching the sovereignty of capital, are in deep systemic crisis. It is more than legitimacy crises; it is about degeneration into authoritarian and neofascist politics (Williams and Satgar eds, 2021). The US military-industrial-security complex is now driving an agenda for a new Cold War with Russia and China, while the US public has no say over this plutocratic foreign and national security direction. Biden has also increased US military spending to $800 billion, unleashing further emissions on the world given the high carbon footprint of the US military, from point emissions in producing military technologies to waging warfare. The Russian offensive and the US proxy war in Ukraine not only intensifies this spiral, but also reinforces a global food shock (largely due to climate impacts on globalised value chains) that began in 2021, which has been amplified by supply-side constraints in wheat, fertiliser and cooking oil. The spike in food prices is also compounded by the spike in global oil prices. China has its own financialised overaccumulation challenges such as its huge housing bubble bursting (the Evergrande problem). Volatility in its stock exchanges and being ensnared increasingly into global rivalries with the US all add up to a possible conflict that can lead to mutual economic destruction, given how interlocked China and the US are in economic terms (trade, debt, investment).¹³ The convergence of anti-war (including anti-nuclear, anti-

---

11 Adam B. Smith, '2021 US billion-dollar weather and climate disasters in historical context'. Climate.gov, 24 January 2022, https://www.climate.gov/news-features/blogs/beyond-data/2021-us-billion-dollar-weather-and-climate-disasters-historical.

12 'Extreme weather and climate events heighten humanitarian needs in Madagascar and around the world'. ReliefWeb, 25 February 2022, https://reliefweb.int/report/madagascar/extreme-weather-and-climate-events-heighten-humanitarian-needs-madagascar-and.

13 Graham Allison, Nathalie Kiersznowski and Charlotte Fitzek, 'The great economic rivalry: China vs the US'. Belfer Center, 23 March 23, https://www.belfercenter.org/publication/great-economic-rivalry-china-vs-us.

chemical and anti-biological weapons), climate justice and food sovereignty forces in this moment is crucial.

We must situate the struggles for socio-economic and socio-ecological survival in South Africa and subsequent decades in this context of global political, economic and environmental instability.

The South African climate justice project

In April 2022, South Africa experienced a flash flood primarily located in the province of KwaZulu-Natal (KZN), killing close to 500 people, destroying nearly 4000 homes, displacing more than 40,000 people and affecting over six thousand schools. The cost of the damage is estimated at R17 billion. This flash flood comes on the heels of the worst drought in the history of the country (from 2014 to 2021), tornadoes, flash flooding (including in 2017, 2019, and late 2021 in KZN), landslides, and wildfires. The ANC government has not learned any lessons from these climate extremes and has not placed South Africa on a trajectory towards a deep, just transition. Instead, it has had a discursive approach to climate policy and multilateral negotiations for almost three decades, while continuing to support and expand a carbon-based minerals-energy complex. As the twelfth-highest carbon emitter in the world and with its intensive use of coal since the late nineteenth century, South Africa should have been trailblazing in terms of systemic adaptation and decarbonisation.

In 2018, when the UN issued its 1.5°C report, the initial core of organisations that make up the Climate Justice Charter (CJC) movement, over 60 organisations including trade unions, called on the South African president and parliament to convene an emergency sitting of parliament to deliberate on the science and climate policy implications of the report, given that South Africa is heating at twice the global average, which, if this were to continue to increase in linear fashion, would place it at a 3°C increase with a global 1.5°C overshoot.[14] The government ignored this call to place the country on a climate emergency footing to deal with climate-induced weather extremes. Subsequent calls made during South Africa's drought and in engagements with South Africa's parliament for mainstreaming a climate emergency response were also ignored.[15] In this context,

---

14 'Open letter to President Cyril Ramaphosa: Demand for emergency parliamentary sitting on UN 1.5°C report'. SAFSC, 23 October 2018, https://www.safsc.org.za/open-letter-to-president-cyril-ramaphosa-demand-for-emergency-parliamentary-sitting-on-un-1-5c-report/.

15 See media releases of the SAFSC, https://www.safsc.org.za/category/media2/.

the CJC movement has charged the president, his Cabinet, the premier of KZN, the mayor of eThekwini (Durban) and the deputy chairperson of the Climate Commission with culpable homicide for the loss of lives during the recent flooding. This refers to illegal and negligent action. This move by the CJC movement is an unprecedented attempt to secure climate justice utilising criminal law and has received extensive media coverage in the South African context.

The CJC movement has to be located within the making of global climate justice politics. There have been two cycles of climate justice resistance (from 2004 to 2015, then from 2015 to 2020). The second cycle of resistance spawned 1°C movements such as #NODAPL, Extinction Rebellion, Sunrise Movement, #FridaysForFuture, indigenous peoples' resistance to the destruction of the Amazon and the SAFSC. The SAFSC emerged during the worst drought in the history of South Africa. It mobilised with drought-impacted communities against high food prices and hunger. These basic needs of communities became the basis to link the climate crisis and injustice. In 2015, the SAFSC convened a hunger tribunal with trade unions, faith-based communities and the South African Human Rights Commission and picketed outside the JSE.[16] In 2016, it hosted drought speak-outs with drought-affected communities, built a campaign around #FoodPricesMustFall and led a bread march through the streets of Johannesburg.[17] In 2018, it developed a People's Food Sovereignty Act, which it took to South Africa's parliament and seven government departments demanding adoption.[18] All these concerns about climate extremes, a heating country and the need for systemic transformation were ignored by the ANC state.

By 2019, the SAFSC began working actively on a CJC process for South Africa. It convened dialogues with drought-affected communities, media, trade unions, social and environmental justice organisations, climate scientists, youth and children; activists were invited to write articles; conference platforms were created; and eventually a draft of the CJC was published online for public comment for the first half of 2020. It was finally launched by South Africa's

---

16 'Memorandum of demands to the Johannesburg Stock Exchange (JSE)'. SAFSC, 23 October 2018, https://www.safsc.org.za/hello-world/.

17 'Press release: statement from the national co-ordinating committee meeting'. SAFSC, 16 March 2018, https://www.safsc.org.za/wp-content/uploads/2016/03/SAFSC_NCC_Press-Release_11-March-2016.pdf.

18 'National peoples drought speak out and bread march memorandum'. 16 May 2016, https://www.safsc.org.za/national-peoples-drought-speak-out-and-bread-march-memorandum/; 'Press release: The ANC government is the national disaster in the water crisis'. SAFSC, 12 February 2018, https://www.safsc.org.za/press-release-the-anc-government-is-the-national-disaster-in-the-water-crisis-feb-2018/.

leading ecosocialist feminists on 28 August 2020.

Today, the CJC movement is endorsed by 261 organisations and is still growing.[19] The CJC was handed over to South Africa's parliament on 16 October 2020, World Food Day, with the demand that it be adopted as per section 234 of the South African Constitution, which provides for such charters. While this has not been conceded yet, the CJC is now a rallying point across progressive civil society, providing greater ideological coherence and a pluri-vision for what a democratic ecosocialist South Africa could look like. This is not a blueprint but an aspirational framework, a signpost, of where the country should go if we are to survive a climate-driven world.

The CJC is anti-capitalist, ecofeminist and decolonial; it is ultimately about emancipatory ecology. This distinguishes it from climate modernising capitalist approaches or deep ecology approaches, which tend to assume that green capitalism (markets, technology and finance) will solve the climate crisis and blame humans for the ecological crises of our time. Emancipatory ecology recognises that (i) humans are dependent on nature as socio-ecological beings; (ii) nature, like workers, is a source of value; and (iii) nature has limits. Moreover, the sources of knowledge in such an approach centre the tacit knowledge of the subaltern (workers, peasants, indigenous peoples, grassroots women and the victims of carbon capitalism more generally). Hence, the CJC embodies the aspirations of key subaltern forces shaping South African society. It contains transformative goals, principles to guide the deep, just transition, 14 systemic alternatives, a conception of a people-driven climate justice state and a strong commitment to renewing commoning practices and radical pan-Africanism, as part of building global solidarities (Satgar, 2022: 181–197).

In the light of the continuity of the ecofascist project globally and in South Africa, the CJC movement has entered a new strategic phase of campaigning.[20] In its strategic perspective document entitled 'What next for the Climate Justice Charter movement?', the CJC movement advances the following crucial aspects of a transformative political orientation:

- A theory of change centred on defending the commons and advancing deep transformation through democratic systemic reforms as part of accelerating and deepening the just transition: Democratic systemic reforms represent a constitutive form of power from below and can be calibrated as weak, strong, and transformative based on political contingencies and the relations

---

19 https://cjcm.org.za/endorse.
20 'What next for the CJCM?' CJC movement, https://cjcm.org.za/media/posts/3d0345f5-ec23-464c-8861-9e9ff2489cb9.

of forces. The politics of democratic systemic reforms will come to the fore in the context of pushing for the rapid phase out of fossil fuels; advancing decarbonisation in communities, workplaces and sectors; developing democratic plans to address climate risks; and advancing transformative regeneration in the context of climate shocks and state failure.

- Strategic transformation through a climate justice political project and developing policy content for an accelerated and deep, just transition from below: Currently, the CJC movement is busy developing the systemic alternatives in the charter into policies for South Africa's deep, just transition. The first policy on a universal basic income has been developed based on an intensive universal BIG campaign (the #UBIGNOW campaign during the Covid-19 pandemic) and in-depth economic modeling. Policies on the water commons, rights of nature, zero waste, socially owned renewable energy, and food sovereignty will be developed this year through public engagements.[21] In addition, the CJC movement is working on a macro-economic Climate Justice Deal for the country. This has involved collaboration with various heterodox economists.

- Crucial programmatic and tactical priorities: Currently, the CJC movement has an umbrella campaign 'to accelerate and deepen the just transition' and through this platform is building convergences and solidaristic actions, including working with communities leading food sovereignty pathway building, frontline organisations standing up to offshore oil and gas extraction, organisations campaigning against nuclear power, developing a people's just transition planning tool (which will inform a campaign for the rapid phase out of fossil fuels), working with communities facing water crises and building a legal network for climate justice. The CJC movement in South Africa is not about importing or downloading a template for its struggle and strategic politics. It is building on and going beyond traditions of mass politics prevalent in the South African context. In coming months, the CJC movement will take the leap to become a formal mass-based member-driven organisation of movements, community organisations and individuals grounded in local organising. It will also be debating and clarifying how to ensure that South Africa's 2024 national elections are climate justice elections.

---

21 'Policies'. CJC movement, https://cjcm.org.za/policies.

Challenges to planetise the movement to end ecocidal capitalism

The CJC movement, like climate justice forces in other parts of the world, is attempting to scale up and intensify a third cycle of climate justice resistance (2020 to the present), but it faces certain common challenges. These include:

- Going beyond single issue, symbolic and apocalyptic climate politics. The climate crisis is multifaceted and cannot be overcome in a piecemeal manner. Neither can it be overcome by mere performative denunciation, shaming and endless critique. Symbolic climate politics has reached its limits. We are running out of time and climate justice forces have to present concrete answers to accelerate and deepen the just transition. They have to assail power structures, contest power and lead from above and from below with concrete answers. We are now in the era of climate elections. This does not mean narrow electoralism or endless bottom-up building. Working strategically with this complexity is the only antidote to the other extreme of apocalyptic climate politics that debilitates transformative praxis with its doomsday discourses and paralysis talk. The world needs inspirational examples and political tipping point interventions that democratically leapfrog societies beyond carbon capitalism.

- Climate justice activism has to be about transpolitics, ensuring workers go beyond narrow economistic demands, feminists beyond women's oppression and environmentalists beyond specific environmental problems. Bridges have to be built, convergences cemented and a common programmatic solidarity has to be engendered as part of tackling the dangerous climate contradiction while addressing class exploitation and multiple oppressions. We all have to be intersectional as well as anti-capitalist.

- Climate justice politics has to go beyond crowd politics, theatre outside climate summits and national cloning of international trends. Though transnational solidarities are important, this is no substitute for national movement building, which has to take centre stage in the third cycle of resistance. Powerful national movements have to be supported, encouraged and institutionalised systematically. There are no shortcuts given the scale and pace of transformation, and the urgency of calling for accelerated and deep, just transitions now. Such movements have to build capacities to create new ecological societies, advance climate justice projects and through democratic systemic reforms start realising the making of democratic ecofeminist-socialist societies now.

- Finally, climate justice forces have to rally and actively support the building of a climate justice bloc of governments, workers, peoples and movements. More active solidarities have to be built that cut across the global South and North to ensure climate pariahs can be undermined from within and from outside. Most importantly, such a bloc has to accelerate the realisation of a global deep, just transition and the making of a new planetary climate emergency institutional architecture for a world entering permanent crisis and uncertainty.

A shorter version of this article was published in the *Monthly Review*, 74, 3, July–August 2022.

Transformative Politics and the New Global Left Imaginary

Alternatives to Neoliberal Globalisation

Introduction

FOR MORE THAN THREE DECADES, neoliberal globalisation has been resisted but yet it has not disappeared and still holds sway as a class project of finance and transnationalising capital. At the same time, the forms of resistance challenging neoliberal globalisation have been variegated, sometimes episodic and generally seem like disjointed flashpoints. This chapter seeks to give analytical coherence to the forms of resistance against neoliberal globalisation and the alternatives that have been championed. The starting point is recognising the internal contradictions of a crisis-ridden neoliberal globalisation project, which is at the same time being constituted and advanced by material forms of power centred on corporations and the US state. Despite financialised booms and busts marking the history of neoliberalism and deeper systemic instability due to the power of finance, as witnessed between 2007 and 2009 in the US and globally, crisis has been institutionalised within the global political economy. The forms of class power buttressing and reproducing neoliberal globalisation need to be understood in order to appreciate the challenges confronting alternatives to neoliberal globalisation.

Moreover, this contribution explores and elaborates on a Marxist and neo-Gramscian approach to global resistance and the alternatives being championed as part of these struggles. While recognising the labour-capital dialectic in Marx and Gramsci's emphasis on aggregating power on the terrain of civil society, these theoretical approaches are developed further to locate resistance conjuncturally (in relation to the neoliberal class project) and within cycles of resistance. In a sense, a broader optic is developed to understand the agency of contemporary resistance while also being more historically specific. This chapter delineates forms of counter-hegemonic resistance to neoliberal globalisation. Such an analysis demonstrates that struggles are occurring on a wide range of fronts and are imbricated in challenging various contradictions of contemporary capitalism thus affirming a post-neoliberal imagination that is anti-capitalist and transformative.

Counter-hegemonic resistances, while affirming crucial alternative possibilities and pathways, are still contingent. They are in the process of being realised and have been expressed through three cycles of resistance, over the past three decades, that have not been able to displace neoliberal globalisation on a global scale. Instead, inequality and climate crises are worsening. Moreover, right-wing forces that are part of ethno-nationalist movements, religious fundamentalist forces, pro-neoliberal parties and authoritarian societies are also contesting to shape the direction of the crisis-ridden neoliberal global political economy in the current conjuncture. Finally, this chapter concludes by situating the limits and challenges facing transformative alternatives. As counter-hegemonic class projects, new horizons of thinking have been opened up, together with capacities and political practices. However, the challenge of capitalist class power reproducing neoliberal globalisation still remains, albeit being contested at this moment in history by a broader array of right-wing forces.

Neoliberalisms and class power

The history of neoliberalism reveals it to be more than a set of ideas about championing markets. Instead, it is a capitalist class project seeking to remake the global economy through restructuring the state, national economy, state–civil society relations, ecological relations and international relations. It has impacted on both the centre and peripheries of global capitalism. The question of how it became a class project remaking the global political economy has given rise to various explanatory approaches. For some analysts, it was a mental model that diffused to different parts of the world from the centres (Roy et al., 2007). Klein (2007) argues that the ascendance of neoliberalism has to do with the advent of disaster capitalism. This means a capitalism introduced in the context of coups, climate shocks, wars and deepening economic crisis. Disaster capitalism harnesses a shock-and-awe approach to imposing an inherently unstable form of financialised capitalism. For other analysts, neoliberalism as a class project reflected a conjunctural shift in which capitalist class power was being remade.[1] This was informed by the over-accumulation crisis of the early 1970s, the end of the Gold Standard, the emergence of the Organization of the Petroleum

---

1   There is a vast body of literature affirming this analytical approach. See Plehwe et al. (2006), Leys (2008) and Gill and Cutler (2014).

Exporting Countries (OPEC), the call for a New International Economic Order by newly independent states in the global South and the vicissitudes of the Cold War, including the rise of military dictatorships as in Chile, the ascendance of Reagan and Thatcher in the 1980s and the fall of the Soviet Union.

In this conjuncture, the rise of neoliberalism as a class project remade the global political economy such that the twentieth-century left projects and imaginations were completely defeated. Besides Sovietised socialism (and all its copies), social democracy and revolutionary nationalism were also pushed back. The Fordist mode of accumulation gave way to a globalised, flexible and post-Fordist mode. The division of labour was remade and trade union power has been increasingly undermined through precariatisation. State–civil society relations have also been remade in the context of structurally adjusting societies to the imperatives of transnationalising capital. For the US, this has meant globalising the power of the dollar–Wall Street regime and remaking finance as a crucial coefficient of US imperial power (Gowan, 1999). In this context, neoliberalism has taken on various meanings and valences in different institutional settings. Within the IMF and World Bank, for instance, neoliberalism went through various iterations from debt-based adjustment in the 1980s and 1990s, to post-2000 approaches centred on good governed states and poverty reduction approaches. This is different from the competitiveness-centred neoliberalism of the WEF, for instance (Carrol and Carson, 2006). Moreover, in national contexts neoliberalism has been mutating and articulating with national ideologies in complex ways. Neoliberalism has had to speak in local vernaculars, drawing on local political traditions, while affirming its core ideological tenets to achieve deep globalisation. In South Africa, this has certainly been the case with the ruling ANC talking the language of NDR while implementing neoliberal structural reforms consistently over the past two decades. Essentially, neoliberalism can only be understood in the plural as neoliberalisms and it is a class project to achieve the deep globalisation of societies while reproducing the power of transnational capital and the US imperial state. Below is an attempt to map various forms of neoliberal class power at work in advancing neoliberalism as a class project. These forms of power work through social forces and are expressed through political and ideological practices (see Table 1).

Table 1: Typology of neoliberal power

Forms of Capital's Class Power	Social Forces Constituting Forms of Class Power	Political and Ideological Practice
Structural power	Corporations, multilateral institutions	Use of market power, global mobility and regulatory standards
Direct power	Super lobbies, business organisations	Financial influence on policy, politicians and parties
Discursive power	Think tanks, sections of the media, academics, social media	Legitimises neoliberal discourses and ideas, while also constructing counter narratives to alternatives
Constitutional power	Political parties, judiciaries, technocrats in the state	Treaties, new constitutions and laws that reshape the role and functions of the state in keeping with marketisation
Imperial power	US State and its allies	Diplomacy, standard setting, coercive power (through coups and military interventions) and active undermining of alternatives

Power in a capitalist society is relational and is constituted in the capital-labour relationship. Power does not automatically grow out of capital's ownership of material resources. Instead, capital uses its ownership of material resources to constitute power through various social practices. Empirically, there are five forms of capitalist class power reproducing neoliberal globalisation.[2] These forms of power have remade national, regional and global political economies. Put differently, states, accumulation strategies, state–civil society relations and international relations have been remade to incorporate the financial- and market-centred imperatives of neoliberal globalisation. Various social forces, from corporations, multilateral institutions, business organisations, political

---

2   Gill (2003: 93–108), a neo-Gramscian theorist, develops in his work the idea of structural and direct power of capital. Much later with Cutler (2014) he introduces constitutional power. I expand on this to include discursive and imperial power.

parties, judiciaries, technocrats, the US state and its allies, have all played a role in advancing financialised market reforms while undermining any alternatives that threaten this class project.

The first form of constituted class power is structural power. This relates to the control corporations have of market share, value chains and their global mobility. This gives transnational corporations leverage over states to bargain conditions and terms for investments. Regulatory standards set by multilateral institutions also ensure property relations and risk to capital is always mitigated. For instance, intellectual property rights regimes are promoted through the WTO. The second form of constituted class power can be termed direct power. This entails the use of finance to buy out policy agendas through enlisting political support through politicians and parties. For instance, in the US super lobbies bring together the power of big corporations in particular sectors of the economy to shape various policies in pharmaceuticals, food, finance and military procurement. This skews decision-making and resource allocations.

The third form of constituted class power is discursive power. Discursive power has been about building capacities to shape narratives and discourses that legitimate neoliberal globalisation and concomitant reforms as solutions to national economic challenges, while at the same time, discrediting alternatives. The role of think-tanks, sections of the media, academics and social media has been central in this regard (Carroll and Carson, 2006). A good example is the WEF, made up of the thousand most powerful corporations in the world. The WEF is also a think-tank for transnational capital and its knowledge tools such as its *Competitiveness Reports* or its Davos forum deliberations are constantly transmitted into global public spheres. Its discourses are framed as in the interest of the global and national economies.

The fourth form of constituted class power is about constitutionalising the legal arrangements that lock in and deepen neoliberal market reforms. New constitutions, part of the third democratisation wave, since 1974 have locked in the independence of the reserve banks of most countries to manage inflation targeting as the core of monetary policy, for instance. Regional treaties like the Lisbon Treaty have been crucial in locking in neoliberal reforms within the EU. This has had serious implications for the redistribution of power between European states and the EU. The fifth form of constituted power is imperial power wielded through the most powerful capitalist state in the interstate system, the US state (Soederberg, 2004a) and its allies. This has entrenched and secured the reproduction of neoliberal globalisation as a class project. The US as the dominant capitalist state has effectively utilised various coefficients of power to reproduce the Washington Consensus since the end of the Cold War. For countries like Venezuela, championing twenty-first-century socialism, the US actively supported a coup against one of its democratically elected presidents in 2002 and it has continued to try to destabilise Venezuela (Wilpert, 2007).

In counterfactual terms, if these five forms of class power were not constituted then the neoliberal class project cannot be reproduced. These forms of power have enabled and facilitated the neoliberal class project, despite its failures as expressed through inequality, unemployment, underdevelopment, climate crisis and precariatisation.

Historical capitalism, conjunctures and counter-hegemonic resistance

Capitalism is a historical system or civilisation. While thinkers like Marx have understood capitalism in terms of its abstract laws of accumulation, historical capitalism has been shaped by different dynamics in different historical periods. What follows is a periodisation of capitalist civilisation (Satgar, 2015b: 28–29). Each of the stages of historical capitalism delineated here can be further delineated into conjunctures and phases based on historical, political, geographic and economic contingencies. Conjunctures and phases shape these stages of capitalism and will be elaborated on further below. For our immediate purposes, the important point relates to the making and existence of capitalist civilisation and more specifically recognition that this takes place through particular non-teleological historical stages.

Capitalist civilisation has been constituted over the past 500 years and has been marked by three major historical stages that include developments in the forms of imperial power, technological development, ideational shifts and struggles from below:

1. Mercantile accumulation (1400s–1800s) involved a prototype of capitalism linked to slavery, colonial conquest, trade and exchange. Sea-based expansion takes off in this period, supported through merchant capital and empires such as the Spanish, Dutch and British. The Reformation happens in Europe which challenges the control of the Roman Catholic Church, the Dutch Revolution (1566–1609), English Revolution (1637–1660), and the Enlightenment (c.1650–1800) all shape this stage of expansion;

2. Monopoly industrial accumulation (c.1750s–1980) involved struggles against land enclosures, technological innovation such as the steam engine, the emergence of factories and increasing concentration and centralisation of capital. Colonial expansion continued but was also rolled back by the American Revolution (1775–1783), the Slave Revolution in Haiti (1791–1804) and the Bolivarian Revolution (1810–1830) against Spanish rule in South America. The French Revolution (1789–1794) also shakes up the heartlands of capitalism. Mid-Victorian competitive capitalism gives way to national monopolies. The Italian nation state is founded (1859–1870), Germany is unified (1864–1871), the American Civil War (1861–1865), the Paris Commune (1871), the Scramble for Africa (1870–1914) and the first Great Depression (1873–96) happen. National monopolies displace competition into national rivalries. The period sees World War I (1914–1918), the second Great Depression (1929–1941), World War 2 (1939–1945) and the end of British hegemony and the Ottoman Empire. The Mexican Revolution (1910–1920) and a wave of socialist revolutions including Russia (1917), China (1949), and Cuba (1959) and national liberation struggles shape the peripheries. US-centred hegemony, the Cold War (1947–1991), Fordism, the Keynesian welfare state and the end of colonialism also determine the character of this stage;
3. Transnational techno-financial accumulation (1973 to the present) emerges as social democracy reaches its limits and stagflation kicks in (1973); there is a wave of struggle (1968–1975) in Western Europe, Prague and the US. The US suffers a defeat in Vietnam and the Nicaraguan Revolution (1979) takes place. There is a shift to containerisation, information and communications technology, post-Fordism and global financialised restructuring. Transnational class structures emerge, the Cold War ends, formal political apartheid ends in South Africa (1994), democratisation sweeps through Africa, parts of Asia, Latin America and the former Soviet Union, while US hegemony is tenuous but increasingly centred on financialised expansion and military power. Power is increasingly diffused with the rise of regional state-society complexes such as China and Russia and since 9/11 the war on terror expands. Global rivalries come to the fore in this phase as systemic crisis tendencies deepen. Anti-neoliberal and anti-globalisation movements emerge as central to rolling back neoliberalisation and saving planetary life.

In the twentieth century, the dominant form of social-democratic capitalism, in the West, was organised through a social contract encompassing the welfare state, Fordist accumulation and mass consumption. Imperial power also buttressed this class project. Moreover, social democracy as a class project defined a conjuncture for Western democracies. This meant social and political forces in these societies operated within a consensus to manage and lead these societies to achieve the values, goals and institutional basis of these class projects. Economic, political and military relations of force were conditioned by these class projects; social democracy was a terrain of struggle for social forces. In this context, hegemonic and counter-hegemonic struggles emerged, based on the building of class and social alliances, within rival historic blocs. Hegemony was never permanent and democratic conditions allowed for rivalries. This also meant that each conjuncture, with its own class project, went through various phases. Social democracy in the West as a class project lasted for about three decades since post-World War 2 and was contested by socialists, liberals and communists, each bringing different class and social interests to the fore to shape social democracy. In the end, social democracy was co-opted by neoliberalism.

Neoliberalism emerged as a hegemonic class project through the political ascendance of Reagan and Thatcher in the 1980s (Gallas, 2016). They valorised possessive individualism (for Thatcher society was over), competition and the power of markets. A programme of social engineering was unleashed, which destroyed the main ideological planks of social democracy. The neoliberal conjuncture in turn has been through various phases and defining moments of struggle. The first phase (1980–1990) was marked by the hegemonic response of neoliberalism to the economic crisis. Unions were pushed back in the US and the UK, revolutionary nationalisms in the peripheries were defeated through debt-based financing and the Cold War arms race was used effectively to outspend the Soviet Bloc and bankrupt it. The second phase (1990–2007) ensured the deepening and expansion of liberalised financial markets; the Washington Consensus was exported with post-Cold War triumphalism as the end of history and through shock therapy in places like Russia; social democracy was completely co-opted as 'third-way' neoliberalism; neoliberal crisis management was used to open up economies in Asia; free trade areas expanded; and poverty reduction, good governance agendas and the millennium development goals became central to modest redistributive efforts to ensure trickle down from above in countries of the global South. The third phase (2007 to the present) is characterised by a general crisis and stagnation. Bail-outs for banks and finance institutions maintained the power of finance, austerity measures kicked in to pass on costs of the crisis to workers and the poor, inequality and precariousness led to major fault-lines in neoliberal Europe including the British decision to leave the EU through Brexit, and ethno-nationalist movements, racist border regimes and authoritarian politics established themselves in various countries. Neofascism is on the rise in a world that is still committed to neoliberal capitalism.

Counter-hegemonic resistance to neoliberalism has been both defensive and offensive. This is for two reasons. First, neoliberalism, as a class project, has been about ensuring the state, economy, society and ecological relations are subsumed by the market. The role of capital to organise all these spheres has been enabled by the power of capital. This means the commodifying logic of neoliberal capitalism has no limits. Defending the gains of the welfare state or decent work has been a crucial defensive struggle to place limits on neoliberal capitalism. As a result, these struggles have also been about defending alternatives. Second, neoliberalisation, as a process of marketising everything, has engendered new contradictions as a crisis-ridden neoliberalism has pressed ahead. Many of these contradictions cannot be resolved by neoliberalism as they are central to its reproduction. Inequality and climate change are two crucial examples. This, in turn, has enabled more offensive struggles to emerge to advance counter-hegemonic alternatives.

Forms of counter-hegemonic resistance and alternatives

Counter-hegemonic resistance to neoliberal globalisation (see Table 2) has expressed itself around various contradictions within the financialised form of capitalism engendered. This has happened at different levels of the global political economy, sometimes in national, regional or global spaces.[3] Moreover, different forms of social agency have to come to the fore ranging from movements, communities, activist groups, policy NGOs, public intellectuals, trade unions and even governments. Some have transnational, cross-country or just international reach. The types of alternatives that have emerged are shaped by the contradiction being confronted. In the case of defensive struggles against neoliberal power, alternatives have been more about defending gains made historically. For example, anti-commodification struggles have been about defending public goods like health, education and welfare. Gender oppression has led to affirmation of rights against discrimination, for instance.

---

3   There is a vast literature on the agentic forces, resistance practices, levels of contestation and alternatives that have been championed. See Houtart and Polet (2001), Fisher and Ponniah (2003), Cavanagh and Mander (2004) and Carroll and Sarker (2016).

Anti-exploitation struggles have confronted precarious work with demands to affirm worker rights and decent work. Offensive struggles against neoliberal class power have engendered systemic alternatives from below and above. From below, social forces have championed pathways for solidarity economies, food sovereignty, energy democracy, clean energy public transport systems and more as part of system change in the context of the climate crisis. These systemic alternatives are about advancing a deep, just transition to sustain life in the context of the climate crisis. On the other hand, some offensive struggles from above constituted fully fledged class projects in opposition to the neoliberal class project. This has entailed rejecting deep globalisation while managing relations with global capitalism on the terms of national and regional interests. Venezuela's rejection of the Free Trade Area of the Americas, an extension of the North American Free Trade Agreement (NAFTA), is one example. At the same time, the increasing role of Merosur (the Southern Common Market) and ALBA (Bolivarian Alliance for the Peoples of our America) in defining regionalisation in opposition to the free trade model of NAFTA are also instructive.

Table 2: Counter-Hegemonic Resistance and Alternatives

Form of Resistance	Social Forces	Alternatives to Neoliberalism
Anti-commodification	Movements, communities, activist groups, policy NGOs	Public goods, defense of the commons and people's land
Anti-oppression	Communities, movements, activist groups, policy NGOs, public intellectuals, trade unions	Anti-discrimination, solidarity, affirming rights, recognise unpaid labour, gender consciousness, economic inclusion
Anti-exploitation	Trade unions, worker committees, activist groups, policy NGOs	Decent work, insourcing, worker rights

Form of Resistance	Social Forces	Alternatives to Neoliberalism
Anti-extractivism	Communities, cross country networks, movements, activist groups, policy NGOs	No to mining, 'keep the coal and fossil fuel in the ground', divestment, polluter pays
Confronting global power	Movements, transnational networks, activist groups, international policy NGOs, public intellectuals	Reform of multilateral institutions, scrap debt, development not free trade
Advancing deep just transitions through systemic alternatives	Community organisations, networks, movements, trade unions, policy NGOS, parties	Food Sovereignty, solidarity economy, climate jobs, basic income grant, socially owned renewable energy, clean energy public transport systems
Counter-hegemonic deglobalisation/ delinking	Governments, parties, alliances, movements, policy NGOs, communities, public intellectuals	Reclaim sovereignty, alternative accumulation models, new regional blocs and deep democracy

Counter-hegemonic struggles are forms of resistance that have to be understood as part of cycles of resistance (see Figure 1). While individual struggles are important, whether defensive or offensive, such struggles need to be located in a larger framework of understanding resistance. Generally, counter-hegemonic struggles are given a national or particular salience. However, as part of confronting neoliberal globalisation over three decades, certain struggles have shaped the conjuncture. This means such struggles have given momentum to political forces and have shifted relations of force to some extent against capital, have inspired other struggles, incited a broader imagination; and have laid the basis for political capacities to be developed for more transformation.

Figure 1: Three Cycles of Counter-Hegemonic Resistance and Alternatives

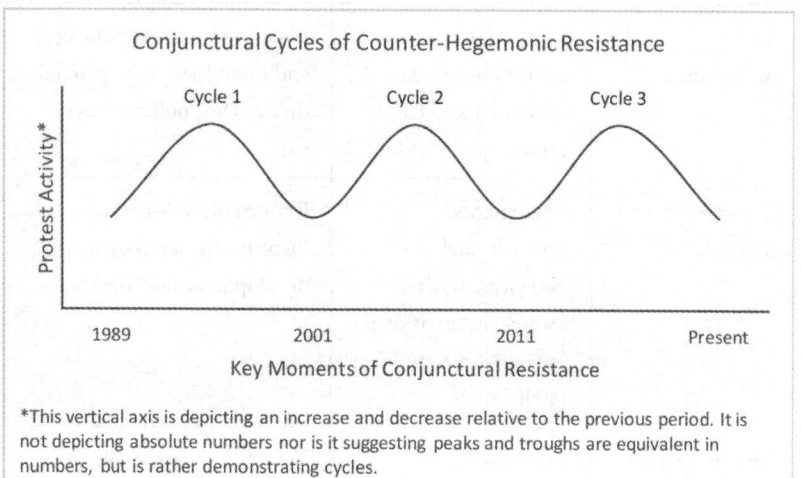

*This vertical axis is depicting an increase and decrease relative to the previous period. It is not depicting absolute numbers nor is it suggesting peaks and troughs are equivalent in numbers, but is rather demonstrating cycles.

Cycle 1: 1989–2001

The first cycle of resistance begins with the Caracazo in Venezuela in 1989, which was against the imposition of an IMF-led structural adjustment programme, particularly increases in the price of gasoline and transport (Robertson, 2014). Hundreds were killed in the week of mass protests. In this context, Hugo Chavez emerged as a coup leader. The rise of the Zapatistas in 1994 against NAFTA and their declaration of war against the Mexican state, heralded the emergence of a movement that was willing to consider armed struggle defensively to protect land and ensure indigenous control of local resources (Collier and Quarateillo, 2005). The Zapatistas went on also to use civil resistance tactics creatively. In 1996, in Kerala, India, the left in power decentralised 40% of the provincial state budget, as part of the People's Campaign for Democratic Decentralisation and laid the basis for a participatory form of local governance (Parayil, 2000). In the same year, indigenous movements in Ecuador also openly challenged and created a crisis for the neoliberal state.

In South Africa, in 1998, the TAC succeeded in securing HIV treatment to prevent mother-to-child transmission and secured a legal victory to compel the South African state to decommodify AIDS drugs and produce generics. This was a challenge for global pharmaceutical corporations. The rise of transnational activism made its mark in 1999 when Seattle became the theatre of mass street protests against the newly formed WTO and its liberalising approach to global trade (Mertes, 2004). In the same year water wars began in Bolivia against transnational and privatised control. This struggle had dramatic consequences for the realignment of forces in Bolivia, particularly the indigenous movement. In 2001, Argentina's economy collapsed, after two decades of intense neoliberalisation, mass street politics brought down several governments while workers took over stressed or abandoned factories, neighbourhood assemblies emerged, and new movements of the unemployed also shaped pathways for alternatives (Starr, 2005).

Case study: From water wars to a new constitution for Bolivia, 2000 (counter-hegemonic de-globalisation)

Bolivia has a long history of left resistance and mass politics. In the twentieth century, this was marked by a programmatic and strategic politics centred on class, nation and, much later, democracy. Underpinning this was the power of organised workers in trade unions who, in turn, provided programmatic support to left parties that represented their interests. Nationalisation and land reform have been crucial ideological pillars of the left project. At the same time, Bolivia has a majority indigenous population, which has never ruled their society since colonialism. However, from the 1980s this began to change as indigenous peasant farmers and communities started to organise their own mass organisations.

Bolivia also experienced rampant neoliberalisation and indigenous resistance was crucial against this. One of the most iconic and decisive battles was against the privatisation of a water utility in the city of Cochabamba in 2000 (Dangl, 2007). Famously, this is also known as the water war. This struggle was waged by an amalgam of democratic mass forces, brought together by the Co-ordinator for the Defence of Water and Life. This coalition married forms of networked and direct democracy among various social forces. The struggles that ensued against Bechtel, a US transnational, given a contract by the Bolivian government to privatise the water system, led to a reversal of this arrangement. The mass mobilisation and pressure from this also realigned political forces in Bolivia and gave momentum for the organisations in this struggle to demand a constituent assembly to secure a constitution that affirmed direct and representative democracy. While the story of Bolivia does not end here, it does reveal how democratic mass agency can defend vital resources central to the needs of a society against neoliberal commodification. However, in the Bolivian case the rise of the Movement for Socialism and Evo Morales to the presidency in 2005 threw up many challenges. First, the space for independent mass organising. Second, the disabling effect of state-centric practices through a post-neoliberal state. Third, the challenge of keeping democratic practices alive.

Cycle 2: 2001–2011

The formation of the WSF in 2001 gave a major boost to transnational activism (Fisher and Ponniah, 2003). It provided a space for the solidarity of national and transnational social movements and advanced an emancipatory utopian imagination that strengthened various systemic alternatives to neoliberal globalisation and affirmed an alternate globalisation practice in various national contexts. At the same time, various left and centre-left governments were elected into power in different countries in Latin America (Brazil, Venezuela, Bolivia and Uruguay, for instance) and this inaugurated what has been termed the pink tide (Sader, 2011). These governments were not united in their approach to resisting neoliberalism, but were certainly wanting to affirm national and regional development priorities. For Brazil's Workers' Party (PT) government, this was about a neo-developmentalism that included more redistributive reforms, active industrial policy and limited land reform while maintaining a globalised posture. For Venezuela's government, this was about a break with neoliberalism and the advance of a twenty-first-century socialism. In 2003, based on the momentum developed by the solidarity economy network in Brazil, the Brazilian Forum for Solidarity Economy was established. Together, with the Secretariat for the Solidarity Economy in government, Brazil began trailblazing a new way forward for self-managed and democratic enterprises to achieve a structural space of their own in the Brazilian economy.

Another crucial systemic alternative championed by La Via Campesina gained further momentum with the adoption of the Nyeleni Declaration of 2007, by 500 delegates from 80 countries, who committed to advancing food sovereignty. This is an alternative to food security and corporate control of food systems. The year 2009 intensified protests against the financial crisis in Iceland, also referred to as the pots and pans revolution. This led to the largest protests in Icelandic history, the fall of a right-wing government and eventually led to a new constitution. Given the deepening crisis of climate change multilateral negotiations, with Obama hijacking the process in Copenhagen and shifting more countries to a pledge and review approach, Bolivia hosted the World People's Conference on Climate Change and the Rights of Mother

Earth in April 2010. This catalysed the climate justice movement, affirmed the patriarchal nature of climate injustice and provided a platform for various systemic alternatives to be championed. Bolivia attempted to lock industrialised countries into a climate debt framework to legally compel them to bring down their emissions, while affirming the rights of mother Earth for all living creatures. In 2010 several movements came to the fore in the uprisings in Arab and North African countries (Hanieh, 2013).

Case study: Climate jobs, 2001 (systemic alternative)

The one million climate jobs campaign emerged out of the organising efforts of eight trade unions in the UK. As a campaign, there was a strong realisation about the need to connect the climate crisis to the challenge of high levels of unemployment, particularly among youth. The proposal envisaged the decarbonisation of work through renewable energy, efforts to increase the energy efficiency of homes and public buildings by insulating them, the implementation of cheap, clean public transport, and the development of green skills through training programmes. The research agenda of the campaign has scanned and mapped the carbon-based sectors of the UK economy and has tried to demonstrate alternative pathways for climate jobs. The first research report was published in 2009 and a more recent report has been put out in 2014. For trade unions, this has entailed having discussions about the science of climate change, the challenges of a heating world and thinking about practical solutions like climate jobs. Union structures have also been invited to adopt motions in support of the campaign.

The campaign platform has grown to also tackle fossil fuel extraction, disinvestment and aviation. For trade unions, this has placed them at the centre of climate justice struggles. The campaign had its first event, a protest against Bush's rejection of the Kyoto Protocol in 2001, and since 2005 they have held an annual march for climate. Moreover, the campaign for climate jobs was then embraced by South Africa in 2011 by an environmental, labour and social movements coalition. A similar process of research, trade union education and public engagement has emerged in South Africa (Ashley, 2018). In short, the climate jobs alternative is about decent work, while seeking to bring down carbon emissions and address the climate crisis as part of the deep, just transition. It is an idea whose time has come, but is plagued by one big challenge. This relates to winning government support, resources, and policy commitment to roll out climate jobs.

Cycle 3: 2011 to the present

The year 2011 witnessed a massive upsurge of mass resistance against authoritarian and neoliberal regimes in the Arab world. Some have referred to this as the Arab Spring. Assemblies in Tahrir Square, in Egypt, also had a knock-on effect globally (Mason, 2012). In Spain, the Indignados (also known as the anti-austerity movement), grew out of various youth and social networks and occupied squares in Spain from 15 May (Della Porta, 2015). They challenged the high unemployment rates and precariousness amongst youth in a crisis-ridden Spanish economy. This struggle also spawned a left party, PODEMOS, which contributed to the end of two-party control in the Spanish political system. In April in India, an anti-corruption movement rose using non-violent tactics like fasts and demanded reforms to give citizens more power to hold government officials accountable. Systemic corruption in India needed to be confronted with greater transparency, accountability and citizens' power. The civil resistance of this movement rolled on for months, even into 2012. Coming out of this movement was the formation of the Common Person's Party. In September 2011, the Occupy Wall Street movement took off in Zuccotti Park (Chomsky, 2012). This occupation garnered symbolic power against the power of finance on Wall Street. After the Zuccotti Park Assembly was shut down by the authorities in early November, #Occupy gained expression in local struggles against foreclosure, student debt and continued to challenge banks and corporations. The meme: we are the 99% versus the 1%, was globalised and drew attention to the deep inequalities in the US and globally.

In South Africa, the climate justice movement, gathered in the People's Space, alongside the UN COP17, also made a compelling case for system change. Moreover, the crisis of multilateral negotiations, the commitment to false solutions and the lack of systemic alternatives were confirmed in this COP. Climate justice forces were increasingly looking to national spaces to advance deep, just transitions. Continued state violence against African Americans and systemic racism gave rise to the #BlackLivesMatter (BLM) network in 2013. BLM is considered the new civil rights movement in the US. Powerful student protests rocked South Africa in 2015 with demands for decolonisation, decommodification and #insourcing. The Dakota Access Pipeline project, with its ambitions to move fossil fuels across various communities, evoked massive grassroots resistance. The Standing Rock Sioux community established an encampment, in April 2016, as a point of convergence of resistance, attracting thousands of supporters. Standing Rock has become an icon of indigenous peoples struggling against ecocidal fossil capital in different parts of the Americas. On 23 June 2016, an overwhelming majority of British citizens chose to leave the EU. This came to be known as Brexit. It is generally understood as a deeply nationalist response to a failed project of neoliberal regionalisation. However, in the complex cauldron of UK politics, the British Labour Party is going through a grassroots-driven resurgence led by left leader Jeremy Corbyn. Across the Atlantic, Bernie Sanders has continued to build a new deal style movement within US society.

Case study: #FeesMustFall, 2015–2017 (anti-commodification)

The #FeesMustFall protests in South Africa took off in October of 2015 (Booysen, 2016). This was preceded by decades of financial exclusions at universities in South Africa as a result of creeping cuts in state funding. Neoliberal macro-economic management put a massive squeeze on universities, such that cost-cutting and fee-based financing became central to how universities functioned. The protests demanded free and quality education, insourcing of outsourced workers and epistemological decolonisation. On the last demand, students wanted an education that spoke to the realities of their societies and drew on thinkers, theories and disciplinary knowledge informed by South African society. After three years of struggle, the #FeesMustFall movement successfully secured insourcing of university service staff at some universities, like the University of the Witwatersrand, a declaration by the national government that free higher education would be introduced and major decolonising initiatives at numerous universities around curriculum, culture, and changing names of buildings. #FeesMustFall united university constituencies in 2015 and became a symbolic rallying point across society. However, by 2016 and into 2017 the use of violent tactics, particularly the demand for universities to shut down, was met with strong force by the state, including the incarceration of numerous student activists and securitisation of many university campuses. Public support was also lost for students in the context of the firebombing of libraries and university buildings.

In many ways, the student struggle became a battleground between the ruling party and opposition parties, some of whom tried to instrumentalise the student struggle.[4] However, reclaiming the public university in the context of rampant commercialising of public enterprises, reforms promoting marketisation and in the context of a society that has been on a neoliberal trajectory for over 20 years, while inequalities have been worsening, is a

---

4   See   https://mg.co.za/article/2017-04-04-the-effs-wrecking-ball-politics-is-fascist-rather-than-left.

massive victory. But, this victory is accompanied by three challenges. First, to ensure the state provides the necessary resources for higher education in general (including training colleges) and such measures are phased in so that universities are not undermined. Second, solidaristic action with trade unions more broadly to win insourcing of labour across the economy. Third, advancing intellectual decolonisation recognises that there is a universalistic aspect to knowledge; that is, knowledge does not belong to a particular race group but is human knowledge. Resisting the commodification of higher education is about defending a public good for the benefit of society. Neoliberalism stands against the needs of society and for privatising everything including education. This reinforces exclusion and inequality.

Limits to counter-hegemonic alternatives

While counter-hegemonic resistance has spawned various alternatives to neoliberal globalisation, this has not been sufficient to ensure the success of these alternatives. At the same time, as inequality and climate crises intersect, such transformative alternatives are not necessarily being embraced as the way forward for societies. In this regard, various limits stand in the way of realising such alternatives. The first limit, already alluded to, is the forms of capitalist power that reproduce neoliberal globalisation. Despite neoliberalism inducing the worst economic crisis in the history of modern capitalism (2007–2009), sometimes referred to as the Great Financial Crisis, it has not been displaced or even abandoned by dominant forces. Instead, the forms of class power underpinning neoliberal globalisation – structural, direct, discursive, constitutional and imperial – have continued to buttress neoliberalism. The outcome of the recent economic crisis was further austerity and a squeeze on workers, the precarious and the poor. Banks were bailed out, bonuses were given to CEOs of investment houses, the US ensured global co-ordination of macro-economic policies through G20 countries and the underlying financial dynamics that caused the crisis have not been addressed. The world is now expecting the next big financialised bubble to grow and burst.

The second limit on the realisation of counter-hegemonic alternatives is the emergence of an ethno-nationalist and religious right wing. The precariousness and deep inequality that has accompanied three decades of marketisation of societies have made sections of many societies extremely desperate. In this context fear-mongering, nationalist fervour and othering are used to realign political constituencies. Combined with a post-truth public sphere, media spectacle and rampant populism, new right-wing forces are emerging against neoliberal globalisation. This is happening in Europe, the US itself with Trump giving rise to white nationalism, in India, and in Israel. This is also converging with a turn to authoritarianism in countries like Russia, Turkey, Philippines and Brazil. In many ways this can be explained as an outcome of failed neoliberalisation and the emergence of market democracies that have not worked.

The third limit on realising counter-hegemonic alternatives has to do with the constitution of a new mass politics to champion counter-hegemonic alternatives. While such a politics is agentially diverse and challenging jaded notions of political subjectivity, it has not been able to institutionalise itself and generate democratic leadership for society in most instances. Some of these forms of resistance are issue centred, localised, and in some cases movement centred but have not built sufficient capacities for scale and mass support. Put simply, the social forces championing such alternatives have not been able to generate a counter-hegemonic class project. This does not mean being state-centric but it does mean constituting alternatives from below as part of building new forms of mass power (direct, structural, movement, symbolic and constitutional) that can transform the state. Hence, the state is also a site of contestation to deepen space and create conditions for more. In a sense, the challenge is to be with, against and beyond the state from below without surrendering the logic and momentum for change from below.

A corollary to this point relates to a fourth limit. This has got to do with ensuring the democratic thrust in the counter-hegemonic alternatives emerging from energy democracy, food sovereignty, rights of nature, solidarity economies and more grow out of a deeply democratic institutional practice. Many of these alternatives are premised on the realisation of deep democracy as part of a post-neoliberal imagination. This is contrary to the shallow market democracies of neoliberalism that privilege the sovereignty of capital over state and society. Moreover, this democratising impulse is a fundamental challenge to the authoritarian forces also rising on the right. However, the limit it faces is the ability of the social forces championing such alternatives to ensure a deep anti-authoritarianism in their own practice. Many social forces are democratic, but have to build deep democratic institutional cultures and an internal reality of genuine democracy to even realise their own alternatives. This is a necessary condition for such social forces to also be democratising forces in a world that is increasingly becoming authoritarian and neo-fascist.

Chapter in Ino Rossi (ed.), *Challenges of Globalization and Prospects for an Inter-Civilizational World Order*. Springer: Cham, Switzerland, 2020.

*Co-operative Development and
Worker Co-operatives*

NUM Worker Co-Ops are Dead!
Long Live Worker Co-Ops?

KATE PHILIP'S ARTICLE IN *South African Labour Bulletin* about the viability of worker co-operatives in South Africa attempts to immunise her perspective from critique by arguing from the standpoint of a grounded, practical understanding of what can work in present-day South Africa. This is reflected in her title: 'A reality check: Worker co-ops in South Africa' and in her argument which is permeated with scepticism about worker co-operatives. However, there is a disconnect between the past NUM co-operative experience from 1987 to early 1990s and present-day South Africa. Philip speaks to us from outside the struggle to build co-operatives today: realism in her perspective is abstract prescription without being genuinely self-critical about the past.

History of co-ops versus NUM experience

We should not make the mistake of reducing the NUM experience of worker co-ops to the defining moment for co-operative development in the way Philip lays out her argument.

In a recent attempt to compile a comprehensive list of publications about co-op models and practices in South Africa, COPAC found 110 publications. Documented by institutions like SALDRU and the Koinonia Centre, this list tells of attempts to build worker/producer co-operatives in the 1970s and 1980s before the NUM experience. Besides union attempts at co-op development, during the militant 1980s community initiatives to build worker co-ops as on the Cape Flats were also taking place and were documented. Many of these publications also point to experiences of non-worker co-operatives engaged in finance, housing, agriculture and so on. They also point to the problems and challenges that non-worker co-operatives were experiencing under conditions of apartheid and state repression. This is important because Philip suggests that non-worker co-operatives (for instance, credit unions, housing and consumer co-operatives) are almost without problems and hence more viable than worker co-operatives.

Another striking feature of this publication list is that South Africa has a long and rich history of co-operatives. This history shows racial division given our past. However, the duality of white and black co-operatives should not take away from the need to learn from the entire history of co-op development in South Africa. The oldest co-operative established in the white community was registered as the Pietermaritzburg Consumers Co-operative in 1892. In addition, the history of black co-ops goes back as far as 1906. An activist at the University of KwaZulu-Natal is currently writing a history of co-ops in South Africa and her work is revealing a critical role played by Mahatma Gandhi, priests, Govan Mbeki and Dora Tamana among others in promoting co-ops in the first half of the twentieth century. To ignore this broader history and what it means for building worker and non-worker co-operatives in present-day South Africa means we are denying an attempt to learn from successes, failures and mistakes made during a racialised but common history. Most importantly, it means we reproduce a racial duality in the present, something that is also implicit in the logic of Philip's argument.

Throwing out the baby with the bath water

One of the main problems raised by Philip against worker co-operatives relates to the nature of their management structures. In particular, she highlights the failure of the NUM co-ops to delegate managerial authority. This is an important point. However, let's not assume that all South African worker co-operatives work with the NUM model of self-management. The problem of failed internal management in these 30 NUM co-ops is just that: a failure of the NUM model of worker co-operatives and not a problem of worker co-ops in general. Moreover, the lack of clarity on asset ownership in a worker co-operative suggests a shortcoming in Philip's understanding of co-op principles as defined in the South African legal framework and internationally.

The legal definition and principles of a co-operative are straightforward about ownership: assets of a co-operative are jointly owned. The assets are indivisible and not linked to member share contributions. In other words, the capital sourced from a member contributes to the internal capital pool of the co-operative and on leaving the member is paid the value contributed. This has nothing to do with asset values or profitability in the co-operative. The flip-side of this question of ownership relates to whether an asset of a co-operative can be sold and whether members can individually benefit from this. An asset of the co-operative whether donated or purchased is the asset of an independent, legal entity, the co-operative, with full powers in law to deal with the sale or purchase of assets according to its constitutional principles or bylaws. In most instances, these provide for a decision-making procedure, normally a special vote among members to dispense with the asset and its proceeds. This is not a confusion in the worker co-op model, as Philip suggests, but the minimum required to maintain the identity of a co-operative and to distinguish its institutional form.

However, in the real world no matter how intelligently the management arrangements and ownership principles are institutionalised, a host of other conditions internally and externally could conspire against the success of a co-operative. Hence the issues raised by Philip in relation to the NUM worker co-operatives force us to ask deeper questions about how these co-ops were designed, capacitated and institutionalised as a model. In this regard Philip's version of what went wrong with the NUM co-operatives is incomplete: it hides more than it reveals. It prompts the following questions: (i) Was there sufficient thought given to the institutional arrangements such that self-management was institutionalised in an efficacious way (it is not enough to refer to Italy and Spain now as best practice)? (ii) Was proper education done with members about collective and member rights such that member understanding and discipline was achieved? (iii) What was the role of the union in this situation? Did it assist or impede the development of the co-operatives? (iv) What mistakes did the NUM and the Mineworkers Development Agency make in this process? (v) How did the state respond to the NUM co-operatives? In short, let's not generalise about worker co-ops in South Africa, including their limits and potential, based on the NUM experience and without understanding in a rigorous and honest way the particular contextual factors that might have contributed to its failures.

New context, new conditions, new challenges

Another disturbing aspect of Philip's argument is how she selectively appropriates part of a COPAC research report to suit her argument. The 2005 COPAC study finds conclusively that most co-ops in Gauteng were initiated by the state and state support in crucial areas like finance, training and access to markets was not forthcoming. This COPAC study recognised that under post-apartheid conditions the state had to come into co-operative development. Given the poverty and underdevelopment facing most communities the state was crucial in providing enabling conditions for co-op development. However, based on the research, it was very clear that the state was not complimenting autonomous co-operative development in the name of Broad-Based Black

Economic Empowerment (B-BBEE), but instead was failing to respond to the start-up and growth needs of these co-ops. It was actually pushing these co-operatives back into poverty. Philip does not recognise this bigger argument and conclusion of the COPAC report as she merely works with the observation about co-operatives failing. Her failure to go into the explanation within the report also reflects her disconnect from current realities around co-op development.

Further, she fails to recognise that post-apartheid co-op development is happening in the context of important state policy and legal reform for co-operative development. Despite some weaknesses, this framework for co-op development is progressive and affirms three crucial assumptions: (i) the state will complement co-operative development in an enabling way; (ii) co-operatives have a distinct identity from other forms of social or economic enterprise; and (iii) co-operative development requires a co-operative movement from below. During the time of the NUM co-operatives this policy support framework for co-operatives did not exist. At the same time, the South African co-operative development policy framework reflects a global shift towards affirming the identity of co-operatives as distinct from capitalist businesses or state- controlled enterprises. In this regard COSATU's role in securing this framework through national policymaking processes and international engagements are crucial. This includes International Labour Organization (ILO) processes which produced a revised standard for co-operatives encapsulated in Recommendation 193 (2002).

To make the post-apartheid co-operative framework work the assumptions underpinning it have to be realised. As implementation is taking place, shortcomings are also coming through. In this regard, training for co-op managers and more specialised training for co-operatives is not provided for. These needs for co-operatives are getting lost in the SETA system and therefore there is a need to enhance the policy support framework through a national co-operatives college, for example. In addition, the racial integration of the co-operative sector is inhibited by the BEE approach. In many instances the co-operation pattern from below between black and white co-operatives challenges a BEE approach from the standpoint of co-operative empowerment. Also, tax reform for post-apartheid co-operatives has to be seriously thought about to improve what we have.

Conclusion

There are many positive opportunities and exciting challenges facing worker and non-worker co-operatives in post-apartheid South Africa. Increasingly our debates about co-operatives must speak to these opportunities and challenges while being informed by history and the ongoing struggle to defend the identity of co-ops. Trade unions, and the working class more broadly, need to claim the post-apartheid co-operative development framework as theirs, grounded in the experiences of the NUM co-operatives and more. In doing this we have to recognise that co-operatives have both strengths and weaknesses. Philip has a lot to teach us about these, but she also has a lot to learn as we struggle to deepen the conditions for successful post-apartheid co-operative development.

South African Labour Bulletin 31(3), July/August 2007.

A Co-operative Movement Response to the Crisis of Civilisation: Choosing to Sustain Life!

Introduction

THE DEVELOPMENT OF THE ICA (International Co-operative Alliance) 'Blueprint for a co-operative decade' (2020) comes to the fore at a crucial historical moment. There is a great deal of uncertainty and flux in the world; dogmatic ideas that have held sway for the past three decades are unhinging, complex global challenges loom large and the global political economy is in transition. The blueprint frames a much-needed integrated strategic vision, which serves as a compass to navigate the difficult world we live in and guide the ship of ethical values and principles defining co-operative identity today. However, even with the guiding role of the blueprint the journey for co-operatives over the next few years requires an awareness of the challenges and practical strategic choices to ensure they become:

- the acknowledged leader in economic, social and environmental sustainability;
- the model preferred by people; and
- the fastest growing form of enterprise.

The crucial challenge is to recognise the co-operative option and its growth is not another version of what exists or something slightly better, but rather it is an alternative. Such a perspective is developed in this contribution from the standpoint of critical and green global political economy.

The crisis of capitalist civilisation and the growth machine

For the past 500 years the world has been remade into a planetary capitalist system. This has been a violent process involving colonialism, genocide, slavery, debt-based control of developing countries and domination of the world by powerful countries. However, over the past three decades and with the demise of the Soviet-controlled Second World, the global economy has been restructured to ensure the vision, values (individualism, markets and greed) and policies (liberalisation, privatisation and financialisation) to bring to the fore a truly planetary capitalist civilisation. This process of restructuring has been referred to as neoliberalisation, which places global finance at the centre of the global economy. Put differently, global finance is now central to the systemic logic of the global economy. This means whole societies, economic sectors and even states, have been remade to manage the risk to finance and the finance-controlled firm.

This experiment in remaking global capitalism has produced a crisis-ridden form of neoliberal capitalism and capitalist civilisation. As high finance prevailed over global accumulation and imposed its speculative rationality, the global capitalist economy has blown out, crashing economies from the Mexican peso crisis (1994), Asian crisis (1997), Brazil and Russia (1998), Dot com (2000) and Argentina (2001) to the present global crisis.

Financialised over-accumulation marks the crisis tendencies of neoliberal capitalism. However, the present crisis, with its origins in the US housing market crisis beginning in 2007, cannot be merely understood as a crisis of financial accumulation or the Great Financial Crisis. Such an understanding perpetuates the idea that by simply fixing financial markets the crisis can be overcome. This reduces the crises of capitalism to a singular crisis and fuels a simplistic understanding of capitalism: that is, capitalism has all the answers or it always overcomes crises. Such a perspective fails to appreciate the extent to which neoliberal financialisation is not just about speculation in financial markets, but is a systemic logic driving global accumulation. It is a crisis of financial markets (booms and busts), of sectors in the global economy (from housing to manufacturing), of those cities and countries integrated into this logic, of a project of transnational finance and, most importantly, a systemic crisis. The latter dimension of the crisis is most serious. The logic of financialisation undermines the conditions necessary to reproduce life on Planet Earth (human and non-human). This includes the interlocking of financialised chaos with resource peak (not just oil), climate change, food crises (such as skyrocketing food prices in 2007–2008) and the securitisation of politics (such that authoritarian and undemocratic state practices are increasingly apparent). High finance does not have solutions to these challenges, except more financialisation (that is, more of the same).

The consequences of the crisis of capitalist civilisation today are dire. While it has created a plutocratic elite (the super-rich 1%), it has brought forth a new form of barbarism, leading to our self-annihilation. As a species we are destroying ourselves, other life forms and the conditions that sustain planetary life. This has amounted to the following:

- A tendency towards genocide – as expressed through the structural violence unleashed by an economy that privileges profits for finance-controlled firms over lives. Crucial examples are the suicides of over 200,000 Indian farmers in the context of liberalisation, 10 million people who die globally from hunger every year, and many others from lack of access to medication for treatable diseases like HIV/AIDS, malaria, diarrhoea and tuberculosis. The end of wage earning, through increasing and in some cases permanent unemployment, also imperils human reproduction. Moreover, we condemn future generations to endure structural violence as we undermine other life giving conditions on the planet.
- Overshooting planetary limits – this includes increasing ocean acidification (which is linked to climate change and confirmed by the recently released fifth assessment report of the IPCC). The proposed boundary is 2.75, but the current level is 2.90. Species loss is proposed at 10 per million but the current rate is greater than 100 per million. (The International Union for Conservation of Nature (IUCN) suggests rather conservatively that over 17,000 plants and animals are at risk of extinction.) The proposed boundary limit for excess nitrogen to avoid ecological degradation is 35 million tonnes; the current output is 121 million tonnes.
- Destruction of lifegiving conditions – by 2025 two-thirds of the world's population is likely to face water scarcity. With current climate change trends, including breaking the threshold of 400 parts per million of greenhouse gases in the atmosphere, we are moving rapidly to a 2°C or more temperature increase on the planet. We are heading for climate breakdown according to the fifth IPCC assessment report. Various tipping point indicators indicate this and include: the melting of the Arctic ice sheet which is releasing immense amounts of methane gas (the deadliest greenhouse gas); increasing sea levels (currently at 3 mm per year or an inch per decade); a rapid decrease in mountain glaciers; warming of the oceans (where it is estimated that about 90% of heat accumulated on the planet is located); devastating droughts; extreme summer and winter temperatures with negative effects on crop yields as average planetary temperatures rise; and rapid destruction of rainforests which is destroying the green lungs of the planet.

Africa is hardest hit and is the epicentre of the crisis of capitalist civilisation. It is where HIV/AIDS is ravaging communities, where climate change impacts are expected to be the worst (some analysts suggest Africa will experience the hottest temperatures and currently Namibia is experiencing the worst drought in its history with over 800,000 people requiring food aid) and where the scramble for minerals, fossil fuels and farming land is all part of a new wave of destructive extractivism and dispossession. For advocates of economic growth this means Africa is experiencing an economic boom, with mainly African petro-states averaging about 5% growth rates.

Central to capitalist civilisation is the role of growth measured in GDP, which measures the value of income (goods and services) less the cost of producing this output (for example, raw materials and labour). It is the most powerful measurement tool and number in the world that determines economic policy-making. However, this Frankenstein number, as it has been referred to, was initially invented in the interwar years to assist the US government understand the impact of economic policies. It was also used in war planning, and after World War 2 became the most powerful economic policy tool in the capitalist world. In the US context, it also counts military expenditure as part of measuring growth. The growth machine is constantly cranked up and encouraged by policy-makers, politicians and business to keep the juggernaut of production, consumption and investment going. It is a proxy for more wealth creation for an elite. In the midst of the current crisis, more growth has been set as a primary policy objective. However, from the standpoint of the crisis of civilisation this means deepening crisis and greater barbarism. More growth means genocide, breaching planetary limits and destroying conditions that sustain life. In short, economic growth does not take into account the real cost to human life and the planet.

The international co-operative movement at a crossroads

The global crisis has, in a sense, enhanced the appeal of co-operatives. The co-operative advantage has been accentuated in global common sense. This is also expressed through the 'Blueprint for a co-operative decade' which recognises the opportunity to make the co-operative case. However, it is important to recognise that the co-operative movement also faces difficult challenges in the context of a world controlled by high finance. It has been contested by high finance and at times brought into discourses that render co-operatives merely another business form, emptied of their deeper social character. In many parts of the world the global capitalist civilisation has reduced co-operatives to small and medium enterprises, social enterprises, another way of making money and as entities functional to the making of competition states that withdraw from directing economic development. This has negative consequences for the space for developing genuine co-operatives, as well as co-operative autonomy and identity.

At the same time, the dramatic economic power of co-operatives in some parts of the world and in some sectors of national economies has also challenged co-operative identity. Many co-operatives have to make difficult decisions to adjust to market pressures, competition and economic restructuring as part of globalisation. This has prompted mergers, complex interlocks, financial stake holding and generally a consolidation of market power. In this context, while experimenting with new practices where necessary, the sustainability of internally democratic and member-driven practices have also been lost as co-operatives become globalising giants. In developing countries, the end of state control has posed a challenge of building a tradition and practice of member-driven co-operatives, which brings forth new challenges for responsive co-operative education from below.

Another crucial challenge facing the co-operative movement today has got to do with a narrow understanding of the co-operative form; that is, it is both a social institution and a business. Merely reducing co-operatives to these two dimensions misses the deeper movement character of co-operatives. It fails to recognise that genuine co-operatives are about linking, solidarity and working together. Since the formation of the ICA there has been a strong emphasis on vertically based national movements. Going forward over the next decade requires the ICA to also recognise that co-operative movements have different shapes and forms, in national contexts. In particular, the rise of new social movements over the past three decades – unemployed people's movement, landless people's movements, the Occupy movement, climate justice networks, for example – which also promote co-operative development, prompts the ICA to recognise that the agency for co-operative development in the world has emerged from different social forces. Such movements are potentially crucial allies of the international co-operative movement. A genuine effort has to be made by the ICA to reach out to these movements.

Finally, and flowing from the previous point, is a recognition that even in its origins in the nineteenth century co-operative philosophy has been divided between two ideological currents: ameliorative and transformative. Over the past few decades, both these currents of co-operation have come to the fore in a context in which the radical utopian imagination renews itself. In the WSF there has been a consistent affirmation of the notion 'Another world is possible'. This rallying slogan with its powerful anticipatory message nourishes a powerful commitment to the transformative impulse of co-operation expressed through the idea of the solidarity economy. Currently, in the ICA, the space for the transformative impulse to drive co-operative development is uncertain. Ideally, the ICA needs to ensure both ameliorative and transformative impulses of co-operative development feed-off, support and democratically challenge each other in order to advance co-operative growth over the next few years. A genuine unity, based on diversity, of the co-operative movement in the twenty-first century is required to confront the crisis of capitalist civilisation.

Growing the co-operative movement as an alternative: Possible ways forward to realise the 2020 'Blueprint for a co-operative decade'

The propositions that follow are meant to inform the ongoing debate on realising the 'Blueprint for a co-operative decade', while affirming the co-operative movement and option as an alternative. This means situating the envisaged growth of the co-operative movement in a different paradigm. Some elements of this paradigm are contained in the blueprint and some are not.

Advancing co-operatives to sustain life

The irrationality of economic growth cannot drive co-operative growth. As an economic measurement and policy tool, it is blind to the real consequences of capitalist civilisation on human life and the planet. Moral and ethical considerations do not feature in the growth machine. It is in this context that the prioritisation of sustainability in the blueprint is welcomed. The role of economic, social and environmental factors in mediating the growth of co-operatives potentially places the co-operative movement in the lead in terms of challenging the world to think differently about how we produce, consume, use finance and live. It potentially holds the prospect of shifting attitudes away from merely thinking in terms of economic wealth, and engendering a conversation about a different conception of wealth.

The real wealth we have are renewable resources on the planet, life-giving conditions and human beings as a creative force. In other words, sustainability as a driver of co-operative growth could open a way to shift focus to protecting the natural and creative human commons; that is, place co-operatives at the centre of sustaining life. It also enables the co-operative movement to join a conversation taking place in the world about a deep and just transition to a low- or zero-carbon economy prioritising renewable energy, the role of carbon debt, the rights of nature (or living well discourse), climate jobs and ecological restructuring of societies. These are issues being debated by transnational climate justice movements and networks to find genuine solutions to climate change. The ICA and its member organisations need to also actively engage the international climate justice movement in a conversation about these issues to clarify the place and role of sustainable co-operative development in the just transition.

Co-operative identity and power

Generally co-operative identity is defined by its ethical values and principles. When these values and principles are institutionalised, this makes for a powerful expression of symbolic power; there is a recognisable difference in the internal relations and practices of a co-operative as compared to other institutions. However, for co-operative growth to accelerate, the global co-operative movement has to become self-aware of the other facets of power inherent in the model and which accentuate its identity.

Thus, beyond symbolic power, co-operatives also have three other types of power: structural power such that they control parts of a market or an economy; movement power based on the networked links, member densities and collective capacities inside the movement; and direct power, which refers to the capacity of the movement to shape public opinion through advocacy, mass campaigning and marketing.

Together these four forms of power (structural, movement, direct and symbolic) are a crucial strategic thrust through which to advance the growth of co-operatives over the next few years. This also means the co-operative movement has to become much more self-aware of its capacity to advance a transformative politics from below in society and in the world. It is only through such a conscious politics that the co-operative movement can confront the crisis of civilisation and sustain life.

Affirming co-operative democracy as transformative democracy

While the blueprint prioritises an emphasis on participation to drive the growth of co-operatives and strengthen co-operative identity, this particular imperative has to be contextualised to appreciate its wider importance. Essentially, the crisis of civilisation is not just underpinned by the narrowing of democracy and a democratic deficit but there is a conscious attempt to subordinate democracy to markets. In other words, market democracy has become the master narrative of what is democracy. This means the state must prioritise the interests of markets and corporations over citizens' needs, democratic accountability is narrowed and electoral contestation is certainly not a guarantee of social justice, policy change and transformation. Thus, market democracy hollows out democracy and concentrates power amongst a few, or the 1% in society. In this context, the importance of economic democracy in a co-operative cannot be underestimated. In fact, the democratic skills, capacities, practice and impulse of co-operatives becomes increasingly important to renew democracy from below to ensure it is deepened. The co-operative form, conscious of its different facets of power, can be the harbinger of direct, participatory and a new kind of accountable electoral democracy; a transformative democracy. This is a crucial antidote to a form of democracy – market democracy – that is in its essence anti-democratic.

Ending hunger for one billion: Advancing global food sovereignty

The genocidal consequences of the crisis of capitalist civilisation are reflected in the most tragic number at the heart of this: one billion hungry people. And as some commentators have pointed out there are also an additional two billion who are food insecure. The global political economy of transnational corporate controlled food is a crime against humanity. Moreover, in the context of climate change and breakdown, the hunger question will become increasingly important and has to be addressed now to ensure we sustain life. This means going beyond food security (merely ensuring enough food is produced to feed a society) and the criminality of large food corporations, and ensuring the food system is reclaimed by the hungry. Thus, the crucial challenge facing the co-operative movement is ensuring the right to food of the one billion, and food insecure more generally, is affirmed through securing food sovereignty. The idea of food sovereignty is championed by important and networked peasant and small-scale farmer movements across the world, to ensure food production, distribution and consumption is placed back in the hands of citizens and communities. This has also been endorsed by the United Nations Conference on Trade and Development (UNCTAD) in its 2013 report entitled 'Wake up before it's too late'. These small-scale farmer movements are currently fighting one of the most important battles on the planet to prevent the destruction of small-scale farming by transnational corporations. This is better known as the last great dispossession and is mainly taking place in the global South. At the same time, many co-operatives are also responsible for food production and control distribution chains. It is time the international co-operative movement opens up a dialogue between these co-operatives and the movement of small-scale farmers to strengthen a global alliance for food sovereignty. It is time to ensure by 2020 that there is zero hunger on the planet, there is a reduction in carbon emissions from agriculture, farming is grounded in agro-ecological methods and is controlled by communities, cities, towns and villages to ensure adaptation to climate change. This can only happen through championing and realising food sovereignty in the world now.

Co-operative Growth for the 21st Century, edited by Bruno Roelants. Geneva: International Co-operative Alliance, 2013.

Solidarity Economy

With, Against and Beyond the State: A Solidarity Economy Through a Movement of Movements

THE SOLIDARITY ECONOMY alternative has emerged in the post-apartheid context. It is an example of transformative politics, which is about constituting new forms of power, changing property relations and enabling counter-logics to private profiteering from below. Emancipatory and anti-capitalist in its orientation, it is new and post-neoliberal, post-social democratic and post-national liberation. The solidarity economy alternative is rooted in South African left thought and has been evolving its own theoretical framework while learning from international experiences, as it engages in grassroots practice.

Contrary to state-centric developmentalism, which controls grassroots logics, or market fundamentalism (neoliberalism), which seeks to subordinate the state to the market, the solidarity economy alternative has a more distinctive approach to the state. The notion of democratic systemic reform captures how solidarity economy agentic forces think about and approach the role of the state. Democratic systemic reform seeks to bring together democratic grassroots power, deep system transformation and embedded state reform into the process of building solidarity economy logics. This idea is clarified in this chapter, as part of characterising practice in South Africa, as it relates to how solidarity economy forces have been converging with the state from below.

In addition, this chapter highlights how solidarity economy forces have critiqued and distanced themselves from some of the practices of the South African state. The state's hybridising of nationalism with discursive elements that skew co-operative development in the direction of market-centred accumulation, failed financing approaches and top-down movement building have been critically engaged within solidarity economy perspectives. Moreover, this chapter affirms the solidarity economy as a grassroots impulse championed by a movement of movements. The making of the solidarity economy as a movement of movements is historicised while mapping the variegated social forms leading this process from below. In this sense, the solidarity economy is beyond the state in building its logics and practices from below. Finally, this chapter concludes with the challenges facing the solidarity economy as a movement of movements.

The solidarity economy as transformative politics

The emergence of the solidarity economy in South Africa was facilitated by three important conditions: (i) the end of institutionalised and regulated apartheid; (ii) the crisis of South Africa's neoliberalised political economy; and (iii) grassroots anti-capitalist emancipatory organising (Satgar 2014b: 207–223). Juxtaposing it conceptually assists with understanding what it is: the solidarity economy is not a fixed and abstract definition mainly centred on particular enterprise forms – for instance, non-profit NGOs or co-operatives. Institutional forms are important for the solidarity economy, but these do not in themselves clarify what it is. Moreover, the solidarity economy is not a residual third sector in a mixed economy in which small and medium enterprises have to find niches. It is not an add-on to the dominant capitalist logic. Finally, the solidarity economy is not a blueprint or ideal utopia. It does not have all the details worked out about how an alternative economy should work.

The solidarity economy is an emancipatory and anti-capitalist grassroots alternative. It seeks exits, departure points, escapes and breakthroughs beyond the ecocidal logic of contemporary capitalism to sustain life. Moreover, its practices are coloured by a utopian imagination. The COPAC and the various social forces its works with have embraced an open-ended notion articulated as follows:

> [The solidarity economy] is a collective humanist response and democratic alternative from below to the crisis we face. It draws on our common humanity as the basis for solidarity action. More concretely, the solidarity economy is a voluntary process organised through collective struggle and conscious choice to establish a new pattern of democratic production, consumption and living that promotes the realisation of human needs and environmental justice (Satgar, 2009a: 18).

From this contingent and open-ended conception, we derive a process-centred vision, which is grounded in ongoing learning. The dialectic of practice and knowledge creation is constantly at work to learn from the past – successes, failures, innovation and problem-solving – to develop a shared knowledge commons to advance systemic transformation. Moreover, values and principles are crucial to guide institutional forms, such as worker co-operatives, co-operative banks, community trusts and other socialised forms, which might emerge. This vision is grounded in realising ethical values (caring, sharing, self-reliance, honesty, democracy, equality, learning, ecological consciousness, social justice and openness) and principles (solidarity, collective ownership, self-management, control of capital, ecocentric, community benefit and participatory democracy).[1] This simply means all social forms, practices and relational dynamics that emerge in the solidarity economy should seek to take forward these values and principles. Finally, the solidarity economy is about a democratising logic from below, at different scales – from households, communities, villages, towns, cities and country scales. Such a logic seeks to intersect, work with and aggregate other anti-capitalist practices, such as transition towns, participatory planning and food sovereignty, as discussed elsewhere in this volume. As a contingent practice, the solidarity economy is not reducible to one institutional form or practice, as it seeks to engender a critical mass and transformative grassroots pathways from these various scales. The logic of its vision and values-centred practices, self-organised and driven from below, is with, against and beyond the state.

Beyond the contingent practices and vision-centred process of what constitutes the solidarity economy, it is also about a distinctive kind of politics. This is different from the twentieth-century instrumentalist politics of Soviet vanguardism, social democracy or even national liberation. In South Africa today, the utopian Marxist impulse of solidarity economy activism was inspired by the thought of Rick Turner, but has now grown beyond this (Satgar, 2014b). Turner's thought gave the emancipatory politics of the solidarity economy crucial elements. In his *The Eye of the Needle*, first published in 1972, the elements of a utopian Marxist method can be discerned (Turner, 2015). It emphasised inspiring the imagination of the collective struggle, so as to dream a life beyond oppression. This is shared by contemporary solidarity economy forces, but the conception of a collective imagination is centred around three crucial ideas today: a solidarity society, democratic ecosocialism and deep, just transition. This realisation out of collective struggle is reaching for a more holistic conception of transformation that takes into account the full lived experience of oppression under post-apartheid capitalism. This means economics, culture, politics, geography, science, technology and the everyday are crucial as sites of resistance and spaces for advancing the solidarity economy. Moreover, these concepts construct a visionary narrative that speaks to the challenge of overcoming the

---

[1] Satgar (2009a). At the first International Solidarity Economy conference convened in South Africa these values and principles were engaged with as part of visioning exercises done in groups. These workshop groups generated a gallery of artwork highlighting the various possibilities and ways in which these values can be realised at the grassroots (COPAC 2012).

most dangerous systemic contradiction, engendered by corporate capital and its ecocidal logic, namely the climate crisis (Satgar, 2018b).

Turner's method also emphasised that the present was history, which meant that it was socially constructed and could be remade. For Turner, social analysis was crucial for understanding the social and power relations that came together in the apartheid social order. The present had to be historicised, so as to understand that it was not naturalised. Today, solidarity economy activism has developed a conception of the political economy of a neoliberalised South Africa, and its articulation with global crisis dynamics, of the globalised industrial food system, seed systems and water. This is a work in progress, but it is about understanding how the development of capitalism in South Africa, including the deepening of neoliberalisation through financial and market power in the post-apartheid period, has created a crisis of production and social reproduction in the present. Unemployment, hunger, water challenges, systemic crises (including the climate crisis) and capitalist power are now increasingly within the political economy perspectives of solidarity economy activism, so as to understand these contradictions and how to develop activist responses for solidarity economy alternatives.[2]

Finally, in the application of his utopian Marxist approach, Turner envisaged alternatives. From his normative and historical social analysis of society, he affirmed a crucial connection between consciousness, human values and social institutions. He believed strongly in the values of non-racialism, non-sexism, human freedom, equality, participatory democracy and ecological justice. Such values had to be reflected in the alternative mechanisms and institutions that could reconstitute society. This included participatory planning and worker control, for instance. However, in contemporary South Africa, two crucial breakthroughs have been made that take us beyond Turner. The first is the issue of solidarity economy pathways from below to realise processes, values-centred visions and institutional forms. The grounding of these pathways in everyday lived realities, conditions of oppression and conscious activism to overcome the socially constructed contradictions of South African and global capitalism are central to the transformative politics of the solidarity economy. This also entails being open to the variegated intervention and initiation points of the solidarity economy. In some instances, this could be a few households, sometimes an enterprise, or a community or a

---

2   In this regard, see various solidarity economy activist tools with this emphasis: Satgar, 2009a; COPAC, 2014, 2015, 2016, 2017.

movement. However, this is a conscious process of building capacity, raising consciousness, getting organised and constructing values-based institutional mechanisms.

The second issue relates to anti-authoritarian and transformative movement building from below to advance the solidarity economy. Compared to trade unions that were central to Turner's practice, emerging solidarity economy institutional forms are advancing values-centred practices, visions and pathways, which are more complex. These are taking the form of networked relations between solidarity economy enterprises, households, support organisations and movements around solidarity economy practices. These relations in power terms are symbiotic, platform-based and horizontal. Moreover, movement building cannot be understood in the singular, but rather in terms of a plurality of convergent and networked forms. In many ways, the solidarity economy is emerging as a movement of movements. This expression of self-agency for emancipation is consistent with Turner's rejection of political vanguard parties, such as communist parties, but it is emerging as unique institutional forms in contemporary South Africa. This is developed further below.

The solidarity economy and the state: The challenge of democratic systemic reform

The modern history of the solidarity economy locates its emergence in the first half of the nineteenth century at a time when workers were searching for alternatives to the brutalising and super-exploitative conditions of industrial capitalism. It was a context that also gave rise to socialism and communism as modern ideologies, alongside liberalism. Capitalism was also experiencing boom and bust cycles, with workers bearing the brunt. It is in the midst of this experience that workers also occupied factories, attempted takeovers and inaugurated modern co-operativism. Since its inception, modern co-operativism has bifurcated either into a more reformist or ameliorative approach regarding the negative impacts of capitalism and a more transformative approach seeking to transform capitalism and go beyond it interstitially. The solidarity economy impulse has its roots in this history and transformative approach. However, into the twentieth century the solidarity economy and bottom-up co-operative development was overtaken by state-led development (Williams, 2014). This expressed itself in modernising state socialism, social democracy and revolutionary nationalism in the peripheries of capitalism. States used co-operatives as part of top-down instrumentalised change and, as a result, regulation in most instances was invasive and undermining of the bottom-up impulse of member-driven co-operatives and movements. In other instances, co-operative regulation supported a mixed economy as part of an embedded approach to economic relations. Capital was taxed, locked in with exchange controls and had to contend with alternative logics for social provisioning. Co-operative movements in these contexts found niches, but struggled to maintain their values, institutional practices and identities as genuine member-driven co-operatives. Neoliberalisation, with its emphasis on market competition, has had debilitating impacts in this regard.

Over the past three decades of neoliberalisation in the global political economy, market imperatives to shore up the power of financial and transnational capital have taken root. Old forms of embedded regulation have been jettisoned and in their place market regulation and reform have emerged. In this process state-economy relations have been remade, so that the state has been reconstructed to merely limit risk to capital (Satgar, 2014a). Market regulation is always about ensuring the state has a minimal role, while capital is incentivised to ensure seamless integration with global markets for trade, finance and production. Capital's structural power has been increased relative to states and other economic forces in this process. This has also had an impact on co-operative regulation, so that heavy state-directed co-operative development has been rolled back and, instead, co-operatives have now been positioned in relation to market relations and treated like any other competitive enterprise. While member-driven co-operatives have emerged in this context, their survival challenges have been exacerbated by deep globalisation into markets. Co-operative forms are crucial for the solidarity economy, given the socialised power and property relations in such institutions. However, market regulation approaches to co-operatives undermine their capacity to secure an alternative logic to meet social needs.

Post-apartheid South Africa's approach to co-operative regulation did not escape market-centred regulation and reform. This is because the state in post-apartheid South Africa embraced neoliberal economic policy and has maintained this for over 20 years of ANC rule (Satgar and Williams, 2011a). This is despite an attempt by co-operatives and broader progressive civil society to ensure that co-operative reform is about democratic systemic reform. Such a form of reform ensures the impulse of co-operative development and solidarity economy is driven from below, while the state plays an enabling role.

Put differently, democratic systemic reform is about creating the conditions for the state to protect, enable and strategically support co-operatives and ultimately a solidarity economy logic driven from below. In practice, this would mean the state responds to the initiatives, pathways and efforts by solidarity economy forces to transform production, consumption, saving and conditions to sustain life. The state does not lead, but ensures its power is harnessed for transformation from below.

In 2001, this was largely the vision and thrust of the co-operative and progressive civil society engagement with the state at the first conference convened by these forces (COPAC, 2001). It built on the people-driven emphasis in the RDP of the ruling ANC and it managed to secure a co-operative reform consistent with international standards and norms, but the emphasis on deepening democratic systemic reform was undermined. Instead of the state agreeing to a dedicated co-operative ministry, operationalising the participatory council (also known as the Co-operatives Board in the Act of 2005) and ensuring co-operative movement development happens from below, it has chosen to instrumentalise co-operative development. There have been at least three failed attempts at state-led movement building thus far. Millions of rands of taxpayers' money have been lost and are not fully accounted for. The current amendments to the Co-operatives Act (6 of 2013), further entrench this approach to movement building, bolstered by the provision for one legally sanctioned co-operative apex structure in South Africa.

Moreover, the Co-operative Banks Act of 2008 is also an attempt at democratic systemic reform. This Act attempts to structurally diversify the financial system in South Africa, which is currently held hostage by four big banks. It is a crucial democratic systemic reform to counter the financialisation of the South African economy and to ensure citizens have an alternative institutional option for their incomes and savings. This Act largely emanates from the efforts of the SACP to promote democratisation of the financial sector.[3] Important institutional and regulatory progress has been taken forward in this regard. However, the potential of this democratic systemic reform has not been fully explored. This is largely a function of the location of the Co-operative Banks Development Agency (CBDA) within the Treasury, which is extremely conservative and merely concerned about limiting systemic threats to the corporate banking system and not wanting co-operative banks to really

---

3   See Satgar (2000), which contributed to the debate in the SACP on the role of co-operative banks.

take off. As a result, the CBDA is constrained in how it proactively promotes co-operative banks as a democratic systemic alternative. The challenge for the CBDA is to reach out to small-scale farmers, trade unions, communities requiring housing, universities and grassroots movements, so that these forces own and drive the building of co-operative banks as part of a democratic systemic reform.

The SAFSC has been at the forefront of championing a pathway for food sovereignty. This is a direct challenge to the corporate-controlled and globalised food system, which is both causing and failing to address the food crisis. Part of the innovation regarding food sovereignty in the South African context has been the connection made with solidarity economy. In this regard, the People's Food Sovereignty Act, adopted at a People's Parliament, is a crucial example of a democratic systemic reform that would require the state to play a role in enabling the systemic diversification of the food system, so that citizens' power from below could be constituted for land, seeds, water, production, consumption and democratic planning of the food system (SAFSC, 2018a). The People's Act envisages a transformative role for the state, which would create conditions, institutions and mechanisms to deepen democratic systemic reform of the food system. As it stands, the South African state is locked into a pathological and globalised food system, while ignoring the importance of food sovereignty pathways to feed households, communities, villages, towns and cities. Nonetheless, the food sovereignty alternative is taking root from below and is linked to advancing the solidarity economy.

The emerging solidarity economy alternative in South Africa envisages and in fact requires a role for the state. It seeks to work with the state, but not on terms that are controlling and instrumentalising. Moreover, this is contrary to market reform and instead is about a democratic approach to regulation. Transformative solidarity economy activism is positing democratic systemic reform that would reclaim, transform and redirect the state from below. This is consistent with the deep, just transition, solidarity society and democratic ecosocialist imagination informing the solidarity economy forces and their transformative struggles.

The solidarity economy critique of the government's approach to co-operative development

The solidarity economy critique of the government's approach to co-operative development is still evolving. Many of the concerns relating to realising democratic systemic reform, raised above, echo in sharper differences in terms of the state's ideological and practical policy approaches to co-operative development. These practices have been critiqued and solidarity economy forces have also kept distance from such state approaches. These include the ideological conflation of co-operatives with a capitalist approach to nation building. This undermines the social character and member-driven and constitutive power of co-operatives as an alternative logic to meet societal needs. In this regard, the incorporation of co-operative development into BEE discourses has married co-operative development to transactional politics, get-rich-quick schemes and brazen corruption.[4] While there have been attempts by the government and the ruling party to inflect this as B-BBEE, the social interests and corrupting agendas at work are clearly visible. If co-operative development were genuinely embedded in a democratic systemic reform approach, this would have allowed co-operatives from below to assert their own voices, identities and power to drive co-operative development, rather than being hijacked by these dubious political agendas.

In addition, central to post-apartheid nation building has been the two economies discourse. Introduced by Thabo Mbeki, this top-down perspective and metaphor was used to locate co-operatives into a fast-track incubation approach to take co-operative beneficiaries from the underdeveloped second economy into the globally competitive first economy. This was consistent with the neoliberalisation of African nationalism and its attempts to deregulate small business development. Co-operatives were to be treated like any other business. This has proved disastrous, with a number of co-operatives being easily registered and the government boasting quantitative growth, while most people involved in these institutions did not even know what co-operatives are. Financing was a challenge, there was a lack of proper groundwork planning (such as education, model design, feasibility assessments, co-operative business planning and constitution development) and general capacity building to develop viable member-driven co-operatives was absent.

Another crucial factor in the state's involvement is how co-operative development finance has been channelled to co-operatives. There are two important institutional financing options that can enable co-operatives to control finance. The first is through internal mechanisms to build up capital pools. This includes share equity, re-investment of surplus and member loans.

---

4   Over the years, COPAC has researched the deleterious impacts of these policy thrusts on co-operatives (see COPAC, 2005, 2006, 2010).

The second is through external sources, but based on a clearly defined co-operative business plan. Such a plan recognises how income generation in the co-operative, supported by external financing, will strengthen its capacities. External sources can include state finance for start-up and working capital, loans from financing institutions and donor support. The South African state has not encouraged co-operatives to build internal capital pools and neither has its financing been geared to the specific needs of each co-operative. Instead, the state has merely followed a one-size-fits-all approach to start-up capital. Many co-operatives are desperate for working capital, including worker co-operatives (Satgar and Williams, 2011b). This challenge has not been addressed by the state, condemning co-operatives to survivalist pathways. Moreover, if there is a donor relationship, co-operatives have not been enabled to control the finance or to determine their own income-generation strategies. Banks, generally, are not friendly to co-operatives.

Finally, the South African government has entrenched a top-down movement-building approach, including through the 2013 amendments to the Co-operatives Act of 2005. This challenge was alluded to above, but it is an important issue and has prompted solidarity economy forces to debate very seriously how to find their own way from below, while engaging the state on their own terms, without getting co-opted, corrupted or controlled.[5] The push from the government, as part of the 2013 amendments to the Co-operatives Act of 2005, provides for only one national apex structure for co-operatives. Such a structure would also be driven by state regulations. This is the worst kind of instrumentalisation of co-operatives and is contrary to freedom of association guaranteed by the Constitution. Moreover, it denies the organic aggregating and networking capacities of co-operatives themselves. In short, the state has closed off its practice from recognising alternative modes of organising from below, including various solidarity economy networks and movements. The top-down logic of state-led co-operative movement building fails to be responsive to alternative approaches that could emanate from community organisations, campaigns, grassroots NGOs and other movements such as trade unions.

---

5   COPAC has facilitated four national assemblies of movements, community organisations and solidarity economy forces to engage with relevant issues, such as their practices, including their relationships with the state. These assemblies occurred in 2011, 2013, 2014 and 2016. The outcomes from these assemblies are available at http://www.copac.org.za (accessed 19 March 2018).

Advancing the solidarity economy through a movement of movements

Despite the anti-democratic, instrumentalising and top-down logic of state co-operative movement building, solidarity economy processes and practices have been evolving at the grassroots in South Africa. Such processes of variegated movement building have been advancing solidarity economy practices at the frontlines of community development processes, through co-operatives, support organisations, education NGOs, as part of movements and in labour struggles. A rough periodisation follows below.

Moment 1 (2007–2010): Learning from international experiences and Ivory Park

The first crucial experience of pioneering and developing solidarity economy practices built on the momentum coming out of joint efforts to advance a participatory approach to build an ecocity in Ivory Park township centred on an ecovillage, co-operatives and transformative community organising (Satgar, 2014b). This involved the community of Ivory Park, the Ecocity Trust and COPAC. COPAC has worked with the community since 1999 and established several co-operatives in the first wave of co-operative development, prior to the Co-operatives Act of 2005 and other state co-operative policy. Important successes and failures were experienced as part of developing organic farming, waste recycling, construction, consumer and bicycle co-operatives. The first wave of co-operative development pivoted on the ecovillage. This was complicated by the controlling role of the ANC in the community. Nonetheless, a second wave of organic co-operative development took place in Ivory Park. Co-operatives emerged in poultry, bakeries and other activities.

In the meantime, COPAC invested in learning from international experiences of co-operative development and the solidarity economy. This began intensively in 2007 after it was recognised that the state was going down a disastrous path for co-operative development. COPAC conducted study tours to different parts of the continent, participated in WSF processes dealing with the solidarity economy and researched experiences in Italy, Brazil, Venezuela, Argentina and the US.[6] This produced valuable research and activist tools to translate the solidarity economy into South African conditions. Ivory Park became a crucial learning space, with a pilot process to test solidarity economy

---

6   In this regard, see COPAC (2008), which discusses successful co-operatives in South Africa and elsewhere on the continent.

mapping, institutional tools and dialogic practice (COPAC, 2011). This yielded important momentum, but was arrested by the destructive role of the ANC in the area. In 2010 COPAC made a call for convergence among progressive social forces to advance the solidarity economy and movement in South Africa.

Moment 2 (2010–2014): Inventing a South African practice and building a knowledge commons

COPAC created the first learning and conversation platform through a conference in 2011. Valuable perspectives, conceptual ideas and debates ensued. A publication was also produced, drawing on international and South African insights, entitled *The Solidarity Economy Alternative: Emerging Theory and Practice*. This volume theorises, through a comparative dialogue, solidarity economy practices and potential pathways in South Africa.

COPAC has been very conscious of not pushing a top-down movement-building approach. Instead, together with others converging in the solidarity economy space, the emphasis has been on creating a knowledge commons to share experiences, innovative practices, popular consciousness raising and developing participatory tools for grassroots transformative organising. In this regard, four solidarity economy assemblies were hosted with movements and grassroots forces from 2011 till 2016, three dedicated activist schools were hosted on the solidarity economy and worker co-operatives, an activist-driven newsletter, *Solidarity Economy News*, was established,[7] site work took place in 15 communities in partnership with organisations and movements, and the Worker Co-operative Campaign – including a crucial tool for establishing worker co-operatives (COPAC, 2015) – and the SAFSC were launched.

In this bottom-up transformative organising process, the solidarity economy impulse found its place in various struggles and among various social forces. First, among community-based movements, the examples that stand out are the various unemployed people's movements in Gauteng, North West, KwaZulu-Natal and Grahamstown. Training took place with these movements on solidarity economy process building and worker co-operative development. Second, trade unions played an important role in championing solidarity economy practices, particularly worker co-operative development. In this regard, the efforts by NUMSA to buy out a recycling plant in 2009, when

---

7   The first *Solidarity Economy News* was produced in 2012 and it has continued, with 18 issues having been produced at the time of writing. See http://copac.org.za/category/newsletters/ (accessed 19 March 2018).

workers were facing retrenchment, are instructive. While the worker takeover failed, NUMSA ended up establishing a worker co-operative for retrenched workers called Sihlahla Muri (Satgar and Williams, 2011b). This built on NUMSA's experience of supporting worker co-operative development as part of union strategy in the 1980s. However, this post-apartheid experiment was short-lived because of the lack of support from local government for a recycling space, the theft of the workers' truck used for waste pick-up, and the failure of NUMSA to build in-house capacity to provide solidarity to this pilot. The other trade union experience in this moment was the Mineline Factory occupation in 2010 (Satgoor, 2014). This factory occupation stalled the liquidation of this factory, built solidarity among various forces and held out the prospect for a worker takeover in which the workers could have established a worker co-operative to run the factory. However, after months of struggle, the IDC committed to establishing a new worker-run factory, but in the end reneged on this commitment after the workers agreed to the liquidation of the old assets.

Third was the development of community-led approaches to the solidarity economy. In this regard, the work of a community NGO called Ntaba ka Ndoda Heritage and Development Centre stands out, as well as the Bulungula Incubator.[8] Both these organisations are in the rural Eastern Cape and pioneered their own approaches to community development, but also adopted elements of the solidarity economy. In the case of Ntaba ka Ndoda, they have developed a cultural programme, engaged in community planning and introduced solidarity economy and food sovereignty into their transformative practices. A lot of learning from Ntaba ka Ndoda practice has been crucial for community approaches to solidarity economy development in the Eastern Cape and beyond. Fourth has been the role of education and support organisations that have embraced solidarity economy approaches. The role of the Workers' College in Durban has been crucial. It has trained a number of students, across various communities in Durban, to advance solidarity economy theory and practices.[9] The other crucial organisation has been the Ecumenical Service for Socio-Economic Transformation (ESSET), which works with informal trade organisations. In 2013–2014 ESSET introduced a programme to improve the livelihoods of informal women traders through co-operatives (Steyn, 2015).

---

8   *Solidarity Economy News* 1 (2012), http://www.copac.org.za/files/Solidarity%20Economy%20 Newsletter%20No%201.pdf (accessed 20 March 2018).

9   *Solidarity Economy News* 8 (2014), http://www.copac.org.za/files/Solidarity%20Economy%20 Newsletter%20No%208.pdf (accessed 20 March 2018).

Today, ESSET is poised to develop an informal women traders' network based on solidarity economy approaches in Lesotho, Swaziland, Zambia and South Africa. The University of Pretoria also launched the Human Economy Programme during this period and has also focused on solidarity approaches. The Human Economy Programme has continued to engage with solidarity economy approaches.[10]

Moment 3 (2014 to the present): Deepening solidarity economy pathways from below

In this moment, solidarity economy approaches evolved to deepen contributions from COPAC, community-based movements, trade unions, community-led approaches and education and support organisations. In addition, the role of campaigns, such as the SAFSC, and co-operatives themselves in promoting the solidarity economy are crucial dimensions in the variegated grassroots impulses championing the solidarity economy. In this regard, the role of the Fingerprint Worker Co-operative is extremely important.

COPAC played an essential role in 2014, as part of a coalition of organisations concerned with the food crisis in South Africa. This culminated in a conference in late 2014 centred on the right to food that laid the basis for the formation of the SAFSC. For COPAC and other solidarity economy partners, this campaign was consistent with a commitment to marry the solidarity economy with food sovereignty since the first international solidarity economy conference hosted in 2011. COPAC served as the secretariat to the SAFSC national co-ordinating committee from 2015 to 2017. In addition, COPAC has continued supporting the solidarity economy through maintaining the newsletter *Solidarity Economy News*, hosting *SAFSC News*, developing numerous activist tools (such as a food sovereignty guide, a seed guide, a People's Food Sovereignty Act and a Water Sovereignty Guide),[11] working with partners at Wits University to promote food sovereignty and the solidarity economy to achieve an ecocentric university and establishing a solidarity economy movements' webpage for grassroots-driven co-operatives.[12] Furthermore, COPAC has pursued a transformative politics research agenda, producing this volume; a book on the climate crisis, which features food sovereignty and the solidarity economy

---

10 A draft version of this chapter was shared with a workshop entitled 'The Struggle for Economic Democracy in Africa', hosted by the Human Economy Programme, 7–9 March 2018, at the University of Pretoria.
11 These tools are all available at http://www.copac.org.za and http://www.safsc.org.za (accessed 20 March 2018).
12 See http://www.sem.org.za (accessed 20 March 2018).

as a crucial systemic alternative for the deep, just transition (Satgar, 2018b; Bennie and Satgoor, 2018); a planned book on food sovereignty; a third book envisaged on the solidarity economy and transformative politics; and has made international links (including in the US, Italy, Spain and Argentina) with regard to worker co-operative development through the Real Utopias project headed by Professor Erik Olin Wright.

In terms of community-based movements, the South African Waste Pickers Association (SAWPA) has also taken forward solidarity economy approaches through establishing worker co-operatives. SAWPA has, through its own initiative, studied worker co-operatives, including through a study tour to Brazil. As a result, it established several worker co-operatives in different parts of South Africa. Through working with COPAC, it has strengthened its own capacity to support and develop its worker co-operative model (Chamane, 2016). Currently SAWPA is expanding worker co-operative development as part of its commitment to zero waste and it is challenging the state and corporate control of waste recycling in South Africa. The South African Council of Churches has also begun searching for new discourses on empowering a citizen-led democracy. At a conference in 2017, it adopted an economic perspective document that affirmed the importance of the climate crisis and the need for a deep, just transition, including food sovereignty and the solidarity economy (South African Council of Churches, 2017).

Trade unions have continued to support solidarity economy approaches in response to the informalisation and precariousness of work. The newly formed SAFTU has had dialogue with various organisations committed to alternative economy approaches, including COPAC, informal traders and Street-Net International. SAFTU has publicly called for community mining co-operatives, as part of nationalisation, to support small-scale informal miners (Mokati, 2017). Education and support organisations have also increasingly placed the solidarity economy on their agendas. The Global Labour University Programme at Wits University offers a social theory course to all trade unions in South Africa. Since 2017, there has been a dedicated focus on systemic alternatives, including the solidarity economy.

Moreover, the Centre for Education Rights and Transformation at the University of Johannesburg has done research on grassroots alternatives and has connected this with thinking about the commons, living well and the solidarity economy (DVV International, 2017). Oxfam South Africa has a dedicated programme elaborating on the notion of the people's economy. This includes a focus on the solidarity economy. In early 2018, Oxfam South Africa hosted a workshop with a dedicated focus on co-operatives and the solidarity economy as part of developing a concerted strategy and programme. Various co-operatives and education and support NGOs are involved.

Community-led approaches to solidarity economy development have continued to produce innovative attempts at aggregating solidarity economy with other transformative practices to create grassroots logics for change. The Kwazakhele township transition initiative, in the Eastern Cape, is another important example. It brings together a focus on the climate crisis, the needs of the community and the importance of systemic alternatives. Similarly, the Earthrise Trust has, since 2014, been championing a development initiative in Rustlers Valley on a farm (Earthrise Trust, 2014). It has developed an innovative model of land reform, which has given use rights to local villagers who have organised themselves into a co-operative to farm allocated land, spawned co-operatives in brick making, built a community crèche, experimented with alternative land use planning with the local community involving a communal organisation, and has a community-run conferencing facility promoting alternative dialogues for transformation.[13]

Finally, the SAFSC has innovatively brought together the idea of food sovereignty and the solidarity economy in its intellectual discourses and practices (Bennie and Satgoor, 2018). As a campaigning platform, the SAFSC is a loose alliance of organisations from the agrarian sector, climate justice, food justice and solidarity economy movements. Launched in 2015, the SAFSC has consistently translated and given substance to a South African approach to food sovereignty. Through its hunger tribunal, drought speak-outs, bread marches, food sovereignty festivals, water sovereignty dialogues and activist schools, it has evolved an alternative perspective on land and agricultural transformation. This is encapsulated in the People's Food Sovereignty Act, shared with several government ministries in 2017 and, in early 2018, handed over to a representative of parliament at a people's dialogue in Cape Town. The SAFSC orientation and the People's Food Sovereignty Act are about advancing a democratically controlled food system from below through households, communities, villages, towns and cities as part of the deep, just transition to survive climate shocks. The bottom-up pathways it envisages link food sovereignty, solidarity economy, water sovereignty, control of seeds and small-scale farming and democratic planning. Various pilot pathways are underway in urban and rural spaces.[14]

---

13   Interview with Gino Govender, trustee of Earthrise Trust, 10 December 2017.
14   *SAFSC News* 9 (2017): 8–15, https://gallery.mailchimp.com/6eb374fe9b580101982b7b47c/

Challenges for solidarity economy as a movement of movements

As a movement of movements, with different grassroots approaches and institutional forms championing the solidarity economy, there are also various challenges. Plurality is an advantage, but it also imposes limits.

First, solidarity economy practices and pathways from below provide a crucial strength, but such networked connections must be deepened. Embedded and localised linkages between production, consumption, finance and democratic planning reflect a constitutive form of power at work. Such forms of power enable a break with the dominant capitalist logic and system. These forms of power include structural (securing space for provisioning in a socialised market), movement (membership), direct (active campaigning) and symbolic power (living examples). Each of these enables scale and depth to be achieved. However, such forms of power have to be developed through institution building, capacity and training. At the same time, these forms of power have to intersect with other systemic alternatives. This means solidarity economy practice needs to work with food sovereignty, zero waste, co-operative banks, participatory planning, climate jobs and more. This is about a transformative activism pushing beyond its limits and constantly seeking to innovate in terms of solidarity economy relations and logics.

A second important challenge is ongoing learning and sharing through the solidarity economy knowledge commons. The case studies in this volume illustrate this and face-to-face sharing in activist schools, learning exchanges, documentaries, online sharing and learning tools, such as newsletters, are all crucial.[15] Such practices construct a collective intellectual knowledge, produced in innovative transformative practices and mutual learning loops. This enables various pathways to emerge among small-scale farmers, waste pickers, trade unions, co-operatives and NGOS, for instance. All these variegated social forces need to deepen solidarity relations to share and diffuse their practices for others to learn from, as they meet various social needs at the frontlines of struggle.

A third challenge is how solidarity economy forces ensure more effective engagement with the state. Currently capitalist states merely meet the needs of capital through protecting private ownership, providing risk-free investment

---

files/92e4fcab-a92b-41f6-90f2-fec8887ee2a8/SAFSC_newsletter_9_.compressed.pdf (accessed 20 March 2018).

15 Online resources include the SAFSC webpage at http://www.safsc.org.za and the Solidarity Economy Movements' webpage at http://www.sem.org.za (accessed 20 March 2018).

conditions, building infrastructure, deregulation and even financial incentives, for instance. The stick is bent too much towards corporate interests and market regulation, even in South Africa. For solidarity economy movements, this poses various challenges in the state relationship. Thus far solidarity economy movements' engagement with the state has been with, against and beyond. But each of these thrusts need to be deepened where necessary. It is essential to ensure recognition from the state, so as to work with it to deepen democratic systemic reform, such as co-operative banking or developing a worker co-operatives Act and policy, for instance. Also participatory mechanisms in current co-operative legislation, such as the Co-operative Council provided to replace the Co-operative Board in the Co-operatives Act of 2005, need to be driven from below. This cannot merely be the preserve of the state-sanctioned co-operative movement. In addition, solidarity economy movements have to challenge the weaknesses of the state regarding co-operative development. Critique, debate and even mass opposition to some of the practices of the state that push back or undermine solidarity economy practices need to be mobilised. Most importantly, solidarity economy movements need to be ahead of the state on the ground in its capacity, power and pathway building. The solidarity economy idea and practice does not belong to the state. It is a people's idea, for the people and by the people. The state is merely there to provide strategic support to this organic logic from below.

Chapter in *Cooperatives in South Africa: Advancing Solidarity Economy Pathways from Below*, edited by Vishwas Satgar. Pietermaritzburg: UKZN Press, 2019.

Food Sovereignty

Break the Food Chain to Build Our Humanity

FOOD IS ESSENTIAL TO THE human condition. Food politics have shaped world history. It was central to the shift from nomadic to settled societies 10,000 years ago, in the making of plantation slavery, voyages of discovery for spices in the East, in remaking an antagonistic relationship with nature through industrial farming and in influencing revolutions from the French and Russian to the more recent Arab Spring.

We imperil society if we ignore food crises and politics

Are service delivery protests food riots in essence? Is the spate of xenophobic attacks a reflection of desperation by the hungry? In a country with 14 million people going to bed hungry, 45.6% of the population food insecure and a poor household spending 80% of its income on food, hunger cannot be ignored in understanding these violent outbursts.

The scale of hunger in South Africa makes us a dehumanised, divided and conflict-prone society. It exposes income inequalities and a cardinal failure of the mainly white-controlled, export-led industrial food system. Yet these contradictions have been rendered non-antagonistic by our narratives of the rainbow nation, although hunger has certainly caused, and is a precipitating factor in, social conflict. Hunger may not be determining in every instance but it certainly contributes. It must be brought into our analyses of what is going on in the growing number of flashpoints engulfing our society.

The drought devastating the maize crop, though commonly understood to be part of South Africa's drought cycle, can no longer be understood outside of climate change shifts taking place because of global warming. Extreme weather occurrences, a result of climate change, are manifesting on the African continent with massive flooding across a number of countries in 2012 and the displacement of six million people in Nigeria alone. With Africa likely to experience the worst effects of climate change, arid and semi-arid land is expected to increase in coming years from 5% to 8%, and water stress is predicted to affect 75 million to 250 million people by 2020.

Vast loss of arable land

In southern Africa there is likely to be a loss of vast tracts of arable land. Climate scientists expect an increase of temperatures at twice the global rate. Basically, there is a correlation of extreme weather patterns and worsening farming output that must be more seriously studied in an effort to adapt South Africa's agricultural system to climate change. For many, a techno-fix such as genetically modified organisms (GMOs) will deal with climate change. In 2014, 86% of maize under cultivation was GMOs; this did not stop the drought from having devastating impacts.

The science of industrial farming is about simplifying complex natural processes to control nature. At the same time, industrial agriculture is one of the largest consumers of South Africa's limited water supply. Climate change brings both complexity and resource challenges that globalised industrial agriculture will have difficulties dealing with. Hence the imperative for a new ecological approach to agricultural production that is more easily adaptable and grounded in values to sustain life.

Most of us take the food on our plates for granted. While we stuff ourselves, we don't consider that one in three children under the age of five are malnourished. We don't ask questions about the nutritional value of the food we consume, who produced it and where it comes from. Yet the food most of us consume is directly related to many pathologies in our society, from growing obesity to food-related illnesses such as diabetes, high blood pressure, strokes and heart disease, as a result of nutritionally deficient diets. Cheap food has been marketed as fast, good and glamorous. For many in our society with low incomes, this choice is out of necessity. This makes the poor in our society victims of food poisoning by design.

The School of Public Health at the University of the Witwatersrand can prove that a chicken drumstick sold by a leading fast-food retailer has twice the amount of salt and calories and three times the amount of fat as the same drumstick in the US.

Broken food system

This past week a set of scenarios dealing with the future of the South African food system was launched at Wits by the Southern African Food Lab. These scenarios confirm the existence of a broken food system and the need for new ways. Though timely, these scenarios cannot avert a confrontation with South

Africa's corporate-controlled food system. In the context of the unhinging political consensus that has shaped the transition to the post-apartheid order and the growing existential threat of climate change, the food crisis could destroy South Africa – or it could assist in redefining a new system.

The food crisis married to authoritarian populist gestures such as land grabs, called for by the EFF, will lead us into a race war. Moreover, it would not be any different from the ANC government's failed land reform, which has raised expectations but has been thin on building sustainability. An alternative approach to the food crisis is grounded in a transformative politics from below, being advanced at the grassroots in South Africa and inspired by rising global movements championing food sovereignty.

Food sovereignty seeks to harness our democracy's potential and is central in ensuring we create conditions to survive climate change with a deep, just transition. It is an alternative to the narrow notion of food security, inadequate to deal with the depth of the food crisis emanating from the corporate-controlled food system, which makes greedy corporations enablers of the right to food. South Africa is one of 20 countries with a justiciable right to food in its Constitution, which requires the enactment of a food sovereignty Act to realise the transformative potential of the Constitution. This is a crucial demand of the newly formed SAFSC and alliance. At its recent founding meeting, the campaign committed itself to focus on increasing food prices and land as part of agrarian transformation. South Africa has escalating food prices and food inflation.

Food riots

Between 2006 and 2008, and 2010 and 2012, this was a global trend leading to food riots in parts of the world. Given the globalised nature of corporate agriculture, including in South Africa, food prices are driven by multiple causal factors, according to many food analysts, including the Food and Agriculture Organization (FAO). They suggest that speculation on US commodities markets, climate change and oil prices are among these factors. The recent decline in oil prices raised the expectation of a downward adjustment in food prices, particularly staples such as bread, but this has not happened.

Despite the sophistication of these analytical models, they are symptomatic in understanding food pricing challenges and assume a globalised market-driven approach to prices as unquestionable, despite the volatility and instability such markets induce. The food price challenge is essentially about food corporations' greed and the absence of a regulatory role for the state to protect our common interest. South Africa's escalating food prices can be curtailed if the state is able to regulate food prices.

The degree and mechanisms underpinning this intervention need to be debated in South Africa. At the same time, there are grassroots alternatives that are transparent and grounded in ethical values such as trust, transparency, environmental justice, democracy and community need. Buying co-operatives, community markets, co-operative bakeries and some farm stalls are all transformative alternatives dealing with pricing differently. These food sovereignty institutions must connect and replicate as part of the emerging solidarity economy in South Africa to ensure producers and consumers can control pricing.

Sign of dispossession

Land in South Africa is imbued with various meanings but most salient is its place in history as a sign of the dispossession of the majority. The frontier wars of dispossession, the infamous 1913 Natives' Land Act and subsequent laws are crucial markers in this painful history. The ANC state has failed dismally to address this historic injustice. From the standpoint of food sovereignty, land is central to our understanding of life, food and culture. Hence, a people's tribunal on land reform to expose the shortcomings of the ANC state and people's land audits will be used to bring idle, unused and common spaces under cultivation through agro-ecology, a farming practice that places sustaining life and ecological systems at the centre of farming practices.

Communities, but mainly women, protecting indigenous edible plants, managing seed banks for generations and defending healthy food cultures from going extinct will be celebrated as part of advancing food sovereignty. In short, the mainly white corporate-controlled food system in South Africa, from farm to plate, is maintaining supply for the few. It is in many ways toxic and is also in crisis.

Food sovereignty is a way for South Africa to critique globalised industrial agriculture and introduce a rights-based discourse and an ecological alternative. The transformative just transition to survive climate change and bring out the best of our humanity has begun here, from below.

Mail & Guardian, 12 March 2015.

South Africa's Food System in Dire Straits

THE SAFSC THIS WEEK led a bread march against hunger through the streets of Johannesburg. In a highly unequal society, studies on the survival strategies of poor households reveal how bread and a brew of sugar and water is what keeps many people alive.

At the same time, bread is a big money-spinner for producers and retailers. Bread profiteering was rife in 2007 and 2010 among producers. Premier Foods, Pioneer Foods, Tiger Brands and Foodcorp were found guilty by the Competition Commission of manipulating wheat and maize milling operations and were rebuked in the Constitutional Court for their abhorrent conduct.

This was also in the context of globalised food system price shocks from 2006 to 2008 and from 2010 to 2011, which made it a complex issue. Today, South Africa's globalised food system is going through its third price shock in less than a decade. All measurements of food prices are showing a dramatic increase in inflation, with year-on-year price increases of staple foods. The increase for January 2015 to January this year was 14.6%.

The biggest increases have been in mealie meal, samp, cooking oil and potatoes, all of which are staples for the poorest people in the country. However, bread prices have also been increasing. A loaf of brown bread (700g) increased by 5.73% and a loaf of white increased by 5.34%. The big food retailers are trying to make this price increase acceptable by setting these prices below food inflation increases (food inflation for March was at 9.5%, higher than headline inflation of 6.5%) and are hiding behind the weak exchange rate for imported wheat to justify bread price increases. In this context, Grain SA has blown the whistle and is arguing that imported wheat is cheaper and therefore bread prices should actually be declining. To understand the extent of the profiteering, more information is needed. People's power through disciplined and non-violent action is crucial to secure an investigation by the public protector and the Human Rights Commission of bread profiteering, which is denying many citizens their right to food. This investigation is one of the main demands of the bread march against hunger, alongside a call for bread and food prices – especially staple foods – to fall.

Such a demand is not unreasonable, given the massive profit made by food retailers in South Africa. Most show an annual profit of more than R1 billion. One owner – Christo Wiese of Shoprite – is the third-wealthiest person in South Africa and is worth about R25 billion. Wealth from food corporations is increasingly concentrated, while most workers in the food system are outsourced and badly paid. The bread march against hunger will also call for an end to outsourcing and for decent work for food industry workers.

Food price increases cannot be uncoupled from the drought ravaging South Africa. Within the first few months of this year, food inflation undermined the ameliorative effect of social grants, and is not only making malnutrition a problem (one in five children in the country are experiencing malnutrition, according to the Global Nutrition Report), but adding to learning disabilities among children. Moreover, drought is exposing the deeper problems of a corporate-controlled food system and a state that is incapable of responding adequately. In South Africa, according to government estimates, about 14.1 million people went to bed hungry before the drought and about 46% of the population was food insecure, revealing a major paradox of our globalised food system. With food prices increasing and the state response coming up short, the number of hungry people has certainly increased.

The state is not tracking and measuring this. Most political parties have not taken the drought seriously, except the DA, which wants a national disaster declared, mainly to protect the interests of commercial farmers. The severity of a drought largely depends on preparedness and the institutional readiness of a society to respond. A drought becomes a disaster because of the capabilities a society has to deal with it. South Africa's response to the climate crisis is being tested in this drought. The drought, which is part of a meteorological pattern that will certainly recur, is revealing how the government is completely unprepared to use the Disaster Management Act.

In his state of the nation address this year, President Jacob Zuma was silent on the global climate crisis and devoid of any seriousness about the drought and its effects. In a country in which most of our water resources are already allocated, mainly to globalised farming, and with increasing water pollution by mining corporations, water management should be a national priority, and the drought should be declared a national crisis to ensure we build greater resilience and sustainability. South Africa's food system was failing the country before the drought. As we enter a world of climate crisis, the insanity of killing ourselves through using fossil fuels is even more apparent.

City Press, 15 May 2016.

Food Sovereignty: The Viable Alternative to ANC and EFF Land Solutions

ALTHOUGH JACOB ZUMA has fallen, South Africa has not escaped the miasma of a Zumafied parliament. His reign represented the degeneration of political leadership and the serious weakening of democracy. ANC and EFF support for a motion to amend the Constitution to advance land expropriation without compensation reflects the absence of deep and serious political debate in our democracy.

One would have expected that, post-Zuma, the ANC would reach for a modicum of engaged deliberation on such a fundamental question, which has to be addressed in a manner that takes the country forward. Moreover, the ANC was not blindsided by the EFF's motion, which was merely confirming its December conference position and the ANC Youth League's own documents that predate the EFF's formation. Both the ANC and EFF authoritarian populist positions share one thing in common. For them land grabs are about revenge. To address the wrongs of colonial and racist dispossession, white farmers must be punished. Some would argue further that Nelson Mandela's reconciliation politics have failed. Yet, as academic and author Sabelo Ndlovu-Gatsheni points out, the paradigm of war in modern Western society, based on the logic of racial division and coloniality, was rejected by Mandela and instead there was a deep decolonial impulse in his ethical approach to reconciliation through his paradigm of peace. Like all political practices, it was grounded in immanent possibility. There were paths taken and not taken. It also means that, as a political resource, Mandela's reconciliatory practice can be put to work to achieve more radical outcomes.

The new anti-white racism of the EFF is shared by the ANC. In this instance, the ANC is clearly far from Mandela but even further away from the principle of non-racialism, including radical non-racialism that advocates fundamental transformation. What the ANC stands for at the level of principle is increasingly unclear. Post-Zuma the ANC's trust deficit with South Africa is still widening.

To be a vengeful racist addressing the land grievance comes with its dangers. Such an approach presumes that all white farmers (about 35,000) are supremacists and must be treated as such. A sharp, racialised antagonism is created with white farmers and more generally white South Africa. A volatile racial fault-line is constructed in our discourse, which can take on a life of its own in everyday politics. The grammar of race war, militant posturing, racial innuendo and symbolic violence sets the stage for confrontation. Julius Malema and the EFF, of course, are not the only ones with a capacity for racial violence. White South Africa, particularly conservative Afrikaners, are armed and therefore the potential for deadly political conflagration is a possibility. A race war in South Africa, over the land, simply means we all lose.

At the same time, there are differences between the EFF and the ANC positions. The EFF views the state as a custodian of all land, providing use rights to individuals and corporations for a maximum of 25 years, subject to renewal. Although the language of small-scale farming is evoked, the EFF has not given it much thought. It is very likely big farmers would emerge in their revolving-door framework to access land use. The state is also meant to support small-scale farmers with procurement opportunities and protections. Ultimately the EFF views small-scale commercial agriculture as a viable prospect in the context of export to the wider African market.

Though the EFF proposal is shot through with inconsistencies, it is primarily about state-supported capitalist agriculture that could compete and displace peasant agriculture in the wider African context. This is a far cry from pan-African solidarity with Africa's peasantry. There will be winners and losers in the EFF's proposal. For the ANC, agrarian transformation is primarily about supporting small-scale farmers to become viable commercial enterprises in the first economy and for export markets. Agri-hubs, extension services and financing are geared towards this pathway. In this policy framework there have been and will continue to be winners and losers.

Yet does one have to be a revengeful racist to address historical injustices such as land dispossession? Radical non-racialism, which is not anti-white but anti-white supremacy, is another principled political position from which to engage the race, class, gender and ecological dynamics of South Africa's unjust food system. This principle informs the campaigning platform of the SAFSC, which is made up of organisations from the agrarian sector, climate justice, food justice and solidarity economy movements.

Formed out of a conference on the right to food in late 2014 and launched in 2015, the campaign has consistently translated and given substance to a

South African approach to food sovereignty. Through its hunger tribunal, drought speak-outs, bread marches, food sovereignty festivals, water sovereignty dialogues and activist schools it has evolved an alternative perspective on land and agricultural transformation. This is encapsulated in a People's Food Sovereignty Act, adopted at a People's Parliament in 2016, shared with several government ministries last year and recently handed over to a representative of parliament at a people's dialogue in Cape Town. The People's Food Sovereignty Act is an example of prefigurative practice. It provides a compass to build food sovereignty pathways from below through households, villages, towns and cities. It envisages a citizen-driven process but supported by the state, to build a democratic, just and sustainable food system. The Act is also an example of democratic systemic reform, which sets out fundamental differences with the ANC and EFF's approach to land reform.

First, agricultural land must be treated as having a social and ecological function. This means chemical, industrial and mono-industrial farming is not the way forward for agriculture. Instead, agro-ecological practices need to be prioritised to produce in harmony with ecosystems, water constraints and more indigenised diets.

Second, small-scale farmers need to be given conditional-use rights of a maximum of two hectares of land as part of the commons but subject to the imperatives of democratic planning. This prevents the over-concentration of land and allows for more than 30 million small-scale farmers to be created in South Africa. The land for this commons will come from the state, religious organisations, communal tenure systems, the private sector and from deconcentrating commercial farms.

Third, the deconcentration of commercial farms must be handled in accordance with the Constitution, as part of a transition, involving a land audit and with a commitment to fair compensation to historically white farmers. A national food sovereignty fund is envisaged, which will be the mechanism to secure funds from South African capital, not the individual taxpayer, to buy out white commercial farmers over a 20-year-period and provide capital to small-scale farmers. Finance, industries, retailers, mining companies and every fraction of (white) capital must contribute to this fund, given the benefits they accrued under apartheid and in the post-apartheid context. This is the gesture of nation building required to advance genuine reconciliation.

Fourth, the state is envisaged as playing an enabling role to ensure food sovereignty is realised as a democratic systemic reform driven from below. This includes a procurement role, a pedagogical role, a regulatory role against dominant commercial food interests, a custodial role of the land commons together with a national food sovereignty council and local communal councils. It is also envisaged the state will support a democratic planning mechanism to plan the water, land, seed, production and consumption issues around a food-sovereign system. This is crucial in a climate-driven world. As opposed to the ANC and the EFF, the food sovereignty proposition envisages an alternative food system controlled by small-scale farmers and consumers but deeply embedded in society. A food-sovereign system will enable South Africa to confront the pathologies of a corporate-controlled food system (such as hunger, unhealthy food choices and globalised diets) while also enduring climate shocks.

Mail & Guardian, 15 March 2018.

Civil Society: The State has Failed and Cannot be Trusted, Let Us Help Solve the Hunger Crisis

THE STORY OF THE South African state is a litany of failure and broken promises, but a new story is still possible if our government manages to wake up and co-ordinate a national response of solidarity with civil society and business to bring about systemic transformation to avert a deepening humanitarian crisis.

Stories told among people are important for constructing the imaginary and a collective identity, for shared meanings and for truth telling. The story we are going to share after the Covid-19 pandemic will certainly not be about a responsive, effective and caring state. In fact, the South African state as custodian of public finances, embodiment of collective will and torch bearer of human rights is currently a pariah in our midst.

The state's criminalisation of some of its citizens prior to Covid-19 is now compounded by a deepening legitimacy crisis. The list of its failings is long:
- local government audits revealing only 20 out of 257 governments having clean audits;
- brazen capture of personal protective equipment contracts by the politically connected;
- hospital services collapsing in parts of the country;
- overreach of prohibitory regulation to deal with smoking and alcohol;
- increasing structural unemployment with more poor and low-skilled women (at least two out of three million, according to a recent study) being the shock absorbers of this crisis;
- water needs of many communities remaining unmet due to decades of failed water governance – including during the worst drought in the history of the country; and
- hunger ravaging numerous communities.

These realities upend the certainties of national liberation thought which justify lapses in ethical conduct or failed policies as mere aberrations in the long march to achieve the common good through the National Democratic Revolution. Well, there is no common good when such politics have brought society to the point of complete destruction. A poignant academic definition of social collapse is this: a failure to meet the basic needs of people amounts to social collapse. This is the dominant narrative emerging in South Africa: a society falling apart and a government incapable of rising to the challenge of protecting society.

President Cyril Ramaphosa's indecisive leadership of South Africa is falling short of what the country needs. It is not him alone, but a ruling party muddling along, with all its contradictory impulses and dangerous tendencies. His approach is to give expression to this mélange of views on how South Africa should be governed, thus ensuring the political party apparatus of the ANC-led alliance prevails, rather than transparent, inclusive, open and democratic policy-making in the interests of the country. In the end, the country is held hostage to obscurantist political practices.

Leninism did not prepare Marxist-Leninists for pandemics, let alone the complexities of the world we live in, and so they remain firmly perched in the shadows of the ANC, eagerly trying to make themselves relevant. The neoliberals are obsessed with managing the optics of financial markets which override any concerns for human life.

In this political drama the nationalists are using this state of exception as an excuse for law and order approaches to mitigate addictions, such as smoking and alcoholism. In the process they are literally missing the point that there are deeper causes and reforms this government failed to introduce prior to Covid-19, including tighter regulation of the tobacco and alcohol industries, given the externalised social costs of these industries that the taxpayer has to carry. The solutions from this regime don't square off with the complexity of the crisis we are living through, which consists of multiple and interconnected socio-ecological crises occurring at once. This involves a climate crisis-induced drought (the first of many to come), a failing globalised economy, a corrupt state and widespread social violence – and now Covid-19.

The common approach of ANC governance has been about controlling citizens from above with crumbs and the big stick and generally letting capital do as it pleases, while creating opportunities for the enrichment of a few through the state. This has not worked before Covid-19, and it is certainly not working now to address the challenges of confronting an unequal South Africa overrun by the pandemic.

Before Covid-19, South Africa was exhausted by naïve promises of foreign investment being the answer to all its problems, by brazen and widespread corruption, and by rulers' disdain for the needs of the people. There is fatigue, anger, desperation and disillusionment in everyday life as Covid-19 takes its toll. Roaring tides of historical change are churning in spaces of social mobilisation to mitigate the negative impact of the lockdown in communities.

Many understand there is more harm than good coming from the governing party. The spell of the pot of gold at the end of Madiba's rainbow does not work any longer. Thus, many are stepping forward with the assumption that the ANC cannot be trusted, let alone be responsible for rising to the challenges of our time. The simple truth is that it has failed, on the terms of its own ideals, its programmatic commitments and in its leadership of society.

The deepening hunger crisis

In the midst of Covid-19, hunger has become worse. In the absence of support from the state and the Solidarity Fund, thousands of communities have attempted to mitigate the hunger crisis through donor-supported food distribution, community kitchens, sharing food and living off the commons – through subsistence fishing for example.

In a study done by the National Food Crisis Forum[1] convened by the SAFSC, a snapshot of community-led food relief efforts suggests a minimum of 206 of these initiatives reach about 53,100 people per week, with the cumulative costs being about R67,688.80 per week and a unit supplied on average costing R340.14: either a hot meal, food parcel, seeds, cash or voucher.

Today, many of these communities are experiencing serious constraints in their food relief efforts. Local donor support is drying up. Low incomes in communities are also having an effect. Organisations doing this work are buckling under pressures and the need in communities is outstripping local relief. Starvation has already taken human life in the community of Waterworks near Lenasia and will continue to do so.

Appeals have been made to the government and to the Solidarity Fund to consider a nationally co-ordinated response to the hunger crisis. This simply means democratising the government's disaster management approach to Covid-19 by bringing in active civil society organisations at national, provincial and local level to address the worsening crisis.

This is a rather obvious move the government could have initiated, especially considering the president's constant rhetoric of social compacting. Addressing the hunger crisis together as government, the Solidarity Fund,

---

1 https://www.safsc.org.za/press-release-second-meeting-of-national-food-crisis-forum/.

progressive civil society and business would demonstrate solidarity in practice and will be more effective. Failing this the UN human rights machinery, including its World Food Programme and Special Rapporteur on the Right to Food, will have to be approached to trigger humanitarian assistance for many facing starvation in the country. Furthermore, given the fragmented and limited welfare grant system in South Africa, the demand for a substantive and universal BIG as the linchpin of our welfare architecture has gained widespread support across progressive civil society and in the public sphere.

If South Africa were to hold a referendum on this idea, it would probably win overwhelming support and get higher voter turnouts than during elections. The SAFSC recently hosted the leading expert in the world on universal income, Guy Standing, for a public webinar on the case for such a measure. While he reflected on numerous examples and lessons, his message overwhelmingly was simply this: South Africa cannot afford not to have such an income transfer, and not just as a temporary relief measure, but rather to address deep structural inequalities.

A recent measure of income inequality suggests 10% of income earners have 65% of national income. This means the billionaires in our society live at the expense of all of us. South Africa is an unviable society because a minority just has too much, and that simply has to end. #UBIGNOW, carefully designed, not eroding but improving existing transfers, and based on redistribution from the wealthy, envisions a systemic transformation that can cushion society, ensure a people-led recovery and be a crucial mechanism to mitigate multiple systemic crises. Its time has come.

In short, co-ordinating a national response to the hunger crisis and speedily introducing a non-means-tested universal income grant transfer now for all living in South Africa, including documented migrants and refugees, could be the solidarity story we tell as a society after Covid-19. The government has to wake up and understand that society is too big to fail – it must be protected now.

Daily Maverick, 18 August 2020.

Universal Basic Income Grant

The South African Precariat, Covid-19 and #BIGNOW

CURRENTLY, THERE ARE 95 countries on the planet that have vibrant campaigns for universal BIG. A global coalition of these campaigns has also called on the UN secretary-general to support a BIG agenda for the planet, to complement existing public benefits and goods. Such requests have been reinforced by the Pope, who on Easter weekend also called for a BIG. With economies shut due to Covid-19 or cranking back up slowly, unemployment skyrocketing and income loss in households, having cash in the hands of citizens to meet basic needs is crucial. With labour movements weakened by over three decades of financialisation, deregulation and liberalisation, citizens are at the mercy of neoliberal ruling classes. The spectrum ranges from Hindu fundamentalist fascism in India, to white nationalist Trumpism in the US to Afro-neoliberalism in South Africa.

What is at stake is self-evident: society is too big to fail. These ruling classes are now facing a historical test in which market-centric pragmatism and more financialisation policies will not be adequate to redress the scale and depth of social suffering. US unemployment is worse than it was in the 2007–2009 crisis. The ILO (2020) has drawn attention to the imperative of comprehensive and adequate social protection measures to accompany Covid-19 public health responses. South Africa has particular features of precarity that existed before the Covid-19 pandemic, and that have been at the heart of its crisis of socio-ecological reproduction. These have worsened under one of the strictest lockdowns in the world. South Africa's lockdown is based on household confinement for the entire population and government-determined essential service economic activity, informed by public health guidelines, at lockdown level 5. This was accompanied by a total ban on exercising in public, and on purchasing alcohol and cigarettes. This lasted for five weeks. Currently government has articulated a lockdown approach of five levels, allowing an expansion at level 4 of essential service economic activity, exercise time from 6 am to 9 am daily, and prohibitions on alcohol and smoking. Level 3 regulations are slightly softer and looser, and this logic extends to level 2 and ultimately level 1 at which point public health guidelines guide social behaviour, all economic activity is meant to be opened up and there are no social controls on big gatherings. The country can revert to level 5 and within this framework some areas of the country can be isolated as hot-spots. A maze of irrational regulations has accompanied each level of lockdown thus far: such as an elaborate system of registering and obtaining permission for community-led food relief efforts at level 4, or criminalisation of thousands of small-scale subsistence fishers while fishing corporations and trawlers have legal permission to continue devastating ocean ecosystems. Many of South Africa's leading epidemiologists, virologists and public health experts have raised concerns about the over-regulation driving this lockdown approach. The ANC government, which has failed for over two decades to lift the African majority out of poverty, joblessness and the grip of inequality, has suddenly stepped up with a newfound concern for the wellbeing and health of the country's citizens. The draconian lockdown has been hailed by the WHO as consistent with the urgency of the situation. However, not enough attention has been paid to the socio-economic mitigation measures that could blunt the horrific social pain caused by the lockdown.

Covid-19 and the socio-economic death of the precariat

South Africa has had stubborn and high structural unemployment, above 20% throughout most of the post-apartheid period; in 2019 the narrow unemployment rate stood at 29% and the expanded rate stood at 38.5%.[1] It is clear that almost 40% of the working age population (about 10 million people) are excluded from generating and sharing in the wealth created in the society. This group of permanently unemployed persons is only one fraction of the precariat.

The second fraction of the precariat and the broader working class comprises the short-term unemployed (about 1.9 million). These are workers who are locked into temporary work, part-time work, labour-broking relationships and other forms of subcontracting. For these workers there are no labour law protections; they are extremely vulnerable and face a high risk of losing earning capacity at any time.

South Africa's economy has a third fraction of the precariat and the broader working class linked to another structural feature, commonly referred to as the

---

1   The narrow rate refers to how many people in the labour force are out of a job but looking for work. The expanded rate additionally includes anybody who is out of a job, wants a job but has given up looking for work.

second economy or in labour market and development studies literature as the informal sector. This includes about 3 million people – 2.6 million engaged in informal trading and about 60,000 to 90,000 waste reclaimers. The latter group saves municipalities about R750 million a year in landfill costs. They live from day to day.

The fourth fraction of the South African working class and precariat are those who have some long-term employment but who earn a wage below R4125 per month and who do not have benefits such as health and unemployment insurance. This figure represents a minimum wage poverty line; it means that workers have to earn this amount or more to ensure that they can bring themselves and their dependents out of poverty. According to the National Minimum Wage project at the University of the Witwatersrand, about 5.5 million workers earned below this amount per month in 2015 (NMW Research Initiative, 2015).[2] They were mainly domestic, agricultural and construction workers. Moreover, their wages supported families ranging from four to ten dependents.

On 26 March 2020 the South African government imposed a level 5 lockdown. Most of the economy was locked down except telecommunications, corporate-controlled food, online banking, health facilities and energy. For the South African precariat this meant increases in the ranks of the unemployed, and instant loss of income and wage-earning capacity. This is a precariat that is trapped in poverty and low wages, and is highly indebted to survive. For the past two months, about 20 million people have had to face a situation with close to nothing to sustain their families. Unemployment is increasing and hunger is widespread. The squeeze on the precariat has thrown up a discourse about how the hunger pandemic may well kill more people rather than Covid-19.

Managing the desperation of the precariat

With the socio-economic crisis among South Africa's precariat already a nightmare before Covid-19, the lived experience under the lockdown can only be described as desperate. The government imposed a lockdown on one of the most unequal countries in the world, and the public health response was not balanced with an appropriate socio-economic response. Besides post-apartheid

---

2   South Africa introduced a Minimum Wage Act in 2018, which was implemented in 2019. The legal minimum wage threshold was changed in 2020 to R20.76 per hour, a 3.8% increase on the previous R20 per hour. Moreover, domestic workers would now receive R15.57 per hour and farm workers R18.68. None of these minimum wage determinations assist workers break out of wage poverty.

economic restructuring being guided by financialised imperatives to ensure an externalised economy deeply connected to global financial markets, South Africa's state has also been ravaged by widespread looting. This has created serious fiscal constraints on the state. In response and just before Covid-19, the Afro-neoliberal finance minister announced an austerity budget, including cutbacks in health expenditure, to deal with this fiscal crisis.

With Covid-19, Afro-neoliberal reason morphed into epidemiological reason (Satgar, 2020a). This means that trickle-down economics and its assumptions of individualising and marketising social problems continued to prevail. This is best understood as epidemiological neoliberalism to manage the desperation of the precariat. This has been apparent as level 5 lockdown kicked in. While unemployment benefits were triggered, this was mainly for workers in formal employment and who have employers that have registered for such benefits. For most of South Africa's precariat such benefits are out of reach.

Moreover, with a corrupt and fiscally constrained Afro-neoliberal state leading the Covid-19 response, it chose early on to mobilise and instrumentalise social solidarity. It crowd-sourced and privatised the frontline response to Covid-19. Individuals and corporations were invited to contribute financially to a Solidarity Fund, seeded with R150 million state funding. This provided an opportunity for billionaires, not subject to an effective wealth tax, to step up to save the nation. We now had to be grateful for their donations and generosity. The Solidarity Fund, together with the Department of Social Development, has distributed just over a million food parcels over the past two months; based on an assumed four persons per household, which equates to 4 million people reached. Such parcels are designed to last for two weeks and have been shown to be nutritionally deficient (Vermeulen et al., 2020). Food parcels have been inadequate to meet the food needs of the 20 million members of the precariat. The media has reported on several hunger flashpoints ranging from street protests to attacks on supermarkets, and even hijackings of food trucks. At the tail end of the level 5 lockdown, the government announced a stimulus package of R500 billion. Most progressive political economists argue this was not a stimulus package, with no new money injected into the economy, but instead a stabilisation package largely based on reprioritising existing fiscal resources (COPAC, 2020).

Within this framework R50 billion was allocated to increases in social grants, including a new Covid-19 relief grant for the unemployed of R350 per person per month for the next six months. This grant is below the food poverty line of R547 per month. At the moment, food prices are going up, and an essential basket of goods now costs R3470.92. It also lasts two weeks rather than three weeks (Pietermaritzburg Economic Justice and Dignity, 2020). The costs of a basic basket of hygiene products is R694.74. Besides R350 being inadequate to ensure a nutritious diet and to meet the hygiene needs of a person, this grant, like others, is shared within poor households that have anywhere between four and ten people. With more people eating and living together under lockdown in poor households, such meagre resource transfers are not going to make a fundamental difference. The epidemiological neoliberalism of the ANC state is not a proportionate response to the suffering of the precariat.

A #BIGNOW for South Africa

It is in this context that a substantive, non-means-tested and universal BIG is necessary in South Africa – anywhere from R3500 to R4500 per person per month (Satgar, 2020b). This should be paid to everyone living in South Africa, including migrants and refugees. As a co-founder and activist in the SAFSC, we are working with numerous allies, leading a #BIGNOW campaign endorsed by unemployed peoples' organisations, informal traders, trade unions and numerous high-profile NGOs (SAFSC, 2020). Many argue that the time has come for systemic change to break the precariat out of poverty and dependency on wage work, and to provide a security cushion to all in society, to ensure a recovery from Covid-19 led by the working class, and to provide a mechanism to enable the working class to lead a deep, just transition to confront the climate crisis. The epidemiological neoliberalism of the ANC state is threatening both the public health response to Covid-19 and the future of South Africa's democracy. The #BIGNOW will end the unbearable lived experience of the precariat and ensure an emancipatory future.

Global Labour Journal 11, 2, May 2020.

The Climate Justice Charter Pluri-Vision

No Short Cuts for a Deep, Just Transition: Towards a Climate Justice Charter for South Africa
with Jane Cherry, Courtney Morgan and Aaisha Domingo

Introduction

THE PURPOSE OF THIS article is to make clear that the fight for a deep, just transition is a crucial part of the working-class struggle. This article also highlights some examples and tools that two organisations are using to strengthen solidarity within civil society. In particular, we focus on the COPAC and the SAFSC's CJC process for South Africa. Both these organisations, through their grassroots-driven activism, recognise the need to urgently build systemic alternatives and solidarity between progressive civil society actors, movements, trade unions and other working-class formations. The time to build alternatives and alliances is necessary now more than ever in the face of worsening climate crisis-linked shocks and extreme weather events, which are and will continue to hit the poor and the working class the hardest.

The deep roots of the climate crisis

The climate crisis is affecting every sphere of life and its effects are beginning to worsen. The world has recorded the hottest temperatures ever over the past three years. Extreme weather events like hurricanes in the Americas, wildfires across Europe, typhoons in Asia, flooding in India, droughts on our continent, including South Africa, stand out. Sea levels are also rising, placing many low-lying communities, populous coastal cities and island states in jeopardy.

Climate change is the result of 150 years of carbon (coal, oil and gas) driven industrialisation. The rich industrial countries owe the world a climate debt. China and India are also now on this carbon treadmill. All the science is telling us that if we want to stop a 2°C overshoot, we have to stop extracting carbon now. If we breach 2°C, runaway global warming is a likely outcome. This will undermine the conditions that sustain life on Planet Earth, for humans and other life forms. We are currently at over 1°C increase since before the Industrial Revolution and are already experiencing the impacts of catastrophic climate change. South Africa, as a water-scarce country, will have more regular and longer droughts in a climate driven world.

For the past 20 years the UN has not provided transformative solutions for the climate crisis. Instead, market solutions like carbon markets, carbon offsets, geoengineering and expensive nuclear have been promoted. The US has refused a regulated approach to bring down carbon emissions. Instead, it has stalled, obstructed, delayed, weakened and has now undermined the multilateral approach to climate change. After 20 years of failed multilateral negotiations, the world is sitting with an ineffective Paris Agreement. Today the US under Trump is poised to eclipse Russia and Saudi Arabia as the main producer of fossil fuels in the world. This gives licence to more fracking, tar sands and carbon extraction. Currently, carbon still dominates the global energy mix and renewables are not taking off, according to the IEA. A sector like globalised agriculture contributes about 40% of global carbon emissions and is also not part of the decarbonising conversation. Petro states, carbon capital, finance capital, imperial power and the failed UN system are causing the climate crisis and are driving us into the age of the Anthropocene in which capitalism is endangering planetary conditions that sustain life.

Who will be affected?

Climate change marries social and climate inequality. This means climate shocks like droughts have greater impacts on the working class and poor. For example, the recent drought in Cape Town had a severe impact on the natural environment, but its economic impacts were felt by workers. One of the economic impacts was that food prices went up significantly because of how the droughts affected crop growth, making some basic food items such as bread unaffordable for many working-class families. Farm workers were also affected by the drought, because instead of using water- saving techniques, and cutting back in other ways, in the interest of profit, many farm owners fired and evicted their farm workers. Water costs also went up to police consumption through day zero while the rich bought water, developed boreholes or went on holiday. In the case of farmers (who control most of South Africa's water) they held on to most of what they had.

The food and water crises, especially the ones seen in Cape Town recently, were made worse by privatisation and mismanagement. With these failures, and in the face of the climate crisis, food and water resources will become even more scarce, therefore making it even more expensive and less readily available to the most vulnerable. Work will also become increasingly precarious. This means that climate justice is an important aspect of the working-class struggle, and it is imperative that trade unions take this up and champion this cause. Climate justice is, at its core, a working-class struggle.

The energy sector in South Africa is also facing a major crisis. The major mining houses have now re-invented themselves as global corporations. Along with the collapse of commodity prices these corporations are pushing major restructuring efforts, with tens of thousands of jobs being lost. In addition, South Africa's current energy policy commits to a carbon-intensive future. The shift to a decarbonised and climate justice path will not be the outcome of polite lobbying of government ministers and policy makers. To achieve this, we must form a new working-class led political bloc drawn from organised labour; community-based social movements representing the unemployed; community organisations; environmental justice organisations; and the new intellectuals of the radicalising student movement. Trade unions will play a critical role in this. Climate change will most negatively affect the poor and workers. This means that trade unions (at least their members) will have the most to lose by ignoring climate change.

Below we introduce two organisations in South Africa that are strengthening the building blocks of this new political bloc as they develop tools and processes to train and mobilise communities around climate justice struggles towards a deep, just transition.

The solution: A deep, just transition

COPAC and the SAFSC are championing grassroots-driven approaches to address the climate crises and promote a deep, just transition in South Africa. COPAC was established in 1999 as a grassroots development NGO. It has identified the food, water and climate crises as three of the most important challenges of our time. In response to the systemic nature of these crises, COPAC believes that the only sustainable way forward is for us to advance systemic solutions towards a deep, just transition.

A deep, just transition involves a complete break from fossil fuels, and a transition to a low or zero carbon society done in a manner that limits the negative impact on workers and communities. Further the deep, just transition isn't only about energy and climate jobs, but it is about food, transport, water and all major social systems. For COPAC, the deep, just transition is about sustaining life now and into the future.

But how can a deep, just transition be achieved? What are these systemic solutions? Drawing from COPAC's experience in the development sector for 19 years, coupled with international examples and theory, it has realised that a deep, just transition must come from below by a people-led push for alternatives. Examples of this include food, seed, water and energy sovereignty, the solidarity economy, indigenous knowledge systems, socially owned renewable energy and climate jobs. COPAC's recent endeavours actively promote two of these alternatives, namely food sovereignty pathways and water sovereignty, as discussed below.

Grassroots-led alternatives: Food and water sovereignty

In 2014, COPAC, together with the Foundation for Human Rights and other grassroots NGOs, hosted interprovincial dialogues on the right to food. Out of these dialogues the idea of a food sovereignty campaign was established, one that would provide a platform to unite movements, sectors, communities and organisations championing food sovereignty. This platform was realised in early 2015 with the launch of the SAFSC as a loose alliance.

Despite limited resources of member organisations, SAFSC has had a notable impact in the food sovereignty sphere in South Africa as it has initiated a number of activities at national and local levels. It hosted a hunger tribunal (2015), national bread march and drought speak out (2016), drafted a People's Food Sovereignty Act and launched it at a people's parliament (2017), engaged government departments with the Act (2017) and hosted national and local activist schools (2015–2018). The drought, its links to climate change and its disproportinate impacts on workers and the poor have been central to these campaign interventions. Hence the SAFSC is now championing food sovereignty pathways to feed communities, villages, towns and cities in this new phase of its activism.

In March 2018 COPAC co-ordinated a dialogue with parliament, SAFSC and local water activists on the water crisis and People's Food Sovereignty Act in Cape Town. This engagement was guided by two grassroots tools developed by COPAC and SAFSC, namely the Act and an activist guide on water sovereignty. In addition, dialogues were kicked off in Mitchells Plain, Elsies River and Rylands with local activists and community organisations.

Grassroots activist tools are one of the key ways that COPAC seeks to promote popular education and activist training in communities. These tools encourage deeper understanding about the systemic nature of the various crises we face. They also seek to combine progressive ideas from international examples with local struggles and solutions. Building grassroots capacities to overcome these crises is one key step towards a deep, just transition.

One notable tool is COPAC's activist guide on water sovereignty, entitled 'Building people's power for water sovereignty'. The purpose of the guide is to democratise knowledge on water so that people can be empowered to become water activists who can work in their communities to build sustainable local solutions to the crisis. COPAC aims to go further with this tool and process, and reach beyond local formations to build alliances and momentum for a grassroots-driven climate justice charter process, as discussed below.

The people's climate justice charter process: Building momentum and alliances with civil society for a just transition

What started out as a water charter process is now about a CJC for South Africa, given the connections between climate, energy, water, food, production, consumption and finance that has emerged in numerous dialogues. In coming months, a participatory process will evolve through a series of dialogues across South Africa. It will also be a grassroots-led process that will provide a platform for input from environmental justice organisations, grassroots movements, affected communities, working-class organisations, unions and citizens using social media. The CJC will be launched at a people's assembly in 2019. Through this process, COPAC and SAFSC aim to build a strong red-green alliance for climate justice in South Africa that can transform the state into a climate emergency state and create the space for systemic transformation from below.

No shortcuts towards a deep, just transition

It is clear that solutions to the climate, food and water crisis cannot come from the current capitalist system. There are in fact no short cuts. More climate shocks mean more misery for the working class and the poor. COPAC and SAFSC believe that it is imperative that progressive civil society works together to form a new working-class-led political bloc. The climate-crisis-induced water and food crises affect us all and the struggle should be first and foremost the struggle of the poor and working classes. COPAC and SAFSC recognise this and invite input from all organisations, unions and working-class formations to join them in this long, difficult, but life-sustaining journey towards a deep, just transition. Without mobilising united working-class and popular power, the climate crisis will destroy South Africa. We need to act now.

South African Labour Bulletin 42, 3 (September/October 2018).

Annexure: Additional Resources for Transformative Activism

Activist resources

- Activist guide: 'People's planning for a deep just transition'. Johannesburg: COPAC. 2022, https://cjcm.org.za/tools/download/b2ce473a-87ab-467a-95e6-b167693bcca7.
- Animation: 'Food sovereignty: let's feed ourselves: starting your own agroecology food garden', 2022, https://youtu.be/OSCo5TZauso.
- Climate Justice Charter, 2020, https://cjcm.org.za/tools/category/636cf30c-bf23-4719-91e4-6b5cc21f9fff.
- Activist guide: 'Climate justice through land justice: a food sovereignty activist guide, Johannesburg: COPAC, 2019, https://cjcm.org.za/tools/download/cb6b898c-9946-4630-ac6d-4b2eb2f67dd1.
- Animation: 'Water is ours: it's time to fight for water sovereignty', 2018, https://youtu.be/VI3M53bi8RQ.
- People's Food Sovereignty Act 2017 and 2018, https://cjcm.org.za/tools/download/1260738d-6b64-4d21-b81d-d8b47600c917.
- Activist guide: 'Building people's power for water sovereignty: an activist guide, Johannesburg: COPAC, 2017, https://cjcm.org.za/tools/download/ec79364c-9b3c-475c-a912-fd9e89f5ce62.
- Animation: 'The hidden story behind hunger: why we need food sovereignty and climate justice', 2016, https://youtu.be/AYHybn0QdYA.
- Activist guide: Advancing food sovereignty through seed saving: an activist guide. Johannesburg: COPAC, 2016 , https://cjcm.org.za/tools/download/c39abc63-515e-4022-a62c-d1f1c7eb0805.

- Activist guide: 'Food sovereignty for the right to food: a guide for grassroots activism'. Johannesburg: COPAC, https://cjcm.org.za/tools/download/b9f6a2e2-8e56-491a-bec5-bf7cafe779d3.
- Activist guide: 'Create work through worker co-operatives: a guide for grassroots activism'. Johannesburg: COPAC, 2015, https://cjcm.org.za/tools/download/cafc6c89-57ed-428b-8b9b-0c384571fd7d.
- Activist guide: 'Building a solidarity economy movement: a guide for grassroots activism'. Johannesburg: COPAC, https://cjcm.org.za/tools/download/797bfe53-f4ec-408d-aeb5-b38abcbfef7b.

Edited volumes

- *New Frontiers for Socialism in the 21st Century* edited by Vishwas Satgar and Langa Zita, 2009. https://copac.org.za/wp-content/uploads/2017/10/New-Frontiers-for-Socialism-Booklet.pdf.
- *People's and Workers' Climate Justice Charter Futures for South Africa: Accelerate the Deep Just Transition Now* edited by Vishwas Satgar, Jane Cherry and Awande Buthelezi. Cape Town: African Sun Media, 2023, https://books.google.co.za/books?id=tSrFEAAAQBAJ&newbks=0&source=gbs_navlinks_s.

Democratic Marxism series

- Volume 1: *Marxisms in the 21st Century: Crisis, Critique and Struggle* edited by Vishwas Satgar and Michelle Williams, 2013, https://library.oapen.org/handle/20.500.12657/41793.
- Volume 2: *Capitalism's Crises: Class Struggles in South Africa and the World* edited by Vishwas Satgar, 2015, https://library.oapen.org/handle/20.500.12657/41794.
- Volume 3: *The Climate Crisis: South African and Global Democratic Ecosocialist Alternatives* edited by Vishwas Satgar, 2018, https://library.oapen.org/handle/20.500.12657/29462.
- Volume 4: *Racism after Apartheid: Challenges for Marxism and Anti-Racism* edited by Vishwas Satgar, 2019, https://library.oapen.org/handle/20.500.12657/25726.
- Volume 5: *BRICS and the New American Imperialism: Global Rivalry and Resistance* edited by Vishwas Satgar, 2020, https://library.oapen.org/handle/20.500.12657/22401.

- Volume 6: *Destroying Democracy: Neoliberal Capitalism and the Rise of Authoritarian Politics* edited by Vishwas Satgar and Michelle Williams, 2021, https://library.oapen.org/handle/20.500.12657/50256.
- Volume 7: *Emancipatory Feminism in the Time of Covid-19: Transformative Resistance and Social Reproduction* edited by Vishwas Satgar and Ruth Ntlokotse, 2023, https://library.oapen.org/handle/20.500.12657/64100.

Bibliography

Achar, G. 2013. *Marxism, Orientalism, Cosmopolitanism*. Chicago: Haymarket.
Ackerman, D. 1995. *A Natural History of Love*. New York: Vintage Books.
Adams, T.F. and Hansen, G.B. 1993. *Putting Democracy to Work: A Practical Guide for Starting and Managing Worker-Owned Business*. San Francisco: Burrett-Koehler Publishers.
Adler, G. 2000. *Engaging the State and Business: The Labour Movement and Co-determination in Contemporary South Africa*. Johannesburg: Witwatersrand University Press.
Adler, G. and Webster, E. 2000. 'Introduction: Consolidating democracy in a liberalising world: Trade unions and democratisation in South Africa' in *Trade Unions and Democratisation in South Africa, 1985–1997* edited by Glenn Adler and Eddie Webster. Johannesburg: Witwatersrand University Press.
African National Congress. 1994. *The Reconstruction and Development Programme (RDP)*. Johannesburg: Umanyano Publications.
African National Congress. 2007. 'Strategy and tactics of the ANC: Building a national democratic society', https://www.anc1912.org.za/adopted-strategy-and-tactics-of-the-anc/ (accessed 17 January 2024).
Aguilar, D.D. 2015. 'Intersectionality' in *Marxism and Feminism* edited by S. Mojab. London: Zed Books.
Alexander, P. 2010. 'Rebellion of the poor: South Africa's service delivery protests – A preliminary analysis'. *Social Movement Studies* 27 (123).
Allen, M.A. 2006. *Globalisation, Negotiation, and the Failure of Transformation in South Africa: Revolution at a Bargain*. New York: Palgrave.
Amin, N. and Bernstein, H. 1995. 'The role of agricultural co-operatives in agriculture and rural development' Land and Agriculture Policy Centre policy paper 32.

Amin, S. 1970. *Accumulation on a World Scale: A Critique of the Theory of Underdevelopment.* New York: Monthly Review Press.
——. 1989. *Eurocentricism.* London: Zed Books.
——. 1990. *Delinking: Towards a Polycentric World.* London: Zed Books.
——. 1992. *Empire of Chaos.* New York: Monthly Review Press.
——. 1994. *Re-reading the Post War Period: An Intellectual Itinerary.* New York: Monthly Review Press.
——. 1996. *Capitalism in the Age of Globalisation.* London: Zed Books.
——. 2006. *Beyond US Hegemony.* London: Zed Books.
——. 2009. 'Interview – Samir Amin' in *New Frontiers for Socialism in the 21st Century: Conversations on a Global Journey* edited by Vishwas Satgar and Langa Zita. Johannesburg: COPAC: 229–268.
——. 2020. 'Towards the fifth international?' in *BRICS and the New American Imperialism: Global Rivalry and Resistance* edited by V. Satgar. Johannesburg: Wits University Press: 148–166.
Amsden, A. 1989. *Asia's Next Giant: South Korea and Late Industrialization.* New York: Oxford University Press.
——. 2001. *The Rise of the 'Rest': Challenges to the West from Late Industrializing Economies.* New York: Oxford University Press.
Anderson, K.B. 2010. *Marx at the Margins: On Nationalism, Ethnicity and Non-Western Societies.* Chicago: University of Chicago Press.
——. 2020. *Class, Gender, Race and Colonialism: The 'Intersectionality' of Marx.* Quebec: Daraja Press and Monthly Review Essays.
Anghie, A. 2005. *Imperialism, Sovereignty, and the Making of International Law.* Cambridge: Cambridge University Press.
Angus, I. (ed.). 2010. *The Global Fight for Climate Justice: Anticapitalist Responses to Global Warming and Environmental Destruction.* Halifax, Nova Scotia: Fernwood Publishing.
Anibal, Q. 2013. 'Coloniality and modernity/rationality' in *Globalization and the Decolonial Option* edited by W.D. Mignolo and A. Escobar. London: Routledge: 22–32.
Anievas, A., Manchanda, N. and Shilliam, R. (eds). 2015. *Race and Racism in International Relations: Confronting the Global Colour Line.* London: Routledge.
Apte, A.P. 1988. 'The role of dairy co-operatives schemes in rural development in India, in *Who Shares?: Co-operatives and Rural Development* edited by D.W. Attwood and B.S. Baviskar. Delhi: Oxford University Press.

Arruzza, C. 2013. *Dangerous Liaisons: The Marriages and Divorces of Marxism and Feminism*. London: Merlin Press.

Ashley, B. 2018. 'Climate jobs at two minutes to midnight' in *The Climate Crisis: South African and Global Democratic Eco-Socialist Alternatives* edited by V. Satgar. Johannesburg: Wits University Press: 272–292.

Ashworth, L.M. 2014. *A History of International Thought: From the Origins of the Modern State to Academic International Relations*. London: Routledge.

Atkinson, D. 2007. 'Taking to the streets: Has developmental local government failed in South Africa?' in *The State of The Nation: South Africa* edited by Sakhele Buhlungu et al. Johannesburg: HSRC Press.

Attwood, D.W. and Baviskar, B.S. 1988. *Who Shares?: Cooperatives and Rural Development*. Delhi: Oxford University Press.

Bahro, R. 1978. *The Alternative in Eastern Europe*. London: Verso.

———. 1982. *Socialism and Survival*. London: Heretic Books.

———. 1986. *Building the Green Movement*. London: GMP Publishers.

Bakker, I. 2007. 'Social reproduction and the constitution of a gendered political economy'. *New Political Economy* 12(4): 541–556.

Baskin, J. and Satgar, V. 1996. 'Assessing the new LRA: A framework for regulated flexibility' in *Against the Current: Labour and Economic Policy in South Africa* edited by Jeremy Baskin. Johannesburg: Ravan Press.

Bassey, N. 2012. *To Cook a Continent: Destructive Extraction and the Climate Crisis in Africa*. Cape Town: Pambazuka Press.

Baviskar, B.S. 1988. 'Dairy co-operatives and rural development in Gujarat' in *Who Shares?: Co-operatives and Rural Development* edited by D.W. Attwood and B.S. Baviskar. Delhi: Oxford University Press.

Bennie, A. and Satgoor, A. 2018. 'Deepening the just transition through food sovereignty and the solidarity economy' in *The Climate Crisis: South African and Global Democratic Eco-Socialist Alternatives* edited by V. Satgar. Johannesburg: Wits University Press: 1–28.

Benton, T. 1996. *The Greening of Marxism*. New York: Guilford Press.

Bernstein, H. 1999. *Memory against Forgetting: Memoirs from a Life in South African Politics 1938–1964*. Johannesburg: Penguin.

Bessis, S. 2003. *Western Supremacy: The Triumph of an Idea?* London: Zed Books.

Bezuidenhout, A. and Tshoaedi, M. (eds). 2017. *Labour Beyond COSATU: Mapping the Rupture in South Africa's Labour Landscape*. Johannesburg: Wits University Press.

Bhattacharya, T. 2017a. 'How not to skip class: social reproduction of labour and the global working class' in *Social Reproduction Theory: Remapping Class, Recentering Oppression* edited by T. Bhattacharya. London: Pluto Books: 68–93.

Bhattacharya, T. (ed.). 2017b. *Social Reproduction Theory: Remapping Class, Recentering Oppression*. London: Pluto Books.

Bilgin, P. and Morton. A.D. 2002. 'Historicising representations of "failed states": Beyond the Cold War annexation of the social sciences'. *Third World Quarterly* 23(1): 55–80.

Blackledge, P. 2012. *Marxism and Ethics: Freedom, Desire and Revolution*. New York: SUNY Press.

Bohrer, A.J. 2022. 'Marxism and intersectionality: A critical historiography' in *Marx Matters* edited by D. Fasenfest. Leiden: Brill: 242–268.

Bond, P. 2000. *Elite Transition: From Apartheid to Neoliberalism in South Africa*. London: Pluto Press.

———. 2001. 'South Africa's agenda in 21st century global governance'. *Review of African Political Economy* 28(89): 415–428.

———. 2004. 'The ANC's "left turn" and South African sub-imperialism'. *Review of African Political Economy* 31(102): 599–616.

———. 2012. *Politics of Climate Change: Paralysis Above, Movement Below*. Pietermaritzburg: University of KwaZulu-Natal Press.

Bond, P., Dada. R. and Erion, G. (eds). 2009. *Climate Change, Carbon Trading and Civil Society: Negative Returns on South African Investments*. Pietermaritzburg: University of KwaZulu-Natal Press.

Booysen, S. (ed.). 2016. *Fees Must Fall: Student Revolt, Decolonisation and Governance in South Africa*. Johannesburg: Wits University Press.

Brand, U. and Wissen, M. 2021. *The Imperial Mode of Living: Everyday Life and the Ecological Crisis of Capitalism*. London: Verso Books.

Brown, H.A. 2012. *Marx on Gender and the Family: A Critical Study*. Leiden: Brill.

BuaNews. 2008. 'Investment Council endorses electricity strategy'. Online,19 May.

Buhlungu, S. 2010. *A Paradox of Victory: COSATU and the Democratic Transformation in South Africa*. Pietermaritzburg: University of KwaZulu-Natal Press.

Buhlungu, S. et al. (eds). 2006. *State of the Nation: South Africa 2005–2006*. Cape Town: HSRC Press.

———. 2007. *State of the Nation: South Africa 2007*. Cape Town: HSRC Press.

Buhlungu, S. and Webster, E. 2006. 'Work restructuring and the future of labour in South Africa' in *State of the Nation: South Africa 2005–2006* edited by Sakhela Buhlungu et al. Cape Town: HSRC Press: 248–269.

Burkett, P. 2006. *Marxism and Ecological Economics: Toward a Red-Green Political Economy*. Leiden: Brill.

——. 2014. *Marx and Nature: A Red and Green Perspective*. Chicago: Haymarket Books.

Callenbach, E. 1999. *Ecology: A Pocket Guide*. Himayatnagar, Hyderabad: Universities Press.

Carmody, P. 2002. 'Between globalisation and (post)apartheid: The political economy of restructuring in South Africa'. *Journal of Southern African Studies* 28(2): 255–275.

Carroll, W.K. 2020. 'Fossil capital, imperialism and the global corporate elite' in *BRICS and the New American Imperialism: Global Rivalry and Resistance* edited by V. Satgar. Johannesburg: Wits University Press: 30–57.

Carroll, W.K. and Carson, W. 2006. 'Neoliberalism, capitalist class formation and the global network of corporations and policy groups' in *Neoliberal Hegemony: A Global Critique* edited by D. Plehwe, B. Walpen and G. Neunhöffer. London: Routledge: 51–69.

Carroll, W.K. and Sarker, K. (eds). 2016. *A World to Win: Contemporary Social Movements and Counter-Hegemony*. Manitoba: Arbeiter Ring Publishing.

Cassim, R. 2006. 'Reflections on South Africa's first wave of economic reforms' in *The Development Decade?: Economic and Social Change in South Africa, 1994–2004* edited by V. Padayachee. Cape Town: HSRC Press: 55–85.

Cassim, R. and Zarenda, H. 2004. 'South Africa's trade policy paradigm: Evolution or involution?' in *South Africa's Foreign Policy 1994–2004: Apartheid Past, Renaissance Future* edited by Elizabeth Sidiropoulos. Johannesburg: South African Institute of International Affairs: 105–118.

Cavanagh, J. and Mander, J. (eds). 2004. *Alternatives to Economic Globalization: A Better World is Possible*. San Francisco: Berrett-Koehler Publishers.

Chakrabarty, C. 2000. *Provincialising Europe: Postcolonial Thought and Historical Difference*. Princeton, N.J.: Princeton University Press.

Chamane, M 2016. 'Worker co-operatives: Big yes for South African Waste Pickers Association'. *Solidarity Economy News* 14: 11, http://copac.org.za/wp-content/uploads/2017/10/Newsletter-14-1.pdf (accessed 20 March 2018).

Chang, H-J. 2002. *Kicking Away the Ladder: Development Strategy in Historical*

Perspective. London: Anthem Press.

Chibber, V. 2003. *Locked in Place: State-Building and Late Industrialization in India*. Princeton, N.J.: Princeton University Press.

Chinguno, C. et al. (eds). 2017. *Rioting and Writing: Diaries of Wits Fallists*. Johannesburg: Society, Work and Development Institute.

Chomsky, N. 2012. *Occupy*. London: Penguin.

Claassens, A. 2015. 'Law, land and custom, 1913–2014: What is at stake today?' in *Land Divided Land Restored: Land Reform in South Africa for the 21st Century* edited by Ben Cousins and Cherryl Walker. Johannesburg: Jacana Media.

Cock, J. 2006. 'Breadwinners and losers: Power relations in the wheat to bread commodity chain'. Unpublished paper, South African Sociological Association Conference, University of the Witwatersrand.

Collier, G.A. and Quarateillo, E.L. 2005. *Basta!: Land and the Zapatista Rebellion in the Chiapas*. Oakland: Food First Books.

COPAC. 2001. *Co-operative Movement Conference Report, 24th and 25th June 2001*. Johannesburg: COPAC.

——. 2005. *Co-operatives in Gauteng (A Quantitative Study): Broad Based BEE or Push Back into Poverty*. Johannesburg: COPAC.

——. 2006. *Co-operative Support Institutions in the Gauteng Co-operative Sector (Case Studies): Enabling Support or Dependent Development?* Johannesburg: COPAC.

——. 2008. *The Passion of the People: Successful Co-operative Experiences in Africa*. Johannesburg: COPAC.

——. 2010. *Co-operating for Transformation: Co-operative Case Studies from Amathole District, Eastern Cape*. Johannesburg: COPAC.

——. 2011. *Building the Solidarity Economy and Movement in Ivory Park: Mapping Research Report*. Johannesburg: COPAC.

——. 2012. *Beyond the Social Economy: Capitalism's Crises and the Solidarity Economy Alternative: Conference Report of the First International Solidarity Economy Conference in South Africa, 28–28 October 2011*. Johannesburg: COPAC.

——. 2014. *Food Sovereignty for the Right to Food: A Guide for Grassroots Activism*. Johannesburg: COPAC.

——. 2015. *Create Work through Worker Co-operatives: A Guide for Grassroots Activism*. Johannesburg: COPAC.

——. 2016. *Advancing Food Sovereignty through Seed Saving: An Activist Guide*. Johannesburg: COPAC.

——. 2017. *Building People's Power for Water Sovereignty: An Activist Guide*.

Johannesburg: COPAC.

———. 2020. 'Webinar: unpacking the COVID-19 stimulus package', 11 May 2020, https://www.youtube.com/watch?v=_B3GROOttp0&feature=youtu.be (accessed 27 May 2020).

Cornelissen, S. 2010. 'The economic impact of South Africa's 2010 World Cup: Ex ante ambitions and possible ex post realities'. *New South African Review* 1: 87–103.

Cox, R. 1994. 'Gramsci, hegemony, and international relations: An essay in method' in *Gramsci, Historical Materialism and International Relations* edited by S. Gill. New York: Cambridge University Press: 49–66.

Crutzen, P.J. 2002. 'Geology of mankind'. *Nature* 415: 23.

Crutzen, P.J. and Stoermer, E.F. 2000. 'The "Anthropocene"'. *Global Change Newsletter* 41: 17.

Cutler, A.C. 2014. 'New constitutionalism and the commodity' in *New Constitutionalism and World Order* edited by S. Gill and A.C. Cutler. Cambridge: Cambridge University Press.

Dangl, B. 2007. *The Price of Fire: Resource Wars and Social Movements in Bolivia*. Oakland: AK Press.

Daniel, J., Naidoo, V. and Naidu, S. 2003. 'The South Africans have arrived: Post-apartheid corporate expansion into Africa' in *State of the Nation: South Africa 2003–2004* edited by John Daniel, Adam Habib and Roger Southall. Cape Town: HSRC Press: 368–390.

Darby, M. 2016. 'Scientists: window for avoiding 1.5C global warming "closed"'. *Climate News*, 29 June, http://www.climatechangenews.com/2016/06/29/scientists-window-for-avoiding-1-5c-global-warming-closed/ (accessed 17 August 2017).

Davis, P. 1995. 'Co-operative management and co-operative purpose: Values, principles and objectives for co-operatives into the 21st century'. Leicester: Management Centre, Faculty of Social Sciences, University of Leicester.

Davis, P. 1996. 'Facilitating co-operative management development'. *Co-op Dialogue* 4(4).

De Angelis, M. 2019. 'Commons' in *Pluriverse: A Post-Development Dictionary* edited by Ashish Kothari et al. Chennai: Tulika Books.

Della Porta, D. 2015. *Social Movements in Times of Austerity: Bringing Capitalism Back into Protest Analysis*. Cambridge: Polity Press.

Democratic Left Front. 2011. 'Another South Africa and World is Possible! conference report, University of the Witwatersrand'.

Department of Finance. 1996. 'Growth employment and redistribution strategy (summary document)': 1–2.

Dlamini, J. 2014. *Askari: The Story of Collaboration and Betrayal in the Anti-Apartheid Struggle*. Johannesburg: Jacana Media.

Drijfhout, S. 2015. 'What climate "tipping points" are – and how they could suddenly change our planet'. *The Conversation*, 9 December, https://theconversation.com/what-climate-tipping-points-are-and-how-theycould-suddenly-change-our-planet-49405 (accessed 17 August 2017).

Dumais, M. 1997. 'Global dimensions of agricultural co-operatives'. *ICA Review* 90(4).

Dussel, E. 1995. *The Invention of the Americas: Eclipse of 'the Other' and the Myth of Modernity*. London: Continuum.

——. 2003. *Philosophy of Liberation*. Eugene: Wipf & Stock.

——. 2013. *Ethics of Liberation in the age of Globalization and Exclusion*. Durham: Duke University Press.

DVV International. 2017. *Remaking the World*. Cape Town: DVV International.

Earthrise Trust. 2014. *The Rustlers Valley Farm Development Initiative*. Ficksburg: Earthrise Trust.

Emission Database for Global Atmospheric Research (EDGAR). 2016. 'Emissions time series', http://edgar.jrc.ec.europa.eu/overview.php?v=CO2ts1990-2015&sort=des2 (accessed 27 November 2017).

Engels, F. 1843 [1959]. *Outlines of a Critique of Political Economy*. Moscow: Progress Publishers.

Engels, F. 1934 [1986]. *Dialectics of Nature*, translated from the German by Clemens Dutt. Moscow: Progress Publishers.

Erasmus, Z. 2017. *Race Otherwise: Forging a New Humanism for South Africa*. Johannesburg: Wits University Press.

Evans, P. 1995. *Embedded Autonomy: States and Industrial Transformation*. Princeton, N.J.: Princeton University Press.

——. 2005. 'Neoliberalism as a political opportunity: constraint and innovation in contemporary development strategy' in *Putting Development First: The Importance of Policy Space in the WTO and IFIs* edited by K. Gallagher. London: Zed Books: 195–215.

——. 2010. 'Constructing the 21st century developmental state: Potentialities and pitfalls' in *Constructing a Democratic Developmental State in South Africa: Potentials and Challenges* edited by Omano Edigheji. Cape Town: HSRC Press: 37–58.

Everatt, D. 2009. *The Origins of Non-Racialism: White Opposition to Apartheid in the 1950s*. Johannesburg: Wits University Press.

Fakier, K. and Cock, J. 2009. 'A gendered analysis of the crisis of social reproduction in contemporary South Africa'. *International Feminist Journal of Politics* 11(3): 353–371.

Fakier, K., Mulinari, D. and Räthzel, N. 2020. *Marxist-Feminist Theories and Struggles Today*. London: Zed Books.

Ferguson, J. 2006. *Global Shadows: Africa in the Neo Liberal World Order*. Durham: Duke University Press.

——. 2020. *Women and Work: Feminism, Labour and Social Reproduction*. London: Pluto Press.

Fine, B. 1995. 'Privatisation and the RDP: A critical assessment'. *Transformation* 27: 1–23.

——. 2010. 'Can South Africa be a developmental state?' in *Constructing a Democratic Developmental State in South Africa: Potentials and Challenges* edited by Omano Edigheji. Cape Town: HSRC Press: 169–182.

Fisher, W.F. and Ponniah, T. (eds). 2003. *Another World is Possible: Popular Alternatives to Globalization at the World Social Forum*. Halifax, Nova Scotia: Fernwood Publishing.

Forrest, K. 2011. *Metal That Will Not Bend: National Union of Metalworkers of South Africa 1980–1995*. Johannesburg: Wits University Press.

Forslund, D. and Reddy, N. 2015. 'Wages and the struggle against income inequality' in *COSATU in Crisis: The Fragmentation of an African Trade Union Federation* edited by Vishwas Satgar and Roger Southall. Johannesburg: KMM Publishers.

Foster, J.B. 2008. 'The dialectics of nature and Marxist ecology' in *Dialectics for the New Century* edited by Bertell Ollman and Tony Smith. New York: Palgrave Macmillan.

——. 2000. *Marx's Ecology: Materialism and Nature*. New York: Monthly Review Press.

Foster, J.B. and Clark, B. 2016. 'Marx's ecology and the left' *Monthly Review* 68(2), http://monthlyreview.org/2016/06/01/marxs-ecology-and-the-left/.

Fraser, N. 2015. 'Legitimation crisis?: On the political contradictions of financialised capitalism'. *Critical Historical Studies* 2(2): 157–189.

——. 2017. 'Crisis of care?: On the social-reproductive contradictions of contemporary capitalism' in *Social Reproduction Theory: Remapping Class,*

Recentering Oppression edited by T. Bhattacharya. London: Pluto Books: 21–36.

——. 2021. 'Climates of capital'. *New Left Review* 127 (Jan.–Feb.): 94–127.

Frederikse, J. 1990. *The Unbreakable Thread: Non-Racialism in South Africa*. Johannesburg: Ravan Press.

Friedman, S. and Reitzes, M. 1995. 'Democratic selections?: Civil society and development in South Africa's new democracy'. *Development Bank of Southern Africa Development Paper 75*, https://www.dbsa.org/sites/default/files/media/documents/2022-11/Democratic%20Selections%20Civil%20Society%20and%20Dev%20and%20South%20Africans%20New%20Democracy%20-1995.pdf.

Fripp, C. 2014. 'South Africa is the 12th highest CO_2 emitter, and it's killing us', 19 August, www.htxt.co.za/2014/08/19/south-africa-is-the-12th-highest-co2-emitter-and-its-killing-us/ (accessed 20 September 2020).

Gallas, A. 2016. *The Thatcherite Offensive: A Neo-Poulantzian Analysis*. Chicago: Haymarket Books.

Gamble, A. and Kelly, G. 1996. 'The new politics of ownership'. *New Left Review* 1/220, Nov-Dec.

Gelb, S. 1991. *South Africa's Economic Crisis: An Overview*. Cape Town: David Phillip.

——. 2005. 'An overview of the South African economy' in *State of the Nation: South Africa 2004–2005* edited by John Daniel, Jessica Lutchman and Roger Southall. Cape Town: HSRC Press: 367–400.

——. 2006. *A South African Developmental State: What is Possible?* Johannesburg: Edge Institute.

Gelb, S. and Black, A. 2004. 'Globalisation in a middle-income economy: FDI, production and the labour market in South Africa' in *Labour and the Globalisation of Production* edited by William Milberg. London: Palgrave: 215–248.

George, S. 1988. 'Co-operatives and Indian dairy policy: More Anand than pattern' in *Who Shares?: Co-operatives and Rural Development* edited by D.W. Attwood and B.S. Baviskar. Delhi: Oxford University Press.

Geras, N. 1983. *Marx and Human Nature: Refutation of a Legend*. London: Verso Books.

Gill, S. 1994. 'Structural change and global political economy: Globalizing elites and the emerging world order' in *Global Transformation: Challenges to the State System* edited by Y. Sakamoto. Tokyo: United Nations University Press: 169–199.

——. 2003. *Power and Resistance in the New World Order*. New York: Palgrave MacMillan.

Gill, S. and Cutler, A.C. (eds). 2014. *New Constitutionalism and World Order*. Cambridge: Cambridge University Press.

Glaser, D. 2013. 'Retrospect: Seven theses about Africa's Marxist regimes' in *Marxisms in the Twenty-First Century: Crisis, Critiques and Struggles* edited by M. Williams and V. Satgar. Johannesburg: University of the Witwatersrand Press.

Gore, T. 2020. 'Confronting carbon inequality: Putting climate justice at the heart of the Covid-19 recovery', https://policy-practice.oxfam.org/resources/confronting-carbon-inequality-putting-climate-justice-at-the-heart-of-the-covid-621052/.

Gottfried, H. 2015. *The Reproductive Bargain: Deciphering the Enigma of Japanese Capitalism*. Leiden: Brill.

Gotz, G.A. 2000. 'Shoot anything that flies, claim anything that falls: Labour and the changing definition of the reconstruction and development programme' in *Trade Unions and Democratisation in South Africa, 1985–1997* edited by Glenn Adler and Eddie Webster. Johannesburg: Witwatersrand University Press.

Gowan, P. 1999. *The Global Gamble: Washington's Faustian Bid for World Dominance*. London: Verso.

Grovogui, S.N. 1996. *Sovereigns, Quasi Sovereigns, and Africans: Race and Self-Determination in International Law*. Minnesota: University of Minnesota Press.

Habib, A. 2003. 'State-civil society relations in post-apartheid South Africa' in *The State of the Nation, South Africa 2003–2004* edited by John Daniel, Adam Habib and Roger Southall. Johannesburg: HSRC Press.

Hall, R. and Kepe, T. 2017. 'Elite capture and state neglect: New evidence on South Africa's land reform'. *Review of African Political Economy* 44(151): 122–130.

Hall, S. 1980. 'Race articulation and societies structured in dominance' in *Sociological Theories: Race and Colonialism*. Paris: UNESCO: 305–345.

Hall, S. 1982. 'Gramsci's concept of hegemony' in *Gramsci's Political Thought: An Introduction* edited by R. Simon. London: Lawrence and Wishart.

Hallowes, D. 2011. *Toxic Futures: South Africa in the Crises of Energy, Environment and Capital*. Pietermaritzburg: University of KwaZulu-Natal Press.

Halperin, S. 2006. 'International relations theory and the hegemony of Western conceptions of modernity' in *Decolonizing International Relations* edited by B. Gruffydd Jones. Lanham: Rowman & Littlefield: 43–64.

Hanieh, A. 2013. *Lineages of Revolt: Issues of Contemporary Capitalism in the Middle East*. Chicago: Haymarket Books.

Harnecker, M. 2015. *A World to Build: New Paths toward Twenty-First Century Socialism*. New York: Monthly Review Press.

Harrison, G. 2010. *Neoliberal Africa: The Impact of Global Social Engineering*. London: Zed Books.

Harvey, C., Gronewold, N. and E&E News. 2019. 'CO_2 emissions will break another record in 2019'. *Scientific American*, 4 December, www.scientificamerican.com/article/co2-emissions-will-break-another-record-in-2019/ (accessed 23 September 2020).

Harvey, E. 2021. *The Great Pretenders: Race and Class under ANC Rule*. Auckland Park: Jacana Media.

Harvey, F. 2019. 'Climate crisis linked to at least 15 $1bn-plus disasters in 2019'. *Guardian*, 27 December, www.theguardian.com/world/2019/dec/27/climate-crisis-linkedto-at-least-15-1bn-plus-disasters-in-2019 (accessed 23 September 2020).

Held, D. and McGrew, A. 1994. 'Globalization and the liberal democratic state' in *Global Transformation: Challenges to the State System* edited by Y. Sakamoto. Tokyo: United Nations University Press: 57–84.

Heller, P. and Ntlokonkulu, L. 2001. *A Civic Movement, or a Movement of Civics?: The South African National Civic Organisation (SANCO) in the Post-apartheid Period*. Johannesburg: Centre for Policy Studies.

Hirsch, A. 2005. *Season of Hope: Economic Reform under Mandela and Mbeki*. Pietermaritzburg: University of KwaZulu-Natal Press.

Hitti, N. 1994. 'The internationalization of the state in the Middle East' in *Global Transformation: Challenges to the State System* edited by Y. Sakamoto. Tokyo: United Nations University Press: 85–106.

Hornborg, A. 2013. *Global Ecology and Unequal Exchange: Fetishism in a Zero-Sum World*. London: Routledge.

Houtart, F. and Polet, F. (eds). 2001. *The Other Davos: The Globalization of Resistance to the World Economic System*. London: Zed Books.

Hussi, P. et al. 1993. *The Development of Co-operatives and other Rural Organisations: The Role of the World Bank*. Washington: World Bank.

Hyden, G. 1988. 'Approaches to co-operative development: Blueprint versus greenhouse' in *Who Shares?: Co-operatives and Rural Development* edited by

D.W. Attwood and B.S. Baviskar. Delhi: Oxford University Press.

Intergovernmental Panel on Climate Change (IPCC). 2014. 'Climate change 2014, synthesis report: contribution of working groups I, II and III to the fifth assessment report of the Intergovernmental Panel on Climate Change'. Geneva: IPCC.

——. 2022. 'Climate change 2022: Impacts, adaptation and vulnerability. Working Group II contribution to the sixth assessment report of the IPCC', https://report.ipcc.ch/ar6wg2/pdf/IPCC_AR6_WGII_FinalDraft_FullReport.pdf (accessed 7 March 2022).

Intergovernmental Science-Policy Platform on Biodiversity and Ecosystem Services (IPBES). 2019. 'Summary for policymakers of the global assessment report on biodiversity and ecosystem services of the Intergovernmental Science-Policy Platform on Biodiversity and Ecosystem Services' edited by S. Díaz et al. Bonn: IPBES Secretariat, https://doi.org/10.5281/zenodo.3553579.

International Labour Organisation (ILO). 1996. 'Creating a favourable climate and conditions for co-operative development in central and eastern Europe'. Geneva: Co-operative Branch, International Labour Office.

——. 2020. 'Covid-19: social protection responses to the crisis', 24 April 2020, https://www.ilo.org/global/about-the-ilo/multimedia/video/institutional-videos/WCMS_742703/lang--en/index.htm (accessed 27 May 2020).

Itkonen, R. 1996. 'My views on co-operative corporate governance'. *Review of International Co-operation* 89(4).

Jaffee, G. 1990. 'Worker co-operatives: their emergence, problems and potential' in *Worker Participation* edited by M. Anstey. Cape Town: Juta.

Jara, M. 2013. 'Critical reflections on the crisis and limits of ANC "Marxism"' in *Marxisms in the Twenty-First Century: Crisis, Critiques and Struggles* edited by M. Williams and V. Satgar. Johannesburg: University of the Witwatersrand Press.

——. 2014. 'The solidarity economy response to the agrarian crisis in South Africa' in *The Solidarity Economy Alternative: Emerging Theory and Practice* edited by V. Satgar. Pietermaritzburg: University of KwaZulu-Natal Press: 227–248.

Jessop, B. 1990. *State Theory: Putting Capitalist States in their Place*. Oxford: Polity Press.

Joffe, A. et al. 1993. 'Meeting the global challenge: A framework for industrial revival in South Africa' in *South Africa and the World Economy in the 1990s* edited by Pauline H. Barker, Alex Boraine and Warren Krafchik. Cape Town: David Phillip: 91–126.

Johnson, C. 1982. *Miti and the Japanese Miracle: The Growth of Industrial Policy, 1925–1975*. Redwood City: Stanford University Press.

Jones, B.G. 2006. 'Introduction: international relations, Eurocentricism, and imperialism' in *Decolonizing International Relations* edited by B. Gruffydd Jones. Lanham: Rowman & Littlefield: 1–22.

——. 2013. 'Slavery, finance and international political economy: Postcolonial reflections' in *Postcolonial Theory and International Relations: A Critical Introduction* edited by S. Seth. London: Routledge: 49–69.

Kamo, T. 1994. 'The internationalization of the state: the case of Japan' in *Global Transformation: Challenges to the State System* edited by Y. Sakamoto. Tokyo: United Nations University Press: 107–133.

Kathrada, A. 2004. *Memoirs*. Cape Town: Zebra Press.

Kiernan, V. 1995 [1969]. *The Lords of Human Kind: European Attitudes to other Cultures in the Imperial Age*. London: Serif.

Klein, N. 2007. *The Shock Doctrine: The Rise of Disaster Capitalism*. London: Penguin Books.

——. 2014. *This Changes Everything*. London: Penguin Books.

Kovel, J. 2003. *The Enemy of Nature: The End of Capitalism or the End of the World*. New Delhi: Tulika Books.

Layfield, D. 2008. *Marxism and Environmental Crises*. Bury St Edmunds: Arena Books.

Lee, C.K. 2014. 'A Chinese developmental state: Miracle or mirage?' in *The End of the Developmental State?* edited by M. Williams. Pietermaritzburg: University of KwaZulu-Natal Press.

Levine, D.J. 2012. *Recovering International Relations: The Promise of Sustainable Critique*. Oxford: Oxford University Press.

Leys, C. 2008. *Total Capitalism: Market Politics, Market State*. New Delhi: Three Essays Collective.

Li, M. 2016. *China and the 21st Century Crisis*. London: Pluto Press.

Linebaugh, P. 2014. *Stop, Thief! The Commons, Enclosures and Resistance*. Oakland: pm Press.

Linklater, A. 2007. *Critical Theory and World Politics: Citizenship, Sovereignty and Humanity*. London: Routledge.

Lodge, T. 2021. *Red Road to Freedom: A History of the South African Communist*

Party 1921–2021. Johannesburg: Jacana Media.

Loriaux, M. 1999. 'The French developmental state as myth and moral ambition' in *The Developmental State* edited by M. Woo-Cumings. Ithaca: Cornell University Press: 235–275.

Louis, M. 1995. 'Agricultural co-operatives in Zimbabwe: A vehicle for rural democratisation?' in *Democracy, Civil Society and the State* edited by L. Sachikonye. Harare: SAPES Trust.

Löwy, M. 2006. *Fire Alarm: Reading Walter Benjamin's 'On the Concept of History'*. London: Verso.

Luxemburg, R. 2003 [1913]. *The Accumulation of Capital: A Contribution to the Economic Theory of Imperialism*. London: Routledge.

Makgetla, N. 2004. 'The post-apartheid economy', *Review of African Political Economy* 100: 263–281.

———. 2010. 'The international economic crisis and employment in South Africa: Development or decline?' *New South African Review* 1: 65–86.

Mandela, N. 1994. *Long Walk to Freedom: The Autobiography of Nelson Mandela*. New York: Little, Brown.

Mangcu, X. 2015. 'What moving beyond race can actually mean: Towards a joint culture' in *The Colour of our Future* edited by Xolela Mangcu. Johannesburg: Wits University Press: 1–16.

Marais, H. 2001. *South Africa, Limits to Change: The Political Economy of Transition*. London: Zed Books.

———. 2011. *South Africa Pushed to the Limit: The Political Economy of Change*. Cape Town: UCT Press.

Marx, K. 1976 [1867]. *Capital: A Critique of Political Economy, volume one*. London: Penguin.

———. 1978 [1885]. *Capital: A Critique of Political Economy, volume two*. London: Penguin.

———. 1981 [1959]. *Economic and Philosophic Manuscripts of 1844*. Moscow: Progress Publishers.

———. 1991 [1894]. *Capital: A Critique of Political Economy, volume three*. London: Penguin.

———. 1996 [1875]. *Critique of the Gotha Programme*. Beijing: Foreign Language Press.

Marx, K. and Engels, F. 1998. *The German Ideology*. New York: Prometheus Books.

———. 2002 [1888]. *The Communist Manifesto*. London: Penguin.

Marya, R. and Patel, R. 2021. *Inflamed: Deep Medicine and the Anatomy of Injustice*. New York: Farar Straus and Giroux.

Maslennikov, V. 1983. *The Co-operative Movement in Asia and Africa*. Moscow: Progress Publishers.

Mason, P. 2012. *Why it's Still Kicking Off Everywhere: The New Global Revolutions*. London: Verso.

McClintock, A. 2013 [1993]. 'The angel of progress: Pitfalls of the term "post-colonialism"' in *Colonial Discourse and Post-colonial Theory: A Reader* edited by P. Williams and L. Chrisman. London: Routledge.

McKibben, B. 2016. 'Recalculating the climate math'. *New Republic*, 22 September, https://newrepublic.com/article/136987/recalculating-climate-math (accessed 17 August 2017).

McKinley, D. 2015. 'It's all about power and money: The present state of the ANC'. *Pambazuka News*, 16 October, https://www.pambazuka.org/governance/it%E2%80%99s-all-about-power-and-money-present-state-anc.

McNally, D. 2017. 'Intersections and dialectics: Critical reconstructions in social reproduction theory' in *Social Reproduction Theory: Remapping Class, Recentering Oppression* edited by T. Bhattacharya. London: Pluto Books.

Meer, I. 2002. *A Fortunate Man*. Cape Town: Zebra Press.

Mertes, T. (ed.). 2004. *A Movement of Movements: Is Another World Really Possible?* London: Verso.

Mies, M. and Shiva, V. 2014. *Ecofeminism*. 2nd edition. London: Zed Books.

Mignolo, W.D. 2010. 'Introduction: coloniality of power and decolonial thinking' in *Globalisation and the Decolonial Option* edited by W.D. Mignolo and A. Escobar. London: Routledge: 1–21.

Mignolo, W.D. and Walsh, C.E. 2018. *On Decoloniality: Concepts, Analytics and Praxis*. Durham: Duke University Press.

Mishra, V. and Hodge, B. 2013 [1993]. 'What is post(-)colonialism?' in *Colonial Discourse and Post-colonial Theory: A Reader* edited by P. Williams and L. Chrisman. London: Routledge.

Mkandawire, T. 2001. 'Thinking about developmental states in Africa'. *Cambridge Journal of Economics* 25: 289–313.

Mlambo-Ngcuka, P. 2006. 'Media briefing: background document: A catalyst for Accelerated and Shared Growth-South Africa', South African government document, 6 February.

Mngxitama, A., Alexander, A. and Gibson, N.C. (eds). 2008. *Biko Lives!: Contesting the Legacies of Steve Biko*. New York: Palgrave Macmillan.

Mohammed, S. 2010. 'The state of the South African economy'. *New South African Review* 1: 39–64.

Mojab, M. (ed.). 2015. *Marxism and Feminism*. London: Zed Books.

Mokati, N. 2017. 'SAFTU says it is intent on protecting workers' rights'. *IOL*, 22 May, https://www.iol.co.za/news/politics/saftu-says-it-is-intent-onprotecting-workers-rights-9280193 (accessed 20 March 2018).

Morana, M., Dussel, E. and Jauregui, C.A. (eds). 2008. *Coloniality at Large: Latin America and the Postcolonial Debate*. Durham: Duke University Press.

Morena, E., Krause, D. and Stevis, D. 2020. *Just Transitions: Social Justice in the Shift Towards a Low Carbon World*. London: Pluto Press.

Morera, E. 1990. *Gramsci's Historicism*. London: Routledge.

Mosoetsa, S. 2011. *Eating from One Pot: The Dynamics of Survival in Poor South African Households*. Johannesburg: Wits University Press.

Munck, R. 1988. *The New International Labour Studies: An Introduction*. London: Zed Books.

Mzala. 1988. 'Revolutionary theory on the national question in South Africa' in *The National Question in South Africa* edited by M. van Diepen. London: Zed Books: 30–55.

Naidoo, P. 2010. 'Indigent management: A strategic response to the struggles of the poor in post-apartheid South Africa'. *New South African Review* 1: 156–159.

National Minimum Wage (NMW) Research Initiative. 2015. 'The working poor: National minimum wage in South Africa'. *Fact sheet* 2, October, http://nationalminimumwage.co.za/wp-content/uploads/2016/03/NMW-RI-Fact-Sheet-2.pdf (accessed 27 May 2020).

National Union of Metalworkers (NUMSA). 2014. 'Resolutions adopted at NUMSA Special National Congress, 16–20 December, 2013'.

Nattrass, N. 2003. 'The state of the economy: a crisis of employment' in *State of the Nation: South Africa 2003–2004* edited by John Daniel, Adam Habib and Roger Southall. Cape Town: HSRC Press: 141–157.

Ndletyana, M. 2007. 'Municipal elections 2006: Protests, independent candidates and cross border municipalities' in *The State of the Nation, South Africa* edited by Sakhele Buhlungu et al. Johannesburg: HSRC Press.

Ndlovu-Gatsheni, S.J. 2021. 'Revisiting Marxism and decolonisation through the legacy of Samir Amin'. *Review of African Political Economy* 48(167): 50–65.

Ndlovu-Gatsheni, S.J. and Zondi, S. (eds). 2016. *Decolonizing the University,*

Knowledge Systems and Disciplines in Africa. Durham: Carolina Academic Press.

Nigam, A. 2020. *Decolonizing Theory: Thinking across Traditions*. London: Bloomsbury.

Oakeshott, R. 1973. 'Mondragon: Spain's oasis of democracy.' *Observer*, 21 January.

Oakeshott, R. 1978. *The Case for Workers' Co-ops*. London: Routledge & Kegan Paul.

O'Connor, J. 1996. 'The second contradiction of capitalism' in *The Greening of Marxism* edited by T. Benton. New York: Guilford Press: 197–221.

Padayachee, V. 1994. 'Debt, development and democracy: The IMF in post-apartheid South Africa'. *Review of African Political Economy* 62: 585–597.

Pahuja, S. 2011. *Decolonising International Law: Development, Economic Growth and the Politics of Universality*. Cambridge: Cambridge University Press.

Palan, R., Abbot, J. and Deans, P. 1999. *State Strategies in the Global Political Economy*. London: Pinter.

Panitch, L., Albo, G. and Chibber, V. 2012. 'The question of strategy'. *Socialist Register* Vol. 49, 2013.

Parayil, G. (ed.). 2000. *Kerala: The Development Experience: Reflections on Sustainability and Replicability*. London: Zed Books.

Patel, A.S. 1988. 'Co-operative dairying and rural development in Gujarat' in *Who Shares?: Cooperatives and Rural Development* edited by D.W. Attwood and B.S. Baviskar. Delhi: Oxford University Press.

Pekka, H. et al. 1993. 'The development of co-operatives and other rural organisations'. *World Bank technical paper* 199.

Pepper, D. 1993. *Ecosocialism: From Deep Ecology to Social Justice*. London: Routledge.

Philip, T.K. 1987. 'Producer co-operatives in South Africa'. *SWOP Labour Studies Research Report* 4, https://vital.seals.ac.za/vital/access/manager/Repository/vital:30391?site_name=GlobalView&exact=sm_creator%3A%22Philip%2C+T+Kate%22&sort=sort_ss_title%2F

——. 2007. 'A reality check: Worker coops in South Africa'. *South African Labour Bulletin* 31(3).

Pietermaritzburg Economic Justice and Dignity (PMBEJD). 2020. 'Covid-19: families living on low incomes may be spending 30% more on food than they did two months ago'. *PMBEJD Research Report*, 26 May, https://pmbejd.org.za/wp-content/uploads/2020/05/PMBEJD-Research-Report-26052020.pdf (accessed 27 May 2020).

Piketty, T. 2014. *Capital in the Twenty-First Century*. Cambridge, Mass: Belknap Press.

Pityana, N.B. et al. (eds). 1991. *Bounds of Possibility: The Legacy of Steve Biko and Black Consciousness*. Cape Town: David Philip.

Plehwe, D., Walpen, B. and Neunhöffer, G. (eds). 2006. *Neoliberal Hegemony: A Global Critique*. London: Routledge.

Polanyi, K. 1944 [2001]. *The Great Transformation: The Political and Economic Origins of our Time*. Boston: Beacon Press.

Quijano, A. 2013 [2010]. 'Coloniality and modernity/rationality' in *Globalization and the Decolonial Option* edited by W.D. Mignolo and A. Escobar. London: Routledge.

Rajapatirana, S. 1998. 'The local to the global market: the challenges for small and medium sized enterprises'. International Co-operative Information Centre.

Reddy, E.S. (comp.). 1991. *Monty Speaks: Speeches of Dr G.M. (Monty) Naicker 1945–1963*. Durban: Madiba Publishers.

Rich, N. 2019. *Losing Earth: The Decade We Could Have Stopped Climate Change*. New York: Picador.

Robertson, E. 2014. 'Venezuela marks 25 years since "Caracazo" uprising against neoliberalism'. *Venezuelanalysis*, https://venezuelanalysis.com/news/10431 (accessed 30 April 2018).

Rogelj, J. et al. 2016. 'Paris Agreement climate proposals need a boost to keep warming well below 2°C'. *Nature* 534: 631–639.

Rosenberg, J. 1994. *The Empire of Civil Society: A Critique of the Realist Theory of International Relations*. London: Verso.

Roy, R.K., Denzau, A.T. and Willett, T.D. 2007. *Neoliberalism: National and Regional Experiments with Global Ideas*. London: Routledge.

Rumney, R. 2005. 'Who owns South Africa: An analysis of the state and private ownership patterns' in *State of the Nation: South Africa 2004–2005* edited by John Daniel, Jessica Lutchman and Roger Southall. Cape Town: HSRC Press: 401–422.

Sader, E. 2011. *The New Mole: Paths of the Latin American Left*. London: Verso.

Said, E. 1979. *Orientalism*. New York: Vintage Books.

Saito, K. 2017. *Karl Marx's Eco-socialism: Capital, Nature, and the Unfinished Critique of Political Economy*. New York: Monthly Review Press.

Sakamoto, Y. (ed.). 1994. *Global Transformation: Challenges to the State System*. Tokyo: United Nations University Press.

Salleh, A. 1994. 'Nature, women, labour, capital: living the deepest contradiction' in *Is Capitalism Sustainable?: Political Economy and the Politics of Ecology* edited by M. O'Connor. New York: Guilford Press: 106–124.

Sarkar, S. 1999. *Eco Socialism or Eco Capitalism?: A Critical Analysis of Humanity's Fundamental Choices*. New Delhi: Orient Longman.

Sassoon, A. 1982. 'Passive revolution and the politics of reform' in *Approaches to Gramsci* edited by A.S. Sassoon. London: Writers and Readers.

Satgar, V. 2000. 'Co-operative banks in South Africa: a brief survey'. *African Communist* 155: 50–57.

——. 2008. 'Neoliberalised South Africa: Labour and the roots of passive revolution'. *Labour, Capital and Society/Travail, Capital et Société* 41(2): 38–69.

——. 2009a. *Building a Solidarity Economy Movement: A Guide for Grassroots Activism*. Johannesburg: COPAC.

——. 2009b. 'Global capitalism and the neoliberalisation of Africa' in *A New Scramble for Africa?: Imperialism, Investment and Development* edited by Roger Southall and Henning Melber. Pietermaritzburg: University of KwaZulu-Natal Press: 35–55.

——. 2009c. 'Reflections: the age of barbarism' in *New Frontiers for Socialism in the 21st Century – Conversations on a Global Journey* edited by V. Satgar and L. Zita. Johannesburg: COPAC.

——. 2012. 'Beyond Marikana: The post-apartheid South African state'. *Africa Spectrum* 47(2–3): 33–62.

——. 2014a. 'The crises of global capitalism and the solidarity economy alternative' in *The Solidarity Economy Alternative: Emerging Theory and Practice* edited by V. Satgar. Pietermaritzburg: University of KwaZulu-Natal Press: 1–34.

——. 2014b. 'The solidarity economy alternative in South Africa: Prospects and challenges' in *The Solidarity Economy Alternative: Emerging Theory and Practice* edited by V. Satgar. Pietermaritzburg: University of KwaZulu-Natal Press: 199–226.

——. 2014c. 'South Africa's green developmental state?' in *The End of the Developmental State?* edited by M. Williams. Pietermaritzburg: University of KwaZulu-Natal Press: 126–153.

——. (ed.) 2015a. *Capitalism's Crises: Class Struggles in South Africa and the World*. Johannesburg: Wits University Press.

——. 2015b. 'From Marx to the systemic crises of capitalist civilization' in *Capitalism's Crises: Class Struggles in South Africa and the World* edited by V.

Satgar. Johannesburg: Wits University Press.

——. 2015c. 'Marxism and the crisis of labour in post-apartheid South Africa' in *COSATU in Crisis: The Fragmentation of an African Trade Union Federation* edited by V. Satgar and R. Southall. Johannesburg: KMM Publishers: 134–161.

——. 2018a. 'The Anthropocene and imperial ecocide: prospects for just transitions' in *The Climate Crisis: South African and Global Democratic Eco-Socialist Alternatives* edited by V. Satgar. Johannesburg: Wits University Press: 47–68.

——. (ed.). 2018b. *The Climate Crisis: South African and Global Democratic Eco-Socialist Alternatives*. Johannesburg: Wits University Press.

——. 2020a. 'Covid-19, the climate crisis and lockdown: An opportunity to end the war with nature', *Daily Maverick*, 25 March 2020, https://www.dailymaverick.co.za/article/2020-03-25-covid-19-the-climate-crisis-and-lockdown-an-opportunity-to-end-the-war-with-nature/ (accessed 27 May 2020).

——. 2020b. 'Covid-19 and the case for a citizens' basic income grant in South Africa', *Daily Maverick*, 15 April 2020, https://www.dailymaverick.co.za/opinionista/2020-04-15-covid-19-and-thecase-for-a-citizens-basic-income-grant-in-south-africa/ (accessed 27 May 2020).

——. 2021. 'The rise of ecofascism' in *Destroying Democracy: Neoliberal Capitalism and the Rise of Authoritarian Politics* edited by Michelle Williams and Vishwas Satgar. Johannesburg: Wits University Press, 2021: 25–48.

——. 2022. 'Marx, the commons and democratic eco-socialism' in *Marx Matters* edited by D. Fasenfest. Leiden: Brill: 181–197.

Satgar, V. and Cherry, J. 2019. 'Climate and food inequality: The South African Food Sovereignty Campaign response'. *Globalisations* 17(2).

Satgar, V. and Cock, J. 2022. 'Ecosocialist activism and movements in South Africa' in *The Routledge Handbook on Ecosocialism* edited by L. Brownhill et al. London: Routledge: 179–188.

Satgar V. and Southall, R. 2015. *COSATU in Crisis: The Fragmentation of an African Trade Union Federation*. Johannesburg: KMM Publishers.

Satgar, V. and Williams, M. 2011a. 'Co-operatives and nation building in post-apartheid South Africa: Contradictions and challenges' in *The Hidden Alternative: Co-operative Values Past, Present and Future* edited by A. Webster et al. Manchester: University of Manchester Press: 177–202.

Satgar, V. and Williams, M. 2011b. 'Co-operatives and worker ownership in South

Africa'. *New South African Review* edited by J. Daniel et al. Johannesburg: Wits University Press: 202–220.

Satgoor, A. 2014. 'The Mineline factory occupation: Pathway to the solidarity economy' in *The Solidarity Economy Alternative: Emerging Theory and Practice* edited by V. Satgar. Pietermaritzburg: University of KwaZulu-Natal Press: 279–298.

Saul, J. 2013. 'Socialism and southern Africa' in *Marxisms in the Twenty-First Century: Crisis, Critiques and Struggles* edited by M. Williams and V. Satgar. Johannesburg: University of the Witwatersrand Press.

Saurin, J. 2006. 'International relations as the imperial illusion; or, the need to decolonize' in *Decolonizing International Relations* edited by B. Gruffydd Jones. Lanham: Rowman & Littlefield.

Sayer, S. 2003 [1998]. *Marxism and Human Nature*. London: Routledge.

Scholes, B., Engelbrecht, F. and Vogel, C. 2020. 'Climate change: Effective action based on enhanced understanding'. Emancipatory Futures Studies, Climate Science Think Piece, Wits, www.safsc.org.za/wp-content/uploads/2020/06/Climate-Science-Doc_ June-2020.pdf (accessed 23 September 2020).

Seekings, J. 2000. *The UDF: A History of the United Democratic Front in South Africa, 1983–1991*. Cape Town: David Phillip.

Serge, V. 1992. *Memoirs of a Revolutionary*. Oxford: Oxford University Press.

Shilliam, R. (ed.). 2011. *International Relations and Non-Western Thought: Imperialism, Colonialism and Investigations of Global Modernity*. London: Routledge.

Shiva, V. 1988 [2016]. *The Violence of the Green Revolution: Third World Agriculture, Ecology and Politics*. Lexington: University Press of Kentucky.

——. 2015 [2005]. *Earth Democracy: Justice, Sustainability and Peace*. Berkeley: North Atlantic Books.

——. 2015. *Who Really Feeds the World?* London: Zed Books.

——. 2016 [1988]. *Staying Alive: Women, Ecology and Development*. Berkeley: North Atlantic Books.

——. 2020 [1997]. *Reclaiming the Commons: Biodiversity, Indigenous Knowledge and the Rights of Mother Earth*. Santa Fe: Synergetic Press.

Shiva, V. and Mies, M. 2014 [1993]. *Eco-feminism*. London: Zed Books.

Shiva, V. and Moser, M. 1995. *Biopolitics: A Feminist and Ecological Reader on Biotechnology*. London: Zed Books.

Shroff, F.M. 2000. 'Ayurveda: Mother of indigenous health knowledge' in

Indigenous Knowledge in Global Contexts: Multiple Readings of Our World edited by George J. Sefa Dei, Budd L. Hall and Dorothy Goldin Rosenburg. Toronto: University of Toronto Press.

Simangan, D. 2020. 'Literature review: Where is the Anthropocene?: International relations in a new geological epoch'. *International Affairs* 96: 211–224.

Simons, R.A. 2004. *All My Life and All My Strength*. Johannesburg: STE Publishers.

Sisulu, E. 2002. *Walter and Albertina Sisulu: In our Lifetime*. Cape Town: David Philip.

Soederberg, S. 2004a. 'American imperialism and new forms of disciplining the non-integrating gap'. *Research in Political Economy* 21: 31–60.

——. 2004b. *The Politics of the New Financial Architecture: Reimposing Neoliberal Domination in the Global South*. New York: Zed Books.

Soederberg, S., Menz, G. and Cerny, P. (eds). 2005. *Internalizing Globalisation: The Rise of Neoliberalism and the Decline of National Varieties of Capitalism*. New York: Palgrave Macmillan.

Sole, S. 2005. 'The state of corruption and accountability' in *State of The Nation: South Africa 2004–2005* edited by John Daniel, Jessica Lutchman and Roger Southall. Cape Town: HSRC Press: 86–111.

South African Communist Party (SACP). 1989. The Path to Power: Programme of the South African Communist Party. https://www.sahistory.org.za/sites/default/files/The%20Path%20to%20Power%201989.pdf

South African Council of Churches (SACC). 2017. 'Towards a just economic transition to meet people's needs and sustain life'. Draft discussion document of the Economic Transformation Working Group.

South African Food Sovereignty Campaign (SAFSC). 2018a. 'People's Food Sovereignty Act, No. 1 of 2018', http://www.safsc.org.za/wp-content/uploads/2017/11/FS-Act-no.1-of-2018.pdf (accessed 20 March 2018).

——. 2018b. 'Open letter to President Cyril Ramaphosa: demand for an emergency sitting of parliament to deliberate on the recently issued UN report on 1.5°C increase in planetary temperature and its implications for South African climate change policy', www.safsc.org.za/open-letter-to-president-cyril-ramaphosa-demand-for-emergency-parliamentary-sitting-on-un-1-5c-report/ (accessed 23 September 2020).

——. 2020. 'Earth Day message: advancing climate justice and food sovereignty: a response to President Ramaphosa's R500 billion stimulus', 22 April 2020, https://www.safsc.org.za/wp-content/uploads/2020/04/FInal-Earth-Day-Message_22Apr2020.pdf (accessed 27 May 2020).

Southall, R. 2005. 'Black empowerment and corporate capital' in *The State of the Nation: South Africa 2004–2005* edited by John Daniel, Roger Southall and Jessica Lutchman. Johannesburg: HSRC Press.

——. 2006. 'Black empowerment and present limits to a more democratic capitalism in South Africa' in *The State of the Nation: South Africa 2005–2006* edited by Sakhele Buhlungu et al. Johannesburg: HSRC.

——. 2007. 'The ANC, black economic empowerment and state-owned enterprise' in *The State of the Nation, South Africa 2007* edited by Sakhele Buhlungu et al. Johannesburg: HSRC Press.

——. 2013. *Liberation Movements in Power: Party and State in Southern Africa*. Pietermaritzburg: University of KwaZulu-Natal Press.

——. 2016. 'White monopoly capital: good politics, bad sociology, worse economics', http://theconversation.com/white-monopoly-capital-good-politics-bad-sociology-worse-economics-77338 (accessed 27 November 2017).

Spaul, H. 1965. *The Co-operative Movement in the World Today*. London: Barrie and Rockliff.

Srinivas, B. 1993. *Worker Takeover in Industry: The Kamani Tubes Experiment*. New Delhi: Sage Publications.

Stanway, D. 2019. 'China plans 226 GW of new coal power projects: Environmental groups'. Reuters, 19 September, fr.reuters.com/article/us-climate-change-china-coal-idUSKBN1W40HS (accessed 23 September 2020).

Starr, A. 2005. *Global Revolt: A Guide to the Movements Against Globalization*. London: Zed Books.

Statistics South Africa. 2017a. 'Quarterly Labour Force Survey: Quarter 3, 2007', http://www.statssa.gov.za/publications/P0211/ P02113rdQuarter2017.pdf (accessed 27 November 2017).

——. 2017b. 'Poverty trends in South Africa: An examination of absolute poverty between 2006 and 2015', http://www. statssa.gov.za/publications/Report-03-10-06/Report-03-10-062015.pdf (accessed 27 November 2017).

Steffen, W. et al. 2015. 'The trajectory of the Anthropocene: The great acceleration'. *Anthropocene Review* 2: 81–98.

Steyn, E. 2015. 'Improving the livelihoods of poor female informal traders through the formation of women's co-operatives'. *Solidarity Economy News*

11: 11–12, http://copac.org.za/wp-content/uploads/2017/10/Solidarity-Economy-Newsletter-No11.pdf (accessed 20 March 2018).

Strange, S. 1994. 'The structure of finance in the world' in *Global Transformation: Challenges to the State System* edited by Y. Sakamoto. Tokyo: United Nations University Press: 228–249.

Suttner, R. and Cronin, J. 1986. *30 Years of the Freedom Charter*. Johannesburg: Ravan Press.

Terreblanche, S. 2012. *Lost in Transformation: South Africa's Search for a New Future since 1986*. Johannesburg: KMM Review Publishing.

Therborn, G. 2018 [2008]. *From Marxism to Post-Marxism?* London: Verso.

Tokar, B. 2010. *Toward Climate Justice: Perspectives on the Climate Crisis and Social Change*. Porsgrunn: Communalism Press.

Turner, B.S. 2014 [1978]. *Marx and the End of Orientalism*. London: Routledge.

Turner, R. 2015 [1972]. *The Eye of the Needle: Towards Participatory Democracy in South Africa*. London: Seagull Books.

United Nations Framework Convention on Climate Change (UNFCCC). 2015. 'Adoption of the Paris Agreement: Proposal by the president' (FCCC/CP/2015/L.9/Rev.1).

UN REPORT, 1987, *Our Common Future SACP 1989*

Van Diepen, M. (ed.) 1988. *The National Question in South Africa*. London: Zed Books.

Vermeulen, H, Schönfeldt, H. C. and Muller, C. 2020. 'Food aid parcels not nutritionally balanced'. *New Frame*, 26 May, https://www.newframe.com/food-aid-parcels-notnutritionallybalanced/?fbclid=IwAR22x97d_57tLJJUHogavuQj7LZyWIh18gh7674X3Ep8N2dLt (accessed 27 May 2020); and *Global Labour Journal* 11(2): 177.

Vogel, L. 2013. *Marxism and the Oppression of Women: Towards a Unitary Theory*. Chicago: Haymarket Books.

Von Holdt, K. 2013. 'The transition to the violent democracy'. *Review of African Political Economy* 40(138).

Wainwright, H. 1994. *Arguments for a New Left: Answering the Free Market Right*. Oxford: Blackwell.

Waldmeir, P. 1997. *The Anatomy of a Miracle: The End of Apartheid and the Birth of the New South Africa*. London: Viking.

Wall, D. 2010. *The Rise of the Green Left: Inside the Worldwide Ecosocialist Movement*. London: Pluto Press.

Wallerstein, I. 2006. *European Universalism: The Rhetoric of Power*. New York:

New Press.

Webster, D. 2019. 'Unemployment in South Africa is worse than you think'. *Mail & Guardian*, 5 August, https://mg.co.za/article/2019-08-05-unemployment-in-south-africa-is-worse-than-youthink (accessed 27 May 2020).

Webster, E. and Pampallis, K. 2017. *The Unresolved National Question: Left Thought under Apartheid*. Johannesburg: Wits University Press.

Whyte, F.W. and Whyte, K.K. 1991. *Making Mondragon: The Growth and Dynamics of the Worker Co-operative Complex*. Ithaca: ILR Press.

Williams, M. 2008. *The Roots of Participatory Democracy: Democratic Communists in South Africa and Kerala, India*. London: Palgrave.

——. 2014. 'The solidarity economy and social transformation' in *The Solidarity Economy Alternative: Emerging Theory and Practice* edited by V. Satgar. Pietermaritzburg: University of KwaZulu-Natal Press: 37–63.

Williams, M. and Satgar, V. (eds). 2021. *Destroying Democracy: Neoliberal Capitalism and the Rise of Authoritarian Politics*. Johannesburg: Wits University Press.

Williams, R. 1983. *Keywords: A Vocabulary of Culture and Society*. New York: Oxford University Press.

Wilpert, G. 2007. *Changing Venezuela by Taking Power: The History and Policies of the Chávez Government*. London: Verso.

Woo-Cumings, M. 1999. 'Introduction: Chalmers Johnson and the politics of nationalism and development' in *The Developmental State* edited by Meredith Woo-Cumings. Ithaca: Cornell University Press: 1–32.

World Bank. 1997. *The State in a Changing World*. Washington, D.C.: World Bank.

World Commission on Environment and Development. 1987. *Our Common Future*. Oxford: Oxford University Press.

World Economic Forum (WEF). 2006. *Global Competitiveness Report*. Geneva: WEF.

World Vision. 2019. 'The number of people affected by hunger in southern Africa "will stretch around the world"'. World Vision, 7 November, reliefweb.int/report/ angola/number-people-affected-hunger-southern-africa-will-stretch-around-world (accessed 23 September 2020).

Zuma, J. 2012. 'State of the Nation Address', 2 March.

Index

A

Abahlali baseMjondolo 136
Accelerated and Shared Growth Initiative for South Africa (ASGISA) 132, 160
accumulation 1–2, 22–23, 27, 34, 85, 103, 109, 110–112, 114–117, 119, 128, 140, 143, 145, 148–151, 157, 159–162, 165–166, 170, 213, 238, 242, 249, 253, 278, 292–294, 324, 326, 344, 373, 413, 431, 453, 472–474, 476
    BEE 162
    capitalist 88, 103, 141, 147, 159, 251, 294, 296, 302, 322, 326, 340, 414, 439, 445
    carbon-based 296, 373
    Chinese 174, 461
    export-led 119, 128
    financialised 262, 281, 499
    global 130, 150, 264, 322, 417–418, 499
    globalised 262, 457
    import-substitution 128, 156
    industrial 423
    male-dominated 264
    market-centred 509
    mercantile 476
    monopoly industrial 477
    neoliberal 262
    primitive 280, 446, 448
    racialised 225, 264, 291
    transnational techno-financial 477
activism 4–5, 36, 183, 185–186, 281, 320, 352, 388, 420, 553, 556
    climate justice 375, 385, 387, 422, 466
    solidarity economy 511–512
    transnational 261, 482, 484
    transformative 525
activist(s) 3, 5, 8–11, 13, 21, 34–35, 122–123, 136, 192, 197, 215, 240, 248, 260, 266, 282, 288, 301, 319, 330, 340–341, 343, 345, 351–353, 355, 358, 365, 394, 463, 479, 480–481, 487, 494, 519–520, 522, 524–525, 537, 556–557
Africa(n) 1–2, 18, 21, 39, 63, 76, 104, 113–114, 116, 129, 140, 147, 149, 162, 200, 209–210, 224, 230, 240, 249, 256, 263, 269, 282, 287, 312, 317–318, 339, 347–348, 350, 354, 357–358, 367–368, 377, 385–386, 388–398, 405, 415, 434, 477, 485, 501, 529
African Food Sovereignty Alliance 358
Africa Forum 154, (see also 'World Economic Forum (WEF)')
African National Congress (ANC) 1–3, 6, 8–9, 17, 19, 24–28, 30, 32, 34–36, 50, 96, 103, 108–110, 114, 117, 121–124, 130–131, 133, 135–139, 143–144, 148, 157, 161–162, 176–181, 188, 190, 192–195, 197, 199, 202–205, 208–215, 220–221, 223, 227, 231, 239–240, 247–248, 256–257, 260–268, 270, 284–287, 289–291, 293–295, 297, 299–300, 346, 356, 365, 367–368, 370–371, 375–378, 385, 387, 389, 392–393, 406–408, 430, 435, 462–463, 473, 514–515, 519–520,

531–532, 535–538, 541, 546, 549
African Union (AU) 154, 357, 383, 405
Africanism 198
Afrikaner 7, 115, 295, 536
Afro-neoliberal(ism) 2, 4, 24, 26–27, 30–31, 34, 111–112, 114–115, 118–122, 126–134, 140, 146–147, 149–151, 154–157, 159, 162, 187, 250–252, 284–285, 290, 292–294, 367–371, 545, 548
agricultural complex 75
agriculture 424, 530
   corporate-controlled 321
   export-led 294, 346, 388
   industrial 530, 532
   globalised 319, 322, 379, 385, 530
   state-supported, capitalist 536
   white male-dominated 319
   women-controlled 319
Aguilar, Delia 330
AIDS denialism 220, 408
Amazon 312–313, 347, 373–374, 463
American Civil War 477
American Revolution 477
Amin, Idi 224
Amin, Samir 61, 282–283, 306–307, 314, 316–318
   Capitalism in the Age of Globalisation 318
   Empire of Chaos 318
   Eurocentrism 307, 317
Amendment Act 76
American dream 216, 218
ANC Polokwane conference (2007) 177–178, 196, 244, 265, 294
ANC-led Alliance 1–3, 9, 12, 18, 20, 24, 33, 36, 84, 97, 114, 119, 121–125, 127, 143, 150, 176, 185–186, 193, 198, 209–211, 224–225, 242, 247, 250, 257–258, 262–268, 270, 284, 290–293, 297–300, 367–369, 431, 540 (see also 'Tripartite Alliance')
ANC–SAPC faction 262
ANC–SACP–COSATU Alliance 261 (see also 'ANC-led Alliance' and 'Tripartite Alliance')
ANC Women's League 197
ANC Youth League 19, 247, 535

anti-ANC 207
anti-apartheid 1, 9, 11, 16–17, 116, 122–124, 127, 240, 277, 280–281, 307
anti-authoritarian 271, 489, 513
anti-capitalism 32, 34, 302, 333, 413, 421
anti-capitalist 16, 21, 23, 38, 48, 52, 91–93, 130, 182, 208, 240, 254, 266, 282, 287–288, 330–331, 341–342, 422, 424, 464, 466, 471, 509–511
anti-climate justice 385
anti-climate science 385
anti-colonial(ism) 10–11, 21, 278, 280, 307
anti-constitutionalism 196, 206, 225
anti-corruption 215, 486
anti-democratic 208, 217, 219, 225, 367, 369–370, 505, 519
anti-ecological 438, 441–442
anti-establishment 207
anti-Eurocentric 34, 314, 321
anti-globalisation 281, 319, 477
anti-humanism 39
anti-imperial(ism) 11, 16, 21, 180, 199, 280, 402
anti-neoliberal 477
anti-oppression 38, 302, 331, 438, 447, 480
anti-parliamentarianism 206
Anti-Privatisation Forum 212, 265
anti-racism 16, 277–278, 302, 324, 436
anti-racist 34, 280, 284, 426
anti-Semitism 206
anti-socialist 173
anti-systemic 271, 282, 428
anti-white 289
anti-white supremacy 287–289, 536
anti-Zuma 268
Anthropocene 21, 29, 33, 36, 296, 304–306, 309–314, 319–321, 344, 363, 413–414, 418, 429–430, 554
anthropocentric 39, 93, 201, 300, 304, 313, 379, 423, 438, 442, 446
anthropogenic effects 310
apartheid 1–3, 7–11, 13, 16–17, 30, 36, 47–48, 59, 67, 76, 88, 109, 113–117, 119, 122–123, 131, 133, 135, 138–139, 142, 144, 148, 156, 175, 184, 192, 200, 209, 224–225, 249–250, 257, 260–261,

263–264, 281, 283, 285–288, 291, 293, 295, 299, 302, 312, 359, 368, 391, 405, 430, 477, 493, 510, 512, 537
Arab Spring 2, 193, 257, 260–261, 486, 529
Arja Samaj 10
armed struggle 10, 13
arms deal 29, 158, 161, 176, 204, 262
Asia 63, 279, 316, 347, 405, 415, 477–478, 553
Asian crisis 499
Asian tigers 141
Association of Mineworkers and Construction Union (AMCU) 211, 267
autarky 317
autonomous worker self-management 45–46, 54, 55 (see also 'workplace forum, autonomous self-management')

B

Bahro, Rudolf 423
    The Alternative in Eastern Europe 423
Bakker, Isabel 327
balance of payments 57, 115, 120
balkanisation 25
Banks Act 80
bantustan 263
barbarism 165–168, 171, 182, 186–187, 500–501
Basic Conditions of Employment Act 30
basic income grant (BIG) 201, 222, 354, 366, 433, 481, 545, 549
    universal 229, 269, 302, 465, 542–543
Bay of Pigs 112
BEE charters 131, 161
Benjamin, Walter 4, 5
    The Concept of History 4
Bhattacharya, Tithi 325, 327–328, 330–331
Biden, Joe 219, 222, 227, 328, 357–358, 380, 388, 403–404, 457, 461
bill of rights 48
Biko, Steve 288, 289
biodiversity 309, 320–322, 328, 439–440
biopiracy 320
bioregionalism 92
biotech companies 320
black business associations 131, 161
black capitalist class 127, 130, 132–133,
292, 294 (see also 'Black Economic Empowerment (BEE)')
black consciousness (BC) 198, 284, 288–289
    academic 288–289
    Africanist 288, 290
    populist 288–289
Black Consciousness movement 270, 288
Black Economic Commission 131, 161
Black Economic Empowerment (BEE) 2, 27, 129–132, 157, 160–162, 175–178, 197, 210, 247, 257, 285, 292–293, 496, 517
    market-driven 292
    state-driven 292
black elite 247
black farmers 76
    small 294–295
black identity 289
#BlackLivesMatter (BLM) 486
black middle class 213, 289, 294
#BlackMonday 295 (see also 'white farmers')
Black Students Society 10 (see also 'University of Natal')
black swan event 373–374
black working class 295
BLUE IQ 85, 99
Bolivarian Alliance for the Peoples of our America (ALBA) 480
Bolivarian Revolution 477
Bolsheviks 169, 171–172
Bretton Woods institutions 119, 131, 151, 244
Brexit 404, 459, 479, 487
BRICS (Brazil, Russia, India, China, South Africa) 210, 405, 458
Broad-Based Black Economic Empowerment (B-BBEE) 495–496, 517
Broad-Based Black Economic Empowerment Act 131, 161
Building Socialism Now 96 (see also 'South African Communist Party (SACP)')
Bulungula Incubator 521
bureaucratisation 122, 126–127, 172
bureaucratised 125–126, 139, 293
burial society 97 (see also 'co-operative movement')

Bush, George 485
Buthelezi, Mangosuthu 153, 221

C

cadre 79, 114, 119, 123, 126, 151, 197, 239, 264, 266
Cancun Summit 251
capital 2, 22, 27, 31, 34, 36, 39, 50, 58, 64, 67, 74, 78–80, 91, 111, 115–116, 118, 120, 125, 129, 132, 145, 147, 155, 157, 183, 211, 222, 237, 244, 246, 251–253, 256, 292, 296, 298, 322, 325–326, 328, 332, 341, 344–346, 370, 435, 438, 448, 450, 453, 461, 474–475, 477, 479, 481, 489, 494, 514, 537, 540
    Afrikaner 116
    banking 115
    big 22
    black 292, 368
    carbon 348, 351, 355, 429–430, 450, 455–456
    commercial 115
    corporate 512
    domestic 154, 158, 291
    finance 132, 146, 148, 153, 167, 251, 368, 458
    financial 148, 214, 514
    fossil 418, 487
    global 153, 291, 318
    globalised 188, 262
    industrial 59, 115
    mercantile 278
    mining 188
    monopoly 2, 12, 16, 109–111, 117, 121, 128, 130, 132, 134, 148, 175, 318, 454
    short-term 105
    transnational(ising) 86, 111–112, 121, 127–128, 132, 134, 140, 144–145, 147–150, 152–155, 159, 162, 166–167, 180, 213–214, 231, 238, 250–251, 253, 262, 322, 340–341, 368, 471, 473, 475, 514
    white 207, 292, 537
    white monopoly 17, 36, 114, 121, 131, 144, 161–162, 264
    working 247
capital flight 116, 148
capital-intensive 152
capitalism 2, 5, 10–13, 16–17, 20, 22, 29, 33, 34, 36–38, 51, 77, 83, 86–87, 90–92, 94–96, 98–99, 112–113, 165–169, 180, 182, 207, 214, 230–232, 239–240, 242–243, 253–255, 258, 261, 264, 270, 278–283, 287, 289–290, 293, 296, 298–299, 302, 311, 322–326, 328–331, 373–374, 377, 419, 421–425, 427, 431, 435, 437–441, 443, 445–448, 450–451, 453, 458, 460, 472, 476–477, 488, 510, 512–513, 554
    African 254
    American 17, 218
    Anglo-American 244
    apartheid 252
    authoritarian state 28
    carbon(-based) 36, 39, 232, 297, 301, 311–312, 333, 359, 372, 374, 375, 429–430, 432, 434, 438–439, 451, 453–454, 464, 466
    Chinese 373, 423
    competitive 318, 326
    domestic 109
    ecocidal 7, 23, 37, 273, 283, 297, 300–302, 322, 329, 332, 373, 430, 453–455, 466
    ecofascist 283, 436, 454–456, 459–460
    financialised 323, 326, 327–328, 330, 375, 448, 472, 479
    fossil 421
    free market 243
    global 1, 33, 77, 127, 133, 162, 165–169, 175, 182, 186–187, 238, 253, 282–283, 292, 297–298, 301, 305, 318, 328, 347, 453–454, 472, 480, 499, 512
    global monopoly 318
    globalising 49, 175, 240, 251, 262, 264, 268, 270, 291, 413, 422, 435
    green 340, 342, 418, 464
    green climate 300, 301
    industrial 86, 439, 441, 513
    Keynesian-welfare 260
    liberal 330, 342, 448
    mercantile 318

monopoly 109, 130, 149, 160, 264, 280
national 116, 148–151
neoliberal(ised) 121, 149, 166–167,
  230–232, 237, 257–258, 268, 292,
  308, 352, 479, 499
post-apartheid 20, 133, 149, 237, 290,
  298, 511
racial 27, 280, 299
shock therapy 12
South African 111, 133, 264, 268, 299,
  301
state(-managed) 170, 175–179, 181,
  183, 185, 207, 243, 247, 254, 326,
  330, 448
transnational 111, 115, 132, 146, 149,
  150–151, 160, 254, 317, 344
Western 180, 278
capitalism crisis 23, 165–166, 230–231, 233,
  235, 258, 266, 323, 326–328, 340, 422,
  454, 498–499, 501
  global 245
capitalist 1, 7, 11, 22, 29, 34, 36, 39, 46, 48,
  52, 63, 66, 69, 83, 91–92, 97, 115–116,
  132, 141, 150, 206, 247, 249, 251, 257,
  262, 278, 280, 285, 290, 301, 303, 308,
  317, 329, 332, 344, 346, 379, 391, 416,
  418, 420, 424, 429, 441, 454, 458, 464,
  472, 476, 499, 501, 510, 512, 517, 525
  carbon 297, 300, 391, 450
  competitive 418
  expansion 278
  global 339, 341
  green 341, 430
  Western 4
  white male 218
capitalist civilisation crisis 498–499,
  501–503, 505
capitalist growth economics 91
capitalist restructuring 145
capitalist society 51, 474
capitalist state 22
capitalist system 86, 89, 98, 317, 329, 421,
  445, 498, 557
  global(ised) 374, 417
  world 86, 91–92, 95
carbon budget (aka carbon space) 311, 346, 417

carbon emissions 297, 309–312, 322,
  343–344, 348–349, 354, 363, 365,
  377, 381–382, 385, 388, 404, 416–417,
  429–430, 435, 455–456, 458, 461–462,
  485, 506, 554
carbon footprint 32, 404, 430, 461
carbon-intensive 39, 297, 458, 555
carbon market 346, 349, 554
carbon tax 382
carbon trading 340, 344, 418
Cele, Bheki 221
centralism 124, 237
Centre for Education Rights and
  Transparency 523
Centre for Small Business Promotion 160
  (see also 'Department of Trade and
  Industry (DTI)')
Chavez, Hugo 482
Chinese Communist Party 28, 174
civil rights movement 219
civil society 32, 50, 52, 56, 80, 114, 119,
  121–128, 139, 151, 177, 183, 186, 193,
  210–212, 215, 222, 228–229, 233,
  263, 265, 285, 339, 340–342, 352, 358,
  377, 382, 384, 407, 420, 464, 471–474,
  514–515, 539, 541–542, 553, 557
civilisational crisis 251, 252
classical revolution 27
clean development mechanism (CDM) 343
clean energy 29, 398, 481
climate 5, 343
  global 310
Climate Action Network 420
climate change 5, 156, 163, 168–169, 189,
  193, 200, 202, 296, 298, 302, 310,
  339–344, 346, 348, 355, 363–366, 374,
  382, 384, 386, 395, 407, 413–416, 419,
  425, 429, 431–433, 438, 460, 484–485,
  499–501, 504–506, 529–532, 553–556
climate conscious 40
climate crisis (see 'crisis')
climate debt 340, 343, 388, 398, 417, 485,
  553
climate denialism 218, 232, 281, 381, 418
climate geography 38
climate hotspot 350, 384, 396

climate injustice 3, 335, 361, 364–365, 375, 384, 397, 461, 463, 485
climate jobs 201, 265, 269, 283, 302, 346, 353–354, 366, 393, 398, 420, 433, 481, 485, 504, 525, 556
Climate Jobs Campaign 266
climate justice 21, 29, 36–37, 233, 312, 314, 339, 343–344, 347–349, 352–355, 359, 364–366, 371, 375, 385–387, 389, 398–399, 404, 408, 419–420, 425, 429–430, 433, 436, 438, 441, 450–451, 455, 462–467, 485–486, 502, 504, 524, 536, 555, 557
Climate Justice Charter (CJC) 21, 32, 36, 313, 333, 347–348, 350–356, 375, 379, 381–386, 389, 396–398, 408, 433, 450, 452, 462, 463–466, 551, 553, 557
Climate Justice Charter Movement (CJCM) 37, 464
Climate Justice Deal 465
climate scientists 348, 354, 374, 380, 383–384, 396, 414, 429, 450, 463, 530
climate shocks 201, 227–228, 297–298, 304, 313–314, 322, 328, 333, 349–350, 363, 365, 370, 375, 378, 380–382, 387, 396–397, 399, 404, 421, 430, 433–434, 455, 460, 465, 472, 524, 538, 554, 557
climate war 364
Clinton, Bill 217
carbon dioxide (CO_2) 395, 425
coalition(s) 50, 207, 485
Cochabamba Declaration (2010) 312
co-determination 45–48, 50–51, 54–56, 118
Coega Industrial Development Zone 156
Cold War 1, 17–18, 22, 63, 83, 112, 166–167, 216–217, 219, 243, 256, 281, 317, 400, 402–404, 473, 476–478
 new 400, 461
collective bargaining 30, 45, 47, 117, 120, 248
colonial 6, 16, 39, 67, 86, 225, 278–281, 287, 293, 299, 305, 307, 315, 379, 390–391, 439, 446, 476–477, 535
colonialism 36, 209, 224, 264, 278, 299, 302, 331, 443, 446, 448, 477, 483, 498
colonialism of a special type 87, 144, 263, 280, 299, 391, 393

colonialist 47
coloniality 22, 304–305, 307–314, 319, 321, 535
colonisation 349
Coloured People's Congress 9
Colvin, Louise 26
Combahee River Collective 331
Commission for Conciliation, Mediation and Arbitration (CCMA) 54
commoning 355, 436, 439, 441, 443, 448–452
commons, the 437–452, 455, 464, 480, 504, 510, 520, 525, 537, 538, 541
communism 141, 427, 513
communist 3, 15, 16, 25–26, 83, 179, 259, 261, 371, 449, 478
Communist League 280
communist parties 513
Communist Party 58, 165, 172, 180
Communist Party of South Africa (CPSA) 280, 287, 299
community food security forum 97
community organisation(s) 4, 126, 352, 396, 465, 481, 518, 555
compensatory and contingency financing facility (CFF) 119, 151
competition state (aka internationalised state) 127, 146
Conference of the Democratic Left (CDL) 253, 255
Conference of the Parties (COP) 21, 36, 339–343, 349, 388, 396, 407, 415, 455, 457–458, 486
Congress Alliance 285
Congress of Democrats 9
Congress of South African Trade Unions (COSATU) 17–20, 25, 30, 47–48, 50–51, 57, 95, 108–110, 117, 118, 120–121, 124, 137, 142–143, 196, 211, 221, 256–257, 262, 266–267, 286, 293, 342, 397, 496
Congress of the People (1955) 285, 286
Congress of the People (COPE) 142, 177, 265
Congress Party 57
conservatism 217

consumerist 26
Constitution, the 30, 36, 125–126, 177, 179, 188, 194, 214, 225, 257, 293, 355–356, 383, 396, 464, 518, 531, 535, 537
Constitutional Court 60, 136, 197–198, 226, 533
constitutional crisis 209
constitutional right(s) 226, 407
constitutionalism 111, 291
    liberal 292
    transformative 206, 292
Convention for a Democratic South Africa (CODESA) 47, 201, 346
co-operative(s) 31–32, 35, 53, 55, 62–81, 91, 160, 239, 240, 244, 247–248, 354, 449, 494–498, 501–504, 506, 510, 514–515, 517–519, 521, 524–525, 532
    agricultural 67, 74–76, 157
    arts and crafts 79
    black 494, 496
    capitalist 78
    consumer 80
    district 72
    federal 64
    financial services 80
    formal 65
    grain 75, 76
    grassroots-driven 522
    informal 65
    labour and technology 78
    non-worker 493–494, 497
    organic farming 79
    primary 64, 67, 69
    producer 493
    secondary 64, 68, 76, 79
    sectoral 64
    village 72, 524
    waste recycling 79
    white 494, 496
    worker 427, 491, 493–494, 496, 510, 518, 520–521, 523, 526
    worker-owned 63, 65–66, 71–72, 78
Co-operative and Policy Alternative Centre (COPAC) 28, 31–32, 35, 187, 246, 351, 353, 382, 493, 495–496, 510, 517–520, 522–523, 553, 555–558

Solidarity Economic News 520, 522
The Solidarity Economy Alternative: Emerging Theory and Practice 520
co-operative autonomy 502
co-operative bank 31, 67, 78–80, 515–516, 525
Co-operative Banks Act 31
Co-operative Banks Development Agency (CBDA) 515–516
Co-operative (Developing Countries) Recommendation 64
co-operative development 31, 69, 491, 493–497, 502–504, 509, 513–517, 519–520, 523, 526
co-operative identity 504–505
co-operative model 493, 495, 504, 523
co-operative movement 69, 70, 72, 77–81, 97–98, 498, 501–504, 514, 526
    global 69, 501, 504–506
    socialist 63, 77–78, 80
    state 519
co-operative movement networks 68
Co-operatives Act 31, 35, 75, 81, 515, 518–519, 526
Co-operatives Bill 80–81
Corbyn, Jeremy 487
corporate capture 258
corrupt(ion) 5–6, 18, 34, 59–60, 74, 137, 161–162, 176–177, 186, 193, 196–197, 200, 203, 213–215, 220, 250, 262, 265, 267, 285, 290, 292, 294, 298, 354, 376, 393, 395, 397, 408, 434, 442, 486, 517–518, 540, 548
Covid-19 3, 5–7, 217–219, 227, 322, 328, 333, 352, 354, 357–358, 372–374, 377–381, 384, 393, 400, 437, 450, 457, 459–460, 465, 539–542, 545, 547–549
Creecy, Barbara 370, 389
credit rating agencies 27, 155, 214, 370, 434
credit union 80
criminal justice system 177
crisis 1, 3, 36, 39, 203, 221, 227, 229, 329, 378, 478–479, 501
    accumulation 145–146
    capitalism 169, 231, 252, 258, 282, 323, 326, 328, 340, 453–454, 499

capitalist 230, 499
capitalist civilisation 499–501
civilisational 35, 231, 243, 250–251, 322
climate 3, 6, 22, 35–38, 215, 232,
    281, 284, 296–301, 304, 308, 310,
    312–313, 321, 328, 333, 343–344,
    346–353, 355–357, 359, 364–366,
    370, 372, 374, 375, 378–381,
    383–385, 388, 391, 396–398, 400,
    404–408, 413–415, 417–418,
    420, 423, 425, 428, 430, 432, 450,
    455–457, 460, 463–464, 466, 472,
    476, 480, 485, 512, 522–524, 534,
    540, 549, 553–555, 557–558
conjunctural 250–251, 281, 328, 340
ecological 301, 327, 340, 352, 464
economic 228, 378–379, 472
energy 555
financial markets 499
financial system 242, 417
fiscal 548
food 201, 388, 499, 531, 554–555, 557
food system 328, 352
global (see 'global economic crisis')
global financial (see 'global economic crisis')
globalisation 251
housing market 499
humanitarian 228
hunger 201, 228–229, 541
higher education 34, 203, 205 (see also 'National Education Crisis Forum')
intersecting 332
legitimacy 3, 210, 213, 215, 294, 328, 341
liberal democracy 205, 228, 230, 254, 328
market democracy 219,
modernity 316
moral 357
nation-building 225
national liberation left politics 260, 262
neoliberalism 240, 244, 251, 281, 479, 499
non-racial democracy 225
non-racialism 284–285, 290

political 357
sectoral 499
social ecological 227
socio-ecological reproduction 333, 329, 347, 377, 545
South African left 261
social reproduction 264, 326, 329
structural 242, 250,
systemic 231, 282, 319, 328, 352, 373–374, 378, 453–454, 499, 512
transnational financial 499
water 364, 554–555, 557
Cronin, Jeremy 27, 175–177, 179–181, 184, 187
cronyism 192, 198
Crutzen, Paul 343–344

D

Dadoo, Yusuf 19, 26
Dakota Access Pipeline project 486
Davis, Angela 331
De Klerk, F.W. 153, 226
debt standstill 116
debt trap 104
decarbonisation 296, 349, 365, 378, 385–386, 397, 407, 418, 433, 457, 462, 465, 554
decolonial 34, 38, 224–225, 273, 304–310, 312–316, 319–321, 333, 443, 448, 451, 464, 485, 535
decolonisation 34, 207, 214, 265, 289, 302, 308, 317, 436, 486–488
decolonial–Marxist–ecofeminism 23, 34
de-globalisation 459, 483
    financial 268
dehumanisation 11, 16, 135, 225, 291, 312
de-industrialisation 27, 53, 106, 144, 167, 346, 454
de-industrialised plant 55
demilitarisation 83
democracy 1, 11–12, 17, 21, 25–26, 30, 34, 49–51, 62, 109, 114, 119, 133, 138, 152, 155, 173, 177–178, 182–183, 188–191, 193, 195, 198–199, 206, 213–216, 219, 226–227, 230, 232–233, 238–239, 244, 250–252, 254, 256, 258–259, 263, 265, 271, 290, 309, 320, 327, 341, 346, 369, 401, 406, 408, 423, 426–428,

432, 434–436, 449, 481, 483, 505, 511, 531–532, 535, 549
American 216, 219
associational 252
carbon 367, 370–371, 434, 442
citizen-led 523
constitutional 1, 26–27, 192, 194, 198, 218, 227, 257, 263, 367, 406
co-operative 504
deep 28, 287, 302
Earth 319–321
economic 320, 505
electoral 109, 122, 133–134, 190, 317, 505
energy 489
failing 193
free market 52
global 341
industrial 45
liberal 2, 230, 290, 292–293, 328, 341
market 1, 2, 26–27, 32, 34, 37, 41, 103, 188–189, 191, 217, 219, 231, 233, 253, 281, 401, 434–435, 454, 461, 489, 505
mature 196, 257
non-racial 225, 286
participatory 114, 122, 126–127, 183–184, 188, 193, 252, 258, 511–512
political 192
popular 144
post-apartheid 260, 263–264, 368
post-Zuma 215
representative 193, 252–253, 341, 426
rural 265
South African 162, 189, 191, 199, 254, 367–368
transformative 188, 190–191, 256, 294, 504–505
democracy from below 193
democratic advance 124
Democratic Alliance (DA) 178, 188, 192, 207, 385, 534
democratic collective 244
Democratic Communist Party of South Africa 184
democratic corporatist state 110, 113–114, 117–122, 125–128, 133, 142
democratic eco(feminist) socialism 37
democratic ecosocialism 29, 37–38, 187, 302–303, 409, 411, 422–429, 432, 436–437, 450, 452, 511 (see also 'ecosocialism')
democratic ecosocialist 3, 23, 28–29, 33, 35, 37, 182, 184, 333, 342, 414, 421–422, 426, 428, 432–433, 436, 438, 450, 454–455, 464, 516 (see also 'ecosocialist')
democratic government 139
Democratic Left Front (DLF) 28, 35, 193, 266
Democratic Marxism series 21, 29, 33–34, 230, 428
democratic political order 52
democratic state 25, 48, 127
democratic systemic reforms 23–24, 30–31, 34–35, 37–38, 229, 333, 378, 383, 411, 433, 436, 451, 455, 464–466, 513–517, 526, 537
democratic thinking 49
democratic transition 18, 30
democratisation 23, 45–46, 49–51, 53–54, 56, 59, 83, 137, 217, 222, 230–231, 233, 244, 321, 333, 341, 398, 477, 515
workplace 45, 51, 53
Denel 157
Department of Labour 256
Department of Social Development 228
Department of Trade and Industry (DTI) 81, 119–120, 160, 247
'Support measures for the enhancement of the international competitiveness of South Africa's industry sector' 119
Department of Trade, Industry and Co-operatives 81
dependency theory 316
deracialisation 18, 120, 130–132, 159–161, 175, 247
deracialised 16, 110, 117, 131, 133, 210, 264, 291, 294
deradicalisation 2, 186, 330
deregulation 30, 127, 145
developing country 91, 417

development corridors 155
Development Facilitation Act 60
development industry 59
development planning 57–59, 62
development planning commission 59–60, 62
developmental state 28, 139–144, 147, 150–152, 162, 174, 247, 292, 370
    capitalist 141
developmentalism 141–142, 509
Disaster Management Act 228, 377–378, 534
division of labour 146, 322, 423, 444, 446, 473
    political 271
Dlamini, Bathabile 197
Dlamini, Sdumo 31
Dussel, Enrique 306–307, 314–316
    Ethics of Liberation: In the Age of Globalisation and Exclusion 316
    Philosophy of Liberation 307, 315
    The Invention of the Americas: Eclipse of 'the Other' and the Myth of Modernity 316

E

E3G 395
Earth system 37, 304, 314, 320, 381, 383, 407, 415, 438–440, 450
    stable 306, 383
Earth system science 304, 310
Earthrise Trust 524
East Asia 127, 141, 143, 373
Eastern Cape 397, 408, 521, 524
Eastern Europe 167, 173, 243, 404
ecocidal 5, 36, 298–299, 301, 321, 374, 379, 413, 436–437, 439, 441, 453, 510, 512
ecocidal destruction 305
ecocide 34, 275, 284, 288, 296–298, 300–302, 312, 346, 440, 446, 453
    climate 429, 430
    imperial 419
Ecocity Trust project 29, 35, 79, 519
ecofascism 34, 232–233, 319, 419, 457–458, 461, 464
ecofeminism 319–321
ecofeminist 306, 319, 323, 329, 333, 352, 425, 464
ecohousing 35, 407

ecohumanism 16
eco-imperialism 296
ecological 306, 308, 310–311, 319, 322–323, 327, 329, 346, 391, 423–426, 441, 443, 445, 447, 460, 466, 530, 536
ecological consciousness 191
ecological crisis 38, 168, 183, 251, 297, 301, 327, 340, 352
    social 227
    world 90
ecological debt 314
ecological destruction 296, 299, 322, 347, 369
ecological footprint 92
ecological justice 35, 347, 419, 512
ecological oppression 305
ecological relations 302, 305, 331–332
ecological science 319
ecologist 436
ecology 329, 422, 424, 427, 432, 436, 443–444
    emancipatory 382, 399, 438, 443, 445–447, 450–451, 464
    Marxist 329–330, 373, 422–425, 431, 437, 442–444, 450, 453
    materialist 422
economic determinism 94
Economic Freedom Fighters (EFF) 26, 28, 34, 191, 197, 205–208, 232, 266, 268, 290, 295, 369, 385, 531, 535–538
economic growth 91, 115–116, 158, 178, 501, 503
economistic 46–47, 113, 466
economy 87, 89, 106, 119, 146, 148, 150, 155–156, 159–160, 167, 188, 200, 209–210, 233, 238, 245, 281, 291–292, 297, 318, 328, 343, 368, 376, 378, 500
    advanced capitalist 71, 104
    agrarian 294
    agro-food 157
    apartheid 116
    capitalist 290
    carbon-based 353, 485, 504
    carbon-intensive 430
    cash 91
    community-controlled 98

competitive 128, 151
developed formal 89
disarticulated 152
domestic 111
enclave 128, 149, 152
export-led 118, 128, 152
external 98
fossil fuel 420
global 91, 133, 158, 162, 313, 318, 322, 372, 400, 403, 456, 460, 472, 475, 499, 549
global capitalist 52, 149, 210, 499
green 202, 349
internationalised 110
local community 91
local township 87
market 70, 281
mixed 143, 510
national 68, 167, 475
productive 210
real 242
rural 67
rural agricultural 74, 76
solidarity 21, 32, 201, 233, 247–248, 258, 265, 302, 352, 366, 433, 436, 451, 480–481, 489, 503, 509–526, 532, 536
South African 30, 45, 106, 111, 116, 119–121, 129, 134, 143, 148, 152, 156–157, 160–162, 246, 250–251, 515
Soviet 170
structurally fragmented 152
subsistence 333
ecosocialism, 238, 434
ecosocialist 166, 435
ecosystem(s) 5, 37–38, 283, 296–297, 305, 316, 322, 373, 380–381, 384, 395, 401, 406, 427, 431, 440, 537
ecovillage 92, 96, 519
Ecumenical Service for Socio-Economic Transformation (ESSET) 521–522
election(s) 48, 122, 177, 180, 188–189, 192–195, 207, 216, 219, 250, 253, 387
1994 democratic 109, 124, 194
2009 general 177–179, 194
2014 general 214, 265, 267
2016 local government 211, 214
2024 general 389, 465
Electoral Commission of South Africa (IEC) 194
electoral contestation 25, 175, 190, 268
emancipation 327
employment equity 131, 161
Employment Equity Act 30
empowerment 131, 161, 175, 186, 288, 327, 496
energy sovereignty 283
Engels, Friedrich 93–94, 324, 441–442
    Anti-Dühring 93
    Dialectics of Nature 93
    Outlines of a Critique of Political Economy 441
    The Communist Manifesto 13, 278–279, 448
Enlightenment, the 278, 319, 476 (see also 'Hegel, Georg Wilhelm Friedrich')
entrepreneur 160
environmental injustice 183
environmental justice 510, 532, 557
environmental movement 93, 348
environmentalism 427, 442
Erwin, Alec 119
Eskom 157, 298, 353, 388
ethics of care 12–13, 16, 32, 38, 40, 358, 379 (see also 'Marx')
ethics of liberation 314, 316
Eurocentricism 317, 448
Europe 2, 156, 244, 259, 277, 280–281, 314, 316–318, 328, 355, 372, 388, 395, 403, 405, 435, 475–476, 479, 489, 553
exceptionalism 263
    South African 145, 147–148, 162, 263
exchange control(s) 105, 116, 148, 155, 269, 514
exclusion(ary) 2, 89, 290
expansionism 167–168
export-led growth 106, 150
export-led industrialisation 61
expropriation 52
exteriority 315
Extinction Rebellion 385, 463

F

failed state 147, 297, 308
fascism 2, 4, 34, 206–208, 217, 230, 232, 243, 251, 374, 402, 545
   new global 251
fascist 197, 205–206, 208, 230–231, 345
Federation of Unions of South Africa (FEDUSA) 397
#FeesMustFall 11, 26, 34, 203, 205, 212, 214, 260, 268, 289, 487
feminism 34, 238, 322–324, 330, 332–333
   black 288
   black American 330
   ecosocialist 330, 333
   emancipatory 322–323, 327, 330–333
   intersectional 323, 327, 330
   liberal 324, 332
   Marxist 12, 331
   popular 331
   socialist 330–331
feminist(s) 9, 37, 214, 324, 399, 426, 434, 466
   ecosocialist 331, 464
   intersectional 323, 330–331
   Marxist 323, 326, 328, 330–331, 447–448
   socialist 323–324
feudalism 279, 448
Fifth International of Peoples and Workers 318, 340
finance 213, 244, 281, 322, 400, 418, 457, 471, 486, 501
   global 292, 368, 499
   global corporate 217
   globalised 198, 281
   international 418
   start-up 518
   transnational 499
   working capital 518
financial crisis (see 'global economic crisis')
financial intermediation 242
financial markets 103, 146, 152, 167, 244, 291, 499, 540
   globalised 231, 548
   international 127
   liberalised 478

financial system 515
financialisation 145, 231, 233, 268, 292, 319, 323, 328, 331, 349, 374, 434, 460, 471, 477, 488, 499, 515, 545
Fingerprint Worker Co-operative 522
First, Ruth 19, 26
First World 61
Fischer, Bram 19, 26
Food and Agriculture Organization (FAO) 531
food (in)security 98, 157, 167, 200, 484, 505, 529, 531, 534
food justice 352, 536
food relief 228
food riots 531
food sovereignty 4, 21, 29, 35, 190, 201, 223, 228, 233, 258, 265, 269, 283, 295, 302, 318– 320, 333, 346, 352, 355, 365, 378, 388, 398, 419–420, 425–426, 436, 441, 451, 462, 465, 480, 481, 484, 489, 505–506, 511, 516, 521–525, 527, 531–532, 535, 537–538, 556
Food Sovereignty Alliance 346
food stress 228
food system 352, 505, 512, 515–516, 524, 530, 533–534, 536, 538
   corporate-controlled 531, 534
   export-led 529
   globalised 533–534
   sustainable 537
   white-controlled 529, 532
foreign direct investment (FDI) 116, 129, 151–152, 155–156, 158, 369
foreign exchange 130, 155
foreign investment 89, 106, 540
foreign investors 27, 139
fossil fuels 157, 218, 296, 311–312, 321, 342, 345–346, 348, 350, 365, 372, 376, 378–380, 382, 386, 391–392, 396–397, 400, 404–406, 413, 417–420, 425, 429–430, 434, 438, 455–458, 461, 465, 481, 485–486, 501, 534, 554–555
Foundation for Human Rights 556
Framework for South Africa's response to the international economic crisis 246
Fraser, Nancy 326–328, 330–331, 448

free market 36, 52, 57, 59–62, 292, 459
Free State 75
free trade area 478
Free Trade Area of the Americas 480
Freedom Charter 27, 130, 139, 142, 228, 237–238, 249, 257, 270, 285–287, 290, 300, 385 (see also 'African National Congress (ANC)')
Freedom Front Plus 385
French Revolution 172, 477, 529
#FridaysForFuture 385, 463 (see also 'Thunberg, Greta')
Front for Socio-Economic Transformation (aka Popular Movement for Transformation) 97

G

G7 48, 132, 153, 168
G8 132, 153
G20 131–132, 153, 251, 253, 456, 488
Gandhi, Indira 319
Gandhi, Mahatma 494
Gandhi Foundation 385
Gatsheni, Sabelo Ndlovu 225
Gauteng 16, 20, 25, 29, 35, 85, 88–89, 96, 98–99, 196, 245, 371, 495, 520
Gauteng Manufacturing Advisory Centre (GAUMAC) 99
Gautrain 29, 158
General Agreement on Tariffs and Trade (GATT) 120
genetically modified organisms (GMOs) 530
geoecological markers 309
geopolitics 22, 167, 210, 218, 256, 306, 308, 311, 313, 315, 318, 357–359, 387, 401, 404, 417–418, 454
climate 388
German Revolution (1848)
Glasgow Financial Alliance for Net Zero 458
Global Climate Coalition 456
global competitiveness rankings 154 (see also 'World Economic Forum (WEF)')
global crisis (see 'global economic crisis')
global economic crisis 152–153, 158, 167–168, 201, 217, 242–243, 245, 281, 327, 372, 400, 435, 488, 499, 501, 545
global economic integration 403

global financial crisis (see 'global economic crisis')
global financial markets 251
global financial system 132, 153, 242, 417
global market(s) 1, 146, 150–151, 213
global North 21, 39, 69, 90, 217, 231, 282, 297, 306, 311, 317–318, 320, 322–323, 332, 343, 354, 382, 386, 416, 429, 437, 467
Global Nutrition Report 534
global political order 48
global South 21, 34, 48, 52, 90, 92, 217, 231, 240, 281, 305–306, 308, 311, 313–314, 317–318, 321–322, 332–333, 347, 349, 357, 367, 386, 402, 430, 436, 437, 442, 454, 456, 467, 473, 478, 506
global terror 82, 84
global warming 95, 168, 301, 363, 392, 397, 429, 437, 529, 553
globalisation 1, 5, 17–18, 26, 33, 48, 52, 110, 114, 116, 119, 121, 129, 133–134, 140, 144, 148, 151, 156, 162, 166–167, 175, 199, 200, 217, 219, 243, 250–251, 253, 264, 268, 285, 290, 292–293, 296, 298, 317–319, 322, 328, 343, 350, 367–368, 370, 372, 400, 417, 419, 435, 439, 458, 471, 473, 484, 502, 514, 531
neoliberal 471–472, 474–476, 481, 488–489
Gold Standard 115, 374, 435, 472
Goldberg, Denis 196, 197
Gorbachev, Mikhail 401, 403
Gordhan, Pravin 212, 215, 367
governance 59, 145, 155, 174, 225, 478
democratic 118
neoliberal global 311
participatory 98
Government of National Unity (GNU) 119, 124–125, 151, 291
gradualism 22
Grain SA 533
Gramsci, Antonio 8, 24, 110, 112–113, 115, 122, 125, 153, 352, 471
Revolutionary Thoughts in the Twentieth Century 8
Selections from the Prison Notebooks 8

grassroots 24, 31–32, 35, 45, 50, 58, 122, 139, 158, 182–184, 186, 188, 193–194, 247, 255, 266–267, 286, 301, 313, 321, 332, 341, 355, 420–421, 426, 428, 451, 464, 486–487, 509– 511, 516, 518–520, 522–525, 531–532, 553, 555–557
Great Depression 242, 251, 328, 477
great financial crash (see 'global economic crisis')
Great Financial Crisis (see 'global economic crisis')
Green Climate Fund 388
green commune 92
green growth 346
green jobs 346
Green New Deal 349, 381
greenhouse approach 69
greenhouse effect 414, 430 (see also 'climate change')
greenhouse gases (GHG) 168, 310, 347, 374, 382, 406, 414–415, 417, 425, 429, 500
Greenhouse project 29, 32
gross domestic product (GDP) 129, 155, 158, 229, 298, 416, 460, 501
gross national product (GNP) 245
Growth, Employment and Redistribution (GEAR) 27, 103, 121, 148, 151, 155, 262
Guevara, Che 12–13
Gulf War 403
Gupta empire 197
Gupta Leaks 214, 294
Gwala, Harry 18

H

Haitian Revolution 21
Hani, Chris 1, 15, 18–19, 26, 123, 256
Harvey, Ebrahim 18
Hayek, Friedrich 243
  The Road to Serfdom 243
healthcare system 6–7
  public 6
Hegel, Georg Wilhelm Friedrich 278
Higher Education Convention 205
Higher Education Crisis Conference 34
Higher Education Crisis process 34
historicise 113–114, 140, 147, 151, 326, 509, 512

HIV/AIDS 3, 183, 358, 366, 482, 500–501
Holocene 296, 304, 309, 312, 314, 363, 414
horizontalism 21
Human Economy Programme 522
human rights 135, 226, 295, 309, 402, 539, 542
Human Sciences Research Council 178
humanism 16, 238, 289
  emancipatory 224–226
  political 289
  radical 16
  revolutionary 330
humanist 285, 288
humanitarian crisis 228
hunger crisis 539, 541–542

I

imperial 17, 37, 83, 147, 199, 225, 260, 264, 283, 291, 296, 307–309, 311–312, 314–315, 347, 365, 379, 382, 416, 430, 453, 456, 473, 475, 478
imperialism 34, 86, 141, 239, 264, 278, 282, 306, 311, 318, 321, 327, 331, 439, 476
  classic 311
  global hegemonic 86
imperialist 99, 199
import restrictions 58
import substitution industrialisation (ISI) 58
Income Tax Act 75, 76
independent judiciary 48
indigenous cultures 320
industrial bargaining forum 47
industrial belt 47
industrial(ised) country 91, 168, 296, 349, 414, 416–417, 429–430, 485, 553
industrial development (see 'industrialisation')
Industrial Development Corporation (IDC) 246, 521
industrial development zones 155
industrial relations 30, 45–47, 49–50, 54, 120, 267
industrial restructuring 50, 53, 118, 143
Industrial Strategy Project (ISP) 118, 142
industrialisation 27–28, 60, 81, 95, 103, 106, 109, 142, 170, 293, 298, 370, 417, 442
  carbon-driven 553

catch-up 141, 413
ecocentric 144, 156
ecocidal 300
ecologically destructive 143, 282
export-led 27, 61, 157
fossil fuel-driven 417
globalised 417
import-substitution 58, 60–61, 110, 115, 133, 151–152, 156–157
inward-looking 109
state-led 143
industrialising country 297, 417
inflation 104–106, 115–116, 121, 146, 148, 155, 533
inflation targeting 155, 475
influx control 117
informal sector 547
informal settlements 136, 183, 190
inheritance tax 32
Inkatha Freedom Party (IFP) 178, 221
integrated development plan (IDP) 97–98
integrated resource plan (IRP) 365, 391
intellectual property rights 320, 357, 459, 475
interest rates 105–106, 155
real 105
Intergovernmental Panel on Climate Change (IPCC) 310, 347, 350, 355, 380, 387, 395–396, 404, 407, 432, 435, 450, 456, 461, 500
Climate Impacts, Adaptation and Vulnerability 404
International Commission on Stratigraphy 310
International Co-operative Alliance (ICA) 63–64, 498, 502–504
International Criminal Court 226
International Energy Agency (IEA) 455, 554
International Labour Organization (ILO) 63–64, 496
International Monetary Fund (IMF) 21, 27, 48, 57, 119, 131–132, 148, 150–151, 153–154, 253, 282, 435, 473, 482
Economic policies for a new South Africa 119, 151
International Panel of Bio-diversity and Eco-system Services 439
international relations 83, 140, 153, 219, 226, 249, 277–279, 285, 291, 295, 304–310, 313–314, 321, 401, 416, 472, 474
international relations theory 307–309
International Renewable Energy Agency 392
international trade regime 231
International Tribunal in Defence of the Rights of Nature 345
International Transport Workers Federation 283
International Union for Conservation of Nature (IUCN) 500
International Working Men's Association (aka First International) 280, 449
internationalism 16, 218, 233, 277, 281–283, 317–318, 341
anti-capitalist 283
internationalist 281, 358
intersectionality 11, 23, 289–290, 322, 327, 330–332, 466
investment treaties 155
bilateral 130
Inyanda National Land Movement 212
Ivory Park Township Ecovillage 31–32, 35

J

Jara, Mazibuko 20
Jim, Irvin 33, 369
Johannesburg Stock Exchange (JSE) 36, 88, 128, 131, 161, 351, 463
Jordan, Pallo 8, 210
July 2021 violence 2–3, 25, 220, 221
just transition 193, 201, 270, 283, 333, 343, 346, 348, 353–354, 356, 370, 392, 398, 407, 418, 428, 433, 456–457, 516
deep, 22, 24, 32, 37–39, 284, 301–302, 313, 333, 348–351, 354–356, 366, 370, 383, 385, 388–389, 397–398, 419, 421, 432–433, 441, 450–452, 455, 459, 462, 464–467, 480–481, 485–486, 504, 511, 523–524, 531, 537, 549, 553, 555–558
transformative 346, 419, 421–422, 532
justice 40, 82–83, 138, 189
environmental 351, 355
global 84
intergenerational 40, 297

K

Kamani Tubes Experiment 66
Kasrils, Ronnie 26, 193–194, 197
Kathrada, Ahmed 196–197, 212, 215
Kathrada Foundation 385
Kautsky, Karl 169
Keynesian 124
Khula Enterprise Finance Ltd 160
Koinonia Centre 493
Ku Klux Klan 231
Kwazakhele township transition initiative 524
KwaZulu-Natal 3, 18–19, 25, 31, 125, 161, 178, 220, 226–227, 256, 350, 394, 397, 407–408, 462–463, 520
Kyoto Protocol 168, 349, 414, 416, 456, 485

L

La Via Campesina 190, 358, 425, 484
labour 120, 142, 213–214, 258, 286, 291–293, 325, 329, 347, 351, 353–355, 392, 419, 424, 431, 441, 445–447, 449, 474, 488, 519
    care 326, 329, 333, 447
    organised 347
    reproductive 324, 330
    wage 89, 326
labour absorption 152
labour law 45–46, 117
labour market 19, 30, 88, 106, 120, 203, 231, 244, 454
    apartheid 30
    gendered 19
    racialised 19, 291
labour movement 47, 110, 117, 118, 142, 231, 257, 259, 545
    deradicalised 3
    organised 133
labour productivity 152
labour relations 293, 445
Labour Relations Act (LRA) 30–31, 45–46, 54–55, 106, 118, 120
Land Bank 75–76, 161, 396
land expropriation without compensation 535
land market 244
Landless People's Movement 212, 265
Latin America 2, 17, 21, 193, 217, 230, 244, 257–258, 261, 305, 314–316, 318, 339, 347, 402, 405, 415, 477, 484
Latin Bank Act 75
Le Pen, Marine 208
left 17, 21, 28–29, 32, 52, 80, 83, 118, 162–163, 166, 175, 179–181, 187, 196, 207–208, 211, 213, 230–231, 233, 237–238, 240, 242–244, 250, 253, 258–261, 268–269, 271, 315, 484
    anti-authoritarian 261
    authoritarian 253–254
    democratic 180, 182, 184–187, 242–244, 249, 253–255, 257
    global 184, 271, 282
    labour 266
    Marxist 266
    national liberation 253–254, 261–262, 264
    new 265
    new global 21, 32, 238, 240, 243, 258, 469
    postcolonial 240, 256
    post-national liberation 267–268
    socialist labour 258
    South African 240, 260–261, 269
    Trotskyist 266, 299
    twentieth century 23
left opposition 172
left parties 483
left politics 1, 8, 21, 23, 29, 33–34, 180–181, 183–185, 187, 238, 239, 241, 258, 260–261, 270, 282, 284, 288, 339
    post-social democratic 4, 180
    post-Soviet 4, 180
    transformative 4, 21
left renewal 19–20, 24, 30, 32–33, 37, 235, 259, 261
left thinking 27, 509
leftist 3
Lenin, Vladimir 23–24, 95, 169–170, 318
Leninism 540
Leninist 23
lesbian, gay, bisexual, transgender, intersexed (LGBTI) 265

lesbian, gay, bisexual, transgender, queer (LGBTQ+) 368
Li, Minqi 423, 436
  China and the 21st Century Crisis 423
liaison committee 48
liberalisation 119, 127, 145, 151, 243, 294, 499–500, 545
  capital account 155
  exchange control 105, 116, 148, 155
  financial 281
  import 120
  tariff 120–121, 148, 151 (see also 'tariff reform')
  trade 106, 151–152, 154, 459
liberalism 34, 186, 288, 306, 513
liberation 261, 286, 299, 314–315
  post-national 4
liberation movement 119, 139, 144–145, 151, 260–261
  ANC-led 109, 257, 300
liberation philosophy 314–316
liberation struggle 192, 196, 215, 288, 291, 477
liberation tax (see 'Black Economic Empowerment (BEE)')
liberation theology 314
Life Esidemeni tragedy 3, 371, 408
Lipton, Merle 10
  Capitalism and Apartheid: South Africa 1910 to 1984 10
Lisbon Treaty 475
local development forum 126
local economic development (LED) 29, 78–79, 85, 87, 89–90
  self-reliant 97–98
  socialist 86, 92, 96–99
  sustainable 85, 91, 96
local government 97, 129, 133, 155, 207, 268, 298, 521, 539
  developmental 97
localisation 91–92
Lonmin (see 'Marikana massacre')
love 12, 14, 39–40
  authentic 16
  bourgeois 15
  communal 14
  idealised 14
  moral 14
  radical 13
  teenage 14
  vanguard 13
Luxembourg, Rosa 166, 169, 439, 453
  The Accumulation of Capital: A Contribution to the Economic Theory of Imperialism 439, 453

M

Madiba (see 'Mandela, Nelson')
Madladla-Routledge, Nozizwe 26, 193–194
Madonsela, Thuli 214
Maize Board 76
majoritarianism 3
Malema, Julius 188, 191, 197, 208, 290, 295, 369, 536
Mamdani, Mahmood 224
  Neither Settler Nor Native: The Making and Unmaking of Permanent Minorities 224
Mandela, Nelson (aka Madiba) 8, 27, 117, 126, 151, 153, 178, 212–213, 222, 224–228, 257, 285, 287, 346, 386, 535, 541
  Long Walk to Freedom 228
Mandela Day 25, 224
Mandela factor 109, 117, 125–126, 291
Mandela Foundation 34, 385
Mantashe, Gwede 371, 389–393, 396–399
Manuel, Trevor 108, 131, 251
Maputo Corridor project 61
Marikana Campaign for Justice 266
Marikana massacre 2, 26, 28, 34, 135–139, 162, 188, 193, 197, 211, 214, 220, 256, 262, 267, 408
marketisation 144–145, 231–322, 326–327, 372, 374, 434–435, 474, 479, 487–488
Marx, Karl 12–13, 16, 33–34, 93–94, 169, 277—283, 324–325, 329–331, 423–424, 431, 437–438, 441–452, 471, 476
  Early Writings 93
  Economic and Philosophical Manuscripts 93, 444
  Capital 93, 278, 445–447
  The Communist Manifesto 13, 278–279, 448

Marx's theory of history 16
Marxism 4, 8, 12, 15, 17–21, 32–35, 47, 94, 166, 169, 174, 182, 237–238, 277, 280, 299, 324, 413, 423–425, 438, 441, 443–444, 448, 451
   anthropocentric 445
   classical 325, 422
   democratic 317
   ecological 333, 424
   productivist 29, 423, 424, 442, 445
   post-productivist 329, 413
   Promethean 300, 413, 438, 441, 443
   revolutionary 12
   Second International 170
   South African 173, 182, 185, 280
   Soviet(ised) 170, 271
Marxism–Leninism 8, 18–20, 24–25, 29, 33, 79, 169–170, 173–174, 181–182, 413
Marxist 15, 18–19, 21, 34, 46, 49, 94–95, 166, 173, 182, 230, 237, 282, 296–297, 299, 316, 323, 327, 422, 424, 427, 442, 471, 511–512
Marxist historiography 27
Marxist politics 16
Marxist–Leninist 4, 33, 110, 169–170, 206, 540
Marxist–Leninist–Maoist 422
mass action 47, 186, 199, 355
mass consciousness 36
mass consumerism 296
mass demobilisation 127
Mass Democratic Movement 11
mass mobilisation 123–124, 200, 212, 244, 260, 267
mass movement 10, 173, 184, 233, 286, 301
mass power 23, 36, 123, 169, 184, 212, 261, 271, 291, 293, 347, 420, 489
mass protests 127
materialism 4, 181–182, 280, 299, 424, 441–442
Mbeki, Govan 494
Mbeki, Thabo 2, 20, 125, 143, 151, 154, 159, 175–177, 187, 196, 198, 209, 213, 243, 265, 285, 517
Mboweni, Tito 376
mercantilism 264

Metal Electrical Workers Union of South Africa (MEWUSA) 245
metropolitan council 89
Mexican Revolution 477
Middle East 460
Mies, Maria 331
   Ecofeminism 319
migration 159, 295
militarism 4, 29, 40, 83–84, 86, 167
minerals–energy complex (MEC) 109, 128, 147, 156, 297, 300, 369, 382, 385, 391, 394, 435, 462
Mineworkers Development Agency 495
Minimum Wage Act 547
Mlambo-Ngcuka, Phumzile 160
Modern co-operativism 513
monetarism 155
money supply 155
monopoly corporation 48, 477
Moosa, Valli 408
Moser, Ingunn
   Biopolitics: A Feminist and Ecological Reader on Biotechnology 319
Motor Industry Development Programme 152
movement of movements 21, 509, 513, 519, 525
Mpumalanga 162
Mugabe, Robert 209
multiculturalism 126
multilateral(ism) 151, 153, 218, 297, 301, 304, 357, 377, 413, 418, 430, 450, 455–456, 462, 474–475, 481, 484, 486, 554
multinational 48
multi-parties 48
multi-party government 125
municipal council 89, 161
municipal government 89

N

Naidoo, Jay 118
Natal Indian Congress (NIC) 8
National Aeronautics and Space Administration (NASA) 301, 414
national consciousness 9, 135, 142
National Co-operative Association

(NCASA) 77–78, 80
National Democratic Revolution (NDR) 3, 18, 24, 95–97, 99, 101, 110, 128, 250, 264, 297, 300, 473, 539
national democratic state 47, 56
National Development Council 58
National Development Plan (NDP) 189, 346, 365–366, 434–435
National Economic Development and Labour Council (NEDLAC) 59–60, 118, 121, 126, 142–143, 248, 258
National Economic Forum 117
National Education Crisis Forum 205
National Food Crisis Forum 228, 541
national government 129, 155, 179, 364, 487
National Health Insurance scheme 7
National Indian Congress (NIC) 8
National Indian Congress–Transvaal Indian Congress (NIC–TIC) 8
National Labour and Economic Development Institute (NALEDI) 19, 30–31, 32, 57, 118, 397 (see also 'COSATU')
national liberation 4, 16, 18, 24, 35, 109–110, 115, 121, 124–125, 133–134, 139, 142, 144, 149, 162, 173, 180–181, 185, 187, 197, 222, 227, 233, 240, 243, 250, 257, 263, 266–268, 284–285, 290–293, 295, 298–300, 368–369, 431, 511, 539
national liberation leadership 123
national liberation left 3, 18, 24, 27
national liberation movement 18, 28, 35, 109–110, 121, 142, 185–186, 209, 264, 281, 368
national liberation politics 3, 19
national liberation revolution 20
national liberation struggle 7, 19, 180, 185, 280, 285, 287, 292–293, 300–301
National Manpower Commission 117
National Minimum Wage Project 547
National Party 117, 263
National Prosecuting Authority (NPA) 138, 177, 198, 221
National Small Business Council 160
National Union of Metalworkers of South Africa (NUMSA) 33, 35, 118, 193, 214, 256–259, 266–267, 269, 286, 346, 520, 521
National Union of Mineworkers (NUM) 267, 286, 392, 397, 493–497
nationalisation 28, 52, 130, 207, 242, 247, 257, 259, 483, 523
nationalism 2, 9, 28, 40, 141–142, 177, 179–181, 187, 206, 263, 281, 291–293, 509
  African 2, 26, 30, 224, 263, 284, 292–293, 295, 298, 340, 367, 404–405, 436, 517
  Afrikaner 287
  ANC-centred 18, 24, 263
  anti-colonial 260
  Arab 317
  Bandung revolutionary 317–318
  black 290
  coloured 2
  exclusionary 2, 22, 39, 232, 333, 457, 460
  exclusivist 232
  extreme white 2
  liberal 218
  nativist 232
  non-racial 142, 286
  post-apartheid 285
  racist 457
  rainbow 285, 291
  revanchist 218, 402
  resource 284–285, 297, 301, 365, 370–371
  revolutionary 3, 17, 24, 33, 109, 121, 141–142, 224, 260, 268–269, 271, 287, 431, 436, 473, 478, 513
  state-centred 284
  white 232, 489
  white supremacist 401
  Zulu 176, 178, 220
nationalist 2, 25, 487, 540
  African 26, 290, 295
  Afrikaner 281
  patriarchal white 232
  revolutionary 237, 261, 269, 280, 422, 427, 442
  right-wing 372, 472, 488

social democratic 237
nationally determined commitments 416, 457
natural relations 329, 379
nature 329
Natives' Land Act 532
Nature–women–labour 329
Nazi 231
Nazi Holocaust 312
Nehru-Mahalonobis model 58 (see also 'development planning')
neo-apartheid 26
neo-authoritarianism 232
neocolonial 317
neo-corporatism 177
neo-corporatist 126, 174, 258
neo-developmentalism 484
neofascism 4, 24, 34, 39, 41, 216, 218, 231–232, 479
   black 2
   white 219
neo-fascist 22, 26, 217, 230–232, 282, 328, 369, 489
neo-Gramscian 471, 474
neo-Hinduism 10, 13
neo-Keynesian 328
neoliberalisation 1, 2, 17, 21, 109–110, 133, 142–144, 147, 175, 238, 252, 256, 260, 264–265, 267, 477, 479, 483, 489, 499, 512, 514, 517
   authoritarian 26, 281
neoliberal(ism) 2, 4, 17, 20, 22, 24, 27, 30, 41, 57, 70–71, 77, 89, 110, 113–118, 128, 139–140, 142–149, 155, 159, 162, 167, 174–175, 188, 196, 207, 213, 231, 233, 240, 243–244, 249, 251–252, 254, 260–261, 264, 266–267, 281–282, 285, 291, 298, 324, 328, 330, 332, 339, 347, 368, 374–377, 379, 418, 454, 456–458, 471–474, 476, 478–480, 484, 486–487, 509, 512, 540, 545, 549
   centre-right 458
   green 340–341, 346, 419–420, 434
   hard-right 230, 458
   structural 154
   transformative 472
   transnational 109, 111, 120–121, 127, 133, 145, 148, 151, 153, 156, 249, 251, 264, 291
neo-Malthusianism 39, 457
neo-mercantilist 210
neo-pluralist 46
neo-Stalinist 166, 173–177, 180–181, 187, 242, 250
New Industrial Policy Framework 160
New International Economic Order 473
New International of Workers and Peoples 282, 28
New Partnership for Africa's Development (NEPAD) 154
Nicaraguan Revolution 477
Nkandla 197, 203, 262, 294
Nkomati Accord 256
Nobel Peace Prize 226
#NODAPL 463
non-capitalist 448, 450, 453
non-governmental organisation (NGO) 31–32, 95, 108, 192–193, 212, 240, 339, 352, 355, 479–481, 510, 518–519, 521, 524–525, 549, 555–556
non-racial(ism) 11, 15, 19, 25, 38, 124–125, 139, 142, 173, 192, 221, 223–225, 227, 257, 263, 270, 284, 286–287, 289–292, 294, 298, 301, 535
   radical 284, 285–293, 295, 302, 365, 535–536
non-renewable resources 90
non-Western 307, 309
North America 156
North American Free Trade Agreement (NAFTA) 480
North Atlantic Treaty Organization (NATO) 167, 402–405, 454
North–South relations 304–306, 309, 313–314, 316, 319–321
North West 520
Ntaba ka Ndoda Heritage and Development Centre 521
Ntsika Enterprise Promotion Agency 160
Nuclear Test Ban Treaty 401
Nyeleni Declaration of 2007 484
Nzimande, Blade 18, 20, 25, 29, 175–181, 184, 187, 204

O

Obama, Barack 188, 191, 217, 281, 311, 417–418, 430, 484
#OceansNotOil campaign 398
Occupy movement 193, 502
Occupy Wall Street movement 486
Oilgate 161
Operation Phakisa 297, 393
Operation Vula 9,
opposition 178, 188, 194–195, 206, 258, 268, 487
oppression 14, 17, 33, 53, 59, 142, 182–183, 187, 233, 239–240, 249, 252, 255, 279–281, 285, 288–289, 294, 299–301, 305, 315, 324, 330–332, 352, 398, 427, 432, 460, 511–512
   apartheid 290
   colonial 315
   intersectional 330
   racial(ised) 280, 287, 289, 291, 299
   women's 280, 300, 323–324, 331, 466, 479
oppressive rule 135
Organisation for Economic Co-operation and Development (OECD) 130, 155, 434
Organization of the Petroleum Exporting Countries (OPEC) 472–473
Oxfam South Africa 523

P

Pan African Student Movement 290
pan-Africanism 263, 317–318, 333, 398, 451, 464, 536
pan-European 309
paramilitarism 206
parastatal 115–116, 128–129, 133, 148, 156–157, 160, 376, 393
Parenti Christian 344
   Tropic of Chaos: Climate Change and the New Geography of Violence 344
Paris Agreement (see 'United Nations (UN) Paris Agreement')
Paris Commune 280, 449, 477
paternal managerialism 74
paternalistic 147

patriarchal 89, 263, 322, 329, 379, 485
patriarchy 1, 196, 264, 319, 324, 330, 332
patronage 32, 127, 178, 190, 218, 262, 265, 271
Pax Americana 311
Pax Britannia 311
People's Food Sovereignty Act 35, 228, 351, 378, 463, 516, 522, 524, 537, 556
#PeoplesVaccine 358, 359
pink tide 484
pluralism 306, 340
plutocracy 401, 403, 461, 499
Polanyi, Karl 243, 435, 439
   The Great Transformation: The Political and Economic Origins of Our Time 243, 374, 435, 439
polycrisis 36, 39 (see also 'crisis')
policy 59, 122, 143, 145, 147, 154, 167, 202, 208, 219, 222, 294–295, 346, 382
   affirmative action 56
   austerity 376, 454, 478, 488, 548
   basic needs 61
   BEE 131–132, 161–162
   climate 363, 387, 389, 398, 462
   climate change economic 219, 356
   climate crisis 371
   co-operative 80, 519
   economic 48, 50, 57, 62, 129–131, 188, 193, 219, 242, 368, 501, 514
   energy 555
   fiscal 104, 117–118, 129, 155, 158
   foreign 129
   foreign exchange 105
   immigration 219
   income 106, 248
   industrial 45, 118–119, 144, 160, 354, 484
   interest rate 105
   labour market 45
   land reform 67
   market-oriented 103
   monetarist 103, 127, 145, 148, 434
   monetary 105, 116–118, 121, 146, 148, 154–155, 475
   neoliberal 143, 514
   neo-mercantilist 116

post-apartheid 300
procurement 160
pro-poor 159
state 69–70, 73, 142–143, 368
trade 61, 118, 120
policy dialogue 205
policy tools 141
political agenda 233
political consciousness 11, 13, 15, 123, 186
political crisis 209
political ecology 35, 310–311, 313, 321
    global 313
political economist 306
political economy 10, 27, 59, 69, 87, 110–113, 115, 130, 133, 147, 149, 162, 167, 183, 200, 230, 243, 258, 269–270, 280, 284, 299, 302, 416, 429, 443, 445–447, 451, 512
    capitalist 425
    ecofeminist 329
    global 145–146, 149, 153, 162, 168, 281, 310–311, 313, 349, 368, 454–455, 471–473, 479–498, 505, 514
    green 498
    growth-driven 299
    international 115
    national 474
    neo-Gramscian global 140
    neoliberalised 510
    neo-Marxist 426
    racist 292
    regional 474
    transnational 111
political education 19–20, 25, 27, 57, 174, 186, 258
political elite 47
political freedom 10
political leadership 9, 173
political movement 116
political praxis 10, 156
political relations 124, 287,
political settlement 117, 121
political sociology 24
politics 2, 4, 22–23, 33, 96, 112–113, 122, 128, 135, 176, 185–186, 195, 201, 206, 213, 232, 239–240, 268, 294, 310, 326, 328, 332, 341, 347, 355, 511
Africanist 295
anti-ecocide 302
anti-mass-based 112
anti-oppression 453
anti-systemic 422
anti-war 405, 461
authoritarian 125, 232, 332, 479, 499
climate 337, 456, 466
climate justice 35, 347, 352, 355, 372, 383, 420–421, 463, 466
big man 308
copycat 203
corporatist 118
counter-hegemonic generative 24
crowd 11, 355
democratic 193, 256
democratic left 182–183, 186, 301
democratic socialist 18
ecofascist class 455
electoral 290
elite 134
environmental justice 29, 35, 332
food sovereignty 425, 529
generative 239, 240
global 226, 400
global climate 455
grassroots 36
hegemonic 114
identity 33, 231–232
institutional 127
just transition 348
labour 245, 257
left (see 'left politics')
market-led 202
Marxist 169
mass 25, 269–270, 285, 301, 354, 465, 489
national 207
national liberation 25, 28, 33, 187, 220, 237, 260, 264, 266–268, 286, 367
neofascist 26, 461
neoliberal 267, 332
new transformative 271
non-racial 290
oppositional 96, 205

parliamentary 50
performative 3
populist 125, 268
post-apartheid 138, 240
post-national liberation 237, 240, 284
president-centred 213
pressure group 96
programmatic 142, 182–183
reactionary 179
resistance 8
revolutionary 23, 169
right (see 'right politics')
shopfloor 257
social democratic 22, 120, 175, 258
social democratic reform 22
socialist 181–183, 185
South African 180, 186, 197, 206, 208, 250, 253, 293
static 238
strategic 8, 17, 258, 323, 327, 454
student 205, 289
top-down 112
transactional 285, 517
trans-feminist 327
transformative 4, 21, 24, 30, 32, 34–35, 37–39, 271, 289, 301, 348, 350, 353, 413, 433, 469, 504, 507, 510, 512, 522, 523, 531
transformative intersectional 38
transformative left 4, 23, 30, 33
transformative strategic 23, 37
transitional 115
union 248
vanguardist 262, 513
white nationalist 231
women's 332
working-class 262, 325
youth 193
politics of dominance 114, 128
pollution 90, 296, 322, 333, 344, 354, 371, 383, 392, 407, 425, 427, 431, 437, 440, 442, 460, 534
popular power 184
populism 174, 176–177, 180, 187, 196, 202, 237, 250, 355, 378, 488
authoritarian 197–198, 204, 207, 209

ethnic 209
fiscal 210
patriarchal 209
populist 178, 203, 205, 242, 261, 289–290, 293, 295, 531, 535
post-anthropocentric 38
post-apartheid 9–10, 18–19, 24, 27, 30–31, 34, 36–37, 88, 109–111, 113–116, 119, 121–122, 128, 130, 134–135, 139–142, 144–145, 147–151, 157, 162, 175, 181, 183–185, 187, 200, 203, 210–212, 215, 237, 239–240, 247–251, 256, 258, 262–263, 265, 267, 270, 284–285, 288, 291–293, 367, 430–431, 434, 495–497, 509, 512, 514, 517, 520, 531, 537, 546–547
post-capitalist 243, 254, 423, 449
post-carbon 433
post-Cold War 318, 478
postcolonial 147, 237–238, 256, 307–308, 317
post-imperial 38, 309, 314, 321
postmodernism 33
post-Napoleonic 277
post-national liberation 509
post-neoliberal 243, 269, 471, 484, 489, 509
post-productivist 38
post-social democratic 509
post-US-dominated 243
post-World War 2 326, 478
pots and pans revolution 484
praxis 16–20, 23–24, 30, 34, 38, 238, 278, 315–316, 439
left 240
mass 17
transformative 7, 16, 19, 26, 31–32, 37, 39–40, 466
transformative left 21
transformative political 33
Presidential Climate Commission 36, 463
President's Conference on Small Business 160
President's International Investment Council 154
pro-apartheid 122
productivism 7, 279, 294, 299, 381, 451

technotopian 39
productivist 4, 24, 431
productivity 325
Programme of Action (POA) 85
pro-socialist 240
Protection of State Information Act 193
provincial government 129, 133, 155, 179
Public Finance Management Act 161
public transport 29, 87, 99, 201, 302, 346, 398, 420, 433, 480–481, 485
Putin, Vladimir 328, 400, 402–403

R

racial 14, 136, 142, 187, 217, 219–220, 223, 232, 239, 249, 281, 289, 291, 308, 313, 494, 496
racialisation 26
racialised 9, 13, 115, 119, 128, 134, 138, 142, 147, 151, 156–157, 226, 264–265, 285, 287–288, 290–291, 293–295, 302, 311, 322, 351–352, 430, 432, 446, 448, 494
racism 1–2, 11, 144, 176, 206, 217, 224–225, 251, 257, 264, 278, 288, 290, 293, 295, 299, 307, 330, 432, 446
   anti-white 535
   global 264
   white 198
racist 11, 26, 33–34, 173, 186, 217, 224, 278, 281, 288–290, 294, 302, 368, 372, 379, 479, 535
rainbow nation 291–292, 294, 529, 541
rainbowism 284, 290–291, 294, 368
Ramaphosa, Cyril 25, 213–215, 220, 222, 224, 365, 367, 369–371, 385, 407, 458, 462, 540
Reagan, Ronald 217, 473, 478
realism 306
   critical 306
realist theory 307
reconciliation 46, 117, 291, 535, 537
   national 125, 257
   racial 226
Reconstruction and Development Programme (RDP) 48–49, 59, 61, 103, 106–107, 118–119, 124, 126, 142, 151, 157, 228, 258, 515
Red October campaign 29

red–green alliance 347, 350, 353, 356, 419, 421, 433, 434
redistribution 103, 142, 175, 452, 542
   state-led 142, 215
reducing emissions from deforestation and forest degradation (REDD+) 343
reductionism 94, 441
   class 324, 330
reductionist 46
reform(s) 21–23, 30, 50, 114, 116, 119, 141, 153–154, 160, 258, 423
   agrarian 69
   co-operative 80, 515
   democratic systemic 23–24, 30–31, 34–35, 37–38, 229, 333, 378, 383, 411, 433, 436, 451, 455, 464–466, 513–517, 526, 537
   economic 111, 117, 132
   electoral 219
   exchange control 121
   financialised market 442, 475
   labour law 49
   labour market 19, 30, 117–118, 120, 142, 175
   land 53, 58, 157, 247, 294–295, 483–484, 524, 531–532, 537
   local government 123
   market 516
   neo-apartheid 114, 116–117
   neoliberal 116, 127–128, 131–132, 475
   policy 50, 132, 496
   radical 50
   revolutionary 92, 96, 98
   redistributive 213, 484
   social democratic 22, 24
   structural 50, 56, 473
   tariff 117, 151
   tax 496
   value added tax 117
reformism 23, 111 (see also 'passive revolution')
regional bloc 318
regionalisation 259, 480, 487
#RememberKhwezi 214
renewable energy 91, 99, 201, 298, 302, 346, 349, 354–355, 366, 389, 392–393, 398,

419–420, 433, 435–436, 441, 451, 457, 465, 481, 485, 504, 554, 556
rent-seeking 60, 292
reproduction 3, 34, 89, 132–133, 144, 167, 251, 262, 300, 305, 323, 325–328, 331, 379, 441, 448, 454, 476, 479
    biological 325
re-racialised 263, 270, 294–295
resistance 1, 10–12, 16, 21, 26, 37, 117, 123, 200, 211, 214, 231, 258, 260–261, 263, 265–267, 269, 271, 280–283, 308, 312, 323, 332, 339, 352, 425, 447, 450, 460, 463, 471–472, 476, 479, 481–483, 488–489, 511
    civil 212, 486
    global 21, 34, 282, 419, 471
    mass 10–11, 17, 286, 290, 359, 486
    transformative 258
revanchism 232
revolution 21–24, 49, 56, 110–113, 176, 203, 209, 220, 258, 277, 423
    counter 112, 230
    democratic 51, 339
    green 74, 319
    passive 109–115, 121, 128, 130, 132–134, 175, 179, 185 (see also 'reformism')
    white 74
    worker 22
revolutionary 13, 20, 23, 28, 41, 50, 72, 94, 112, 166, 169, 171, 203–204, 260, 269, 279, 300, 368
    change 300
    conscious 13
    counter 177
    nationalist 72
#Rhodes Must Fall movement 268, 289
right 130, 134, 217–218, 230, 232, 328, 332
    democratic 257
    extreme 22, 230–231, 328
    extreme white 26
right politics 26, 332
Right Livelihood Award 319
Right2Know Campaign 212, 265, 269
rights-of-nature alternative 345–346
Rio UN Conference (1992) (aka Local Agenda 21) 91
Rivonia trial 225
Robben Island 8
Rodrik, Dani 434, 459
Rome Statute 226
rural development 72, 74, 76
Russia–Ukraine war 400, 403–405, 454, 457, 459, 461
Russian Revolution (1917) 8, 21–22, 24, 49, 112, 169, 170, 172–173, 269, 427, 529

S

SACP Conference on Socialism and Sustainable Local Economic Development 29
Said, Edward 307
    Orientalism 307
Salleh, Ariel 331
sanctions 115–116, 156, 281, 403
Sanders, Bernie 358, 487
Satgar, Vishwas
    COSATU in Crisis: The Fragmentation of an African Trade Union Federation 31
    Destroying Democracy: Neoliberal Capitalism and the Rise of Authoritarian Politics 2
    New Frontiers for Socialism in the 21st Century: Conversations on a Global Journey 20, 182, 187
#SaveSouthAfrica 215
Schreiner, Olive 280
Scorpions 177
Second World 48, 70, 499
sector education and training authority (SETA) 99, 496
separation of powers 48, 59, 216
Serge, Victor 172
    Memoirs of a Revolutionary 172
service delivery 89, 265, 269, 294, 529
Seven Day War 18
Sharpeville massacre 3
Shiva, Vandana 306, 314, 319–321, 331
    Biopolitics: A Feminist and Ecological Reader on Biotechnology 319
    Ecofeminism 319
    Reclaiming the Commons: Biodiversity,

Indigenous Knowledge and the Rights of Mother Earth 320
Staying Alive: Women, Ecology and Development 319
The Violence of the Green Revolution: Third World Agriculture, Ecology and Politics 319
shoras 47
Sisulu, Walter 8
Slave Revolution 477
Slovo, Joe 8, 18, 24–27, 29, 170, 174, 237
Slums Act 136
small and medium enterprises (SMEs) 81, 105, 160, 502, 510
small, medium and micro enterprise 62
small-scale farmers 190, 388, 505–506, 516, 524–525, 536–537
social actor 140
social agency 128
social contract 118, 201–202, 217, 228, 389, 478
social democracy 4, 24, 50, 120, 181, 237–238, 254, 259–261, 269, 271, 287, 422, 431, 436, 473, 477–478, 511, 513
left 109
social democrat(ic) 16–17, 20, 22–24, 30–31, 50–52, 118, 142, 233, 239, 261, 268, 442, 477
Social Democratic Party 280
social development 58, 95
social dialogue 205
social enterprise 244
social grants 158, 178, 534, 542, 548
social injustice 135
social justice 53, 140, 191, 193, 265, 348, 351, 353, 385, 505, 511
social movement 93, 207, 261, 484
social partner 90, 118
social protection 327
social relief grants 222
social reproduction 22, 158, 264, 295, 322, 325–329, 333, 447, 459, 512
social reproduction theory (SRT) 322–331, 447
social sciences 304–305, 306, 310
social theory 33, 441

socialisation 53, 56, 247
socialism 9, 13, 16, 19–20, 22, 24, 30, 33, 38, 49–50, 52–53, 56, 79, 85, 93, 95, 97–98, 110, 134, 166, 169, 170, 172–176, 182, 196, 237–238, 257, 259, 267, 269–271, 279, 286, 421–423, 427–428, 434–438, 450, 476, 484, 513
African 317, 427
anarchist 238
authoritarian state 12
centrally planned 170
Chinese 12
democratic 12, 20, 28
democratic eco(feminist) 37
Marxist 92–95, 99, 173, 422
nationalist 436
Nehruvian 427, 436
postcolonial 319
post-Stalinist 237
productivist 436, 438, 450
re-Stalinised 237
scientific 317
South African 270
Soviet(ised) 11, 17, 27, 29, 48, 52, 109, 121, 142, 169, 237, 242, 268, 287, 436, 473
Stalinist 95, 170, 180, 237–238
state-centric 56, 423, 450–451
worker-controlled 261
socialist 35, 48–49, 51, 63, 77–78, 85, 92, 94, 96–97, 99, 103, 130, 150, 169, 176, 180–181, 279–280, 283, 299, 317, 399, 426–427, 431, 433, 478
ecofeminist 329, 466
Fabian 427
Socialist and Revolutionary workers Party 369 (see also 'Jim, Irvin')
socialist pluralism 182
socialist renewal 24–25, 27–29, 32, 169, 174–176, 180–182, 184, 186, 187
socialist transformation 96
socio-ecological reproduction 319, 322, 329–330, 347, 369, 377, 439, 448, 452, 545
socio-ecological reproduction theory (SERT) 323, 327, 329–331, 333, 347, 349

Sociology of Work Project (SWOP) 118
Solidarity Economy Movement 189–190, 191, 346
Solidarity Fund 222, 228–229, 377, 541, 548
solidary society 511,
Sonlit, Rebecca, 345
   A Paradise Built in Hell: The Extraordinary Communities That Arise in Disaster 345
South Africa 1–5, 7, 10–12, 14–21, 25–29, 32, 34–35, 37, 45–49, 51–52, 56–57, 59–63, 66–67, 71–72, 74, 77, 81, 83, 87, 93, 95–96, 103–105, 109–142, 144–145, 148–156, 158–162, 170, 173–175, 177–178, 180–185, 187–190, 192, 194–197, 200–201, 203–214, 220–228, 230, 232, 237–240, 243–245, 247–255, 257–271, 277, 280, 284–286, 288–303, 313, 340–342, 346–348, 350–356, 358–359, 363–365, 367–370, 373, 376–389, 392–394, 396–399, 405, 407–409, 414, 421, 429–432, 434–435, 438, 450–455, 458–459, 462–465, 473, 477, 482, 485–487, 493–494, 497, 509–516, 518–520, 522–524, 526, 529–535, 538–540, 542, 545–548, 553–555, 558
South African Airways 157
South African Clothing and Textile Workers Union (SACTWU) 118
South African Coloured People's Organisation 285
South African Communist Party (SACP) 8–9, 16–20, 24–29, 31–32, 35, 43, 48–50, 52, 57, 63, 77–81, 85, 96–99, 103, 108–109, 121–123, 125, 144, 163, 173–184, 186–187, 196–197, 206, 211, 214–215, 221, 247, 256, 261, 266, 280, 299–300, 369, 515
   African Communist 19, 25, 27, 30–31, 49, 56, 62, 81
South African Congress of Democrats 285–286
South African Congress of Trade Unions (SACTU) 123
South African Council of Churches 523
South African Credit and Co-operative League (SACCOL) 80
South African dream 249, 250
South African Federation of Trade Unions (SAFTU) 211, 397, 523
South African Food Sovereignty Campaign (SAFSC) 21, 32, 35–36, 212, 228, 351–353, 356, 378, 381, 384–385, 396, 462–463, 516, 520, 522, 524–525, 531, 533, 536, 541–542, 549, 553, 555–558
South African Human Rights Commission (SAHRC) 227, 351, 463, 533
South African Indian Congress 285
South African National Civic Organisation (SANCO) 123, 124
South African Reserve Bank (SARB) 155
South African Waste Pickers Association (SAWPA) 523
South Asia 349, 373
Southall, Roger
   COSATU in Crisis: The Fragmentation of an African Trade Union Federation 31
South-East Asia 349
southern Africa 104, 209, 256, 313, 348, 350, 381, 395, 408, 530
Southern African Food Lab 530
Southern Africa Labour and Development Research Unit (SALDRU) 430, 434, 493
Southern African Clothing and Textile Workers' Union (SACTWU) 397
Southern Common Market (Mercosur) 480
sovereign debt 158
sovereignty 17, 48
Soviet Revolution 95, 170
Soviet Bloc 423, 478
Soviet Union 9, 17–19, 22, 29, 58, 63, 95, 170, 173, 237, 260, 423, 473, 477
Soweto uprising (1976) 3, 11, 286
Spanish-American war 167
Special Conference on State Power (2005) 196
Special Rapporteur on the Right to Food 542
Stalin, Joseph 95, 169, 171–172, 217, 243, 298, 442
Stalinisation 20, 174

Stalinism 170
Stalinist 28, 172, 181, 369
Standing Rock (Sioux) resistance 312, 385, 486
state capture 161, 209, 294, 298
state centric 139, 142, 174, 238, 254, 269, 287, 449
state centricism 27–28
state-owned enterprise 203, 215, 298
state ownership 52–53, 56
state power 25, 29, 135, 175, 196, 238
State Power Conference (2005) 25–26
statism 237
statist 24, 97, 116, 150, 174, 182, 317
stokvels 97 (see also 'co-operative movement')
Street-Net International 523
Student Representative Council (SRC) 204
structural adjustment 104, 317, 454
structural adjustment programme (SAP) 57–58, 482
structuralism 306
sub-imperialism 149
sub-prime housing market crisis 167, 242
sub-Saharan Africa 67
subsistence 319–321, 325
Sunrise Movement 463
supremacist 39, 218
    Trumpian white nationalist 219, 545
    white 232, 278, 285, 287, 302, 308, 390, 536
supremacy 314
    Western 314
    white male 390
sustainable development 31, 79, 90–91

T

Tamana, Dora 494
tariff 58, 106–107, 152
taxation 104, 107, 222–223, 229, 269, 298
techno-industrialism 5
Telkom 157
Thatcher, Margaret 379, 473, 478
Third Communist International 49
Third World 46, 61, 66, 68–70, 116, 237, 317
Thunberg, Greta 385
totalitarianism 206, 282
totality 315

township 4, 31–32, 35, 86–90, 97–99, 123, 136, 183, 245
township economy 87, 97–98
trade 92, 244, 251, 278, 418, 476, 483, 514
trade and industrial strategy 85
trade-related aspects of intellectual property (TRIPS) waiver 357–358
trade-related investment measures (TRIMS) 130, 155 (see also 'World Trade Organization (WTO)')
trade union(s) (see 'union(s)')
trade unionism (see 'unionism')
trade unionist (see 'unionist')
Traditional Authorities Bill 193
traditional leaders 263
transformation 18, 27, 48, 50–51, 56, 97, 112, 142, 189, 238, 240, 248, 257–259, 261, 267, 292, 298, 464–466, 481, 505, 511
    agrarian 294, 524, 531, 536
    agro-ecological 352, 388, 506, 532, 537
    democratic 206, 421
    ecological 423, 436
    economic 124, 139, 154, 192, 215, 285
    fundamental 121, 134, 186, 293, 433, 535
    global 238, 339
    local 92–93
    post-apartheid 121
    progressive 140
    radical 175
    radical economic 292–294, 369
    revolutionary 50, 279
    rural 79
    social 50, 121, 237, 241
    socio-ecological 350
    state-led 142
    structural 144, 162, 247
    systemic 23, 270, 296, 348, 354, 356, 397, 419, 452, 463, 509–510, 539
transformation from below 48, 70, 176, 181, 248, 271, 303, 350, 398, 515, 531, 557
transformative change 1, 231, 269–270, 398, 428
transformative movement 36–37
transformative political orientation 20
transformative power 191, 303

transformative strategy 49, 271
transformative vision 52–53
transition 9, 22, 25–26, 31, 38, 47, 70, 118, 142, 185, 279–280, 367, 369–370, 388, 423, 498
    democratic 11, 50, 110, 114, 116, 130, 144, 156, 261, 448, 451, 531
    democratic ecosocialist 23, 28, 301
    ecological 156
    economic 61
    energy 391–392, 397
    negotiated 117
    political 46, 49, 111
    renewable energy 370
    socialist 49, 51, 96–97
    state-centric 451
transnational 46, 88, 110, 114, 116, 128, 145, 151, 153–154, 340–341, 484
transnational corporation/firm 37, 129, 133, 146, 152, 190, 283, 475, 505–506,
    global 133
transnational fraction(ation) 128–130, 133–134, 150, 175
transnationalisation 2, 27, 109, 119, 121, 140, 145, 156, 160, 341
Transnet 157, 160
Travelgate 161
Treatment Action Campaign (TAC) 212, 265, 482
tricameral parliament 11
Tripartite Alliance 9, 34, 108, 118, 123, 177, 194, 213 (see also 'ANC-led Alliance')
Trotsky, Leon 431
Trotskyism 28
Trotskyist 4, 20, 24, 27–28, 181, 280
Trudeau, Justin 458
Trump, Donald 208, 216–219, 231–232, 281, 297, 311, 332, 348, 366, 372, 376, 381, 403, 417–419, 430, 434, 459, 489
Truth and Reconciliation Commission (TRC) 126, 291

U

#UBIGNOW 223, 229, 465, 542, 545 (see also 'basic income grant (BIG)')
#BIGNOW for South Africa 459
ubuntu 420

Unemployed People's Movement (UPM) 137, 194
unilateralism 218
union(s) 4, 16, 24, 29, 31, 33, 47–48, 50–51, 54–55, 58, 66, 78, 95, 117–118, 123, 133, 176, 184, 186, 196, 211, 214, 240, 245, 248, 256, 258–259, 267, 271, 282–283, 286–287, 293, 295, 332, 347–348, 351, 353–354, 356, 358–359, 366, 369, 385, 396–398, 419, 421, 433, 462–463, 473, 478–481, 483, 485, 488, 493, 497, 513, 516, 520–523, 525, 549, 553, 555, 557–558
union investment company 175–176
union movement 45, 54, 60, 174, 177, 179, 287, 397
    black 287, 293
    left-wing 110
union unity 50
unionism 51, 293
    black 11, 286
    business 33, 248, 355
    modern industrial 257
    strategic 50–52
    transformative 45, 49, 51–52, 54, 56, 355
unionist 9, 20, 30, 353
United Democratic Front (UDF) 8–11, 17, 122–123, 126, 184, 200, 240, 286–287
United Democratic Left Front 184
United Front 214, 266–267, 269, 271, 346
United Nations (UN) 82–83, 253, 301, 304, 318, 341, 347, 349, 367, 377, 380, 386, 388, 405–407, 413, 415, 417, 420, 425, 430, 455–456, 462, 554
United Nations (UN) Paris Agreement 297, 348, 365, 388, 407, 415–419, 430, 456–458, 554
United Nations (UN) Charter 402
United Nations–Conference of the Parties (UN–COP) (see 'Conference of the Parties (COP)')
United Nations Conference on Trade and Development (UNCTAD) 505
United Nations (UN) Environmental Programme 440
    Making Peace with Nature 440

United Nations (UN) Food Summit 388
United Nations Framework Convention on
    Climate Change (UNFCCC) 339, 348,
    414
United States (US) supremacy 166–168
universal basic grant 223
universalism 309
University of Johannesburg 137, 523
University of KwaZulu-Natal 203
University of Natal 10
University of the Witwatersrand (aka Wits
    University) 29, 34, 99, 204–205, 289,
    487, 522–523, 530, 547
    *Emancipatory Futures Studies in the
        Anthropocene* project 21, 29, 33, 36

V
vaccines 357
vaccine apartheid 357, 359, 459
vanguardism 237, 254, 339, 434, 511
    national liberation 262
vanguardist 239, 259, 261, 268, 271, 300,
    413, 428
Vavi, Zwelinzima 137, 267
Vogel, Lise 324, 325–327
    *Marxism and the Oppression of Women:
        Towards a Unitary Theory* 324
voluntarist agreement 54
Von Holdt, Karl 45–46, 50
    South African Labour Bulletin 45
Vukani–Sidikiwe campaign 26, 192–193, 214
Vulnerable 20 (V20) group of countries
    415–416

W
Washington Consensus 57, 61, 149, 476, 478
Water Sovereignty Guide 522, 557
wealth tax 32, 202, 382
weapons of mass destruction 83, 168
web of life 6, 38, 251–252
welfare state 22, 127, 143, 323, 442, 477–479
West(ern), the 48, 52, 59–60, 113, 127, 147,
    279, 306–309, 312, 317, 373, 400, 422,
    436, 442, 448, 478, 535
Western Cape 364, 384, 396
Western countries 22, 116, 210, 357
white farmers 295, 536

white middle class 330
white South Africa 536
Williams, Michelle
    *Destroying Democracy: Neoliberal
        Capitalism and the Rise of
        Authoritarian Politics* 2 *Roots of
        Participatory Democracy: Democratic
        Communists in Kerala, India and
        South Africa* 174, 181
Williams, Raymond 426
    Keywords 426
Wits University (see 'University of the
    Witwatersrand')
Wolpe, Harold 185, 280
WoMin African Alliance 333, 358
worker control 46–47, 49–56, 71, 173, 245,
    247–248, 258–259, 286, 354, 447, 512
Worker Co-operation Campaign 520
worker movement 50–51, 53
worker ownership 51–54, 56, 71, 247
workers from below 47
workers' council 47
workers' parties 16
working class action 97
workplace forum 45–47, 51, 54–55, 60, 118
    autonomous self-management 55–56
works committee 48
World Bank 21, 27, 48, 57, 63, 108, 119, 127,
    131–132, 144, 150–151, 153–154, 253,
    282, 340, 370–371, 430, 434–435, 473
World Commission on Environment and
    Development (aka UN Commission or
    Brundtland Commission) 90, 91
    Our Common Future 90
World Cup 158, 161, 204, 266, 291
World Economic Forum (WEF) 127,
    150–151, 153–154, 251, 253, 473, 475
World Food Programme 542
World Health Organization (WHO) 358, 546
World Meteorological Organization (WMO)
    301, 363, 414
World People's Conference on Climate
    Change and the Rights of Mother Earth
    484–485
World Social Forum (WSF) 21, 184, 243,
    261, 282, 318, 339–341, 484, 503, 519

World Summit on Sustainable Development (WSSD) 35, 91, 95
World Trade Organization (WTO) 21, 27, 120, 150–151, 153–155, 244, 253, 282, 320, 357–358, 435, 475, 483
World War 1 22, 243, 306, 374, 435, 453, 477
World War 2 17, 22, 72, 141, 219, 260, 306, 310, 328, 373–374, 435, 477, 501
World War 3 400, 435

X
Xi, Jinping 328

Y
Young Communist League 20

Z
Zimbabwe land grabs 295
Zimbabwe moment 209, 212
Zita, Langa 45, 51
   New Frontiers for Socialism in the 21st Century: Conversations on a Global Journey 20, 182, 187
Zondo Commission 367
Zuma, Jacob 25–26, 34, 143, 151, 154–155, 160–162, 176–180, 188, 191, 196–199, 206, 208–215, 220–222, 226, 243, 260, 262, 264–266, 285, 290, 292, 294, 342, 366–367, 369, 371, 376, 393–394, 534–535
Zumafication 20, 25–26, 163, 196, 214, 225, 266, 294
Zumafied 20, 198, 535
#ZumaMustGo 26, 198–199, 214